The Principles of Psychology

by William James

Authorized Edition

in two volumes
Volume Two

Dover Publications
Garden City, New York

This authorized Dover edition, first published in
1950, is an unabridged and unaltered republication
of the work first published by Henry Holt and
Company in 1890. This edition is published by
special arrangement with Henry Holt and Company.

International Standard Book Number

ISBN-13: 978-0-486-20382-9
ISBN-10: 0-486-20382-4

Manufactured in the United States by LSC Communications Book LLC
20382436   2021
www.doverpublications.com

CONTENTS.

CHAPTER XXI.

CHAPTER XXII.

CHAPTER XXIII.

CHAPTER XXIV.

CHAPTER XXV.

CHAPTER XXVI.

CHAPTER XXVII.

CHAPTER XXVIII.

PSYCHOLOGY.

CHAPTER XVII.

SENSATION.

AFTER inner perception, outer perception! The next three chapters will treat of the processes by which we cognize at all times the present world of space and the material things which it contains. And first, of the process called Sensation.

SENSATION AND PERCEPTION DISTINGUISHED.

The words Sensation and Perception do not carry very definitely discriminated meanings in popular speech, and in Psychology also their meanings run into each other. Both of them name processes in which we cognize an objective world; both (under normal conditions) need the stimulation of incoming nerves ere they can occur; Perception always involves Sensation as a portion of itself; and Sensation in turn never takes place in adult life without Perception also being there. They are therefore names for different cognitive *functions*, not for different sorts of mental *fact*. The nearer the object cognized comes to being a simple quality like 'hot,' 'cold,' 'red,' 'noise,' 'pain,' apprehended irrelatively to other things, the more the state of mind approaches pure sensation. The fuller of relations the object is, on the contrary; the more it is something classed, located, measured, compared, assigned to a function, etc., etc.; the more unreservedly do we call the state of mind a perception, and the relatively smaller is the part in it which sensation plays.

Sensation, then, so long as we take the analytic point of

*view, differs from Perception only in the extreme simplicity of its
object or content.** Its function is that of mere *acquaintance*
with a fact. Perception's function, on the other hand, is
knowledge *about* † a fact; and this knowledge admits of
numberless degrees of complication. But in both sensation and perception we perceive the fact as an *immediately
present outward reality,* and this makes them differ from
'thought' and 'conception,' whose objects do not appear
present in this immediate physical way. *From the physio-*

---

* Some persons will say that we never have a really simple object or
content. My definition of sensation does not require the simplicity to be
absolutely, but only relatively, extreme. It is worth while in passing,
however, to warn the reader against a couple of inferences that are often
made. One is that because we gradually learn to analyze so many qualities we ought to conclude that there are no really indecomposable feelings
in the mind. The other is that because the processes that produce our sensations are multiple, the sensations regarded as subjective facts must also
be compound. To take an example, to a child the taste of lemonade comes
at first as a simple quality. He later learns both that many stimuli and
many nerves are involved in the exhibition of this taste to his mind, and
he also learns to perceive separately the sourness, the coolness, the sweet,
the lemon aroma, etc., and the several degrees of strength of each and all
of these things,—the experience falling into a large number of aspects,
each of which is abstracted, classed, named, etc., and all of which appear
to be the elementary sensations into which the original 'lemonade flavor'
is decomposed. It is argued from this that the latter never was the simple
thing which it seemed. I have already criticised this sort of reasoning
in Chapter VI (see pp. 170 ff.). The mind of the child enjoying the simple
lemonade flavor and that of the same child grown up and analyzing it are
in two entirely different conditions. Subjectively considered, the two
states of mind are two altogether distinct sorts of fact. The later mental
state says 'this is the *same flavor (or fluid)* which that earlier state perceived as simple,' but that does not make the two states themselves identical.
It is nothing but a case of learning more and more *about* the same topics
of discourse or things.—Many of these topics, however, must be confessed
to resist all analysis, the various colors for example. He who sees blue and
yellow 'in' a certain green means merely that when green is confronted
with these other colors he sees relations of *similarity.* He who sees abstract
'color' in it means merely that he sees a similarity between it and all the
other objects known as colors. (Similarity itself cannot ultimately be accounted for by an identical abstract element buried in all the similars, as
has been already shown, p. 492 ff.) He who sees abstract paleness, intensity, purity, in the green means other similarities still. These are all outward determinations of that special green, knowledges *about* it, *zufällige An-
sichten,* as Herbart would say, not *elements* of its composition. Compare
the article by Meinong in the Vierteljahrschrift für wiss. Phil., xii. 324.

† See above, p. 221.

*logical point of view both sensations and perceptions differ from
'thoughts'* (in the narrower sense of the word) *in the fact that
nerve-currents coming in from the periphery are involved in their
production. In perception these nerve-currents arouse voluminous associative or reproductive processes in the cortex; but when
sensation occurs alone, or with a minimum of perception, the accompanying reproductive processes are at a minimum too.*

I shall in this chapter discuss some general questions
more especially relative to Sensation. In a later chapter
perception will take its turn. I shall entirely pass by the
classification and natural history of our special 'sensations,' such matters finding their proper place, and being
sufficiently well treated, in all the physiological books.*

THE COGNITIVE FUNCTION OF SENSATION.

A pure sensation is an abstraction; and when we adults
talk of our 'sensations' we mean one of two things: either
certain *objects,* namely simple *qualities* or *attributes* like
hard, hot, pain; or else those of our thoughts in which
acquaintance with these objects is least combined with
knowledge about the relations of them to other things. As
we can only think or talk about the relations of objects
with which we have *acquaintance* already, we are forced to
postulate a function in our thought whereby we first become
aware of the *bare immediate natures* by which our several
objects are distinguished. This function is sensation.
And just as logicians always point out the distinction
between substantive terms of discourse and relations found
to obtain between them, so psychologists, as a rule, are
ready to admit this function, of the vision of the terms or
matters meant, as something distinct from the knowledge
about them and of their relations *inter se.* Thought with
the former function is sensational, with the latter, intellectual. Our earliest thoughts are almost exclusively sensational. They merely give us a set of *thats,* or *its,* of subjects

---

* Those who wish a fuller treatment than Martin's Human Body affords
may be recommended to Bernstein's 'Five Senses of Man,' in the International Scientific Series, or to Ladd's or Wundt's Physiological Psychology.
The completest compendium is L. Hermann's Handbuch der Physiologie,
vol. III.

of discourse, with their relations not brought out.   The first
time we see *light*, in Condillac's phrase we *are* it rather
rather than see it.   But all our later optical knowledge is
about what this experience gives.   And though we were
struck blind from that first moment, our scholarship in the
subject would lack no essential feature so long as our memory remained.   In training-institutions for the blind they
teach the pupils as much *about* light as in ordinary schools.
Reflection, refraction, the spectrum, the ether-theory, etc.,
are all studied.   But the best taught born-blind pupil of
such an establishment yet lacks a knowledge which the
least instructed seeing baby has.   They can never show him
what light is in its 'first intention'; and the loss of that
sensible knowledge no book-learning can replace.   All this
is so obvious that we usually find sensation 'postulated'
as an element of experience, even by those philosophers who
are least inclined to make much of its importance, or to
pay respect to the knowledge which it brings.*

---

* " The sensations which we *postulate* as the signs or occasions of our
perceptions " (A. Seth: Scottish Philosophy, p. 89).   " Their existence is
supposed only because, without them, it would be impossible to account
for the complex phenomena which are directly present in consciousness "
(J. Dewey: Psychology, p. 34).   Even as great an enemy of Sensation as
T. H. Green has to allow it a sort of hypothetical existence under protest.
" Perception presupposes feeling " (Contemp. Review, vol. xxxi. p. 747).
Cf. also such passages as those in his Prolegomena to Ethics, §§ 48, 49.—
Physiologically, the sensory and the reproductive or associative processes
may wax and wane independently of each other.   Where the part directly
due to stimulation of the sense-organ preponderates, the thought has a
sensational character, and differs from other thoughts in the sensational
direction.   Those thoughts which lie farthest in that direction we call *sen-*
sations, for practical convenience, just as we call *conceptions* those which
lie nearer the opposite extreme.   But we no more have conceptions pure
than we have pure sensations.   Our most rarefied intellectual states involve
some bodily sensibility, just as our dullest feelings have some intellectual
scope.   Common-sense and common psychology express this by saying
that the mental state is composed of distinct fractional *parts*, one of which
is sensation, the other conception.   We, however, who believe every
mental state to be an integral thing (p. 276) cannot talk thus, but must
speak of the degree of sensational or intellectual character, or function, of
the mental state.   Professor Hering puts, as usual, his finger better upon
the truth than any one else.   Writing of visual perception, he says : " It
is inadmissible in the present state of our knowledge to assert that first
and last the same retinal picture arouses exactly the same *pure sensation*,

But the trouble is that most, if not all, of those who admit it, admit it as a fractional *part* of the thought, in the old-fashioned atomistic sense which we have so often criticised.

Take the pain called toothache for example. Again and again we feel it and greet it as the same real item in the universe. We must therefore, it is supposed, have a distinct pocket for it in our mind into which it and nothing else will fit. This pocket, when filled, is the sensation of toothache; and must be either filled or half-filled whenever and under whatever form toothache is present to our thought, and whether much or little of the rest of the mind be filled at the same time. Thereupon of course comes up the paradox and mystery: If the knowledge of toothache be pent up in this separate mental pocket, how can it be known *cum alio* or brought into one view with anything else? This pocket knows nothing else; no other part of the mind knows toothache. The knowing of toothache *cum alio* must be a miracle. And the miracle must have an Agent. And the Agent must be a Subject or Ego ' out of time,'—and all the rest of it, as we saw in Chapter X. And then begins the well-worn round of recrimination between the sensationalists and the spiritualists, from which we are saved by our determination from the outset to accept the psychological point of view, and to admit knowledge whether of simple toothaches or of philosophic systems as an ultimate fact. There are realities and there are ' states of mind,' and the latter know the former; and it is just as wonderful for a state of mind to be a ' sensation ' and know a simple pain as for it to be a thought and know a system

---

but that this sensation, in consequence of practice and experience, is differently *interpreted* the last time, and elaborated into a different perception from the first. For the only real *data* are, on the one hand, the physical picture on the retina,—and that is both times the same; and, on the other hand, the resultant state of consciousness (*ausgelöste Empfindungscomplex*) —and that is both times distinct. *Of any third thing, namely, a pure sensation thrust between the retinal and the mental pictures, we know nothing. We can then, if we wish to avoid all hypothesis, only say that the nervous apparatus reacts upon the same stimulus differently the last time from the first, and that in consequence the consciousness is different too.*" (Hermann's Hdbch., III. I. 567-8.)

of related things.* But there is no reason to suppose that
when different states of mind know different things about
the same toothache, they do so by virtue of their all *containing* faintly or vividly the original pain. Quite the reverse. The by-gone sensation of my gout was painful, as
Reid somewhere says ; the *thought* of the same gout as by-
gone is pleasant, and in no respect resembles the earlier
mental state.

Sensations, then, first make us acquainted with innumerable things, and then are replaced by thoughts which
know the same things in altogether other ways. And
Locke's main doctrine remains eternally true, however
hazy some of his language may have been, that

"though there be a great number of considerations wherein things may
be compared one with another, and so a multitude of relations ; yet
they all *terminate in*, and are concerned about, those simple ideas †
either of sensation or reflection, which I think to be the whole materials
of all our knowledge. . . . The simple ideas we receive from sensation
and reflection are the *boundaries* of our thoughts ; beyond which, the
mind whatever efforts it would make, is not able to advance one jot ; nor
can it make any discoveries when it would pry into the nature and
hidden causes of those ideas." ‡

The nature and hidden causes of ideas will never be
unravelled till the *nexus* between the brain and consciousness is cleared up. All we can say now is that sensations
are *first* things in the way of consciousness. Before conceptions can come, sensations must have come ; but before
sensations come, no psychic fact need have existed, a nerve-
current is enough. If the nerve-current be not given,
nothing else will take its place. To quote the good Locke
again :

"It is not in the power of the most exalted wit or enlarged understanding, by any quickness or variety of thoughts, to invent or frame

---

* Yet even writers like Prof. Bain will deny, in the most gratuitous
way, that sensations know anything. "It is evident that the lowest or
most restricted form of sensation does not contain an element of knowledge. The mere state of mind called the sensation of scarlet is not knowledge, although a necessary preparation for it." 'Is not knowledge *about*
scarlet' is all that Professor Bain can rightfully say.

† By simple ideas of sensation Locke merely means sensations.

‡ Essay c. H. U., bk. II. ch. XXIII. § 29 ; ch. XXV. § 9.

one new simple idea [i.e. sensation] in the mind. . . . I would have any one try to fancy any taste which had never affected his palate, or frame the idea of a scent he had never smelt ; and when he can do this, I will also conclude that a blind man hath ideas of colors, and a deaf man true distinct notions of sounds." *

The brain is so made that all currents in it run one way. Consciousness of some sort goes with all the currents, but it is only when new currents are entering that it has the sensational *tang*. And it is only then that consciousness directly *encounters* (to use a word of Mr. Bradley's) a reality outside itself.

The difference between such encounter and all conceptual knowledge is very great. A blind man may know all *about* the sky's blueness, and I may know all *about* your toothache, conceptually ; tracing their causes from primeval chaos, and their consequences to the crack of doom. But so long as he has not felt the blueness, nor I the toothache, our knowledge, wide as it is, of these realities, will be hollow and inadequate. Somebody must *feel* blueness, somebody must *have* toothache, to make human knowledge of these matters real. Conceptual systems which neither began nor left off in sensations would be like bridges without piers. Systems about fact must plunge themselves into sensation as bridges plunge their piers into the rock. Sensations are the stable rock, the *terminus a quo* and the *teminus ad quem* of thought. To find such termini is our aim with all our theories—to conceive first when and where a certain sensation may be had, and then to have it. Finding it stops discussion. Failure to find it kills the false conceit of knowledge. Only when you deduce a possible sensation for me from your theory, and give it to me when and where the theory requires, do I begin to be sure that your thought has anything to do with truth.

Pure sensations can only be realized in the earliest days of life. They are all but impossible to adults with memories and stores of associations acquired. Prior to all impressions on sense-organs the brain is plunged in deep sleep and consciousness is practically non-existent. Even the first weeks

---

* *Op. cit.* bk. ii. ch. ii. § 2.

after birth are passed in almost unbroken sleep by human infants. It takes a strong message from the sense-organs to break this slumber. In a new-born brain this gives rise to an absolutely pure sensation. But the experience leaves its 'unimaginable touch' on the matter of the convolutions, and the next impression which a sense-organ transmits produces a cerebral reaction in which the awakened vestige of the last impression plays its part. Another sort of feeling and a higher grade of cognition are the consequence; and the complication goes on increasing till the end of life, no two successive impressions falling on an identical brain, and no two successive thoughts being exactly the same. (See above, p. 230 ff.)

The first sensation which an infant gets is for him the Universe. And the Universe which he later comes to know is nothing but an amplification and an implication of that first simple germ which, by accretion on the one hand and intussusception on the other, has grown so big and complex and articulate that its first estate is unrememberable. In his dumb awakening to the consciousness of *something there,* a mere *this* as yet (or something for which even the term *this* would perhaps be too discriminative, and the intellectual acknowledgment of which would be better expressed by the bare interjection 'lo!'), the infant encounters an object in which (though it be given in a pure sensation) all the 'categories of the understanding' are contained. *It has objectivity, unity, substantiality, causality, in the full sense in which any later object or system of objects has these things.* Here the young knower meets and greets his world; and the miracle of knowledge bursts forth, as Voltaire says, as much in the infant's lowest sensation as in the highest achievement of a Newton's brain. The physiological condition of this first sensible experience is probably nerve-currents coming in from many peripheral organs at once. Later, the one confused Fact which these currents cause to appear is perceived to be many facts, and to contain many qualities.* For as the currents vary, and the brain-paths

---

* "So far is it from being true that we necessarily have as many feelings in consciousness at one time as there are inlets to the sense then played upon, that it is a fundamental law of pure sensation that each momentary

are moulded by them, other thoughts with other 'objects' come, and the 'same thing' which was apprehended as a present *this* soon figures as a past *that*, about which many unsuspected things have come to light. The principles of this development have been laid down already in Chapters XII and XIII, and nothing more need here be added to that account.

"THE RELATIVITY OF KNOWLEDGE."

To the reader who is tired of so much *Erkenntnisstheoric* I can only say that I am so myself, but that it is indispensable, in the actual state of opinions about Sensation, to try to clear up just what the word means. Locke's pupils seek to do the impossible with sensations, and against them we must once again insist that sensations 'clustered together' cannot build up our more intellectual states of mind. Plato's earlier pupils used to admit Sensation's existence, grudgingly, but they trampled it in the dust as something corporeal, non-cognitive, and vile.* His latest followers

---

state of the organism yields but one feeling, however numerous may be its parts and its exposures. . . . To this original Unity of consciousness it makes no difference that the tributaries to the single feeling are beyond the organism instead of within it, in an outside object with several sensible properties, instead of in the living body with its several sensitive functions. . . . The unity therefore is not made by 'association' of several components; but the plurality is formed by *dissociation* of unsuspected varieties within the unity; the substantive thing being no product of synthesis, but the residuum of differentiation." (J. Martineau: A Study of Religion (1888), p. 192–4.) Compare also F. H. Bradley, Logic, book i. chap. ii.

* Such passages as the following abound in anti-sensationalist literature: "Sense is a kind of dull, confused, and stupid perception obtruded upon the soul from without, whereby it perceives the alterations and motions within its own body, and takes cognizance of individual bodies existing round about it, but does not clearly comprehend what they are nor penetrate into the nature of them, it being intended by nature, as Plotinus speaks, not so properly for *knowledge* as for the *use of the body*. For the soul suffering under that which it perceives by way of *passion* cannot master or *Conquer* it, that is to say, know or understand it. For so Anaxagoras in Aristotle very fitly expresses the nature of knowledge and intellection under the notion of *Conquering*. Wherefore it is necessary, since the mind understands all things, that it should be free from mixture and passion, for this end, as Anaxagoras speaks, that it may be able to *master and conquer* its objects, that is to say, to *know and understand* them. In like manner Plotinus, in his book of Sense and Memory, makes to *suffer* and to *be conquered* all one, as also to *know* and to *conquer;* for which reason he concludes that

seem to seek to crowd it out of existence altogether. The
only reals for the neo-Hegelian writers appear to be *relations*, relations without terms, or whose terms are only
speciously such and really consist in knots, or gnarls of
relations finer still *in infinitum.*

"Exclude from what we have considered real all qualities constituted by relation, we find that none are left." "Abstract the many
relations from the one thing and there is nothing. . . . Without the
relations it would not exist at all." * "The single feeling is nothing

---

that which suffers doth not know. . . . Sense that suffers from external
objects lies as it were prostrate under them, and is overcome by them.
. . . Sense therefore is a certain kind of drowsy and somnolent perception of that passive part of the soul which is as it were asleep in the body,
arid acts concretely with it. . . . It is an energy arising from the body and
a certain kind of drowsy or sleeping life of the soul blended together
with it. The perceptions of which compound, or of the soul as it were half
asleep and half awake, are confused, indistinct, turbid, and encumbered
cogitations very different from the energies of the noetical part, . . . which
are free, clear, serene, satisfactory, and awakened cogitations. That is to
say, knowledges." Etc., etc., etc. (R. Cudworth: Treatise concerning
Eternal and Immutable Morality, bk III. chap. II.) Similarly Malebranche: "THÉODORE.—Oh, oh, Ariste! God knows pain, pleasure, warmth,
and the rest. But he does not feel these things. He knows pain, since he
knows what that modification of the soul is in which pain consists. He
knows it because he alone causes it in us (as I shall presently prove), and he
knows what he does. In a word, he knows it because his knowledge has
no bounds. But he does not feel it, for if so he would be unhappy. To
know pain, then, is not to feel it.   ARISTE.—That is true. But to feel it
is to know it, is it not?   THÉODORE.—No indeed, since God does not feel
it in the least, and yet he knows it perfectly. But in order not to quibble
about terms, if you will have it that to feel pain is to know it, agree at least
that it is not to know it clearly, that it is not to know it by light and by
evidence—in a word, that it is not to know its nature; in other words and to
speak exactly, it is not to know it at all. To feel pain, for example, is to
feel ourselves unhappy without well knowing either what we are or what
is this modality of our being which makes us unhappy. . . . Impose silence
on your senses, your imagination, and your passions, and you will hear the
pure voice of inner truth, the clear and evident replies of our common master. Never confound the evidence which results from the comparison of
ideas with the liveliness of the sensations which touch and thrill you. The
livelier our sensations and feelings (*sentiments*) are, the more darkness do
they shed. The more terrible or agreeable are our phantoms, and the more
body and reality they appear to have, the more dangerous are they and fit
to lead us astray." (Entretiens sur la Métaphysique, 3me Entretien, *ad
init.*) Malebranche's Theodore prudently does not try to explain how
God's 'infinite felicity' is compatible with his not feeling joy.

* Green: Prolegomena, §§ 20, 28.

real." "On the recognition of relations as constituting the *nature* of ideas, rests the possibility of any tenable theory of their reality."

Such quotations as these from the late T. H. Green* would be matters of curiosity rather than of importance, were it not that sensationalist writers themselves believe in a so-called 'Relativity of Knowledge,' which, if they only understood it, they would see to be identical with Professor Green's doctrine. They tell us that the relation of sensations to each other is something belonging to their essence, and that no one of them has an absolute content:

"That, e.g., black can only be felt in contrast to white, or at least in distinction from a paler or a deeper black; similarly a tone or a sound only in alternation with others or with silence; and in like manner a smell, a taste, a touch, only, so to speak, *in statu nascendi*, whilst, when the stimulus continues, all sensation disappears. This all seems at first sight to be splendidly consistent both with itself and with the facts. But looked at more closely, it is seen that neither is the case." †

---

* Introd. to Hume, §§ 146, 188. It is hard to tell just what this apostolic human being but strenuously feeble writer means by relation. Sometimes it seems to stand for system of related fact. The ubiquity of the 'psychologist's fallacy' (see p. 196) in his pages, his incessant leaning on the confusion between the thing known, the thought that knows it, and the farther things known about that thing and about that thought by later and additional thoughts, make it impossible to clear up his meaning. Compare, however, with the utterances in the text such others as these: "The waking of Self-consciousness from the sleep of sense is an absolute new beginning, and nothing can come within the 'crystal sphere' of intelligence except as it is determined by intelligence. What sense is to sense is nothing for thought. What sense is to thought, it is as determined *by* thought. There can, therefore, be no 'reality' in sensation to which the world of thought can be referred." (Edward Caird's Philosophy of Kant, 1st ed. pp. 393-4.) "When," says Green again, "feeling a pain or pleasure of heat, I perceive it to be connected with the action of approaching the fire, am I not perceiving a relation *of which one constituent, at any rate, is a simple sensation? The true answer is, No.*" "Perception, in its simplest form . . . —perception as the first sight or touch of an object in which nothing but what is seen or touched is recognized—*neither is nor contains sensation*" (Contemp. Rev., XXXI. pp. 746, 750.) "Mere sensation is in truth a phrase that represents no reality." "Mere feeling, then, as a mat̲ter unformed by thought, has no place in the world of facts, in the cosmos of possible experience." (Prolegomena to Ethics, §§ 46, 50.)—I have expressed myself a little more fully on this subject in Mind, x. 27 ff.

† Stumpf: Tonpsychologie, I. pp. 7, 8. Hobbes's phrase, *sentire semper idem et non sentire ad idem recidunt*, is generally treated as the original statement of the relativity doctrine. J. S. Mill (Examn. of Hamilton, p. 6)

The two leading facts from which the doctrine of universal relativity derives its wide-spread credit are these:

1) The *psychological fact* that so much of our actual knowledge *is* of the relations of things—even our simplest sensations in adult life are habitually referred to classes as we take them in; and

2) The *physiological fact* that our senses and brain must have periods of change and repose, else we cease to feel and think.

Neither of these facts proves anything about the presence or non-presence to our mind of absolute qualities with which we become sensibly acquainted. Surely not the psychological fact; for our inveterate love of relating and comparing things does not alter the intrinsic qualities or nature of the things compared, or undo their absolute givenness. And surely not the physiological fact; for the length of time during which we can feel or attend to a quality is altogether irrelevant to the intrinsic constitution of the quality felt. The time, moreover, is long enough in many instances, as sufferers from neuralgia know.* And the doctrine of relativity, not proved by these facts, is flatly disproved by other facts even more patent. So far are we from not knowing (in the words of Professor Bain) "any one thing by itself, but only the difference between it and another thing," that if this were true the whole edifice of our knowledge would collapse. If all we felt were the *difference* between the *C* and *D*, or *c* and *d*, on the musical scale, that being the same in the two pairs of notes, the pairs themselves would be the same, and language could get along without substantives. But Professor Bain does not mean seriously what he says, and we need spend no more time on this vague and popular form of the doctrine.† The facts which seem to hover before the minds

---

and Bain (Senses and Intellect, p. 321; Emotions and Will, pp. 550, 570–2; Logic, ɪ. p. 2; Body and Mind, p. 81) are subscribers to this doctrine. Cf. also J. Mill's Analysis, J. S. Mill's edition, ɪɪ. 11, 12.

* We can steadily hear a note for half an hour. The differences between the senses are marked. Smell and taste seem soon to get fatigued.

† In the popular mind it is mixed up with that entirely different doctrine of the ' Relativity of Knowledge ' preached by Hamilton and Spencer. This doctrine says that our knowledge is relative *to us*, and is not of the

of its champions are those which are best described under the head of a physiological law.

THE LAW OF CONTRAST.

I will first enumerate the main facts which fall under this law, and then remark upon what seems to me their significance for psychology.*

[Nowhere are the phenomena of contrast better exhibited, and their laws more open to accurate study, than in connection with the sense of sight. Here both kinds—simultaneous and successive—can easily be observed, for they are of constant occurrence. Ordinarily they remain unnoticed, in accordance with the general law of economy which causes us to select for conscious notice only such elements of our object as will serve us for æsthetic or practical utility, and to neglect the rest; just as we ignore the double images, the *mouches volantes*, etc., which exist for everyone, but which are not discriminated without careful attention. But by attention we may easily discover the general facts involved in contrast. We find that *in general the color and brightness of one object always apparently affect the color and brightness of any other object seen simultaneously with it or immediately after.*

In the first place, if we look for a moment at any surface and then turn our eyes elsewhere, the complementary color and opposite degree of brightness to that of the first surface tend to mingle themselves with the color and the brightness of the second. This is *successive contrast.* It finds its explanation in the fatigue of the organ of sight, causing it to respond to any particular stimulus less and less readily the longer such stimulus continues to act. This is shown clearly in the very marked changes which occur in case of continued fixation of one particular point of any field. The field darkens slowly, becomes more and more indistinct, and finally, if one is practised enough in holding the eye per-

---

object as the latter is in itself. It has nothing to do with the question which we have been discussing, of whether our objects of knowledge contain absolute terms or consist altogether of relations.

* What follows in brackets, as far as p. 27, is from the pen of my friend and pupil Mr. E. B. Delabarre.

fectly steady, slight differences in shade and color may entirely disappear. If we now turn aside the eyes, a negative after-image of the field just fixated at once forms, and mingles its sensations with those which may happen to come from anything else looked at. This influence is distinctly evident only when the first surface has been 'fixated' without movement of the eyes. It is, however, none the less present at all times, even when the eye wanders from point to point, causing each sensation to be modified more or less by that just previously experienced. On this account successive contrast is almost sure to be present in cases of simultaneous contrast, and to complicate the phenomena.

A *visual image is modified not only by other sensations just previously experienced, but also by all those experienced simultaneously with it, and especially by such as proceed from contiguous portions of the retina.* This is the phenomenon of *simultaneous contrast.* In this, as in successive contrast, both brightness and hue are involved. A bright object appears still brighter when its surroundings are darker than itself, and darker when they are brighter than itself. Two colors side by side are apparently changed by the admixture, with each, of the complement of the other. And lastly, a gray surface near a colored one is tinged with the complement of the latter.*

The phenomena of simultaneous contrast in sight are so complicated by other attendant phenomena that it is diffi-

---

* These phenomena have close analogues in the phenomena of contrast presented by the temperature-sense (see W. Preyer in Archiv f. d. ges. Phys., Bd. xxv. p. 79 ff.). Successive contrast here is shown in the fact that a warm sensation appears warmer if a cold one has just previously been experienced ; and a cold one colder, if the preceding one was warm. If a finger which has been plunged in hot water, and another which has been in cold water, be both immersed in lukewarm water, the same water appears cold to the former finger and warm to the latter. In simultaneous contrast, a sensation of warmth on any part of the skin tends to induce the sensation of cold in its immediate neighborhood ; and *vice versâ.* This may be seen if we press with the palm on two metal surfaces of about an inch and a half square and three-fourths inch apart ; the skin between them appears distinctly warmer. So also a small object of exactly the temperature of the palm appears warm if a cold object, and cold if a warm object, touch the skin near it.

cult to isolate them and observe them in their purity. Yet it is evidently of the greatest importance to do so, if one would conduct his investigations accurately. Neglect of this principle has led to many mistakes being made in accounting for the facts observed. As we have seen, if the eye is allowed to wander here and there about the field as it ordinarily does, successive contrast results and allowance must be made for its presence. It can be avoided only by carefully fixating with the well-rested eye a point of one field, and by then observing the changes which occur in this field when the contrasting field is placed by its side. Such a course will insure pure simultaneous contrast. But even thus it lasts in its purity for a moment only. It reaches its maximum of effect immediately after the introduction of the contrasting field, and then, if the fixation is continued, it begins to weaken rapidly and soon disappears ; thus undergoing changes similar to those observed when any field whatever is fixated steadily and the retina becomes fatigued by unchanging stimuli. If one continues still further to fixate the same point, the color and brightness of one field tend to spread themselves over and mingle with the color and brightness of the neighboring fields, thus substituting ' *simultaneous induction* ' for simultaneous contrast.

Not only must we recognize and eliminate the effects of successive contrast, of temporal changes due to fixation, and of simultaneous induction, in analyzing the phenomena of simultaneous contrast, but we must also take into account *various other influences which modify its effects.* Under favorable circumstances the contrast-effects are very striking, and did they always occur as strongly they could not fail to attract the attention. But they are not always clearly apparent, owing to various disturbing causes which form no exception to the laws of contrast, but which have a modifying effect on its phenomena. When, for instance, the ground observed has many distinguishable features—a *coarse grain, rough surface, intricate pattern,* etc.—the contrast effect appears weaker. This does not imply that the effects of contrast are absent, but merely that the resulting sensations are overpowered by the many other stronger sensations which entirely occupy the attention. On such a ground a faint negative after-image—undoubtedly due to retinal modifications—may become invisible; and even weak objective differences in color may become imperceptible. For example, a faint spot or grease-stain on woollen cloth, easily seen at a distance, when the fibres are not distinguishable, disappears when closer examination reveals the intricate nature of the surface.

Another frequent cause of the apparent absence of contrast is the presence of narrow dark intermediate fields, such as are formed by *bordering a field with black lines, or by the shaded contours of objects.* When such fields interfere with the contrast, it is because black and white can absorb much color without themselves becoming clearly colored; and because such lines separate other fields too far for them to distinctly influence one another. Even weak objective differences in color may be made imperceptible by such means.

A third case where contrast does not clearly appear is where the *color of the contrasting fields is too weak or too intense,* or where there is *much difference in brightness between the two fields.* In the latter case, as can easily be shown, it is the contrast of brightness which interferes with the color-contrast and makes it imperceptible. For this reason contrast shows best between fields of about equal brightness. But the intensity of the color must not be too great, for then its very darkness necessitates a dark contrasting field which is too absorbent of induced color to allow the contrast to appear strongly. The case is similar if the fields are too light.

To obtain the best contrast-effects, therefore, the contrasting fields should be near together, should not be separated by shadows or black lines, should be of homogeneous texture, and should be of about equal brightness and medium intensity of color. Such conditions do not often occur naturally, the disturbing influences being present in case of almost all ordinary objects, thus making the effects of contrast far less evident. To eliminate these disturbances and to produce the conditions most favorable for the appearance of good contrast-effects, various experiments have been devised, which will be explained in comparing the rival theories of explanation.

There are *two theories—the psychological and the physiological*—which attempt to explain the phenomena of contrast.

Of these the *psychological one* was the first to gain prominence. *Its most able advocate has been Helmholtz. It explains contrast as a* DECEPTION OF JUDGMENT. In ordinary life our sensations have interest for us only so far as they give us practical knowledge. Our chief concern is to recognize objects, and we have no occasion to estimate exactly their absolute brightness and color. Hence we gain no facility in so doing, but neglect the constant changes in their shade, and are very uncertain as to the exact degree of their brightness or tone of their color. When objects are near one another "we are inclined to consider those differences which are clearly and surely perceived as greater than those which appear uncertain in perception or which must be judged by aid of memory," * just as we see a medium-sized man taller than he really is when he stands beside a short man. Such deceptions are more easily possible in the judgment of small differences than of large ones; also where there is but one element of difference instead of many. In a large number of cases of contrast, in all of which a whitish spot is surrounded on all sides by a colored surface—Meyer's experiment, the mirror experiment, colored shadows, etc., soon to be described—the contrast is produced, according to Helmholtz, by the fact that "a colored illumination or a transparent colored covering appears to be spread out over the field, and observation does not show directly that it fails on the white spot." † We therefore believe that we see the latter through the former color. Now

"Colors have their greatest importance for us in so far as they are properties of bodies and can serve as signs for the recognition of bodies. . . . We have become accustomed, in forming a judgment in regard to the colors of bodies, to eliminate the varying brightness and

---

* Helmholtz, Physiolog. Optik, p. 392.
† *Loc. cit.* p. 407.

color of the illumination. We have sufficient opportunity to investigate the same colors of objects in full sunshine, in the blue light of the clear sky, in the weak white light of a cloudy day, in the reddish-yellow light of the sinking sun or of the candle. Moreover the colored reflections of surrounding objects are involved. Since we see the same colored objects under these varying illuminations, we learn to form a correct conception of the color of the object in spite of the difference in illumination, i.e. to judge how such an object would appear in white illumination ; and since only the constant color of the object interests us, we do not become conscious of the particular sensations on which our judgment rests. So also we are at no loss, when we see an object through a colored covering, to distinguish what belongs to the color of the covering and what to the object. In the experiments mentioned we do the same also where the covering over the object is not at all colored, because of the deception into which we fall, and in consequence of which we ascribe to the body a false color, the color complementary to the colored portion of the covering." *

We think that we see the complementary color through the colored covering,—for these two colors together would give the sensation of white which is actually experienced. If, however, in any way the white spot is recognized as an independent object, or if it is compared with another object known to be white, our judgment is no longer deceived and the contrast does not appear.

"As soon as the contrasting field is recognized as an independent body which lies above the colored ground, or even through an adequate tracing of its outlines is seen to be a separate field, the contrast disappears. Since, then, the judgment of the spatial position, the material independence, of the object in question is decisive for the determination of its color, it follows that the contrast-color arises not through an act of sensation but through an act of judgment." †

In short, the apparent change in color or brightness through contrast is due to no change in excitation of the organ, to no change in sensation; but in consequence of a false judgment the unchanged sensation is wrongly interpreted, and thus leads to a changed *perception* of the brightness or color.

In opposition to this theory has been developed one which attempts to explain all cases of contrast as depend-

---

* *Loc. cit.* p. 408.
† *Loc. cit.* p. 406.

ing purely on *physiological action of the terminal apparatus of vision.* *Hering is the most prominent supporter of this view.* By great originality in devising experiments and by insisting on rigid care in conducting them, he has been able to detect the faults in the psychological theory and to practically establish the validity of his own. Every visual sensation, he maintains, is correlated to a physical process in the nervous apparatus. Contrast is occasioned, not by a false idea resulting from unconscious conclusions, but by the fact that the excitation of any portion of the retina—and the consequent sensation—depends not only on its own illumination, but on that of the rest of the retina as well.

"If this psycho-physical process is aroused, as usually happens, by light-rays impinging on the retina, its nature depends not only on the nature of these rays, but also on the constitution of the entire nervous apparatus which is connected with the organ of vision, and on the state in which it finds itself." *

When a limited portion of the retina is aroused by external stimuli, the rest of the retina, and especially the immediately contiguous parts, tends to react also, and in such a way as to produce therefrom the sensation of the opposite degree of brightness and the complementary color to that of the directly-excited portion. When a gray spot is seen alone, and again when it appears colored through contrast, the objective light from the spot is in both cases the same. Helmholtz maintains that the neural process and the corresponding *sensation* also remain unchanged, but are differently *interpreted ;* Hering, that the neural process and the sensation are themselves changed, and that the 'interpretation' is the direct conscious correlate of the altered retinal conditions. According to the one, the contrast is psychological in its origin ; according to the other, it is purely physiological. In the cases cited above where the contrast-color is no longer apparent—on a ground with many distinguishable features, on a field whose borders are traced with black lines, etc.,—the psychological theory, as we have seen, attributes this to the fact that under these circumstances we judge the smaller patch of color to be an

---

* E. Hering, in Hermann's Handbuch d. Physiologie, III. 1, p. 565.

independent object on the surface, and are no longer deceived in judging it to be something over which the color of the ground is drawn. The physiological theory, on the other hand, maintains that the contrast-effect is still produced, but that the conditions are such that the slight changes in color and brightness which it occasions become imperceptible.

The two theories, stated thus broadly, may seem equally plausible. Hering, however, has conclusively proved, by experiments with after-images, that the process on one part of the retina does modify that on neighboring portions, under conditions where deception of judgment is impossible.* A careful examination of the facts of contrast will show that its phenomena must be due to this cause. *In all the cases which one may investigate it will be seen that the upholders of the psychological theory have failed to conduct their experiments with sufficient care.* They have not excluded successive contrast, have overlooked the changes due to

---

* Hering : 'Zur Lehre vom Lichtsinne.'—Of these experiments the following (found on p. 24 ff.) may be cited as a typical one : "From dark gray paper cut two strips 3–4 cm. long and ¼ cm. wide, and lay them on a background of which one half is white and the other half deep black, in such a way that one strip lies on each side of the border-line and parallel to it, and at least 1 cm. distant from it. Fixate ½ to 1 minute a point on the border-line between the strips. One strip appears much brighter than the other. Close and cover the eyes, and the negative after-image appears. . . . The difference in brightness of the strips in the after-image is in general much greater than it appeared in direct vision. . . . This difference in brightness of the strips by no means always increases and decreases with the difference in brightness of the two halves of the background. . . . A phase occurs in which the difference in brightness of the two halves of the background entirely disappears, and yet both after-images of the strips are still very clear, one of them brighter and one darker than the background, which is equally bright on both halves. Here can no longer be any question of contrast-effect, because the *conditio sine qua non* of contrast, namely, the differing brightness of the ground, is no longer present. This proves that the different brightness of the after-images of the strips must have its ground in a different state of excitation of the corresponding portions of the retina, and from this follows further that both these portions of the retina were differently stimulated during the original observation ; for the different after-effect demands here a different fore-effect. . . . In the original arrangement, the objectively similar strips appeared of different brightness, because both corresponding portions of the retina were truly differently excited."

steady fixation, and have failed to properly account for the various modifying influences which have been mentioned above. We can easily establish this if we examine the most striking experiments in simultaneous contrast.

Of these one of the best known and most easily arranged is that known as *Meyer's experiment.* A scrap of gray paper is placed on a colored background, and both are covered by a sheet of transparent white paper. The gray spot then assumes a contrast-color, complementary to that of the background, which shines with a whitish tinge through the paper which covers it. Helmholtz explains the phenomenon thus :

> "If the background is green, the covering-paper itself appears to be of a greenish color. If now the substance of the paper extends without apparent interruption over the gray which lies under it, we think that we see an object glimmering through the greenish paper, and such an object must in turn be rose-red, in order to give white light. If, however, the gray spot has its limits so fixed that it appears to be an independent object, the continuity with the greenish portion of the surface fails, and we regard it as a gray object which lies on this surface." *

The contrast-color may thus be made to disappear by tracing in black the outlines of the gray scrap, or by placing above the tissue paper another gray scrap of the same degree of brightness, and comparing together the two grays. On neither of them does the contrast-color now appear.

Hering † shows clearly that this interpretation is incorrect, and that the disturbing factors are to be otherwise explained. In the first place, the experiment can be so arranged that we could not possibly be deceived into believing that we see the gray through a colored medium. Out of a sheet of gray paper cut strips 5 mm. wide in such a way that there will be alternately an empty space and a bar of gray, both of the same width, the bars being held together by the uncut edges of the gray sheet (thus presenting an appearance like a gridiron). Lay this on a colored background—e.g. green—cover both with transparent paper, and above all put a black frame which covers all the edges, leaving visible only the bars, which are now alternately

---

* Helmholtz, Physiolog. Optik, p. 407.
† In Archiv f. d. ges. Physiol., Bd. XLI. S. 1 ff.

green and gray. The gray bars appear strongly colored by contrast, although, since they occupy as much space as the green bars, we are not deceived into believing that we see the former through a green medium. The same is true if we weave together into a basket pattern narrow strips of green and gray and cover them with the transparent paper.

Why, then, if it is a true sensation due to physiological causes, and not an error of judgment, which causes the contrast, does the color disappear when the outlines of the gray scrap are traced, enabling us to recognize it as an independent object? In the first place, it does not necessarily do so, as will easily be seen if the experiment is tried. The contrast-color often remains distinctly visible in spite of the black outlines. In the second place, there are many adequate reasons why the effect should be modified. Simultaneous contrast is always strongest at the border-line of the two fields; but a narrow black field now separates the two, and itself by contrast strengthens the whiteness of both original fields, which were already little saturated in color; and on black and on white, contrast-colors show only under the most favorable circumstances. Even weak objective differences in color may be made to disappear by such tracing of outlines, as can be seen if we place on a gray background a scrap of faintly-colored paper, cover it with transparent paper and trace its outlines. Thus we see that it is not the recognition of the contrasting field as an independent object which interferes with its color, but rather a number of entirely explicable physiological disturbances.

The same may be proved in the case of holding above the tissue paper a second gray scrap and comparing it with that underneath. To avoid the disturbances caused by using papers of different brightness, the second scrap should be made exactly like the first by covering the same gray with the same tissue paper, and carefully cutting a piece about 10 mm. square out of both together. To thoroughly guard against successive contrast, which so easily complicates the phenomena, we must carefully prevent all previous excitation of the retina by colored light. This may be done by arranging thus: Place the sheet of tissue paper on a glass pane, which rests on four supports; under the paper put the first gray scrap. By means of a wire, fasten the second gray scrap 2 or 3 cm. above the glass plate. Both scraps appear exactly alike, except at the edges. Gaze now at both scraps, with eyes not exactly accommodated, so that they appear near one another, with a very narrow space between. Shove now a colored field (green) underneath the glass plate, and the contrast appears at once on both scraps. If it appears less clearly on the upper scrap, it is because of its bright and dark edges, its inequalities, its grain, etc. When the accommodation is exact, there is no essential change, although then on the upper scrap the bright edge on the side toward the light, and the dark edge on the shadow side, disturb somewhat. By continued fixation the contrast becomes weaker and finally yields to simultaneous induction, causing the scraps to become indistinguishable from the ground. Remove the green field and both scraps become green, by successive induction. If the eye moves about freely these last-named phenomena do not appear, but the contrast continues indefinitely and becomes stronger. When Helmholtz found that the contrast on the lower scrap disappeared, it was evidently because he then really held the eye fixed. This experiment may be disturbed by holding the upper scrap wrongly and by the differences in brightness of its edges, or by other inequalities, but not by that recognizing of it 'as an independent body lying above the colored ground,' on which the psychological explanation rests.

In like manner the claims of the psychological explanation can be shown to be inadequate in other cases of contrast. Of frequent use are revolving disks, which are especially efficient in showing good contrast-phenomena, because all inequalities of the ground disappear and leave a perfectly homogeneous surface. On a white disk are arranged colored sectors, which are interrupted midway by narrow black fields in such a way that when the disk is revolved the white becomes mixed with the color and the black, forming a colored disk of weak saturation on which appears a gray ring. The latter is colored by contrast with the field which surrounds it. Helmholtz explains the fact thus :

"The difference of the compared colors appears greater than it really is either because this difference, when it is the only existing one and draws the attention to itself alone, makes a stronger impression than when it is one among many, or because the different colors of the surface are conceived as alterations of the one ground-color of the surface such as might arise through shadows falling on it, through colored reflexes, or through mixture with colored paint or dust. In truth, to produce an objectively gray spot on a green surface, a reddish coloring would be necessary." *

This explanation is easily proved false by painting the disk with narrow green and gray concentric rings, and giving each a different saturation. The contrast appears though there is no ground-color, and no longer a single difference, but many. The facts which Helmholtz brings forward in support of his theory are also easily turned against him. He asserts that if the color of the ground is too intense, or if the gray ring is bordered by black circles, the contrast becomes weaker; that no contrast appears on a white scrap held over the colored field; and that the gray ring when compared with such scrap loses its contrast-color either wholly or in part. Hering points out the inaccuracy of all these claims. Under favorable conditions it is impossible to make the contrast disappear by means of black enclosing lines, although they naturally form a disturbing element; increase in the saturation of the field, if disturbance through increasing brightness-contrast is to be avoided, demands a darker gray field, on which contrast-colors are less easily perceived ; and careful use of the white scrap leads to entirely different results. The contrast-color does appear upon it when it is first placed above the colored field; but if it is carefully fixated, the contrast-color diminishes very rapidly both on it and on the ring, from causes already explained. To secure accurate observation, all complication through successive contrast should be avoided thus : first arrange the white scrap, then interpose a gray screen between it and the disk, rest the eye, set the wheel in motion, fixate the scrap, and then have the screen re-

---

* Helmholtz, *loc. cit.* p. 412.

moved. The contrast at once appears clearly, and its disappearance through continued fixation can be accurately watched.

Brief mention of a few other cases of contrast must suffice. The so-called mirror experiment consists of placing at an angle of 45° a green (or otherwise colored) pane of glass, forming an angle with two white surfaces, one horizontal and the other vertical. On each white surface is a black spot. The one on the horizontal surface is seen through the glass and appears dark green, the other is reflected from the surface of the glass to the eye, and appears by contrast red. The experiment may be so arranged that we are not aware of the presence of the green glass, but think that we are looking directly at a surface with green and red spots upon it; in such a case there is no deception of judgment caused by making allowance for the colored medium through which we think that we see the spot, and therefore the psychological explanation does not apply. On excluding successive contrast by fixation the contrast soon disappears as in all similar experiments.*

Colored shadows have long been thought to afford a convincing proof of the fact that simultaneous contrast is psychological in its origin. They are formed whenever an opaque object is illuminated from two separate sides by lights of different colors. When the light from one source is white, its shadow is of the color of the other light, and the second shadow is of a color complementary to that of the field illuminated by both lights. If now we take a tube, blackened inside, and through it look at the colored shadow, none of the surrounding field being visible, and then have the colored light removed, the shadow still appears colored, although 'the circumstances which caused it have disappeared.' This is regarded by the psychologists as conclusive evidence that the color is due to deception of judgment. It can, however, easily be shown that the persistence of the color seen through the tube is due to fatigue of the retina through the prevailing light, and that when the colored light is removed the color slowly disappears as the

---

* See Hering : Archiv. f. d. ges. Physiol., Bd. xli. S. 358 ff.

equilibrium of the retina becomes gradually restored. When successive contrast is carefully guarded against, the simultaneous contrast, whether seen directly or through the tube, never lasts for an instant on removal of the colored field. The physiological explanation applies throughout to all the phenomena presented by colored shadows. *

If we have a small field whose illumination remains constant, surrounded by a large field of changing brightness, an increase or decrease in brightness of the latter results in a corresponding apparent decrease or increase respectively in the brightness of the former, while the large field seems to be unchanged. Exner says:

" This illusion of sense shows that we are inclined to regard as constant the dominant brightness in our field of vision, and hence to refer the changing difference between this and the brightness of a limited field to a change in brightness of the latter."

The result, however, can be shown to depend not on illusion, but on actual retinal changes, which alter the sensation experienced. The irritability of those portions of the retina lighted by the large field becomes much reduced in consequence of fatigue, so that the increase in brightness becomes much less apparent than it would be without this diminution in irritability. The small field, however, shows the change by a change in the contrast-effect induced upon it by the surrounding parts of the retina.†

The above cases show clearly that *physiological processes, and not deception of judgment, are responsible for contrast of color.* To say this, however, is not to maintain that our perception of a color is never in any degree modified by our judgment of what the particular colored thing before us may be. We have unquestionable illusions of color due to wrong inferences as to what object is before us. Thus Von Kries‡ speaks of wandering through evergreen forests covered with snow, and thinking that through the interstices of the boughs he saw the deep blue of pine-clad mountains, cov-

---

* Hering: Archiv f. d. ges. Physiol., Bd. xl. S. 172 ff. ; Delabarre : American Journal of Psychology, ii. 636.

† Hering: Archiv f. d. ges. Physiol., Bd. xli. S. 91 ff.

‡ Die Gesichtsempfindungen u. ihre Analyse, p. 128.

ered with snow and lighted by brilliant sunshine ; whereas what he really saw was the white snow on trees near by, lying in shadow]. *

Such a mistake as this is undoubtedly of psychological origin. It is a wrong *classification* of the appearances, due to the arousal of intricate processes of association, amongst which is the suggestion of a different hue from that really before the eyes. In the ensuing chapters such illusions as this will be treated of in considerable detail. But it is a mistake to interpret the simpler cases of contrast in the light of such illusions as these. These illusions can be rectified in an instant, and we then wonder how they could have been. They come from insufficient attention, or from the fact that the impression which we get is a sign of more than one possible object, and can be interpreted in either way. In none of these points do they resemble simple color-contrast, which *unquestionably is a phenomenon of sensation immediately aroused.*

I have dwelt upon the facts of color-contrast at such great length because they form so good a text to comment on in my struggle against the view that sensations are immutable psychic things which coexist with higher mental functions. Both sensationalists and intellectualists agree that such sensations exist. They *fuse,* say the pure sensationalists, and *make* the higher mental function; they *are combined* by activity of the Thinking Principle, say the intellectualists. I myself have contended that they *do not exist* in or alongside of the higher mental function when that exists. The things which arouse them exist; and the higher mental function also knows these same things. But just as its knowledge of the things supersedes and displaces their knowledge, so it supersedes and displaces them, when it comes, being as much as they are a direct resultant of whatever momentary brain-conditions may obtain. The psychological theory of contrast, on the other hand, holds the sensations still to exist in themselves unchanged before the mind, whilst the 'relating activity' of the latter

---

* Mr. Delabarre's contribution ends here.

deals with them freely and settles to its own satisfaction what each shall be, in view of what the others also are. Wundt says expressly that the Law of Relativity is "not a law of sensation but a law of Apperception;" and the word Apperception connotes with him a higher intellectual spontaneity.* This way of taking things belongs with the philosophy that looks at the *data* of sense as something earthborn and servile, and the 'relating of them together' as something spiritual and free. Lo! the spirit can even change the intrinsic quality of the sensible facts themselves if by so doing it can relate them better to each other! But (apart from the difficulty of seeing how changing the sensations should relate them better) is it not manifest that the relations are part of the 'content' of consciousness, part of the 'object,' just as much as the sensations are? Why ascribe the former exclusively to the *knower* and the latter to the *known?* The *knower* is in every case a unique pulse of thought corresponding to a unique reaction of the brain upon its conditions. All that the facts of contrast show us is that the *same real thing* may give us quite different sensations when the conditions alter, and that we must therefore be careful which one to select as the thing's truest representative.

There are many other facts beside the phenomena of contrast which prove that *when two objects act together on us the sensation which either would give alone becomes a different sensation.* A certain amount of skin dipped in hot water gives the perception of a certain heat. More skin immersed makes the heat much more intense, although of course the water's heat is the same. A certain extent as well as intensity, in the quantity of the stimulus is requisite for any quality to be felt. Fick and Wunderli could not distinguish heat from touch when both were applied through a

---

* Physiol. Psych., I. 351, 458–60. The full inanity of the law of relativity is best to be seen in Wundt's treatment, where the great ' *allgemeiner Gesetz der Beziehung,*' invoked to account for Weber's law as well as for the phenomena of contrast and many other matters, can only be defined as a tendency *to feel all things in relation to each other!* Bless its little soul! But why does it change the things so, when it thus feels them in relation?

hole in a card, and so confined to a small part of the skin. Similarly there is a *chromatic minimum* of size in objects. The image they cast on the retina must needs have a certain extent, or it will give no sensation of color at all. Inversely, more intensity in the outward impression may make the subjective object more extensive. This happens, as will be shown in Chapter XIX, when the illumination is increased: The whole room expands and dwindles according as we raise or lower the gas-jet. It is not easy to explain any of these results as illusions of judgment due to the inference of a wrong objective cause for the sensation which we get. No more is this easy in the case of Weber's observation that a thaler laid on the skin of the forehead feels heavier when cold than when warm; or of Szabadföldi's observation that small wooden disks when heated to 122° Fahrenheit often feel heavier than those which are larger but not thus warmed;* or of Hall's observation that a heavy point moving over the skin seems to go faster than a lighter one moving at the same rate of speed.†

Bleuler and Lehmann some years ago called attention to a strange idiosyncrasy found in some persons, and consisting in the fact that impressions on the eye, skin, etc., were accompanied by distinct sensations of *sound.‡ Colored hearing* is the name sometimes given to the phenomenon, which has now been repeatedly described. Quite lately the Viennese aurist Urbantschitsch has proved that these cases are only extreme examples of a very general law, and that all our sense-organs influence each other's sensations.§ The hue of patches of color so distant as not to be recognized was immediately, in U.'s patients, perceived when a tuning-fork was sounded close to the ear. Sometimes, on the contrary, the field was darkened by the sound. The acuity of vision was increased, so that letters too far off to be read could be read when the tuning-fork was heard. Urbantschitsch, varying his experiments, found that their

---

* Ladd: Physiol. Psych., p. 348.
† Mind, x. 567.
‡ Zwangsmässige Lichtempfindung durch Schall (Leipzig, 1881).
§ Pflüger's Archiv, XLII. 154.

results were mutual, and that sounds which were on the
limits of audibility became audible when lights of various
colors were exhibited to the eye. Smell, taste, touch, sense
of temperature, etc., were all found to fluctuate when lights
were seen and sounds were heard. Individuals varied much
in the degree and kind of effect produced, but almost every
one experimented on seems to have been in some way
affected. The phenomena remind one somewhat of the
' dynamogenic' effects of sensations upon the strength of
muscular contraction observed by M. Féré, and later to be
described. The most familiar examples of them seem to be
the increase of *pain* by noise or light, and the increase of
nausea by all concomitant sensations. Persons suffering in
any way instinctively seek stillness and darkness.

Probably every one will agree that the best way of for-
mulating all such facts is physiological : it must be that the
cerebral process of the first sensation is reinforced or otherwise altered by the other current which comes in. No one,
surely, will prefer a psychological explanation *here.* Well,
it seems to me that *all* cases of mental reaction to a plurality of stimuli must be like these cases, and that the physiological formulation is everywhere the simplest and the
best. When simultaneous red and green light make us see
yellow, when three notes of the scale make us hear a chord,
it is not because the sensations of red and of green and of
each of the three notes enter the mind as such, and there
' combine' or 'are combined by its relating activity' into
the yellow and the chord, it is because the larger sum of
light-waves and of air-waves arouses new cortical processes,
to which the yellow and the chord directly correspond.
Even when the sensible qualities of things enter into the
objects of our highest thinking, it is surely the same. Their
several *sensations* do not continue to exist there tucked
away. They are *replaced* by the higher thought which,
although a different psychic unit from them, knows the
same sensible qualities which they know.

The principles laid down in Chapter **VI** seem then to
be corroborated in this new connection. *You cannot build
up one thought or one sensation out of many; and only direct*

experiment can inform us of what we shall perceive when we get many stimuli at once.

THE 'ECCENTRIC PROJECTION' OF SENSATIONS.

We often hear the opinion expressed that all our sensations at first appear to us as subjective or internal, and are afterwards and by a special act on our part 'extradited' or 'projected' so as to appear located in an outer world. Thus we read in Professor Ladd's valuable work that

" Sensations . . . are psychical states *whose place*—so far as they can be said to have one—*is the mind.* The transference of these sensations from mere mental states to physical processes located in the periphery of the body, or to qualities of things projected in space external to the body, is a mental act. It may rather be said to be a mental *achievement* [cf. Cudworth, above, as to knowledge being *conquering*], for it is an act which in its perfection results from a long and intricate process of development. . . . Two noteworthy stages, or ' epoch-making' achievements in the process of elaborating the presentations of sense, require a special consideration. These are ' *localization*,' or the transference of the composite sensations from mere states of the mind to processes or conditions recognized as taking place at more or less definitely fixed points or areas of the body; and ' *eccentric projection* ' (sometimes called ' eccentric perception ') or the giving to these sensations an objective existence (in the fullest sense of the word ' objective ') as qualities of objects situated within a field of space and in contact with, or more or less remotely distant from, the body." *

It seems to me that there is not a vestige of evidence for this view. It hangs together with the opinion that our sensations are originally devoid of all spatial content, † an opinion which I confess that I am wholly at a loss to understand. As I look at my bookshelf opposite I cannot frame to myself an idea, however imaginary, of any feeling which I could ever possibly have got from it except the feeling of

---

* Physiological Psychology, 385, 387. See also such passages as that in Bain : The Senses and the Intellect, pp. 364–6.

† ·· Especially must we avoid all attempts, whether avowed or concealed, to account for the *spatial* qualities of the presentations of sense by merely describing the qualities of the simple sensations and the modes of their combination. It is position and extension in space which constitutes the very peculiarity of the objects as *no longer* mere sensations or affections of the mind. As sensations, they are neither *out* of ourselves nor possessed of the qualities indicated by the word spread-out." (Ladd, *op. cit.* p. 391.)

the same big extended sort of outward fact which I now perceive. So far is it from being true that our first way of feeling things is the feeling of them as subjective or mental, that the exact opposite seems rather to be the truth. Our earliest, most instinctive, least developed kind of consciousness is the objective kind; and only as reflection becomes developed do we become aware of an inner world at all. Then indeed we enrich it more and more, even to the point of becoming idealists, with the spoils of the outer world which at first was the only world we knew. But subjective consciousness, aware of itself as subjective, does not at first exist. Even an attack of pain is surely felt at first objectively as something in space which prompts to motor reaction, and to the very end it is located, not in the mind, but in some bodily part.

" A sensation which should not awaken an impulse to move, nor any tendency to produce an outward effect, would manifestly be useless to a living creature. On the principles of evolution such a sensation could never be developed. Therefore every sensation originally refers to something external and independent of the sentient creature. Rhizopods (according to Engelmann's observations) retract their pseudopodia whenever these touch foreign bodies, even if these foreign bodies are the pseudopodia of other individuals of their own species, whilst the mutual contact of their own pseudopodia is followed by no such contraction. These low animals can therefore already feel an outer world—even in the absence of innate ideas of causality, and probably without any clear consciousness of space. In truth the conviction that something exists outside of ourselves does not come from thought. It comes from sensation; it rests on the same ground as our conviction of our own existence. . . . If we consider the behavior of new-born animals, we never find them betraying that they are first of all conscious of their sensations as purely subjective excitements. We far more readily incline to explain the astonishing certainty with which they make use of their sensations (and which is an effect of adaptation and inheritance) as the result of an inborn intuition of the outer world. . . . Instead of starting from an original pure subjectivity of sensation, and seeking how this could possibly have acquired an objective signification, we must, on the contrary, begin by the possession of objectivity by the sensation and then show how for reflective consciousness the latter becomes interpreted as an effect of the object, how in short the original immediate objectivity becomes changed into a remote one." *

---

* A. Riehl: Der Philosophischer Kriticismus, Bd. ii. Theil ii. p. 64.

Another confusion, much more common than the denial of all objective character to sensations, is the assumption that they are all originally located *inside the body* and are projected outward by a secondary act. This secondary judgment is always false, according to M. Taine, so far as the place of the sensation itself goes. But it happens to *hit* a real object which is at the point towards which the sensation is projected; so we may call its result, according to this author, a *veridical hallucination.** The word Sensation, to

---

* On Intelligence, part II. bk. II. chap. II. §§ VII, VIII. Compare such statements as these : "The consequence is that when a sensation has for its usual condition the presence of an object more or less distant from our bodies, and experience has once made us acquainted with this distance, we shall situate our sensation at this distance.—This, in fact, is the case with sensations of hearing and sight. The peripheral extremity of the acoustic nerve is in the deep-seated chamber of the ear. That of the optic nerve is in the most inner recess of the eye. But still, in our present state, we never situate our sensations of sound or color in these places, but without us, and often at a considerable distance from us. . . . All our sensations of color are thus projected out of our body, and clothe more or less distant objects, furniture, walls, houses, trees, the sky, and the rest. This is why, when we afterwards reflect on them, we cease to attribute them to ourselves; they are alienated and detached from us, so far as to appear different from us. Projected from the nervous surface in which we localize the majority of the others, the tie which connected them to the others and to ourselves is undone. . . . Thus, all our sensations are wrongly situated, and the red color is no more extended on the arm-chair than the sensation of tingling is situated at my fingers' ends. They are all situated in the sensory centres of the encephalon; all appear situated elsewhere, and a common law allots to each of them its apparent situation." (Vol. II. pp. 47–53.)—Similarly Schopenhauer : "I will now show the same by the sense of sight. The immediate *datum* is here limited to the sensation of the retina which, it is true, admits of considerable diversity, but at bottom reverts to the impression of light and dark with their shades, and that of colors. This sensation is through and through subjective, that is, inside of the organism and under the skin." (Schopenhauer : Satz vom Grunde, p. 58.) This philosopher then enumerates *seriatim* what the Intellect does to make the originally subjective sensation objective: 1) it turns it bottom side up; 2) it reduces its doubleness to singleness; 3) it changes its flatness to solidity; and 4) it projects it to a distance from the eye. Again: "*Sensations* are what we call the impressions on our senses, in so far as they come to our consciousness as states of our own body, especially of our nervous apparatus; we call them *perceptions* when we form out of them the representation of outer objects." (Helmholtz: Tonempfindungen, 1870, p. 101.) —Once more : "Sensation is always accomplished in the psychic centres, but it manifests itself at the excited part of the periphery. In other words,

begin with, is constantly, in psychological literature, used as if it meant one and the same thing with the *physical impression* either in the terminal organs or in the centres, which is its antecedent condition, and this notwithstanding that by sensation we mean a mental, not a physical, fact. But those who expressly mean by it a mental fact still leave to it a physical *place*, still think of it as objectively inhabiting the very neural tracts which occasion its appearance when they are excited; and then (going a step farther) they think that it must *place itself* where *they* place it, or be subjectively sensible of that place as its habitat in the first instance, and afterwards have to be *moved* so as to appear elsewhere.

All this seems highly confused and unintelligible. Consciousness, as we saw in an earlier chapter (p. 214) cannot properly be said to *inhabit* any place. It has dynamic relations with the brain, and cognitive relations with everything and anything. From the one point of view *we* may say that a sensation is in the same place with the brain (if we like), just as from the other point of view we may say that it is in the same place with whatever quality it may be cognizing. But the supposition that a sensation primitively *feels either itself or its object to be in the same place with the brain* is absolutely groundless, and neither *a priori* probability nor facts from experience can be adduced to show that such a deliverance forms any part of the original cognitive function of our sensibility.

Where, then, do we feel the objects of our original sensations to be ?

Certainly a child newly born in Boston, who gets a sensation from the candle-flame which lights the bedroom, or from his diaper-pin, does not feel either of these objects to

---

one is conscious of the phenomenon in the nervous centres, . . . but one perceives it in the peripheric organs. This phenomenon depends on the experience of the sensations themselves, in which there is a *reflection* of the subjective phenomenon and a tendency on the part of perception to return as it were to the external cause which has roused the mental state because the latter is connected with the former." (Sergi: Psychologie Physiologique (Paris, 1888), p. 189.)—The clearest and best passage I know is in Liebmann: Der Objective Anblick (1869), pp. 67–72, but it is unfortunately too long to quote.

be situated in longitude 72° W. and latitude 41° N. He
does not feel them to be in the third story of the house. He
does not even feel them in any distinct manner to be to the
right or the left of any of the other sensations which he
may be getting from other objects in the room at the same
time. He does not, in short, know anything *about* their
space-relations to anything else in the world. The flame
fills its own place, the pain fills its own place ; but as yet
these places are neither identified with, nor discriminated
from, any other places. That comes later. For the places
thus first sensibly known are elements of the child's space-
world which remain with him all his life ; and by memory
and later experience he learns a vast number of things *about*
those places which at first he did not know. But to the
end of time certain places of the world remain defined for
him as the places *where those sensations were*; and his only
possible answer to the question *where anything is* will be to
say '*there*,' and to name some sensation or other like those
first ones, which shall identify the spot. Space *means* but
the aggregate of all our possible sensations. There is no
duplicate space known *aliunde*, or created by an 'epoch-
making achievement' into which our sensations, originally
spaceless, are dropped. They *bring* space and all its places
to our intellect, and do not derive it thence.

By his body, then, the child later means simply *that place
where* the pain from the pin, and a lot of other sensations
like it, were or are felt. It is no more true to say that he
locates that pain in his body, than to say that he locates his
body in that pain. Both are true : that pain is part of what
he *means by the word body*. Just so by the outer world the
child means nothing more than *that place where* the candle-
flame and a lot of other sensations like it are felt. He no
more locates the candle in the outer world than he locates
the outer world in the candle. Once again, he does both ;
for the candle is part of what he *means* by 'outer world.'

This (it seems to me) will be admitted, and will (I trust)
be made still more plausible in the chapter on the Perception of Space. But the later developments of this perception are so complicated that these simple principles get

easily overlooked. One of the complications comes from the fact that things *move*, and that the original object which we feel them to be splits into two parts, one of which remains as their whereabouts and the other goes off as their quality or nature. We then contrast where they *were* with where they *are*. If *we* do not move, the sensation of *where they were* remains unchanged; but we ourselves presently move, so that that also changes; and 'where they were' becomes no longer the actual sensation which it was originally, but a sensation which we merely conceive as possible. Gradually the system of these possible sensations, takes more and more the place of the actual sensations. 'Up' and 'down' become 'subjective' notions; east and west grow more 'correct' than 'right' and 'left' etc.; and things get at last more 'truly' located by their relation to certain ideal fixed co-ordinates than by their relation either to our bodies or to those objects by which their place was originally defined. *Now this revision of our original localizations is a complex affair; and contains some facts which may very naturally come to be described as translocations whereby sensations get shoved farther off than they originally appeared.*

Few things indeed are more striking than the changeable distance which the objects of many of our sensations may be made to assume. A fly's humming may be taken for a distant steam-whistle; or the fly itself, seen out of focus, may for a moment give us the illusion of a distant bird. The same things seem much nearer or much farther, according as we look at them through one end or another of an opera-glass. Our whole optical education indeed is largely taken up with assigning their proper distances to the objects of our retinal sensations. An infant will grasp at the moon; later, it is said, he projects that sensation to a distance which he knows to be beyond his reach. In the much quoted case of the 'young gentleman who was born blind,' and who was 'couched' for the cataract by Mr. Chesselden, it is reported of the patient that "when he first saw, he was so far from making any judgment about distances, that he thought all objects whatever touched his eyes (as he expressed it) as what he felt did his skin." And other patients born blind, but relieved by surgical operation, have been described as bringing their hand close to their eyes to feel for the objects which they at first saw, and only gradually stretching out their hand when they found that no contact occurred. Many have concluded from these facts that our earliest visual objects must seem in immediate contact with our eyes.

But tactile objects also may be affected with a like ambiguity of situation.

If one of the hairs of our head be pulled, we are pretty accurately sensible of the direction of the pulling by the movements imparted to the head.* But the feeling of the pull is localized, not in that part of the hair's length which the fingers hold, but in the scalp itself. This seems connected with the fact that our hair hardly serves at all as a tactile organ. In creatures with *vibrissæ*, however, and in those quadrupeds whose whiskers are tactile organs, it can hardly be doubted that the feeling is projected out of the root into the shaft of the hair itself. We ourselves have an approach to this when the beard as a whole, or the hair as a whole, is touched. We perceive the contact at some distance from the skin.

When fixed and hard appendages of the body, like the teeth and nails, are touched, we feel the contact where it objectively is, and not deeper in, where the nerve-terminations lie. If, however, the tooth is loose, we feel two contacts, spatially separated, one at its root, one at its top.

From this case to that of a hard body not organically connected with the surface, but only accidentally in contact with it, the transition is immediate. With the point of a cane we can trace letters in the air or on a wall just as with the finger-tip; and in so doing feel the size and shape of the path described by the cane's tip just as immediately as, without a cane, we should feel the path described by the tip of our finger. Similarly the draughtsman's immediate perception seems to be of the point of his pencil, the sur-

---

* This is proved by Weber's device of causing the head to be firmly pressed against a support by another person, whereupon the direction of traction ceases to be perceived.

geon's of the end of his knife, the duellist's of the tip of his rapier as it plunges through his enemy's skin. When on the middle of a vibrating ladder, we feel not only our feet on the round, but the ladder's feet against the ground far below. If we shake a locked iron gate we feel the middle, on which our hands rest, move, but we equally feel the stability of the ends where the hinges and the lock are, and we seem to feel all three at once.* And yet the place where the contact is *received* is in all these cases the skin, whose sensations accordingly are sometimes interpreted as objects on the surface, and at other times as objects a long distance off.

We shall learn in the chapter on Space that our feelings of our own movement are principally due to the sensibility of our rotating *joints.* Sometimes by fixing the attention, say on our elbow-joint, we can feel the movement in the joint itself; but we always are simultaneously conscious of the path which during the movement our finger-tips describe through the air, and yet these same finger-tips themselves are in no way physically modified by the motion. A blow on our ulnar nerve behind the elbow is felt both there and in the fingers. Refrigeration of the elbow produces pain in the fingers. Electric currents passed through nerve-trunks, whether of cutaneous or of more special sensibility (such as the optic nerve), give rise to sensations which are vaguely localized beyond the nerve-tracts traversed. Persons whose legs or arms have been amputated are, as is well known, apt to preserve an illusory feeling of the lost hand or foot being there. Even when they do not have this feeling constantly, it may be occasionally brought back. This sometimes is the result of exciting electrically the nerve-trunks buried in the stump.

"I recently faradized," says Dr. Mitchell, "a case of disarticulated shoulder without warning my patient of the possible result. For two years he had altogether ceased to feel the limb. As the current affected the brachial plexus of nerves he suddenly cried aloud, 'Oh the hand,— the hand!' and attempted to seize the missing member. The phantom

---

* Lotze: Med. Psych., 428–433; Lipps: Grundtatsachen des Seelenlebens, 582.

I had conjured up swiftly disappeared, but no spirit could have more amazed the man, so real did it seem." *

Now the apparent position of the lost extremity varies. Often the foot seems on the ground, or follows the position of the artificial foot, where one is used. Sometimes where the arm is lost the elbow will seem bent, and the hand in a fixed position on the breast. Sometimes, again, the position is non-natural, and the hand will seem to bud straight out of the shoulder, or the foot to be on the same level with the knee of the remaining leg. Sometimes, again, the position is vague; and sometimes it is ambiguous, as in another patient of Dr. Weir Mitchell's who

"lost his leg at the age of eleven, and remembers that the foot by degrees approached, and at last reached the knee. When he began to wear an artificial leg it reassumed in time its old position, and he is never at present aware of the leg as shortened, unless for some time he talks and thinks of the stump, and of the missing leg, when . . . the direction of attention to the part causes a feeling of discomfort, and the subjective sensation of active and unpleasant movement of the toes. With these feelings returns at once the delusion of the foot as being placed at the knee."

All these facts, and others like them, can easily be described as if our sensations might be induced by circumstances to migrate from their *original locality* near the brain or near the surface of the body, and to appear farther off; and (under different circumstances) to return again after having migrated. But a little analysis of what happens shows us that this description is inaccurate.

The objectivity with which each of our sensations originally comes to us, the roomy and spatial character which is a primitive part of its content, is not in the first instance relative to any other sensation. The first time we open our eyes we get an optical object which is *a place*, but which is not yet *placed* in relation to any other object, nor identified with any place otherwise known. It is a place with which so far we are only *acquainted*. When later we know that this same place is in 'front' of us, that only means that we have learned something *about* it, namely, that it is *congruent with that*

---

* Injuries to Nerves (Philadelphia, 1872), p. 350 ff.

other place, called 'front,' which is given us by certain sensations of the arm and hand or of the head and body.   But
at the first moment of our optical experience, even though
we already had an acquaintance with our head, hand, and
body, we could not possibly know anything about their
relations to this new seen object.   It could not be immediately located in respect of *them.*   How its place agrees with
the places which their feelings yield is a matter of which
only later experience can inform us; and in the next
chapter we shall see with some detail how later experience
does this by means of discrimination, association, selection,
and other constantly working functions of the mind.   When,
therefore, the baby grasps at the moon, that does not mean
that what he sees fails to give him the sensation which he
afterwards knows as distance; it means only that he has
not learned at what *tactile or manual distance* things which appear at that *visual distance* are.*   And when a person just
operated for cataract gropes close to his face for far-off
objects, that only means the same thing.   All the ordinary
optical signs of differing distances are absent from the poor
creature's sensation anyhow.   His vision is monocular
(only one eye being operated at a time); the lens is gone,
and everything is out of focus; he feels photophobia, lachry-
mation, and other painful resident sensations of the eyeball
itself, whose place he has long since learned to know in
tactile terms; what wonder, then, that the first tactile reaction which the new sensations provoke should be one
associated with the tactile situation of the organ itself?
And as for his assertions about the matter, what wonder,
again, if, as Prof. Paul Janet says, they are still expressed
in the tactile language which is the only one he knows.
" *To be touched* means for him to receive an impression without first making a movement."   His eye gets such an
impression now; so he can only say that the objects are
'touching it.'

    " All his language, borrowed from touch, but applied to the objects
of his sight, make us think that he perceives differently from ourselves,

---

    * In reality it probably means only a restless movement of desire, which
he might make even after he had become aware of his impotence to touch
the object.

whereas, at bottom, it is only his different way of talking about the same experience." *

The other cases of translocation of our sensations are equally easily interpreted without supposing any 'projection' from a centre at which they are originally perceived. Unfortunately the details are intricate ; and what I say now can only be made fully clear when we come to the next chapter. We shall then see that we are constantly selecting certain of our sensations as *realities* and degrading others to the status of *signs* of these. When we get one of the signs we think of the reality signified ; and the strange thing is that then the reality (which need not be itself a sensation at all at the time, but only an idea) is so interesting that it acquires an hallucinatory strength, which may even eclipse that of the relatively uninteresting sign and entirely divert our attention from the latter. Thus the sensations to which our joints give rise when they rotate are signs of what, through a large number of other sensations, tactile and optical, we have come to know as the movement of the whole limb. This movement of the whole limb is what we *think of* when the joint's nerves are excited in that way ; and *its* place is so much more important than the joint's place that our sense of the latter is taken up, so to speak, into our perception of the former, and the sensation of the movement seems to diffuse itself into our very fingers and toes. But by abstracting our attention from the suggestion of the entire extremity we can perfectly well perceive the same sensation as if it were concentrated in one spot. We can identify it with a differently located tactile and visual image of 'the joint' itself.

Just so when we feel the tip of our cane against the ground. The peculiar sort of movement of the hand (impossible in one direction, but free in every other) which we experience when the tip touches 'the ground,' is a sign to us of the visual and tactile object which we already

---

* Revue Philosophique, VII. p. 1 ff., an admirable critical article, in the course of which M. Janet gives a bibliography of the cases in question. See also Dunan: *ibid.* XXV. 165-7. They are also discussed and similarly interpreted by T. K. Abbot: Sight and Touch (1864), chapter x.

know under that name. We think of ' the ground ' as being there and giving us the sensation of this kind of movement. The sensation, we say, comes *from* the ground. The ground's place seems to be its place ; although at the same time, and for very similar practical reasons, we think of another optical and tactile object, ' the hand ' namely, and consider that *its* place *also* must be the place of our sensation. In other words, we take an object or sensible content A, and confounding it with another object otherwise known, B, or with two objects otherwise known, B and C, we identify its place with their places. But in all this there is *no 'project-ing '* (such as the extradition-philosophers talk of) of A out of an *original* place ; no primitive location which it first occupied, *away from* these other sensations, has to be con-tradicted ; no natural ' centre,' from which it is expelled, exists. That would imply that A aboriginally came to us in definite local relations with other sensations, for to be *out* of B and C is to be in local relation with them as much as to be *in* them is so. But it was no more out of B and C than it was in them when it first came to us. It simply had nothing to do with them. To say that we feel a sen-sation's seat to be ' in the brain ' or ' against the eye ' or ' under the skin ' is to say as much *about* it and to deal with it in as non-primitive a way as to say that it is a mile off. These are all secondary perceptions, ways of defining the sensation's seat *per aliud.* They involve numberless associations, identifications, and imaginations, and admit a great deal of vacillation and uncertainty in the result.*

I conclude, then, that there is no truth in the ' eccentric pro-jection ' theory. It is due to the confused assumption that the bodily processes which cause a sensation must also be its seat. † But sensations have no seat in this sense. They

---

* The intermediary and shortened locations of the lost hand and foot in the amputation cases also show this. It is easy to see why the phantom foot might continue to follow the position of the artificial one. But I confess that I cannot explain its half way-positions.

† It is from this confused assumption that the time-honored riddle comes, of how, with an upside-down picture on the retina, we can see things right-side up. Our consciousness is *naïvely* supposed to inhabit the

become seats for each other, as fast as experience associates them together; but that violates no primitive seat possessed by any one of them. And though our sensations cannot then so analyze and talk of themselves, yet at their very first appearance quite as much as at any later date are they cognizant of all those qualities which we end by extracting and conceiving under the names of *objectivity, exteriority,* and *extent.* It is surely subjectivity and interiority which are the notions *latest* acquired by the human mind. *

picture and to feel the picture's position as related to other objects of space. But the truth is that the picture is non-existent either as a habitat or as any-thing else, for immediate consciousness. Our notion of it is an enormous-ly late conception. The outer object is given immediately with all those qualities which later are named and determined in relation to other sensa-tions. The 'bottom' of this object is where we see what by touch we afterwards know as our *feet,* the 'top' is the place in which we see what we know as other people's heads, etc., etc. Berkeley long ago made this matter perfectly clear (see his Essay towards a new Theory of Vision, §§ 93–98, 113–118).

* For full justification the reader must see the next chapter. He may object, against the summary account given now, that in a babe's immediate field of vision the various things which appear are located *relatively to each other* from the outset. I admit that *if discriminated,* they would appear so located. But they are parts of the content of one sensation, not sensations separately experienced, such as the text is concerned with. The fully de-veloped 'world,' in which all our sensations ultimately find location, is nothing but an imaginary object framed after the pattern of the field of vision, by the addition and continuation of one sensation upon another in an orderly and systematic way. In corroboration of my text I must refer to pp. 57–60 of Riehl's book quoted above on page 32, and to Uphues: Wahrnehmung und Empfindung (1888), especially the *Einleitung* and pp. 51–61.

CHAPTER XVIII.

IMAGINATION.

Sensations, once experienced, modify the nervous organism, so that copies of them arise again in the mind after the original outward stimulus is gone. No mental copy, however, can arise in the mind, of any kind of sensation which has never been directly excited from without.

The blind may dream of sights, the deaf of sounds, for years after they have lost their vision or hearing; * but the man *born* deaf can never be made to imagine what sound is like, nor can the man *born* blind ever have a mental vision. In Locke's words, already quoted, "the mind can frame unto itself no one new simple idea." The originals of them all must have been given from without. Fantasy, or Imagination, are the names given to the faculty of reproducing copies of originals once felt. The imagination is called 'reproductive' when the copies are literal; 'productive' when elements from different originals are recombined so as to make new wholes.

After-images belong to sensation rather than to imagination; so that the most immediate phenomena of imagination would seem to be those tardier images (due to what the Germans call *Sinnesgedächtniss*) which were spoken of in Vol. I, p. 647,—coercive hauntings of the mind by echoes of unusual experiences for hours after the latter have taken place. The phenomena ordinarily ascribed to imagination, however, are those mental pictures of possible sensible

---

* Prof. Jastrow has ascertained by statistical inquiry among the blind that if their blindness have occurred before a period embraced between the fifth and seventh years the visual centres seem to decay, and visual dreams and images are gradually outgrown. If sight is lost after the seventh year, visual imagination seems to survive through life. See Prof. J.'s interesting article on the Dreams of the Blind, in the New Princeton Review for January 1888.

experiences, to which the ordinary processes of associative thought give rise.

When represented with surroundings concrete enough to constitute a *date*, these pictures, when they revive, form *recollections*. We have already studied the machinery of recollection in Chapter XVI. When the mental pictures are of data freely combined, and reproducing no past combination exactly, we have acts of imagination properly so called.

OUR IMAGES ARE USUALLY VAGUE.

For the ordinary 'analytic' psychology, each sensibly discernible element of the object imagined is represented by its own separate idea, and the total object is imagined by a 'cluster' or 'gang' of ideas. We have seen abundant reason to reject this view (see p. 276 ff.). An imagined object, however complex, is at any one moment thought in one idea, which is aware of all its qualities together. If I slip into the ordinary way of talking, and speak of various ideas 'combining,' the reader will understand that this is only for popularity and convenience, and he will not construe it into a concession to the atomistic theory in psychology.

Hume was the hero of the atomistic theory. Not only were ideas copies of original impressions made on the sense-organs, but they were, according to him, completely adequate copies, and were all so separate from each other as to possess no manner of connection. Hume proves ideas in the imagination to be completely adequate copies, not by appeal to observation, but by *a priori* reasoning, as follows :

"The mind cannot form any notion of quantity or quality, without forming a precise notion of the degrees of each," for " 'tis confessed that no object can appear to the senses; or in other words, that no impression* can become present to the mind, without being determined in its degrees both of quantity and quality. The confusion in which impressions are sometimes involved proceeds only from their faintness and unsteadiness, not from any capacity in the mind to receive any impression, which in its real existence has no particular degree nor proportion. That is a contradiction in terms; and even implies the flattest

* Impression means sensation for Hume.

of all contradictions, *viz.*, that 'tis possible for the same thing both to
be and not to be. Now since all ideas are derived from impressions,
and are nothing but copies and representations of them, whatever is
true of the one must be acknowledged concerning the other. Impressions and ideas differ only in their strength and vivacity. The foregoing conclusion is not founded on any particular degree of vivacity. It
cannot therefore be affected by any variation in that particular. An
idea is a weaker impression; and as a strong impression must necessarily have a determinate quantity and quality, the case must be the
same with its copy or representative." *

The slightest introspective glance will show to anyone
the falsity of this opinion. Hume surely had images of
his own works without seeing distinctly every word and
letter upon the pages which floated before his mind's eye.
His dictum is therefore an exquisite example of the way in
which a man will be blinded by *a priori* theories to the
most flagrant facts. It is a rather remarkable thing, too,
that the psychologists of Hume's own empiricist school
have, as a rule, been more guilty of this blindness than
their opponents. The fundamental *facts* of consciousness
have been, on the whole, more accurately reported by the
spiritualistic writers. None of Hume's pupils, so far as I
know, until Taine and Huxley, ever took the pains to contradict the opinion of their master. Prof. Huxley in his
brilliant little work on Hume set the matter straight in the
following words :

" When complex impressions or complex ideas are reproduced as
memories, it is probable that the copies never give all the details of the
originals with perfect accuracy, and it is certain that they rarely do so.
No one possesses a memory so good, that if he has only once observed
a natural object, a second inspection does not show him something that
he has forgotten. Almost all, if not all, our memories are therefore
sketches, rather than portraits, of the originals—the salient features
are obvious, while the subordinate characters are obscure or unrepre-
sented.

" Now, when several complex impressions which are more or less
different from one another—let us say that out of ten impressions in
each, six are the same in all, and four are different from all the rest—
are successively presented to the mind, it is easy to see what must be
the nature of the result. The repetition of the six similar impressions
will strengthen the six corresponding elements of the complex idea,

* Treatise on Human Nature, part I. § VII.

which will therefore acquire greater vividness ; while the four differing impressions of each will not only acquire no greater strength than they had at first, but, in accordance with the law of association, they will all tend to appear at once, and will thus neutralize one another.

" This mental operation may be rendered comprehensible by considering what takes place in the formation of compound photographs—when the images of the faces of six sitters, for example, are each received on the same photographic plate, for a sixth of the time requisite to take one portrait. The final result is that all those points in which the six faces agree are brought out strongly, while all those in which they differ are left vague ; and thus what may be termed a *generic* portrait of the six, in contradistinction to a *specific* portrait of any one, is produced.

" Thus our ideas of single complex impressions are incomplete in one way, and those of numerous, more or less similar, complex impressions are incomplete in another way ; that is to say, they are *generic*, not *specific*. And hence it follows that our ideas of the impressions in question are not, in the strict sense of the word, copies of those impressions ; while, at the same time, they may exist in the mind independently of language.

" The generic ideas which are formed from several similar, but not identical, complex experiences are what are called *abstract* or *general* ideas ; and Berkeley endeavored to prove that all general ideas are nothing but particular ideas annexed to a certain term, which gives them a more extensive signification, and makes them recall, upon occasion, other individuals which are similar to them. Hume says that he regards this as ' one of the greatest and the most valuable discoveries that has been made of late years in the republic of letters,' and endeavors to confirm it in such a manner that it shall be ' put beyond all doubt and controversy. '

" I may venture to express a doubt whether he has succeeded in his object ; but the subject is an abstruse one ; and I must content myself with the remark, that though Berkeley's view appears to be largely applicable to such general ideas as are formed after language has been acquired, and to all the more abstract sort of conceptions, yet that general ideas of sensible objects may nevertheless be produced in the way indicated, and may exist independently of language. In dreams, one sees houses, trees, and other objects, which are perfectly recognizable as such, but which remind one of the actual objects as seen ' out of the corner of the eye,' or of the pictures thrown by a badly-focussed magic lantern. A man addresses us who is like a figure seen in twilight ; or we travel through countries where every feature of the scenery is vague ; the outlines of the hills are ill-marked, and the rivers have no defined banks. They are, in short, generic ideas of many past impressions of men, hills, and rivers. An anatomist who occupies himself intently with the examination of several specimens of some new kind of animal, in course of time acquires so vivid a conception of its form and struc-

ture that the idea may take visible shape and become a sort of waking
dream. But the figure which thus presents itself is generic, not specific. It is no copy of any one specimen, but, more or less, a mean of
the series ; and there seems no reason to doubt that the minds of children before they learn to speak, and of deaf-mutes, are peopled with
similarly generated generic ideas of sensible objects." *

Are Vague Images ' Abstract Ideas ' ?

The only point which I am tempted to criticise in this
account is Prof. Huxley's *identification of these generic images
with ' abstract or general ideas' in the sense of universal conceptions.* Taine gives the truer view. He writes :

"Some years ago I saw in England, in Kew Gardens, for the first
time, araucarias, and I walked along the beds looking at these strange
plants, with their rigid bark and compact, short, scaly leaves, of a
sombre green, whose abrupt, rough, bristling form cut in upon the fine
softly-lighted turf of the fresh grass-plot. If I now inquire what this
experience has left in me, I find, first, the sensible representation of an
araucaria ; in fact, I have been able to describe almost exactly the form
and color of the plant. But there is a difference between this representation and the former sensations, of which it is the present echo. The
internal semblance, from which I have just made my description, is
vague, and my past sensations were precise. For, assuredly, each of
the araucarias I saw then excited in me a distinct visual sensation ;
there are no two absolutely similar plants in nature ; I observed perhaps
twenty or thirty araucarias ; without a doubt each one of them differed
from the others in size, in girth, by the more or less obtuse angles of its
branches, by the more or less abrupt jutting out of its scales, by the style
of its texture ; consequently, my twenty or thirty visual sensations were
different. But no one of these sensations has completely survived in its
echo ; the twenty or thirty revivals have blunted one another ; thus
upset and agglutinated by their resemblance they are confounded
together, and my present representation is their residue only. This is
the product, or rather the fragment, which is deposited in us, when we
have gone through a series of similar facts or individuals. Of our
numerous experiences there remain on the following day four or five
more or less distinct recollections, which, obliterated themselves, leave
behind in us a simple colorless, vague representation, into which enter
as components various reviving sensations, in an utterly feeble, incomplete, and abortive state.—*But this representation is not the general and
abstract idea. It is but its accompaniment*, and, if I may say so, the
ore from which it is extracted. For the representation, though badly
sketched, is a sketch, the sensible sketch of a distinct individual. . . .
But my abstract idea corresponds to the whole class ; it differs, then,
from the representation of an individual.—Moreover, my abstract idea

* Huxley's Hume, pp. 92-94.

is perfectly clear and determinate ; now that I possess it, I never fail
to recognize an araucaria among the various plants which may be shown
me ; it differs then from the confused and floating representation I have
of some particular araucaria." *

In other words, a blurred picture is just as much a single
mental fact as a sharp picture is ; and *the use of either picture
by the mind to symbolize a whole class of individuals is a new
mental function*, requiring some other modification of consciousness than the mere perception that the picture is
distinct or not. I may bewail the indistinctness of my
mental image of my absent friend. That does not prevent
my thought from meaning *him* alone, however. And I may
mean all mankind, with perhaps a very sharp image of one
man in my mind's eye. The meaning is a function of the
more ' transitive ' parts of consciousness, the ' fringe ' of
relations which we feel surrounding the image, be the latter
sharp or dim. This was explained in a previous place (see
p. 473 ff., especially the note to page 477), and I would not
touch upon the matter at all here but for its historical
interest.

Our ideas or images of past sensible experiences may
then be either distinct and adequate or dim, blurred, and
incomplete. It is likely that the different degrees in which
different men are able to make them sharp and complete
has had something to do with keeping up such philosophic
disputes as that of Berkeley with Locke over abstract ideas.
Locke had spoken of our possessing ' the general idea of a
triangle ' which " must be neither oblique nor rectangle,
neither equilateral, equicrural, nor scalenon, but all and
none of these at once." Berkeley says :

" If any man has the faculty of framing in his mind such an idea of
a triangle as is here described, it is in vain to pretend to dispute him
out of it, nor would I go about it. All I desire is that the reader would
fully and certainly inform himself whether *he* has such an idea or no." †

Until very recent years it was supposed by all philosophers that there was a typical human mind which all individual minds were like, and that propositions of universal
validity could be laid down about such faculties as ' the

---

* On Intelligence (N. Y.), vol. II. p. 139.

† Principles, Introd. § 13. Compare also the passage quoted above,
p. 469

Imagination.' Lately, however, a mass of revelations have poured in, which make us see how false a view this is. There are imaginations, not 'the Imagination,' and they must be studied in detail.

INDIVIDUALS DIFFER IN IMAGINATION.

The first breaker of ground in this direction was Fechner, in 1860. Fechner was gifted with unusual talent for subjective observation, and in chapter XLIV of his 'Psychophysik' he gave the results of a most careful comparison of his own optical after-images, with his optical memory-pictures, together with accounts by several other individuals of their optical memory-pictures.* The result was to show a great

---

* The differences noted by Fechner between after-images and images of imagination proper are as follows :

After-images.	*Imagination-images.*
Feel coercive ;	Feel subject to our spontaneity ;
Seem unsubstantial, vaporous ;	Have, as it were, more body ;
Are sharp in outline ;	Are blurred ;
Are bright ;	Are darker than even the darkest black of the after-images ;
Are almost colorless ;	Have lively coloration ;
Are continuously enduring ;	Incessantly disappear, and have to be renewed by an effort of will. At last even this fails to revive them.
Cannot be voluntarily changed.	Can be exchanged at will for others.
Are exact copies of originals.	Cannot violate the necessary laws of appearance of their originals—e.g., a man cannot be imagined from in front and behind at once. The imagination must walk round him, so to speak ;
Are more easily got with shut than with open eyes ;	Are more easily had with open than with shut eyes ;
Seem to move when the head or eyes move ;	Need not follow movements of head or eyes.
The field within which they appear (with closed eyes) is dark, contracted, flat, close to the eyes, in front, and the images have no perspective ;	The field is extensive in three dimensions, and objects can be imagined in it above or behind almost as easily as in front.
The attention seems directed forwards towards the sense-organ, in observing after-images.	In imagining, the attention feels as if drawn backwards towards the brain.

Finally, Fechner speaks of the impossibility of attending to both after-personal diversity. " It would be interesting," he writes, " to work up the subject statistically ; and I regret that other occupations have kept me from fulfilling my earlier intention to proceed in this way."

Fechner's intention was independently executed by Mr. Galton, the publication of whose results in 1880 may be said to have made an era in descriptive Psychology.

"It is not necessary," says Galton, "to trouble the reader with my early tentative steps. After the inquiry had been fairly started it took the form of submitting a certain number of printed questions to a large number of persons. There is hardly any more difficult task than that of framing questions which are not likely to be misunderstood, which admit of easy reply, and which cover the ground of inquiry. I did my best in these respects, without forgetting the most important part of all—namely, to tempt my correspondents to write freely in fuller explanation of their replies, and on cognate topics as well. These separate letters have proved more instructive and interesting by far than the replies to the set questions.

" The first group of the rather long series of queries related to the illumination, definition, and coloring of the mental image, and were framed thus :

" ' Before addressing yourself to any of the Questions on the opposite page, think of some definite object—suppose it is your breakfast-table as you sat down to it this morning—and consider carefully the picture that rises before your mind's eye.

" ' 1. *Illumination.*—Is the image dim or fairly clear ? Is its brightness comparable to that of the actual scene ?

" ' 2. *Definition.*—Are all the objects pretty well defined at the same time, or is the place of sharpest definition at any one moment more contracted than it is in a real scene ?

" ' 3. *Coloring.*—Are the colors of the china, of the toast, bread-crust, mustard, meat, parsley, or whatever may have been on the table, quite distinct and natural ? '

" The earliest results of my inquiry amazed me. I had begun by questioning friends in the scientific world, as they were the most likely class of men to give accurate answers concerning this faculty of visual-

---

images and imagination-images at once, even when they are of the same object and might be expected to combine. All these differences are true of Fechner ; but many of them would be untrue of other persons. I quote them as a type of observation which any reader with sufficient patience may repeat. To them may be added, as a universal proposition, that afterimages seem larger if we project them on a distant screen, and smaller if we project them on a near one, whilst no such change takes place in mental pictures.

izing, to which novelists and poets continually allude, which has left an abiding mark on the vocabularies of every language, and which supplies the material out of which dreams and the well-known hallucinations of sick people are built.

" To my astonishment, I found that *the great majority of the men of science to whom I first applied protested that mental imagery was unknown to them,* and they looked on me as fanciful and fantastic in supposing that the words ' mental imagery' really expressed what I believed everybody supposed them to mean. They had no more notion of its true nature than a color-blind man, who has not discerned his defect, has of the nature of color. They had a mental deficiency of which they were unaware, and naturally enough supposed that those who affirmed they possessed it were romancing. To illustrate their mental attitude it will be sufficient to quote a few lines from the letter of one of my correspondents, who writes :

" ' These questions presuppose assent to some sort of a proposition regarding the "mind's eye," and the " images" which it sees. . . . This points to some initial fallacy. . . . It is only by a figure of speech that I can describe my recollection of a scene as a " mental image " which I can " see " with my " mind's eye." ' . . . I do not see it . . . any more than a man sees the thousand lines of Sophocles which under due pressure he is ready to repeat. The memory possesses it,' etc.

" Much the same result followed inquiries made for me by a friend among members of the French Institute.

" On the other hand, when I spoke to persons whom I met *in general society,* I found an entirely different disposition to prevail. *Many men and a yet larger number of women, and many boys and girls, declared that they habitually saw mental imagery, and that it was perfectly distinct to them and full of color.* The more I pressed and crossed-questioned them, professing myself to be incredulous, the more obvious was the truth of their first assertions. They described their imagery in minute detail, and they spoke in a tone of surprise at my apparent hesitation in accepting what they said. I felt that I myself should have spoken exactly as they did if I had been describing a scene that lay before my eyes, in broad daylight, to a blind man who persisted in doubting the reality of vision. Reassured by this happier experience, I recommenced to inquire among scientific men, and soon found scattered instances of what I sought, though in by no means the same abundance as elsewhere. I then circulated my questions more generally among my friends and through their hands, and obtained replies . . . from persons of both sexes, and of various ages, and in the end from occasional correspondents in nearly every civilized country.

" I have also received batches of answers from various educational establishments both in England and America, which were made after the masters had fully explained the meaning of the questions, and interested the boys in them. These have the merit of returns derived from a general census, which my other data lack, because I cannot for a moment suppose that the writers of the latter are a haphazard proportion of those to whom they were sent. Indeed I know of some who, disavowing all possession of the power, and of many others who, possessing it in too faint a degree to enable them to express what their experiences really were, in a manner satisfactory to themselves, sent no returns at all. Considerable statistical similarity was, however, observed between the sets of returns furnished by the schoolboys and those sent by my separate correspondents, and I may add that they accord in this respect with the oral information I have elsewhere obtained. The conformity of replies from so many different sources which was clear from the first, the fact of their apparent trustworthiness being on the whole much increased by cross-examination (though I could give one or two amusing instances of break-down), and the evident effort made to give accurate answers, have convinced me that it is a much easier matter than I had anticipated to obtain trustworthy replies to psychological questions. Many persons, especially women and intelligent children, take pleasure in introspection, and strive their very best to explain their mental processes. I think that a delight in self-dissection must be a strong ingredient in the pleasure that many are said to take in confessing themselves to priests.

" Here, then, are two rather notable results : the one is the proved facility of obtaining statistical insight into the processes of other persons' minds, whatever *a priori* objection may have been made as to its possibility ; and the other is that scientific men, as a class, have feeble powers of visual representation. There is no doubt whatever on the latter point, however it may be accounted for. My own conclusion is that an over-ready perception of sharp mental pictures is antagonistic to the acquirement of habits of highly-generalized and abstract thought, especially when the steps of reasoning are carried on by words as symbols, and that if the faculty of seeing the pictures was ever possessed by men who think hard, it is very apt to be lost by disuse. The highest minds are probably those in which it is not lost, but subordinated, and is ready for use on suitable occasions. I am, however, bound to say that the missing faculty seems to be replaced so serviceably by other modes of conception, chiefly, I believe, connected with the incipient motor sense, not of the eyeballs only but of the muscles generally, that *men who declare themselves entirely deficient in the power of seeing mental pictures can nevertheless give lifelike descriptions* of what they have seen, and can otherwise express themselves as if they were gifted with a vivid visual imagination. *They can also become painters of the rank of Royal Academicians.** . . .

---

* [I am myself a good draughtsman, and have a very lively interest in pictures, statues, architecture and decoration, and a keen sensibility to artistic effects. But I am an extremely poor visualizer, and find myself often unable to reproduce in my mind's eye pictures which I have most carefully examined.—W. J.]

"It is a mistake to suppose that sharp sight is accompanied by clear visual memory. I have not a few instances in which the independence of the two faculties is emphatically commented on ; and I have at least one clear case where great interest in outlines and accurate appreciation of straightness, squareness, and the like, is unaccompanied by the power of visualizing. Neither does the faculty go with dreaming. I have cases where it is powerful, and at the same time where dreams are rare and faint or altogether absent. One friend tells me that his dreams have not the hundredth part of the vigor of his waking fancies.

" The visualizing and the identifying powers are by no means necessarily combined. A distinguished writer on metaphysical topics assures me that he is exceptionally quick at recognizing a face that he has seen before, but that he cannot call up a mental image of any face with clearness.

" Some persons have the power of combining in a single perception more than can be seen at any one moment by the two eyes. . . .

" I find that a few persons can, by what they often describe as a kind of touch-sight, visualize at the same moment all round the image of a solid body. Many can do so nearly, but not altogether round that of a terrestrial globe. An eminent mineralogist assures me that he is able to imagine simultaneously all the sides of a crystal with which he is familiar. I may be allowed to quote a curious faculty of my own in respect to this. It is exercised only occasionally and in dreams, or rather in nightmares, but under those circumstances I am perfectly conscious of embracing an entire sphere in a single perception. It appears to lie within my mental eyeball, and to be viewed centripetally.

" This power of comprehension is practically attained in many cases by indirect methods. It is a common feat to take in the whole surroundings of an imagined room with such a rapid mental sweep as to leave some doubt whether it has not been viewed simultaneously. Some persons have the habit of viewing objects as though they were partly transparent ; thus, if they so dispose a globe in their imagination as to see both its north and south poles at the same time, they will not be able to see its equatorial parts. They can also perceive all the rooms of an imaginary house by a single mental glance, the walls and floors being as if made of glass. A fourth class of persons have the habit of recalling scenes, not from the point of view whence they were observed, but from a distance, and they visualize their own selves as actors on the mental stage. By one or other of these ways, the power of seeing the whole of an object, and not merely one aspect of it, is possessed by many persons.

" The place where the image appears to lie differs much. Most persons see it in an indefinable sort of way, others see it in front of the eye, others at a distance corresponding to reality. There exists a power which is rare naturally, but can, I believe, be acquired without much difficulty, of projecting a mental picture upon a piece of paper, and of holding it fast there, so that it can be outlined with a pencil. To this I shall recur.

"Images usually do not become stronger by dwelling on them; the first idea is commonly the most vigorous, but this is not always the case. Sometimes the mental view of a locality is inseparably connected with the sense of its position as regards the points of the compass, real or imaginary. I have received full and curious descriptions from very different sources of this strong geographical tendency, and in one or two cases I have reason to think it allied to a considerable faculty of geographical comprehension.

" The power of visualizing is higher in the female sex than in the male, and is somewhat, but not much, higher in public-school boys than in men. After maturity is reached, the further advance of age does not seem to dim the faculty, but rather the reverse, judging from numerous statements to that effect; but advancing years are sometimes accompanied by a growing habit of hard abstract thinking, and in these cases —not uncommon among those whom I have questioned—the faculty undoubtedly becomes impaired. There is reason to believe that it is very high in some young children, who seem to spend years of difficulty in distinguishing between the subjective and objective world. Language and book-learning certainly tend to dull it.

" The visualizing faculty is a natural gift, and, like all natural gifts, has a tendency to be inherited. In this faculty the tendency to inheritance is exceptionally strong, as I have abundant evidence to prove, especially in respect to certain rather rare peculiarities, . . . which, when they exist at all, are usually found among two, three, or more brothers and sisters, parents, children, uncles and aunts, and cousins.

" Since families differ so much in respect to this gift, we may suppose that races would also differ, and there can be no doubt that such is the case. I hardly like to refer to civilized nations, because their natural faculties are too much modified by education to allow of their being appraised in an off-hand fashion. I may, however, speak of the French, who appear to possess the visualizing faculty in a high degree. The peculiar ability they show in prearranging ceremonials and *fêtes* of all kinds, and their undoubted genius for tactics and strategy, show that they are able to foresee effects with unusual clearness. Their ingenuity in all technical contrivances is an additional testimony in the same direction, and so is their singular clearness of expression. Their phrase ' figurez-vous,' or ' picture to yourself,' seems to express their dominant mode of perception. Our equivalent of ' imagine ' is ambiguous.

.   .   .   .

"I have many cases of persons mentally reading off scores when playing the pianoforte, or manuscript when they are making speeches. One statesman has assured me that a certain hesitation in utterance which he has at times is due to his being plagued by the image of his manuscript speech with its original erasures and corrections. He cannot lay the ghost, and he puzzles in trying to decipher it.

"Some few persons see mentally in print every word that is uttered; they attend to the visual equivalent and not to the sound of the words, and they read them off usually as from a long imaginary strip of paper, such as is unwound from telegraphic instruments."

The reader will find further details in Mr. Galton's 'Inquiries into Human Faculty,' pp. 83–114.* I have myself for many years collected from each and all of my psychology-students descriptions of their own visual imagination ; and found (together with some curious idiosyncrasies) corroboration of all the variations which Mr. Galton reports. As examples, I subjoin extracts from two cases near the ends of the scale. The writers are first cousins, grandsons of a distinguished man of science. The one who is a good visualizer says :

"This morning's breakfast-table is both dim and bright; it is dim if I try to think of it when my eyes are open upon any object; it is perfectly clear and bright if I think of it with my eyes closed.—All the objects are clear at once, yet when I confine my attention to any one object it becomes far more distinct.—I have more power to recall color than any other one thing: if, for example, I were to recall a plate decorated with flowers I could reproduce in a drawing the exact tone, etc. The color of anything that was on the table is perfectly vivid.—There is very little limitation to the extent of my images: I can see all four sides of a room, I can see all four sides of two, three, four, even more rooms with such distinctness that if you should ask me what was in any particular place in any one, or ask me to count the chairs, etc., I could do it without the least hesitation.—The more I learn by heart the more clearly do I see images of my pages. Even before I can recite the lines I see them so that I could give them very slowly word for word, but my mind is so occupied in looking at my printed image that I have no idea of what I am saying, of the sense of it, etc. When I first found myself doing this I used to think it was merely because I knew the lines imperfectly; but I have quite convinced myself that I really do see an image. The strongest proof that such is really the fact is, I think, the following:

"I can look down the mentally seen page and see the words that *commence* all the lines, and from any one of these words I can continue

---

* See also McCosh and Osborne, Princeton Review, Jan. 1884. There are some good examples of high development of the Faculty in the London Spectator, Dec. 28, 1878, pp. 1631, 1634, Jan. 4, 11, 25, and March 18, 1879.

the line. I find this much easier to do if the words begin in a straight line than if there are breaks. Example:

Étant fait . . . . .
Tous . . . . .
A des . . . . .
Que fit . . . . .
Céres . . . . .
    Avec . . . . .
Un fleur . . . . .
    Comme . . . . .
(*La Fontaine* 8. IV.)"

The poor visualizer says :

" My ability to form mental images seems, from what I have studied of other people's images, to be defective, and somewhat peculiar. The process by which I seem to remember any particular event is not by a series of distinct images, but a sort of panorama, the faintest impressions of which are perceptible through a thick fog.—I cannot shut my eyes and get a distinct image of anyone, although I used to be able to a few years ago, and the faculty seems to have gradually slipped away. —In my most vivid dreams, where the events appear like the most real facts, I am often troubled with a dimness of sight which causes the images to appear indistinct.—To come to the question of the breakfast-table, there is nothing definite about it. Everything is vague. I cannot say *what* I see. I could not possibly count the chairs, but I happen to know that there are ten. I see nothing in detail.—The chief thing is a general impression that I cannot tell exactly what I do see. The coloring is about the same, as far as I can recall it, only very much washed out. Perhaps the only color I can see at all distinctly is that of the table-cloth, and I could probably see the color of the wall-paper if I could remember what color it was."

A person whose visual imagination is strong finds it hard to understand how those who are without the faculty can think at all. *Some people undoubtedly have no visual images at all worthy of the name,** and instead of *seeing* their breakfast-table, they tell you that they *remember* it or *know* what was on it. This knowing and remembering takes

* Take the following report from one of my students : "I am unable to form in my mind's eye any visual likeness of the table whatever. After many trials, I can only get a hazy surface, with nothing on it or about it. I can see no variety in color, and no positive limitations in extent, while I cannot see what I see well enough to determine its position in respect to my eye, or to endow it with any quality of size. I am in the same position as to the word *dog*. I cannot see it in my mind's eye at all ; and so cannot tell whether I should have to run my eye along it, if I did see it."

place undoubtedly by means of verbal images, as was explained already in Chapter IX, pp. 265–6.

The study of Aphasia (see p. 54) *has of late years shown
how unexpectedly great are the differences between individuals in
respect of imagination.* And at the same time the discrepancies between lesion and symptom in different cases of
the disease have been largely cleared up. In some individuals the habitual ' thought-stuff,' if one may so call it,
is visual; in others it is auditory, articulatory, or motor;
in most, perhaps, it is evenly mixed. The same local cerebral
injury must needs work different practical results in persons who differ in this way. In one it will throw a much-
used brain-tract out of gear; in the other it may affect an
unimportant region. A particularly instructive case was
published by Charcot in 1883.* The patient was

Mr. X., a merchant, born in Vienna, highly educated, master of
German, Spanish, French, Greek, and Latin. Up to the beginning of
the malady which took him to Professor Charcot, he read Homer at
sight. He could, starting from any verse out of the first book of the
Iliad, repeat the following verses without hesitating, by heart. Virgil
and Horace were familiar. He also knew enough of modern Greek for
business purposes. Up to within a year (from the time Charcot saw
him) he enjoyed an exceptional *visual* memory. He no sooner thought
of persons or things, but features, forms, and colors arose with the
same clearness, sharpness, and accuracy as if the objects stood before
him. When he tried to recall a fact or a figure in his voluminous
polyglot correspondence, the letters themselves appeared before him
with their entire content, irregularities, erasures and all. At school he
recited from a mentally seen page which he read off line by line and
letter by letter. In making computations, he ran his mental eye down
imaginary columns of figures, and performed in this way the most
varied operations of arithmetic. He could never think of a passage in
a play without the entire scene, stage, actors, and audience appearing
to him. He had been a great traveller. Being a good draughtsman,
he used to sketch views which pleased him; and his memory always
brought back the entire landscape exactly. If he thought of a conversation, a saying, an engagement, the place, the people, the entire scene
rose before his mind.

His *auditory memory* was always deficient, or at least secondary.
He had no taste for music.

---

* Progrès Médical, 21 juillet. I abridge from the German report of
the case in Wilbrand: Die Seelenblindheit (1887).

A year and a half previous to examination, after business-anxieties, loss of sleep, appetite, etc., he noticed suddenly one day an extraordinary change in himself. After complete confusion, there came a violent contrast between his old and his new state. Everything about him seemed so new and foreign that at first he thought he must be going mad. He was nervous and irritable. Although he saw all things distinct, he had entirely lost his memory for forms and colors. On ascertaining this, he became reassured as to his sanity. He soon discovered that he could carry on his affairs by using his memory in an altogether new way. He can now describe clearly the difference between his two conditions.

Every time he returns to A., from which place business often calls him, he seems to himself as if entering a strange city. He views the monuments, houses, and streets with the same surprise as if he saw them for the first time. Gradually, however, his memory returns, and he finds himself at home again. When asked to describe the principal public place of the town, he answered, "I know that it is there, but it is impossible to imagine it, and I can tell you nothing about it." He has often drawn the port of A. To-day he vainly tries to trace its principal outlines. Asked to draw a minaret, he reflects, says it is a square tower, and draws, rudely, four lines, one for ground, one for top, and two for sides. Asked to draw an arcade, he says, "I remember that it contains semi-circular arches, and that two of them meeting at an angle make a vault, but how it *looks* I am absolutely unable to imagine." The profile of a man which he drew by request was as if drawn by a little child; and yet he confessed that he had been helped to draw it by looking at the bystanders. Similarly he drew a shapeless scribble for a tree.

He can no more remember his wife's and children's faces than he can remember the port of A. Even after being with them some time they seem unusual to him. He forgets his own face, and once spoke to his image in a mirror, taking it for a stranger. He complains of his loss of feeling for colors. "My wife has black hair, this I know; but I can no more recall its color than I can her person and features." This visual amnesia extends to dating objects from his childhood's years—paternal mansion, etc., forgotten.

No other disturbances but this loss of visual images. Now when he seeks something in his correspondence, he must rummage among the letters like other men, until he meets the passage. He can recall only the first few verses of the Iliad, and must *grope* to read Homer, Virgil, and Horace. Figures which he adds he must now whisper to himself. He realizes clearly that he must help his memory out with auditory images, which he does with effort. *The words and expressions which he recalls seem now to echo in his ear, an altogether novel sensation for him.* If he wishes to learn by heart anything, a series of phrases for example, he must *read them several times aloud,* so as to impress his ear. When later he repeats the thing in question, the sensation of inward hearing which precedes articulation rises up in his mind. This feeling was formerly unknown to him. He speaks French fluently; but affirms that he can no longer think in French; but must get his French words by translating them from Spanish or German, the languages of his childhood. He dreams no more in visual terms, but only in words, usually Spanish words. A certain degree of verbal blindness affects him—he is troubled by the Greek alphabet, etc *

If this patient had possessed the auditory type of imagination from the start, it is evident that the injury, whatever it was, to his centres for optical imagination, would have affected his practical life much less profoundly.

" *The auditory type,*" says M. A. Binet,† " *appears to be rarer than the visual.* Persons of this type imagine what they think of in the language of sound. In order to remember a lesson they impress upon their mind, not the look of the page, but the sound of the words. They reason, as well as remember, by ear. In performing a mental addition they repeat verbally the names of the figures, and add, as it were, the sounds, without any thought of the graphic signs. Imagination also takes the auditory form. ' When I write a scene,' said Legouvé to Scribe, ' I *hear ;* but you *see.* In each phrase which I write, the voice of the personage who speaks strikes my ear. *Vous, qui êtes le théâtre même,* your actors walk, gesticulate before your eyes ; I am a *listener,* you a *spectator.*'—' Nothing more true,' said Scribe ; ' do you know where I am when I write a piece ? In the middle of the parterre.' It is clear that the *pure audile,* seeking to develop only a single one of his faculties, may, like the pure visualizer, perform astounding feats of memory—Mozart, for example, noting from memory the *Miserere* of the Sistine Chapel after two hearings ; the deaf Beethoven, composing and inwardly repeating his enormous symphonies. On the other hand, the man of auditory type, like the visual, is exposed to serious dangers ; for if he lose his auditory images, he is without resource and breaks down completely.

" It is possible that persons with hallucinations of hearing, and in-

---

* In a letter to Charcot this interesting patient adds that his character also is changed : "I was formerly receptive, easily made enthusiastic, and possessed a rich fancy. Now I am quiet and cold, and fancy never carries my thoughts away. . . . I am much less susceptible than formerly to anger or sorrow. I lately lost my dearly-beloved mother; but felt far less grief at the bereavement than if I had been able to see in my mind's eye her physiognomy and the phases of her suffering, and especially less than if I had been able to witness in imagination the outward effects of her untimely loss upon the members of the family."

† Psychologie du Raisonnement (1886), p. 25.

dividuals afflicted with the mania that they are victims of persecution, may all belong to the auditory type ; and that the predominance of a certain kind of imagination may predispose to a certain order of hallucinations, and perhaps of delirium.

" The *motor type* remains—perhaps the most interesting of all, and certainly the one of which least is known. Persons who belong to this type [*les moteurs*, in French, *motiles*, as Mr. Galton proposes to call them in English] make use, in memory, reasoning, and all their intellectual operations, of images derived from movement. In order to understand this important point, it is enough to remember that ' all our perceptions, and in particular the important ones, those of sight and touch, contain as integral elements the movements of our eyes and limbs ; and that, if movement is ever an essential factor in our really seeing an object, it must be an equally essential factor when we see the same object in imagination ' (Ribot).* For example, the complex impression of a ball, which is there, in our hand, is the resultant of optical impressions of touch, of muscular adjustments of the eye, of the movements of our fingers, and of the muscular sensations which these yield. When we imagine the ball, its idea must include the images of these muscular sensations, just as it includes those of the retinal and epidermal sensations. They form so many *motor images.* If they were not earlier recognized to exist, that is because our knowledge of the muscular sense is relatively so recent. In older psychologies it never was mentioned, the number of senses being restricted to five.

" There are persons who remember a drawing better when they have followed its outlines with their finger. Lecoq de Boisbaudran used this means in his artistic teaching, in order to accustom his pupils to draw from memory. He made them follow the outlines of figures with a pencil held in the air, forcing them thus to associate muscular with visual memory. Galton quotes a curious corroborative fact. Colonel Moncrieff often observed in North America young Indians who, visiting occasionally his quarters, interested themselves greatly in the engravings which were shown them. One of them followed with care with the point of his knife the outline of a drawing in the Illustrated London News, saying that this was to enable him to carve it out the better on his return home. In this case the motor images were to

---

* [I am myself a very poor visualizer, and find that I can seldom call to mind even a single letter of the alphabet in purely retinal terms. I must trace the letter by running my mental eye over its contour in order that the image of it shall have any distinctness at all. On questioning a large number of other people, mostly students, I find that perhaps half of them say they have no such difficulty in seeing letters mentally. Many affirm that they can see an entire word at once, especially a short one like ' dog,' with no such feeling of creating the letters successively by tracing them with the eye.—W. J.]

reinforce the visual ones. The young savage was a *motor*.* . . . When one's motor images are destroyed, one loses one's remembrance of movements, and sometimes, more curiously still, one loses the power of executing them. Pathology gives us examples in motor aphasia, agraphia, etc. Take the case of agraphia. An educated man, knowing how to write, suddenly loses this power, as a result of cerebral injury. His hand and arm are in no way paralytic, yet he cannot write. Whence this loss of power ? He tells us himself : he no longer knows how. He has forgotten how to set about it to trace the letters, he has lost the memory of the movements to be executed, he has no longer the motor images which, when formerly he wrote, directed his hand. . . . Other patients, affected with word-blindness, resort to these motor images precisely to make amends for their other deficiency. . . . An individual affected in this way cannot read letters which are placed before his eyes, even although his sight be good enough for the purpose. This loss of the power of reading by sight may, at a certain time, be the only trouble the patient has. Individuals thus mutilated succeed in reading by an ingenious roundabout way which they often discover themselves : it is enough that they should trace the letters with their finger to understand their sense. What happens in such a case ? How can the hand supply the place of the eye ? The motor image gives the key to the problem. If the patient can read, so to speak, with his fingers, it is because in tracing the letters he gives himself a certain number of muscular impressions which are those of writing. In one word, the patient reads by writing (Charcot): the feeling of the graphic movements suggests the sense of what is being written as well as sight would." †

The imagination of a blind-deaf mute like Laura Bridgman must be confined entirely to tactile and motor material. *All blind persons must belong to the 'tactile' and 'motile' types* of the French authors. When the young man whose cataracts were removed by Dr. Franz was shown different geometric figures, he said he " had not been able to form from them the idea of a square and a disk until he perceived a sensation of what he saw in the points of his fingers, as if he really touched the objects." ‡

Professor Stricker of Vienna, who seems to have the motile form of imagination developed in unusual strength,

---

* It is hardly needful to say that in modern primary education, in which the blackboard is so much used, the children are taught their letters, etc., by all possible channels at once, sight, hearing, and movement.

† See an interesting case of a similar sort, reported by Farges, in l'Encéphale, 7me Année, p. 545.

‡ Philosophical Transactions, 1841, p. 65.

has given a very careful analysis of his own case in a couple of monographs with which all students should become familiar.* His recollections both of his own movements and of those of other things are accompanied invariably by distinct muscular feelings in those parts of his body which would naturally be used in effecting or in following the movement. In thinking of a soldier marching, for example, it is as if he were helping the image to march by marching himself in his rear. And if he suppresses this sympathetic feeling in his own legs, and concentrates all his attention on the imagined soldier, the latter becomes, as it were, paralyzed. In general his imagined movements, of whatsoever objects, seem paralyzed the moment no feelings of movement either in his own eyes or in his own limbs accompany them.† The movements of articulate speech play a predominant part in his mental life.

"When after my experimental work I proceed to its description, as a rule I reproduce in the first instance only words, which I had already associated with the perception of the various details of the observation whilst the latter was going on. For speech plays in all my observing so important a part that I ordinarily clothe phenomena in words as fast as I observe them." ‡

Most persons, on being asked *in what sort of terms they imagine words,* will say 'in terms of hearing.' It is not until their attention is expressly drawn to the point that they find it difficult to say whether auditory images or motor images connected with the organs of articulation predominate. A good way of bringing the difficulty to consciousness is that proposed by Stricker: Partly open your mouth and then imagine any word with labials or dentals in it, such as 'bubble,' 'toddle.' Is your image under these conditions distinct? To most people the image is at first 'thick,' as the sound of the word would be if they tried to pronounce it with the lips parted. Many can never imagine the words

---

* Studien über die Sprachvorstellungen (1880), and Studien über die Bewegungsvorstellungen (1882).

† Prof. Stricker admits that by practice he has succeeded in making his eye-movements 'act vicariously' for his leg-movements in imagining men walking.

‡ Bewegungsvorstellungen, p. 6.

clearly with the mouth open; others succeed after a few
preliminary trials. The experiment proves how dependent
our verbal imagination is on actual feelings in lips, tongue,
throat, larynx, etc.

"When we recall the impression of a word or sentence, if we do not
speak it out, we feel the twitter of the organs just about to come to
that point. The articulating parts—the larynx, the tongue, the lips—
are all sensibly excited; a *suppressed articulation is in fact the material of our recollection*, the intellectual manifestation, the *idea* of
speech." *

The open mouth in Stricker's experiment not only prevents actual articulation of the labials, but our feeling of
its openness keeps us from imagining their articulation,
just as a sensation of glaring light will keep us from
strongly imagining darkness. In persons whose auditory
imagination is weak, the articulatory image seems to constitute the whole material for verbal thought. Professor
Stricker says that in his own case no auditory image enters
into the words of which he thinks.† Like most psychologists, however, he makes of his personal peculiarities a rule,
and says that verbal thinking is normally and universally an exclusively motor representation. *I* certainly get
auditory images, both of vowels and of consonants, in
addition to the articulatory images or feelings on which
this author lays such stress. And I find that numbers of
my students, after repeating his experiments, come to this
conclusion. There is *at first* a difficulty due to the open
mouth. That, however, soon vanishes, as does also the
difficulty of thinking of one vowel whilst continuously
sounding another. What probably remains true, however,
is that most men have a less auditory and a more articulatory verbal imagination than they are apt to be aware of.

* Bain : Senses and Intellect, p. 339.
† Studien über Sprachvorstellungen, 28, 31, etc. Cf. pp. 49–50, etc.
Against Stricker, see Stumpf, Tonpsychol., 155–162, and Revue Philosophique, xx. 617. See also Paulhan, Rev. Philosophique, xvi. 405.
Stricker replies to Paulhan in vol. xviii. p. 685. P. retorts in vol. xix.
p. 118. Stricker reports that out of 100 persons questioned he found only
one who had *no* feeling in his lips when silently thinking the letters M B,
P; and out of 60 only *two* who were conscious of no internal articulation
whilst reading (pp. 59–60).

Professor Stricker himself has acoustic images, and can imagine the sounds of musical instruments, and the peculiar voice of a friend. A statistical inquiry on a large scale, into the variations of acoustic, tactile, and motor imagination, would probably bear less fruit than Galton's inquiry into visual images. A few monographs by competent observers, like Stricker, about their own peculiarities, would give much more valuable information about the diversities which prevail.*

Touch-images are very strong in some people. The most vivid touch-images come when we ourselves barely escape local injury, or when we see another injured. The place

---

* I think it must be admitted that some people have no vivid substantive images in *any* department of their sensibility. One of my students, an intelligent youth, denied so pertinaciously that there was *anything* in his mind *at all* when he thought, that I was much perplexed by his case. I myself certainly have no such vivid play of nascent movements or motor images as Professor Stricker describes. When I seek to represent a row of soldiers marching, all I catch is a view of stationary legs first in one phase of movement and then in another, and these views are extremely imperfect and momentary. Occasionally (especially when I try to stimulate my imagination, as by repeating Victor Hugo's lines about the regiment,

> " Leur pas est si correct, sans tarder ni courir,
> Qu'on croit voir des ciseaux se fermer et s'ouvrir,")

I seem to get an instantaneous glimpse of an actual movement, but it is to the last degree dim and uncertain. All these images seem at first as if purely retinal. I think, however, that rapid eye-movements accompany them, though these latter give rise to such slight feelings that they are almost impossible of detection. Absolutely no leg-movements of my own are there ; in fact, to call such up arrests my imagination of the soldiers. My optical images are in general very dim, dark, fugitive, and contracted. It would be utterly impossible to *draw* from them, and yet I perfectly well distinguish one from the other. My auditory images are excessively inadequate reproductions of their originals. I have *no* images of taste or smell. Touch-imagination is fairly distinct, but comes very little into play with most objects thought of. Neither is all my thought verbalized; for I have shadowy schemes of relation, as apt to terminate in a nod of the head or an expulsion of the breath as in a definite word. On the whole, vague images or sensations of movement inside of my head towards the various parts of space in which the terms I am thinking of either lie or are momentarily symbolized to lie together with movements of the breath through my pharynx and nostrils, form a by no means inconsiderable part of my *thought-stuff*. I doubt whether my difficulty in giving a clearer account is wholly a matter of inferior power of introspective attention, though that doubtless plays its part. Attention, *ceteris paribus*, must always be inferior in proportion to the feebleness of the internal images which are offered it to hold on to.

may then actually tingle with the imaginary sensation—
perhaps not altogether imaginary, since goose-flesh, pal-
ing or reddening, and other evidences of actual muscular
contraction in the spot may result.

" An educated man," says a writer who must always be quoted when
it is question of the powers of imagination,* "told me once that on
entering his house one day he received a shock from crushing the finger
of one of his little children in the door. At the moment of his fright
he felt a violent pain in the corresponding finger of his own body,
and this pain abode with him three days."

The same author makes the following discrimination,
which probably most men could verify:

" On the skin I easily succeed in bringing out suggested sensations
wherever I will. But because it is necessary to protract the mental effort I can only awaken such sensations as are in their nature prolonged,
as warmth, cold, pressure. Fleeting sensations, as those of a prick, a
cut, a blow, etc., I am unable to call up, because I cannot imagine them
ex abrupto with the requisite intensity. The sensations of the former
order I can excite upon any part of the skin; and they may become so
lively that, whether I will or not, I have to pass my hand over the place
just as if it were a real impression on the skin." †

Meyer's account of his own visual images is very interesting; and with it we may close our survey of differences between the normal powers of imagining in different individuals.

" With much practice," he says, " I have succeeded in making it
possible for me to call up subjective visual sensations at will. I tried
all my experiments by day or at night with closed eyes. At first it
was very difficult. In the first experiments which succeeded the whole
picture was luminous, the shadows being given in a somewhat less strong
bluish light. In later experiments I saw the objects dark, with
bright outlines, or rather I saw outline drawings of them, bright on a
dark ground. I can compare these drawings less to chalk drawings on
a blackboard than to drawings made with phosphorus on a dark wall
at night, though the phosphorus would show luminous vapors which
were absent from my lines. If I wished, for example, to see a face,
without intending that of a particular person, I saw the outline of a
profile against the dark background. When I tried to repeat an ex-

---

* Geo. Herm. Meyer, Untersuchungen üb. d. Physiol. d. Nervenfaser
(1843), p. 233. For other cases see Tuke's Influence of Mind upon Body,
chaps. II and VII.

† Meyer, *op. cit.* p. 238.

periment of the elder Darwin I saw only the edges of the die as bright lines on a dark ground. Sometimes, however, I saw the die really white and its edges black ; it was then on a paler ground. I could soon at will change between a white die with black borders on a light field, and a black die with white borders on a dark field ; and I can do this at any moment now. After long practice . . . these experiments succeeded better still. I can now call before my eyes almost any object which I please, as a subjective appearance, and this in its own natural color and illumination. I see them almost always on a more or less light or dark, mostly dimly changeable ground. Even known faces I can see quite sharp, with the true color of hair and cheeks. It is odd that I see these faces mostly in profile, whereas those described [in the previous extract] were all full-face. Here are some of the final results of these experiments :

" 1) Some time after the pictures have arisen they vanish or change into others, without my being able to prevent it.

" 2) When the color does not integrally belong to the object, I cannot always control it. A face, e.g., never seems to me blue, but always in its natural color ; a red cloth, on the other hand, I can sometimes change to a blue one.

" 3) I have sometimes succeeded in seeing pure colors without objects; they then fill the entire field of view.

" 4) I often fail to see objects which are not known to me, mere fictions of my fancy, and instead of them there will appear familiar objects of a similar sort; for instance, I once tried to see a brass sword-hilt with a brass guard, instead of which the more familiar picture of a rapier-guard appeared.

" 5) Most of these subjective appearances, especially when they were bright, left after-images behind them when the eyes were quickly opened during their presence. For example, I thought of a silver stir-rup, and after I had looked at it a while I opened my eyes and for a long while afterwards saw its after-image.

" These experiments succeeded best when I lay quietly on my back and closed my eyes. I could bear no noise about me, as this kept the vision from attaining the requisite intensity. The experiments succeed with me now so easily that I am surprised they did not do so at first, and I feel as though they ought to succeed with everyone. The important point in them is to get the image sufficiently intense by the exclusive direction of the attention upon it, and by the removal of all disturbing impressions." *

The negative after-images which succeeded upon Meyer's imagination when he opened his eyes are a highly interesting, though rare, phenomenon. So far as I know there is

---

* Meyer, *op. cit.* pp. 238–41.

only one other published report of a similar experience.* It
would seem that in such a case the neural process corresponding to the imagination must be the entire tract concerned in the actual sensation, even down as far as the
retina. This leads to a new question to which we may
now turn—of what is

THE NEURAL PROCESS WHICH UNDERLIES IMAGINATION?

The commonly-received idea is that it is only a milder
degree of the same process which took place when the
thing now imagined was sensibly perceived. Professor
Bain writes:

"Since a sensation in the first instance diffuses nerve-currents
through the interior of the brain outwards to the organs of expression
and movement,—the persistence of that sensation, after the outward
exciting cause is withdrawn, can be but a continuance of the same diffusive currents, perhaps less intense, but not otherwise different. The
shock remaining in the ear and brain, after the sound of thunder, must
pass through the same circles, and operate in the same way as during
the actual sound. We can have no reason for believing that, in this
self-sustaining condition, the impression changes its seat, or passes into
some new circles that have the special property of retaining it. Every
part actuated *after* the shock must have been actuated *by* the shock,
only more powerfully. With this single difference of intensity, the mode
of existence of a sensation existing after the fact is essentially the same
as its mode of existence during the fact. . . . Now if this be the case
with impressions *persisting* when the cause has ceased, what view are
we to adopt concerning impressions *reproduced* by mental causes alone,
or without the aid of the original, as in ordinary recollection? What
is the manner of occupation of the brain with a resuscitated feeling of
resistance, a smell or a sound? There is only one answer that seems
admissable. *The renewed feeling occupies the very same parts, and in
the same manner, as the original feeling, and no other parts, nor in
any other assignable manner.* I imagine that if our present knowledge
of the brain had been present to the earliest speculators, this is the only

---

* That of Dr. Ch. Féré in the Revue Philosophique, xx. 364. Johannes
Müller's account of hypnagogic hallucinations floating before the eyes for
a few moments after these had been opened, seems to belong more to the
category of spontaneous hallucinations (see his Physiology, London, 1842,
p. 1394). It is impossible to tell whether the words in Wundt's Vorlesungen, I. 387, refer to a personal experience of his own or not; probably
not. *Il va sans dire* that an inferior visualizer like myself can get no such
after-images. Nor have I as yet succeeded in getting report of any from
my students.

hypothesis that would have occurred to them. For where should a past feeling be embodied, if not in the same organs as the feeling when present ? It is only in this way that its identity can be preserved ; a feeling differently embodied would be a different feeling." *

It is not plain from Professor Bain's text whether by the ' same parts ' he means only the same parts *inside the brain,* or the same *peripheral* parts also, as those occupied by the original feeling. The examples which he himself proceeds to give are almost all cases of imagination of *movement,* in which the peripheral organs are indeed affected, for actual movements of a weak sort are found to accompany the idea. This is what we should expect. All currents tend to run forward in the brain and discharge into the muscular system ; and the idea of a movement tends to do this with peculiar facility. But the question remains : Do currents run *backward,* so that if the optical centres (for example) are excited by ' association ' and a visual object is imagined, a current runs *down to the retina* also, and excites that sympathetically with the higher tracts ? In other words, *can peripheral sense-organs be excited from above, or only from without ? Are they excited in imagination ?* Professor Bain's instances are almost silent as to this point. All he says is this :

" We might think of a blow on the hand until the skin were actually irritated and inflamed. The attention very much directed to any part of the body, as the great toe, for instance, is apt to produce a distinct feeling in the part, which we account for only by supposing a revived nerve-current to flow there, making a sort of false sensation, an influence from within mimicking the influences from without in sensation proper.—(See the writings of Mr. Braid, of Manchester, on Hypnotism, etc.)"

If I may judge from my own experience, all feelings of this sort are consecutive upon motor currents invading the skin and producing contraction of the muscles there, the muscles whose contraction gives ' goose-flesh ' when it takes place on an extensive scale. I never get a *feeling* in the skin, however strongly I *imagine* it, until some actual change in the condition of the skin itself has occurred. The truth seems to be that the cases where peripheral

---

* Senses and Intellect, p. 338.

sense-organs are directly excited in consequence of imagination are exceptional rarities, if they exist at all. *In common cases of imagination it would seem more natural to suppose that the seat of the process is purely cerebral, and that the sense-organ is left out.* Reasons for such a conclusion would be briefly these :

1) In imagination the *starting-point* of the process must be in the brain. Now we know that currents usually flow one way in the nervous system ; and for the peripheral sense-organs to be excited in these cases, the current would have to flow backward.

2) There is between imagined objects and felt objects a difference of conscious quality which may be called almost absolute. It is hardly possible to confound the liveliest image of fancy with the weakest real sensation. The felt object has a plastic reality and outwardness which the imagined object wholly lacks. Moreover, as Fechner says, in imagination the attention feels as if drawn backwards to the brain ; in sensation (even of after-images) it is directed forward towards the sense-organ.* The difference between the two processes feels like one of kind, and not like a mere 'more' or 'less' of the same.† If a sensation of sound were only a strong imagination, and an imagination a weak sensation, there ought to be a border-line of experience where we never could tell whether we were hearing a weak sound or imagining a strong one. In comparing a present sensation felt with a past one imagined, it will be remembered that we often judge the imagined one to *have been the stronger* (see above, p. 500, note). This is inexplicable if the imagination be simply a weaker excitement of the sensational process.

To these reasons the following objections may be made : To 1): The current demonstrably *does* flow backward

---

* See above, Vol. II. p. 50, note.

† V. Kandinsky (Kritische u. klinische Betrachtungen im Gebiete der Sinnestäuschungen (Berlin, 1885), p. 135 ff.) insists that in even the live-liest pseudo-hallucinations (see below, Chapter XX), which may be regarded as the intensest possible results of the imaginative process, there is no outward objectivity perceived in the thing represented, and that a *ganzer Abgrund* separates these 'ideas' from true hallucination and objective perception.

down the optic nerve in Meyer's and Féré's negative after-image. Therefore it *can* flow backward; therefore it *may* flow backward in some, however slight, degree, in all imagination.*

To 2): The difference alleged is not absolute, and sensation and imagination *are* hard to discriminate where the sensation is so weak as to be just perceptible. At night hearing a very faint striking of the hour by a far-off clock, our imagination reproduces both rhythm and sound, and it is often difficult to tell which was the last real stroke. So of a baby crying in a distant part of the house, we are uncertain whether we still hear it, or only imagine the sound. Certain violin-players take advantage of this in diminuendo terminations. After the pianissimo has been reached they continue to bow as if still playing, but are careful not to touch the strings. The listener hears in imagination a

---

* It seems to also flow backwards in certain hypnotic hallucinations. Suggest to a 'Subject' in the hypnotic trance that a sheet of paper has a red cross upon it, then pretend to remove the imaginary cross, whilst you tell the Subject to look fixedly at a dot upon the paper, and he will presently tell you that he sees a 'bluish-green' cross. The genuineness of the result has been doubted, but there seems no good reason for rejecting M. Binet's account (Le Magnétisme Animal, 1887, p. 188). M. Binet, following M. Parinaud, and on the faith of a certain experiment, at one time believed, the optical brain-centres and not the retina to be the seat of ordinary negative after-images. The experiment is this: Look fixedly, with one eye open, at a colored spot on a white background. Then close that eye and look fixedly with the *other* eye at a plain surface. A negative after-image of the colored spot will presently appear. (Psychologie du Raisonnement, 1886, p. 45.) But Mr. Delabarre has proved (American Journal of Psychology, II. 326) that this after-image is due, not to a higher cerebral process, but to the fact that the retinal process in the *closed* eye affects consciousness at certain moments, and that its object is then projected into the field seen by the eye which is open. M. Binet informs me that he is converted by the proofs given by Mr. Delabarre.

The fact remains, however, that the negative after-images of Herr Meyer, M. Féré, and the hypnotic subjects, form an exception to all that we know of nerve-currents, if they are due to a refluent centrifugal current to the retina. It may be that they will hereafter be explained in some other way. Meanwhile we can only write them down as a paradox. Sig. Sergi's theory that there is *always* a refluent wave in perception hardly merits serious consideration (Psychologie Physiologique, pp. 99, 189). Sergi's theory has recently been reaffirmed with almost incredible crudity by Lombroso and Ottolenghi in the Revue Philosophique, XXIX. 70 (Jan. 1890).

degree of sound fainter still than the preceding pianissimo.
This phenomenon is not confined to hearing :

"If we slowly approach our finger to a surface of water, we often
deceive ourselves about the moment in which the wetting occurs. The
apprehensive patient believes himself to feel the knife of the surgeon
whilst it is still at some distance." *

Visual perception supplies numberless instances in which
the same sensation of vision is perceived as one object or
another according to the interpretation of the mind. Many
of these instances will come before us in the course of the
next two chapters ; and in Chapter XIX similar illusions
will be described in the other senses. Taken together, all
these facts would force us to admit that *the subjective
difference between imagined and felt objects is less absolute
than has been claimed, and that the cortical processes which
underlie imagination and sensation are not quite as discrete
as one at first is tempted to suppose. That peripheral sensory processes are ordinarily involved in imagination seems
improbable ; that they may sometimes be aroused from the cortex
downwards cannot, however, be dogmatically denied.*

The imagination-process CAN *then pass over into the sensation-process.* In other words, genuine sensations *can* be
centrally originated. When we come to study hallucinations in the chapter on Outer Perception, we shall see that
this is by no means a thing of rare occurrence. At present,
however, we must admit that *normally the two processes do
NOT pass over into each other ;* and we must inquire why.
One of two things must be the reason. Either

1. Sensation-processes occupy a different *locality* from
imagination-processes ; or

2. Occupying the same locality, they have an *intensity*
which under normal circumstances currents from other
cortical regions are incapable of arousing, and to produce
which currents from the periphery are required.

It seems almost certain (after what was said in Chapter
II. pp. 49–51) *that the imagination-process differs from the
sensation-process by its intensity rather than by its locality.*
However it may be with lower animals, the assumption that

----
* Lotze, Med. Psych. p. 509.

ideational and sensorial centres are locally distinct appears
to be supported by no facts drawn from the observation of
human beings. After occipital destruction, the hemianopsia which results in man is sensorial blindness, not mere
loss of optical ideas. Were there centres for crude optical
sensation below the cortex, the patients in these cases
would still feel light and darkness. Since they do not preserve even this impression on the lost half of the field, we
must suppose that there are no centres for vision of any
sort whatever below the cortex, and that the corpora quadri-
gemina and other lower optical ganglia are organs for reflex
movement of eye-muscles and not for conscious sight.
Moreover there are no facts which oblige us to think that,
within the occipital cortex, one part is connected with sensation and another with mere ideation or imagination. The
pathological cases assumed to prove this are all better explained by disturbances of conduction between the optical
and other centres (see p. 50). In bad cases of hemianopsia
the patient's images depart from him together with his sensibility to light. They depart so completely that he does not
even know what is the matter with him. To perceive that
one is blind to the right half of the field of view one must
have an idea of that part of the field's possible existence.
But the defect in these patients has to be revealed to them
by the doctor, they themselves only knowing that there is
' something wrong ' with their eyes. What you have no idea
of you cannot miss ; and their not definitely missing this
great region out of their sight seems due to the fact that their
very idea and memory of it is lost along with the sensation.
A man blind of his eyes merely, sees *darkness.* A man blind
of his visual brain-centres can no more see darkness out of
the parts of his retina which are connected with the brain-
lesion than he can see it out of the skin of his back. He
cannot see at all in that part of the field ; and he cannot
think of the light which he ought to be feeling *there,* for the
very notion of the existence of that particular ' there ' is
cut out of his mind.*

---

* See an important article by Binet in the Revue Philosophique, xxvi.
481 (1888) ; also Dufour, in Revue Méd. de la Suisse Romande, 1889, No.
8. cited in the Neurologisches Centralblatt, 1890, p. 48.

Now if we admit that sensation and imagination are due to the activity of the same centres in the cortex, we can see a very good teleological reason why they should correspond to discrete kinds of process in these centres, and why the process which gives the sense that the object is really there ought normally to be arousable only by currents entering from the periphery and not by currents from the neighboring cortical parts. We can see, in short, why *the sensational process* OUGHT TO *be discontinuous with all normal ideational processes, however intense.* For, as Dr. Münsterberg justly observes :

" Were there not this peculiar arrangement we should not distinguish reality and fantasy, our conduct would not be accommodated to the facts about us, but would be inappropriate and senseless, and we could not keep ourselves alive. . . . That our thoughts and memories should be copies of sensations with their intensity greatly reduced is thus a consequence deducible logically from the natural adaptation of the cerebral mechanism to its environment." *

Mechanically the discontinuity between the ideational and the sensational kinds of process must mean that when the greatest ideational intensity has been reached, an order of *resistance* presents itself which only a new order of force can break through. The current from the periphery is the new order of force required; and what happens after the resistance is overcome is the sensational process. We may suppose that the latter consists in some new and more violent sort of disintegration of the neural matter, which now explodes at a deeper level than at other times.

Now how shall we conceive of the ' resistance ' which prevents this sort of disintegration from taking place, this sort of intensity in the process from being attained, so much of the time ? It must be either an intrinsic resistance, some force of cohesion in the neural molecules themselves; or an extrinsic influence, due to other cortical cells. When we come to study the process of hallucination we shall see that both factors must be taken into account. There is a degree of inward molecular cohesion in our brain-cells which it probably takes a sudden inrush of

---

* Die Willenshandlung (1888), pp. 129–40.

destructive energy to spring apart. Incoming peripheral currents possess this energy from the outset. Currents from neighboring cortical regions might attain to it if they could *accumulate* within the centre which we are supposed to be considering. But since during waking hours every centre communicates with others by association-paths, no such accumulation can take place. The cortical currents which run in run right out again, awakening the next ideas; the level of tension in the cells does not rise to the higher explosion-point; and the latter must be gained by a sudden current from the periphery or not at all.

CHAPTER XIX.

THE PERCEPTION OF 'THINGS.'

PERCEPTION AND SENSATION COMPARED.

A PURE sensation we saw above, p. 7, to be an abstraction never realized in adult life. Any quality of a thing which affects our sense-organs does also more than that: it arouses processes in the hemispheres which are due to the organization of that organ by past experiences, and the result of which in consciousness are commonly described as ideas which the sensation suggests. The first of these ideas is that of the *thing* to which the sensible quality belongs. *The consciousness of particular material things present to sense* is nowadays called *perception.** The consciousness of such things may be more or less complete; it may be of the mere name of the thing and its other essential attributes, or it may be of the thing's various remoter relations. It is impossible to draw any sharp line of distinction between the barer and the richer consciousness, because the moment we get beyond the first crude sensation all our consciousness is a matter of suggestion, and the various suggestions shade gradually into each other, being one and all products of the same psychological machinery of association. In the directer consciousness fewer, in the remoter more, associative processes are brought into play.

---

* The word Perception, however, has been variously used. For historical notices, see Hamilton's Lectures on Metaphysics, II. 96. For Hamilton perception is the consciousness of external objects' (*ib.* 28). Spencer defines it oddly enough as "a discerning of the relation or relations between *states of consciousness* partly presentative and partly representative; which states of consciousness must be themselves known to the extent involved in the knowledge of their relations" (Psychol., § 355).

Perception thus differs from sensation by the consciousness of farther facts associated with the object of the sensation:

"When I lift my eyes from the paper on which I am writing I see the chairs and tables and walls of my room, each of its proper shape and at its proper distance. I see, from my window, trees and meadows, and horses and oxen, and distant hills. I see each of its proper size, of its proper form, and at its proper distance; and these particulars appear as immediate informations of the eye, as the colors which I see by means of it. Yet philosophy has ascertained that we derive nothing from the eye whatever but sensations of color. . . . How, then, is it that we receive accurate information, by the eye, of size and shape and distance? By association merely. The colors upon a body are different, according to its figure, its shape, and its size. But the sensations of color and what we may here, for brevity, call the sensations of extension, of figure, of distance, have been so often united, felt in conjunction, that the sensation of the color is never experienced without raising the ideas of the extension, the figure, the distance, in such intimate union with it, that they not only cannot be separated, but are actually supposed to be seen. The sight, as it is called, of figure, or distance, appearing as it does a simple sensation, is in reality a complex state of consciousness—a sequence in which the antecedent, a sensation of color, and the consequent, a number of ideas, are so closely combined by association that they appear not one idea, but one sensation."

This passage from James Mill * gives a clear statement of the doctrine which Berkeley in his Theory of Vision made for the first time an integral part of Psychology. Berkeley compared our visual sensations to the words of a language, which are but signs or occasions for our intellects to pass to what the speaker means. As the sounds called words have no inward affinity with the ideas they signify, so neither have our visual sensations, according to Berkeley, any inward affinity with the things of whose presence they make us aware. Those things are *tangibles;* their real properties, such as shape, size, mass, consistency, position, reveal themselves only to touch. But the visible signs and the tangible significates are by long custom so " closely twisted, blended, and incorporated together, and the prejudice is so confirmed and riveted in our thoughts by a long tract of time, by the use of language, and want of reflection," † that we think we *see* the whole object, tangible and visible alike, in one simple indivisible act.

---

* Analysis, I. 97.
† Theory of Vision, 51.

Sensational and reproductive brain-processes combined, then, are what give us the content of our perceptions. Every concrete particular material thing is a conflux of sensible qualities, with which we have become acquainted at various times. Some of these qualities, since they are more constant, interesting, or practically important, we regard as essential constituents of the thing. In a general way, such are the tangible shape, size, mass, etc. Other properties, being more fluctuating, we regard as more or less accidental or inessential. We call the former qualities the reality, the latter its appearances. Thus, I hear a sound, and say 'a horse-car'; but the sound is not the horse-car, it is one of the horse-car's least important manifestations. The real horse-car is a feelable, or at most a feelable and visible, thing which in my imagination the sound calls up. So when I get, as now, a brown eye-picture with lines not parallel, and with angles unlike, and call it my big solid rectangular walnut library-table, that picture is not the table. It is not even like the table as the table is for vision, when rightly seen. It is a distorted perspective view of three of the sides of what I mentally *perceive* (more or less) in its totality and undistorted shape. The back of the table, its square corners, its size, its heaviness, are features of which I am conscious when I look, almost as I am conscious of its name. The suggestion of the name is of course due to mere custom. But no less is that of the back, the size, weight, squareness, etc.

Nature, as Reid says, is frugal in her operations, and will not be at the expense of a particular instinct to give us that knowledge which experience and habit will soon produce. Reproduced sights and contacts tied together with the present sensation in the unity of a *thing* with a name, these are the complex objective stuff out of which my actually perceived table is made. Infants must go through a long education of the eye and ear before they can perceive the realities which adults perceive. *Every perception is an acquired perception.**

---

* The educative process is particularly obvious in the case of the ear, for all sudden sounds seem alarming to babies. The familiar noises of

Perception may then be defined, in Mr. Sully's words, as that process by which the mind

"supplements a sense-impression by an accompaniment or escort of revived sensations, the whole aggregate of actual and revived sensations
being solidified or 'integrated' into the form of a percept, that is, an
apparently immediate apprehension or cognition of an object now
present in a particular locality or region of space." *

Every reader's mind will supply abundant examples of the process here described ; and to write them down would be therefore both unnecessary and tedious. In the chapter on Space we have already discussed some of the more interesting ones ; for in our perceptions of shape and position it is really difficult to decide how much of our sense of the ob-
ject is due to reproductions of past experience, and how much to the immediate sensations of the eye. I shall accordingly confine myself in the rest of this chapter to cer-
tain additional generalities connected with the perceptive process.

The first point is relative to that 'solidification' or 'in-
tegration,' whereof Mr. Sully speaks, of the present with the absent and merely represented sensations. Cerebrally taken, these words mean no more than this, that the process aroused in the sense-organ has shot into various paths which habit has already organized in the hemi-
spheres, and that instead of our having the sort of con-
sciousness which would be correlated with the simple sen-
sorial process, we have that which is correlated with this more complex process. This, as it turns out, is the consciousness of that more complex 'object,' the whole 'thing,'
instead of being the consciousness of that more simple object, the few qualities or attributes which actually im-
press our peripheral nerves. This consciousness must have the unity which every 'section' of our stream of thought retains so long as its objective content does not sensibly

---

house and street keep them in constant trepidation until such time as they
have either learned the objects which emit them, or have become blunted
to them by frequent experience of their innocuity.
    * Outlines, p. 153.

change. More than this we cannot say; we certainly ought not to say what usually is said by psychologists, and treat the perception as a sum of distinct psychic entities, the present sensation namely, *plus* a lot of images from the past, all 'integrated' together in a way impossible to describe. The perception is one state of mind or nothing—as I nave already so often said.

In many cases it is easy to compare the psychic results of the sensational with those of the perceptive process. We then see a marked difference in the way in which the impressed portions of the object are felt, in consequence of being cognized along with the reproduced portion, in the higher state of mind. Their sensible quality changes under our very eye. Take the already-quoted catch, *Pas de lieu Rhône que nous:* one may read this over and over again without recognizing the sounds to be identical with those of the words *paddle your own canoe.* As we seize the English meaning the sound itself appears to change. Verbal sounds are usually perceived with their meaning at the moment of being heard. Sometimes, however, the associative irradiations are inhibited for a few moments (the mind being preoccupied with other thoughts) whilst the words linger on the ear as mere echoes of acoustic sensation. Then, usually, their interpretation suddenly occurs. But at that moment one may often surprise a change in the very *feel* of the word. Our own language would sound very different to us if we heard it without understanding, as we hear a foreign tongue. Rises and falls of voice, odd sibilants and other consonants, would fall on our ear in a way of which we can now form no notion. Frenchmen say that English sounds to them like the *gazouillement des oiseaux* —an impression which it certainly makes on no native ear. Many of us English would describe the sound of Russian in similar terms. All of us are conscious of the strong inflections of voice and explosives and gutturals of German speech in a way in which no German can be conscious of them.

This is probably the reason why, if we look at an isolated printed word and repeat it long enough, it ends by assuming an entirely unnatural aspect. Let the reader try this with any word on this page. He will soon begin to wonder if it can possibly be the word he has been using all his life with that meaning. It stares at him from the paper like a glass eye, with no speculation in it. Its body is indeed there, but its soul is fled. It is reduced, by this new way of attending to it, to its sensational nudity. We never before attended to it in this way, but habitually got it clad with its meaning the moment we caught sight of it, and rapidly passed from it to the other words of the phrase. We apprehended it, in short, with a cloud of associates, and thus perceiving it, we felt it quite otherwise than as we feel it now divested and alone.

Another well-known change is when we look at a landscape with our head upside down. Perception is to a certain extent baffled by this manœuvre; gradations of distance and other space-determinations are made uncertain; the reproductive or associative processes, in short, decline; and, simultaneously with their diminution, the colors grow richer and more varied, and the contrasts of light and shade more marked. The same thing occurs when we turn a painting bottom upward. We lose much of its meaning, but, to compensate for the loss, we feel more freshly the value of the mere tints and shadings, and become aware of any lack of purely sensible harmony or balance which they may show.* Just so, if we lie on the floor and look up at the mouth of a person talking behind us. His lower lip here takes the habitual place of the upper one upon our retina, and seems animated by the most extraordinary and unnatural mobility, a mobility which now strikes us because (the associative processes being disturbed by the unaccustomed point of view) we get it as a naked sensation and not as part of a familiar object perceived.

On a later page other instances will meet us. For the present these are enough to prove our point. Once more we find ourselves driven to admit that when qualities of an object impress our sense and we thereupon perceive the object, the sensation as such of those qualities does not

---

* Cf. Helmholtz, Optik, pp. 433, 723, 728, 772 ; and Spencer, Psychology, vol. ii. p. 249, note.

still exist inside of the perception and form a constituent thereof. The sensation is one thing and the perception another, and neither can take place at the same time with the other, because their cerebral conditions are not the same. They may *resemble* each other, but in no respect are they identical states of mind.

PERCEPTION IS OF DEFINITE AND PROBABLE THINGS.

The chief cerebral conditions of perception are the paths of association irradiating from the sense-impression, which may have been already formed. If a certain sensation be strongly associated with the attributes of a certain thing, that thing is almost sure to be perceived when we get the sensation. Examples of such things would be familiar people, places, etc., which we recognize and name at a glance. But *where the sensation is associated with more than one reality*, so that either of two discrepant sets of residual properties may arise, the perception is doubtful and vacillating, and *the most that can then be said of it is that it will be of a* PROBABLE *thing*, of the thing which would most usually have given us that sensation.

In these ambiguous cases it is interesting to note that perception is rarely abortive ; *some* perception takes place. The two discrepant sets of associates do not neutralize each other or mix and make a blur. What we more commonly get is first one object in its completeness, and then the other in its completeness. In other words, *all brain-processes are such as give rise to what we may call* FIGURED *consciousness*. If paths are irradiated at all, they are irradiated in consistent systems, and occasion thoughts of definite objects, not mere hodge-podges of elements. Even where the brain's functions are half thrown out of gear, as in aphasia or dropping asleep, this law of figured consciousness holds good. A person who suddenly gets sleepy whilst reading aloud will read wrong; but instead of emitting a mere broth of syllables, he will make such mistakes as to read ' supper-time ' instead of ' sovereign,' ' overthrow ' instead of ' opposite,' or indeed utter entirely imaginary phrases, composed of several definite words, instead of phrases of the book. So in aphasia : where the disease is mild the patient's mistakes consist in using entire wrong words instead of right ones. It is only in grave lesions that he becomes quite inarticulate. These facts show how subtle is the associative link; how delicate yet how strong that connection among brain-paths which makes any number of them, once excited together, thereafter tend to vibrate as a systematic whole. A small group of elements, '*this*,' common to two systems, A and B, may touch off A or B according as accident decides the next step (see Fig. 47). If it happen that a single point leading from '*this*' to B is momentarily a little more pervious than any leading from '*this*' to A, then that little advantage will upset the equilibrium in favor of the entire system B. The currents will sweep first through that point

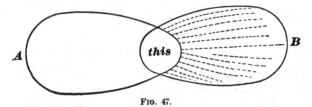

FIG. 47.

and thence into all the paths of B, each increment of advance making A more and more impossible. The thoughts correlated with A and B, in such a case, will have objects different, though similar. The similarity will, however, consist in some very limited feature if the '*this*' be small.

Thus the faintest sensations will give rise to the perception of definite things if only they resemble those which the things are wont to arouse. In fact, a sensation must be strong and distinct in order not to suggest an object and, if it is a nondescript feeling, really to seem one. The auræ of epilepsy, globes of light, fiery vision, roarings in the ears, the sensations which electric currents give rise to when passed through the head, these are unfigured because they are strong. Weaker feelings of the same sort would probably suggest objects. Many years ago, after reading Maury's book, *Le Sommeil et les Rêves*, I began for the first time to observe those ideas which faintly flit through the mind at all times, words, visions, etc., disconnected with the main stream of thought, but discernible to an attention on the watch for them. A horse's head, a coil of rope, an anchor, are, for example, ideas which have come to me unsolicited whilst I have been writing these latter lines. They can often be explained by subtle links of association, often not at all. But I have not a few times been surprised, after noting some such idea, to find, on shutting my eyes, an after-image left on the retina by some bright or dark object recently looked at, and which had evidently suggested the idea. 'Evidently,' I say, because the general shape, size, and position of object thought-of and of after-image were the same, although the idea had details which the retinal image lacked. We shall probably never know just what part retinal after-images play in determining the train of our thoughts. Judging by my own experiences I should suspect it of being not insignificant.*

---

* The more or less geometrically regular phantasms which are produced by pressure on the eyeballs, congestion of the head. inhalation of anæsthetics, etc., might again be cited to prove that faint and vague excitements of sense-organs are transformed into figured objects by the brain. only the facts are not quite clearly interpretable ; and the figuring may possibly be due to some retinal peculiarity, as yet unexplored. Beautiful patterns, which would do for wall-papers, succeed each other when the eyeballs are long pressed. Goethe's account of his own phantasm of a flower is well known. It came in the middle of his visual field whenever he closed his eyes and depressed his head, "unfolding itself and developing from its interior new flowers, formed of colored or sometimes green leaves, not natural but of fantastic forms, and symmetrical as the rosettes of sculptors," etc. (quoted in Müller's Physiology, Baly's tr., p. 1397). The fortification- and zigzag-patterns, which are well-known appearances in the field of view in certain functional disorders, have characteristics (steadiness, coerciveness, blotting out of other objects) suggestive of a retinal origin—this is why the entire class of phenomena treated of in this note seem to me still doubtfully connected with the cerebral factor in perception of which the text treats.—I copy from Taine's book on Intelligence (vol. I. p. 61) the translation of an interesting observation by Prof. M. Lazarus, in which the same effect of an after-image is seen. Lazarus himself proposes the name of 'visionary illusions' for such modifications of ideal pictures by peripheral stimulations.(Lehre von den Sinnestäuschungen, 1867, p. 19). "I was on the Kaltbad terrace at Rigi, on a very clear afternoon, and attempting to make out the Waldbruder, a rock which stands out from the midst of the gigantic wall of mountains surrounding it, on whose summits we see like a crown the glaciers of Titlis, Uri-Rothsdock, etc. I was looking alternately with the naked eye and with a spy-glass ; but could not distinguish it with the naked eye. For the space of six to ten minutes I had gazed steadfastly upon the mountains, whose color varied according

ILLUSIONS.

Let us now, for brevity's sake, treat A and B in Fig. 47 as if they stood for objects instead of brain-processes. And let us furthermore suppose that A and B are, both of them, objects which might probably excite the sensation which I have called '*this*,' but that on the present occasion A and not B is the one which actually does so. If, then, on this occasion '*this*' suggests A and not B, the result is a *correct perception.* But if, on the contrary, '*this*' suggests B and not A, the result is a *false perception,* or, as it is technically called, an *illusion.* But the *process* is the same, whether the perception be true or false.

---

to their several altitudes or declivities between violet, brown, and dark green, and I had fatigued myself to no purpose, when I ceased looking and turned away. At that moment I saw before me (I cannot recollect whether my eyes were shut or open) the figure of an absent friend, like a corpse. . . . I asked myself at once how I had come to think of my absent friend.—In a few seconds I regained the thread of my thoughts, which my looking for the Waldbruder had interrupted, and readily found that the idea of my friend had by a very simple necessity introduced itself among them. My recollecting him was thus naturally accounted for.—But in addition to this, he had appeared as a corpse. How was this ?—At this moment, whether through fatigue or in order to think, I closed my eyes, and found at once the whole field of sight, over a considerable extent, covered with the same corpse-like hue, a greenish-yellow gray. I thought at once that I had here the principle of the desired explanation, and attempted to recall to memory the forms of other persons. And, in fact, these forms too appeared like corpses ; standing or sitting, as I wished, all had a corpse-like tint. The persons whom I wished to see did not all appear to me as sensible phantoms ; and again, when my eyes were open, I did not see phantoms, or at all events only saw them faintly, of no determined color.—I then inquired how it was that phantoms of persons were affected by and colored like the visual field surrounding them, how their outlines were traced, and if their faces and clothes were of the same color. But it was then too late, or perhaps the influence of reflection and examination had been too powerful. All grew suddenly pale, and the subjective phenomenon, which might have lasted some minutes longer, had disappeared.—It is plain that here an inward reminiscence, arising in accordance with the laws of association, had combined with an optical after-image. The excessive excitation of the periphery of the optic nerve. I mean the long-continued preceding sensation of my eyes when contemplating the color of the mountain, had indirectly provoked a subjective and durable sensation, that of the complemenatry color ; and my reminiscence, incorporating itself with this subjective sensation, became the corpse-like phantom I have described."

Note that in every illusion what is false is what is in-ferred, not what is immediately given. The 'this,' if it were felt by itself alone, would be all right, it only becomes misleading by what it suggests. If it is a sensation of sight, it may suggest a tactile object, for example, which later tactile experiences prove to be not there. *The so-called 'fallacy of the senses,' of which the ancient sceptics made so much account, is not fallacy of the senses proper, but rather of the intellect, which interprets wrongly what the senses give.**

So much premised, let us look a little closer at these illusions. They are due to two main causes. *The wrong object is perceived either because*

1) *Although not on this occasion the real cause, it is yet the habitual, inveterate, or most probable cause of 'this;'* or because

2) *The mind is temporarily full of the thought of that object, and therefore 'this' is peculiarly prone to suggest it at this moment.*

I will give briefly a number of examples under each head. The first head is the more important, because it includes a number of constant illusions to which all men are subject, and which can only be dispelled by much experience.

Illusions of the First Type.

One of the oldest instances dates from Aristotle. Cross

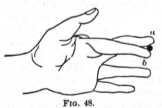

two fingers and roll a pea, pen-holder, or other small object be-tween them. It will seem double. Professor Croom Robertson has given the clearest analysis of this illusion. He observes that if the object be brought into con-

Fig. 48.

tact first with the forefinger and next with the second finger, the two contacts seem to come in at different points of space.

---

* Cf. Th. Reid's Intellectual Powers, essay II. chap. XXII, and A. Binet. in Mind, IX. 206. M. Binet points out the fact that what is fallaciously inferred is always an object of some other sense than the 'this.' 'Optical illusions' are generally errors of touch and muscular sensibility, and the fallaciously perceived object and the experiences which correct it are both tactile in these cases.

The forefinger-touch seems higher, though the finger is really lower ; the second-finger-touch seems lower, though the finger is really higher. "We perceive the contacts as double because we refer them to two distinct parts of space." The touched sides of the two fingers are normally not together in space, and customarily never do touch one thing; the one thing which now touches them, therefore, seems in two places, i.e. seems two things.*

There is a whole batch of illusions which come from optical sensations interpreted by us in accordance with our usual rule, although they are now produced by an unusual object. The *stereoscope* is an example. The eyes see a picture apiece, and the two pictures are a little disparate, the one seen by the right eye being a view of the object taken from a point slightly to the right of that from which the left eye's picture is taken. Pictures thrown on the two eyes by solid objects present this identical disparity. Whence we react on the sensation in our usual way, and perceive a solid. If the pictures be exchanged we perceive a hollow mould of the object, for a hollow mould would cast just such disparate pictures as these. Wheatstone's instrument, the *pseudoscope,* allows us to look at solid objects and see with each eye the other eye's picture. We then perceive the solid object hollow, *if it be an object which might probably be hollow,* but not otherwise. A human face, e.g., never appears hollow to the pseudoscope. In this irregularity of reaction on different objects, some seem hollow, others not; the perceptive process is true to its law, which is *always to react on the sensation in a determinate and figured fashion if possible, and in as probable a fashion as the case admits.* To couple faces and hollow-

---

* The converse illusion is hard to bring about. The points a and b, being normally in contact, mean to us the same space, and hence it might be supposed that when simultaneously touched, as by a pair of callipers, we should feel but one object, whilst as a matter of fact we feel two. It should be remarked, in explanation of this that an object placed between the two fingers in their normal uncrossed position always awakens the sense of *two contacts.* When the fingers are *pressed together* we feel *one object* to be between them. And when the fingers are crossed, and their corresponding points a and b simultaneously *pressed,* we do get something like the illusion of singleness—that is, we get a very doubtful doubleness.

ness violates all our habits of association. For the same
reason it is very easy to make an intaglio cast of a face, or
the painted inside of a pasteboard mask, look convex, instead of concave as they are.

Our sense of the *position* of things with respect to our
eye consists in suggestions of how we must move our hand
to touch them. Certain places of the image on the retina,
certain actively-produced positions of the eyeballs, are
normally linked with the sense of every determinate position which an outer thing may come to occupy. Hence we
perceive the usual position, even if the optical sensation be
artificially brought from a different part of space. Prisms
warp the light-rays in this way, and throw upon the retina
the image of an object situated, say, at spot a of space in the
same manner in which (without the prisms) an object situated at spot b would cast its image   Accordingly we feel
for the object at b instead of a. If the prism be before one
eye only we see the object at b with that eye, and in its
right position a with the other—in other words, we see it
double. If both eyes be armed with prisms with their angle
towards the right, we pass our hand to the right of all objects
when we try rapidly to touch them. And this illusory
sense of their position lasts until a new association is fixed,
when on removing the prisms a contrary illusion at first
occurs. Passive or unintentional changes in the position
of the eyeballs seem to be no more kept account of by the
mind than prisms are; so we spontaneously make no allowance for them in our perception of distance and movements.
Press one of the eyeballs into a strained position with the
finger, and objects move and are translocated accordingly,
just as when prisms are used.

Curious *illusions of movement* in objects occur whenever
the eyeballs move without our intending it. We shall learn
in the following chapter that the original visual feeling of
movement is produced by any image passing over the retina.
Originally, however, this sensation is definitely referred
neither to the object nor to the eyes. Such definite reference grows up later, and obeys certain simple laws. We
believe objects to move: 1) whenever we get the retinal
movement-feeling, but think our eyes are still; and 2) when-

ever we think that our eyes move, but fail to get the retinal movement-feeling. We believe objects to be still, on the contrary, 1) whenever we get the retinal movement-feeling, but think our eyes are moving; and 2) whenever we neither think our eyes are moving, nor get the retinal movement-feeling. Thus the perception of the object's state of motion or rest depends on the notion we frame of our own eye's movement. Now many sorts of stimulation make our eyes move without our knowing it. If we look at a waterfall, river, railroad train, or any body which continuously passes in front of us in the same direction, it carries our eyes with it. This movement can be noticed in our eyes by a by-stander. If the object keep passing towards our left, our eyes keep following whatever moving bit of it may have caught their attention at first, until that bit disappears from view. Then they jerk back to the right again, and catch a new bit, which again they follow to the left, and so on indefinitely. This gives them an oscillating demeanor, slow involuntary rotations leftward alternating with rapid voluntary jerks rightward. But *the oscillations continue* for a while after the object has come to a standstill, or the eyes are carried to a new object, and this produces the illusion that things now move in the opposite direction. For we are unaware of the slow leftward automatic movements of our eyeballs, and think that the retinal movement-sensations thereby aroused must be due to a rightward motion of the object seen; whilst the rapid voluntary rightward movements of our eyeballs we interpret as attempts to pursue and catch again those parts of the object which have been slipping away to the left.

Exactly similar oscillations of the eyeballs are produced in *giddiness*, with exactly similar results. Giddiness is easiest produced by whirling on our heels. It is a feeling of the movement of our own head and body through space, and is now pretty well understood to be due to the irritation of the semi-circular canals of the inner ear.* When,

---

* Purkinje, Mach, and Breuer are the authors to whom we mainly owe the explanation of the feeling of vertigo. I have found (American Journal of Otology. Oct. 1882) that in deaf-mutes (whose semi-circular canals or entire auditory nerves must often be disorganized) there very frequently exists no susceptibility to giddiness or whirling.

after whirling, we stop, we seem to be spinning in the reverse
direction for a few seconds, and then objects appear to continue whirling in the same direction in which, a moment
previous, our body actually whirled. The reason is that
our *eyes normally tend to maintain* their field of view. If we
suddenly turn our head leftwards it is hard to make the
eyes follow. They roll in their orbits rightwards, by a
sort of compensating inertia. Even though we *falsely
think* our head to be moving leftwards, this consequence
occurs, and our eyes move rightwards—as may be observed
in any one with vertigo after whirling. As these movements are unconscious, the retinal movement-feelings which
they occasion are naturally referred to the objects seen.
And the intermittent voluntary twitches of the eyes towards
the left, by which we ever and anon recover them from the
extreme rightward positions to which the reflex movement
brings them, simply confirm and intensify our impression
of a leftward-whirling field of view : we seem to ourselves
to be periodically pursuing and overtaking the objects in
their leftward flight. The whole phenomenon fades out
after a few seconds. And it often ceases if we voluntarily
fix our eyes upon a given point.*

Optical vertigo, as these illusions of objective movement
are called, results sometimes from brain-trouble, intoxications, paralysis, etc. A man will awaken with a weakness
of one of his eye-muscles. An intended orbital rotation
will then not produce its expected result in the way of
retinal movement-feeling—whence false perceptions, of
which one of the most interesting cases will fall to be
discussed in later chapters.

There is an illusion of movement of the opposite sort,
with which every one is familiar at *railway stations.* Habitually, when we ourselves move forward, our entire field of
view glides backward over our retina. When our movement is due to that of the windowed carriage, car, or boat

---

* The involuntary continuance of the eye's motions is not the only cause
of the false perception in these cases. There is also a true negative after-
image of the original retinal movement-sensations, as we shall see in
Chapter XX.

in which we sit, all stationary objects visible through the window give us a sensation of gliding in the opposite direction. Hence, whenever we get this sensation, of a window with *all* objects visible through it moving in one direction, we react upon it in our customary way, and perceive a stationary field of view, over which the window, and we ourselves inside of it, are passing by a motion of our own. Consequently when another train comes alongside of ours in a station, and fills the entire window, and, after standing still awhile, begins to glide away, we judge that it is *our* train which is moving, and that the other train is still. If, however, we catch a glimpse of any part of the station through the windows, or between the cars, of the other train, the illusion of our own movement instantly disappears, and we perceive the other train to be the one in motion. This, again, is but making the usual and probable inference from our sensation.*

Another illusion due to movement is explained by Helmholtz. Most wayside objects, houses, trees, etc., look small when seen out of the windows of a swift train. This is because we perceive them in the first instance unduly near. And we perceive them unduly near because of their extraordinarily rapid parallactic flight backwards. When we ourselves move forward all objects glide backwards, as aforesaid ; but the nearer they are, the more rapid is this apparent translocation. Relative rapidity of passage backwards is thus so familiarly associated with nearness that when we feel it we perceive nearness. But with a given size of retinal image the nearer an object is, the smaller do we judge its actual size to be. Hence in the train, the faster we go, the nearer do the trees and houses seem, and the nearer they seem, the smaller do they look.†

Other illusions are due to the feeling of convergence being wrongly interpreted. When we converge our eyeballs we perceive an *approximation* of whatever thing we may be looking at. Whatever things do approach whilst we look

---

* We never, so far as I know, get the converse illusion at a railroad station and believe the other train to move when it is still.

† Helmholtz : Physiol. Optik, 365.

at them oblige us, so long as they are not very distant, to converge our eyes. Hence approach of the thing is the *probable* objective fact when we feel our eyes converging. Now in most persons the internal recti muscles, to which convergence is due, are weaker than the others; and the entirely passive position of the eyeballs, the position which they assume when covered and looking at nothing in particular, is either that of parallelism or of slight divergence. Make a person look with both eyes at some near object, and then screen the object from *one* of his eyes by a card or book. The chances are that you will see the eye thus screened turn just a little outwards. Remove the screen, and you will now see it turn in as it catches sight of the object again. The other eye meanwhile keeps as it was at first. To most persons, accordingly, all objects seem to *come nearer* when, after looking at them with one eye, both eyes are used; and they seem to *recede* during the opposite change. With persons whose external recti muscles are insufficient, the illusions may be of the contrary kind.

The size of the retinal image is a fruitful source of illusions. Normally, the retinal image grows larger as the object draws near. But the sensation yielded by this enlargement is also given by any object which really grows in size without changing its distance. Enlargement of retinal image is therefore an ambiguous sign. An opera-glass enlarges the moon. But most persons will tell you that she looks smaller through it, only a great deal nearer and brighter. They read the enlargement as a sign of approach; and the perception of approach makes them actually reverse the sensation which suggests it—by an exaggeration of our habitual custom of making allowance of the apparent enlargement of whatever object approaches us, and reducing it in imagination to its natural size. Similarly, in the theatre the glass brings the stage near, but hardly seems to magnify the people on it.

The well-known increased *apparent size of the moon on the horizon* is a result of association and probability. It is seen through vaporous air, and looks dimmer and duskier than when it rides on high; and it is seen over fields, trees,

hedges, streams, and the like, which break up the intervening space and make us the better realize the latter's extent.
Both these causes make the moon seem more distant from
us when it is low ; and as its visual angle grows no less, we
deem that it must be a larger body, and we so perceive it.
It looks particularly enormous when it comes up directly
behind some well-known large object, as a house or tree,
distant enough to subtend an angle no larger than that of
the moon itself.*

The feeling of accommodation also gives rise to false perceptions of size. Usually we accommodate our eyes for an
object as it approaches us. Usually under these circumstances the object throws a larger retinal image. But
believing the object to remain the same, we make allowance
for this and treat the entire eye-feeling which we receive
as significant of nothing but *approach.* When we relax our
accommodation and at the same time the retinal image
grows smaller, the probable cause is always a *receding*
object. The moment we put on convex glasses, however,
the accommodation relaxes, but the retinal image grows
larger instead of less. This is what would happen if our
object, whilst receding, grew. Such a probable object we
accordingly perceive, though with a certain vacillation as
to the recession, for the growth in apparent size is also a
probable sign of approach, and is at moments interpreted
accordingly.—Atropin paralyzes the muscles of accommodation. It is possible to get a dose which will weaken
these muscles without laming them altogether. When a
known near object is then looked at we have to make the
same voluntary strain to accommodate, as if it were a great
deal nearer ; but as its retinal image is not enlarged in proportion to this suggested approach, we deem that it must
have grown smaller than usual. In consequence of this
so-called *micropsy,* Aubert relates that he saw a man apparently no larger than a photograph. But the small size
again made the man seem farther off. The real distance

* Cf. Berkeley's Theory of Vision, §§ 67–79 ; Helmholtz : Physiologische
Optik, pp. 630–1 ; Lechalas in Reuve Philosophique, xxvi. 49.

was two or three feet, and he seemed against the wall of the room.* Of these vacillations we shall have to speak again in the ensuing chapter.†

Mrs. C. L. Franklin has recently described and explained with rare acuteness an illusion of which the most curious thing is that it was never noticed before. Take a single pair of crossed lines (Fig. 49), hold them in a horizontal plane before the eyes, and look along them, at such a distance that with the right eye shut, 1, and with the left eye shut, 2, looks like the projection of a vertical line. Look steadily now at the point of intersection of the lines with both eyes open, and you will see a third line sticking up like a pin through the paper at right angles to the plane of the two first lines. The explanation of this illusion is

FIG. 49.

very simple, but so circumstantial that I must refer for it to Mrs. Franklin's own account.‡ Suffice it that images of the two lines fall on 'corresponding' rows of retinal points, and that the illusory vertical line is the only object capable of throwing such images. A variation of the experiment is this:

"In Fig. 50 the lines are all drawn so as to pass through a common point. With a little trouble one eye can be put into the position of this point—it is only necessary that the paper be held so that, with one eye shut, the other eye sees all the lines leaning neither to the right nor to the left. After a moment one can fancy the lines to be vertical staffs standing out of the plane of the paper. . . . This illusion [says Mrs. Franklin] I take to be of purely mental origin. When a line lies anywhere in a plane passing through the apparent vertical meridian of one eye, and is looked at with that eye only. . . . we have no very good means of knowing how it is directed in that plane. . . . Now of the lines in nature which lie anywhere within such a plane, by far the

---

* Physiol. Optik, p. 602.

† It seems likely that the strains in the *recti* muscles have something to do with the vacillating judgment in these atropin cases. The internal recti contract whenever we accommodate. They squint and produce double vision when the innervation for accommodation is excessive. To see singly, when straining the atropinized accommodation, the contraction of our internal *recti* must be neutralized by a correspondingly excessive contraction of the external *recti*. But this is a sign of the object's recession, etc.

‡ American Journal of Psychology, I. 101 ff.

greater number are vertical lines. Hence we are peculiarly inclined to think that a line which we perceive to be in such a plane is a vertical line. But to see a lot of lines at once, all ready to throw their images

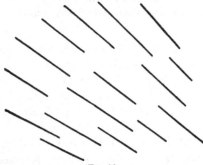

FIG. 50.

upon the vertical meridian, is a thing that has hardly ever happened to us, except when they all have been vertical lines. Hence when that happens we have a still stronger tendency to think that what we see before us is a group of vertical lines."

In other words, we see, as always, the most probable object.

The foregoing may serve as examples of the first type of illusions mentioned on page 86. I could cite of course many others, but it would be tedious to enumerate all the thaumatropes and zoetropes, dioramas, and juggler's tricks in which they are embodied. In the chapter on Sensation we saw that many illusions commonly ranged under this type are, physiologically considered, of another sort altogether, and that associative processes, strictly so called, have nothing to do with their production.

Illusions of the Second Type.

We may now turn to illusions of the second of the two types discriminated on page 86. In this type we perceive a wrong object because our mind is full of the thought of it at the time, and any sensation which is in the least degree connected with it touches off, as it were, a train already laid, and gives us a sense that the object is really before us. Here is a familiar example:

"If a sportsman, while shooting woodcock in cover, sees a bird about the size and color of a woodcock get up and fly through the foliage, not having time to see more than that it is a bird of such a size and color, he immediately supplies by inference the other qualities of a woodcock, and is afterwards disgusted to find that he has shot a thrush. I have done so myself, and could hardly believe that the thrush was the bird I had fired at, so complete was my mental supplement to my visual perception." *

As with game, so with enemies, ghosts, and the like Anyone waiting in a dark place and expecting or fearing strongly a certain object will interpret any abrupt sensation to mean that object's presence. The boy playing ' I spy,' the criminal skulking from his pursuers, the superstitious person hurrying through the woods or past the churchyard at midnight, the man lost in the woods, the girl who tremulously has made an evening appointment with her swain, all are subject to illusions of sight and sound which make their hearts beat till they are dispelled. Twenty times a day the lover, perambulating the streets with his preoccupied fancy, will think he perceives his idol's bonnet before him.

The Proof-reader's Illusion. I remember one night in Boston, whilst waiting for a 'Mount Auburn' car to bring me to Cambridge, reading most distinctly that name upon the signboard of a car on which (as I afterwards learned) 'North Avenue ' was painted. The illusion was so vivid that I could hardly believe my eyes had deceived me. All reading is more or less performed in this way.

" Practised novel- or newspaper-readers could not possibly get on so fast if they had to see accurately every single letter of every word in order to perceive the words. More than half of the words come out of their mind, and hardly half from the printed page. Were this not so, did we perceive each letter by itself, typographic errors in well-known words would never be overlooked. Children, whose ideas are not yet ready enough to perceive words at a glance, read them wrong if they are printed wrong, that is, right according to the way of printing. In a foreign language, although it may be printed with the same letters, we read by so much the more slowly as we do not understand, or are unable promptly to perceive the words. But we notice misprints all the more readily. For this reason Latin and Greek and, still better, Hebrew works are more correctly printed, because the proofs are better corrected, than in German works. Of two friends of mine, one knew much Hebrew, the other little ; the latter, however, gave instruction in

* Romanes, Mental Evolution in Animals, p. 324.

Hebrew in a gymnasium ; and when he called the other to help correct his pupils' exercises, it turned out that he could find out all sorts of little errors better than his friend, because the latter's perception of the words as totals was too swift." *

Testimony to personal identity is proverbially fallacious for similar reasons. A man has witnessed a rapid crime or accident, and carries away his mental image. Later he is confronted by a prisoner whom he forthwith perceives in the light of that image, and recognizes or 'identifies' as a participant, although he may never have been near the spot. Similarly at the so-called 'materializing séances' which fraudulent mediums give : in a dark room a man sees a gauze-robed figure who in a whisper tells him she is the spirit of his sister, mother, wife, or child, and falls upon his neck. The darkness, the previous forms, and the expectancy have so filled his mind with premonitory images that it is no wonder he perceives what is suggested. These fraudulent 'séances' would furnish most precious documents to the psychology of perception, if they could only be satisfactorily inquired into. In the hypnotic trance any suggested object is sensibly perceived. In certain subjects this happens more or less completely after waking from the trance. It would seem that under favorable conditions a somewhat similar susceptibility to suggestion may exist in certain persons who are not otherwise entranced at all.

This suggestibility is greater in the lower senses than in the higher. A German observer writes :

"We know that a weak smell or taste may be very diversely interpreted by us, and that the same sensation will now be named as one thing and the next moment as another. Suppose an agreeable smell of flowers in a room : A visitor will notice it, seek to recognize what it is,

---

* M. Lazarus: Das Leben d. Seele, II (1857), p. 32. In the ordinary hearing of speech half the words we seem to hear are supplied out of our own head. A language with which we are perfectly familiar is understood, even when spoken in low tones and far off. An unfamiliar language is unintelligible under these conditions. If we do not get a very good seat at a foreign theatre, we fail to follow the dialogue ; and what gives trouble to most of us when abroad is not only that the natives speak so fast, but that they speak so indistinctly and so low. The verbal objects for interpreting the sounds by are not alert and ready made in our minds, as they are in our familiar mother-tongue, and do not start up at so faint a cue.

and at last perceive more and more distinctly that it is the perfume of roses—until after all he discovers a bouquet of violets. Then suddenly he recognizes the violet-smell, and wonders how he could possibly have hit upon the roses.—Just so it is with taste. Try some meat whose visible characteristics are disguised by the mode of cooking, and you will perhaps begin by taking it for venison, and end by being quite certain that it is venison, until you are told that it is mutton ; where-upon you get distinctly the mutton flavor.—In this wise one may make a person taste or smell what one will, if one only makes sure that he shall conceive it beforehand as we wish, by saying to him : 'Doesn't that taste just like, etc.?' or 'Doesn't it smell just like, etc.?' One can cheat whole companies in this way ; announce, for instance, at a meal, that the meat tastes 'high,' and almost every one who is not animated by a spirit of opposition will discover a flavor of putrescence which in reality is not there at all.

"In the sense of *feeling* this phenomenon is less prominent, because we get so close to the object that our sensation of it is never incomplete. Still, examples may be adduced from this sense. On superficially feeling of a cloth, one may confidently declare it for velvet, whilst it is perhaps a long-haired cloth ; or a person may perhaps not be able to decide whether he has put on woolen or cotton stockings, and, trying to ascertain this by the feeling on the skin of the feet, he may become aware that he gets the feeling of cotton or wool according as he thinks of the one or the other. When the feeling in our fingers is somewhat blunted by cold, we notice many such phenomena, being then more ex-posed to confound objects of touch with one another." *

High authorities have doubted this power of imagination to falsify present impressions of sense.† Yet it unquestion-ably exists. Within the past fortnight I have been annoyed by a smell, faint but unpleasant, in my library. My annoy-ance began by an escape of gas from the furnace below stairs. This seemed to get lodged in my imagination as a sort of standard of perception; for, several days after the furnace had been rectified, I perceived the 'same smell' again. It was traced this time to a new pair of India rubber shoes which had been brought in from the shop and laid on a table. It persisted in coming to me for several days, however, in spite of the fact that no other member of the family or visitor noticed anything unpleasant. My impres-sion during part of this time was one of uncertainty whether

---

* G. H. Meyer, Untersuchungen, etc., pp. 242–3.

† Helmholtz, P. O. 438. The question will soon come before us **again** in the chapter on the Perception of Space.

the smell was imaginary or real; and at last it faded out. Everyone must be able to give instances like this from the smell-sense. When we have paid the faithless plumber for pretending to mend our drains, the intellect inhibits the nose from perceiving the same unaltered odor, until perhaps several days go by. As regards the ventilation or heating of rooms, we are apt to feel for some time as we think we ought to feel. If we believe the ventilator is shut, we feel the room close. On discovering it open, the oppression disappears.

An extreme instance is given in the following extract:

" A patient called at my office one day in a state of great excitement from the effects of an offensive odor in the horse-car she had come in, and which she declared had probably emanated from some very sick person who must have been just carried in it. There could be no doubt that something had affected her seriously, for she was very pale, with nausea, difficulty in breathing, and other evidences of bodily and mental distress. I succeeded, after some difficulty and time, in quieting her, and she left, protesting that the smell was unlike anything she had ever before experienced and was something dreadful. Leaving my office soon after, it so happened that I found her at the street-corner, waiting for a car: we thus entered the car together. She immediately called my attention to the same sickening odor which she had experienced in the other car, and began to be affected the same as before, when I pointed out to her that the smell was simply that which always emanates from the straw which has been in stables. She quickly recognized it as the same, when the unpleasant effects which arose while she was possessed with another perception of its character at once passed away." *

It is the same with touch. Everyone must have felt the sensible quality change under his hand, as sudden contact with something moist or hairy, in the dark, awoke a shock of disgust or fear which faded into calm recognition of some familiar object? Even so small a thing as a crumb of potato on the table-cloth, which we pick up, thinking it a crumb of bread, feels horrible for a few moments to our fancy, and different from what it is.

Weight or muscular feeling is a sensation; yet who has not heard the anecdote of some one to whom Sir Humphry Davy showed the metal sodium which he had just discovered? "Bless me, how heavy it is!" said the man;

---

* C. F. Taylor, Sensation and Pain, p. 37 (N. Y., 1882).

showing that his idea of what metals as a class ought to be had falsified the sensation he derived from a very light substance.

In the sense of hearing, similar mistakes abound. I have already mentioned the hallucinatory effect of mental images of very faint sounds, such as distant clock-strokes (above, p. 71). But even when stronger sensations of sound have been present, everyone must recall some experience in which they have altered their acoustic character as soon as the intellect referred them to a different source. The other day a friend was sitting in my room, when the clock, which has a rich low chime, began to strike. "Hollo!" said he, "hear that hand-organ in the garden," and was surprised at finding the real source of the sound. I had myself some years ago a very striking illusion of the sort. Sitting reading late one night, I suddenly heard a most formidable noise proceeding from the upper part of the house, which it seemed to fill. It ceased, and in a moment renewed itself. I went into the hall to listen, but it came no more. Resuming my seat in the room, however, there it was again, low, mighty, alarming, like a rising flood or the *avant-courier* of an awful gale. It came from all space. Quite startled, I again went into the hall, but it had already ceased once more. On returning a second time to the room, I discovered that it was nothing but the breathing of a little Scotch terrier which lay asleep on the floor. The note-worthy thing is that as soon as I recognized what it was, I was compelled to think it a different sound, and could not then *hear* it as I had heard it a moment before.

In the anecdotes given by Delbœuf and Reid, this was probably also the case, though it is not so stated. Reid says:

"I remember that once lying abed, and having been put into a fright, I heard my own heart beat; but I took it to be one knocking at the door, and arose and opened the door oftener than once, before I discovered that the sound was in my own breast." (Inquiry, chap. IV. § 1.)

Delbœuf's story is as follows:

"The illustrious P. J. van Beneden, senior, was walking one evening with a friend along a woody hill near Chaudfontaine. 'Don't you hear,' said the friend, 'the noise of a hunt on the mountain?' M. van Beneden listens and distinguishes in fact the giving-tongue of the dogs. They listen some time, expecting from one moment to another to see a deer bound by; but the voice of the dogs seems neither to recede nor approach. At last a countryman comes by, and they ask him who it is that can be hunting at this late hour. But he, pointing to some puddles of water near their feet, replies: 'Yonder little animals are what you hear.' And there there were in fact a number of toads of the species *Bombinator igneus.* . . . This batrachian emits at the pairing season a silvery or rather crystalline note. . . . Sad and pure, it is a voice in nowise resembling that of hounds giving chase." *

The sense of sight, as we have seen in studying Space, is pregnant with illusions of both the types considered. No sense gives such fluctuating impressions of the same object as sight does. With no sense are we so apt to treat the sensations immediately given as mere signs ; with none is the invocation from memory of a *thing,* and the consequent perception of the latter, so immediate. The 'thing' which we perceive always resembles, as we have seen, the object of some absent object of sensation, usually another optical figure which in our mind has come to be the standard of reality ; and it is this incessant reduction of our optical objects to more 'real' forms which has led some authors into the mistake of thinking that the sensations which first apprehend them are originally and natively of any form at all.†

Of accidental and occasional illusions of sight many amusing examples might be given. Two will suffice. One is a reminiscence of my own. I was lying in my berth in a steamer listening to the sailors holystone the deck outside ; when, on turning my eyes to the window, I perceived with perfect distinctness that the chief-engineer of the vessel had entered my state-room, and was standing looking through the window at the men at work upon the guards. Surprised at his intrusion, and also at his intentness and

---

* Examen Critique de la Loi Psychophysique (1883), p. 61.

† Compare A. W Volkmann's essay 'Ueber Ursprüngliches und Erworbenes in den Raumanschauungen,' on p. 139 of his Untersuchungen im Gebiete der Optik ; and Chapter XIII of Hering's contribution to Hermann's Handbuch der Physiologie, vol. III.

immobility, I remained watching him and wondering how long he would stand thus. At last I spoke ; but getting no reply, sat up in my berth, and then saw that what I had taken for the engineer was my own cap and coat hanging on a peg beside the window. The illusion was complete ; the engineer was a peculiar-looking man ; and I saw him unmistakably ; but after the illusion had vanished I found it hard voluntarily to make the cap and coat look like him at all.

The following story, which I owe to my friend Prof. Hyatt, is of a probably not uncommon class :

" During the winter of 1858, while in Venice, I had the somewhat peculiar illusion which you request me to relate. I remember the circumstances very accurately because I have often repeated the story, and have made an effort to keep all the attendant circumstances clear of exaggeration. I was travelling with my mother, and we had taken rooms at a hotel which had been located in an old palace. The room in which I went to bed was large and lofty. The moon was shining brightly, and I remember standing before a draped window, thinking of the romantic nature of the surroundings, remnants of old stories of knights and ladies, and the possibility that even in that room itself love-scenes and sanguinary tragedies might have taken place. The night was so lovely that many of the people were strolling through the narrow lanes or so-called streets, singing as they went, and I laid awake for some time listening to these patrols of serenaders, and of course finally fell asleep. I became aware that some one was leaning over me closely, and that my own breathing was being interfered with; a decided feeling of an unwelcome presence of some sort awakened me. As I opened my eyes I saw, as distinctly as I ever saw any living person, a draped head about a foot or eighteen inches to the right, and just above my bed. The horror which took possession of my young fancy was beyond anything I have ever experienced. The head was covered by a long black veil which floated out into the moonlight, the face itself was pale and beautiful, and the lower part swathed in the white band commonly worn by the nuns of Catholic orders. My hair seemed to rise up, and a profuse perspiration attested the genuineness of the terror which I felt. For a time I lay in this way, and then gradually gaining more command over my superstitious terrors, concluded to try to grapple with the apparition. It remained perfectly distinct until I reached at it sharply with my hand, and then disappeared, to return again, however, as soon as I sank back into the pillow. The second or third grasp which I made at the head was not followed by a reappearance, and I then saw that the ghost was not a real presence, but depended upon the position of my head. If I moved my eyes either to the left or right of the original position occupied by my head when I awakened, the ghost disappeared, and by returning to about the same position, I could make it reappear with nearly the same intensity as at first. I presently satisfied myself by these experiments that the illusion arose from the effect of the imagination, aided by the actual figure made by a visual section of the moonbeams shining through the lace curtains of the window. If I had given way to the first terror of the situation and covered up my head, I should probably have believed in the reality of the apparition, since I have not by the slightest word, so far as I know, exaggerated the vividness of my feelings."

THE PHYSIOLOGICAL PROCESS IN PERCEPTION.

Enough has now been said to prove the general law of perception, which is this, that *whilst part of what we perceive comes through our senses from the object before us, another part* (and it may be the larger part) *always comes* (in Lazarus's phrase) *out of our own head.*

At bottom this is only one case (and that the simplest case) of the general fact that our nerve-centres are an organ for reacting on sense-impressions, and that our hemispheres, in particular, are given us in order that records of our private past experience may co-operate in the reaction. Of course such a general way of stating the fact is vague; and all those who follow the current theory of ideas will be prompt to throw this vagueness at it as a reproach. Their way of describing the process goes much more into detail. The sensation, they say, awakens 'images' of other sensations associated with it in the past. These images 'fuse,' or are 'combined' by the Ego with the present sensation into a new product, the percept, etc., etc. Something so indistinguishable from this in practical outcome is what really occurs, that one may seem fastidious in objecting to such a statement, specially if one have no rival theory of the elementary processes to propose. And yet, if this notion of images rising and flocking and fusing *be* mythological (and we have all along so considered it), why should we entertain it unless confessedly as a mere figure of speech? As such, of course, it is convenient and welcome to pass. But if we try to put an exact meaning into it, all we find is that the brain reacts by paths which previous experiences have worn, and makes us usually perceive the probable thing, i.e., the thing by which on previous occasions the reaction was most frequently aroused.

But we can, I think, without danger of being too speculative, be a little more exact than this, and conceive of a physiological reason why the felt quality of an object changes when, instead of being apprehended in a mere sensation, the object is perceived as a thing. All consciousness seems to depend on a certain slowness of the process in the cortical cells. The rapider currents are, the less feeling they seem to awaken. If a region A, then, be so connected with another region B that every current which enters A immediately drains off into B, we shall not be very strongly conscious of the sort of object that A can make us feel. If B, on the contrary, has no such copious channel of discharge, the excitement will linger there longer ere it diffuses itself elsewhere, and our consciousness of the sort of object that B makes us feel will be strong. Carrying this to an ideal maximum, we may say that if A offer *no* resistance to the transmission forward of the current, and if the current *terminate* in B, then, no matter what causes may initiate the current, we shall get no consciousness of the object peculiar to A, but on the contrary a vivid sensation of the object peculiar to B. And this will be true though at other times the connection between A and B might lie less open, and every current *then* entering A might give us a strong consciousness of A's peculiar object. In other words, just in proportion as associations are habitual, will the qualities of the suggested thing tend to substitute themselves in consciousness for those of the thing immediately there; or, more briefly, *just in proportion as an experience is probable will it tend to be directly felt.* In all such experiences the paths lie wide open from the cells first affected to those concerned with the suggested ideas. A circular after-image on the receding wall or ceiling is actually *seen* as an ellipse, a square after-image of a cross there is seen as slant-legged, etc., because only in the process correlated with the vision of the latter figures do the inward currents find a pause (see the next chapter).

We must remember this when, in dealing with the eye, we come to point out the erroneousness of the principle laid down by Reid and Helmholtz that true sensations can never be changed by the suggestions of experience.

A certain illusion of which I have not yet spoken affords an additional illustration of this. *When we will to execute a movement and the movement for some reason does not occur, unless the sensation of the part's* NOT *moving is a strong one, we are apt to feel as if the movement had actually taken place.* This seems habitually to be the case in anæsthesia of the moving parts. Close the patient's eyes, hold his anæsthetic arm still, and tell him to raise his hand to his head; and when he opens his eyes he will be astonished to find that the movement has not taken place. All reports of anæsthetic cases seem to mention this illusion. Sternberg who wrote on the subject in 1885,* lays it down as a law that the intention to move is the same thing as the feeling of the motion. We shall later see that this is false (Chapter XXV); but it certainly may *suggest* the feeling of the motion with hallucinatory intensity. Sternberg gives the following experiment, which I find succeeds with at least half of those who try it: Rest your palm on the edge of the table with your forefinger hanging over in a position of extreme flexion, and then exert your will to flex it still more. The position of the other fingers makes this impossible, and yet if we do not look to see the finger, we think we feel it move. He quotes from Exner a similar experiment with the jaws: Put some hard rubber or other unindentable obstacle between

---

* In the Proceedings of the American Society for Psychical Research, pp. 253–4. I have tried to account for some of the variations in this consciousness. Out of 140 persons whom I found to feel their lost foot, some did so *dubiously.* "Either they only feel it occasionally, or only when it pains them, or only when they try to move it; or they only feel it when they 'think a good deal about it' and make an effort to conjure it up. When they 'grow inattentive,' the feeling 'flies back' or 'jumps back,' to the stump. Every degree of consciousness. from complete and permanent hallucination down to something hardly distinguishable from ordinary fancy, seems represented in the sense of the missing extremity which these patients say they have. Indeed I have seldom seen a more plausible lot of evidence for the view that imagination and sensation are but differences of vividness in an identical process than these confessions, taking them altogether, contain. Many patients say they can hardly tell whether they feel or fancy the limb. "

your back teeth and bite hard: you think you feel the jaw move and the front teeth approach each other, though in the nature of things no movement can occur.*—The visual suggestion of the path traversed by the finger-tip as the *locus* of the movement-feeling in the joint, which we discussed on page 41, is another example of this semi-hallucinatory power of the suggested thing. Amputated people, as we have learned, still feel their lost feet, etc. This is a necessary consequence of the law of specific energies, for if the central region correlated with the foot give rise to any feeling at all it must give rise to the feeling of a foot.† But the curious thing is that many of these patients can *will the foot to move*, and when they have done so, distinctly *feel the movement to occur*. They can, to use their own language, ' work ' or ' wiggle ' their lost toes. ‡

Now in all these various cases we are dealing with data which in normal life are inseparably joined. Of all possible experiences, it is hard to imagine any pair more uniformly and incessantly coupled than the volition to move, on the one hand, and the feeling of the changed position of the parts, on the other. From the earliest ancestors of ours which had feet, down to the present day, the movement of the feet must always have accompanied the will to move them ; and here, if anywhere, habit's consequences ought to be found.‡ The process of the willing ought, then, to pour into the process of feeling the command effected, and ought to awaken that feeling in a maximal degree provided no other positively contradictory sensation come in at the same time. In most of us, when the will fails of its effect there is a contradictory sensation. We discern a resistance or the unchanged position of the limb. But neither in anæsthesia nor in amputation can there be any contradictory sensation in the foot to correct us ; so imagination has all the force of fact.

---

* Pflüger's Archiv, xxxvii. 1.

† Not all patients have this additional illusion.

‡ I ought to say that in *almost* all cases the volition is followed by actual contraction of muscles in the *stump*.

'APPERCEPTION.'

In Germany since Herbart's time Psychology has always had a great deal to say about a process called *Apperception.** The incoming ideas or sensations are said to be 'apperceived' by 'masses' of ideas already in the mind. It is plain that the process we have been describing as perception is, at this rate, an apperceptive process. So are all recognition, classing, and naming; and passing beyond these simplest suggestions, all farther thoughts about our percepts are apperceptive processes as well. I have myself not used the word apperception because it has carried very different meanings in the history of philosophy,† and 'psychic reaction,' 'interpretation,' 'conception,' 'assimilation,' 'elaboration,' or simply 'thought,' are perfect synonyms for its Herbartian meaning, widely taken. It is, moreover, hardly worth while to pretend to analyze the so-called apperceptive performances beyond the first or perceptive stage, because their variations and degrees are literally innumerable. 'Apperception' is a name for the sum-total of the effects of what we have studied as association; and it is obvious that the things which a given experience will suggest to a man depend on what Mr. Lewes calls his entire psychostatical conditions, his nature and stock of ideas, or, in other words, his character, habits, memory, education, previous experience, and momentary mood. We gain no insight into what really occurs either in the mind or in the brain by calling all these things the 'apperceiving mass,' though of course this may upon occasion be convenient. On the whole I am inclined to think Mr. Lewes's term of 'assimilation' the most fruitful one yet used.‡

Professor H. Steinthal has analyzed apperceptive processes with a sort of detail which is simply burdensome.§

---

* Cf. Herbart, Psychol. als. Wissenschaft, § 125.

† Compare the historical reviews by K. Lange : Ueber Apperception (Plauen, 1879), pp. 12–14; by Staude in Wundt's Philosophische Studien, I. 149; and by Marty in Vierteljsch. f. wiss. Phil., x. 347 ff.

‡ Problems, vol. I. p. 118 ff.

§ See his Einleitung in die Psychologie u. Sprachwissenschaft (1881), p. 166 ff.

His introduction of the matter may, however, be quoted. He begins with an anecdote from a comic paper.

" In the compartment of a railway-carriage six persons unknown to each other sit in lively conversation. It becomes a matter of regret that one of the company must alight at the next station. One of the others says that he of all things prefers such a meeting with entirely unknown persons, and that on such occasions he is accustomed neither to ask who or what his companions may be nor to tell who or what he is. Another thereupon says that he will undertake to decide this question, if they each and all will answer him an entirely disconnected question. They began. He drew five leaves from his note-book. wrote a question on each, and gave one to each of his companions with the request that he write the answer below. When the leaves were returned to him, he turned, after reading them, without hesitation to the others, and said to the first, ' You are a man of science '; to the second, ' You are a sol- dier '; to the third, ' You are a philologer '; to the fourth, ' You are a journalist '; to the fifth, ' You are a farmer.' All admitted that he was right, whereupon he got out and left the five behind. Each wished to know what question the others had received; and behold, he had given the same question to each. It ran thus :

" ' What being destroys what it has itself brought forth ?

" To this the naturalist had answered, ' vital force '; the soldier, ' war '; the philologist, ' Kronos '; the publicist, ' revolution '; the farmer, ' a boar '. This anecdote, methinks, if not true, is at least splendidly well invented. Its narrator makes the journalist go on to say : ' Therein consists the joke. Each one answers the first thing that occurs to him,* and that is whatever is most nearly related to his pur- suit in life. Every question is a hole-drilling experiment, and the an- swer is an opening through which one sees into our interiors.' . . . So do we all. We are all able to recognize the clergyman, the soldier, the scholar, the business man, not only by the cut of their garments and the attitude of their body, but by what they say and how they express it. We guess the place in life of men by the interest which they show and the way in which they show it, by the objects of which they speak, by the point of view from which they regard things, judge them, conceive them, in short by their mode of *apperceiving*. . . .

" Every man has one group of ideas which relate to his own person and interests, and another which is connected with society. Each has his group of ideas about plants, religion, law, art, etc., and more especially about the rose, epic poetry, sermons, free trade, and the like. Thus the mental content of every individual, even of the uneducated

---

* One of my colleagues, asking himself the question after reading the anecdote, tells me that he replied ' Harvard College,' the faculty of that body having voted, a few days previously, to keep back the degrees of members of the graduating class who might be disorderly on class-day night. **W.**

and of children, consists of masses or circles of knowledge of which each lies within some larger circle, alongside of others similarly included, and of which each includes smaller circles within itself. . . . The perception of a thing like a horse . . . is a process between the present horse's picture before our eyes, on the one hand, and those fused or interwoven pictures and ideas of all the horses we have ever seen, on the other; . . . a process between two factors or momenta, of which one existed before the process and was an old possession of the mind (the group of ideas, or concept, namely), whilst the other is but just presented to the mind, and is the immediately supervening factor (the sense-impression). The former apperceives the latter; the latter is apperceived by the former. Out of their combination an apperception-product arises: the knowledge of the perceived being as a horse. The earlier factor is relatively to the later one active and *a priori ;* the supervening factor is given, *a posteriori*, passive. . . . We may then define Apperception as the movement of two masses of consciousness (Vorstellungsmassen) against each other so as to produce a cognition.

" The *a priori* factor we called active, the *a posteriori* factor passive, but this is only relatively true. . . . Although the *a priori* moment commonly shows itself to be the more powerful, apperception-processes can perfectly well occur in which the new observation transforms or enriches the apperceiving group of ideas. A child who hitherto has seen none but four-cornered tables apperceives a round one as a table; but by this the apperceiving mass (' table ') is enriched. To his previous knowledge of tables comes this new feature that they need not be four-cornered, but may be round. In the history of science it has happened often enough that some discovery, at the same time that it was apperceived, i.e. brought into connection with the system of our knowledge, transformed the whole system. In principle, however, we must maintain that, although either factor is both active and passive, the *a priori* factor is almost always the more active of the two." *

This account of Steinthal's brings out very clearly the *difference between our psychological conceptions and what are called concepts in logic.* In logic a concept is unalterable ; but what are popularly called our ' conceptions of things ' alter by being used. The aim of ' Science ' is to attain conceptions so adequate and exact that we shall never need to change them. There is an everlasting struggle in every mind between the tendency to keep unchanged, and the tendency to renovate, its ideas. Our education is a ceaseless compromise between the conservative and the progressive factors. Every new experience must be disposed

---

* *Op. cit.* pp. 166–171.

of under *some* old head. The great point is to find the head
which has to be least altered to take it in. Certain Polyne-
sian natives, seeing horses for the first time, called them
pigs, that being the nearest head. My child of two played
for a week with the first orange that was given him, calling
it a 'ball.' He called the first whole eggs he saw 'potatoes,'
having been accustomed to see his 'eggs' broken into a
glass, and his potatoes without the skin. A folding pocket-
corkscrew he unhesitatingly called 'bad-scissors.' Hardly
any one of us can make new heads easily when fresh experiences come. Most of us grow more and more enslaved to
the stock conceptions with which we have once become
familiar, and less and less capable of assimilating impressions in any but the old ways. Old-fogyism, in short, is the
inevitable terminus to which life sweeps us on. Objects
which violate our established habits of 'apperception' are
simply not taken account of at all ; or, if on some occasion
we are forced by dint of argument to admit their existence,
twenty-four hours later the admission is as if it were not,
and every trace of the unassimilable truth has vanished
from our thought. Genius, in truth, means little more than
the faculty of perceiving in an unhabitual way.

On the other hand, nothing is more congenial, from
babyhood to the end of life, than to be able to assimilate
the new to the old, to meet each threatening violator or
burster of our well-known series of concepts, as it comes
in, see through its unwontedness, and ticket it off as an old
friend in disguise. This victorious assimilation of the new
is in fact the type of all intellectual pleasure. The lust for
it is curiosity. The relation of the new to the old, before
the assimilation is performed, is wonder. We feel neither
curiosity nor wonder concerning things so far beyond us
that we have no concepts to refer them to or standards by
which to measure them.* The Fuegians, in Darwin's voy-

---

* The great maxim in pedagogy is to knit every new piece of knowledge on to a pre-existing curiosity—i.e., to assimilate its matter in some
way to what is already known. Hence the advantage of " comparing all
that is far off and foreign to something that is near home, of making the
unknown plain by the example of the known, and of connecting all the
instruction with the personal experience of the pupil. . . . If the teacher is

age, wondered at the small boats, but took the big ship as a 'matter of course.' Only what we partly know already inspires us with a desire to know more. The more elaborate textile fabrics, the vaster works in metal, to most of us are like the air, the water, and the ground, absolute existences which awaken no ideas. It is a matter of course that an engraving or a copper-plate inscription should possess that degree of beauty. But if we are shown a *pen*-drawing of equal perfection, our personal sympathy with the difficulty of the task makes us immediately wonder at the skill. The old lady admiring the Academician's picture, says to him: "And is it really all done *by hand?*"

IS PERCEPTION UNCONSCIOUS INFERENCE?

A widely-spread opinion (which has been held by such men as Schopenhauer, Spencer, Hartmann, Wundt, Helmholtz, and lately interestingly pleaded for by M. Binet *) will have it that *perception should be called a sort of reasoning operation, more or less unconsciously and automatically performed.* The question seems at first a verbal one, depending on how broadly the term reasoning is to be taken. If, every time a present sign suggests an absent reality to our mind, we make an inference ; and if every time we make an inference we reason ; then perception is indubitably reasoning. Only one sees no room in it for any unconscious part. Both associates, the present sign and the contiguous things which it suggests, are above-board, and no intermediary

---

to explain the distance of the sun from the earth, let him ask . . . 'If anyone there in the sun fired off a cannon straight at you, what should you do?' ' Get out of the way ' would be the answer. ' No need of that,' the teacher might reply. ' You may quietly go to sleep in your room, and get up again, you may wait till your confirmation-day, you may learn a trade, and grow as old as I am,—*then* only will the cannon-ball be getting near, *then* you may jump to one side! See, so great as that is the sun's distance!' " (K. Lange, Ueber Apperception, 1879, p. 76—a charming though prolix little work.)

* A. Schopenhauer, Satz vom Grunde, chap. iv. H. Spencer, Psychol., part vi. chaps. ix, x. E. v. Hartmann, Phil. of the Unconscious (B), chaps. vii, viii. W. Wundt. Beiträge, pp. 422 ff.; Vorlesungen, iv, xiii. H. Helmholtz, Physiol Optik, pp. 430, 447. A. Binet, Psychol. du Raisonnement, chaps. iii, v. Wundt and Helmholtz have more recently ' recanted.' See above, vol i. p. 169 note.

ideas are required. Most of those who have upheld the thesis in question have, however, made a more complex supposition. What they have meant is that perception is a *mediate* inference, and that the middle term is unconscious. When the sensation which I have called ' this ' (p. 83, *supra*) is felt, they think that some process like the following runs through the mind :

> ' This ' is M ;
> but   M is A ;
> therefore   ' this ' is A.*

Now there seem no good grounds for supposing this additional wheelwork in the mind. The classification of ' *this* ' as M is itself an act of perception, and should, if all perception were inference, require a still earlier syllogism for its performance, and so backwards *in infinitum*. The only extrication from this coil would be to represent the process in altered guise, thus:

> ' This ' is *like those;*
> *Those* are A ;
> Therefore ' this ' is A.

The major premise here involves no association by contiguity, no *naming* of *those* as M, but only a suggestion of unnamed similar images, a recall of analogous past sensations with which the characters that make up A were habitually conjoined. But here again, what grounds of fact are there for admitting this recall ? We are quite unconscious of any such images of the past. And the conception of all the forms of association as resultants of the elementary fact of habit-worn paths in the brain makes such images entirely superfluous for explaining the phenomena in point. Since the brain-process of 'this,' the sign of A, has repeatedly been aroused in company with the process of the full object A, direct paths of irradiation from the one to the other must be already established. And although roundabout paths may also be possible, as from 'this' to 'those,' and then

---

* When not all M, but only some M, is A, when, in other words, M is ' undistributed ' the conclusion is liable to error. Illusions would thus be *logical fallacies,* if true perceptions were valid syllogisms. They would draw false conclusions from undistributed middle terms.

from 'those' to 'A' (paths which would lead to practically
the same conclusion as the straighter ones), yet there is no
ground whatever for assuming them to be traversed now,
especially since appearances point the other way. In
explicit reasoning, such paths are doubtless traversed; in
perception they are in all probability closed. So far, then,
from perception being a species of reasoning properly so
called, both it and reasoning are co-ordinate varieties of that
deeper sort of process known psychologically as the association of ideas, and physiologically as the law of habit in
the brain. *To call perception unconscious reasoning is thus
either a useless metaphor, or a positively misleading confusion
between two different things.*

One more point and we may leave the subject of Perception. *Sir Wm. Hamilton thought that he had discovered a
'great law'* which had been wholly overlooked by psychologists, and which, 'simple and universal,' is this: "Knowledge and Feeling,—Perception and Sensation, though always coexistent, are always in the inverse ratio of each
other." Hamilton wrote as if perception and sensation
were two coexistent elements entering into a single state
of consciousness. Spencer refines upon him by contending
that they are two mutually exclusive *states* of consciousness, not two elements of a single state. If sensation be
taken, as both Hamilton and Spencer mainly take it in this
discussion, to mean the feeling of *pleasure* or *pain*, there is
no doubt that the law, however expressed, is true; and that
the mind which is strongly conscious of the pleasantness or
painfulness of an experience is *ipso facto* less fitted to
observe and analyze its outward cause.* Apart from pleasure and pain, however, the law seems but a corollary of the
fact that the more concentrated a state of consciousness is,
the more vivid it is. When feeling a color, or listening to
a tone *per se*, we get it more intensely, notice it better, than
when we are aware of it merely as one among many other
properties of a total object. The more diffused cerebral
excitement of the perceptive state is probably incompatible

---

* See Spencer, Psychol., II. p. 250, note, for a physiological hypothesis
to account for this fact.

with quite as strong an excitement of separate parts as the sensational state comports. So we come back here to our own earlier discrimination between the perceptive and the sensational processes, and to the examples which we gave on pp. 80, 81.*

HALLUCINATIONS.

Between normal perception and illusion we have seen that there is no break, the *process* being identically the same in both. The last illusions we considered might fairly be called hallucinations. We must now consider the false perceptions more commonly called by that name.† In or-

---

* Here is another good example, taken from Helmholtz's Optics, p. 435: "The sight of a man walking is a familiar spectacle to us. We perceive it as a connected whole, and at most notice the most striking of its peculiarities. Strong attention is required, and a special choice of the point of view, in order to feel the perpendicular and lateral oscillations of such a walking figure. We must choose fitting points or lines in the background with which to compare the positions of its head. But if a distant walking man be looked at through an astronomical telescope (which inverts the object), what a singular hopping and rocking appearance he presents ! No difficulty now in seeing the body's oscillations, and many other details of the gait. . . . But, on the other hand, its total character, whether light or clumsy, dignified or graceful, is harder to perceive than in the upright position."

† Illusions and hallucinations must both be distinguished from *delusions*. A delusion is a false opinion about a matter of fact, which need not necessarily involve, though it often does involve, false perceptions of sensible things. We may, for example, have religious delusions, medical delusions, delusions about our own importance, about other peoples' characters, etc., *ad libitum*. The delusions of the insane are apt to affect certain typical forms, often very hard to explain. But in many cases they are certainly theories which the patients invent to account for their abnormal bodily sensations. In other cases they are due to hallucinations of hearing and of sight. Dr. Clouston (Clinical Lectures on Mental Disease, lecture III *ad fin.*) gives the following special delusions as having been found in about a hundred melancholy female patients who were afflicted in this way. There were delusions of

general persecution;	being destitute;
general suspicion;	being followed by the police;
being poisoned;	being very wicked;
being killed;	impending death;
being conspired against;	impending calamity;
being defrauded;	the soul being lost;
being preached against in church;	having no stomach;
being pregnant;	having no inside;

dinary parlance hallucination is held to differ from illusion in that, whilst there is an object really there in illusion, *in hallucination there is no objective stimulus at all.* We shall presently see that this supposed absence of objective stimulus in hallucination is a mistake, and that hallucinations are often only *extremes* of the perception process, in which the secondary cerebral reaction is out of all normal proportion to the peripheral stimulus which occasions the activity. Hallucinations usually appear abruptly and have the character of being forced upon the subject. But they possess various degrees of apparent *objectivity.* One mistake *in limine* must be guarded against. They are often talked of as mental *images* projected outwards by mistake. But where an hallucination is complete, it is much more than a mental image. *An hallucination is a strictly sensational form of consciousness, as good and true a sensation as if there were a real object there.* The object happens not to be there, that is all.

The milder degrees of hallucination have been designated as *pseudo-hallucinations.* Pseudo-hallucinations and hallucinations have been sharply distinguished from each

---

having a bone in the throat;
having lost much money;
being unfit to live;
that she will not recover;
that she is to be murdered;
that she is to be boiled alive;
that she is to be starved;
that the flesh is boiling;
that the head is severed from the body;
that children are burning;
that murders take place around;
that it is wrong to take food;
being in hell;
being tempted of the devil;
being possessed of the devil;
having committed an unpardonable sin;
unseen agencies working;
her own identity;
being on fire;

having neither stomach nor brains;
being covered with vermin;
letters being written about her;
property being stolen;
her children being killed;
having committed theft;
the legs being made of glass;
having horns on the head;
being chloroformed;
having committed murder;
fear of being hanged;
being called names by persons;
being acted on by spirits;
being a man;
the body being transformed;
insects coming from the body;
rape being practised on her;
having a venereal disease;
being a fish;
being dead;
having committed 'suicide of the soul.'

other only within a few years. Dr. Kandinsky writes of their difference as follows :

" In carelessly questioning a patient we may confound his pseudo-hallucinatory perceptions with hallucinations. But to the unconfused consciousness of the patient himself, even though he be imbecile, the identification of the two phenomena is impossible, at least in the sphere of vision. At the moment of having a pseudo-hallucination of sight, the patient feels himself in an entirely different relation to this subjective sensible appearance, from that in which he finds himself whilst subject to a true visual hallucination. The latter is reality itself ; the former, on the contrary, remains' always a subjective phenomenon which the individual commonly regards either as sent to him as a sign of God's grace, or as artificially induced by his secret persecutors . . . If he knows by his *own experience* what a genuine hallucination is, it is quite impossible for him to mistake the pseudo-hallucination for it. . . . A concrete example will make the difference clear :

"Dr. N. L. . . . heard one day suddenly amongst the voices of his persecutors ('coming from a hollow space in the midst of the wall') a rather loud voice impressively saying to him : 'Change your national allegiance.' Understanding this to mean that his only hope consisted in ceasing to be subject to the Czar of Russia, he reflected a moment what allegiance would be better, and resolved to become an English subject. At the same moment he saw a pseudo-hallucinatory lion of natural size, which appeared and quickly laid its fore-paws on his shoulders. He had a lively feeling of these paws as a tolerably painful local pressure (complete hallucination of touch). Then the same voice from the wall said : 'Now you have a lion—now you will rule,' whereupon the patient recollected that the lion was the national emblem of England. The lion appeared to L. very distinct and vivid, but he nevertheless remained conscious, as he afterwards expressed it, that he saw the animal, not with his bodily but with his mental eyes. (After his recovery he called analogous apparitions by the name of ' expressive-plastic ideas.') Accordingly he felt no terror, even though he felt the contact of the claws. . . . Had the lion been a complete hallucination, the patient, as he himself remarked after recovery, would have felt great fear, and very likely screamed or taken to flight. Had it been a simple image of the fancy he would not have connected it with the voices, of whose objective reality he was at the time quite convinced." *

From ordinary images of memory and fancy, pseudo-hallucinations differ in being much more vivid, minute, de-

---

* V. Kandinsky: Kritische u. Klinische Betrachtungen im Gebiete d. Sinnestäuschungen (1885), p. 42.

tailed, steady, abrupt, and spontaneous, in the sense that all feeling of our own activity in producing them is lacking. Dr. Kandinsky had a patient who, after taking opium or haschisch, had abundant pseudo-hallucinations and hallucinations. As he also had strong visualizing power and was an educated physician, the three sorts of phenomena could be easily compared. Although projected outwards (usually not farther than the limit of distinctest vision, a foot or so) the pseudo-hallucinations *lacked the character of objective reality* which the hallucinations possessed, but, unlike the pictures of imagination, it was almost impossible to produce them at will. Most of the 'voices' which people hear (whether they give rise to delusions or not) are pseudo-hallucinations. They are described as '*inner*' voices, although their character is entirely unlike the inner speech of the subject with himself. I know two persons who hear such inner voices making unforeseen remarks whenever they grow quiet and listen for them. They are a very common incident of delusional insanity, and at last grow into vivid hallucinations. The latter are comparatively frequent occurrences in sporadic form; and certain individuals are liable to have them often. From the results of the 'Census of Hallucinations,' which was begun by Edmund Gurney, it would appear that, roughly speaking, one person at least in every ten is likely to have had a vivid hallucination at some time in his life.* The following cases from healthy people will give an idea of what these hallucinations are:

"When a girl of eighteen, I was one evening engaged in a very painful discussion with an elderly person. My distress was so great that I took up a thick ivory knitting-needle that was lying on the mantelpiece of the parlor and broke it into small pieces as I talked. In the midst of the discussion I was very wishful to know the opinion of a brother with whom I had an unusually close relationship. I turned round and saw him sitting at the further side of a centre-table, with his arms folded (an unusual position with him), but, to my dismay, I per-

---

* See Proceedings of Soc. for Psych. Research, Dec. 1889, pp. 7, 183. The International Congress for Experimental Psychology has now charge of the Census, and the present writer is its agent for America.

ceived from the sarcastic expression of his mouth that he was not in sympathy with me, was not 'taking my side,' as I should then have expressed it. The surprise cooled me, and the discussion was dropped.

"Some minutes after, having occasion to speak to my brother, I turned towards him, but he was gone. I inquired when he left the room, and was told that he had not been in it, which I did not believe, thinking that he had come in for a minute and had gone out without being noticed. About an hour and a half afterwards he appeared, and convinced me, with some trouble, that he had never been near the house that evening. He is still alive and well."

Here is another case :

"One night in March 1873 or '74, I cannot recollect which year, I was attending on the sick-bed of my mother. About eight o'clock in the evening I went into the dining-room to fix a cup of tea, and on turning from the sideboard to the table, on the other side of the table before the fire, which was burning brightly, as was also the gas, I saw standing with his hand clasped to his side in true military fashion a soldier of about thirty years of age, with dark, piercing eyes looking directly into mine. He wore a small cap with standing feather ; his costume was also of a soldierly style. He did not strike me as being a spirit, ghost, or anything uncanny, only a living man ; but after gazing for fully a minute I realized that it was nothing of earth, for he neither moved his eyes nor his body, and in looking closely I could see the fire beyond. I was of course startled, and yet did not run out of the room. I felt stunned. I walked out rapidly, however, and turning to the servant in the hall asked her if she saw anything. She said not. I went into my mother's room and remained talking for about an hour, but never mentioned the above subject for fear of exciting her, and finally forgot it altogether, returning to the dining-room, still in forgetfulness of what had occurred, but repeating, as above, the turning from sideboard to table in act of preparing more tea. I looked casually towards the fire, and there I saw the soldier again. This time I was entirely alarmed, and fled from the room in haste. I called to my father, but when he came he saw nothing."

Sometimes more than one sense is affected. The following is a case :

"In response to your request to write out my experience of Oct. 30, 1886, I will inflict on you a letter.

"On the day above mentioned, Oct. 30, 1886, I was in ———, where I was teaching. I had performed my regular routine work for the day, and was sitting in my room working out trigonometrical formulæ. I was expecting every day to hear of the confinement of my wife, and naturally my thoughts for some time had been more or less with her. She was, by the way, in B——, some fifty miles from me.

"At the time, however, neither she nor the expected event was in my mind ; as I said, I was working out trigonometrical formulæ, and I had been working on trigonometry the entire evening. About eleven o'clock, as I sat there buried in sines, cosines, tangents, cotangents, secants, and cosecants, I felt very distinctly upon my left shoulder a touch, and a slight shake, as if somebody had tried to attract my attention by other means and had failed. Without rising I turned my head, and there between me and the door stood my wife, dressed exactly as I last saw her, some five weeks before. As I turned she said : ' It is a little Herman ; he has come.' Something more was said, but this is the only sentence I can recall. To make sure that I was not asleep and dreaming, I rose from the chair, pinched myself and walked toward the figure, which disappeared immediately as I rose. I can give no information as to the length of time occupied by this episode, but I know I was awake, in my usual good health. The touch was very distinct, the figure was absolutely perfect, stood about three feet from the door, which was closed, and had not been opened during the evening. The sound of the voice was unmistakable, and I should have recognized it as my wife's voice even if I had not turned and had not seen the figure at all. The tone was conversational, just as if she would have said the same words had she been actually standing there.

"In regard to myself, I would say, as I have already intimated, I was in my usual good health ; I had not been sick before, nor was I after the occurrence, not so much as a headache having afflicted me.

"Shortly after the experience above described, I retired for the night and, as I usually do, slept quietly until morning. I did not speculate particularly about the strange appearance of the night before, and though I thought of it some, I did not tell anybody. The following morning I rose, not conscious of having dreamed anything, but I was very firmly impressed with the idea that there was something for me at the telegraph-office. I tried to throw off the impression, for so far as I knew there was no reason for it. Having nothing to do, I went out for a walk ; and to help throw off the impression above noted, I walked away from the telegraph-office. As I proceeded, however, the impression became a conviction, and I actually turned about and went to the very place I had resolved not to visit, the telegraph-office. The first person I saw on arriving at said office was the telegraph-operator, who being on terms of intimacy with me, remarked : ' Hello, papa, I've got a telegram for you.' The telegram announced the birth of a boy, weighing nine pounds, and that all were doing well. Now, then, I have no theory at all about the events narrated above ; I never had any such experience before nor since ; I am no believer in spiritualism, am not in the least superstitious, know very little about ' thought-transference,'

' unconscious cerebration,' etc., etc., but I am absolutely certain about what I have tried to relate.

"In regard to the remark which I heard, ' It is a little Herman,' etc., I would add that we had previously decided to call the child, if a boy, *Herman*—my own name, by the way."*

The hallucination sometimes carries a change of the general consciousness with it, so as to appear more like a sudden lapse into a dream. The following case was given me by a man of 43, who had never anything resembling it before :

"While sitting at my desk this A. M. reading a circular of the Loyal Legion a very curious thing happened to me, such as I have never experienced. It was perfectly real, so real that it took some minutes to recover from. It seems to me like a direct intromission into some other world. I never had anything approaching it before save when dreaming at night. I was wide awake, of course. But this was the feeling. I had only just sat down and become interested in the circular, when I seemed to lose myself for a minute and then found myself in the top story of a high building very white and shining and clean, with a noble window immediately at the right of where I sat. Through this window I looked out upon a marvellous reach of landscape entirely new. I never had before such a sense of infinity in nature, such superb stretches of light and color and *cleanness.* I know that for the space of three minutes I was entirely lost, for when I began to come to, so to speak,—sitting in that other world, I debated for three or four minutes more as to which was dream and which was reality. Sitting there I got a faint sense of C.... [the town in which the writer was], away off and dim at first. Then I remember thinking ' Why, I used to live in C....; perhaps I am going back.' Slowly C.... did come back, and I found myself at my desk again. For a few minutes the process of determining where I was was very funny. But the whole experience was perfectly delightful, there was such a sense of brilliancy and clearness and lightness about it. I suppose it lasted in all about seven minutes or ten minutes."

The hallucinations of fever-delirium are a mixture of pseudo-hallucination, true hallucination, and illusion. Those of opium, hasheesh, and belladonna resemble them

---

*This case is of the class which Mr. Myers terms ' veridical.' In a subsequent letter the writer informs me that his vision occurred some five hours *before* the child was born.

in this respect. The following vivid account of a fit of hasheesh-delirium has been given me by a friend :

"I was reading a newspaper, and the indication of the approaching delirium was an inability to keep my mind fixed on the narrative. Directly I lay down upon a sofa there appeared before my eyes several rows of human hands, which oscillated for a moment, revolved and then changed to spoons. The same motions were repeated, the objects changing to wheels, tin soldiers, lamp-posts, brooms, and countless other absurdities. This stage lasted about ten minutes, and during that time it is safe to say that I saw at least a thousand different objects. These whirling images did not appear like the realities of life, but had the character of the secondary images seen in the eye after looking at some brightly-illuminated object. A mere suggestion from the person who was with me in the room was sufficient to call up an image of the thing suggested, while without suggestion there appeared all the common objects of life and many unreal monstrosities, which it is absolutely impossible to describe, and which seemed to be creations of the brain.

"The character of the symptoms changed rapidly. A sort of wave seemed to pass over me, and I became aware of the fact that my pulse was beating rapidly. I took out my watch, and by exercising considerable will-power managed to time the heart-beats, 135 to the minute.

"I could feel each pulsation through my whole system, and a curious twitching commenced, which no effort of the mind could stop.

"There were moments of apparent lucidity, when it seemed as if I could see within myself, and watch the pumping of my heart. A strange fear came over me, a certainty that I should never recover from the effects of the opiate, which was as quickly followed by a feeling of great interest in the experiment, a certainty that the experience was the most novel and exciting that I had ever been through.

"My mind was in an exceedingly impressionable state. Any place thought of or suggested appeared with all the distinctness of the reality. I thought of the Giant's Causeway in Staffa, and instantly I stood within the portals of Fingal's Cave. Great basaltic columns rose on all sides, while huge waves rolled through the chasm and broke in silence upon the rocky shore. Suddenly there was a roar and blast of sound, and the word 'Ishmaral' was echoing up the cave. At the enunciation of this remarkable word the great columns of basalt changed into whirling clothes pins and I laughed aloud at the absurdity.

"(I may here state that the word 'Ishmaral' seemed to haunt my other hallucinations, for I remember that I heard it frequently thereafter.) I next enjoyed a sort of metempsychosis. Any animal or thing that I thought of could be made the being which held my mind. I thought of a fox, and instantly I was transformed into that animal. I could distinctly feel myself a fox, could see my long ears and bushy tail, and by a sort of introvision felt that my complete anatomy was that of a fox. Suddenly the point of vision changed. My eyes seemed to be located at the back of my mouth ; I looked out between the parted lips, saw the two rows of pointed teeth, and, closing my mouth with a snap, saw—nothing.

" I was next transformed into a bombshell, felt my size, weight, and thickness, and experienced the sensation of being shot up out of a giant mortar, looking down upon the earth, bursting and falling back in a shower of iron fragments.

" Into countless other objects was I transformed, many of them so absurd that I am unable to conceive what suggested them. For example, I was a little china doll, deep down in a bottle of olive oil, next moment a stick of twisted candy, then a skeleton inclosed in a whirling coffin, and so on *ad infinitum.*

" Towards the end of the delirium the whirling images appeared again, and I was haunted by a singular creation of the brain, which reappeared every few moments. It was an image of a double-faced doll, with a cylindrical body running down to a point like a peg-top.

" It was always the same, having a sort of crown on its head, and painted in two colors, green and brown, on a background of blue. The expression of the Janus-like profiles was always the same, as were the adornments of the body. After recovering from the effects of the drug I could not picture to myself exactly how this singular monstrosity appeared, but in subsequent experiences I was always visited by this phantom, and always recognized every detail of its composition. It was like visiting some long-forgotten spot and seeing some sight that had faded from the memory, but which appeared perfectly familiar as soon as looked upon.

" The effects of the drug lasted about an hour and a half, leaving me a trifle tipsy and dizzy ; but after a ten-hour sleep I was myself again, save for a slight inability to keep my mind fixed on any piece of work for any length of time, which remained with me during most of the next day."

THE NEURAL PROCESS IN HALLUCINATION.

Examples of these singular perversions of perception might be multiplied indefinitely, but I have no more space. Let us turn to the question of what the physiological process may be to which they are due. It must, of course, consist of an excitement from within of those centres which are active in normal perception, identical in kind and degree with that which real external objects are usually needed to induce. The particular process which currents from the sense-organs arouse would seem under normal circumstances to be arousable in no other way. On p. 72 ff. above, we saw that the centres aroused by incoming peripheral currents are probably identical with the centres used in mere imagination; and that the vividness of the sensational kind of consciousness is probably correlated with a discrete degree of *intensity* in the process therein aroused. Referring the reader back to that passage and to what was more lately said on p. 103 ff., I now proceed to complete my theory of the perceptive process by an analysis of what may most probably be believed to take place in hallucination strictly so called.

We have seen (p. 75) that the free discharge of cells into each other through associative paths is a likely reason why the maximum intensity of function is not reached when the cells are excited by their neighbors in the cortex. At the end of Chapter XXV we shall return to this conception, and whilst making it still more precise, use it for explaining certain phenomena connected with the will. The idea is that the leakage forward along these paths is too rapid for the inner tension in any centre to accumulate to the maximal explosion-point, unless the exciting currents are greater than those which the various portions of the cortex supply to each other. Currents from the periphery are (as it seems) the only currents whose energy can vanquish the supra-ideational resistance (so to call it) of the cells, and cause the peculiarly intense sort of disintegration with which the sensational quality is linked. *If, however, the leakage forward were to stop*, the tension inside certain cells might reach the explosion-point, even though the influence which excited them came only from neighboring cortical parts. Let an empty pail with a leak in its bottom, tipped up against a support so that if it ever became full of water it would upset, represent the resting condition of the centre for a certain sort of feeling. Let water poured into it stand for the currents which are its natural stimulus; then the hole in its bottom will, of course, represent the 'paths' by which it transmits its excitement to other associated cells. Now let two other vessels have the function

of supplying it with water. One of these vessels stands
for the neighboring cortical cells, and can pour in hardly
any more water than goes out by the leak. The pail conse-
sequently never upsets in consequence of the supply from
this source. A current of water passes through it and does
work elsewhere, but in the pail itself nothing but what
stands for *ideational* activity is aroused. The other vessel,
however, stands for the peripheral sense-organs, and supplies a stream of water so copious that the pail promptly
fills up in spite of the leak, and presently *upsets ;* in other
words, *sensational* activity is aroused. But it is obvious that
if the leak were plugged, the slower stream of supply
would also end by upsetting the pail.

To apply this to the brain and to thought, if we take a
series of processes A B C D E, associated together in that
order, and suppose that the current through them is very
fluent, there will be little intensity anywhere until, perhaps,
a pause occurs at E. But the moment the current is blocked
anywhere, say between C and D, the process in C must
grow more intense, and might even be conceived to explode
so as to produce a sensation in the mind instead of an idea.

It would seem that some hallucinations are best to be
explained in this way. We have in fact a regular series of
facts which can all be formulated under the single law that *the
substantive strength of a state of consciousness bears an inverse
proportion to its suggestiveness.* It is the halting-places of
our thought which are occupied with distinct imagery.
Most of the words we utter have no time to awaken images
at all ; they simply awaken the following words. But when
the sentence *stops*, an image dwells for awhile before the
mental eye (see Vol. I. p. 243). Again, whenever the associative processes are reduced and impeded by the approach
of unconsciousness, as in falling asleep, or growing faint, or
becoming narcotized, we find a concomitant increase in the
intensity of whatever partial consciousness may survive. In
some people what M. Maury has called ' hypnagogic ' hallucinations * are the regular concomitant of the process of

---

* Le Sommeil et les Rêves (1865), chaps. III, IV.

falling asleep. Trains of faces, landscapes, etc., pass before the mental eye, first as fancies, then as pseudo-hallucinations, finally as full-fledged hallucinations forming dreams. If we regard association-paths as paths of drainage, then the shutting off of one after another of them as the encroaching cerebral paralysis advances ought to act like the plugging of the hole in the bottom of the pail, and make the activity more intense in those systems of cells that retain any activity at all. The level rises because the currents are not drained away, until at last the full sensational explosion may occur.

The usual explanation of hypnagogic hallucinations is that they are ideas deprived of their ordinary *reductives*. In somnolescence, sensations being extinct, the mind, it is said, then having no stronger things to compare its ideas with, ascribes to these the fulness of reality. At ordinary times the objects of our imagination are reduced to the *status* of subjective facts by the ever-present contrast of our sensations with them. Eliminate the sensations, however, this view supposes, and the 'images' are forthwith 'projected' into the outer world and appear as realities. Thus is the illusion of dreams also explained. This, indeed, after a fashion gives an account of the facts.* And yet it certainly fails to explain the extraordinary vivacity and completeness of so many of our dream-fantasms. The process of 'imagining' must (in these cases at least †) be not merely relatively, but absolutely and in itself more intense than at other times. The fact is, it is not a process of imagining, but a genuine sensational process; and the theory in question is therefore false as far as that point is concerned.

Dr. Hughlings Jackson's explanation of the epileptic seizure is acknowledged to be masterly. It involves

---

* This theory of incomplete rectification of the inner images by their usual reductives is most brilliantly stated by M. Taine in his work on Intelligence, book II. chap. I.

† Not, of course, in all cases, because the cells remaining active are themselves on the way to be overpowered by the general (unknown) condition to which sleep is due.

principles exactly like those which I am bringing forward here. The 'loss of consciousness' in epilepsy is due to the most highly organized brain-processes being exhausted and thrown out of gear. The less organized (more instinctive) processes, ordinarily inhibited by the others, are then exalted, so that we get as a mere consequence of relief from the inhibition, the meaningless or maniacal action which so often follows the attack. *

Similarly the *subsultus tendinorum* or jerking of the muscles which so often startles us when we are on the point

---

* For a full account of Jackson's theories, see his 'Croonian Lectures' published in the Brit. Med. Journ. for 1884. Cf. also his remarks in the Discussion of Dr. Mercier's paper on Inhibition in 'Brain,' xi. 361.

The loss of vivacity in the images in the process of waking, as well as the gain of it in falling asleep, are both well described by M. Taine, who writes (on Intelligence, i. 50, 58) that often in the daytime, when fatigued and seated in a chair, it is sufficient for him to close one eye with a handkerchief, when, " by degrees, the sight of the other eye becomes vague, and it closes. All external sensations are gradually effaced, or cease, at all events, to be remarked ; the internal images, on the other hand, feeble and rapid during the state of complete wakefulness, become intense, distinct, colored, steady, and lasting : there is a sort of ecstasy, accompanied by a feeling of expansion and of comfort. Warned by frequent experience, I know that sleep is coming on, and that I must not disturb the rising vision ; I remain passive, and in a few minutes it is complete. Architecture, landscapes, moving figures, pass slowly by, and sometimes remain, with incomparable clearness of form and fulness of being ; sleep comes on, and I know no more of the real world I am in. Many times, like M. Maury, I have caused myself to be gently roused at different moments of this state, and have thus been able to mark its characters.—The intense image which seems an external object is but a more forcible continuation of the feeble image which an instant before I recognized as internal ; some scrap of a forest, some house, some person which I vaguely imagined on closing my eyes, has in a minute become present to me with full bodily details, so as to change into a complete hallucination. Then, waking up on a hand touching me, I feel the figure decay, lose color, and evaporate ; what had appeared a substance is reduced to a shadow. . . . In such a case, I have often seen, for a passing moment, the image *grow pale*, waste away, and evaporate ; sometimes, on opening the eyes, a fragment of landscape or the skirt of a dress appears still to float over the fire-irons or on the black hearth." This persistence of dream-objects for a few moments after the eyes are opened seems to be no extremely rare experience. Many cases of it have been reported to me directly. Compare Müller's Physiology, Baly's tr., p. 945.

of falling asleep, may be interpreted as due to the rise (in certain lower motor centres) of the ordinary ' tonic ' tension to the explosion-point, when the inhibition commonly exerted by the higher centres falls too suddenly away.

One possible condition of hallucination then stands revealed, whatever other conditions there may be. *When the normal paths of association between a centre and other centres are thrown out of gear, any activity which may exist in the first centre tends to increase in intensity until finally the point may be reached at which the last inward resistance is overcome, and the full sensational process explodes.** Thus it will happen that causes of an amount of activity in brain-cells which would ordinarily result in a weak consciousness may produce a very strong consciousness when the overflow of these cells is stopped by the torpor of the rest of the brain. A slight peripheral irritation, then, if it reaches the centres of consciousness at all during sleep, will give rise to the dream of a violent sensation. All the books about dreaming are full of anecdotes which illustrate this. For example, M. Maury's nose and lips are tickled with a feather while he sleeps. He dreams he is being tortured by having a pitch-plaster applied to his face, torn off, lacerating the skin of nose and lips. Descartes, on being bitten by a flea, dreams of being run through by a sword. A friend tells me, as I write this, of his hair changing its position in his forehead just as he ' dozed off ' in his chair a few days since. Instantly he dreamed that some one had struck him a blow. Examples can be quoted *ad libitum*, but these are enough.†

---

* I say the ' normal ' paths, because hallucinations are not incompatible with *some* paths of association being left. Some hypnotic patients will not only have hallucinations of objects suggested to them, but will amplify them and act out the situation. But the paths here seem excessively narrow, and the reflections which ought to make the hallucination incredible do not occur to the subject's mind. In general, the narrower a train of ' ideas ' is, the vivider the consciousness is of each. Under ordinary circumstances, the entire brain probably plays a part in draining any centre which may be ideationally active. When the drainage is reduced in any way it probably makes the active process more intense.

† M. A. Maury gives a number: *op. cit.* pp. 126–8.

We seem herewith to have an explanation for a certain number of hallucinations. *Whenever the normal forward irradiation of intra-cortical excitement through association-paths is checked, any accidental spontaneous activity or any peripheral stimulation (however inadequate at other times) by which a brain-centre may be visited, sets up a process of full sensational intensity therein.*

In the hallucinations artificially produced in hypnotic subjects, some degree of peripheral excitement seems usually to be required. The brain is asleep as far as its own spontaneous thinking goes, and the words of the ' magnetizer' then awaken a cortical process which drafts off into itself any currents of a related sort which may come in from the periphery, resulting in a vivid objective perception of the suggested thing. Thus, point to a dot on a sheet of paper, and call it 'General Grant's photograph,' and your subject will see a photograph of the General there instead of the dot. The dot gives objectivity to the appearance, and the suggested notion of the General gives it form. Then magnify the dot by a lens; double it by a prism or by nudging the eyeball; reflect it in a mirror; turn it upside down; or wipe it out; and the subject will tell you that the 'photograph' has been enlarged, doubled, reflected, turned about, or made to disappear. In M. Binet's language, * the dot is the outward *point de repère* which is needed to give objectivity to your suggestion, and without which the latter will only produce a *conception* in the subject's mind.† M. Binet has shown that such a periphe-

---

* M. Binet's highly important experiments, which were first published in vol. XVII of the Revue Philosophique (1884), are also given in full in chapter IX of his and Féré's work on 'Animal Maguetism' in the International Scientific Series. Where there is no dot on the paper, nor any other visible mark, the subject's judgment about the 'portrait' would seem to be guided by what he sees happening to the entire sheet.

† It is a difficult thing to distinguish in a hypnotic patient between a genuine sensorial hallucination of something suggested and a conception of it merely, coupled with belief that it is there. I have been surprised at the vagueness with which such subjects will often trace upon blank paper the outlines of the pictures which they say they 'see' thereupon. On the other

ral *point de repère* is used in an enormous number, not only of hypnotic hallucinations, but of hallucinations of the insane. These latter are often *unilateral;* that is, the patient hears the voices always on one side of him, or sees the figure only when a certain one of his eyes is open. In many of these cases it has been distinctly proved that a morbid irritation in the internal ear, or an opacity in the humors of the eye, was the starting point of the current which the patient's diseased acoustic or optical centres clothed with their peculiar products in the way of ideas. *Hallucinations produced in this way are* 'ILLUSIONS'; *and M. Binet's theory, that all hallucinations must start in the periphery, may be called an attempt to reduce hallucination and illusion to one physiological type,* the type, namely, to which normal perception belongs. In every case, according to M. Binet, whether of perception, of hallucination, or of illusion, we get the sensational vividness by means of a current from the peripheral nerves. It may be a mere trace of a current. But that trace is enough to kindle the maximal or supra-ideational process so that the object perceived will have the character of *externality.* What the *nature* of the object shall be will depend wholly on the particular system of paths in which the process is kindled. Part of the thing in all cases comes from the sense-organ, the rest is furnished by the mind. But we cannot by introspection distinguish between these parts; and our only formula for the result is that the brain has *reacted on* the impression in the normal way. Just so in the dreams which we have considered, and in the hallucinations of which M. Binet tells, we can only say that the brain has *reacted* in an abnormal way.

M. Binet's theory accounts indeed for a multitude of cases, but certainly not for all. The prism does not always double

---

hand, you will hear them say that they find no difference between a real flower which you show them and an imaginary flower which you tell them is beside it. When told that one is imaginary and that they must pick out the real one, they sometimes say the choice is impossible, and sometimes they point to the imaginary flower.

the false appearance,* nor does the latter always disappear when the eyes are closed. Dr. Hack Tuke † gives several examples in sane people of well-exteriorized hallucinations which did not respond to Binet's tests; and Mr. Edmund Gurney ‡ gives a number of reasons why intensity in a cortical process may be expected to result from local pathological activity just as much as its peculiar nature does. For Binet, an abnormally or exclusively active part of the cortex gives the *nature* of what shall appear, whilst a peripheral sense-organ alone can give the *intensity* sufficient to make it appear projected into real space. But since this intensity is after all but a matter of degree, one does not see why, under rare conditions, the degree in question *might* not be attained by inner causes exclusively. In that case we should have certain hallucinations centrally initiated alongside of the peripherally initiated hallucinations, which are the only sort that M. Binet's theory allows. *It seems probable on the whole, therefore, that centrally initiated hallucinations can exist.* How often they do exist is another question. The existence of hallucinations which affect more than one sense is an argument for central initiation. For grant that the thing seen may have its starting point in the outer world, the voice which it is heard to utter must be due to an influence from the visual region, i.e. must be of central origin.

Sporadic cases of hallucination, visiting people only once in a lifetime (which seem to be by far the most frequent type), are on any theory hard to understand in detail. They are often extraordinarily complete ; and the fact that many of them are reported as *veridical,* that is, as coinciding with real events, such as accidents, deaths, etc., of the persons seen, is an additional complication of the phenomenon. The first really scientific study of hallucination

---

* Only the other day, in three hypnotized girls, I failed to double an hallucination with a prism. Of course it may not have been a fully-developed hallucination.

† Brain, xi. 441.

‡ Mind, x. 161, 316 ; and Phantasms of the Living (1886), i. 470–488.

in all its possible bearings, on the basis of a large mass of empirical material, was begun by Mr. Edmund Gurney and is continued by other members of the Society for Psychical Research; and the 'Census' is now being applied to several countries under the auspices of the International Congress of Experimental Psychology. It is to be hoped that out of these combined labors something solid will eventually grow. The facts shade off into the phenomena of motor automatism, trance, etc.; and nothing but a wide comparative study can give really instructive results.*

The part played by the peripheral sense-organ in hallucination is just as obscure as we found it in the case of imagination. The things seen often seem opaque and hide the background upon which they are projected. It does not follow from this, however, that the retina is actually involved in the vision. A contrary process going on in the visual centres would prevent the retinal impression made by the outer realities from being felt, and this would in mental terms be equivalent to the hiding of them by the imaginary figure. The negative after-images of mental pictures reported by Meyer and Féré, and the negative after-images of hypnotic hallucinations reported by Binet and others so far constitute the only evidence there is for the retina being involved. But until these after-images are explained in some other way we must admit the possibility of a centrifugal current from the optical centres downwards into the peripheral organ of sight, paradoxical as the course of such a current may appear.

'PERCEPTION-TIME.'

The time which the perceptive process occupies has been inquired into by various experimenters. Some call it perception-time, some choice-time, some discrimination-time. The results have been already given in Chapter XIII (vol. I, p. 523 ff.), to which the reader is consequently referred.

---

* In Mr. Gurney's work, just cited, a very large number of veridical cases are critically discussed.

Dr. Romanes gives an interesting variation of these time-measurements. He found *

"an astonishing difference between different individuals with respect to the rate at which they are able to *read*. Of course reading implies enormously intricate processes of perception both of the sensuous and of the intellectual order ; but if we choose for these observations persons who have been accustomed to read much, we may consider that they are all very much on a par with respect to the amount of practice which they have had, so that the differences in their rates of reading may fairly be attributed to real differences in their rates of forming complex perceptions in rapid succession, and not to any merely accidental differences arising from greater or less facility acquired by special practice.

"My experiments consisted in marking a brief printed paragraph in a book which had never been read by any of the persons to whom it was to be presented. The paragraph, which contained simple statements of simple facts, was marked on the margin with pencil. The book was then placed before the reader open, the page, however, being covered with a sheet of paper. Having pointed out to the reader upon this sheet of paper what part of the underlying page the marked paragraph occupied, I suddenly removed the sheet of paper with one hand, while I started a chronograph with the other. Twenty seconds being allowed for reading the paragraph (ten lines octavo), as soon as the time was up I again suddenly placed the sheet of paper over the printed page, passed the book on to the next reader, and repeated the experiment as before. Meanwhile, the first reader, the moment after the book had been removed, wrote down all that he or she could remember having read. And so on with all the other readers.

"Now the results of a number of experiments conducted on this method were to show, as I have said, astonishing differences in the *maximum* rate of reading which is possible to different individuals, all of whom have been accustomed to extensive reading. That is to say, the difference may amount to 4 to 1 ; or, otherwise stated, in a given time one individual may be able to read four times as much as another. Moreover, it appeared that there was no relationship between slowness of reading and power of assimilation ; on the contrary, when all the efforts are directed to assimilating as much as possible in a given time, the rapid readers (as shown by their written notes) usually give a better account of the portions of the paragraph which have been compassed by the slow readers than the latter are able to give ; and the most rapid reader I have found is also the best at assimilating. I should further say that there is no relationship between rapidity of perception as thus tested and intellectual activity as tested by the general results of intellectual work ; for I have tried the experiment with

---

* Mental Evolution in Animals, p. 136.

several highly distinguished men in science and literature, most of whom I found to be slow readers."*

---

* *Literature.* The best treatment of perception with which I am acquainted is that in Mr. James Sully's book on ' Illusions ' in the International Scientific Series. On hallucinations the literature is large. Gurney, Kandinsky (as already cited), and some articles by Kraepelin in the Vierteljahrschrift für Wissenschaftliche Philosophie, vol. v (1881), are the most systematic studies recently made. All works on Insanity treat of them. Dr. W. W. Ireland's works, ' The Blot upon the Brain ' (1886) and ' Through the Ivory Gate ' (1890) have much information on the subject. Gurney gives pretty complete references to older literature. The most important thing on the subject from the point of view of theory is the article by Mr. Myers on the Demon of Socrates in the Proceedings of the Society for Psychical Research for 1889, p. 522.

CHAPTER XX.

THE PERCEPTION OF SPACE.*

THE FEELING OF CRUDE EXTENSITY.

In the sensations of hearing, touch, sight, and pain we are accustomed to distinguish from among the other elements the element of voluminousness. We call the reverberations of a thunderstorm more voluminous than the squeaking of a slate-pencil; the entrance into a warm bath gives our skin a more massive feeling than the prick of a pin; a little neuralgic pain, fine as a cobweb, in the face, seems less extensive than the heavy soreness of a boil or the vast discomfort of a colic or a lumbago; and a solitary star looks smaller than the noonday sky. In the sensation of dizziness or subjective motion, which recent investigation has proved to be connected with stimulation of the semi-circular canals of the ear, the spatial character is very prominent. Whether the ' muscular sense' directly yields us knowledge of space is still a matter of litigation among psychologists. Whilst some go so far as to ascribe our entire cognition of extension to its exclusive aid, others deny to it all extensive quality whatever. Under these circumstances we shall do better to adjourn its consideration; admitting, however, that it seems at first sight as if we felt something decidedly more voluminous when we contract our thigh-muscles than when we twitch an eyelid or some small muscle in the face. It seems, moreover, as if this difference lay in the feeling of the thigh-muscles themselves.

In the sensations of smell and taste this element of varying vastness seems less prominent but not altogether absent. Some tastes and smells appear less extensive than complex flavors, like that of roast meat or plum pudding, on the one hand, or heavy odors like musk or tuberose, on

---

* Reprinted, with considerable revision, from ' Mind ' for 1887.

the other. The epithet *sharp* given to the acid class would seem to show that to the popular mind there is something narrow and, as it were, streaky, in the impression they make, other flavors and odors being bigger and rounder.

The sensations derived from the inward organs are also distinctly more or less voluminous. Repletion and empti-ness, suffocation, palpitation, headache, are examples of this, and certainly not less spatial is the consciousness we have of our general bodily condition in nausea, fever, heavy drowsiness, and fatigue. Our entire cubic content seems then sensibly manifest to us as such, and feels much larger than any local pulsation, pressure, or discomfort. Skin and retina are, however, the organs in which the space-element plays the most active part. Not only does the maximal vastness yielded by the retina surpass that yielded by any other organ, but the intricacy with which our atten-tion can subdivide this vastness and perceive it to be com-posed of lesser portions simultaneously coexisting along-side of each other is without a parallel elsewhere.* The ear gives a greater vastness than the skin, but is consider-ably less able to subdivide it.†

Now my first thesis is that this element, discernible in each and every sensation, though more developed in some than in others, is the original sensation of space, out of which all the exact knowledge about space that we afterwards come to have is woven by processes of discrimination, association, and selection. 'Extensity,' as Mr. James Ward calls it,‡

---

* Prof. Jastrow has found that invariably we tend to *underestimate* the amount of our skin which may be stimulated by contact with an object when we express it in terms of visual space; that is, when asked to mark on paper the extent of skin affected, we always draw it much too small. This shows that the eye gets as much space-feeling from the smaller line as the skin gets from the larger one. Cf. Jastrow: Mind, xi. 546-7; Ameri-can Journal of Psychology, iii. 53.

† Amongst sounds the graver ones seem the most extensive. Stumpf gives three reasons for this: 1) association with bigger causes; 2) wider reverberation of the hand and body when grave notes are sung; 3) audi-bility at a greater distance. He thinks that these three reasons dispense us from supposing an immanent extensity in the sensation of sound as such. See his remarks in the Tonpsychologie, i. 207-211.

‡ Encyclopædia Britannica, 9th Edition, article Psychology, pp. 46, 53.

on this view, becomes an element in each sensation just as intensity is. The latter every one will admit to be a distinguishable though not separable ingredient of the sensible quality. In like manner extensity, being an entirely peculiar kind of feeling indescribable except in terms of itself, and inseparable in actual experience from some sensational quality which it must accompany, can itself receive no other name than that of *sensational element.*

It must now be noted that *the vastness hitherto spoken of is as great in one direction as in another.* Its dimensions are so vague that in it there is no question as yet of surface as opposed to depth ; 'volume' being the best short name for the sensation in question. *Sensations of different orders are roughly comparable, inter se, with respect to their volumes.* This shows that the spatial quality in each is identical wherever found, for different qualitative elements, e.g. warmth and odor, are incommensurate. Persons born blind are reported surprised at the largeness with which objects appear to them when their sight is restored. Franz says of his patient cured of cataract : "He saw everything much larger than he had supposed from the idea obtained by his sense of touch. Moving, and especially living, objects appeared very large." * Loud sounds have a certain enormousness of feeling. It is impossible to conceive of the explosion of a cannon as filling a small space. In general, sounds seem to occupy all the room between us and their source ; and in the case of certain ones, the cricket's song, the whistling of the wind, the roaring of the surf, or a distant railway train, to have no definite starting point.

In the sphere of vision we have facts of the same order. 'Glowing' bodies, as Hering says, give us a perception "which seems *roomy* (*raumhaft*) in comparison with that of strictly surface color. A glowing iron looks luminous through and through, and so does a flame." † A luminous fog, a band of sunshine, affect us in the same way. As Hering urges :

---

* Philosophical Transactions (1841).

† Hermann's Handb. d. Physiol., Bd. iii. 1, S. 575.

" We must distinguish *roomy* from superficial, as well as distinctly from indistinctly bounded, sensations. The dark which with closed eyes one sees before one is, for example, a roomy sensation. We do not see a black surface like a wall in front of us, but a space filled with darkness, and even when we succeed in seeing this darkness as terminated by a black wall there still remains in front of this wall the dark space. The same thing happens when we find ourselves with open eyes in an absolutely dark room. This sensation of darkness is also vaguely bounded. An example of a distinctly bounded roomy sensation is that of a clear and colored fluid seen in a glass ; the yellow of the wine is seen not only on the bounding surface of the glass ; the yellow sensation fills the whole interior of the glass. By day the so-called empty space between us and objects seen appears very different from what it is by night. The increasing darkness settles not only upon the things but also *between* us and the things, so as at last to cover them completely and fill the space alone. If I look into a dark box I find it *filled* with darkness, and this is seen not merely as the dark-colored sides or walls of the box. A shady corner in an otherwise well-lighted room is full of a darkness which is not only *on* the walls and floor but *between* them in the space they include. Every sensation is there where I experience it, and if I have it at once at every point of a certain roomy space, it is then a voluminous sensation. A cube of transparent green glass gives us a spatial sensation ; an opaque cube painted green, on the contrary, only sensations of surface." *

There are certain quasi-motor sensations in the head when we change the direction of the attention, which equally seem to involve three dimensions. If with closed eyes we think of the top of the house and then of the cellar, of the distance in front of us and then of that behind us, of space far to the right and then far to the left, we have something far stronger than an idea,—an actual feeling, namely, as if something in the head moved into another direction. Fechner was, I believe, the first to publish any remarks on these feelings. He writes as follows :

" When we transfer the attention from objects of one sense to those of another we have an indescribable feeling (though at the same time one perfectly determinate and reproducible at pleasure) of altered direction, or differently localized tension (*Spannung*). We feel a strain forward in the eyes, one directed sideways in the ears, increasing with the degree of our attention, and changing according as we look at an object carefully, or listen to something attentively ; wherefore we speak of *straining the attention*. The difference is most plainly felt when

---

* *Loc. cit.* S. 572.

the attention vibrates rapidly between eye and ear. This feeling localizes itself with most decided difference in regard to the various sense-organs according as we wish to discriminate a thing delicately by touch, taste, or smell.

"But now I have, when I try to vividly recall a picture of memory or fancy, a feeling perfectly analogous to that which I experience when I seek to grasp a thing keenly by eye or ear ; and this analogous feeling is very differently localized. While in sharpest possible attention to real objects (as well as to after-images) the strain is plainly forwards, and, when the attention changes from one sense to another, only alters its direction between the sense-organs, leaving the rest of the head free from strain, the case is different in memory or fancy ; for here the feeling withdraws entirely from the external sense-organs, and seems rather to take refuge in that part of the head which the brain fills. If I wish, for example, to recall a place or person, it will arise before me with vividness, not according as I strain my attention forwards, but rather in proportion as I, so to speak, retract it backwards." *

It appears probable that the feelings which Fechner describes are in part constituted by imaginary semi-circular canal sensations.† These undoubtedly convey the most delicate perception of change in direction; and when, as here, the changes are not perceived as taking place in the external world, they occupy a vague internal space located within the head.‡

---

* Elemente der Psychophysik, II. 475–6.

† See Foster's Text-book of Physiology, bk. III. c. VI. § 2.

‡ Fechner, who was ignorant of the but lately discovered function of the semi-circular canals, gives a different explanation of the organic seat of these feelings. They are probably highly composite. With me, actual movements in the eyes play a considerable part in them, though I am hardly conscious of the peculiar feelings in the scalp which Fechner goes on to describe thus : "The feeling of strained attention in the different sense-organs seems to be only a muscular one produced in using these various organs by setting in motion, by a sort of reflex action, the set of muscles which belong to them. One can ask, then, with what particular muscular contraction the sense of strained attention in the effort to recall something is associated ? On this question my own feeling gives me a decided answer ; it comes to me distinctly not as a sensation of tension in the inside of the head, but as a feeling of strain and contraction in the scalp, with a pressure from outwards in over the whole cranium, undoubtedly caused by a contraction of the muscles of the scalp. This harmonizes very well with the expressions, *sich den Kopf zerbrechen, den Kopf zusammennehmen.* In a former illness, when I could not endure the slightest effort after continuous thought, and had no theoretical bias on this question, the muscles of the scalp, especially those of the back-head, assumed a fairly morbid degree of sensibility whenever I tried to think." (Elem. der Psychophysik, II. 490–91.)

In the skin itself there is a vague form of projection into the third dimension to which Hering has called attention.

"Heat is not felt only against the cutaneous surface, but when communicated through the air may appear extending more or less out from the surface into the third dimension of surrounding space. . . . We can determine in the dark the place of a radiant body by moving the hand to and fro, and attending to the fluctuation of our feeling of warmth. The feeling itself, however, is not projected fully into the spot at which we localize the hot body, but always remains in the neighborhood of the hand."

The interior of one's mouth-cavity feels larger when explored by the tongue than when looked at. The crater of a newly-extracted tooth, and the movements of a loose tooth in its socket, feel quite monstrous. A midge buzzing against the drum of the ear will often seem as big as a butterfly. The spatial sensibility of the tympanic membrane has hitherto been very little studied, though the subject will well repay much trouble. If we approach it by introducing into the outer ear some small object like the tip of a rolled-up tissue-paper lamplighter, we are surprised at the large radiating sensation which its presence gives us, and at the sense of clearness and openness which comes when it is removed. It is immaterial to inquire whether the far-reaching sensation here be due to actual irradiation upon distant nerves or not. We are considering now, not the objective causes of the spatial feeling, but its subjective varieties, and the experiment shows that the same object gives more of it to the inner than to the outer cuticle of the ear. The pressure of the air in the tympanic cavity upon the membrane gives an astonishingly large sensation. We can increase the pressure by holding our nostrils and closing our mouth and forcing air through our Eustachian tubes by an expiratory effort; and we can diminish it by either inspiring or swallowing under the same conditions of closed mouth and nose. In either case we get a large round tridimensional sensation inside of the head, which seems as if it must come from the affection of an organ much larger than the tympanic membrane, whose surface hardly exceeds that of one's little-finger-nail.

The tympanic membrane is furthermore able to render sensible differences in the pressure of the external atmosphere, too slight to be felt either as noise or in this more violent way. If the reader will sit with closed eyes and let a friend approximate some solid object, like a large book, noiselessly to his face, he will immediately become aware of the object's presence and position—likewise of its departure. A friend of the writer, making the experiment for the first time, discriminated unhesitatingly between the three degrees of solidity of a board, a lattice-frame, and a sieve, held close to his ear. Now as this sensation is never used by ordinary persons as a means of perception, we may fairly assume that its felt quality, in those whose attention is called to it for the first time, belongs to it *quâ* sensation, and owes nothing to educational suggestions. But this felt quality is most distinctly and unmistakably one of vague spatial vastness in three dimensions—quite as much so as is the felt quality of the retinal sensation when we lie on our back and fill the entire field of vision with the empty blue sky. When an object is brought near the ear we immediately feel shut in, contracted; when the object is removed, we suddenly feel as if a transparency, clearness, openness, had been made outside of us. And the feeling will, by any one who will take the pains to observe it, be acknowledged to involve the third dimension in a vague, unmeasured state.*

The reader will have noticed, in this enumeration of facts, that *voluminousness of the feeling seems to bear very little relation to the size of the organ that yields it.* The ear and eye are comparatively minute organs, yet they give us feelings of great volume. The same lack of exact proportion between size of feeling and size of organ affected obtains within the limits of particular sensory organs. An object appears smaller on the lateral portions of the retina than it does on the fovea, as may be easily verified by holding the

---

* That the sensation in question is one of tactile rather than of acoustic sensibility would seem proved by the fact that a medical friend of the writer, both of whose *membranæ tympani* are quite normal, but one of whose ears is almost totally deaf, feels the presence and withdrawal of objects as well at one ear as at the other.

two forefingers parallel and a couple of inches apart, and transferring the gaze of one eye from one to the other. Then the finger not directly looked at will appear to shrink, and this whatever be the direction of the fingers. On the tongue a crumb, or the calibre of a small tube, appears larger than between the fingers. If two points kept equidistant (blunted compass- or scissors-points, for example) be drawn across the skin so as really to describe a pair of parallel lines, the lines will appear farther apart in some spots than in others. If, for example, we draw them horizontally across the face, so that the mouth falls between them, the person experimented upon will feel as if they began to diverge near the mouth and to include it in a well-marked ellipse. In like manner, if we keep the compass-

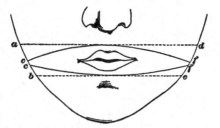

Fig. 51 (after Weber).

points one or two centimetres apart, and draw them down the forearm over the wrist and palm, finally drawing one along one finger, the other along its neighbor, the appearance will be that of a single line, soon breaking into two, which become more widely separated below the wrist, to contract again in the palm, and finally diverge rapidly again towards the finger-tips. The dotted lines in Figs. 51 and 52 represent the true path of the compass-points; the full lines their apparent path.

The same length of skin, moreover, will convey a more extensive sensation according to the manner of stimulation. If the edge of a card be pressed against the skin, the distance between its extremities will seem shorter than that between two compass-tips touching the same terminal points.*

---

* The skin seems to obey a different law from the eye here. If a given retinal tract be excited, first by a series of points, and next by the two

In the eye, intensity of nerve-stimulation seems to increase the *volume* of the feeling as well as its brilliancy. If we raise and lower the gas alternately, the whole room and all the objects in it seem alternately to enlarge and contract. If we cover half a page of small print with a gray glass, the print seen through the glass appears decidedly smaller than that seen outside of it, and the darker the glass the greater the difference. When a circumscribed opacity in front of the retina keeps off part of the light from the portion which it covers, objects projected on that portion may seem but half as large as when their image falls outside of it.* The inverse effect seems produced by certain drugs and anæsthetics. Morphine, atropine, daturine, and cold blunt the sensibility of the skin, so that distances upon it seem less. Haschish produces strange perversions of the general sensibility. Under its influence one's body may seem either enormously enlarged or strangely contracted. Sometimes a single member will alter its proportion to the rest; or one's back, for instance, will appear entirely absent, as if one were hollow behind. Objects comparatively near will recede to a vast distance, a short street assume to the eye an immeasurable perspective. Ether and chloroform

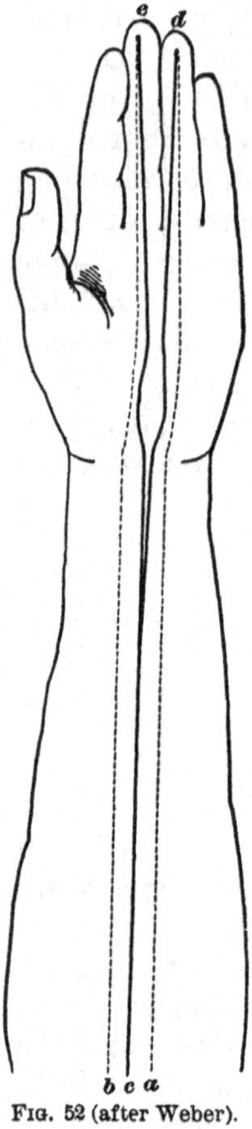

Fig. 52 (after Weber).

extreme points, with the interval between them unexcited, this interval will seem considerably less in the second case than it seemed in the first. In the skin the unexcited interval feels the larger. The reader may easily verify the facts in this case by taking a visiting-card, cutting one edge of it into a saw-tooth pattern, and from the opposite edge cutting out all but the two corners, and then comparing the feelings aroused by the two edges when held against the skin.

* Classen, Physiologie des Gesichtssinnes, p. 114 ; see also A. Riehl, Der Philosophische Kriticismus, II. p. 149.

occasionally produce not wholly dissimilar results. Panum, the German physiologist, relates that when, as a boy, he was etherized for neuralgia, the objects in the room grew extremely small and distant, before his field of vision darkened over and the roaring in his ears began. He also mentions that a friend of his in church, struggling in vain to keep awake, saw the preacher grow smaller and smaller and more and more distant. I myself on one occasion observed the same recession of objects during the beginning of chloroformization. In various cerebral diseases we find analogous disturbances.

Can we assign the physiological conditions which make the elementary sensible largeness of one sensation vary so much from that of another? Only imperfectly. One factor in the result undoubtedly is the number of nerve-terminations simultaneously excited by the outward agent that awakens the sensation. When many skin-nerves are warmed, or much retinal surface illuminated, our feeling is larger than when a lesser nervous surface is excited. The single sensation yielded by two compass-points, although it seems simple, is yet felt to be much bigger and blunter than that yielded by one. The touch of a single point may always be recognized by its quality of sharpness. This page looks much smaller to the reader if he closes one eye than if both eyes are open. So does the moon, which latter fact shows that the phenomenon has nothing to do with parallax. The celebrated boy couched for the cataract by Cheselden thought, after his first eye was operated, " all things he saw extremely large," but being couched of his second eye, said " that objects at first appeared large to this eye, but not so large as they did at first to the other; and looking upon the same object with both eyes, he thought it looked about twice as large as with the first couched eye only, but not double, that we can anyways discover."

The greater extensiveness that the feeling of certain parts of the same surface has over other parts, and that one order of surface has over another (retina over skin, for example), may also to a certain extent be explained by the operation of the same factor. It is an anatomical fact that the most spatially sensitive surfaces (retina, tongue, finger-tips, etc.) are supplied by nerve-trunks of unusual thickness, which must supply to every unit of surface-area an unusually large number of terminal fibres. But the variations of felt extension obey probably only a very rough law of numerical proportion to the number of fibres. A sound is not twice as voluminous to two ears as to one; and the above-cited variations of feeling, when the same surface is excited under different conditions, show that the feeling is a resultant of several factors of which the anatomical one is only the principal. Many ingenious hypotheses have been brought forward to assign the co-operating factors where different conditions give conflicting amounts of felt space. Later we shall analyze some of these cases in detail, but it must be confessed here in advance that many of them resist analysis altogether. *

---

* It is worth while at this point to call attention with some emphasis to the fact that, though the anatomical condition of the feeling *resembles* the feeling itself, such resemblance cannot be taken by our understanding to explain *why* the feeling should be just what it is. We hear it untiringly reiterated by materialists and spiritualists alike that we can see no possible inward reason why a certain brain-process should produce the feeling of redness and another of anger : the one process is no more red than the other is angry, and the coupling of process and feeling is, as far as our understanding goes, a juxtaposition pure and simple. But in the matter of *spatial* feeling, where the retinal patch that produces a triangle in the mind is itself a triangle, it looks at first sight as if the sensation might be a direct cognition of its own neural condition. Were this true, however, our sensation should be one of *multitude* rather than of continuous extent ; for the condition is *number* of optical nerve-termini, and even this is only a remote condition and not an immediate condition. The immediate condition of the feeling is not the process in the retina, but the process in the brain; and the process in the brain may, for aught we know, be as unlike a triangle,—nay, it probably is so,—as it is unlike redness or rage. It is simply a *coincidence* that in the case of space one of the organic conditions, viz., the triangle impressed on the skin or the retina, should lead to a representation in the mind of the subject observed similar to that which it produces in the psychological observer. In no other kind of case is the coincidence found. Even should we admit that we cognize triangles in space because of our immediate cognition of the triangular shape of our excited group of nerve-tips, the matter would hardly be more transparent, for the mystery would still remain, why are we so much better cognizant of triangles on our finger-tips than on the nerve-tips of our back, on our eye than on our ear, and on any of these parts than in our brain ? Thos. Brown very rightly rejects the notion of explaining the shape of the space perceived by the shape of the 'nervous expansion affected.' "If this

THE PERCEPTION OF SPATIAL ORDER.

So far, all we have established or sought to establish is the existence of the vague form or *quale* of spatiality as an inseparable element bound up with the other peculiarities of each and every one of our sensations. The numerous examples we have adduced of the variations of this extensive element have only been meant to make clear its strictly sensational character. In very few of them will the reader have been able to explain the variation by an added intellectual element, such as the suggestion of a recollected experience. In almost all it has seemed to be the immediate psychic effect of a peculiar sort of nerve-process excited; and all the nerve-processes in question agree in yielding what space they do yield, to the mind, in the shape of a simple total vastness, in which, *primitively* at least, no *order of parts* or of *subdivisions* reigns.

Let no one be surprised at this notion of a space without order. There may be a space without order just as there may be an order without space.* And the primitive perceptions of space are certainly of an unordered kind. The order which the spaces first perceived potentially include must, before being distinctly apprehended by the mind, be woven into those spaces by a rather complicated set of intellectual acts. The primordial largenesses which the sensations yield must be *measured and subdivided* by consciousness, and *added* together, before they can form by their synthesis what we know as the real Space of the objective world. In these operations, imagination, association, attention, and selection play a decisive part; and although they nowhere add any new material to the space-data of sense, they so shuffle and manipulate these data and hide

---

alone were necessary, we should have square inches and half inches, and various other forms, rectilinear and curvilinear, of fragance and sound." (Lectures, XXII.)

* Musical tones, e.g., have an order of quality independent either of their space- or time-order. Music comes from the time-order of the notes upsetting their quality-order. In general, if $a\ b\ c\ d\ e\ f\ g\ h\ i\ j\ k$, etc., stand for an arrangement of feelings in the order of their quality, they may assume *any* space-order or time-order, as $d\ e\ f\ a\ h\ g$, etc., and still the order of quality will remain fixed and unchanged.

present ones behind imagined ones that it is no wonder if some authors have gone so far as to think that the sense-data have no spatial worth at all, and that the intellect, since it makes the subdivisions, also gives the spatial quality to them out of resources of its own.

As for ourselves, having found that all our sensations (however as yet unconnected and undiscriminated) are of extensive objects, *our next problem is : How do we* ARRANGE *these at first chaotically given spaces into the one regular and orderly 'world of space' which we now know?*

To begin with, there is no reason to suppose that the several sense-spaces of which a sentient creature may become conscious, each filled with its own peculiar content, should tend, simply *because they are many*, to enter into any definite spatial intercourse with each other, or lie in any particular order of positions. Even in ourselves we can recognize this. Different feelings may coexist in us without assuming any particular spatial order. The sound of the brook near which I write, the odor of the cedars, the comfort with which my breakfast has filled me, and my interest in this paragraph, all lie distinct in my consciousness, but in no sense outside or alongside of each other. Their spaces are interfused and at most fill the same vaguely objective world. Even where the qualities are far less disparate, we may have something similar. If we take our subjective and corporeal sensations alone, there are moments when, as we lie or sit motionless, we find it very difficult to feel distinctly the length of our back or the direction of our feet from our shoulders. By a strong effort we can succeed in dispersing our attention impartially over our whole person, and then we feel the real shape of our body in a sort of unitary way. But in general a few parts are strongly emphasized to consciousness and the rest sink out of notice ; and it is then remarkable how vague and ambiguous our perception of their relative order of location is. Obviously, for the orderly arrangement of a multitude of sense-spaces in consciousness, something more than their mere separate existence is required. What is this further condition?

If a number of sensible extents are to be perceived alongside

*of each other and in definite order they must appear as parts in
a vaster sensible extent which can enter the mind simply and all
at once.* I think it will be seen that the difficulty of estimating correctly the form of one's body by pure feeling
arises from the fact that it is very hard to feel its totality as
a unit at all. The trouble is similar to that of thinking forwards and backwards simultaneously. When conscious of
our head we tend to grow unconscious of our feet, and there
enters thus an element of time-succession into our perception of ourselves which transforms the latter from an act of
intuition to one of construction. This element of constructiveness is present in a still higher degree, and carries
with it the same consequences, when we deal with objective
spaces too great to be grasped by a single look. The relative positions of the shops in a town, separated by many
tortuous streets, have to be thus constructed from data apprehended in succession, and the result is a greater or less
degree of vagueness.

That a sensation *be discriminated as a part* from out of a
larger enveloping space is then the *conditio sine quâ non* of its
being apprehended in a definite spatial order. The problem
of ordering our feelings in space is then, in the first instance,
a problem of discrimination, but not of discrimination pure
and simple; for then not only coexistent sights but coexistent sounds would necessarily assume such order, which
they notoriously do not. Whatever is discriminated will
appear as a small space within a larger space, it is true, but
this is but the very rudiment of order. For the location of
it within that space to become precise, other conditions still
must supervene; and the best way to study what they are
will be to pause for a little and *analyze what the expression
'spatial order' means.*

Spatial order is an abstract term. The concrete perceptions which it covers are figures, directions, positions, magnitudes, and distances. To single out any one of these
things from a total vastness is partially to introduce order
into the vastness. To subdivide the vastness into a multitude of these things is to apprehend it in a completely
orderly way. Now what are these things severally? **To**

begin with, no one can for an instant hesitate to say that some of them are qualities of sensation, just as the total vastness is in which they lie. Take figure: a square, a circle, and a triangle appear in the first instance to the eye simply as three different kinds of impressions, each so peculiar that we should recognize it if it were to return. When Nunnely's patient had his cataracts removed, and a cube and a sphere were presented to his notice, he could at once perceive a difference in their shapes; and though he could not say which was the cube and which the sphere, he saw they were not of the same figure. So of lines: if we can notice lines at all in our field of vision, it is inconceivable that a vertical one should not affect us differently from an horizontal one, and should not be recognized as affecting us similarly when presented again, although we might not yet know the name 'vertical,' or any of its connotations, beyond this peculiar affection of our sensibility. So of angles: an obtuse one affects our feeling immediately in a different way from an acute one. Distance-apart, too, is a simple sensation—the sensation of a line joining the two distant points: lengthen the line, you alter the feeling and with it the distance felt.

Space-relations.

But with distance and direction we pass to the category of space-*relations*, and are immediately confronted by an opinion which makes of all relations something *toto cœlo* different from all facts of feeling or imagination whatsoever. A relation, for the Platonizing school in psychology, is an energy of pure thought, and, as such, is quite incommensurable with the data of sensibility between which it may be perceived to obtain.

We may consequently imagine a disciple of this school to say to us at this point: "Suppose you *have* made a separate specific sensation of each line and each angle, what boots it? You have still the order of directions and of distances to account for; you have still the relative magnitudes of all these felt figures to state; you have their respective positions to define before you can be said to have brought order into your space. And not one of these de-

terminations can be effected except through an act of relating thought, so that your attempt to give an account of
space in terms of pure sensibility breaks down almost at
the very outset. *Position,* for example, can never be a sensation, for it has nothing intrinsic about it; it can only
obtain *between* a spot, line, or other figure and *extraneous
co-ordinates,* and can never be an element of the sensible
datum, the line or the spot, in itself. Let us then confess
that Thought alone can unlock the riddle of space, and
that Thought is an adorable but unfathomable mystery."

Such a method of dealing with the problem has the
merit of shortness. Let us, however, be in no such hurry,
but see whether we cannot get a little deeper by patiently
considering what these space-relations are.

'Relation' is a very slippery word. It has so many
different concrete meanings that the use of it as an abstract
universal may easily introduce bewilderment into our
thought. We must therefore be careful to avoid ambiguity
by making sure, wherever we have to employ it, what its
precise meaning is in that particular sphere of application.
At present we have to do with space-relations, and no others.
Most 'relations' are feelings of an entirely different order
from the terms they relate. The relation of similarity, e.g.,
may equally obtain between jasmine and tuberose, or between Mr. Browning's verses and Mr. Story's; it is itself
neither odorous nor poetical, and those may well be pardoned
who have denied to it all sensational content whatever.
But just as, in the field of quantity, the relation between
two numbers is another number, so *in the field of space the
relations are facts of the same order with the facts they relate.
If these latter be patches in the circle of vision, the former
are certain other patches between them.* When we speak of
the relation of direction of two points toward each other,
we mean simply the sensation of the line that joins the two
points together. *The line is the relation;* feel it and you
feel the relation, see it and you see the relation; nor can
you in any conceivable way think the latter except by imagining the former (however vaguely), or describe or indicate the one except by pointing to the other. And the
moment you have imagined the line, the relation stands

before you in all its completeness, with nothing further to be done. Just so the relation of *direction* between two lines is identical with the peculiar sensation of shape of the space enclosed between them. This is commonly called an angular relation.

If these relations are sensations, no less so are the relations of position. *The relation of position between the top and bottom points of a vertical line is that line,* and nothing else. The relations of position between a point and a horizontal line below it are potentially numerous. There is one more important than the rest, called its distance. This is the sensation, ideal or actual, of a perpendicular drawn from the point to the line.* Two lines, one from each extremity of the horizontal to the point, give us a peculiar sensation of triangularity. This feeling may be said to constitute the *locus* of all the relations of position of the elements in question. *Rightness and leftness, upness and downness, are again pure sensations* differing specifically from each other, and generically from everything else. Like all sensations, they can only be indicated, not described. If we take a cube and label one side *top,* another *bottom,* a third *front,* and a fourth *back,* there remains no form of words by which we can describe to another person which of the remaining sides is *right* and which *left.* We can only point and say *here* is right and *there* is left, just as we should say *this* is red and *that* blue. Of two points seen beside each other at all, one is always affected by one of these feelings, and the other by the opposite; the same is true of the extremities of any line.†

---

* The whole science of geometry may be said to owe its being to the exorbitant interest which the human mind takes in *lines.* We cut space up in every direction in order to manufacture them.

† Kant was, I believe, the first to call attention to this last order of facts. After pointing out that two opposite spherical triangles, two gloves of a pair, two spirals wound in contrary directions, have identical inward determinations, that is, have their parts defined with relation *to each other* by the same law, and so must be *conceived* as identical, he showed that the impossibility of their mutual superposition obliges us to assign to each figure of a symmetrical pair a peculiar difference of its own which can only consist in an *outward* determination or relation of its parts, no longer to each other, but to the whole of an objectively outlying space with its points of the compass given absolutely. This inconceivable difference is perceived only

Thus it appears indubitable that all space-relations except those of magnitude are nothing more or less than pure sensational objects. But *magnitude* appears to outstep this narrow sphere. We have relations of muchness and littleness between times, numbers, intensities, and qualities, as well as spaces. It is impossible, then, that such relations should form a particular kind of simply spatial feeling. This we must admit: the relation of quantity is generic and occurs in many categories of consciousness, whilst the other relations we have considered are specific and occur in space alone. When our attention passes from a shorter line to a longer, from a smaller spot to a larger, from a feebler light to a stronger, from a paler blue to a richer, from a march tune to a galop, the transition is accompanied in the synthetic field of consciousness by a peculiar feeling of difference which is what we call the sensation of *more,*— more length, more expanse, more light, more blue, more motion. This transitional sensation of *more* must be identical with itself under all these different accompaniments, or we should not give it the same name in every case. We get it when we pass from a short vertical line to a long horizontal one, from a small square to a large circle, as well as when we pass between those figures whose shapes are congruous. But when the shapes are congruous our consciousness of the relation is a good deal more distinct, and it is most distinct of all when, in the exercise of our analytic attention, we notice, first, a *part*, and then the *whole*, of a *single* line or shape. Then the *more* of the whole actually sticks out, as a separate piece of space, and is so envisaged. The same exact sensation of it is given when we are able to superpose one line or figure on another. This indispensable condition of exact measurement of the *more* has led some to think that the feeling itself arose in every case from original experiences of superposition. This is

---

"through the relation to right and left, which is a matter of immediate intuition." In these last words (*welches unmittelbar auf Anschauung geht* —Prolegomena, § 12) Kant expresses all that we have meant by speaking of up and down, right and left, as *sensations*. He is wrong, however, in invoking relation to extrinsic total space as essential to the existence of these contrasts in figures. Relation to our own body is enough.

probably not an absolutely true opinion, but for our present purpose that is immaterial. So far as the subdivisions
of a sense-space are to be *measured* exactly against each
other, objective forms occupying one subdivision must
directly or indirectly be superposed upon the other, and
the mind must get the immediate feeling of an outstanding
plus. And even where we only feel one subdivision to be
vaguely larger or less, the mind must pass rapidly between
it and the other subdivision, and receive the immediate sensible shock of the *more.*

*We seem thus to have accounted for all space-relations, and
made them clear to our understanding. They are nothing but
sensations of particular lines, particular angles, particular forms
of transition, or* (in the case of a *distinct more*) *of particular
outstanding portions of space after two figures have been superposed.* These relation-sensations may actually be produced
as such, as when a geometer draws new lines across a figure
with his pencil to demonstrate the relations of its parts,
or they may be ideal representations of lines, not really
drawn. But in either case their entrance into the mind is
equivalent to a more detailed subdivision, cognizance, and
measurement of the space considered. *The bringing of subdivisions to consciousness constitutes, then, the entire process
by which we pass from our first vague feeling of a total
vastness to a cognition of the vastness in detail.* The more
numerous the subdivisions are, the more elaborate and perfect the cognition becomes. But inasmuch as all the subdivisions are themselves sensations, and even the feeling
of 'more' or 'less' is, where not itself a figure, at least a
sensation of transition between two sensations of figure,
it follows, for aught we can as yet see to the contrary,
that *all spatial knowledge is sensational at bottom,* and that,
as the sensations lie together in the unity of consciousness,
no new material element whatever comes to them from a
supra-sensible source.*

---

* In the eyes of many it will have seemed strange to call a relation a
mere line, and a line a mere sensation. We may easily learn a great deal
about any relation, say that between two points: we may divide the line
which joins these, and distinguish it, and classify it, and find out *its* rela-

The bringing of subdivisions to consciousness ! This, then, is our next topic. They may be brought to consciousness under three aspects in respect of their *locality*, in respect of their *size*, in respect of their *shape*.

The Meaning of Localization.

Confining ourselves to the problem of locality for the present, let us begin with the simple case of a sensitive surface, only two points of which receive stimulation from without. How, first, are these two points felt as alongside of each other with an interval of space between them ? We must be conscious of two things for this : of the duality of the excited points, and of the extensiveness of the unexcited interval. The duality alone, although a necessary, is not a sufficient condition of the spatial separation. We may, for instance, discern two sounds in the same place, sweet and sour in the same lemonade, warm and cold, round and pointed contact in the same place on the skin, etc.* In all discrimination the recognition of the duality of two feelings by the mind is the easier the more strongly the feelings are

---

tions by drawing or representing new lines, and so on. But all this further industry has naught to do with our *acquaintance* with the relation itself, in its first intention. So cognized, the relation *is* the line and nothing more. It would indeed be fair to call it something less; and in fact it is easy to understand how most of us come to feel as if the line were a much grosser thing than the relation. The line is broad or narrow, blue or red, made by this object or by that alternately, in the course of our experience; it is therefore independent of any one of these accidents; and so, from viewing it as no one of *such* sensible qualities, we may end by thinking of it as something which cannot be defined except as the negation of all sensible quality whatever, and which needs to be put *into* the sensations by a mysterious act of 'relating thought.'

Another reason why we get to feel as if a space-relation must be something other than the mere feeling of a line or angle is that between two positions we can potentially make any number of lines and angles, or find, to suit our purposes, endlessly numerous relations. The sense of this indefinite potentiality cleaves to our words when we speak in a general way of 'relations of place,' and misleads us into supposing that not even any single one of them can be exhaustively equated by a single angle or a single line.

* This often happens when the warm and cold points, or the round and pointed ones, are applied to the skin within the limits of a single 'Empfindungskreis.'

contrasted in quality. If our two excited points awaken identical qualities of sensation, they must, perforce, appear to the mind as one ; and, not distinguished at all, they are, *a fortiori*, not localized apart. Spots four centimetres distant on the back have no qualitative contrast at all, and fuse into a single sensation. Points less than three thousandths of a millimetre apart awaken on the retina sensations so contrasted that we apprehend them immediately as two. Now these unlikenesses which arise so slowly when we pass from one point to another in the back, so much faster on the tongue and finger-tips, but with such inconceivable rapidity on the retina, what are they? Can we discover anything about their intrinsic nature?

The most natural and immediate answer to make is that they are unlikeness of *place* pure and simple. In the words of a German physiologist,* to whom psychophysics owes much :

" The sensations are from the outset (*von vornherein*) localized. . . . Every sensation as such is from the very beginning affected with the spatial quality, so that this quality is nothing like an external attribute coming to the sensation from a higher faculty, but must be regarded as something immanently residing in the sensation itself."

And yet the moment we reflect on this answer an insuperable logical difficulty seems to present itself. No single *quale* of sensation can, by itself, amount to a consciousness of *position*. Suppose no feeling but that of a single point ever to be awakened. Could that possibly be the feeling of any special *whereness* or *thereness* ? Certainly not. *Only when a second point is felt to arise can the first one acquire a determination of up, down, right or left, and these determinations are all relative to that second point.* Each point, so far as it is *placed*, *is* then only by virtue of what it *is not*, namely, by virtue of another point. This is as much as to say that position has nothing *intrinsic* about it ; and that, although a feeling of absolute bigness may, *a feeling of place cannot, possibly form an immanent element in any single isolated sensation.* The very writer we have quoted has given heed to this objection, for he continues (p. 335) by saying that the

---

* Vierordt, Grundriss der Physiologie, 5te Auflage (1877), pp. 326, 436.

sensations thus originally localized "are only so *in them-selves,* but not in the representation of consciousness, which is not yet present. . . . They are, in the first instance, devoid of all mutual relations with each other." But such a localization of the sensation 'in itself' would seem to mean nothing more than the susceptibility or *potentiality* of being distinctly localized when the time came and other conditions became fulfilled. Can we now discover anything about such susceptibility in itself before it has borne its ulterior fruits in the developed consciousness?

'Local Signs.'

To begin with, every sensation of the skin and every visceral sensation seems to derive from its topographic seat a peculiar shade of feeling, which it would not have in another place. And this feeling *per se* seems quite another thing from the perception of the place. Says Wundt * :

" If with the finger we touch first the cheek and then the palm, exerting each time precisely the same pressure, the sensation shows notwithstanding a distinctly marked difference in the two cases. Similarly, when we compare the palm with the back of the hand, the nape of the neck with its anterior surface, the breast with the back ; in short, any two distant parts of the skin with each other. And moreover, we easily remark, by attentively observing, that spots even tolerably close together differ in respect of the quality of their feeling. If we pass from one point of our cutaneous surface to another, we find a perfectly gradual and continuous alteration in our feeling, notwithstanding the objective nature of the contact has remained the same. Even the sensations of corresponding points on opposite sides of the body, though similar, are not identical. If, for instance, we touch first the back of one hand and then of the other, we remark a qualitative unlikeness of sensation. It must not be thought that such differences are mere matters of imagination, and that we take the sensations to be different because we represent each of them to ourselves as occupying a different place. With sufficient sharpening of the attention, we may, confining ourselves to the quality of the feelings alone, entirely abstract from their locality, and yet notice the differences quite as markedly."

---

*Vorlesungen üb. Menschen- u. Thierseele (Leipzig, 1863), I. 214. See also Ladd's Physiological Psychology, pp. 396–8, and compare the account by G. Stanley Hall (Mind, x. 571) of the sensations produced by moving a blunt point lightly over the skin. Points of cutting pain, quivering, thrilling, whirling, tickling, scratching, and acceleration, alternated with each other along the surface.

Whether these local contrasts shade into each other with absolutely continuous gradations, we cannot say. But we know (continues Wundt) that

"they change, when we pass from one point of the skin to its neighbor, with very different degrees of rapidity. On delicately-feeling parts, used principally for touching, such as the finger-tips, the difference of sensation between two closely approximate points is already strongly pronounced ; whilst in parts of lesser delicacy, as the arm, the back, the legs, the disparities of sensation are observable only between distant spots."

The internal organs, too, have their specific *qualia* of sensation. An inflammation of the kidney is different from one of the liver ; pains in joints and muscular insertions are distinguished. Pain in the dental nerves is wholly unlike the pain of a burn. But very important and curious similarities prevail throughout these differences. Internal pains, whose seat we cannot see, and have no means of knowing unless the character of the pain itself reveal it, are felt *where* they belong. Diseases of the stomach, kidney, liver, rectum, prostate, etc., of the bones, of the brain and its membranes, are referred to their proper position. Nerve-pains describe the length of the nerve. Such localizations as those of vertical, frontal, or occipital headache of intracranial origin force us to conclude that parts which are neighbors, whether inner or outer, may possess by mere virtue of that fact a common peculiarity of feeling, a respect in which their sensations agree, and which serves as a token of their proximity. These *local* colorings are, moreover, so strong that we cognize them as the same, throughout all contrasts of sensible quality in the accompanying perception. Cold and heat are wide as the poles asunder ; yet if both fall on the cheek, there mixes with them something that makes them in *that respect* identical ; just as, contrariwise, despite the identity of cold with itself wherever found, when we get it first on the palm and then on the cheek, some difference comes, which keeps the two experiences for ever asunder.*

---

* Of the anatomical and physiological conditions of these facts we know as yet but little, and that little need not here be discussed. Two principal hypotheses have been invoked in the case of the retina. Wundt (Men-

And now let us revert to the query propounded a moment since: *Can these differences of mere quality in feeling, varying according to locality yet having each sensibly and intrinsically and by itself nothing to do with position, constitute the 'susceptibilities' we mentioned, the conditions of being perceived in position, of the localities to which they belong?* The numbers on a row of houses, the initial letters of a set of words, have no intrinsic kinship with points of space, and yet they are the conditions of our knowledge of where any house is in the row, or any word in the dictionary. Can the modifications of feeling in question be tags or labels of this kind which in no wise originally reveal the position of the spot to which they are attached, but guide us to it by what Berkeley would call a 'customary tie'? Many authors have unhesitatingly replied in the affirmative; Lotze, who in his Medizinische Psychologie* first described the sensations in this way, designating them, thus conceived, as *local-signs.* This term has obtained wide currency in Germany, and *in speaking of the 'LOCAL-SIGN THEORY' hereafter, I shall always mean the theory which denies that there can be in a sensation any element of actual locality, of inherent spatial order,* any tone as

---

schen- u. Thierseele, I. 214) called attention to the changes of color-sensibility which the retina displays as the image of the colored object passes from the fovea to the periphery. The color alters and becomes darker, and the change is more rapid in certain directions than in others. This alteration in general, however, is one of which, *as such,* we are wholly unconscious. We see the sky as bright blue all over, the modifications of the blue sensation being interpreted by us, not as differences in the objective color, but as distinctions in its locality. Lotze (Medizinische Psychologie, 333, 355), on the other hand, has pointed out the peculiar tendency which each particular point of the retina has to call forth that movement of the eyeball which will carry the image of the exciting object from the point in question to the *fovea.* With each separate tendency to movement (as with each actual movement) we may suppose a peculiar modification of sensibility to be conjoined. This modification would constitute the peculiar local tingeing of the image by each point. See also Sully's Psychology, pp. 118–121. Prof. B. Erdman has quite lately (Vierteljahrsschrift f. wiss. Phil., x. 324–9) denied the existence of all evidence for such immanent *qualia* of feeling characterizing each locality. Acute as his remarks are, they quite fail to convince me. On the skin the *qualia* are evident, I should say. Where, as on the retina, they are less so (Kries and Auerbach), this may well be a mere difficulty of discrimination not yet educated to the analysis.

* 1852, p. 331.

it were which cries to us immediately and without further
ado, 'I am *here*,' or 'I am *there*.'

If, as may well be the case, we by this time find ourselves tempted to accept the Local-sign theory in a general
way, we have to clear up several farther matters. If a sign
is to lead us to *the thing* it means, we must have some other
source of knowledge of that thing. Either the thing has
been given in a previous experience of which the sign also
formed part—they are *associated ;* or it is what Reid calls a
'natural' sign, that is, a feeling which, the first time it
enters the mind, evokes from the native powers thereof a
cognition of the thing that hitherto had lain dormant. In
both cases, however, the sign is one thing, and the thing
another. In the instance that now concerns us, *the sign is
a quality of feeling and the thing is a position.* Now we have
seen that the position of a point is not only revealed, but
created, by the existence of other points to which it stands
in determinate *relations.* *If the sign can by any machinery
which it sets in motion evoke a consciousness either of the other
points, or of the relations, or of both, it would seem to fulfil its
function, and reveal to us the position we seek.*

But such a machinery is already familiar to us. It is
neither more nor less than the law of habit in the nervous
system. When any point of the sensitive surface has been
frequently excited simultaneously with, or immediately
before or after, other points, and afterwards comes to be
excited alone, there will be a tendency for its perceptive
nerve-centre to irradiate into the nerve-centres of the other
points. Subjectively considered, this is the same as if we
said that *the peculiar feeling of the first point* SUGGESTS *the
feeling of the entire region with whose stimulation its own excitement has been habitually* ASSOCIATED.

Take the case of the stomach. When the epigastrium
is heavily pressed, when certain muscles contract, etc., the
stomach is squeezed, and its peculiar local sign awakes in
consciousness simultaneously with the local signs of the
other squeezed parts. There is also a sensation of total
vastness aroused by the combined irritation, and *somewhere*
in this the stomach-feeling seems to lie. Suppose that
later a pain arises in the stomach from some non-mechani-

cal cause. It will be tinged by the gastric local sign, and the nerve-centre supporting this latter feeling will excite the centre supporting the dermal and muscular feelings habitually associated with it when the excitement was mechanical. From the combination the same peculiar vastness will again arise. In a word, 'something' in the stomach-sensation 'reminds' us of a total space, of which the diaphragmatic and epigastric sensations also form a part, or, to express it more briefly still, suggests the neighborhood of these latter organs.*

Revert to the case of two excited points on a surface with an unexcited space between them. The general result of previous experience has been that when either point was impressed by an outward object, the same object also touched the immediately neighboring parts. Each point, together with its local sign, is thus associated with a circle of surrounding points, the association fading in strength as the circle grows larger. Each will revive its own circle; but when both are excited together, the strongest revival will be that due to the *combined* irradiation. Now the tract *joining the two excited points* is the only part common to the two circles. And the feelings of this whole tract will therefore awaken with considerable vividness in the imagination when its extremities are touched by an outward irritant. The mind receives with the impression of the two distinct points the vague idea of a line. The twoness of the points comes from the contrast of their local signs: the line comes from the associations into which experience has wrought these latter. If no ideal line arises we have duality without sense of interval; if the line be excited actually rather

---

* Maybe the localization of intracranial pain is itself due to such association as this of local signs with each other, rather than to their qualitative similarity in neighboring parts (*supra*, p. 19); though it is conceivable that association and similarity itself should here have one and the same neural basis. If we suppose the sensory nerves from those parts of the body beneath any patch of skin to terminate in the same sensorial brain-tract as those from the skin itself, and if the excitement of any one fibre tends to irradiate through the whole of that tract, the feelings of all fibres going to that tract would presumably both have a similar intrinsic quality, and at the same time tend each to arouse the other. Since the same nerve-trunk in most cases supplies the skin and the parts beneath, the anatomical hypothesis presents nothing improbable.

than ideally, we have the interval given with its ends, in the form of a single extended object felt. E. H. Weber, in the famous article in which he laid the foundations of all our accurate knowledge of these subjects, *laid it down as the logical requisite for the perception of two separated points, that the mind should, along with its consciousness of them, become aware of an unexcited interval as such. I have only tried to show how the known laws of experience may cause this requisite to be fulfilled.* Of course, if the local signs of the entire region offer but little qualitative contrast *inter se*, the line suggested will be but dimly defined or discriminated in length or direction from other possible lines in its neighborhood. This is what happens in the back, where consciousness can sunder two spots, whilst only vaguely apprehending their distance and direction apart.

The relation of position of the two points *is* the suggested interval or line. Turn now to the simplest case, that of *a single excited spot. How can it suggest its position?* Not by recalling any particular line unless experience have constantly been in the habit of marking or tracing some one line from it towards some one neighboring point. Now on the back, belly, viscera, etc., no such tracing habitually occurs. The consequence is that the only suggestion is that of the whole neighboring circle; i.e., *the spot simply recalls the general region in which it happens to lie.* By a process of successive construction, it is quite true that we can also get the feeling of distance between the spot and some other particular spot. Attention, by reinforcing the local sign of one part of the circle, can awaken a new circle round this part, and so *de proche en proche* we may slide our feeling down from our cheek, say, to our foot. But when we first touched our cheek we had no consciousness of the foot at all.* In the extremities, the lips, the tongue and other mobile parts, the case is different. We there have an instinctive tendency, when a part of lesser discriminative

---

* Unless, indeed, the foot happen to be spontaneously tingling or something of the sort at the moment. The whole surface of the body is always in a state of semi-conscious irritation which needs only the emphasis of attention, or of some accidental inward irritation, to become strong at any point.

sensibility is touched, to move the member so that the touching object glides along it to the place where sensibility is greatest. If a body touches our hand we move the hand over it till the finger-tips are able to explore it. If the sole of our foot touches anything we bring it towards the toes, and so forth. There thus arise lines of habitual passage from all points of a member to its sensitive tip. These are the lines most readily recalled when any point is touched, and their recall is identical with the consciousness of the distance of the touched point from the ' tip.' I think anyone must be aware when he touches a point of his hand or wrist that it is the relation to the finger-tips of which he is usually most conscious. Points on the forearm suggest either the finger-tips or the elbow (the latter being a spot of greater sensibility*). In the foot it is the toes, and so on. A point can only be cognized in its relations to the entire body at once by awakening a *visual* image of the whole body. Such awakening is even more obviously than the previously considered cases a matter of pure association.

This leads us to the eye. On the retina the fovea and the yellow spot about it form a focus of exquisite sensibility, towards which every impression falling on an outlying portion of the field is moved by an instinctive action of the muscles of the eyeball. Few persons, until their attention is called to the fact, are aware how almost impossible it is to keep a conspicuous visible object in the margin of the field of view. The moment volition is relaxed we find that without our knowing it our eyes have turned so as to bring it to the centre. This is why most persons are unable to keep the eyes steadily converged upon a point in space with nothing in it. The objects against the walls of the room

---

* It is true that the inside of the fore-arm, though its discriminative sensibility is often less than that of the outside, usually rises very prominently into consciousness when the latter is touched. Its *æsthetic* sensibility to contact is a good deal finer. We enjoy stroking it from the extensor to the flexor surface around the ulnar side more than in the reverse direction. Pronating movements give rise to contacts in this order, and are frequently indulged in when the back of the fore-arm feels an object against it.

invincibly attract the foveæ to themselves. If we contemplate a blank wall or sheet of paper, we always observe in a moment that we are directly looking at some speck upon it which, unnoticed at first, ended by 'catching our eye.' Thus *whenever an image falling on the point P of the retina excites attention, it more habitually moves from that point towards the fovea than in any one other direction.* The line traced thus by the image is not always a straight line. When the direction of the point from the fovea is neither vertical nor horizontal but oblique, the line traced is often a curve, with its concavity directed upwards if the direction is upwards, downwards if the direction is downwards. This may be verified by anyone who will take the trouble to make a simple experiment with a luminous body like a candle-flame in a dark enclosure, or a star. Gazing first at some point remote from the source of light, let the eye be suddenly turned full upon the latter. The luminous image will necessarily fall in succession upon a continuous series of points, reaching from the one first affected to the fovea. But by virtue of the slowness with which retinal excitements die away, the entire series of points will for an instant be visible as an after-image, displaying the above peculiarity of form according to its situation.* These radiating lines are neither regular nor invariable in the same person, nor, probably, equally curved in different individuals. We are incessantly drawing them between the fovea and every point of the field of view. Objects remain in their peripheral indistinctness only so long as they are unnoticed. The moment we attend to them they grow distinct through one of these motions—which leads to the idea prevalent among uninstructed persons that we see distinctly all parts of the field of view at once. *The result of this incessant tracing of radii is that whenever a local sign P is awakened by a spot of light falling upon it, it recalls forthwith, even though the eyeball be unmoved, the local signs of all the other points which lie between P and the fovea.* It recalls them in imaginary form, just as the normal reflex movement would recall them in vivid form; and with their recall is given a consciousness more or less

---

* These facts were first noticed by Wundt: see his Beiträge, p. 140, 202. See also Lamansky, Pflüger's Archiv, XI. 418.

faint of the whole line on which they lie. In other words, no ray of light can fall on any retinal spot without the local sign of that spot revealing to us, by recalling the line of its most habitual associates, its direction and distance from the centre of the field. The fovea acts thus as the origin of a system of polar co-ordinates, in relation to which each and every retinal point has through an incessantly-repeated process of association its distance and direction determined. Were *P* alone illumined and all the rest of the field dark we should still, even with motionless eyes, know whether *P* lay high or low, right or left, through the *ideal streak*, different from all other streaks, which *P* alone has the power of awakening.*

---

* So far all has been plain sailing, but our course begins to be so tortuous when we descend into minuter detail that I will treat of the more precise determination of locality in a long note. When *P* recalls an ideal line leading to the fovea the line is felt in its entirety and but vaguely ; whilst *P*, which we supposed to be a single star of actual light, stands out in strong distinction from it. The ground of the distinction between *P* and the ideal line which it terminates is manifest—*P* being vivid while the line is faint ; *but why should P hold the particular position it does, at the end of the line, rather than anywhere else—for example, in its middle?* That seems something not at all manifest.

To clear up our thoughts about this latter mystery, let us take the case of an actual line of light, none of whose parts is ideal. The feeling of the line is produced, as we know, when a multitude of retinal points are excited together, each of which *when excited separately* would give rise to *one* of the feelings called local signs. Each of these signs is the feeling of a small space. From their simultaneous arousal we might well suppose a feeling of larger space to result. But why is it necessary that *in* this larger spaciousness the sign *a* should appear always at one end of the line, *z* at the other, and *m* in the middle ? For though the line be a unitary streak of light, its several constituent points can nevertheless break out from it, and become alive, each for itself, under the selective eye of attention.

The uncritical reader, giving his first careless glance at the subject, will say that there is no mystery in this, and that ' of course ' local signs must appear alongside of each other, each in its own place;—there is no other way possible. But the more philosophic student, whose business it is to discover difficulties quite as much as to get rid of them, will reflect that it is conceivable that the partial factors might fuse into a larger space, and yet not each be located within it any more than a voice is *located* in a chorus. He will wonder how, after combining into the line, the points *can* become severally alive again : the separate puffs of a ' sirene ' no longer strike the ear after they have fused into a certain pitch of sound. He will recall the fact that when, after looking at things with one eye closed, we

And with this we can close the first great division of our subject. We have shown that, within the range of

double, by opening the other eye, the number of retinal points affected, the new retinal sensations do not as a rule appear *alongside* of the old ones and additional to them, but merely make the old ones seem larger and nearer. Why should the affection of new points on the *same* retina have so different a result? In fact, he will see no sort of logical connection between (1) the original separate local signs, (2) the line as a unit, (3) the line with the points discriminated in it, and (4) the various nerve-processes which subserve all these different things. He will suspect our local sign of being a very slippery and ambiguous sort of creature. Positionless at first, it no sooner appears in the midst of a gang of companions than it is found maintaining the strictest position of its own, and assigning place to each of its associates. How is this possible? Must we accept what we rejected a while ago as absurd, and admit the points each to have position *in se?* Or must we suspect that our whole construction has been fallacious, and that we have tried to conjure up, out of association, qualities which the associates never contained?

There is no doubt a real difficulty here; and the shortest way of dealing with it would be to confess it insoluble and ultimate. Even if position be not an intrinsic character of any one of those sensations we have called local signs, we must still admit that there is *something about* every one of them that stands for the potentiality of position, and is the *ground* why the local sign, when it gets placed at all, gets placed *here* rather than *there.* If this ' something ' be interpreted as a physiological something, as a mere nerve-process, it is easy to say in a blank way that when it is excited alone, it is an ' ultimate fact ' (1) that a positionless spot will appear; that when it is excited together with other similar processes, but *without* ⌐the process of discriminative attention, it is another ' ultimate fact ' (2) that a unitary line will come; and that the final ' ultimate fact ' (3) is that, when the nerve-process is excited *in combination with* that other process which subserves the feeling of attention, what results will be the line with the local sign inside of it determined to a particular place. Thus we should escape the responsibility of explaining, by falling back on the everlasting inscrutability of the psycho-neural nexus. The moment we call the ground of localization physiological, we need only point out *how,* in those cases in which localization occurs, the physiological process *differs* from those in which it does not, to have done all we can possibly do in the matter. This would be unexceptionable logic, and with it we might let the matter drop, satisfied that there was no self-contradiction in it, but only the universal psychological puzzle of how a new mode of consciousness emerges whenever a fundamentally new mode of nervous action occurs.

But, blameless as such tactics would logically be on our part, let us see whether we cannot push our theoretic insight a little farther. It seems to me we can. We cannot, it is true, give a reason why the line we feel when process (2) awakens should have its own peculiar shape; nor can we explain the essence of the process of discriminative attention. But we can see why, if the brute facts be admitted that a line may have one of its parts singled out by attention at all, and that that part may appear in relation to

every sense, experience takes *ab initio* the spatial form. We have also shown that in the cases of the retina and skin

---

other parts at all, the relation must be *in the line itself,*—for the line and the parts are the only things supposed to be in consciousness. And we can furthermore suggest a reason why parts appearing thus in relation to each other in a line should fall into an immutable order, and each within that order keep its characteristic place.

If a lot of such local signs all have any quality which evenly augments as we pass from one to the other, we can arrange them in an ideal serial order, in which any one local sign must lie below those with more, above those with less, of the quality in question. It must divide the series into two parts,—unless indeed it have a maximum or minimum of the quality, when it either begins or ends it.

Such an ideal series of local signs in the mind is, however, not yet identical with the feeling of a line in space. Touch a dozen points on the skin *successively,* and there seems no necessary reason why the notion of a definite line should emerge, even though we be strongly aware of a gradation of quality among the touches. We may of course symbolically arrange them in a line in our thought, but we can always distinguish between a line symbolically thought and a line directly felt.

But note now the peculiarity of the nerve-processes of all these local signs: though they may give no line when excited successively, when excited *together* they do give the actual sensation of a line in space. The sum of them is the neural process of that line; the sum of their feelings is the feeling of that line; and if we begin to single out particular points from the line, and notice them by their rank, it is impossible to see how this rank can *appear* except as an actual fixed space-position sensibly felt as a bit of the total line. The scale itself appearing as a line, rank in it must appear as a definite part of the line. If the seven notes of an octave, when heard together, appeared to the sense of hearing as an outspread *line* of sound—which it is needless to say they do not—why then no one note could be discriminated without being localized, according to its pitch, *in* the line, either as one of its extremities or as some part between.

But not alone the gradation of their quality arranges the local-sign feelings in a scale. Our *movements* arrange them also in a *time*-scale. Whenever a stimulus passes from point *a* of the skin or retina to point *f,* it awakens the local-sign feelings in the perfectly definite time-order *abcdef.* It cannot excite *f* until *cde* have been successively aroused. The feeling *c* sometimes is preceded by *ab*, sometimes followed by *ba*, according to the movement's direction; the result of it all being that we never feel either *a*, *c*, or *f*, without there clinging to it faint reverberations of the various time-orders of transition in which, throughout past experience, it has been aroused. To the local sign *a* there clings the tinge or tone, the penumbra or fringe, of the transition *bcd.* To *f*, to *c*, there cling quite different tones. Once admit the principle that a feeling may be tinged by the reproductive consciousness of an habitual transition, even when the transition is not made, and it seems entirely natural to admit that, if the transition be habitually in the order *abcdef*, and if *a*, *c*, and *f* be felt separately at all, *a* will be felt with an essential *earliness,* *f* with an essential *lateness,* and that *c* will

every sensible total may be subdivided by discriminative attention into sensible parts, which are also spaces, and into relations between the parts, these being sensible spaces too. Furthermore, we have seen (in a foot-note) that different parts, once discriminated, necessarily fall into a determinate order, both by reason of definite gradations in their quality, and by reason of the fixed order of time-succession in which movements arouse them. But in all this nothing has been said of the comparative *measurement* of one sensible space-total against another, or of the way in which, by summing our divers simple sensible space-experiences together, we end by constructing what we regard as the unitary, continuous, and infinite objective Space of the real world. To this more difficult inquiry we next pass.

THE CONSTRUCTION OF 'REAL' SPACE.

The problem breaks into two subordinate problems .

(1) *How is the subdivision and measurement of the several sensorial spaces completely effected?* and

(2) *How do their mutual addition and fusion and reduction to the same scale, in a word, how does their synthesis, occur?*

I think that, as in the investigation just finished, we found ourselves able to get along without invoking any data but those that pure sensibility on the one hand, and the ordinary intellectual powers of discrimination and recollec-

---

fall between. Thus those psychologists who set little store by local signs and great store by movements in explaining space-perception, would have a perfectly definite time-order, due to motion, by which to account for the definite order of positions that appears when sensitive spots are excited all at once. Without, however, the preliminary admission of the 'ultimate fact' that this collective excitement shall feel like a *line* and nothing else, it can never be explained why the new order should needs be an order of *positions*, and not of merely ideal serial rank. We shall hereafter have any amount of opportunity to observe how thoroughgoing is the participation of motion in all our spatial measurements. Whether the local signs have their respective qualities evenly graduated or not, the feelings of transition must be set down as among the *veræ causæ* in localization. But the gradation of the local signs is hardly to be doubted; so we may believe ourselves really to possess two sets of reasons for localizing any point we may happen to distinguish from out the midst of any line or any larger space.

tion on the other, were able to yield; so here we shall emerge from our more complicated quest with the conviction that all the facts can be accounted for on the supposition that no other mental forces have been at work save those we find everywhere else in psychology: sensibility, namely, for the data; and discrimination, association, memory, and choice for the rearrangements and combinations which they undergo.

1. *The Subdivision of the Original Sense-spaces.*

How are spatial subdivisions brought to consciousness? in other words, How does spatial discrimination occur? The general subject of discrimination has been treated in a previous chapter. Here we need only inquire what are the conditions that make spatial discrimination so much finer in sight than in touch, and in touch than in hearing, smell, or taste.

The first great condition is, that different points of the surface shall differ in the quality of their immanent sensibility, that is, that each shall carry its special local-sign. If the skin felt everywhere exactly alike, a foot-bath could be distinguished from a total immersion, as being smaller, but never distinguished from a wet face. The local-signs are indispensable; two points which have the same local-sign will always be felt as the same point. We do not judge them two unless we have discerned their sensations to be different.* Granted none but homogeneous irritants, that organ would then distinguish the greatest multiplicity of irritants—would count most stars or compass-points, or best compare the size of two wet surfaces—whose local sensibility was the least even. A skin whose sensibility shaded rapidly off from a focus, like the apex of a boil, would be better than a homogeneous integument for spatial perception. The retina, with its exquisitely sensitive fovea, has this peculiarity, and undoubtedly owes to it a great part

* M. Binet (Revue Philosophique, Sept. 1880, page 291) says we judge them locally different as soon as their sensations differ enough for us to distinguish them as qualitatively different when successively excited. This is not strictly true. Skin-sensations, different enough to be discriminated when *successive*, may still fuse locally if excited both at once.

of the minuteness with which we are able to subdivide the total bigness of the sensation it yields. On its periphery the local differences do not shade off very rapidly, and we can count there fewer subdivisions.

But these local differences of feeling, so long as the surface is unexcited from without, are almost null. I canot feel them by a pure mental act of attention unless they belong to quite distinct parts of the body, as the nose and the lip, the finger-tip and the ear; their contrast needs the reinforcement of outward excitement to be felt. In the spatial muchness of a colic—or, to call it by the more spacious-sounding vernacular, of a 'bellyache'—one can with difficulty distinguish the north-east from the south-west corner, but can do so much more easily if, by pressing one's finger against the former region, one is able to make the pain there more intense.

The local differences require then an adventitious sensation, superinduced upon them, to awaken the attention. After the attention has once been awakened in this way, it may continue to be conscious of the unaided difference; just as a sail on the horizon may be too faint for us to notice until someone's finger, placed against the spot, has pointed it out to us, but may then remain visible after the finger has been withdrawn. But all this is true only on condition that separate points of the surface may be *exclusively* stimulated. If the whole surface at once be excited from without, and homogeneously, as, for example, by immersing the body in salt water, local discrimination is not furthered. The local-signs, it is true, all awaken at once; but in such multitude that no one of them, with its specific quality, stands out in contrast with the rest. If, however, a single extremity be immersed, the contrast between the wet and dry parts is strong, and, at the surface of the water especially, the local-signs attract the attention, giving the feeling of a ring surrounding the member. Similarly, two or three wet spots separated by dry spots, or two or three hard points against the skin, will help to break up our consciousness of the latter's bigness. In cases of this sort, where points receiving an identical kind of excitement are, nevertheless, felt to be locally distinct, and the objective irritants are also judged multiple,—e.g., compass-points on skin or stars on retina,—the ordinary explanation is no doubt just, and we judge the outward causes to be multiple because we have discerned the local feelings of their sensations to be different.

Capacity for partial stimulation is thus the second condition favoring discrimination. A sensitive surface which has to be excited in all its parts at once can yield nothing but a sense of undivided largeness. This appears to be the case with the olfactory, and to all intents and purposes with the gustatory, surfaces. Of many tastes and flavors, even simultaneously presented, each affects the totality of its respective organ, each appears with the whole vastness given by that organ, and appears interpenetrated by the rest.*

---

* It may, however, be said that even in the tongue there is a determination of bitter flavors to the back and of acids to the front edge of the organ. Spices likewise affect its sides and front, and a taste like that of alum localizes itself, by its styptic effect on the portion of mucous membrane, which it immediately touches, more sharply than roast pork, for example, which stimulates all parts alike. The pork, therefore, tastes more spacious than the alum or the pepper. In the nose, too, certain smells, of which vinegar may be taken as the type, seem less spatially extended than heavy, suffocating odors, like musk. The reason of this appears to be that the former inhibit inspiration by their sharpness, whilst the latter are drawn into the lungs, and thus excite an objectively larger surface. The ascription of height and depth to certain notes seems due, not to any localization of the sounds, but to the fact that a feeling of vibration in the chest and tension in the gullet accompanies the singing of a bass note, whilst, when we sing high, the palatine mucous membrane is drawn upon by the muscles which move the larynx, and awakens a feeling in the roof of the mouth.

The only real objection to the law of partial stimulation laid down in the text is one that might be drawn from the organ of hearing; for, according to modern theories, the cochlea may have its separate nerve-termini exclusively excited by sounds of differing pitch, and yet the sounds seem all to fill a common space, and not necessarily to be arranged alongside of each other. At most the high note is felt as a thinner, brighter streak against a darker background. In an article on Space, published in the Journal of Speculative Philosophy for January, 1879, I ventured to suggest that possibly the auditory nerve-termini might be "excited all at once by sounds of any pitch, as the whole retina would be by every luminous point if there were no dioptric apparatus affixed." And I added : " Notwithstanding the brilliant conjectures of the last few years which assign different acoustic end-organs to different rates of air-wave, we are still greatly in the dark about the subject ; and I, for my part, would much more confidently reject a theory of hearing which violated the principles advanced in

I should have been willing some years ago to name without hesitation a third condition of discrimination—saying it would be most developed in that organ which is susceptible of the *most various qualities* of feeling. The retina is unquestionably such an organ. The colors and shades it perceives are infinitely more numerous than the diversities of skin-sensation. And it can feel at once white and black, whilst the ear can in nowise so feel sound and silence. But the late researches of Donaldson, Blix, and Goldscheider, * on specific points for heat, cold, pressure, and pain in the skin ; the older ones of Czermak (repeated later by Klug in Ludwig's laboratory), showing that a hot and a cold compass-point are no more easily discriminated as two than two of equal temperature ; and some unpublished experiments of my own—all disincline me to make much of this condition now.† There is, however, one quality of sensa-

---

this article than give up those principles for the sake of any hypothesis hitherto published about either organs of Corti or basilar membrane." Professor Rutherford's theory of hearing, advanced at the meeting of the British Association for 1886, already furnishes an alternative view which would make hearing present no exception to the space-theory I defend, and which, whether destined to be proved true or false, ought, at any rate, to make us feel that the Helmholtzian theory is probably not the last word in the physiology of hearing. Stepano, ff. (Hermann und Schwalbe's Jahresbericht, xv. 404, Literature 1886) reports a case in which more than the upper half of one cochlea was lost without any such deafness to deep notes on that side as Helmholtz's theory would require.

* Donaldson, in Mind, x. 399, 577; Goldscheider, in Archiv f. (Anat. u.) Physiologie; Blix, in Zeitschrift für Biologie. A good résumé may be found in Ladd's Physiol. Psychology, part II. chap. IV. §§ 21-23.

† I tried on nine or ten people, making numerous observations on each, what difference it made in the discrimination of two points to have them alike or unlike. The points chosen were (1) two large needle-heads, (2) two screw-heads, and (3) a needle-head and a screw-head. The distance of the screw-heads was measured from their centres. I found that when the points gave diverse qualities of feeling (as in 3), this facilitated the discrimination, but much less strongly than I expected. The difference, in fact, would often not be perceptible twenty times running When, however, one of the points was endowed with a rotary movement, the other remaining still, the doubleness of the points became much more evident than before. To observe this I took an ordinary pair of compasses with one point blunt, and the movable leg replaced by a metallic rod which could, at any moment, be made to rotate *in situ* by a dentist's drilling-machine, to which it was attached. The compass had then its points applied to the skin at such a distance apart as to be felt as one impression. Suddenly rotating the drill-apparatus then almost always made them seem as two.

tion which is particularly exciting, and that is the *feeling of motion over any of our surfaces*. The erection of this into a separate elementary quality of sensibility is one of the most recent of psychological achievements, and is worthy of detaining us a while at this point.

The Sensation of Motion over Surfaces.

The feeling of motion has generally been assumed by physiologists to be impossible until the positions of *terminus a quo* and *terminus ad quem* are severally cognized, and the successive occupancies of these positions by the moving body are perceived to be separated by a distinct interval of time.* As a matter of fact, however, we cognize only the very slowest motions in this way. Seeing the hand of a clock at XII and afterwards at VI, we judge that it has moved through the interval. Seeing the sun now in the east and again in the west, I infer it to have passed over my head. But we can only *infer* that which we already generically know in some more direct fashion, and it is experimentally certain that we have the feeling of motion given us as a direct and simple *sensation*. Czermak long ago pointed out the difference between seeing the motion of the second-hand of a watch, when we look directly at it, and noticing the fact of its having altered its position when we fix our gaze upon some other point of the dial-plate. In the first case we have a specific quality of sensation which is absent in the second. If the reader will find a portion of his skin—the arm, for example—where a pair of compass-points an inch apart are felt as one impression, and if he will then trace lines a tenth of an inch long on that spot with a pencil-point, he will be distinctly aware of the point's motion and vaguely aware of the direction of the motion. The perception of the motion here is certainly not derived from a pre-existing knowledge that its starting and ending points are separate positions in space, because positions in space ten times wider apart fail to be discriminated as such

---

* This is only another example of what I call ' the psychologist's fallacy '—thinking that the mind he is studying must necessarily be conscious of the object after the fashion in which the psychologist himself is conscious of it.

when excited by the dividers. It is the same with the retina. One's fingers when cast upon its peripheral portions cannot be counted—that is to say, the five retinal tracts which they occupy are not distinctly apprehended by the mind as five separate positions in space—and yet the slightest *movement* of the fingers is most vividly perceived as movement and nothing else. It is thus certain that our sense of movement, being so much more delicate than our sense of position, cannot possibly be derived from it. *A curious observation by Exner* * completes the proof that movement is a primitive form of sensibility, by showing it to be much more delicate than our sense of succession in time. This very able physiologist caused two electric sparks to appear in rapid succession, one beside the other. The observer had to state whether the right-hand one or the left-hand one appeared first. When the interval was reduced to as short a time as 0.044″ the discrimination of temporal order in the sparks became impossible. But Exner found that if the sparks were brought so close together in space that their irradiation-circles overlapped, the eye then felt their flashing as if it were the motion of a single spark from the point occupied by the first to the point occupied by the second, and the time-interval might then be made as small as 0.015″ before the mind began to be in doubt as to whether the apparent motion started from the right or from the left. On the skin similar experiments gave similar results.

Vierordt, at almost the same time,† *called attention to certain persistent illusions, amongst which are these:* If another person gently trace a line across our wrist or finger, the latter being stationary, it will feel to us as if the member were moving in the opposite direction to the tracing point. If, on the contrary, we move our limb across a fixed point, it will be seen as if the point were moving as well. If the reader will touch his forehead with his forefinger kept motionless, and then rotate the head so that the skin of the forehead passes beneath the finger's tip, he will have

---

* Sitzb. der. k. Akad. Wien, Bd. LXXII., Abth. 3 (1875).
† Zeitschrift für Biologie, XII. 226 (1876).

an irresistible sensation of the latter being itself in motion in the opposite direction to the head. So in abducting the fingers from each other; some may move and the rest be still still, but the still ones will feel as if they were actively separating from the rest. These illusions, according to Vierordt, are survivals of a primitive form of perception, when motion was felt as such, but ascribed to the whole content of consciousness, and not yet distinguished as belonging exclusively to one of its parts. When our perception is fully developed we go beyond the mere relative motion of thing and ground, and can ascribe absolute motion to one of these components of our total object, and absolute rest to another. When, in vision for example, the whole background moves together, we think that it is ourselves or our eyes which are moving; and any object in the foreground which may move relatively to the background is judged by us to be still. But primitively this discrimination cannot be perfectly made. The sensation of the motion spreads over all that we see and infects it. Any relative motion of object and retina both makes the object seem to move, and makes us feel ourselves in motion. Even now when our whole object moves we still get giddy; and we still see an apparent motion of the entire field of view, whenever we suddenly jerk our head and eyes or shake them quickly to and fro. Pushing our eyeballs gives the same illusion. We *know* in all these cases what really happens, but the conditions are unusual, so our primitive sensation persists unchecked. So it does when clouds float by the moon. We *know* the moon is still; but we *see* it move even faster than the clouds. Even when we slowly move our eyes the primitive sensation persists under the victorious conception. **If** we notice closely the experience, we find that any object towards which we look appears moving to meet our eye.

But the most valuable contribution to the subject is the paper of G. H. Schneider,* who takes up the matter zoologically, and shows by examples from every branch of the animal kingdom that movement is the quality by which animals most easily attract each other's attention. The in-

---

* Vierteljahrsch. für wiss. Philos., II. 377.

stinct of 'shamming death' is no shamming of death at all, but rather a paralysis through fear, which saves the insect, crustacean, or other creature from being *noticed at all* by his enemy. It is parallelled in the human race by the breath-holding stillness of the boy playing 'I spy,' to whom the seeker is near; and its obverse side is shown in our involuntary waving of arms, jumping up and down, and so forth, when we wish to attract someone's attention at a distance. Creatures 'stalking' their prey and creatures hiding from their pursuers alike show how immobility diminishes conspicuity. In the woods, if we are quiet, the squirrels and birds will actually touch us. Flies will light on stuffed birds and stationary frogs.* On the other hand, the tremendous shock of feeling the thing we are sitting on begin to move, the exaggerated start it gives us to have an insect unexpectedly pass over our skin, or a cat noiselessly come and snuffle about our hand, the excessive reflex effects of tickling, etc., show how exciting the sensation of motion is *per se.* A kitten cannot help pursuing a moving ball. Impressions too faint to be cognized at all are immediately felt if they move. A fly sitting is unnoticed,—we feel it the moment it crawls. A shadow may be too faint to be perceived. As soon as it moves, however, we see it. Schneider found that a shadow, with distinct outline, and directly fixated, could still be perceived when moving, although its objective strength might be but half as great as that of a stationary shadow so faint as just to disappear. With a blurred shadow in indirect vision the difference in favor of motion was much greater—namely, 13.3 : 40.7. If we hold a finger between our closed eyelid and the sunshine we shall not notice its presence. The moment we move it to and fro, however, we discern it. Such visual perception as this reproduces the conditions of sight among the radiates.†

---

* Exner tries to show that the structure of the faceted eye of articulates adapts it for perceiving motions almost exclusively.

† Schneider tries to explain why a sensory surface is so much more excited when its impression moves. It has long since been noticed how much more acute is discrimination of successive than of simultaneous differences. But in the case of a moving impression, say on the retina, we have a sum-

Enough has now been said to show that *in the education of spatial discrimination the motions of impressions across sensory surfaces must have been the principal agent* in breaking up our consciousness of the surfaces into a consciousness of their parts. Even to-day the main function of the peripheral regions of our retina is that of sentinels, which, when beams of light move over them, cry ' Who goes there ? ' and call the fovea to the spot. Most parts of the skin do but perform the same office for the finger-tips. Of course finger-tips and fovea leave *some* power of direct perception to marginal retina and skin respectively. But it is worthy of note that such perception is best developed on the skin of the most movable parts (the labors of Vierordt and his pupils have well shown this) ; and that in the blind, whose skin is exceptionally discriminative, it seems to have become so through the inveterate habit which most of them possess of twitching and moving it under whatever object may touch them, so as to become better acquainted with the conformation of the same. Czermak was the first to notice this. It may be easily verified. Of course *movement of surface under object is (for purposes of stimulation) equivalent to movement of object over surface.* In exploring the shapes and

mation of both sorts of difference ; whereof the natural effect must be to produce the most perfect discrimination of all.

FIG. 53.

In the left-hand figure let the dark spot B move, for example, from right to left. At the outset there is the simultaneous contrast of black and white in B and A. When the motion has occurred so that the right-hand figure is produced, the same contrast remains, the black and the white having changed places. But in addition to it there is a double successive contrast, first in A, which, a moment ago white, has now become black ; and second in B, which, a moment ago black, has now become white. If we make each single feeling of contrast = 1 (a supposition far too favorable to the state of rest), the sum of contrasts in the case of motion will be 3, as against 1 in the state of rest. That is, our attention will be called by a treble force to the difference of color, provided the color begin to move.—(Cf. also Fleischl, Physiologische Optische Notizen, 2te Mittheilung, Wiener Sitzungsberichte, 1882.)

sizes of things by either eye or skin the movements of these organs are incessant and unrestrainable. Every such move-ment draws the points and lines of the object across the surface, imprints them a hundred times more sharply, and drives them home to the attention. The immense part thus played by movements in our perceptive activity is held by many psychologists* to prove that the muscles are them-selves the space-perceiving organ. Not surface-sensibility, but 'the muscular sense,' is for these writers the original and only revealer of objective extension. But they have all failed to notice with what peculiar intensity muscular contractions call surface-sensibilities into play, and that the mere discrimination of impressions (quite apart from any question of measuring the space between them) largely depends on the mobility of the surface upon which they fall. †

---

* Brown, Bain, J. S. Mill, and in a modified manner Wundt, Helmholtz, Sully, etc.

† M. Ch. Dunan, in his forcibly written essay 'l'Espace Visuel et l'Espace Tactile' in the Revue Philosophique for 1888, endeavors to prove that surfaces alone give no perception of extent, by citing the way in which the blind go to work to gain an idea of an object's shape. If surfaces were the percipient organ, he says, " both the seeing and the blind ought to gain an exact idea of the size (and shape) of an object by merely laying their hand flat upon it (provided of course that it were smaller than the hand), and this because of their direct appreciation of the amount of tactile surface affected, and with no recourse to the muscular sense. . . . But the fact is that a person born blind never proceeds in this way to measure ob-jective surfaces. The only means which he has of getting at the size of a body is that of running his finger along the lines by which it is bounded. For instance, if you put into the hands of one born blind a book whose dimensions are unknown to him, he will begin by resting it against his chest so as to hold it horizontal ; then, bringing his two hands together at the middle of the edge opposite to the one against his body, he will draw them asunder till they reach the ends of the edge in question : and then, and not till then, will he be able to say what the length of the object is " (vol. xxv. p. 148). I think that anyone who will try to appreciate the size and shape of an object by simply 'laying his hand flat upon it' will find that the great obstacle is that he *feels the contours* so imperfectly. The moment, however, the hands move, the contours are emphatically and dis-tinctly felt. All perception of shape and size is perception of contours, and first of all these must be made *sharp*. Motion does this ; and the impulse to move our organs in perception is primarily due to the craving which we feel to get our surface-sensations sharp. When it comes to the naming and

2. *The Measurement of the sense-spaces against each other.*

What precedes is all we can say in answer to the problem of discrimination. Turn now to that of measurement of the several spaces against each other, that being the first step in our constructing out of our diverse space-experiences the one space we believe in as that of the real world.

The first thing that seems evident is that we have no *immediate* power of comparing together with any accuracy the extents revealed by different sensations. Our mouth-cavity feels indeed to itself smaller, and to the tongue larger, than it feels to the finger or eye, our tympanic membrane feels larger than our finger-tip, our lips feel larger than a surface equal to them on our thigh. So much comparison is immediate; but it is vague; and for anything exact we must resort to other help.

The great agent in comparing the extent felt by one sensory surface with that felt by another, is superposition—superposition of one surface upon another, and superposition of one outer thing upon many surfaces. Thus are exact equivalencies and common measures introduced, and the way prepared for numerical results.

Could we not superpose one part of our skin upon another, or one object on both parts, we should hardly succeed in coming to that knowledge of our own form which we possess. The original differences of bigness of our different parts would remain vaguely operative, and we should have no certainty as to how much lip was equivalent to so much forehead, how much finger to so much back.

But with the power of exploring one part of the surface by another we get a direct perception of cutaneous equivalencies. The primitive differences of bigness are overpowered when we feel by an immediate sensation that a certain length of thigh-surface is in contact with the entire palm and fingers. And when a motion of the opposite finger-tips draws a line first along this same length of thigh and

---

measuring of objects in terms of some common standard we shall see presently how movements help also; but no more in this case than the other do they help, because the quality of extension itself is contributed by the 'muscular sense.'

then along the whole of the hand in question, we get a new manner of measurement, less direct but confirming the equivalencies established by the first. In these ways, by superpositions of parts and by tracing lines on different parts by identical movements, a person deprived of sight can soon learn to reduce all the dimensions of his body to a homogeneous scale. By applying the same methods to objects of his own size or smaller, he can with equal ease make himself acquainted with their extension stated in terms derived from his own bulk, palms, feet, cubits, spans, paces, fathoms (armspreads), etc. In these reductions it is to be noticed that *when the resident sensations of largeness of two opposed surfaces conflict, one of the sensations is chosen as the true standard and the other treated as illusory. Thus an empty tooth-socket is believed to be* really smaller than the finger-tip which it will not admit, although it may *feel* larger ; and in general it may be said that the hand, as the almost exclusive organ of palpation, gives its own magnitude to the other parts, instead of having its size determined by them. In general, it is, as Fechner says, the extent felt by the more sensitive part to which the other extents are reduced. *

But even though exploration of one surface by another were impossible, we could always measure our various surfaces against each other by applying the same extended object first to one and then to another. We should of course have the alternative of supposing that the object itself waxed and waned as it glided from one place to another (cf. above, p. 141) ; but the principle of simplifying as much as possible our world would soon drive us out of that assumption into the easier one that objects as a rule

---

* Fechner describes (Psychophysik, I. 132) a   method of equivalents ' for measuring the sensibility of the skin. Two compasses are used, one on the part A. another on the part B, of the surface The points on B must be adjusted so that their distance apart appears equal to that between the points on A   With the place A constant, the second pair of points must be varied a great deal for every change in the place B. though for the same A and B the relation of the two compasses is remarkably constant, and con- tinues unaltered for months provided but few experiments are made on each day. If, however, we practise daily their difference grows less, in accordance with the law given in the text

keep their sizes, and that most of our sensations are affected by errors for which a constant allowance must be made.

In the retina there is no reason to suppose that the bignesses of two impressions (lines or blotches) falling on different regions are primitively felt to stand in any exact mutual ratio. It is only when the impressions come from the *same object* that we judge their sizes to be the same. And this, too, only when the relation of the object to the eye is believed to be on the whole unchanged. When the object by moving changes its relations to the eye the sensation excited by its image even on the same retinal region becomes so fluctuating that we end by ascribing no absolute import whatever to the retinal space-feeling which at any moment we may receive. So complete does this overlooking of retinal magnitude become that it is next to impossible to compare the visual magnitudes of objects at different distances without making the experiment of superposition. We cannot say beforehand how much of a distant house or tree our finger will cover. The various answers to the familiar question, How large is the moon?—answers which vary from a cartwheel to a wafer—illustrate this most strikingly. The hardest part of the training of a young draughtsman is his learning to feel directly the retinal (i.e. primitively sensible) magnitudes which the different objects in the field of view subtend. To do this he must recover what Ruskin calls the 'innocence of the eye'—that is, a sort of childish perception of stains of color merely as such, without consciousness of what they mean.

With the rest of us this innocence is lost. *Out of all the visual magnitudes of each known object we have selected one as the* REAL *one to think of, and degraded all the others to serve as its signs.* This 'real' magnitude is determined by æsthetic and practical interests. It is that which we get when the object is at the distance most propitious for exact visual discrimination of its details. This is the distance at which we hold anything we are examining. Farther than this we see it too small, nearer too large. And the larger and the smaller feeling vanish in the act of suggesting this one, their more important *meaning*. As I look along the dining-

table I overlook the fact that the farther plates and glasses
feel so much smaller than my own, for I *know* that they are
all equal in size ; and the feeling of them, which is a present
sensation, is eclipsed in the glare of the knowledge, which
is a merely imagined one.

If the inconsistencies of sight-spaces *inter se* can thus be
reduced, of course there can be no difficulty in equating
sight-spaces with spaces given to touch.   In this equation
it is probably the touch-feeling which prevails as real and
the sight which serves as sign—a reduction made necessary
not only by the far greater constancy of felt over seen
magnitudes, but by the greater practical interest which the
sense of touch possesses for our lives.   As a rule, things
only benefit or harm us by coming into direct contact with
our skin : sight is only a sort of anticipatory touch ; the
latter is, in Mr. Spencer's phrase, the 'mother-tongue of
thought,' and the handmaid's idiom must be translated
into the language of the mistress before it can speak clearly
to the mind.*

Later on we shall see that the feelings excited in the
joints when a limb moves are used as signs of the path
traversed by the extremity.   But of this more anon.   As
for the equating of sound-, smell-, and taste-volumes with
those yielded by the more discriminative senses, they are
too vague to need any remark.   It may be observed of
pain, however, that its size has to be reduced to that of the
normal tactile size of the organ which is its seat.   A finger
with a felon on it, and the pulses of the arteries therein, both
' feel ' larger than we believe they really ' are.'

---

* Prof. Jastrow gives as the result of his experiments this general
conclusion (Am. Journal of Psychology, iii. 53) : "The space-perceptions
of disparate senses are themselves disparate, and whatever harmony
there is amongst them we are warranted in regarding as the result
of experience.   The spacial notions of one deprived of the sense of sight
and reduced to the use of the other space-senses must indeed be different
from our own."   But he continues : "The existence of the striking
disparities between our visual and our other space-perceptions without
confusing us, and, indeed, without usually being noticed, can only be
explained by the tendency to interpret all dimensions *into their visual
equivalents.*"   But this author gives no reasons for saying ' visual ' rather
than ' tactile ;' and I must continue to think that probabilities point the
other way so far as what we call real magnitudes are concerned.

It will have been noticed in the account given that *when two sensorial space-impressions, believed to come from the same object, differ, then* THE ONE MOST INTERESTING, *practically or æsthetically,* IS JUDGED TO BE THE TRUE ONE. This law of interest holds throughout—though a permanent interest, like that of touch, may resist a strong but fleeting one like that of pain, as in the case just given of the felon.

3. *The Summation of the Sense-spaces.*

Now for the next step in our construction of real space : *How are the various sense-spaces added together into a consolidated and unitary continuum ?* For they are, in man at all events, incoherent at the start.

Here again the first fact that appears is that *primitively our space-experiences form a chaos, out of which we have no immediate faculty for extricating them. Objects of different sense-organs, experienced together, do not in the first instance appear either inside or alongside or far outside of each other, neither spatially continuous nor discontinuous, in any definite sense of these words.* The same thing is almost as true of objects felt by different parts of the same organ before discrimination has done its finished work. The most we can say is that all our space-experiences together form an *objective total* and that this *objective total* is vast.

Even now the space inside our mouth, which is so intimately known and accurately measured by its inhabitant the tongue, can hardly be said to have its internal directions and dimensions known in any exact relation to those of the larger world outside. It forms almost a little world by itself. Again, when the dentist excavates a small cavity in one of our teeth, we feel the hard point of his instrument scraping, in distinctly differing directions, a surface which seems to our sensibility vaguely larger than the subsequent use of the mirror tells us it 'really' is. And though the directions of the scraping differ so completely *inter se,* not one of them can be identified with the particular direction in the outer world to which it corresponds. The space of the tooth-sensibility is thus really a little world by itself, which can only become congruent with the outer space-world by farther experiences which shall alter its bulk, identify its directions, fuse its margins, and finally imbed it as a definite part within a definite whole. And even though every joint's rotations should be felt to vary *inter se* as so many differences of direction in a common room; even though the same were true of diverse tracings on the skin, and of diverse tracings on the retina respectively, it would still not follow that feelings of direction, on these different surfaces, are intuitively comparable among each other, or with the other directions yielded by the feelings of the semi-circular canals. It would not follow that we should immediately judge the relations of them all to each other in one space-world.

If with the arms in an unnatural attitude we 'feel' things, we are perplexed about their shape, size, and position. Let the reader lie on his back with his arms stretched above his head, and it will astonish him to find how ill able he is to recognize the geometrical relations of objects placed within reach of his hands. But the geometrical relations here spoken of are nothing but identities recognized between the directions and sizes perceived in this way and those perceived in the more usual ways. The two ways do not fit each other intuitively.

How lax the connection between the system of visual and the system of tactile directions is in man, appears from the facility with which microscopists learn to reverse the movements of their hand in manipulating things on the stage of the instrument. To move the slide to the *seen* left they must draw it to the *felt* right. But in a very few days the habit becomes a second nature. So in tying our cravat, shaving before a mirror, etc., the right and left sides are inverted, and the directions of our hand movements are the opposite of what they seem. Yet this never annoys us. Only when by accident we try to tie the cravat of another person do we learn that there are two ways of combining sight and touch perceptions. Let any one try for the first time to write or draw while looking at the image of his hand and paper in a mirror, and he will be utterly bewildered. But a very short training will teach him to undo in this respect the associations of his previous lifetime.

Prisms show this in an even more striking way. If the eyes be armed with spectacles containing slightly prismatic glasses with their bases turned, for example, towards the right, every object looked at will be apparently translocated to the left; and the hand put forth to grasp any such object will make the mistake of passing beyond it on the left side. But less than an hour of practice in wearing such spectacles rectifies the judgment so that no more mistakes are made. In fact the new-formed associations are already so strong, that when the prisms are first laid aside again the opposite error is committed, the habits of a lifetime violated, and the hand now passed to the right of every object which it seeks to touch.

The primitive chaos thus subsists to a great degree through life so far as our immediate sensibility goes. We feel our various objects and their bignesses, together or in succession; but so soon as it is a question of the order and relations of many of them at once our intuitive apprehension remains to the very end most vague and incomplete. Whilst we are attending to one, or at most to two or three objects, all the others *lapse*, and the most we feel of them is that they still linger on the outskirts and can be caught again by turning in a certain way. Nevertheless *throughout all this confusion we conceive of a world spread out in a perfectly fixed and orderly fashion, and we believe in its existence. The question is : How do this conception and this belief arise ? How is the chaos smoothed and straightened out ?*

Mainly by two operations : Some of the experiences are apprehended to exist out- and alongside of each other, and others are apprehended to interpenetrate each other, and to occupy the same room. In this way what was incoherent and irrelative ends by being coherent and definitely related ; nor is it hard to trace the principles, by which the mind is guided in this arrangement of its perceptions, in detail.

In the first place, following the great intellectual law of economy, we simplify, unify, and identify as much as we possibly can. *Whatever sensible data can be attended to together we locate together. Their several extents seem one extent. The place at which each appears is held to be the same with the place at which the others appear. They become, in short, so many properties of* ONE AND THE SAME REAL THING. This is the first and great commandment, the fundamental 'act' by which our world gets spatially arranged.

In this *coalescence in a 'thing,'* one of the coalescing sensations is held to *be* the thing, the other sensations are taken for its more or less accidental *properties*, or modes of appearance.* The sensation chosen to be the thing essentially is the most constant and practically important of the lot; most often it is hardness or weight. But the hardness or weight is never without tactile bulk; and as we can always see something in our hand when we feel something there, we equate the bulk felt with the bulk seen, and thenceforward this common bulk is also apt to figure as of the essence of the 'thing.' Frequently a shape so figures, sometimes a temperature, a taste, etc.; but for the most part temperature, smell, sound, color, or whatever other phenomena may vividly impress us simultaneously with the bulk felt or seen, figure among the accidents. Smell and sound impress us, it is true, when we neither see nor touch the thing; but they are strongest when we see or touch, so we locate the *source* of these properties within the touched or seen space, whilst the properties themselves we regard as overflowing in a weakened form into the spaces filled by other things. *In all this, it will be observed, the sense-data whose spaces coalesce into one are yielded by different sense-organs.* Such data have no tendency to displace each other from consciousness, but can be attended to together all at once. Often indeed they vary concomitantly and reach a maximum together. We may be sure, therefore, that the general rule of our mind is to locate IN *each other all* sensations which are associated in simultaneous experience, and do not interfere with each other's perception.†

---

* Cf. Lipps on 'Complication,' Grundtatsachen, etc., p. 579.

† Ventriloquism shows this very prettily. The ventriloquist talks without moving his lips, and at the same time draws our attention to a doll, a box, or some other object. We forthwith locate the voice within this object. On the stage an actor ignorant of music sometimes has to sing, or play on the guitar or violin. He goes through the *motions* before our eyes, whilst in the orchestra or elsewhere the music is performed. But because as we listen we see the actor, it is almost impossible not to *hear* the music as if coming from where he sits or stands.

Different impressions on the same sense-organ do interfere with each other's perception, and cannot well be attended to at once. Hence *we do not locate them in each other's spaces, but arrange them in a serial order of exteriority, each alongside of the rest, in a space larger than that which any one sensation brings.* This larger space, however, is an object of conception rather than of direct intuition, and bears all the marks of being constructed piecemeal by the mind. The blind man forms it out of tactile, locomotor, and auditory experiences, the seeing man out of visual ones almost exclusively. As the visual construction is the easiest to understand, let us consider that first.

Every single visual sensation or 'field of view' is limited. To get a new field of view for our object the old one must disappear. But the disappearance may be only partial. Let the first field of view be A B C. If we carry our attention to the limit C, it ceases to be the limit, and becomes the centre of the field, and beyond it appear fresh parts where there were none before : * A B C changes, in short, to C D E. But although the parts A B are lost to sight, yet their image abides in the memory ; and if we think of our first object A B C as having existed or as still existing at all, we must think of it as it was originally presented, namely, as spread out from C in one direction just as C D E is spread out in another. A B and D E can never coalesce in one place (as they could were they objects of different senses) because they can never be perceived at once : we must lose one to see the other. So (the letters standing now for 'things') we get to conceive of the successive fields of things after the analogy of the several things which we perceive in a single field. They must be out- and along-side of each other, and we conceive that their juxtaposed spaces must make a larger space. A B C + C D E must, in short, be imagined to exist in the form of A B C D E or not imagined at all.

We can usually recover anything lost from sight by moving our attention and our eyes back in its direction ; and

---

* Cf. Shand, in Mind, XIII. 340.

through these constant changes every field of seen things comes at last to be thought of as always having a fringe of *other things possible to be seen* spreading in all directions round about it. Meanwhile the movements concomitantly with which the various fields alternate are also felt and remembered ; and gradually (through association) this and that movement come in our thought to suggest this or that extent of fresh objects introduced. Gradually, too, since the objects vary indefinitely in kind, we abstract from their several natures and think separately of their mere extents, of which extents the various movements remain as the only constant introducers and associates. More and more, therefore, do we think of movement and seen extent as mutually involving each other, until at last (with Bain and J. S. Mill) we may get to regard them as synonymous, and say, " What is the *meaning of the word extent,* unless it be possible movement?" * We forget in this conclusion that (whatever intrinsic extensiveness the movements may appear endowed with), that seen spreadoutness which is the pattern of the abstract extensiveness which we imagine came to us originally from the retinal sensation.

The muscular sensations of the eyeball *signify* this sort of visible spreadoutness, just as this visible spreadoutness may come in later experience to *signify* the ' real ' bulks, distances, lengths and breadths known to touch and locomotion.† · To the very end, however, in us seeing men, the quality, the nature, the *sort of thing we mean* by extensiveness, would seem to be the sort of feeling which our retinal stimulations bring.

In one deprived of sight the principles by which the notion of real space is constructed are the same. Skin-feelings take in him the place of retinal feelings in giving

---

* See, e.g., Bain's Senses and Intellect, pp. 366–7, 371.

† When, for example, a baby looks at its own moving hand, it sees one object at the same time that it feels another. Both interest its attention, and it locates them together. But the felt object's size is the more constant size, just as the felt object is, on the whole, the more interesting and important object ; and so the retinal sensations become regarded as its signs and have their ' real space-values ' interpreted in tangible terms.

the quality of lateral spreadoutness, as our attention passes from one extent of them to another, awakened by an object sliding along. Usually the moving object is our hand; and feelings of movement in our joints invariably accompany the feelings in the skin. But the feeling of the skin is what the blind man *means* by his skin ; so the size of the skin-feelings stands as the absolute or real size, and the size of the joint-feelings becomes a sign of these. Suppose, for example, a blind baby with (to make the description shorter) a blister on his toe, exploring his leg with his finger-tip and feeling a pain shoot up sharply the instant the blister is touched. The experiment gives him four different kinds of sensation—two of them protracted, two sudden. The first pair are the movement-feeling in the joints of the upper limb, and the movement-feeling on the skin of the leg and foot. These, attended to together, have their extents identified as one objective space— the hand moves through the same space in which the leg lies. The second pair of objects are the pain in the blister, and the peculiar feeling the blister gives to the finger. Their spaces also fuse ; and as each marks the end of a peculiar movement-series (arm moved, leg stroked), the movement-spaces are *emphatically* identified with each other at *that* end. Were there other small blisters distributed down the leg, there would be a number of these emphatic points ; the movement-spaces would be identified, not only as totals, but point for point. *

---

* The incoherence of the different primordial sense-spaces *inter se* is often made a pretext for denying to the primitive bodily feelings any spatial quality at all. Nothing is commoner than to hear it said : "Babies have originally no spatial perception ; for when a baby's toe aches he does not place the pain in the toe. He makes no definite movements of defence, and may be vaccinated without being held." The facts are true enough ; but the interpretation is all wrong. What really happens is that *the baby does not place his ' toe' in the pain ;* for he knows nothing of his ' toe' as yet. He has not attended to it as a visual object ; he has not handled it with his fingers ; nor have its normal organic sensations or contacts yet become interesting enough to be discriminated from the whole massive feeling of the foot, or even of the leg to which it belongs. In short, the toe is neither a member of the babe's optical space, of his hand-movement space, nor an independent member of his leg-and-foot space. It has actually no mental existence yet save as this little pain-space. What wonder,

Just so with spaces beyond the body's limits. Continuing the joint-feeling beyond the toe, the baby hits another object, which he can still think of when he brings his hand back to its blister again. That object at the end of that joint-feeling means a new place for him, and the more such objects multiply in his experience the wider does the space of his conception grow. If, wandering through the woods to-day by a new path, I find myself suddenly in a glade which affects my senses exactly as did another I reached last week at the end of a different walk, I believe the two identical affections to present the same persisting glade, and infer that I have attained it by two differing roads. The spaces walked over grow congruent by their extremities; though apart from the common sensation which those extremities give me, I should be under no necessity of connecting one walk with another at all. The case in no whit differs when shorter movements are concerned. If, moving first one arm and then another, the blind child gets the same kind of sensation upon the hand, and gets it again as often as he repeats either process, he judges that he has touched the same object by both motions, and concludes that the motions terminate in a common place. From place to place marked in this way he moves, and adding the places moved through, one to another, he builds up his notion of the extent of the outer world. The seeing man's process is identical; only his units, which may be successive bird's-eye views, are much larger than in the case of the blind.

---

then, if the pain seem a little space-world all by itself? But let the pain once associate itself with these other space-worlds, and its space will become part of their space. Let the baby feel the nurse stroking the limb and awakening the pain every time her finger passes towards the toe; let him look on and see her finger on the toe every time the pain shoots up; let him handle his foot himself and get the pain whenever the toe comes into his fingers or his mouth; let moving the leg exacerbate the pain,—and all is changed. The space of the pain becomes identified with that part of each of the other spaces which gets felt when it awakens; and by their identity with *it* these parts are identified with each other, and grow systematically connected as members of a larger extensive whole.

FEELINGS IN JOINTS AND FEELINGS IN MUSCLES.

1. *Feelings of Movement in Joints.*

I have been led to speak of feelings which arise in joints. As these feelings have been too much neglected in Psychology hitherto, in entering now somewhat minutely into their study I shall probably at the same time freshen the interest of the reader, which under the rather dry abstractions of the previous pages may presumably have flagged.

When, by simply flexing my right forefinger on its metacarpal joint, I trace with its tip an inch on the palm of my left hand, is my feeling of the size of the inch purely and simply a feeling in the skin of the palm, or have the muscular contractions of the right hand and forearm anything to do with it? In the preceding pages I have constantly assumed spatial sensibility to be an affair of surfaces. At first starting, the consideration of the 'muscular sense' as a space-measurer was postponed to a later stage. Many writers, of whom the foremost was Thomas Brown, in his *Lectures on the Philosophy of the Human Mind*, and of whom the latest is no less a Psychologist than Prof. Delbœuf,* hold that the consciousness of active muscular motion, aware of its own amount, is the *fons et origo* of all spatial measurement. It would seem to follow, if this theory were true, that two skin-feelings, one of a large patch, one of a small one, possess their difference of spatiality, not as an immediate element, but solely by virtue of the fact that the large one, to get its points *successively* excited, demands more muscular contraction than the small one does. Fixed associations with the several amounts of muscular contraction required in this particular experience would thus ex-

---

* 'Pourquoi les Sensations visuelles sont elles étendues?' in Revue Philosophique, IV. 167.—As the proofs of this chapter are being corrected, I receive the third 'Heft' of Münsterberg's Beiträge zur Experimentellen Psychologie, in which that vigorous young psychologist reaffirms (if I understand him after so hasty a glance) more radically than ever the doctrine that muscular sensation proper is our one means of measuring extension. Unable to reopen the discussion here, I am in duty bound to call the attention of the reader to Herr M.'s work.

plain the apparent sizes of the skin-patches, which sizes would consequently not be primitive data but derivative results.

It seems to me that no evidence of the muscular measurements in question exists; but that all the facts may be explained by surface-sensibility, provided we take that of the joint-surfaces also into account.

The most striking argument, and the most obvious one, which an upholder of the muscular theory is likely to produce is undoubtedly this fact : if, with closed eyes, we trace figures in the air with the extended forefinger (the motions may occur from the metacarpal-, the wrist-, the elbow-, or the shoulder-joint indifferently), what we are *conscious of* in each case, and indeed most acutely conscious of, is the geometric path described by the finger-*tip*. Its angles, its subdivisions, are all as distinctly felt as if seen by the eye ; and yet the surface of the finger-tip receives no impression at all.* But with each variation of the figure, the muscular contractions vary, and so do the feelings which these yield. Are not these latter the sensible data that make us aware of the lengths and directions we discern in the traced line ?

Should we be tempted to object to this supposition of the advocate of perception by muscular feelings, that we have *learned* the spatial significance of these feelings by reiterated experiences of *seeing* what figure is drawn when each special muscular grouping is felt, so that in the last resort the muscular space feelings would be derived from retinal-surface feelings, our opponent might immediately hush us by pointing to the fact that in persons born blind the phenomenon in question is even more perfect than in ourselves.

If we suggest that the blind may have originally traced the figures on the cutaneous surface of cheek, thigh, or palm, and may now remember the specific figure which each present movement formerly caused the skin-surface to perceive, he may reply that the delicacy of the motor percep-

---

* Even if the figure be drawn on a board instead of in the air, the variations of contact on the finger's surface will be much simpler than the peculiarities of the traced figure itself.

tion far exceeds that of most of the cutaneous surfaces ; that, in fact, we can feel a figure traced only in its differentials, so to speak,—a figure which we merely *start* to trace by our finger-tip, a figure which, traced in the same way *on* our finger-tip by the hand of another, is almost if not wholly unrecognizable.

The champion of the muscular sense seems likely to be triumphant *until we invoke the articular cartilages*, as internal surfaces whose sensibility is called in play by every movement we make, however delicate the latter may be.

To establish the part they play in our geometrizing, it is necessary to review a few facts. It has long been known by medical practitioners that, in patients with cutaneous anæsthesia of a limb, whose muscles also are insensible to the thrill of the faradic current, a very accurate sense of the way in which the limb may be flexed or extended by the hand of another may be preserved.* On the other hand, we may have this sense of movement impaired when the tactile sensibility is well preserved. That the pretended feeling of outgoing innervation can play in these cases no part, is obvious from the fact that the movements by which the limb changes its position are passive ones, imprinted on it by the experimenting physician. The writers who have sought a *rationale* of the matter have consequently been driven by way of exclusion to assume the articular surfaces to be the seat of the perception in question. †

That the joint-surfaces are sensitive appears evident from the fact that in inflammation they become the seat of excruciating pains, and from the perception by everyone who lifts weights or presses against resistance, that every increase of the force opposing him betrays itself to his consciousness principally by the starting-out of new feelings or the increase of old ones, in or about the joints. If the structure and mode of mutual application of two articular surfaces be taken into account, it will appear that, granting the surfaces to *be* sensitive, no more favorable mechanical

---

* See for example Duchenne, Electrisation localisée, pp. 727, 770, Leyden; Virchow's Archiv, Bd. xlvii. (1869).

† E.g., Eulenburg, Lehrb. d. Nervenkrankheiten (Berlin), 1878, i. 3.

conditions could be possible for the delicate calling of the
sensibility into play than are realized in the minutely graduated rotations and firmly resisted variations of pressure
involved in every act of extension or flexion.   Nevertheless
it is a great pity that we have as yet no direct testimony,
no expressions from patients with healthy joints accidentally laid open, of the impressions they experience when the
cartilage is pressed or rubbed.

The first approach to direct evidence, so far as I know,
is contained in the paper of Lewinski,* published in 1879.
This observer had a patient the inner half of whose leg
was anæsthetic.   When this patient stood up, he had a
curious illusion about the position of his limb, which disappeared the moment he lay down again : he thought himself *knock-kneed.*   If, as Lewinski says, we assume the inner
half of the joint to share the insensibility of the corresponding part of the skin, then he *ought* to feel, when the
joint-surfaces pressed against each other in the act of
standing, the outer half of the joint most strongly.   But
this is the feeling he would also get whenever it was by any
chance sought to force his leg into a knock-kneed attitude.
Lewinski was led by this case to examine the feet of certain ataxic patients with imperfect sense of position.   He
found in every instance that when the toes were flexed *and
drawn upon* at the same time (the joint-surfaces drawn
asunder) all sense of the amount of flexion disappeared.
On the contrary, when he pressed a toe *in*, whilst flexing it,
the patient's appreciation of the amount of flexion was
much improved, evidently because the artificial increase of
articular pressure made up for the pathological insensibility of the parts.

Since Lewinski's paper an important experimental research by A. Goldscheider † has appeared, which completely
establishes our point.   This patient observer caused his
fingers, arms, and legs to be passively rotated upon their
various joints in a mechanical apparatus which registered
both the velocity of movement impressed and the amount

---

* ' Ueber den Kraftsinn,' Virchow's Archiv, Bd. LXXVII. 134.
† Archiv f. (Anat. u) Physiologie (1889), pp. 369, 540.

of angular rotation. No active muscular contraction took place. The minimal felt amounts of rotation were in all cases surprisingly small, being much less than a single angular degree in all the joints except those of the fingers. Such displacements as these, the author says (p. 490), can hardly be detected by the eye. The point of application of the force which rotated the limb made no difference in the result. Rotations round the hip-joint, for example, were as delicately felt when the leg was hung by the heel as when it was hung by the thigh whilst the movements were performed. Anæsthesia of the skin produced by induction-currents also had no disturbing effect on the perception, nor did the various degrees of pressure of the moving force upon the skin affect it. It became, in fact, all the more distinct in proportion as the concomitant pressure-feelings were eliminated by artificial anæsthesia. When the joints themselves, however, were made artificially anæsthetic the perception of the movement grew obtuse and the angular rotations had to be much increased before they were perceptible. All these facts prove according to Herr Goldscheider, that *the joint surfaces and these alone are the starting point of the impressions by which the movements of our members are immediately perceived.*

Applying this result, which seems invulnerable, to the case of the tracing finger-tip, we see that our perception of the latter gives no countenance to the theory of the muscular sense. *We indubitably localize the finger-tip at the successive points of its path by means of the sensations which we receive from our joints.* But if this is so, it may be asked, why do we feel the figure to be traced, not within the joint itself, but in such an altogether different place? And why do we feel it so much larger than it really is?

I will answer these questions by asking another: Why do we move our joints at all? Surely to gain something more valuable than the insipid joint-feelings themselves. And these more interesting feelings are in the main produced upon the *skin* of the moving part, or of some other part over which it passes, or upon the eye. With movements of the fingers we explore the configuration of all real objects with which we have to deal, our own body as well as foreign things. Nothing that interests us is located in the joint; everything that interests us either *is* some part of our skin, or is something that we see as we handle it. The cutaneously felt and the seen extents come thus to figure as the important things for us to concern ourselves with. Every time the joint moves, even though we neither see, nor feel cutaneously, the reminiscence of skin-events and sights which formerly coincided with that extent of move- ment, ideally awaken as the movement's import, and the mind drops the present sign to attend to the import alone. The joint-sensation itself, as such, does not disappear in the process. A little attention easily detects it, with all its fine peculiarities, hidden beneath its vaster suggestions ; so that really the mind has two space-perceptions before it, congruent in form but different in scale and place, either of which exclusively it may notice, or both at once,—the joint-space which it *feels* and the real space which it *means.*

The joint-spaces serve so admirably as signs because of their capacity for *parallel variation* to all the peculiarities of external motion. There is not a direction in the real world nor a ratio of distance which cannot be matched by some direction or extent of joint-rotation. Joint-feelings, like all feelings, are roomy. Specific ones are contrasted *inter se* as different directions are contrasted within the same extent. If I extend my arm straight out at the shoulder, the rotation of the shoulder-joint will give me one feeling of movement ; if then I sweep the arm forward, the same joint will give me another feeling of movement. Both these movements are felt to happen in space, and differ in specific quality. Why shall not the specificness of the quality just consist in the feeling of a peculiar *direc- tion?* * Why may not the several joint-feelings *be* so many perceptions of movement in so many different directions? That we cannot explain why they *should* is no presumption that they *do* not, for we never can explain why any sense- organ should awaken the sensation it does.

---

* Direction in its ' first intention,' of course ; direction with which so far we merely become *acquainted,* and *about* which we know nothing save perhaps its difference from another direction a moment ago experienced in the same way !

But if the joint-feelings are directions and extents, standing in relation to each other, the task of association in interpreting their import in eye- or skin-terms is a good deal simplified. Let the movement *bc*, of a certain joint, derive its absolute space-value from the cutaneous feeling it is always capable of engendering; then the longer movement *abcd* of the same joint will be judged to have a greater space-value, even though it may never have wholly merged with a skin-experience. So of differences of direction : so much joint-difference = so much skin-difference ; therefore, more joint-difference = more skin-difference. *In fact, the joint-feeling can excellently serve as a map on a reduced scale, of a reality which the imagination can identify at its pleasure with this or that sensible extension simultaneously known in some other way.*

When the joint-feeling in itself acquires an emotional interest,—which happens whenever the joint is inflamed and painful,—the secondary suggestions fail to arise, and the movement is felt where it is, and in its intrinsic scale of magnitude.*

The localization of the joint-feeling in a space simultaneously known otherwise (i.e. to eye or skin), is what is commonly called the *extradition or eccentric projection of the feeling.* In the preceding chapter I said a good deal on this subject; but we must now see a little more closely just what happens in this instance of it. The content of the joint-feeling, to begin with, is an object, and *is* in itself a place. For it to be *placed*, say *in the elbow*, the elbow as seen or handled must already have become another object for the mind,

---

* I have said hardly anything about associations with visual space in the foregoing account, because I wished to represent a process which the blind and the seeing man might equally share. It is to be noticed that the space suggested to the imagination when the joint moves, and projected to the distance of the finger-tip, is not represented as any *specific* skin-tract. What the seeing man imagines is a visible path; what the blind man imagines is rather a generic image, an abstraction from many skin-spaces whose local signs have neutralized each other, and left nothing but their common vastness behind. We shall see as we go on that this generic abstraction of space-magnitude from the various local peculiarities of feeling which accompanied it when it was for the first time felt, occurs on a considerable scale in the acquired perceptions of blind as well as of seeing men.

and with its place as thus known, the place which the joint-feeling fills must coalesce. That the latter should be felt 'in the elbow' is therefore a 'projection' of it into the place of another object as much as its being felt in the finger-tip or at the end of a cane can be. But when we say 'projection' we generally have in our mind the notion of a *there* as contrasted with a *here*. What is the *here* when we say that the joint-feeling is *there?* The 'here' seems to be the spot which the mind has chosen for its own post of observation, usually some place within the head, but sometimes within the throat or breast—not a rigorously fixed spot, but a region from any portion of which it may send forth its various acts of attention. Extradition from either of *these* regions is the common law under which we perceive the whereabouts of the north star, of our own voice, of the contact of our teeth with each other, of the tip of our finger, of the point of our cane on the ground, or of a movement in our elbow-joint.

But *for the distance between the 'here' and the 'there' to be felt, the entire intervening space must be itself an object of perception.* The consciousness of this intervening space is the *sine quâ non* of the joint-feeling's projection to the farther end of it. When it is filled by our own bodily tissues (as where the projection only goes as far as the elbow or finger-tip) we are sensible of its extent alike by our eye, by our exploring movements, and by the resident sensations which fill its length. When it reaches beyond the limits of our body, the resident sensations are lacking, but limbs and hand and eye suffice to make it known. Let me, for example, locate a feeling of motion coming from my elbow-joint in the point of my cane a yard beyond my hand. Either I see this yard as I flourish the cane, and the seen end of it then absorbs my sensation just as my seen elbow might absorb it, or I am blind and imagine the cane as an object continuing my arm, either because I have explored both arm and cane with the other hand, or because I have pressed them both along my body and leg. If I project my joint-feeling farther still, it is by a conception rather than a distinct imagination of the space. I *think:* 'farther,' 'thrice as far,' etc.; and thus get a symbolic image of a distant path at which I point.* But the 'absorption' of the joint-feeling by the distant spot, in whatever terms the latter may be apprehended, is never anything but that coalescence into one 'thing' already spoken of on page 184, of whatever different sensible objects interest our attention at once.

2. *Feelings of Muscular Contraction.*

Readers versed in psychological literature will have missed, in our account thus far, the usual invocation of 'the muscular sense.' This word is used with extreme vagueness to cover all resident sensations, whether of motion or position, in our members, and even to designate the supposed feeling of efferent discharge from the brain. We shall later see good reason to deny the existence of the latter feeling. We have accounted for the better part at least of the resident feelings of motion in limbs by the sensibility of the articular surfaces. The skin and ligaments also must have feelings awakened as they are stretched or squeezed in flexion or extension. And I am inclined to think that *the sensations of our contracting muscles themselves probably play as small a part in building up our exact knowledge of space as any class of sensations which we possess.* The muscles, indeed, play an all-important part, but it is through the remote effect of their contractions on other sensitive parts, not through their own resident sensations being aroused. In other words, *muscular contraction is only indirectly instrumental, in giving us space-perceptions, by its effects on surfaces.* In skin and retina it produces a motion of the stimulus upon the surface; in joints it produces a motion of the surfaces upon each other—such motion being by far the

---

* The ideal enlargement of a system of sensations by the mind is nothing exceptional. Vision is full of it; and in the manual arts, where a workman gets a tool larger than the one he is accustomed to and has suddenly to adapt all his movements to its scale, or where he has to execute a familiar set of movements in an unnatural position of body; where a piano-player meets an instrument with unusually broad or narrow keys; where a man has to alter the size of his handwriting—we see how promptly the mind multiplies once for all, as it were, the whole series of its operations by a constant factor, and has not to trouble itself after that with further adjustment of the details.

most delicate manner of exciting the surfaces in question. One is tempted to doubt whether the muscular sensibility as such plays even a subordinate part as *sign* of these more immediately geometrical perceptions which are so uniformly associated with it as effects of the contraction objectively viewed.

For this opinion many reasons can be assigned. First, it seems *a priori* improbable that such organs as muscles should give us feelings whose variations bear any exact proportion to the spaces traversed when they contract. As G. E. Müller says,* their sensory nerves must be excited either chemically or by mechanical compression whilst the contractions last, and in neither case can the excitement be proportionate to the position into which the limb is thrown. The chemical state of the muscle depends on the *previous* work more than on the actually present contraction ; and the internal pressure of it depends on the resistance offered more than on the shortening attained. *The intrinsic muscular sensations are likely therefore to be merely those of massive strain or fatigue, and to carry no accurate discrimination with them of lengths of path moved through.*

Empirically we find this probability confirmed by many facts. The judicious A. W. Volkman observes † that :

" Muscular feeling gives tolerably fine evidence as to the *existence* of movement, but hardly any direct information about its extent or direction. We are not aware that the contractions of a *supinator longus* have a wider range than those of a *supinator brevis ;* and that the fibres of a bipenniform muscle contract in opposite directions is a fact of which the muscular feeling itself gives not the slightest intimation. Muscle-feeling belongs to that class of general sensations which tell us of our inner states, but not of outer relations ; it does not belong among the space-perceiving senses."

E. H. Weber in his article Tastsinn called attention to the fact that muscular movements as large and strong as those of the diaphragm go on continually without our perceiving them as motion.

G. H. Lewes makes the same remark. When we think of our muscular sensations as movements in space, it is

* Pflüger's Archiv, XLV. 65.
† Untersuchungen im Gebiete der Optik, Leipzig (1863), p. 188.

because we have ingrained with them in our imagination a movement on a surface simultaneously felt.

" Thus whenever we breathe there is a contraction of the muscles of the ribs and the diaphragm. Since we *see* the chest expanding, we know it as a movement and can only think of it as such. But the diaphragm itself is not seen, and consequently by no one who is not physiologically enlightened on the point is this diaphragm thought of in movement. Nay, even when told by a physiologist that the diaphragm moves at each breathing, every one who has not seen it moving downward pictures it as an upward movement, because the chest moves upward." *

A personal experience of my own seems strongly to corroborate this view. For years I have been familiar, during the act of gaping, with a large, round, smooth sensation in the region of the throat, a sensation characteristic of gaping and nothing else, but which, although I had often wondered about it, never suggested to my mind the motion of anything. The reader probably knows from his own experience exactly what feeling I mean. It was not till one of my students told me, that I learned its objective cause. If we look into the mirror while gaping, we see that at the moment we have this feeling the hanging palate *rises* by the contraction of its intrinsic muscles. The contraction of these muscles and the compression of the palatine mucous membrane are what occasion the feeling; and I was at first astonished that, coming from so small an organ, it could appear so voluminous. Now the curious point is this—that no sooner had I learned by the eye its objective space-significance, than I found myself enabled mentally to *feel* it as a movement upwards of a body in the situation of the uvula. When I now have it, my fancy *injects* it, so to speak, with the image of the rising uvula; and it *absorbs* the image easily and naturally. In a word, a muscular contraction gave me a sensation whereof I was unable during forty years to interpret a motor meaning, of which two glances of the eye made me permanently the master. To my mind no further proof is needed of the fact that muscular contraction, merely as such, need not be perceived directly as so much motion through space.

---

* Problems of Life and Mind, prob. VI. chap. IV. § 45.

Take again the contractions of the muscles which make the eyeball rotate. The feeling of these is supposed by many writers to play the chief part in our perceptions of extent. The space seen between two things *means*, according to these authors, nothing but the amount of contraction which is needed to carry the *fovea* from the first thing to the second. But close the eyes and note the contractions in themselves (even when coupled as they still are with the delicate surface sensations of the eyeball rolling under the lids), and we are surprised at finding how vague their space-import appears. Shut the eyes and roll them, and you can with no approach to accuracy tell the outer object which shall first be seen when you open them again.* Moreover, if our eye-muscle-contractions had much to do with giving us our sense of seen extent, we ought to have a natural illusion of which we find no trace. Since the feeling in the muscles grows disproportionately intense as the eyeball is rolled into an extreme eccentric position, all places on the extreme *margin* of the field of view ought to appear farther from the centre than they really are, for the fovea cannot get to them without an amount of this feeling altogether in excess of the amount of actual rotation.† When we turn to the

---

* Volkmann, *op. cit.* p. 189. Compare also what Hering says of the inability in his own case to make after-images seem to move when he rolls his closed eyes in their sockets ; and of the insignificance of his feelings of convergence for the sense of distance (Beiträge zur Physiologie, 1861-2, pp. 31, 141). Helmholtz also allows to the muscles of convergence a very feeble share in producing our sense of the third dimension (Physiologische Optik, 649-59).

† Compare Lipps, Psychologische Studien (1885), p. 18, and the other arguments given on pp. 12 to 27. The most plausible reasons *for* contractions of the eyeball-muscles being admitted as original contributors to the perception of extent, are those of Wundt, Physiologische Psychologie, II. 96-100. They are drawn from certain constant errors in our estimate of lines and angles ; which, however, are susceptible, all of them, of different interpretations (see some of them further on).—Just as my MS. goes to the printer, Herr Münsterberg's Beiträge zur experimentellen Psychologie, Heft 2, comes into my hands with experiments on the measurement of space recorded in it, which, in the author's view, prove the feeling of muscular strain to be a principal factor in our vision of extent. As Münsterberg worked three hours a day for a year and a half at comparing the length of lines, seen with his eyes in different positions ; and as he carefully averaged and ' percented ' 20.000 observations, his conclusion must be listened to with great respect. Briefly it is this, that "our judgments of

muscles of the body at large we find the same vagueness. Goldscheider found that the minimal perceived rotation of

size depend on a comparison of the intensity of the feelings of movement which arise in our eyeball-muscles as we glance over the distance, and which fuse with the sensations of light " (p. 142). The facts upon which the conclusion is based are certain constant errors which Münsterberg found according as the standard or given interval was to the right or the left of the interval to be marked off as equal to it, or as it was above or below it, or stood in some more complicated relation still. He admits that he cannot explain all the errors in detail, and that we "stand before results which seem surprising and not to be unravelled, because we cannot analyze the elements which enter into the complex sensation which we receive." But he has no doubt whatever of the general fact "that the movements of the eyes and the sense of their position when fixed exert so decisive an influence on our estimate of the spaces seen, that the errors cannot possibly be explained by anything else than the movement-feelings and their reproductions in the memory" (pp. 166, 167). It is presumptuous to doubt a man's opinion when you haven't had his experience ; and yet there are a number of points which make me feel like suspending judgment in regard to Herr M.'s *dictum*. He found, for example, a constant tendency to under-estimate intervals lying to the right, and to overestimate intervals lying to the left. He ingeniously explains this as a result of the habit of *reading*, which trains us to move our eyes easily along straight lines from left to right, whereas in looking from right to left we move them in curved lines across the page. As we *measure intervals as straight lines,* it costs more muscular effort to measure from right to left than the other way, and an interval lying to the left seems to us consequently longer than it really is. Now I have been a reader for more years than Herr Münsterberg; and yet with me there is a strongly pronounced error the other way. It is the rightward-lying interval which to me seems longer than it really is. Moreover, Herr M. wears concave spectacles, and looked through them with his *head fixed.* May it not be that some of the errors were due to distortion of the retinal image, as the eye looked no longer through the centre but through the margin of the glass? In short, with all the presumptions which we have seen against muscular contraction being definitely felt as length, I think that there may be explanations of Herr M.'s results which have escaped even his sagacity ; and I call for a suspension of judgment until they shall have been confirmed by other observers. I do not myself doubt that our feeling of seen extent may be *altered* by concomitant muscular feelings. In Chapter XVII (pp. 28–80) we saw many examples of similar alterations, interferences with, or exaltations of, the sensory effect of one nerve-process by another. I do not see why currents from the muscles or eyelids, coming in at the same time with a retinal impression, might not make the latter seem bigger, in the same way that a greater *intensity* in the retinal stimulation makes it seem bigger ; or in the way that a greater extent of surface excited makes the color of the surface seem stronger, or if it be a skin-surface, makes its heat seem greater ; or in the way that the coldness of the dollar on the forehead (in Weber's old experiments) made the dollar seem heavier. But this is a *physiological* way ; and a limb about a joint was no less when the movement was 'active' or produced by muscular contraction than when it was 'passively' impressed.* The consciousness of active movement became so blunt when the joint (alone!) was made anæsthetic by faradization, that it became evident that the feeling of contraction could never be used for *fine* discrimination of extents. And that it was not used for coarse discriminations appeared clear to Goldscheider from certain other results which are too circumstantial for me to quote in detail.† His general conclusion is that we feel our movements exclusively in our articular surfaces, and that our muscular contractions in all probability hardly occasion this sort of perception at all. ‡

My conclusion is that the 'muscular sense' must fall back to the humble position from which Charles Bell raised it, and no longer figure in Psychology as the leading organ in space-perception which it has been so long 'cracked up' to be.

Before making a minuter study of Space as apprehended by the eye, we must turn to see what we can discover of space as known to the blind. But as we do so, let us cast a glance upon the results of the last pages, and ask ourselves once more whether the building up of orderly space-perceptions out of primitive incoherency requires any mental powers beyond those displayed in ordinary intellectual operations. I think it is obvious—granting the spacial *quale* to exist in the primitive sensations—that discrimination, association, addition, multiplication, and division, blending into generic images, substitution of similars, selective emphasis, and abstraction from uninteresting details, are quite capable of giving us all the space-percep-

---

the bigness gained is that of the retinal image after all. If I understand Münsterberg's meaning, it is quite different from this: the bigness belongs to the muscular feelings, as such, and is merely *associated* with those of the retina. *This* is what I deny.

 * Archiv f. (Anat. u.) Physiol. (1889), p. 542.

 † *Ibid.* p. 496.

 ‡ *Ibid.* p. 497. Goldscheider thinks that our muscles do not even give us the feeling of *resistance*, that being also due to the articular surfaces; whilst *weight* is due to the tendons. *Ibid.* p. 541.

tions we have so far studied, without the aid of any mysterious 'mental chemistry' or power of 'synthesis' to create elements absent from the original data of feeling. It cannot be too strongly urged in the face of mystical attempts, however learned, that there is not a landmark, not a length, not a point of the compass in real space which *is* not some *one* of our feelings, either experienced directly as a presentation or ideally suggested by another feeling which has come to serve as its sign. In degrading some sensations to the rank of signs and exalting others to that of realities signified, we smooth out the wrinkles of our first chaotic impressions and make a continuous order of what was a rather incoherent multiplicity. But the *content* of the order remains identical with that of the multiplicity—sensational both, through and through.

HOW THE BLIND PERCEIVE SPACE.

The blind man's construction of real space differs from that of the seeing man most obviously in the larger part which synthesis plays in it, and the relative subordination of analysis. The seeing baby's eyes take in the whole room at once, and discriminative attention must arise in him before single objects are visually discerned. The blind child, on the contrary, must form his mental image of the room by the addition, piece to piece, of parts which he learns to know successively. With our eyes we may apprehend instantly, in an enormous bird's-eye view, a landscape which the blind man is condemned to build up bit by bit after weeks perhaps of exploration. We are exactly in his predicament, however, for spaces which exceed our visual range. We think the ocean as a whole by multiplying mentally the impression we get at any moment when at sea. The distance between New York and San Francisco is computed in days' journeys; that from earth to sun is so many times the earth's diameter, etc.; and of longer distances still we may be said to have no adequate mental image whatever, but only numerical verbal symbols.

But the symbol will often give us the emotional effect of the perception. Such expressions as the abysmal vault of heaven, the endless expanse of ocean, etc., summarize many computations to the imagination, and give the sense of an enormous horizon. So it seems with the blind. They multiply mentally the amount of a distinctly felt freedom to move, and gain the immediate sense of a vaster freedom still. Thus it is that blind men are never without the consciousness of their horizon. They all enjoy travelling, especially with a companion who can describe to them the objects they pass. On the prairies they feel the great openness; in valleys they feel closed in; and one has told me that he thought few seeing people could enjoy the view from a mountain-top more than he. A blind person on entering a house or room immediately receives, from the reverberations of his voice and steps, an impression of its dimensions, and to a certain extent of its arrangement. The tympanic sense noticed on p. 140, *supra,* comes in to help here, and possibly other forms of tactile sensibility not yet understood. Mr. W. Hanks Levy, the blind author of 'Blindness and the Blind' (London), gives the following account of his powers of perception:

"Whether within a house or in the open air, whether walking or standing still, I can tell, although quite blind, when I am opposite an object, and can perceive whether it be tall or short, slender or bulky. I can also detect whether it be a solitary object or a continuous fence; whether it be a close fence or composed of open rails; and often whether it be a wooden fence, a brick or stone wall, or a quick-set hedge. I cannot usually perceive objects if much lower than my shoulder, but sometimes very low objects can be detected. This may depend on the nature of the objects, or on some abnormal state of the atmosphere. The currents of air can have nothing to do with this power, as the state of the wind does not directly affect it; the sense of hearing has nothing to do with it, as when snow lies thickly on the ground objects are more distinct, although the footfall cannot be heard. I seem to perceive objects through the skin of my face, and to have the impressions immediately transmitted to the brain. The only part of my body possessing this power is my face; this I have ascertained by suitable experiments. Stopping my ears does not interfere with it, but covering my face with a thick veil destroys it altogether. None of the five senses have anything to do with the existence of this power, and the circumstances above named induce me to call this unrecognized sense by the name of 'facial perception.' . . . When passing along a street I can distinguish shops from private houses, and even point out the doors and windows, etc., and this whether the doors be shut or open. When a window consists of one entire sheet of glass, it is more difficult to discover than one composed of a number of small panes. From this it would appear that glass is a bad conductor of sensation, or at any rate of the sensation specially connected with this sense. When objects below the face are perceived, the sensation seems to come in an oblique line from the object to the upper part of the face. While walking with a friend in Forest Lane, Stratford, I said, pointing to a fence which separated the road from a field, 'Those rails are not quite as high as my shoulder.' He looked at them, and said they were higher. We. however, measured, and found them about three inches lower than my shoulder. At the time of making this observation I was about four feet from the rails. Certainly in this instance facial perception was more accurate than sight. When the lower part of a fence is brick-work, and the upper part rails, the fact can be detected, and the line where the two meet easily perceived. Irregularities in height, and pro-jections and identations in walls, can also be discovered."

According to Mr. Levy, this power of seeing with the face is diminished by a fog, but not by ordinary dark-ness. At one time he could tell when a cloud obscured the horizon, but he has now lost that power, which he has known several persons to possess who are totally blind. These effects of aqueous vapor suggest immediately that fluctuations in the heat radiated by the objects may be the source of the perception. One blind gentleman, Mr. Kil-burne, an instructor in the Perkins Institution in South Boston, who has the power spoken of in an unusual degree, proved, however, to have no more delicate a sense of tem-perature in his face than ordinary persons. He himself supposed that his ears had nothing to do with the faculty until a complete stoppage of them, not only with cotton but with putty on top of it, by abolishing the perception entirely, proved his first impression to be erroneous. Many blind men say immediately that their ears are concerned in the matter.

Sounds certainly play a far more prominent part in the mental life of the blind than in our own. In taking a walk through the country, the mutations of sound, far and near, constitute their chief delight. And to a great extent their imagination of distance and of objects moving from one distant spot to another seems to consist in thinking how a certain sonority would be modified by the change of place. It is unquestionable that the semi-circular-canal feelings play a great part in defining the points of the compass and the direction of distant spots, in the blind as in us. We *start* towards them by feelings of this sort; and so many directions, so many different-feeling starts.*

The only point that offers any theoretic difficulty is the prolongation into space of the direction, after the start. We saw, ten pages back, that for extradition to occur beyond the skin, the portion of skin in question *and* the space beyond must form a common object for some other sensory surface. The eyes are for most of us this sensory surface; for the blind it can only be other parts of the skin, coupled or not with motion. But the mere gropings of the hands in every direction must end by surrounding the whole body with a sphere of felt space. And this sphere must become enlarged with every movement of locomotion, these movements gaining their space-values from the semi-circular-canal feelings which accompany them, and from the farther and farther parts of large fixed objects (such as the bed, the wainscoting, or a fence) which they bring within the grasp. It might be supposed that a knowledge of space acquired by so many successive discrete acts would always retain a somewhat jointed and so to speak, granulated character. When we who are gifted with sight think of a space too large to come into a single field of view, we are apt to imagine it as composite, and filled with more or less jerky stoppings and startings (think, for instance, of the space from here to San Francisco), or else we reduce the scale symbolically and imagine how much larger on a map the distance would look than others with whose totality we are familiar.

I am disposed to believe, after interrogating many blind persons, that the use of imaginary maps on a reduced scale is less frequent with them than with the rest of us. Possibly the extraordinary changeableness of the visual magnitudes of things makes this habit natural to us, while the fixity of tactile magnitudes keeps them from falling into it. (When the blind young man operated on by Dr. Franz was

---

* "Whilst the memories which we seeing folks preserve of a man all centre round a certain exterior form composed of his image, his height, his gait, in the blind all these memories are referred to something quite different, namely, *the sound of his voice.*" (Dunan, Rev. Phil., xxv. 357.)

shown a portrait in a locket, he was vastly surprised that the face could be put into so small a compass : it would have seemed to him, he said, as impossible as to put a bushel into a pint.) Be this as it may, however, the space which each blind man feels to extend beyond his body is felt by him as one smooth continuum—all trace of those muscular startings and stoppings and reversals which presided over its formation having been eliminated from the memory. It seems, in other words, a generic image of the space-element common to all these experiences, with the unessential particularities of each left out. In truth, *where* in this space a start or a stop may have occurred was quite accidental. It may never occur just there again, and so the attention lets it drop altogether. Even as long a space as that traversed in a several-mile walk will not necessarily appear to a blind man's thought in the guise of a series of locomotor acts. Only where there is some distinct locomotor difficulty, such as a step to ascend, a difficult crossing, or a disappearance of the path, will distinct locomotor images constitute the idea. Elsewhere the space seems continuous, and its parts may even all seem coexistent; though, as a very intelligent blind friend once remarked to me, ' To think of such distances involves probably more mental wear and tear and brain-waste in the blind than in the seeing.' This seems to point to a greater element of successive addition and construction in the blind man's idea.

Our own visual explorations go on by means of innumerable stoppings and startings of the eyeballs. Yet these are all effaced from the final space-sphere of our visual imagination. They have neutralized each other. We can even distribute our attention to the right and left sides simultaneously, and think of those two quarters of space as coexistent. Does the smoothing out of the locomotor interruptions from the blind man's tactile space-sphere offer any greater paradox? Surely not. And it is curious to note that both in him and in us there is one particular locomotor feeling that is apt to assert itself obstinately to the last. We and he alike spontaneously imagine space as lying *in front* of us, for reasons too obvious to enumerate. If we think of the space behind us, we, as a rule, have to

turn round mentally, and in doing so the front space vanishes. But in this, as in the other things of which we have
been talking, individuals differ widely. Some, in imagining a room, can think of all its six surfaces at once. Others
mentally turn round, or, at least, imagine the room in several successive and mutually exclusive acts (cf. p. 54, above).

Sir William Hamilton, and J. S. Mill after him, have
quoted approvingly an opinion of Platner (an eighteenth-
century philosopher) regarding the space-perceptions of
the blind. Platner says :

"The attentive observation of a person born blind . . . has convinced me that the sense of touch by itself is altogether incompetent to
afford us the representation of extension and space. . . . In fact, to
those born blind, time serves instead of space. Vicinity and distance
mean in their mouths nothing more than the shorter or longer time
. . . necessary to attain from some one feeling to some other."

After my own observation of blind people, I should
hardly have considered this as anything but an eccentric
opinion, worthy to pair off with that other belief that color
is primitively seen without extent, had it not been for the
remarkable Essay on Tactile and Visual Space by M. Ch.
Dunan, which appeared in the Revue Philosophique for
1888. This author quotes * three very competent witnesses,
all officials in institutions for the blind [it does not appear
from the text that more than one of them was blind him-
self], who say that blind people *only live in time.* M.
Dunan himself does not share exactly this belief, but he
insists that the blind man's and the seeing man's representation of space have *absolutely naught* in common, and that
we are deceived into believing that what they mean by
space is analogous to what we mean, by the fact that so many
of them are but semi-blind and still think in visual terms,
and from the farther fact that they all *talk* in visual terms
just like ourselves. But on examining M. Dunan's reasons
one finds that they all rest on the groundless logical assumption that the perception of a geometrical form which
we get with our eyes, and that which a blind man gets with

* Vol. xxv. pp. 357–8.

his fingers, must either be absolutely identical or absolutely unlike. They cannot be similar in diversity, "for they are simple notions, and it is of the essence of such to enter the mind or leave it all at once, so that one who has a simple notion at all, possesses it in all its completeness. . . . Therefore, since it is impossible that the blind should have of the forms in question ideas *completely identical* with our seeing ones, it follows that their ideas must be *radically different from and wholly irreducible to our own.*" * Hereupon M. Dunan has no difficulty in finding a blind man who still preserves a crude sensation of diffused light, and who says when questioned that *this light has no extent.* Having 'no extent' appears, however, on farther questioning, to signify merely not enveloping any particular tactile objects, nor being located within their outline; so that (allowing for latitude of expression) the result tallies perfectly with our own view. A relatively stagnant retinal sensation of diffused light, not varying when different objects are handled, would naturally remain an object quite apart. If the word 'extent' were habitually used to denote tactile extent, this sensation, having no tactile associates whatever, would naturally have 'extent' denied of it. And yet all the while it would be *analogous* to the tactile sensations in having the quality of bigness. Of course it would have no *other* tactile qualities, just as the tactile objects have no other optical qualities than bigness. All sorts of analogies obtain between the spheres of sensibility. Why are 'sweet' and 'soft' used so synonymously in most languages? and why are both these adjectives applied to objects of so many sensible kinds. Rough sounds, heavy smells, hard lights, cold colors, are other examples. Nor does it follow from such analogies as these that the sensations compared need be composite and have some of their parts identical. We saw in Chapter XIII that likeness and difference are an elementary relation, not to be resolved in every case into a mixture of absolute identity and absolute heterogeneity of content (cf. Vol. I, pp. 492–3).

I conclude, then, that although in its more superficial

---

* P. 135.

determinations the blind man's space is very different from our space, yet a deep analogy remains between the two. 'Big' and 'little,' 'far' and 'near,' are similar contents of consciousness in both of us. But the *measure* of the bigness and the farness is very different in him and in ourselves. He, for example, can have no notion of what we mean by objects appearing smaller as they move away, because he must always conceive of them as of their constant tactile size. Nor, whatever analogy the two extensions involve, should we expect that a blind man receiving sight for the first time should recognize his new-given optical objects by their familiar tactile names. Molyneux wrote to Locke:

"Suppose a man born blind, and now adult, and taught by his touch to distinguish between a cube and a sphere, . . . so as to tell, when he felt one and the other, which is the cube, which the sphere. Suppose then the cube and sphere placed on a table an l the blind man to be made to see ; query, whether by his sight, before he touched them, he could now distinguish and tell which is the globe, which the cube ?"

This has remained in literature as 'Molyneux's query.' Molyneux answered 'No.' And Locke says :*

" I agree with this thinking gentleman whom I am proud to call my friend, and am of opinion that the blind man at first sight would not be able to say which was the globe, which the cube, whilst he only saw them ; though he could unerringly name them by his touch and certainly distinguish them by the difference of their figures felt."

This opinion has not lacked experimental confirmation. From Chesselden's case downwards, patients operated for congenital cataract have been unable to name at first the things they saw. " So, Puss, I shall know you another time," said Chesselden's patient, after catching the cat, looking at her steadfastly, and setting her down. Some of this incapacity is unquestionably due to general mental confusion at the new experience, and to the excessively unfavorable conditions for perception which an eye with its lens just extirpated affords. That the analogy of inner nature between the retinal and tactile sensations goes beyond mere extensity is proved by the cases where the patients were the most intelligent, as in the young man operated on by Dr. Franz,

* Essay conc. Hum. Und., bk. II. chap. IX. § 8.

who named circular, triangular, and quadrangular figures at first sight.*

VISUAL SPACE.

It is when we come to analyze minutely the conditions of *visual* perception that difficulties arise which have made psychologists appeal to new and *quasi*-mythical mental powers. But I firmly believe that even here exact investigation will yield the same verdict as in the cases studied hitherto. This subject will close our survey of the facts; and if it give the result I foretell, we shall be in the best of positions for a few final pages of critically historical review.

If a common person is asked how he is enabled to see things as they are, he will simply reply, by opening his eyes and looking. This innocent answer has, however, long since been impossible for science. There are various paradoxes and irregularities about *what* we appear to perceive under seemingly identical optical conditions, which immediately raise questions. To say nothing now of the time-honored conundrums of why we see upright with an inverted retinal picture, and why we do not see double; and to leave aside the whole field of color-contrasts and ambiguities, as not directly relevant to the space-problem,—it is certain that the same retinal image makes us see quite differently-sized and differently-shaped objects at different times, and it is equally certain that the same ocular movement varies in its perceptive import. It ought to be possible, were the act of perception completely and *simply* intelligible, to assign for every distinct judgment of size, shape, and position a distinct optical modification of some kind as its occasion. And the connection between the two ought to be so constant that, given the same modification, we should always have the same judgment. But if we

---

* Philosophical Transactions, 1841. In T. K. Abbot's Sight and Touch there is a good discussion of these cases. Obviously, positive cases are of more importance than negative. An under-witted peasant, Noé M., whose case is described by Dr. Dufour of Lausanne (Guérison d'un Aveuge-Né, 1876) is much made of by MM. Naville and Dunan; but it seems to me only to show how little *some* people can deal with new experiences in which others find themselves quickly at home. This man could not even tell whether one of his first objects of sight moved or stood still (p. 9).

study the facts closely *we soon find no such constant connection between either judgment and retinal modification, or judgment and muscular modification, to exist.* The judgment seems to result from the combination of retinal, muscular and intellectual factors with each other ; and any one of them may occasionally overpower the rest in a way which seems to leave the matter subject to no simple law.

The scientific study of the subject, if we omit Descartes, began with Berkeley, and the particular perception he analyzed in his New Theory of Vision was that of distance or depth. Starting with the physical assumption that a difference in the distance of a point can make no difference in the nature of its retinal image, since "distance being a line directed endwise to the eye, it projects only one point in the fund of the eye—which point remains invariably the same, whether the distance be longer or shorter," he concluded that distance could not possibly be a visual sensation, but must be an intellectual 'suggestion' from 'custom' of some non-visual experience. According to Berkeley this experience was tactile. His whole treatment of the subject was excessively vague,—no shame to him, as a breaker of fresh ground,—but as it has been adopted and enthusiastically hugged in all its vagueness by nearly the whole line of British psychologists who have succeeded him, it will be well for us to begin our study of vision by refuting his notion that depth cannot possibly be perceived in terms of purely visual feeling.

The Third Dimension.

Berkeleyans unanimously assume that no retinal sensation can primitively be of volume ; if it be of extension at all (which they are barely disposed to admit), it can be only of two-, not of three-, dimensional extension. At the beginning of the present chapter we denied this, and adduced facts to show that all objects of sensation are voluminous in three dimensions (cf. p. 136 ff.). It is impossible to lie on one's back on a hill, to let the empty abyss of blue fill one's whole visual field, and to sink deeper and deeper into the merely sensational mode of consciousness regarding it, without feeling that an indeterminate, palpitating, circling depth is as indefeasibly one of its attributes as its breadth. We may artificially exaggerate this sensation of depth. Rise and look from the hill-top at the distant view ; represent to yourself as vividly as possible the distance of the uttermost horizon ; and then *with inverted head* look at the same. There will be a startling increase in the perspective, a most sensible recession of the maximum distance ; and as you raise the head you can actually see the horizon-line again draw near.*

Mind, I say nothing as yet about our estimate of the 'real' amount of this depth or distance. I only want to confirm its existence as a natural and inevitable optical consort of the two other optical dimensions. The field of view is always a *volume*-unit. Whatever be supposed to be its absolute and 'real' size, the relative sizes of its dimensions are functions of each other. Indeed, it happens perhaps most often that the breadth- and height-feeling take their absolute measure from the depth-feeling. If we plunge our head into a wash-basin, the felt nearness of the bottom makes us feel the lateral expanse to be small. If, on the contrary, we are on a mountain-top, the distance of the horizon carries with it in our judgment a proportionate

---

* What may be the physiological process connected with this increased sensation of depth is hard to discover. It seems to have nothing to do with the parts of the retina affected, since the mere inversion of the picture (by mirrors, reflecting prisms, etc.), without inverting the head, does not seem to bring it about ; nothing with sympathetic axial rotation of the eyes, which might enhance the perspective through exaggerated disparity of the two retinal images (see J. J. Müller, 'Raddrehung u. Tiefendimension,' Leipzig Acad. Berichte, 1875, page 124), for one-eyed persons get it as strongly as those with two eyes. I cannot find it to be connected with any alteration in the pupil or with any ascertainable strain in the muscles of the eye, sympathizing with those of the body. The exaggeration of distance is even greater when we throw the head over backwards and contract our superior recti in getting the view, than when we bend forward and contract the inferior recti. Making the eyes diverge slightly by weak prismatic glasses has no such effect. To me, and to all whom I have asked to repeat the observation, the result is so marked that I do not well understand how such an observer as Helmholtz, who has carefully examined vision with inverted head, can have overlooked it. (See his Phys. Optik, pp. 433, 723, 728, 772.) I cannot help thinking that anyone who can explain the exaggeration of the depth-sensation in this case will at the same time throw much light on its normal constitution.

height and length in the mountain-chains that bound it to
our view. But as aforesaid, let us not consider the question of absolute size now,—it must later be taken up in a
thorough way. Let us confine ourselves to the way in
which the three dimensions which are seen, get their values
fixed *relatively to each other.*

Reid, in his Inquiry into the Human Mind, has a section
'Of the Geometry of Visibles,' in which he assumes to
trace what the perceptions would be of a race of 'Idomenians' reduced to the sole sense of sight. Agreeing with
Berkeley that sight alone can give no knowledge of the third
dimension, he humorously deduces various ingenious absurdities in their interpretations of the material appearances before their eyes.

Now I firmly believe, on the contrary, that one of Reid's
Idomenians would frame precisely the same conception of
the external world that we do, if he had our intellectual
powers.* Even were his very eyeballs fixed and not movable like ours, that would only retard, not frustrate, his
education. For the *same object*, by alternately covering in
its lateral movements different parts of his retina, would
determine the mutual equivalencies of the first two dimensions of the field of view; and by exciting the physiological
cause of his perception of depth in various degrees, it would
establish a scale of equivalency between the first two and
the third.

First of all, one of the sensations given by the object
is chosen to represent its 'real' size and shape, in accordance with the principles laid down on pp. 178 and 179.
*One sensation measures the 'thing' present, and the 'thing' then
measures the other sensations.* The peripheral parts of the
retina are equated with the central by receiving the image
of the same object. This needs no elucidation in case the

* "In Froriep's Notizen (1838, July), No. 133, is to be found a detailed
account, with a picture, of an Esthonian girl, Eva Lauk, then fourteen
years old, born with neither arms nor legs, which concludes with the
following words: 'According to the mother, her intellect developed quite
as fast as that of her brother and sisters; in particular, she came as quickly
to a right judgment of the size and distance of visible objects, although,
of course, she had no use of hands.'" (Schopenhauer, Welt als Wille, II.
44.)

object does not change its distance or its front. But suppose, to take a more complicated case, that the object is a
stick, seen first in its whole length, and then rotated round
one of its ends; let this fixed end be the one near the eye.
In this movement the stick's image will grow progressively
shorter; its farther end will appear less and less separated laterally from its fixed near end; soon it will be
screened by the latter, and then reappear on the opposite
side, and finally on that side resume its original length.
Suppose this movement to become a familiar experience;
the mind will presumably react upon it after its usual fashion (which is that of unifying all data which it is in any
way possible to unify), and consider it the movement of a
constant object rather than the transformation of a fluctuating one. Now, the *sensation of depth* which it receives during the experience is awakened more by the far than by the
near end of the object. But how much depth? What shall
measure its amount? Why, at the moment the far end is
ready to be eclipsed, the difference of its distance from the
near end's distance must be judged equal to the stick's
whole length; but that length has already been judged
equal to a certain optical sensation of breadth. *Thus we
find that given amounts of the visual depth-feeling become signs
of fixed amounts of the visual breadth-feeling. The measurement of distance is, as Berkeley truly said, a result of suggestion and experience. But visual experience alone is adequate
to produce it, and this he erroneously denied.*

Suppose a colonel in front of his regiment at dress-
parade, and suppose he walks at right angles towards the
midmost man of the line. As he advances, and surveys
the line in either direction, he looks more and more *down*
it and less and less *at* it, until, when abreast of the midmost man, he feels the end men to be *most* distant; then
when the line casts hardly any lateral image on his retina
at all, what distance shall he judge to be that of the end
men? Why, half the length of the regiment as it was
originally seen, of course; but this length was a moment
ago a retinal object spread out laterally before his sight.
He has now merely equated a retinal depth-feeling with a
retinal breadth-feeling. If the regiment moved, and the

colonel stood still, the result would be the same. In such
ways as these a creature endowed with eyes alone could
hardly fail of measuring out all three dimensions of the
space he inhabited. And we ourselves, I think, although
we *may* often 'realize' distance in locomotor terms
(as Berkeley says we must always do), yet do so no less
often in terms of our retinal map, and always in this way
the more spontaneously. Were this not so, the three visual
dimensions could not possibly feel to us as homogeneous as
they do, nor as commensurable *inter se.*

*Let us then admit distance to be at least as genuinely optical
a content of consciousness as either height or breadth. The
question immediately returns, Can any of them be said in any
strictness to be optical sensations?* We have contended all
along for the affirmative reply to this question, but must
now cope with difficulties greater than any that have assailed us hitherto.

Helmholtz and Reid on Sensations.

A sensation is, as we have seen in Chapter XVII,
the mental affection that follows most immediately upon
the stimulation of the sense-tract. Its antecedent is directly physical, no psychic links, no acts of memory, inference, or association intervening. Accordingly, if we suppose the nexus between neural process in the sense-organ,
on the one hand, and conscious affection, on the other, to
be by nature uniform, *the same process ought always to give
the same sensation ;* and conversely, *if what seems to be a sensation varies whilst the process in the sense-organ remains unchanged, the reason is presumably that it is really not a sensation but a higher mental product, whereof the variations depend
on events occurring in the system of higher cerebral centres.*

Now the *size* of the field of view varies enormously in all
three dimensions, without our being able to assign with any
definiteness the process in the visual tract on which the
variation depends. We just saw how impossible such
assignment was in the case where turning down the head
produces the enlargement. In general, the maximum feeling of depth or distance seems to take the lead in determining the apparent magnitude of the whole field, and the

two other dimensions seem to follow. If, to use the former instance, I look close into a wash-basin, the lateral extent of the field shrinks proportionately to its nearness. If I look from a mountain, the things seen are vast in height and breadth, in proportion to the farness of the horizon. But *when we ask what changes in the eye determine how great this maximum feeling of depth or distance* (which is undoubtedly felt as a unitary vastness) *shall be, we find ourselves unable to point to any one of them as being its absolutely regular concomitant.* Convergence, accommodation, double and disparate images, differences in the parallactic displacement when we move our head, faintness of tint, dimness of outline, and smallness of the retinal image of objects named and known, are all processes that have *something to do* with the perception of ' far ' and of ' near ' ; but the effect of each and any one of them in determining such a perception at one moment may at another moment be reversed by the presence of some other sensible quality in the object, that makes us, evidently by reminding us of past experience, judge it to be at a different distance and of another shape. If we paint the inside of a pasteboard-mask like the outside, and look at it with one eye, the accommodation- and parallax-feelings are there, but fail to make us see it hollow, as it is. Our mental knowledge of the fact that human faces are always convex overpowers them, and we directly perceive the nose to be nearer to us than the cheek instead of farther of.

The other organic tokens of farness and nearness are proved by similar experiments (of which we shall ere long speak more in detail) to have an equally fluctuating import. They lose all their value whenever the collateral circumstances favor a strong intellectual conviction that the object presented to the gaze is *improbable*—cannot be either *what* or *where* they would make us perceive it to be.

Now the query immediately arises : *Can the feelings of these processes in the eye, since they are so easily neutralized and reversed by intellectual suggestions, ever have been direct sensations of distance at all?* Ought we not rather to assume, since the distances which we see *in spite* of them are conclusions from past experience, that the distances which we see *by means* of them are equally such conclusions? Ought we not, in short, to say unhesitatingly that distance must be an intellectual and not a sensible content of consciousness? and that each of these eye-feelings serves as a mere signal to awaken this content, our intellect being so framed that sometimes it notices one signal more readily and sometimes another?

Reid long ago (Inquiry, c. VI. sec. 17) said:

" It may be taken for a general rule that things which are produced by custom may be undone or changed by disuse or by contrary custom. On the other hand, it is a strong argument that an effect is not owing to custom, but to the constitution of nature, when a contrary custom is found neither to change nor to weaken it."

More briefly, a way of seeing things that can be un-learned was presumably learned, and only what we cannot unlearn is instinctive.

This seems to be Helmholtz's view, for he confirms Reid's maxim by saying in emphatic print:

" No elements in our perception can be sensational which may be overcome or reversed by factors of demonstrably experimental origin. Whatever can be overcome by suggestions of experience must be re-garded as itself a product of experience and custom. If we follow this rule it will appear that only *qualities* are sensational, whilst almost all *spatial* attributes are results of habit and experience." *

This passage of Helmholtz's has obtained, it seems to me, an almost deplorable celebrity. The reader will please observe its very radical import. Not only would he, and does he, for the reasons we have just been ourselves con-sidering, deny distance to be an optical sensation; but, extending the same method of criticism to judgments of size, shape, and direction, and finding no single retinal or muscular process in the eyes to be indissolubly linked with any one of these, he goes so far as to say that all optical space-perceptions whatsoever must have an intellectual

---

* Physiol. Optik, p. 438. Helmholtz's reservation of ' qualities' is in-consistent. Our judgments of light and color vary as much as our judg-ments of size, shape, and place, and ought by parity of reasoning to be called intellectual products and not sensations. In other places he does treat color as if it were an intellectual product.

origin, and a content that no items of visual sensibility can account for.*

As Wundt and others agree with Helmholtz here, and as their conclusions, if true, are irreconcilable with all the sensationalism which I have been teaching hitherto, it clearly devolves upon me to defend my position against this new attack. But as this chapter on Space is already so overgrown with episodes and details, I think it best to reserve the refutation of their general principle for the next chapter, and simply to assume at this point its untenability. This has of course an arrogant look; but if the reader will bear with me for not very many pages more, I shall hope to appease his mind. Meanwhile I affirm confidently that *the same outer objects actually* FEEL *different to us according as our brain reacts on them in one way or another by making us perceive them as this or as that sort of thing.* So true is this that one may well, with Stumpf,† reverse Helmholtz's query, and ask: "What would become of our sense-perceptions in case experience were *not* able so to transform them?" Stumpf adds: "All wrong perceptions that depend on peculiarities in the organs are more or less perfectly corrected by the influence of imagination following the guidance of experience."

If, therefore, among the facts of optical space-perception (which we must now proceed to consider in more detail) we find instances of an identical organic eye-process, giving us different perceptions at different times, in consequence of different collateral circumstances suggesting different objective facts to our imagination, we must not hastily conclude, with the school of Helmholtz and Wundt, that the organic eye-process pure and simple, without the collateral circumstances, is incapable of giving us any sensation of a spatial kind at all. We must rather seek to discover *by what means* the circumstances can so have transformed a space-sensation, which, but for their presence, would probably have been felt in its natural purity. And I may as well say

---

* It is needless at this point to consider what Helmholtz's views of the nature of the intellectual space-yielding process may be. He vacillates—we shall later see how.

† *Op. cit.* p. 214.

now in advance that we shall find the means to be nothing more or less than association—*the suggestion to the mind of optical objects not actually present*, but more habitually associated with the 'collateral circumstances' than the sensation which they now displace and being imagined now with a quasi-hallucinatory strength. But before this conclusion emerges, it will be necessary to have reviewed the most important facts of optical space-perception, in relation to the organic conditions on which they depend. Readers acquainted with German optics will excuse what is already familiar to them in the following section.*

---

* Before embarking on this new topic it will be well to shelve, once for all, the problem of what is the physiological process that underlies the distance-feeling. Since one-eyed people have it, and are inferior to the two-eyed only in measuring its gradations, it can have no exclusive connection with the double and disparate images produced by binocular parallax. Since people with closed eyes, looking at an after-image, do not usually see it draw near or recede with varying convergence, it cannot be simply constituted by the convergence-feeling. For the same reason it would appear non-identical with the feeling of accommodation. The differences of apparent parallactic movement between far and near objects as we move our head cannot constitute the distance-sensation, for such differences may be easily reproduced experimentally (in the movements of visible spots against a background) without engendering any illusion of perspective. Finally, it is obvious that visible faintness, dimness, and smallness *are* not *per se* the feeling of visible distance, however much in the case of well-known objects they may serve as signs to suggest it.

A certain maximum distance-value, however, being given to the field of view of the moment, whatever it be, the feelings that accompany the processes just enumerated become so many *local signs* of the gradation of distances within this maximum depth. They help us to subdivide and measure it. Itself, however, is felt as a unit, a total distance-value, determining the vastness of the whole field of view, which accordingly appears as an abyss of a certain volume. And the question still persists, what neural process is it that underlies the sense of this distance-value?

Hering, who has tried to explain the gradations within it by the interaction of certain native distance-values belonging to each point of the two retinæ, seems willing to admit that the *absolute* scale of the space-volume within which the natively fixed relative distances shall appear is *not* fixed, but determined each time by 'experience in the widest sense of the word ' (*Beiträge*, p. 344). What he calls the *Kernpunkt* of this space-volume is the point we are momentarily fixating. The absolute scale of the whole volume depends on the absolute distance at which this *Kernpunkt* is judged to lie from the person of the looker. "By an alteration of the localization of the *Kernpunkt*, the *inner* relations of the seen space are nowise altered ; this space in its totality is as a fixed unit, so to speak, displaced with re-

Let us begin the long and rather tedious inquiry by the most important case. Physiologists have long sought for

---

spect to the self of the looker" (p. 345). But what constitutes the localization of the *Kernpunkt* itself at any given time, except ' Experience,' i.e., higher cerebral and intellectual processes, involving memory, Hering does not seek to define.

Stumpf, the other sensationalist writer who has best realized the difficulties of the problem, thinks that the primitive sensation of distance must have an immediate physical antecedent, either in the shape of "an organic alteration accompanying the process of accommodation, or else given directly in the specific energy of the optic nerve." In contrast with Hering, however, he thinks that it is the *absolute* distance of the spot fixated which is thus primitively, immediately, and physiologically given, and not the relative distances of other things about this spot. These, he thinks, are originally seen in what, broadly speaking, may be termed one plane with it. Whether the distance of this plane, considered as a phenomenon of our primitive sensibility, be an invariable datum, or susceptible of fluctuation, he does not, if I understand him rightly, undertake dogmatically to decide, but inclines to the former view. For him then, as for Hering, higher cerebral processes of association, under the name of ' Experience,' are the authors of fully one-half part of the distance-perceptions which we at any given time may have.

Hering's and Stumpf's theories are reported for the English reader by Mr. Sully (in Mind, III. pp. 172–6). Mr. Abbott, in his Sight and Touch (pp. 96–8), gives a theory which is to me so obscure that I only refer the reader to its place, adding that it seems to make of distance a fixed function of retinal sensation as modified by focal adjustment. Besides these three authors I am ignorant of any, except Panum, who may have attempted to define distance as in any degree an immediate sensation. And with them the direct sensational share is reduced to a very small proportional part, in our completed distance-judgments.

Professor Lipps, in his singularly acute Psychologische Studien (p. 69 ff.),argues, as Ferrier, in his review of Berkeley (Philosophical Remains, II. 330 ff.), had argued before him, that it is *logically impossible* we should perceive the distance of anything from the eye by sight; for a *seen* distance can only be between *seen* termini ; and one of the termini, in the case of distance from the eye, is the eye itself, which is not seen. Similarly of the distance of two points behind each other : the near one *hides* the far one, no space is seen between them. For the space between two objects to be *seen,* both must appear *beside* each other, then the space in question will be *visible.* On no other condition is its visibility possible. The conclusion is that things can properly be seen only in what Lipps calls a surface, and that our knowledge of the third dimension must needs be conceptual, not sensational or visually intuitive.

But no arguments in the world can prove a feeling which actually exists to be impossible. The feeling of depth or distance, of farness or awayness, does actually exist as a fact of our visual sensibility. All that Professor Lipps's reasonings prove concerning it is that it is not linear in

a simple law by which to connect the seen direction and distance of objects with the retinal impressions they produce. Two principal theories have been held of this matter, the 'theory of identical points,' and the 'theory of projection,'—each incompatible with the other, and each beyond certain limits becoming inconsistent with the facts.

The Theory of Identical Points.

This theory starts from the truth that on both retinæ an impression on the upper half makes us perceive an object as below, on the lower half as above, the horizon; and

 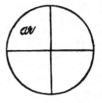

Fig. 54.

on the right half an object to the left, on the left half one to the right, of the median line. Thus each quadrant of one retina corresponds as a whole to the *similar* quadrant of

---

its character, or in its immediacy fully homogeneous and consubstantial with the feeling of literal distance between two seen termini; in short, that there are *two* sorts of optical sensation, each inexplicably due to a peculiar neural process. The neural process is easily discovered, in the case of lateral extension or spreadoutness, to be the number of retinal nerve-ends affected by the light; in the case of protension or mere farness it is more complicated and, as we have concluded, is still to seek. The two sensible qualities unite in the primitive visual bigness. The measurement of their various amounts against each other obeys the general laws of all such measurements. We discover their equivalencies by means of objects, apply the same units to both, and translate them into each other so habitually that at last they get to seem to us even quite similar in kind. This final appearance of homogeneity may perhaps be facilitated by the fact that in binocular vision two points situated on the prolongation of the optical axis of *one* of the eyes, so that the near one hides the far one, are by the *other* eye seen laterally apart. Each eye has in fact a foreshortened lateral view of the other's line of sight. In The London Times for Feb. 8, 1884, is an interesting letter by J. D. Dougal, who tries to explain by this reason why two-eyed rifle-shooting has such advantages over shooting with one eye closed.

the other; and within two similar quadrants, *al* and *ar* for
example, there should, if the correspondence were consist-
ently carried out, be geometrically similar points which, if
impressed at the same time by light emitted from the same
object, should cause that object to appear in the same direction to either eye. Experiment verifies this surmise. If
we look at the starry vault with parallel eyes, the stars all
seem single; and the laws of perspective show that under
the circumstances the parallel light-rays coming from each
star must impinge on points within either retina which *are*
geometrically similar to each other. The same result may
be more artificially obtained. If we take two exactly similar pictures, smaller, or at least no larger, than those on an
ordinary stereoscopic slide, and if we look at them as
stereoscopic slides are looked at, that is, at one with each
eye (a median partition confining the view of either eye to
the picture opposite it), we shall see but one flat picture,
all of whose parts appear sharp and single.* Identical
points being impressed, both eyes see their object in the
same direction, and the two objects consequently coalesce
into one.

The same thing may be shown in still another way.
With fixed head converge the eyes upon some conspicuous
objective point behind a pane of glass; then close either
eye alternately and make a little ink-mark on the glass,
'covering' the object as seen by the eye which is momentarily open. On looking now with both eyes the ink-marks
will seem single, and in the same direction as the objective
point. Conversely, let the eyes converge on a single ink-

---

* Just so, a pair of spectacles held an inch or so from the eyes seem
like one large median glass. The faculty of seeing stereoscopic slides single
without an instrument is of the utmost utility to the student of physiological optics, and persons with strong eyes can easily acquire it. The
only difficulty lies in dissociating the degree of accommodation from the
degree of convergence which it usually accompanies. If the right picture
is focussed by the right eye, the left by the left eye, the optic axes must
either be parallel or converge upon an imaginary point some distance
behind the plane of the pictures, according to the size and distance apart
of the pictures. The accommodation, however, has to be made for the
plane of the pictures itself, and a near accommodation with a far-off convergence is something which the ordinary use of our eyes never teaches us
to effect.

spot on the glass, and then by alternate shutting of them let it be noted what objects behind the glass the spot covers to the right and left eye respectively. Now with both eyes open, both these objects and the spot will appear in the same place, one or other of the three becoming more distinct according to the fluctuations of retinal attention.*

Now what is the direction of this common place? The only way of defining the direction of an object is by *pointing to it.* Most people, if asked to look at an object over the horizontal edge of a sheet of paper which conceals their hand and arm, and then to point their finger at it (raising the hand gradually so that at last a finger-tip will appear above the sheet of paper), are found to place the finger not between either eye and the object, but between the latter and the root of the nose, and this whether both eyes or either alone be used. Hering and Helmholtz express this by saying that we judge of the direction of objects as they would appear to an imaginary cyclopean eye, situated between our two real eyes, and with its optical axis bisecting the angle of convergence of the latter. Our two retinæ act, according to Hering, as if they were superposed in the place of this imaginary double-eye; we see by the corresponding points of each, situated far asunder as they really are, just as we *should* see if they were superposed and could both be excited together.

The judgment of objective singleness and that of identical direction seem to hang necessarily together. And that of identical direction seems to carry with it the necessity of a common origin, between the eyes or elsewhere, from which all the directions felt may seem to be estimated. This is why the cyclopean eye is really a fundamental part of the formulation of the theory of identical retinal points, and why Hering, the greatest champion of this theory, lays so much stress upon it.

It is an immediate consequence of the law of identical pro-

---

* These two observations prove the law of identical direction only for objects which excite the foveæ or lie in the line of direct looking. Observers skilled in indirect vision can, however, more or less easily verify the law for outlying retinal points.

*jection of images on geometrically similar points that images
which fall upon geometrically* DISPARATE *points of the two retinœ
should be projected in* DISPARATE *directions, and that their objects
should consequently appear in* TWO *places, or* LOOK DOUBLE.
Take the parallel rays from a star falling upon two eyes
which converge upon a near object, O, instead of being
parallel, as in the previously instanced case. If SL and SR
in Fig. 55 be the parallel rays, each of them will fall upon
the nasal half of the retina which it strikes.

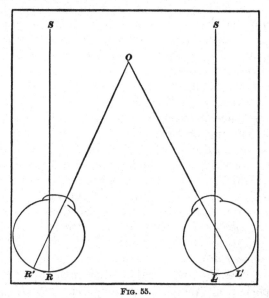

FIG. 55.

But the two nasal halves are disparate, geometrically
symmetrical, not geometrically *similar.* The image on the
left one will therefore appear as if lying in a direction leftward of the cyclopean eye's line of sight; the image of the
right one will appear far to the right of the same direction.
The star will, in short, be seen double,—' homonymously '
double.

Conversely, if the star be looked at directly with parallel
axes, O will be seen double, because its images will affect
the outer or cheek halves of the two retinæ, instead of one
outer and one nasal half. The position of the images will
here be reversed from that of the previous case. The right

eye's image will now appear to the left, the left eye's to the right—the double images will be ' heteronymous.'

The same reasoning and the same result ought to apply where the object's place with respect to the direction of the two optic axes is such as to make its images fall not on non-similar retinal halves, but on non-similar parts of similar halves. Here, of course, the directions of projection will be less widely disparate than in the other case, and the double images will appear to lie less widely apart.

Careful experiments made by many observers according to the so-called haploscopic method confirm this law, and show that *corresponding points, of single visual direction,* exist upon the two retinæ. For the detail of these one must consult the special treatises.

Note now an important consequence. If we take a stationary object and allow the eyes to vary their direction and convergence, a purely geometrical study will show that there will be some positions in which its two images impress corresponding retinal points, but more in which they impress disparate points. The former constitute the so-called horopter, and their discovery has been attended with great mathematical difficulty. Objects or parts of objects which lie in the eyes' horopter at any given time cannot appear double. *Objects lying out of the horopter would seem, if the theory of identical points were strictly true, necessarily and always to appear double.*

Here comes the first great conflict of the identity-theory with experience. Were the theory true, we ought all to have an intuitive knowledge of the horopter as the line of distinctest vision. Objects placed elsewhere ought to seem, if not actually double, at least blurred. And yet no living man makes any such distinction between the parts of his field of vision. To most of us the whole field appears single, and it is only by rare accident or by special education that we ever catch a glimpse of a double image. In 1838, Wheatstone, in his truly classical memoir on binocular vision and the stereoscope,* showed that the disparateness of the

---

* This essay, published in the Philosophical Transactions, contains the germ of almost all the methods applied since to the study of optical perception. It seems a pity that England, leading off so brilliantly the modern

points on which the two images of an object fall does not within certain limits affect its seen singleness at all, but rather the *distance* at which it shall appear. Wheatstone made an observation, moreover, which subsequently became the bone of much hot contention, in which he strove to show that not only might disparate images fuse, but images on corresponding or identical points might be seen double.*

I am unfortunately prevented by the weakness of my own eyes from experimenting enough to form a decided personal opinion on the matter. It seems to me, however, that the balance of evidence is against the Wheatstonian interpretation, and that disparate points may fuse, without identical points for that reason ever giving double images. The two questions, "Can we see single with disparate points?" and "Can we see double with identical points?" although at the first blush they may appear, as to Helmholtz they appear, to be but two modes of expressing the same inquiry, are in reality distinct. The first may quite well be answered affirmatively and the second negatively.

Add to this that the experiment quoted from Helmholtz above by no means always succeeds, but that many individuals place their finger between the object and *one* of their eyes, oftenest the right;† finally, observe that the

---

epoch of this study, should so quickly have dropped out of the field. Almost all subsequent progress has been made in Germany, Holland, and, *longo intervallo*, America.

* This is no place to report this controversy, but a few bibliographic references may not be inappropriate. Wheatstone's own experiment is in section 12 of his memoir. In favor of his interpretation see Helmholtz, Phys. Opt., pp. 737-9; Wundt, Physiol. Psychol., 2te Aufl. p. 144; Nagel, Sehen mit zwei Augen, pp. 78-82. Against Wheatstone see Volkmann. Arch. f. Ophth., v. 2-74, and Untersuchungen, p. 266; Hering, Beiträge zur Physiologie, 29-45, also in Hermann's Hdbch. d. Physiol., Bd. III. 1 Th. p. 435; Aubert, Physiologie d. Netzhaut, p. 322; Schön, Archiv f. Ophthal., XXIV. 1. pp. 56-65; and Donders, *ibid.* XIII 1. p. 15 and note.

† When we see the finger the whole time, we usually put it in the line joining object and left eye if it be the left finger, joining object and right eye if it be the right finger. Microscopists, marksmen, or persons one of whose eyes is much better than the other, almost always refer directions to a single eye, as may be seen by the position of the shadow on their face when they point at a candle-flame.

identity-theory, with its Cyclopean starting point for all lines of direction, gives by itself no ground for the *distance* on any line at which an object shall appear, and has to be helped out in this respect by subsidiary hypotheses, which, in the hands of Hering and others, have become so complex as easily to fall a prey to critical attacks ; and it will soon seem as if *the law of identical seen directions by corresponding points, although a simple formula for expressing concisely many fundamental phenomena, is by no means an adequate account of the whole matter of retinal perception.**

The Projection-Theory.

Does the theory of projection fare any better? This theory admits that each eye sees the object in a different direction from the other, along the line, namely, passing from the object through the middle of the pupil to the retina. A point directly fixated is thus seen on the optical axes of both eyes. There is only one point, however, which these two optical axes have in common, and that is the point to which they converge. Everything directly looked at is seen at this point, and is thus seen both single and at its proper distance. It is easy to show the incompatibility of this theory with the theory of identity. Take an objective point (like O in Fig. 50, when the star is looked at) casting its images R' and L' on geometrically dissimilar parts of the two retinæ and affecting the outer half of each eye. On the identity-theory it ought necessarily to appear double, whilst on the projection-theory there is no reason whatever why it should not appear single, provided only it be located by the judgment on each line of visible direc-

---

* Professor Joseph Le Conte, who believes strongly in the identity-theory, has embodied the latter in a pair of laws of the relation between positions seen single and double, near or far, on the one hand, and convergences and retinal impressions, on the other, which, though complicated, seems to me by far the best descriptive formulation yet made of the normal facts of vision. His account is easily accessible to the reader in his volume 'Sight' in the International Scientific Series, bk. II. c. 3, so I say no more about it now, except that it does not solve any of the difficulties we are noting in the identity-theory, nor account for the other fluctuating perceptions of which we go on to treat.

tion, neither nearer nor farther than its point of intersection with the other line.

Every point in the field of view ought, in truth, if the pro-jection-theory were uniformly valid, to appear single, entirely irrespective of the varying positions of the eyes, for from every point of space two lines of visible direction pass to the two retinæ; and at the intersection of these lines, or just where the point is, there, according to the theory, it should appear. *The objection to this theory is thus precisely the reverse of the objection to the identity-theory. If the latter ruled, we ought to see most things double all the time. If the projection-theory ruled, we ought never to see anything double. As a matter of fact we get too few double images for the iden-tity-theory, and too many for the projection-theory.*

The partisans of the projection-theory, beginning with

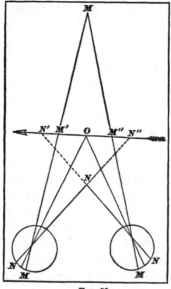

Fig. 56.

Aguilonius, have always explained double images as the result of an erroneous judgment of the *distance* of the object, the images of the latter being projected by the imagination along the two lines of visible direction either nearer or farther than the point of intersection of the latter. A diagram will make this clear.

Let O be the point looked at, **M** an object farther, and **N** an object nearer, than it. Then **M** and **N** will send the lines of visible direction **MM** and **NN** to the two retinæ. If **N** be judged as far as O, it must necessarily lie where the two lines of visible direction **NN** intersect the plane of the arrow, or in two places, at **N'** and at **N''**. If **M** be judged as near as O, it must for the same reason form two images at **M'** and **M''**.

It is, as a matter of fact, true that we often misjudge the distance in the way alleged. If the reader will hold his forefingers, one beyond the other, in the median line, and fixate them alternately, he will see the one not looked at, double ; and he will also notice that it appears nearer to the plane of the one looked at, whichever the latter may be, than it really is. Its changes of apparent size, as the convergence of the eyes, alter also prove the change of apparent distance. The distance at which the axes converge seems, in fact, to exert a sort of attraction upon objects situated elsewhere. Being the distance of which we are most acutely sensible, it invades, so to speak, the whole field of our perception. If two half-dollars be laid on the table an inch or two apart, and the eyes fixate steadily the point of a pen held in the median line at varying distances between the coins and the face, there will come a distance at which the pen stands between the left half-dollar and the right eye, and the right half-dollar and the left eye. The two half-dollars will then coalesce into one ; and this one will show its apparent approach to the pen-point by seeming suddenly much reduced in size.*

Yet, in spite of this tendency to inaccuracy, we are never actually mistaken about the half-dollar being behind the pen-point. It may not seem far enough off, but still it is farther than the point. In general it may be said that where the objects are known to us, no such illusion of distance occurs in any one as the theory would require. And in some observers, Hering for example, it seems hardly to occur at all. If I look into infinite distance and get my finger in double images, they do not seem infinitely far off.

---

* Naturally it takes a smaller object at a less distance to cover by its image a constant amount of retinal surface.

To make objects at different distances seem equidistant, careful precautions must be taken to have them alike in appearance, and to exclude all outward reasons for ascribing to the one a different location from that ascribed to the other. Thus Donders tries to prove the law of projection by taking two similar electric sparks, one behind the other on a dark ground, one seen double ; or an iron rod placed so near to the eyes that its double images seem as broad as that of a fixated stove-pipe, the top and bottom of the objects being cut off by screens, so as to prevent all suggestions of perspective, etc. The three objects in each experiment seem in the same plane.*

Add to this the impossibility, recognized by *all* observers, of ever seeing double with the *foveæ*, and the fact that authorities as able as those quoted in the note on Wheatstone's observation deny that they can see double then with identical points, and we are forced to conclude that *the projection-theory, like its predecessor, breaks down. Neither formulates exactly or exhaustively a law for all our perceptions.*

Ambiguity of Retinal Impressions.

What does each theory try to do ? To make of seen location a fixed function of retinal impression. Other facts may be

FIG. 57.

brought forward to show how far from fixed are the perceptive functions of retinal impressions. We alluded a while ago to the extraordinary ambiguity of the retinal image as a revealer of magnitude. Produce an after-image of the sun and look at your finger-tip : it will be smaller than your nail. Project it on the table, and it will be as big as a strawberry ; on the wall, as large as a plate ; on yonder mountain, bigger than a house. And yet it is an unchanged

---

* Archiv f. Ophthal., Bd. XVII. Abth. 2, pp. 44–6 (1871).

retinal impression. Prepare a sheet with the figures shown
in Fig. 57 strongly marked upon it, and get by direct fixation a distinct after-image of each.

Project the after-image of the cross upon the upper left-
hand part of the wall, it will appear as in Fig. 58 ; on the
upper right-hand it will appear as in Fig. 59. The circle

FIG. 58.   FIG. 59.

similarly projected will be distorted into two different
ellipses. If the two parallel lines be projected upon the
ceiling or floor far in front, the farther ends will diverge ;
and if the three parallel lines be thrown on the same surfaces, the upper pair will seem farther apart than the lower.

Adding certain lines to others has the same distorting
effect. In what is known as Zöllner's pattern (Fig. 60), the
long parallels tip towards each other the moment we draw
the short slanting lines over them yet their retinal images

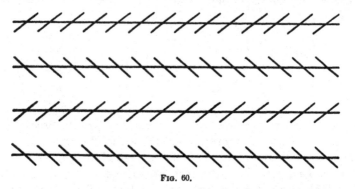

FIG. 60.

are the same they always were. A similar distortion of
parallels appears in Fig 61.

Drawing a square inside the circle (Fig. 52) gives to the
outline of the latter an indented appearance where the
square's corners touch it. Drawing the radii inside of one

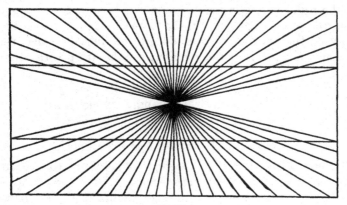

Fig. 61.

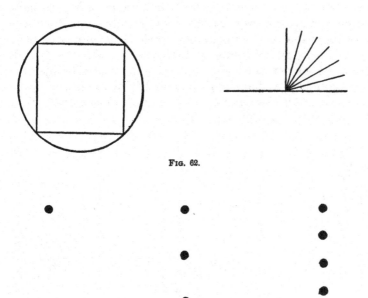

Fig. 62.

Fig. 63.

of the right angles in the same figure makes it seem larger than the other. In Fig. 63, the retinal image of the space between the extreme dots is in all three lines the same, yet it seems much larger the moment it is filled up with other dots.

In the stereoscope certain pairs of lines which look single under ordinary circumstances immediately seem double when we add certain other lines to them.*

Ambiguous Import of Eye-movements.

These facts show the indeterminateness of the space-import of various *retinal impressions.* Take now the *eye's movements,* and we find a similar vacillation. When we follow a moving object with our gaze, the motion is 'voluntary'; when our eyes oscillate to and fro after we have made ourselves dizzy by spinning around, it is 'reflex'; and when the eyeball is pushed with the finger, it is 'passive.' Now, in all three of these cases we get a feeling from the movement as it effects itself. But the objective perceptions to which the feeling assists us are by no means the same. In the first case we may see a stationary field of view with one moving object in it; in the second, the total field swimming more or less steadily in one direction; in the third, a sudden jump or twist of the same total field.

The feelings of convergence of the eyeballs permit of the same ambiguous interpretation. When objects are near we converge strongly upon them in order to see them; when far, we set our optic axes parallel. But the exact degree of convergence fails to be felt; or rather, being felt, fails to tell us the absolute distance of the object we are regarding. Wheatstone arranged his stereoscope in such a way that the size of the retinal images might change without the convergence altering; or conversely, the convergence might change without the retinal image altering. Under these circumstances, he says,† the object seemed to approach or recede in the first case, without altering its size; in the second, to change its size without altering its distance—just

---

* A. W. Volkmann, Untersuchungen, p. 253.
† Philosophical Transactions, 1852, p. 4.

the reverse of what might have been expected. Wheatstone adds, however, that ' fixing the attention ' converted each of these perceptions into its opposite. The same perplexity occurs in looking through prismatic glasses, which alter the eyes' convergence. We cannot decide whether the object has come nearer, or grown larger, or both, or neither; and our judgment vacillates in the most surprising way. We may even make our eyes diverge, and the object will none the less appear at a finite distance. When we look through the stereoscope, the picture seems at no determinate distance. These and other facts have led Helmholtz to deny that the feeling of convergence has any very exact value as a distance-measurer.*

With *the feelings of accommodation* it is very much the same. Donders has shown † that the apparent magnifying power of spectacles of moderate convexity hardly depends at all upon their enlargement of the retinal image, but rather on the relaxation they permit of the muscle of accommodation. This suggests an object farther off, and consequently a much larger one, since its retinal size rather increases than diminishes. But in this case the same vacillation of judgment as in the previously mentioned case of convergence takes place. The recession made the object seem larger, but the apparent growth in size of the object now makes it look as if it came nearer instead of receding. The effect thus contradicts its own cause. Everyone is conscious, on first.putting on a pair of spectacles, of a doubt whether the field of view draws near or retreats.‡

There is still *another deception, occurring in persons who have had one eye-muscle suddenly paralyzed.* This deception

---

* Physiol. Optik, 649–664. Later this author is led to value convergence more highly. Arch. f. (Anat. u.) Physiol. (1878), p. 322.

† Anomalies of Accommodation and Refraction (New Sydenham Soc. Transl., London, 1864), p. 155.

‡ These strange contradictions have been called by Aubert ' secondary ' deceptions of judgment. See Grundzüge d. Physiologischen Optik (Leipzig, 1876), pp. 601, 615, 627. One of the best examples of them is the small size of the moon as first seen through a telescope. It is larger and brighter, so we see its details more distinctly and judge it nearer. But because we judge it so much nearer we think it must have grown smaller. Cf. Charpentier in Jahresbericht, x. 430.

has led Wundt to affirm that the eyeball-feeling proper, the incoming sensation of effected rotation, tells us only of the direction of our eye-movements, but not of their whole extent.* For this reason, and because not only Wundt, but many other authors, think the phenomena in these partial paralyses demonstrate the existence of a feeling of innervation, a feeling of the outgoing nervous current, opposed to every afferent sensation whatever, it seems proper to note the facts with a certain degree of detail.

Suppose a man wakes up some morning with the external rectus muscle of his right eye half paralyzed, what will be the result? He will be enabled only with great effort to rotate the eye so as to look at objects lying far off to the right. Something in the effort he makes will make him feel as if the object lay much farther to the right than it really is. If the left and sound eye be closed, and he be asked to touch rapidly with his finger an object situated towards his right, he will point the finger to the right of it. The current explanation of the 'something' in the effort which causes this deception is that it is the sensation of the outgoing discharge from the nervous centres, the 'feeling of innervation,' to use Wundt's expression, requisite for bringing the open eye with its weakened muscle to bear upon the object to be touched. If that object be situated 20 degrees to the right, the patient has now to innervate as powerfully to turn the eye those 20 degrees as formerly he did to turn the eye 30 degrees. He consequently believes as before that he *has* turned it 30 degrees ; until, by a newly-acquired custom, he learns the altered spatial import of all the discharges his brain makes into his right abducens nerve. The 'feeling of innervation,' maintained to exist by this and other observations, plays an immense part in the space-theories of certain philosophers, especially Wundt. I shall elsewhere try to show that the observations by no means warrant the conclusions drawn from them, and that the feeling in question is probably a wholly fictitious entity.† Meanwhile it suffices to point out that even those who set most store by it are compelled, by the

---

* Revue Philosophique, III. 9, p. 220.
† See Chapter XXIV.

readiness with which the translocation of the field of view becomes corrected and further errors avoided, to admit that the precise space-import of *the supposed sensation of outgoing energy is as ambiguous and indeterminate as that of any other of the eye-feelings we have considered hitherto.*

I have now given what no one will call an understatement of the facts and arguments by which it is sought to banish the credit of directly revealing space from each and every kind of eye-sensation taken by itself. The reader will confess that they make a very plausible show, and most likely wonder whether my own theory of the matter can rally from their damaging evidence. But the case is far from being hopeless; and the introduction of a discrimination hitherto unmade will, if I mistake not, easily vindicate the view adopted in these pages, whilst at the same time it makes ungrudging allowance for all the ambiguity and illusion on which so much stress is laid by the advocates of the intellectualist-theory.

The Choice of the Visual Reality.

We *have* native and fixed optical space-sensations; *but experience leads us to select certain ones from among them to be the exclusive bearers of reality : the rest become mere signs and suggesters of these.* The factor of *selection,* on which we have already laid so much stress, here as elsewhere is the solving word of the enigma. If Helmholtz, Wundt, and the rest, with an ambiguous retinal sensation before them, meaning now one size and distance, and now another, had not contented themselves with merely saying:—The size and distance are not this sensation, they are something beyond it which it merely calls up, and whose own birthplace is afar —in 'synthesis' (Wundt) or in 'experience' (Helmholtz) as the case may be ; if they had gone on definitely to ask and definitely to answer the question, What are the size and distance in their proper selves ? they would not only have escaped the present deplorable vagueness of their space-theories, but they would have seen that the objective spatial attributes ' signified ' are simply and solely *certain other optical sensations now absent,* but which the present sensations suggest.

What, for example, is the slant-legged cross which we think we see on the wall when we project the rectangular after-image high up towards our right or left (Figs. 58 and 59)? Is it not in very sooth a retinal sensation itself? An imagined sensation, not a felt one, it is true, but none the less essentially and originally sensational or retinal for that, —the sensation, namely, which we should receive if a 'real' slant-legged cross stood on the wall *in front of us* and threw its image on our eye. That image is not the one our retina now holds. Our retina now holds the image which a cross of square shape throws when in front, but which a cross of the slant-legged pattern *would* throw, provided it were actually on the wall in the distant place at which we look. Call this actual retinal image the 'square' image. The square image is then one of the innumerable images the slant-legged cross can throw. Why should another one, and that an absent one, of those innumerable images be picked out to represent exclusively the slant-legged cross's 'true' shape? Why should that absent and imagined slant-legged image displace the present and felt square image from our mind? Why, when the objective cross gives us so many shapes, as it varies its position, should we think we feel the true shape only when the cross is directly in front? And when that question is answered, how can the absent and represented feeling of a slant-legged figure so successfully intrude itself into the place of a presented square one?

Before answering either question, let us be doubly sure about our facts, and see how true it is that *in our dealings with objects we always do pick out one of the visual images they yield, to constitute the real form or size.*

The matter of size has been already touched upon, so that no more need be said of it here. As regards shape, almost all the retinal shapes that objects throw are perspective 'distortions.' Square table-tops constantly present two acute and two obtuse angles; circles drawn on our wall-papers, our carpets, or on sheets of paper, usually show like ellipses; parallels approach as they recede; human bodies are foreshortened ; and the transitions from one to another of these altering forms are infinite and continual. Out of the flux, however, one phase always stands prominent. It is the form the object has when we see it easiest and best : and that is when our eyes and the object both are in what may be called *the normal position.* In this position our head is upright and our optic axes either parallel or symmetrically convergent ; the plane of the object is perpendicular to the visual plane ; and if the object is one containing many lines it is turned so as to make them, as far as possible, either parallel or perpendicular to the visual plane. In this situation it is that we compare all shapes with each other ; here every exact measurement and decision is made.*

It is very easy to see why the normal situation should have this extraordinary pre-eminence. First, it is the position in which we easiest hold anything we are examining in our hands ; second, it is a turning-point between all right- and all left-hand perspective views of a given object ; third, it is the only position in which symmetrical figures seem symmetrical and equal angles seem equal ; fourth, it is often that starting-point of movements from which the eye is least troubled by axial rotations, by which *superposition* † of the retinal images of different lines and different parts of the same line is easiest produced, and consequently by which the eye can make the best comparative measurements in its sweeps. All these merits single the normal position out to be chosen. No other point of view offers so many æsthetic and practical advantages. Here we believe we see the object as it *is ;* elsewhere, only as it seems. Experience and custom soon teach us, however, that the seeming appearance passes into the real one by continuous gradations. They teach us, moreover, that seeming and being may be strangely interchanged. Now a real circle may slide into a seeming ellipse ; now an ellipse may, by sliding in the same direction, become a seeming circle ; now

---

* The only exception seems to be when we expressly wish to abstract from particulars, and to judge of the general 'effect.' Witness ladies trying on new dresses with their heads inclined and their eyes askance ; or painters in the same attitude judging of the ' values ' in their pictures.

† The importance of Superposition will appear later on.

a rectangular cross grows slant-legged; now a slant-legged one grows rectangular.

Almost any form in oblique vision may be thus a derivative of almost any other in 'primary' vision; and we must learn, when we get one of the former appearances, to translate it into the appropriate one of the latter class; we must learn of what optical 'reality' it is one of the optical signs. Having learned this, we do but obey that law of economy or simplification which dominates our whole psychic life, when we attend exclusively to the 'reality' and ignore as much as our consciousness will let us the 'sign' by which we came to apprehend it. The signs of each probable real thing being multiple and the thing itself one and fixed, we gain the same mental relief by abandoning the former for the latter that we do when we abandon mental images, with all their fluctuating characters, for the definite and unchangeable *names* which they suggest. The selection of the several 'normal' appearances from out of the jungle of our optical experiences, to serve as the real sights of which we shall think, is psychologically a parallel phenomenon to the habit of thinking in words, and has a like use. Both are substitutions of terms few and fixed for terms manifold and vague.

Sensations which we Ignore.

This service of sensations as mere signs, to be ignored when they have evoked the other sensations which are their significates, was noticed first by Berkeley and remarked in many passages, as the following:

"Signs, being little considered in themselves, or for their own sake, but only in their relative capacity and for the sake of those things whereof they are signs, it comes to pass that the mind overlooks them, so as to carry its attention immediately on to the things signified . . . which in truth and strictness are not *seen*, but only *suggested* and *apprehended* by means of the proper objects of sight which alone are seen." (Divine Visual Language, § 12.)

Berkeley of course erred in supposing that the thing suggested was not even *originally* an object of sight, as the sign now is which calls it up. Reid expressed Berkeley's principle in yet clearer language:

"The visible appearances of objects are intended by nature only as signs or indications, and the mind passes instantly to the things sig-

nified, without making the least reflection upon the sign, or even perceiving that there is any such thing. . . . The mind has acquired a confirmed and inveterate habit of inattention to them (the signs). For
they no sooner appear than, quick as lightning, the thing signified succeeds and engrosses all our regard. They have no name in language ;
and although we are conscious of them when they pass through the
mind, yet their passage is so quick and so familiar that it is absolutely
unheeded ; nor do they leave any footsteps of themselves, either in the
memory or imagination." (Inquiry, chap. v. §§ 2, 3.)

If we review the facts we shall find every grade of non-
attention between the extreme form of overlooking mentioned by Reid (or forms even more extreme still) and complete conscious perception of the sensation present. Sometimes it is literally impossible to become aware of the latter.
Sometimes a little artifice or effort easily leads us to discern
it together, or in alternation, with the 'object' it reveals.
Sometimes the present sensation is held to *be* the object or
to reproduce its features in undistorted shape, and *then*, of
course, it receives the mind's full glare.

The deepest inattention is to subjective optical sensations, strictly so called, or those which are not signs of
outer objects at all. Helmholtz's treatment of these phenomena, *muscœ volitantes*, negative after-images, double
images, etc., is very satisfactory. He says :

" We only attend with any ease and exactness to our sensations in so
far forth as they can be utilized for the knowledge of outward things ;
and we are accustomed to neglect all those portions of them which have
no significance as regards the external world. So much is this the case
that for the most part special artifices and practice are required for
the observation of these latter more subjective feelings. Although it
might seem that nothing should be easier than to be conscious of one's
own sensations, experience nevertheless shows that often enough either a
special talent like that showed in eminent degree by Purkinje, or accident or theoretic speculation, are necessary conditions for the discovery
of subjective phenomena. Thus, for example, the blind spot on the
retina was discovered by Mariotte by the theoretic way ; similarly by
me the existence of 'summation'-tones in acoustics. In the majority
of cases accident is what first led observers whose attention was especially exercised on subjective phenomena to discover this one or that ;
only where the subjective appearances are so intense that they interfere with the perception of objects are they noticed by all men alike.
But if they have once been discovered it is for the most part easy for
subsequent observers who place themselves in proper conditions and
bend their attention in the right direction to perceive them. But in

many cases—for example, in the phenomena of the blind spot, in the discrimination of over-tones and combination-tones from the ground-tone of musical sounds, etc.—such a strain of the attention is required, even with appropriate instrumental aids, that most persons fail. The very after-images of bright objects are by most men perceived only under exceptionally favorable conditions, and it takes steady practice to see the fainter images of this kind. It is a commonly recurring experience that persons smitten with some eye-disease which impairs vision suddenly remark for the first time the *muscæ volitantes* which all through life their vitreous humor has contained, but which they now firmly believe to have arisen since their malady ; the truth being that the latter has only made them more observant of all their visual sensations. There are also cases where one eye has gradually grown blind, and the patient lived for an indefinite time without knowing it, until, through the accidental closure of the healthy eye alone, the blindness of the other was brought to attention.

"Most people, when first made aware of binocular double images, are uncommonly astonished that they should never have noticed them before, although all through their life they had been in the habit of seeing singly only those few objects which were about equally distant with the point of fixation, and the rest, those nearer and farther, which constitute the great majority, had always been double.

"We must then *learn* to turn our attention to our particular sensations, and we learn this commonly only for such sensations as are means of cognition of the outer world. Only so far as they serve this end have our sensations any importance for us in ordinary life. Subjective feelings are mostly interesting only to scientific investigators ; were they remarked in the ordinary use of the senses, they could only cause disturbance. Whilst, therefore, we reach an extraordinary degree of firmness and security in objective observation, we not only do not reach this where subjective phenomena are concerned, but we actually attain in a high degree the faculty of overlooking these altogether, and keeping ourselves independent of their influence in judging of objects, even in cases where their strength might lead them easily to attract our attention." (Physiol. Optik, pp. 431-2.)

Even where the sensation is not merely subjective, as in the cases of which Helmholtz speaks, but is a sign of something outward, we are also liable, as Reid says, to overlook its intrinsic quality and attend exclusively to the image of the ' thing ' it suggests. But here everyone *can* easily notice the sensation itself if he will. Usually we see a sheet of paper as uniformly white, although a part of it may be in shadow. But we can in an instant, if we please, notice the shadow as local color. A man walking towards us does not usually seem to alter his size ; but we can, by setting our attention in a peculiar way make him appear to do so. The whole education of the artist consists in his learning to see the presented signs as well as the represented things. No matter what the field of view *means*, he sees it also as it *feels*—that is, as a collection of patches of color bounded by lines—the whole forming an optical diagram of whose intrinsic proportions one who is not an artist has hardly a conscious inkling. The ordinary man's attention passes *over* them to their import; the artist's turns back and dwells *upon* them for their own sake. 'Don't draw the thing as it *is*, but as it *looks !* ' is the endless advice of every teacher to his pupil; forgetting that what it 'is' is what it would also 'look,' provided it were placed in what we have called the 'normal' situation for vision. In this situation the sensation as 'sign' and the sensation as 'object' coalesce into one, and there is no contrast between them.

Sensations which seem Suppressed.

But a great difficulty has been made of certain peculiar cases which we must now turn to consider. They are *cases in which a present sensation, whose existence is supposed to be proved by its outward conditions being there, seems absolutely suppressed or changed by the image of the 'thing' it suggests.*

This matter carries us back to what was said on p. 218. The passage there quoted from Helmholtz refers to these cases. He thinks they conclusively disprove the original and intrinsic spatiality of any of our retinal sensations; for if such a one, actually present, had an immanent and essential space-determination of its own, that might well be added to and overlaid or even momentarily eclipsed by suggestions of its signification, but how could it possibly be altered or completely *suppressed* thereby? Of actually present sensations, he says, being *suppressed* by suggestions of experience—

" We have not a single well-attested example. In all those illusions which are provoked by *sensations* in the absence of their usually exciting objects, the mistake never vanishes by the better understanding of the object really present, and by insight into the cause of deception. Phosphenes provoked by pressure on the eyeball, by traction on the entrance of the optic nerve, after-images, etc., remain projected into their apparent place in the field of vision, just as the image projected from a mirror's surface continues to be seen *behind* the mirror, although we *know* that to all these appearances no outward reality corresponds. True enough, we can remove our attention, and keep it removed, from sensations that have no reference to the outer world, those, e.g., of the weaker after-images, and of entoptic objects, etc. . . . But what would become of our perceptions at all if we had the power not only of ignoring, but of *transforming into their opposites,* any part of them that differed from that outward experience, the image of which, as that of a present reality, accompanies them in the mind?" *

And again :

"On the analogy of all other experience, we should expect that the conquered feelings would persist to our perception, even if only in the shape of recognized illusions. But this is not the case. One does not see how the assumption of originally spatial sensations can explain our optical cognitions, when in the last resort those who believe in these very sensations find themselves obliged to assume that they are *overcome* by our better judgment, based on experience."

These words, coming from such a quarter, necessarily carry great weight. But the authority even of a Helmholtz ought not to shake one's critical composure. And the moment one abandons abstract generalities and comes to close quarters with the particulars, I think one easily sees that no such conclusions as those we have quoted follow from the latter. But profitably to conduct the discussion *we must divide the alleged instances into groups.*

(*a*) With Helmholtz, *color-perception* is equally with space-perception an intellectual affair. The so-called simultaneous color-contrast, by which one color modifies another alongside of which it is said, is explained by him as an unconscious inference. In Chapter XVII we discussed the color-contrast problem ; the principles which applied to its solution will prove also applicable to part of the present problem. In my opinion, Hering has definitely proved that, when one color is laid beside another, it modifies the sensation of the latter, not by virtue of any mere mental suggestion, as Helmholtz would have it, but by actually exciting a new nerve-process, to which the modified feeling of color immediately corresponds. The explanation is physiological, not psychological. The transformation of

---

* Physiol. Optik, p. 817.

the original color by the inducing color is due to the disappearance of the physiological conditions under which the
first color was produced, and to the induction, under the
new conditions, of a genuine new sensation, with which the
'suggestions of experience' have naught to do.

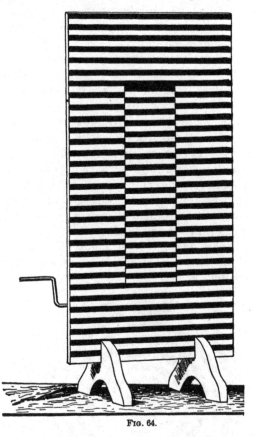

Fig. 64.

That processes in the visual apparatus propagate themselves laterally, if one may so express it, is also shown by
the *phenomena of contrast which occur after looking upon
motions* of various kinds.   Here are a few examples.   If,
over the rail of a moving vessel, we look at the water rushing along the side, and then transfer our gaze to the deck, a
band of planks will appear to us, moving in the opposite

direction to that in which, a moment previously, we had
been seeing the water move, whilst on either side of this
band another band of planks will move as the water did.
Looking at a waterfall, or at the road from out of a car-
window in a moving train, produces the same illusion, which
may be easily verified in the laboratory by a simple piece
of apparatus. A board with a window five or six inches
wide and of any convenient length is supported upright on
two feet. On the back side of the board, above and below
the window, are two rollers, one of which is provided with
a crank. An endless band of any figured stuff is passed
over these rollers (one of which can be so adjusted on its
bearings as to keep the stuff always taut and not liable to
slip), and the surface of the front board is also covered with
stuff or paper of a nature to catch the eye. Turning the
crank now sets the central band in continuous motion,
whilst the margins of the field remain really at rest, but
after a while appear moving in the contrary way. Stopping
the crank results in an illusory appearance of motion in
reverse directions all over the field.

A disk with an Archimedean spiral drawn upon it,
whirled round on an ordinary rotating machine, produces
still more startling effects.

Fig. 65.

"If the revolution is in the direction in which the spiral line
approaches the centre of the disk the entire surface of the latter seems
to expand during revolution and to contract after it has ceased ; and

vice versâ if the movement of revolution is in the opposite direction. If in the former case the eyes of the observers are turned from the rotating disk towards any familiar object—e.g. the face of a friend—the latter seems to contract or recede in a somewhat striking manner, and to expand or approach after the opposite motion of the spiral." *

An elementary form of these motor illusions seems to be the one described by Helmholtz on pp. 568–571 of his Optik. The motion of anything in the field of vision along an acute angle towards a straight line sensibly distorts

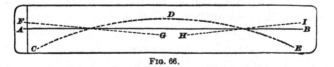

FIG. 66.

that line. Thus in Fig. 66: Let AB be a line drawn on paper, CDE the tracing made over this line by the point of a compass steadily followed by the eye, as it moves. As the compass-point passes from C to D, the line appears to move downwards; as it passes from D to E, the line appears to move upwards; at the same time the whole line seems to incline itself in the direction FG during the first half of the compass's movement; and in the direction HI during its last half; the change from one inclination to another being quite distinct as the compass-point passes over D.

Any line across which we draw a pencil-point appears to be animated by a rapid movement of its own towards the pencil-point. This apparent movement of both of two things in relative motion to each other, even when one of them is absolutely still, reminds us of the instances quoted

---

* Bowditch and Hall, in Journal of Physiology, vol. III. p. 299. Helmholtz tries to explain this phenomenon by unconscious rotations of the eyeball. But movements of the eyeball can only explain such appearances of movements as are the same over the whole field. In the windowed board one part of the field seems to move in one way, another part in another. The same is true when we turn from the spiral to look at the wall —the *centre* of the field alone swells out or contracts, the margin does the reverse or remains at rest. Mach and Dvorak have beautifully proved the impossibility of eye-rotations in this case (Sitzungsber. d. Wiener Akad., Bd. LXI.). See also Bowditch and Hall's paper as above, p. 300.

from Vierordt on page 188, and seems to take us back to a primitive stage of perception, in which the discriminations we now make when we feel a movement have not yet been made. If we draw the point of a pencil through 'Zöllner's pattern' (Fig. 60, p. 232), and follow it with the eye, the whole figure becomes the scene of the most singular apparent unrest, of which Helmholtz has very carefully noted the conditions. The illusion of Zöllner's figure vanishes entirely, or almost so, with most people, if they steadily look at one point of it with an unmoving eye; and the same is the case with many other illusions.

Now all these facts taken together seem to show—vaguely it is true, but certainly—*that present excitements and after-effects of former excitements may alter the result of processes occurring simultaneously at a distance from them in the retina* or other portions of the apparatus for optical sensation. In the cases last considered, the moving eye, as it sweeps the fovea over certain parts of the figure, seems thereby to determine a modification in the feeling which the *other* parts confer, which modification is the figure's 'distortion.' It is true that this statement explains nothing. It only keeps the cases to which it applies from being explained spuriously. *The spurious account of these illusions is that they are intellectual, not sensational, that they are secondary, not primary, mental facts.* The distorted figure is said to be one which the mind is led to *imagine,* by falsely drawing an unconscious inference from certain premises of which it is not distinctly aware. And the imagined figure is supposed to be strong enough to suppress the perception of whatever real sensations there may be. But Helmholtz, Wundt, Delbœuf, Zöllner, and all the advocates of unconscious inference are at variance with each other when it comes to the question what these unconscious premises and inferences may be.

That small angles look proportionally larger than larger ones is, in brief, the fundamental illusion to which almost all authors would reduce the peculiarity of Fig. 67, as of Figs. 60, 61, 62 (pp. 232, 233). This peculiarity of small angles is by Wundt treated as the case of a filled space seeming larger than an empty one, as in Fig. 68 ; and this, according to both Delbœuf and Wundt, is owing to the fact that more muscular innervation is needed for the eye to traverse a filled space than an empty one, because the points and lines

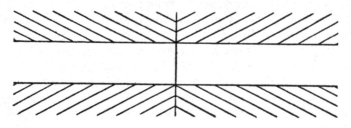

FIG. 67.

in the filled space inevitably arrest and constrain the eye, and this makes us feel as if it were doing more work, i.e. traversing a longer distance.* When, however, we recol-

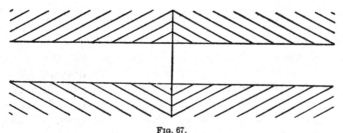

FIG. 68.

lect that muscular movements are positively proved to have *no* share in the waterfall and revolving-spiral illusions, and that it is hard to see how Wundt's and Delbœuf's particular form of muscle-explanation can possibly apply to the compass-point illusion considered a moment ago, we must conclude that these writers have probably exaggerated, to say the least, the reach of their muscle-explanation in the case

---

* Bulletins de l'Acad. de Belgique, XXI. 2; Revue Philosophique, VI. pp. 223–5; Physiologische Psychologie, 2te Aufl. p. 103. Compare Münsterberg's views, Beiträge, Heft 2, p. 174.

of the subdivided angles and lines. Never do we get such strong muscular feelings as when, against the course of nature, we oblige our eyes to be still; but fixing the eyes on one point of the figure, so far from making that part of the latter seem larger, dispels, in most persons, the illusion of these diagrams altogether.

As for Helmholtz, he invokes, to explain the enlargement of small angles,* what he calls a '*law of contrast*' between directions and distances of lines, analogous to that between colors and intensities of light. Lines cutting another line make the latter seem more inclined away from them than it really is. Moreover, clearly recognizable magnitudes appear greater than equal magnitudes which we but vaguely apprehend. But this is surely a sensationalistic law, a native function of our seeing-apparatus. Quite as little as the negative after-image of the revolving spiral could such contrast be deduced from any association of ideas or recall of past objects. The principle of contrast is criticised by Wundt, † who says that by it small spaces ought to appear to us smaller, and not larger, than they really are. Helmholtz might have retorted (had not the retort been as fatal to the uniformity of his own principle as to Wundt's) that if the muscle-explanation were true, it ought not to give rise to just the opposite illusions in the skin. We saw on p. 141 that subdivided spaces appear shorter than empty ones upon the skin. To the instances there given add this: Divide a line on paper into equal halves, puncture the extremities, and make punctures all along one of the halves; then, with the finger-tip on the opposite side of the paper, follow the line of punctures; the empty half will seem much longer than the punctured half. This seems to bring things back to unanalyzable laws, by reason of which our feeling of size is determined differently in the skin and in the retina, even when the objective conditions are the same. Hering's explanation of Zöllner's figure is to be found in Hermann's Handb. d. Physiologie, III. 1. p. 579. Lipps ‡ gives another reason

---

* Physiol. Optik, pp. 562–71.

† Physiol. Psych., pp. 107–8.

‡ Gruñdtatsachen des Seelenlebens, pp. 526–30.

why lines cutting another line make the latter seem to bend away from them more than is really the case. If, he says, we draw (Fig. 69) the line *pm* upon the line *ab*, and follow the latter with our eye, we shall, on reaching the point *m*, tend for a moment to slip off *ab* and to follow *mp*, without distinctly realizing that we are not still on the main line. This makes us feel as if the remainder *mb* of the main line were bent a little away from its original direction. The illusion is apparent in the shape of a seeming

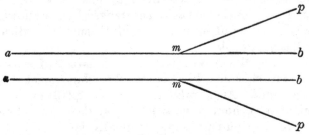

FIG. 69.

approach of the ends *b, b,* of the two main lines. This to my mind would be a more satisfactory explanation of this class of illusions than any of those given by previous authors, were it not again for what happens in the skin.

Considering all the circumstances, I feel justified in discarding his entire batch of illusions as irrelevant to our present inquiry. Whatever they may prove, they do not prove that our visual percepts of form and movement may not be sensations strictly so called. They much more probably fall into line with the phenomena of irradiation and of color-contrast, and with Vierordt's primitive illusions of movement. They show us, if anything, a realm of sensations in which our habitual experience has not yet made traces, and which persist in spite of our better knowledge, *un*suggestive of those other space-sensations which we all the time know from extrinsic evidence to constitute the real space-determinations of the diagram. Very likely, if these sensations were as frequent and as practically important as they now are insignificant and rare, we should end by substituting their significates—the real space-values of the diagrams—for them. These latter we should then seem to see directly, and the illusions would disappear like that of the size of a tooth-socket when the tooth has been out a week.

(*b*) *Another batch of cases which we may discard is that of double images.* A thoroughgoing anti-sensationalist ought to deny all native tendency to see double images when disparate retinal points are stimulated, because, he should say, most people never get them, but *see* all things single which experience has led them to believe to *be* single. "Can a doubleness, so easily neutralized by our knowledge, ever be a datum of sensation at all?" such an anti-sensationalist might ask.

To which the answer is that it *is* a datum of sensation, but a datum which, like many other data, must first be *discriminated.* As a rule, no sensible qualities are discriminated without a motive.* And those that later we learn to discriminate were originally felt confused. As well pretend that a voice, or an odor, which we have learned to pick out, is no sensation now. One may easily acquire skill in discriminating double images, though, as Hering somewhere says, it is an art of which one cannot become master in one year or in two. For masters like Hering himself, or Le Conte, the ordinary stereoscopic diagrams are of little use. Instead of combining into one solid appearance, they simply cross each other with their doubled

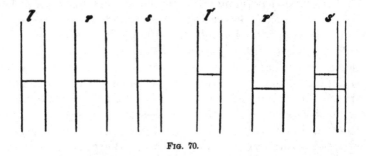

Fig. 70.

lines. Volkmann has shown a great variety of ways in which the addition of secondary lines, differing in the two

---

* Cf. *supra*, p. 515 ff.

fields, helps us to see the primary lines double. The effect is analogous to that shown in the cases which we despatched a moment ago, where given lines have their space-value changed by the addition of new lines, without our being able to say why, except that a certain mutual adhesion of the lines and modification of the resultant feeling takes place by psychophysiological laws. Thus, if in Fig. 70, *l* and *r* be crossed by an horizontal line at the same level, and viewed stereoscopically, they appear as a single pair of lines, *s*, in space. But if the horizontal be at different levels, as in *l'*, *r'*, three lines appear, as in *s'*.*

Let us then say no more about double images. All that the facts prove is what Volkmann says,† that, although there may be sets of retinal fibres so organized as to give an impression of two separate spots, yet the excitement of other retinal fibres may inhibit the effect of the first excitement, and prevent us from actually making the discrimination. Still farther retinal processes may, however, bring the doubleness to the eye of attention; and, once there, it is as genuine a sensation as any that our life affords.‡

(*c*) *These groups of illusions being eliminated,* either as cases of defective discrimination, or as changes of one space-sensation into another when the total retinal process changes, *there remain but two other groups to puzzle us.* The first is that of the after-images distorted by projection on to oblique planes; the second relates to the instability of our judgments of relative distance and size by the eye, and includes especially what are known as pseudoscopic illusions.

---

* See Archiv f. Ophthalm., v. 2, 1 (1859), where many more examples are given.

† Untersuchungen, p. 250 ; see also p. 242.

‡ I pass over certain difficulties about double images, drawn from the perceptions of a few squinters (e.g. by Schweigger, Klin. Untersuch über das Schielen, Berlin, 1881 ; by Javal, Annales d'Oculistique, LXXXV. p. 217), because the facts are exceptional at best and very difficult of interpretation. In favor of the sensationalistic or nativistic view of one such case, see the important paper by Von Kries, Archiv f. Ophthalm., XXIV. 4, p. 117.

The phenomena of the first group were described on page 232. A. W. Volkmann has studied them with his accustomed clearness and care. * Even an imaginarily inclined wall, in a picture, will, if an after-image be thrown upon it, distort the shape thereof, and make us *see* a form of which our after-image would be the natural projection on the retina, were that form laid upon the wall. Thus a signboard is painted in perspective on a screen, and the eye, after steadily looking at a rectangular cross, is turned to the painted signboard. The after-image appears as an oblique-legged cross upon the signboard. It is the converse phenomenon of a perspective drawing like Fig. 71, in which

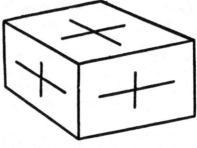

Fig. 71.

really oblique-legged figures are seen as rectangular crosses.

The unstable judgments of relative distance and size were also mentioned on pp. 231–2. Whatever the size may be of the retinal image which an object makes, the object is seen as of its own normal size. A man moving towards us is not sensibly perceived to *grow*, for example; and my finger, of which a single joint may more than conceal him from my view, is nevertheless seen as a much smaller object than the man. As for distances, it is often possible to make the farther part of an object seem near and the nearer part far. A human profile in intaglio, looked at steadily with one eye, or even both, soon appears irresistibly as a bas-relief. The inside of a common pasteboard mask, painted like the outside, and viewed with one eye in a direct light, also looks convex instead of hollow. So strong is the illu-

---

* Physiologische Untersuchungen im Gebiete der Optik, v.

sion, after long fixation, that a friend who painted such a
mask for me told me it soon became difficult to see how to
apply the brush. Bend a visiting-card across the middle,
so that its halves form an angle of 90° more or less; set it
upright on the table, as in Fig. 72, and view it with one eye.

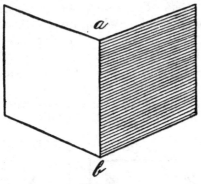

FIG. 72.

You can make it appear either as if it opened towards you
or away from you. In the former case, the angle *ab* lies

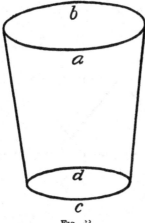

FIG. 73.

upon the table, *b* being nearer to you than *a*; in the latter
case *ab* seems vertical to the table—as indeed it really is—
with *a* nearer to you than *b*.* Again, look, with either one or

* Cf. E. Mach, Beiträge zur Analyse der Empfindungen, p. 87.

two eyes, at the opening of a wine-glass or tumbler (Fig. 73), held either above or below the eye's level. The retinal image of the opening is an oval, but we can see the oval in either of two ways,—as if it were the perspective view of a circle whose edge *b* were farther from us than its edge *a* (in which case we should seem to be looking down on the circle), or as if its edge *a* were the more distant edge (in which case we should be looking up at it through the *b* side of the glass). As the manner of seeing the edge changes, the glass itself alters its form in space and looks straight or seems bent towards or from the eye,* according as the latter is placed beneath or above it.

Plane diagrams also can be conceived as solids, and that in more than one way. Figs. 74, 75, 76, for example, are am-

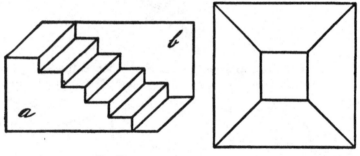

FIG. 74.　　　　　　　　　FIG. 75.

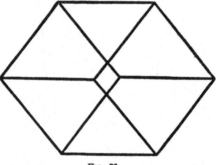

FIG. 76.

biguous perspective projections, and may each of them remind us of two different natural objects. Whichever of these

---

* Cf. V. Egger, Revue Philos., xx. 488.

objects we conceive clearly at the moment of looking at the figure, we seem to *see* in all its solidity before us. A little practice will enable us to flap the figures, so to speak, backwards and forwards from one object to the other at will. We need only attend to one of the angles represented, and imagine it either solid or hollow—pulled towards us out of the plane of the paper, or pushed back behind the same—and the whole figure obeys the cue and is instantaneously transformed beneath our gaze.*

The peculiarity of all these cases is the ambiguity of the perception to which the fixed retinal impression gives rise. With our retina excited in exactly the same way, whether by after-image, mask or diagram, we *see* now this object and now that, as if the retinal image *per se* had no essential space-import. Surely if form and length were originally retinal sensations, retinal rectangles ought not to become acute or obtuse, and lines ought not to alter their relative lengths as they do. If *relief* were an optical feeling, it ought not to flap to and fro, with every optical condition unchanged. Here, if anywhere, the deniers of space-sensation ought to be able to make their final stand.†

It must be confessed that their plea is plausible at first sight. But it is one thing to throw out retinal sensibility altogether as a space-yielding function the moment we find an ambiguity in its deliverances, and another thing to examine candidly the conditions which may have brought the ambiguity about. The former way is cheap, wholesale, shallow; the latter difficult and complicated, but full of instruction in the end. Let us try it for ourselves.

In the case of the diagrams 72, 73, 74, 75, 76, the real object, lines meeting or crossing each other on a plane, is

---

* Loeb (Pflüger's Archiv, xl. 274) has proved that muscular changes of adaptation in the eye for near and far distance are what determine the form of the relief.

† The strongest passage in Helmholtz's argument against sensations of space is relative to these fluctuations of seen relief: "Ought one not to conclude that if sensations of relief exist at all, they must be so faint and vague as to have no influence compared with that of past experience? Ought we not to believe that the perception of the third dimension may have arisen *without* them, since we now see it taking place as well *against* them as *with* them?" (Physiol. Optik. p. 817.)

replaced by an *imagined solid which we describe as seen.
Really it is not seen but only so vividly conceived as to
approach a vision of reality.* We feel all the while, however,
that the solid suggested is not solidly there. *The reason*
why one solid may seem more easily suggested than
another, and *why it is easier in general to perceive the
diagram solid than flat, seems due to probability.** Those
lines have countless times in our past experience been
drawn on our retina by solids for once that we have seen
them flat on paper. And hundreds of times we have
looked down upon the upper surface of parallelopipeds,
stairs and glasses, for once that we have looked upwards
at their bottom—hence we see the solids easiest as if from
above.

Habit or probability seems also to govern the illusion of
the intaglio profile, and of the hollow mask. We have *never*
seen a human face except in relief—hence the case with
which the present sensation is overpowered. Hence, too,
the obstinacy with which human faces and forms, and
other extremely familiar convex objects, refuse to appear
hollow when viewed through Wheatstone's pseudoscope.
Our perception seems wedded to certain total ways of
seeing certain objects. The moment the object is suggested
at all, it takes possession of the mind in the fulness of its
stereotyped habitual form. This explains the suddenness
of the transformations when the perceptions change. The
object shoots back and forth completely from this to that
familiar thing, and doubtful, indeterminate, and composite
things are excluded, apparently because we are *unused* to
their existence.

When we turn from the diagrams to the actual folded
visiting-card and to the real glass, the imagined form seems
fully as real as the correct one. The card flaps over; the
glass rim tilts this way or that, as if some inward spring
suddenly became released in our eye. In these changes the
actual retinal image receives different *complements from the
mind.* But the remarkable thing is that the complement

---

* Cf. E. Mach, Beiträge, etc., p. 90, and the preceding chapter of the
present work, p. 86 ff.

and the image combine so completely that the twain are one flesh, as it were, and cannot be discriminated in the result. If the complement be, as we have called it (on pp. 237–8), a set of imaginary absent eye-sensations, they seem no whit less vividly there than the sensation which the eye now receives from without.

The case of the after-images distorted by projection upon an oblique plane is even more strange, for the imagined perspective figure, lying in the plane, seems less to combine with the one a moment previously seen by the eye than to suppress it and take its place.* The point needing explanation, then, in all this, is how it comes to pass that, when imagined sensations are usually so inferior in vivacity to real ones, they should in these few experiences prove to be almost or quite their match.

The mystery is solved when we note the class to which all these experiences belong. They are 'perceptions' of definite 'things,' definitely situated in tridimensional space. The mind uniformly uses its sensations to *identify things by.* The sensation is invariably apperceived by the idea, name, or 'normal' aspect (p. 238) of the *thing.* The peculiarity of the *optical* signs of things is their extraordinary mutability. A 'thing' which we follow with the eye, never doubting of its physical identity, will change its retinal image incessantly. A cross, a ring, waved about in the air, will pass through every conceivable angular and elliptical form. All the while, however, as we look at them, we hold fast to the perception of their 'real' shape, by mentally combining the pictures momentarily received with the notion of peculiar positions in space. It is not the cross and ring pure and simple which we perceive, but the cross *so held*, the ring *so held.* From the day of our birth we have sought every hour of our lives to *correct* the apparent form of things, and trans-

---

* I ought to say that I seem always able to see the cross rectangular at will. But this appears to come from an imperfect absorption of the rectangular after-image by the inclined plane at which the eyes look. The cross, with me, is apt to detach itself from this and then look square. I get the illusion better from the circle, whose after-image becomes in various ways elliptical on being projected upon the different surfaces of the room, and cannot then be easily made to look circular again.

late it into the real form by keeping note of the way they are placed or held. In no other class of sensations does this incessant correction occur. What wonder, then, that the notion ' so placed ' should invincibly exert its habitual corrective effect, even when the object with which it combines is only an after-image, and make us perceive the latter under a changed but more ' real ' form ? The ' real ' form is also a sensation conjured up by memory ; but it is one so *probable,* so *habitually* conjured up when we have just this combination of optical experiences, that it partakes of the invincible freshness of reality, and seems to break through that law which elsewhere condemns reproductive processes to being so much fainter than sensations.

Once more, *these cases form an extreme. Somewhere, in the list of our imaginations of absent feelings, there must be found the vividest of all. These optical reproductions of real form are the vividest of all.* It is foolish to reason from cases lower in the scale, to prove that the scale can contain no such extreme cases as these ; and particularly foolish since we can definitely see why these imaginations ought to be more vivid than any others, whenever they recall the forms of habitual and probable things. These latter, by incessantly repeated presence and reproduction, will plough deep grooves in the nervous system. There will be developed, to correspond to them, paths of least resistance, of unstable equilibrium, liable to become active in their totality when any point is touched off. Even when the objective stimulus is imperfect, we shall still *see* the full convexity of a human face, the correct inclination of an angle or sweep of a curve, or the distance of two lines. Our mind will be like a polyhedron, whose facets are the attitudes of perception in which it can most easily rest. These are worn upon it by *habitual* objects, and from one of these it can pass only by tumbling over into another.*

Hering has well accounted for the sensationally vivid character of these habitually reproduced forms. He says,

---

* In Chapter XVIII, p. 74. I gave a reason why imaginations *ought* not to be as vivid as sensations. It should be borne in mind that that reason does not apply to these complemental imaginings of the real shape of things actually before our eyes.

after reminding us that every visual sensation is correlated to a physical process in the nervous apparatus :

"If this psychophysical process is aroused, as usually happens, by light-rays impinging on the retina, its form depends not only on the nature of these rays, but on the constitution of the entire nervous apparatus which is connected with the organ of vision, and on the *state* in which it finds itself. The same stimulus may excite widely different sensations according to this state.

" The constitution of the nervous apparatus depends naturally in part upon innate predisposition ; but the *ensemble* of effects wrought by stimuli upon it in the course of life, whether these come through the eyes or from elsewhere, is a co-factor of its development. To express it otherwise, involuntary and voluntary experience and exercise assist in determining the material structure of the nervous organ of vision, and hence the ways in which it may react on a retinal image as an outward stimulus. That experience and exercise should be possible at all in vision is a consequence of the reproductive power, or memory, of its nerve-substance. Every particular activity of the organ makes it more suited to a repetition of the *same ;* ever slighter touches are required to make the repetition occur. The organ habituates itself to the repeated activity. . . .

" Suppose now that, in the first experience of a complex sensation produced by a particular retinal image, certain portions were made the special objects of attention. In a repetition of the sensible experience it will happen that notwithstanding the identity of the outward stimulus these portions will be more easily and strongly reproduced ; and when this happens a hundred times the inequality with which the various constituents of the complex sensation appeal to consciousness grows ever greater.

" Now in the present state of our knowledge we cannot assert that in both the first and the last occurrence of the retinal image in question the same *pure sensation* is provoked, but that the mind *interprets* it differently the last time in consequence of experience ; for the only *given* things we know are on the one hand the retinal image which is both times the same, and on the other the mental percept which is both times different ; of a third thing, such as a pure sensation, interpolated between image and percept, we know nothing. We ought, therefore, if we wish to avoid hypotheses, simply to say that the nervous apparatus reacts the last time differently from the first, and gives us in consequence a different group of sensations.

" But not only by repetition of the same retinal image, but by that of similar ones, will the law obtain. Portions of the image common to the successive experiences will awaken, as it were, a stronger echo in the nervous apparatus than other portions. Hence it results that *reproduction is usually elective :* the more strongly reverberating parts of the picture yield stronger feelings than the rest. This may result in the latter being quite overlooked and, as it were, eliminated from perception. It may even come to pass that instead of these parts eliminated by election a feeling of entirely different elements comes to consciousness— elements not objectively contained in the stimulus. A group of sensations, namely, for which a strong tendency to reproduction has become, by frequent repetition, ingrained in the nervous system will easily revive as a *whole* when, not its whole retinal image, but only an essential part thereof, returns. In this case we get some sensations to which no adequate stimulus exists in the retinal image, and which owe their being solely to the reproductive power of the nervous apparatus. This is *complementary (ergänzende) reproduction.*

"Thus a few points and disconnected strokes are sufficient to make us see a human face, and without specially directed attention we fail to note that we see much that really is not drawn on the paper. Attention will show that the outlines were deficient in spots where we thought them complete. . . . The portions of the percept supplied by complementary reproduction depend, however, just as much as its other portions, on the reaction of the nervous apparatus upon the retinal image, indirect though this reaction may, in the case of the supplied portions, be. And so long as they are present, we have a perfect right to call them sensations, for they differ in no wise from such sensations as correspond to an actual stimulus in the retina. Often, however, they are not persistent; many of them may be expelled by more close observation, but this is not proved to be the case with all. . . . In vision with one eye . . . the distribution of parts within the third dimension is essentially the work of this complementary reproduction, i.e. of former experience. . . . When a certain way of localizing a particular group of sensations has become with us a second nature, our better knowledge, our judgment, our logic, are of no avail. . . . Things actually diverse may give similar or almost identical retinal images; e.g., an object extended in three dimensions, and its flat perspective picture. In such cases it often depends on small accidents, and especially on our will, whether the one or the other group of sensations shall be excited. . . . We can see a relief hollow, as a mould, or *vice versâ;* for a relief illuminated from the left can look just like its mould illuminated from the right. Reflecting upon this, one may infer from the direction of the shadows that one has a relief before one, and the idea of the relief will guide the nerve-processes into the right path, so that the *feeling* of the relief is suddenly aroused. . . . Whenever the retinal image is of such a nature that two diverse modes of reaction on the part of the nervous apparatus are, so to speak, equally, or nearly equally, imminent, it must depend on small accidents whether the one or the other reaction is realized. In these cases our previous knowledge often has a decisive effect, and helps the correct perception to victory. The bare idea of the right object is itself a feeble reproduction which with the help of the proper retinal picture develops into clear and lively sensation. But if there be not already in the nervous apparatus a disposition to the production of that percept which our judgment tells us is right, our knowledge strives in vain to conjure up the feeling of it; we then know that we see something to which no reality corresponds, but we see it all the same." *

Note that no object not probable, no object which we are not incessantly practised in reproducing, can acquire this vividness in imagination. Objective corners are ever changing their angles to the eyes, spaces their apparent size, lines their distance. But by no transmutation of position in space does an objective straight line appear bent, and only in one position out of an infinity does a broken line look straight. Accordingly, it is impossible by projecting the after-image

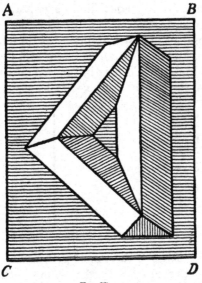

Fig. 77.

of a straight line upon two surfaces which make a solid angle with each other to give the line itself a sensible 'kink.' Look with it at the corner of your room: the after-image, which may overlap all three surfaces of the corner, still continues straight. Volkmann constructed a complicated surface of projection like that drawn in Fig. 77, but he found it impossible so to throw a straight after-image upon it as to alter its visible form.

---

* Hermann's Handb. der Physiologie. III. 1, p. 565–71.

One of the situations in which we oftenest see things is spread out on the ground before us. We are incessantly drilled in making allowance for *this* perspective, and reducing things to their real form in spite of optical foreshortening. Hence if the preceding explanations are true, we ought to find this habit inveterate. The *lower* half of the retina, which habitually sees the *farther* half of things spread out on the ground, ought to have acquired a habit of enlarging its pictures by imagination, so as to make them more than equal to those which fall on the upper retinal surface; and this habit ought to be hard to escape from, even when both halves of the object are equidistant from the eye, as in a vertical line on paper. Delbœuf has found, accordingly, that if we try to bisect such a line we place the point of division about $\frac{1}{16}$ of its length too high.*

Similarly, a square cross, or a square, drawn on paper, should look higher than it is broad. And that this is actually the case, the reader may verify by a glance at Fig. 78.

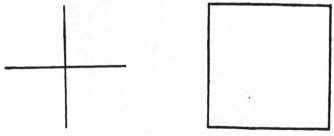

FIG. 78.

For analogous reasons the upper and lower halves of the letter S, or of the figure 8, hardly seem to differ. But when turned upside down, as ς, ႘, the upper half looks much the larger.†

---

* Bulletin de l'Académie de Belgique, 2me Série, xix. 2.

† Wundt seeks to explain all these illusions by the relatively stronger ' feeling of innervation ' needed to move the eyeballs upwards,—a careful study of the muscles concerned is taken to prove this,—and a consequently greater estimate of the distance traversed. It suffices to remark, however, with Lipps, that were the innervation all, a column of S's placed on top of each other should look each larger than the one below it, and a weather-cock on a steeple gigantic, neither of which is the case. Only the halves of *the same object* look different in size, because the customary correction

Hering has tried to explain our exaggeration of small angles in the same way. We have more to do with right angles than with any others : right angles, in fact, have an altogether unique sort of interest for the human mind. Nature almost never begets them, but we think space by means of them and put them everywhere. Consequently obtuse and acute ones, liable always to be the images of right ones foreshortened, particularly easily revive right ones in memory. It is hard to look at such figures as *a, b, c,* in Fig. 79, without seeing them in perspective, as

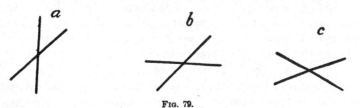

FIG. 79.

approximations, at least, to foreshortened rectangular forms. *

At the same time the genuine sensational form of the lines before us can, in all the cases of distortion by suggested perspective, be felt correctly by a mind able to abstract from the notion of perspective altogether. Individuals differ in this abstracting power. Artistic training improves it, so that after a little while errors in vertical bisection, in estimating height relatively to breadth, etc., become impossible. In other words, we learn to take the optical sensation before us *pure.* †

_____

for foreshortening bears only on the relations of the parts of special *things* spread out before us. Cf. Wundt, Physiol. Psych., 2te Aufl. ii. 96–8 ; Th. Lipps, Grundtatsachen, etc., p. 535.

* Hering would partly solve in this way the mystery of Figs. 60, 61, and 67. No doubt the explanation partly applies ; but the strange cessation of the illusion when we fix the gaze fails to be accounted for thereby.

† Helmholtz has sought (Physiol. Optik, p. 715) to explain the divergence of the apparent vertical meridians of the two retinæ, by the manner in which an identical line drawn on the ground before us in the median plane will throw its images on the two eyes respectively. The matter is too technical for description here ; the unlearned reader may be referred for it to J. Le Conte's Sight in the Internat. Scient. Series, p. 198 ff. But, for the benefit of those to whom *verbum sat*, I cannot help saying that it seems to me that the *exactness* of the relation of the two meridians—whether diver-

We may then sum up our study of illusions by saying that they in no wise undermine our view that every spatial determination of things is originally given in the shape of a sensation of the eyes. They only show how very potent certain *imagined* sensations of the eyes may become.

These sensations, so far as they bring definite forms to the mind, appear to be retinal exclusively. The movements of the eyeballs play a great part in educating our perception, it is true; but they have nothing to do with *constituting* any one feeling of form. Their function is limited to *exciting* the various feelings of form, by tracing retinal streaks; and to *comparing* them, and *measuring* them off against each other, by applying different parts of the retinal surface to the same objective thing. Helmholtz's analysis of the facts of our '*measurement of the field of view*' is, bating a lapse or two, masterly, and seems to prove that the movements of the eye have had some part in bringing our sense of retinal equivalencies about—*equivalencies*, mind, of different retinal forms and sizes, not forms and sizes themselves. *Superposition* is the way in which the eye-movements accomplish this result. An object traces the line AB on a peripheral tract of the retina. Quickly we move the eye so that the same object traces the line *ab* on a central tract. Forthwith, to our mind, AB and *ab* are judged equivalent. But, as Helmholtz admits, the equivalence-judgment is independent of the way in which we may feel the form and length of the several retinal pictures themselves:

"The retina is like a pair of compasses, whose points we apply in succession to the ends of several lines to see whether they agree or not in length. All we need know meanwhile about the compasses is that the distance of their points remains unchanged. What that distance is, and what is the shape of the compasses, is a matter of no account."*

gent or not, for their divergence differs in individuals and often in one individual at diverse times—precludes its being due to the mere habitual falling-off of the image of one objective line on both. Le Conte, e.g., measures their position down to a sixth of a degree, others to tenths. This indicates an organic identity in the sensations of the two retinæ, which the experience of median perspective horizontals may roughly have agreed with, but hardly can have engendered. Wundt explains the divergence as usual, by the *Innervationsgefühl* (*op. cit.* II. 99 ff.).

* Physiol. Optik, p. 547.

*Measurement implies a stuff to measure. Retinal sensa-
tions give the stuff; objective things form the yard-stick; motion does the measuring operation;* which can, of course, be
well performed only where it is possible to make the same
object fall on many retinal tracts. This is practically impossible where the tracts make a wide angle with each
other. But there are certain directions in the field of view,
certain retinal lines, along which it is particularly easy to
make the image of an object slide. The object then becomes a 'ruler' for these lines, as Helmholtz puts it,*
making them seem straight throughout if the object looked
straight to us in that part of them at which it was most
distinctly seen.

But all this need of superposition shows how devoid of
exact space-import the feelings of movement are *per se*. As
we compare the space-value of two retinal tracts by superposing them successively upon the same objective line, so
we also have to compare the space-value of objective angles
and lines by superposing them on the same retinal tract.
Neither procedure would be required if our eye-movements
were apprehended immediately, by pure muscular feeling
or innervation, for example, as distinct lengths and directions in space. To compare retinal tracts, it would then
suffice simply to notice how it feels to move *any* image over
them. And two objective lines could be compared as
well by moving different retinal tracts along them as by
laying them along the same. It would be as easy to com-

---

* "We can with a short ruler draw a line as long as we please on a
plane surface by first drawing one as long as the ruler permits, and then
sliding the ruler somewhat along the drawn line and drawing again, etc.
If the ruler is exactly straight, we get in this way a straight line. If it is
somewhat curved we get a circle. Now, instead of the sliding ruler we
use in the field of sight the central spot of distinctest vision impressed with
a linear sensation of sight, which at times may be intensified till it becomes
an after-image. We follow, in looking, the direction of this line, and in
so doing we slide the line along itself and get a prolongation of its length.
On a plane surface we can carry on this procedure on any sort of a straight
or curved ruler, but in the field of vision there is for each direction and
movement of the eye only one sort of line which it is possible for us to
slide along in its own direction continually." These are what Helmholtz
calls the 'circles of direction' of the visual field—lines which he has
studied with his usual care. Cf. Physiol. Optik, p. 548 ff.

pare non-parallel figures as it now is to judge of those which are parallel.* Those which it took the same amount of movement to traverse would be equal, in whatever direction the movement occurred.

GENERAL SUMMARY.

With this we may end our long and, I fear to many readers, tediously minute survey. The facts of vision form a jungle of intricacy; and those who penetrate deeply into physiological optics will be more struck by our omissions than by our abundance of detail. But for students who may have lost sight of the forest for the trees, I will recapitulate briefly the points of our whole argument from the beginning, and then proceed to a short historical survey, which will set them in relief.

All our sensations are positively and inexplicably extensive wholes.

The sensations contributing to space-*perception* seem exclusively to be the surface of skin, retina, and joints. 'Muscular' feelings play no appreciable part in the generation of our feelings of form, direction, etc.

The total bigness of a cutaneous or retinal feeling soon becomes subdivided by discriminative attention.

Movements assist this discrimination by reason of the peculiarly exciting quality of the sensations which stimuli moving over surfaces arouse.

Subdivisions, once discriminated, acquire definite relations of position towards each other within the total space. These 'relations' are themselves feelings of the subdivisions that intervene. When these subdivisions are not the seat of stimuli, the relations are only reproduced in imaginary form.

The various sense-spaces are, in the first instance, incoherent with each other; and primitively both they and their subdivisions are but vaguely comparable in point of bulk and form.

The *education* of our space-perception consists largely of two processes—reducing the various sense-feelings to a

---

* Cf. Hering in Hermann's Handb. der Physiol., III. 1, pp. 553–4.

common *measure,* and *adding them together* into the single all-including space of the real world.

Both the measuring and the adding are performed by the aid of *things.*

The imagined aggregate of positions occupied by all the actual or possible, moving or stationary, things which we know, is our notion of 'real' space—a very incomplete and vague conception in all minds.

The *measuring* of our space-feelings against each other mainly comes about through the successive arousal of different ones by the same *thing,* by our selection of certain ones as feelings of its *real* size and shape, and by the degradation of others to the status of being merely *signs* of these.

For the successive application of the same thing to different space-giving surfaces motion is indispensable, and hence plays a great part in our space-education, especially in that of the eye. Abstractly considered, the motion of the object over the sensitive surface would educate us quite as well as that of the surface over the object. But the self-mobility of the organ carrying the surface *accelerates* immensely the result.

In completely educated space-perception, the present sensation is usually just what Helmholtz (Physiol. Optik, p. 797) calls it, 'a sign, the interpretation of whose meaning is left to the understanding.' But the understanding is exclusively reproductive and never productive in the process; and its function is limited to the recall of previous space-sensations with which the present one has been associated and which may be judged more real than it.

Finally, this reproduction may in the case of certain visual forms be as vivid, or almost so, as actual sensation is.

The third dimension forms an original element of all our space-sensations. In the eye it is subdivided by various discriminations. The more distant subdivisions are often shut out altogether, and, in being suppressed, have the effect of diminishing the absolute space-value of the total field of view.*

---

* This shrinkage and expansion of the absolute space-value of the total optical sensation remains to my mind the most obscure part of the whole

HISTORICAL.

Let us now close with a brief historical survey. The first achievement of note in the study of space-perception was Berkeley's theory of vision. This undertook to establish two points, first that *distance* was not a visual but a tactile form of consciousness, suggested by visual signs ; secondly, that there is no one quality or 'idea' common to the sensations of touch and sight, such that prior to experience one might possibly anticipate from the look of an object anything about its felt size, shape, or position, or from the touch of it anything about its look.

In other words, that primitively chaotic or semi-chaotic condition of our various sense-spaces which we have demonstrated, was established for good by Berkeley; and he bequeathed to psychology the problem of describing the manner in which the deliverances are harmonized so as all to refer to one and the same extended world.

His disciples in Great Britain have solved this problem after Berkeley's own fashion, and to a great extent as we have done ourselves, by the ideas of the various senses suggesting each other in consequence of Association. But, either because they were intoxicated with the principle of association, or because in the number of details they lost their general bearings, they have forgotten, as a rule, to state *under what sensible form the primitive spatial experiences are found* which later became associated with so many other sensible signs. Heedless of their master Locke's precept, that the mind can frame unto itself no one new simple idea, they seem for the most part to be trying to *explain the extensive quality itself*, account for it, and evolve it, by the mere association together of feelings which originally possessed it not. They first evaporate the nature of extension by making it tantamount to mere 'coexistence,' and then they explain coexistence as being the same thing as *succession*, provided it

---

subject. It is a real optical sensation, seeming introspectively to have nothing to do with locomotor or other suggestions. It is easy to say that 'the Intellect produces it,' but what does that mean? The investigator who will throw light on this one point will probably clear up other difficulties as well.

be an extremely rapid or a reversible succession. Space-perception thus emerges without being anywhere postulated. The only things postulated are unextended feelings and time. Says Thomas Brown (lecture XXIII.): " I am inclined to re-verse exactly the process commonly supposed ; and instead of deriving the measure of time from extension, to derive the knowledge and original measure of extension from time." Brown and both the Mills think that retinal sensations, colors, in their primitive condition, are felt with no extension and that the latter merely becomes inseparably associated with them. John Mill says : " Whatever may be the retinal impression conveyed by a line which bounds two colors, I see no ground for thinking that by the eye alone we could acquire the conception of what we now mean when we say that one of the colors is outside [beside] the other." *

Whence does the extension come which gets so insepa-rably associated with these non-extended colored sensations? From the ' sweep and movements ' of the eye—from mus-cular feelings. But, as Prof. Bain says, if movement-feel-ings give us any property of things, " it would seem to be not space, but time." † And John Mill says that " the idea of space is, at bottom, one of time." ‡ Space, then, is not to be found in any elementary sensation, but, in Bain's words, " as a quality, it has no other origin and no other meaning than the *association* of these different [non-spatial] motor and sensitive effects." §

This phrase is mystical-sounding enough to one who understands association as *producing* nothing, but only as knitting together things already produced in separate ways. The truth is that the English Associationist school, in trying to show how much their principle can accomplish, have altogether overshot the mark and espoused a kind of theory in respect to space-perception which the general tenor of their philosophy should lead them to abhor. Really there are but three possible kinds of theory concerning space. Either (1) there is no spatial *quality* of sensation at all, and

---

* Examination of Hamilton, 3d ed. p. 283.
† Senses and Intellect, 3d ed. p. 183.
‡ Exam. of Hamilton, 3d ed. p. 283.
§ Senses and Intellect, p. 372.

space is a mere symbol of succession ; or (2) there is an *extensive quality given* immediately in certain particular sensations ; or, finally, (3) there is a *quality produced* out of the inward resources of the mind, to envelop sensations which, as given originally, are not spatial, but which, on being cast into the spatial form, become united and orderly. This last is the Kantian view. Stumpf admirably designates it as the 'psychic stimulus' theory, the crude sensations being considered as goads to the mind to put forth its slumbering power.

Brown, the Mills, and Bain, amid these possibilities, seem to have gone astray like lost sheep. With the 'mental chemistry' of which the Mills speak—precisely the same thing as the 'psychical synthesis' of Wundt, which, as we shall soon see, is a principle expressly intended to do what Association can never perform—they hold the third view, but again in other places imply the first. And, between the impossibility of getting from mere association anything not contained in the sensations associated and the dislike to allow spontaneous mental productivity, they flounder in a dismal dilemma. Mr. Sully joins them there in what I must call a vague and vacillating way. Mr. Spencer of course is bound to pretend to 'evolve' all mental qualities out of antecedents different from themselves, so that we need perhaps not wonder at his refusal to accord the spatial quality to any of the several elementary sensations out of which our space-perception grows. Thus (Psychology, II. 168, 172, 218):

" No idea of extension can arise from a *simultaneous* excitation " of a multitude of nerve-terminations like those of the skin or the retina, since this would imply a " knowledge of their relative positions "—that is, " a pre-existent idea of a special extension, which is absurd." " No relation between *successive* states of consciousness gives in itself any idea of extension." " The muscular sensations accompanying motion are quite distinct from the notions of space and time associated with them."

Mr. Spencer none the less inveighs vociferously against the Kantian position that space is produced by the mind's own resources. And yet he nowhere denies space to be a specific affection of consciousness different from time !

Such incoherency is pitiful. The fact is that, at bottom, all these authors are really 'psychical stimulists,' or Kantists. The space they speak of is a super-sensational mental product. This position appears to me thoroughly mythological. But let us see how it is held by those who know more definitely what they mean. Schopenhauer expresses the Kantian view with more vigor and clearness than any-one else. He says:

" A man must be forsaken by all the gods to dream that the world we see outside of us, filling space in its three dimensions, moving down the inexorable stream of time, governed at each step by Causality's invariable law,—but in all this only following rules which we may prescribe for it in advance of all experience,—to dream, I say, that such a world should stand there outside of us, quite objectively real with no complicity of ours, and thereupon by a subsequent *act*, through the instrumentality of mere sensation, that it should enter our head and reconstruct a duplicate of itself as it was outside. For what a poverty-stricken thing is this mere sensation ! Even in the noblest organs of sense it is nothing more than a local and specific feeling, susceptible within its kind of a few variations, but always strictly subjective and containing in itself nothing objective, nothing resembling a perception. For sensation of every sort is and remains a process in the organism itself. As such it is limited to the territory inside the skin and can never, accordingly, *per se* contain anything that lies outside the skin or outside ourselves. . . . Only when the Understanding . . . is roused to activity and brings its sole and only form, the *law of Causality*, into play, only then does the mighty transformation take place which makes out of subjective sensation objective intuition. The Understanding, namely, grasps by means of its innate, *a priori*, ante-experiential form, the given sensation of the body as an *effect* which as such must necessarily have a *cause*. At the same time the Understanding summons to its aid the form of the outer sense which similarly lies already preformed in the intellect (or brain), and which is Space, in order to locate that cause outside of the organism. . . . In this process the Understanding, as I shall soon show, takes note of the most minute peculiarities of the given sensation in order to construct in the outer space a cause which shall completely account for them. This operation of the Understanding is, however, not one that takes place discursively, reflectively, *in abstracto*, by means of words and concepts ; but is intuitive and immediate. . . . Thus the Understanding must first create the objective world ; never can the latter, already complete *in se*, simply promenade into our heads through the senses and organic apertures. For the senses yield us nothing further than the raw material which must be first elaborated into the objective conception of an orderly physical world-system by means of the aforesaid simple forms of Space, Time, and Causality. . . . Let me show the great chasm between sensation and perception by showing how raw the material is out of which the fair structure is upreared. Only two senses serve objective perception : touch and sight. They alone furnish the data on the basis whereof the Understanding, by the process indicated, erects the objective world. . . . These data in themselves are still no perception ; that is the Understanding's work. If I press with my hand against the table, the sensation I receive has no analogy with the idea of the firm cohesion of the parts of this mass : only when my Understanding passes from the sensation to its cause does it create for itself a body with the properties of solidity, impenetrability, and hardness. When in the dark I lay my hand on a surface, or grasp a ball of three inches diameter, in either case the same parts of the hand receive the impression : but out of the different contraction of the hand in the two cases my Understanding constructs the form of the body whose contact caused the feeling, and confirms its construction by leading me to move my hand over the body. If one born blind handles a cubical body, the sensations of his hand are quite uniform on all sides and in all directions,—only the corners press upon a smaller part of his skin. In these sensations, as such, there is nothing whatever analogous to a cube. But from the felt resistance his Understanding infers immediately and intuitively a cause thereof, which now presents itself as a solid body; and from the movements of exploration which the arms made whilst the feelings of the hands remained constant he constructs, in the space known to him *a priori*, the body's cubical shape. Did he not bring with him ready-made the idea of a cause and of a space, with the laws thereof, there never could arise, out of those successive feelings in his hand, the image of a cube. If we let a string run through our closed hand, we immediately construct as the cause of the friction and its duration in such an attitude of the hand, a long cylindrical body moving uniformly in one direction. But never out of the pure sensation in the hand could the idea of movement, that is, of change of position in space by means of time, arise : such a content can never lie in sensation, nor come out of it. Our Intellect, antecedently to all experience, must bear in itself the intuitions of Space and Time, and therewithal of the possibility of motion, and no less the idea of Causality, to pass from the empirically given feeling to its cause, and to construct the latter as a so moving body of the designated shape. For how great is the abyss between the mere sensation in the hand and the ideas of causality, materiality, and movement through Space, occurring in Time! The feeling in the hand, even with different contacts and positions, is something far too uniform and poor in content for it to be possible to construct out of *it* the idea of Space with its three dimensions, of the action of bodies on each other, with the properties of extension, impenetrability, cohesion, shape, hardness, softness, rest, and motion—in short, the foundations of the objective world. This is only possible through Space, Time, and Causality . . . being preformed in the Intellect itself, . . . from whence it again follows that the perception of the external world is essentially an intellectual process, a work of the Understanding, *to which sensation furnishes merely the occasion*, and the data to be interpreted in each particular case." *

I call this view mythological, because I am conscious of no such Kantian machine-shop in my mind, and feel no call to disparage the powers of poor sensation in this merciless way. I have no introspective experience of mentally producing or creating space. My space-intuitions occur not in two times but in one. There is not one moment of passive inextensive sensation, succeeded by another of active extensive perception, but the form I see is as immediately felt as the color which fills it out. That the higher parts of the mind come in, who can deny ? They add and subtract, they compare and measure, they reproduce and abstract. They inweave the space-sensations with intellectual relations ; but *these* relations are the same when they obtain between the elements of the space-system as when they obtain between any of the other elements of which the world is made.

The essence of the Kantian contention is that there are not *spaces*, but *Space*—one infinite continuous *Unit*—and that our knowledge of *this* cannot be a piecemeal sensational affair, produced by summation and abstraction. To which the obvious reply is that, if any known thing bears on its front the *appearance* of piecemeal construction and abstraction, it is this very notion of the infinite unitary space of the world. It is a *notion*, if ever there was one ; and no intuition. Most of us apprehend it in the barest symbolic abridgment : and if perchance we ever do try to make it more adequate, we just add one image of sensible extension to another until we are tired. Most of us are obliged to turn round and drop the thought of the space in front of us when we think of that behind. And the space represented as near to us seems more minutely subdivisible than that we think of as lying far away.

The other prominent German writers on space are also ' psychical stimulists.' Herbart, whose influence has been widest, says ' the resting eye sees no space,'† and ascribes

---

* Vierfache Wurzel des Satzes vom zureichenden Grunde, pp. 52–7.

† Psychol. als Wissenschaft, § 111.

visual extension to the influence of movements combining
with the non-spatial retinal feelings so as to form gradated
series of the latter. A given sensation of such a series
reproduces the idea of its associates in regular order, and
its idea is similarly reproduced by any one of them with
the order reversed. Out of the fusion of these two contrasted reproductions comes the form of space*—Heaven
knows how.

The obvious objection is that mere serial order is a *genus,*
and space-order a very peculiar species of that *genus ;* and
that, if the terms of reversible series became by that fact
coexistent terms in space, the musical scale, the degrees of
warmth and cold, and all other ideally graded series ought
to appear to us in the shape of extended corporeal aggregates,—which they notoriously do not, though we may of
course *symbolize* their order by a spatial scheme. W.
Volkmann von Volkmar, the Herbartian, takes the bull here
by the horns, and says the musical scale *is* spatially extended, though he admits that its space does not belong to
the real world.† I am unacquainted with any other Herbartian so bold.

To Lotze we owe the much-used term 'local sign.' He
insisted that space could not emigrate directly into the
mind from without, but must be *reconstructed* by the soul ;
and he seemed to think that the first reconstructions of it
by the soul must be super-sensational. But why sensations themselves might not be the soul's *original* spatial re-
constructive acts Lotze fails to explain.

Wundt has all his life devoted himself to the elaboration
of a space-theory, of which the neatest and most final expression is to be found in his Logik (II. 457–60). He says :

"In the eye, space-perception has certain constant peculiarities
which prove that no single optical sensation by itself possesses the extensive form, but that everywhere in our perception of space heterogene-

---

* Psychol. als Wissenschaft, § 113.

† Lehrbuch d. Psychol., 2te Auflage, Bd. II. p. 66. Volkmann's fifth
chapter contains a really precious collection of historical notices concerning space-perception theories.

ous feelings combine. If we simply suppose that luminous sensations *per se* feel extensive, our supposition is shattered by that influence of movement in vision which is so clearly to be traced in many normal errors in the measurement of the field of view. If we assume, on the other hand, that the movements and their feelings are alone possessed of the extensive quality, we make an unjustified hypothesis, for the phenomena compel us, it is true, to accord an influence to movement, but give us no right to call the retinal sensations indifferent, for there are no visual ideas without retinal sensations. If then we wish rigorously to express the given facts, we can ascribe a spatial constitution only to *combinations* of retinal sensations with those of movement."

Thus Wundt, dividing theories into 'nativistic' and 'genetic,' calls his own a genetic theory. To distinguish it from other theories of the same class, he names it a 'theory of complex local signs.'

"It supposes two systems of local signs, whose relations—taking the eye as an example—we may think as . . . the measuring of the manifold local-sign system of the retina by the simple local-sign system of the movements. In its psychological nature this is a process of associative synthesis : it consists in the fusion of both groups of sensations into a product, whose elementary components are no longer separable from each other in idea. In melting wholly away into the product which they create they become consciously undistinguishable, and the mind apprehends only their resultant, the intuition of space. Thus there obtains a certain analogy between this psychic synthesis and that chemical synthesis which out of simple bodies generates a compound that appears to our immediate perception as a homogeneous whole with new properties."

Now let no modest reader think that if this sounds obscure to him it is because he does not know the full context ; and that if a wise professor like Wundt can talk so fluently and plausibly about 'combination' and 'psychic synthesis,' it must surely be because those words convey a so much greater fulness of positive meaning to the scholarly than to the unlearned mind. Really it is quite the reverse ; *all* the virtue of the phrase lies in its mere sound and skin. Learning does but make one the more sensible of its inward unintelligibility. Wundt's 'theory' is the flimsiest thing in the world. It starts by an untrue assumption, and then corrects it by an unmeaning phrase. Retinal sensations *are* spatial ; and were they not, no amount of 'synthesis' with equally spaceless motor sensations could

intelligibly make them so. Wundt's theory is, in short,
but an avowal of impotence, and an appeal to the inscrutable powers of the soul.* It confesses that we cannot
analyze the constitution or give the genesis of the spatial
quality in consciousness. But at the same time it says the
antecedents thereof are psychical and not cerebral facts.
In calling the quality in question a *sensational* quality, our
own account equally disclaimed ability to analyze it, but
said its antecedents were cerebral, not psychical—in other
words, that it was a *first* psychical thing. This is merely
a question of probable fact, which the reader may decide.

And now what shall be said of Helmholtz? Can I find
fault with a book which, on the whole, I imagine to be one
of the four or five greatest monuments of human genius in
the scientific line? If truth impels I must fain try, and
take the risks. It seems to me that Helmholtz's genius
moves most securely when it keeps close to particular facts.
At any rate, it shows least strong in purely speculative
passages, which in the Optics, in spite of many beauties,
seem to me fundamentally vacillating and obscure. The
'empiristic' view which Helmholtz defends is that the
space-determinations we perceive are in every case products of a process of unconscious inference.† The inference is similar to one from induction or analogy. ‡ We always see that form before us which *habitually* would have
caused the sensation we now have. § But the latter sensation can never be intrinsically spatial, or its intrinsic space-
determinations would never be overcome as they are so
often by the 'illusory' space-determinations it so often
suggests.‖ Since the illusory determination can be traced
to a suggestion of Experience, the 'real' one must also be
such a suggestion: so that *all* space intuitions are due sole-

* Why talk of 'genetic theories'? when we have in the next breath to
write as Wundt does: "If then we must regard the intuition of space as a
product that simply emerges from the conditions of our mental and physical organization, nothing need stand in the way of our designating it as one
of the *a priori* functions with which consciousness is endowed." (Logik,
II. 460.)

† P. 430.   ‡ Pp. 430, 449.   § P. 428.   ‖ P. 442.

ly to Experience.* The only psychic activity required for this is the association of ideas.†

But how, it may be asked, can association produce a space-quality not in the things associated? How can we by induction or analogy infer what we do not already generically know? Can 'suggestions of experience' reproduce elements which no particular experience originally contained? This is the point by which Helmholtz's 'empiristic' theory, as a *theory*, must be judged. No theory is worthy of the name which leaves such a point obscure.

Well, Helmholtz does so leave it. At one time he seems to fall back on inscrutable powers of the soul, and to range himself with the 'psychical stimulists.' He speaks of Kant as having made the essential step in the matter in distinguishing the content of experience from that form—space, course—which is given it by the peculiar faculties of the mind. ‡ But elsewhere, again, § speaking of sensationalistic theories which would connect spatially determinate feelings *directly* with certain neural events, he says it is better to assume only such simple psychic activities as we *know* to exist, and gives the association of ideas as an instance of what he means. Later,‖ he reinforces this remark by confessing that he does not see how any neural process *can* give rise without antecedent experience to a ready-made (*fertige*) perception of space. And, finally, in a single momentous sentence, he speaks of sensations of *touch* as if they might be the original material of our space-percepts—which thus, from the optical point of view, 'may be assumed as *given*.'¶

Of course the eye-man has a right to fall back on the skin-man for help at a pinch. But doesn't this means that he is a mere eye-man and not a complete psychologist? In other words, Helmholtz's Optics and the 'empiristic theory' there professed are not to be understood as attempts at answering the *general* question of how space-consciousness enters the mind. They simply deny that it enters with the

---

* Pp. 442, 818.   † P. 798. Cf. also Popular Scientific Lectures, pp. 301–3.
‡ P. 456; see also 428, 441.   § P. 797.   ‖ P. 812.
¶ Bottom of page 797.

first optical sensations.* Our own account has affirmed stoutly that it enters *then ;* but no more than Helmholtz have we pretended to show *why.* Who calls a thing a first sensation admits he has no theory of its production. Helmholtz, though all the while without an articulate theory, makes the world think he has one. He beautifully traces the immense part which reproductive processes play in our vision of space, and never—except in that one pitiful little sentence about touch—does he tell us just what it is they reproduce. He limits himself to denying that they reproduce originals of a visual sort. And so difficult is the subject, and so magically do catch-words work on the popular-scientist ear, that most likely, had he written 'physiological' instead of 'nativistic,' and 'spiritualistic' instead of 'empiristic' (which synonyms Hering suggests), numbers of his present empirical evolutionary followers would fail to find in his teaching anything worthy of praise. But since he wrote otherwise, they hurrah for him as a sort of second Locke, dealing another death-blow at the old bugaboo of 'innate ideas.' His 'nativistic' adversary Hering, they probably imagine,—Heaven save the mark!— to be a scholastic in modern disguise.

After Wundt and Helmholtz, the most important anti-sensationalist space-philosopher in Germany is Professor Lipps, whose deduction of space from an order of non-spatial differences, continuous yet separate, is a wonderful piece of subtlety and logic. And yet he has to confess that continuous differences form in the first instance only a logical series, which *need* not appear spatial, and that wherever it does so appear, this must be accounted a 'fact,' due merely 'to the nature of the soul.' †

Lipps, and almost all the anti-sensationalist theorists except Helmholtz, seem guilty of that confusion which Mr.

---

* In fact, to borrow a simile from Prof. G. E. Müller (Theorie der sinnl. Aufmerksamkeit, p. 38), the various senses bear in the Helmholtzian philosophy of perception the same relation to the 'object' perceived by their means that a troop of jolly drinkers bear to the landlord's bill, when no one has any money, but each hopes that one of the rest will pay.

† Grundtatsachen des Seelenlebens (1883), pp. 480, 591-2. Psychologische Studien (1885), p. 14.

Shadworth Hodgson has done so much to clear away, viz., the confounding the analysis of an idea with the means of its production. Lipps, for example, finds that every space we think of can be broken up into positions, and concludes that in some undefined way the several positions must have pre-existed in thought before the aggregate space could have appeared to perception. Similarly Mr. Spencer, defining extension as an ' aggregate of relations of coexistent position,' says " every cognition of magnitude is a cognition of relations of position," * and " no idea of extension can arise from the simultaneous excitation " of many nerves " unless there is a knowledge of their relative positions."† Just so Prof. Bain insists that the very *meaning* of space is scope for movement, ‡ and that therefore distance and magnitude *can* be no original attributes of the eye's sensibility. Similarly because movement is analyzable into positions occupied at successive moments by the mover, philosophers (e.g. Schopenhauer, as quoted above) have repeatedly denied the possibility of *its* being an immediate sensation. We have, however, seen that it is the most immediate of all our space-sensations. Because it can only occur in a definite direction the impossibility of perceiving it without perceiving its direction has been decreed—a decree which the simplest experiment overthrows. § It is a case of what I have called the 'psychologist's fallacy ': mere acquaintance with space is treated as tantamount to every sort of knowledge about it, the conditions of the latter are demanded of the former state of mind, and all sorts of mythological processes are brought in to help. ‖ As well might one say that because the world consists of all its parts, there-

---

* Psychology, II. p. 174.

† *Ibid.* p. 168.

‡ Senses and Intellect, 3d ed. pp. 366–75.

§ Cf. Hall and Donaldson in Mind, x. 559.

‖ As other examples of the confusion, take Mr. Sully : " The *fallacious assumption* that there can be an idea of distance in general, apart from particular distances" (Mind, III. p. 177) ; and Wundt: " An indefinite localization, which waits for experience to give it its reference to real space, stands in contradiction with the very idea of localization, which means the reference to a determinate point of space " (Physiol. Psych., 1te Aufl. p. 480).

fore we can only apprehend it at all by having unconsciously summed these up in our head. It is the old idea of our actual knowledge being drawn out from a pre-existent potentiality, an idea which, whatever worth it may metaphysically possess, does no good in psychology.

My own sensationalistic account has derived most aid and comfort from the writings of Hering, A. W. Volkmann, Stumpf, Leconte, and Schön. All these authors allow ample scope to that Experience which Berkeley's genius saw to be a present factor in all our visual acts. But they give Experience some grist to grind, which the *soi-disant* 'empiristic' school forgets to do. Stumpf seems to me the most philosophical and profound of all these writers; and I owe him much. I should doubtless have owed almost as much to Mr. James Ward, had his article on Psychology in the Encyclopædia Britannica appeared before my own thoughts were written down. The literature of the question is in all languages very voluminous. I content myself with referring to the bibliography in Helmholtz's and Aubert's works on Physiological Optics for the visual part of the subject, and with naming in a note the ablest works in the English tongue which have treated of the subject in a *general* way.*

---

* G. Berkeley: Essay towards a new Theory of Vision ; Samuel Bailey: A Review of Berkeley's Theory of Vision (1842) ; J. S. Mill's Review of Bailey, in his Dissertations and Disquisitions, vol. II ; Jas. Ferrier: Review of Bailey, in 'Philosophical Remains,' vol. II ; A. Bain: Senses and Intellect, 'Intellect,' chap. I ; H. Spencer: Principles of Psychology, pt. VI. chaps. XIV, XVI ; J. S. Mill: Examination of Hamilton, chap. XIII (the best statement of the so-called English empiricist position) ; T. K. Abbott: Sight and Touch, 1861 (the first English book to go at all minutely into *facts;* Mr. Abbott maintaining retinal sensations to be originally of space in three dimensions) ; A. C. Fraser: Review of Abbott, in North British Review for Aug. 1864 ; another review in Macmillan's Magazine, Aug. 1866 ; J. Sully: Outlines of Psychology, chap. VI ; J. Ward: Encyclop. Britannica, 9th Ed., article 'Psychology,' pp. 53–5 ; J. E. Walter: The Perception of Space and Matter (1879) —I may also refer to a 'discussion' between Prof. G. Croom Robertson, Mr. J. Ward, and the present writer, in Mind, vol. XIII.—The present chapter is only the filling out with detail of an article entitled 'The Spatial Quale,' which appeared in the Journal of Speculative Philosophy for January 1879 (XIII. 64).

CHAPTER XXI.*

THE PERCEPTION OF REALITY.

BELIEF.

EVERYONE knows the difference between imagining a thing and believing in its existence, between supposing a proposition and acquiescing in its truth. In the case of acquiescence or belief, the object is not only apprehended by the mind, but is held to have reality. Belief is thus the mental state or function of cognizing reality. As used in the following pages, 'Belief' will mean every degree of assurance, including the highest possible certainty and conviction.

There are, as we know, two ways of studying every psychic state. First, the way of analysis: What does it consist in? What is its inner nature? Of what sort of mind-stuff is it composed? Second, the way of history: What are its conditions of production, and its connection with other facts?

Into the first way we cannot go very far. *In its inner nature, belief, or the sense of reality, is a sort of feeling more allied to the emotions than to anything else.* Mr. Bagehot distinctly calls it the 'emotion' of conviction. I just now spoke of it as acquiescence. It resembles more than anything what in the psychology of volition we know as consent. Consent is recognized by all to be a manifestation of our active nature. It would naturally be described by such terms as 'willingness' or the 'turning of our disposition.' What characterizes both consent and belief is the cessation of theoretic agitation, through the advent of an idea which is inwardly stable, and fills the mind solidly to the exclusion of contradictory ideas. When this is the case, motor effects are apt to follow. Hence the states of

---

* Reprinted, with additions, from 'Mind' for July 1869.

consent and belief, characterized by repose on the purely intellectual side, are both intimately connected with subsequent practical activity. This inward stability of the mind's content is as characteristic of disbelief as of belief. But we shall presently see that we never disbelieve anything except for the reason that we believe something else which contradicts the first thing.* Disbelief is thus an incidental complication to belief, and need not be considered by itself.

The true opposites of belief, psychologically considered, *are doubt and inquiry, not disbelief.* In both these states the content of our mind is in unrest, and the emotion engendered thereby is, like the emotion of belief itself, perfectly distinct, but perfectly indescribable in words. Both sorts of emotion may be pathologically exalted. One of the charms of drunkenness unquestionably lies in the deepening of the sense of reality and truth which is gained therein. In whatever light things may then appear to us, they seem more utterly what they are, more 'utterly utter' than when we are sober. This goes to a fully unutterable extreme in the nitrous oxide intoxication, in which a man's very soul will sweat with conviction, and he be all the while unable to tell what he is convinced of at all.† The pathological state opposed to this solidity and deepening has been called the questioning mania (*Grübelsucht* by the Germans). It is sometimes found as a substantive affection, paroxysmal or chronic, and consists in the inability to rest in any conception, and the need of having it confirmed and explained. 'Why do I stand here where I stand?' 'Why is a glass a glass, a chair a chair?' 'How is it that men are only of the size they are? Why not as big as houses,' etc., etc.‡

---

* Compare this psychological fact with the corresponding logical truth that all negation rests on covert assertion of something else than the thing denied. (See Bradley's Principles of Logic, bk. i. ch. 3.)

† See that very remarkable little work, 'The Anæsthetic Revelation and the Gist of Philosophy,' by Benj. P. Blood (Amsterdam, N. Y., 1874). Compare also Mind, vii. 206.

‡ "To one whose mind is healthy thoughts come and go unnoticed; with me they have to be faced, thought about in a peculiar fashion, and then disposed of as finished, and this often when I am utterly wearied and would be at peace; but the call is imperative. This goes on to the hin-

There is, it is true, another pathological state which is as far removed from doubt as from belief, and which some may prefer to consider the proper contrary of the latter state of mind. I refer to the feeling that everything is hollow, unreal, dead. I shall speak of this state again upon a later page. The point I wish to notice here is simply that belief and disbelief are but two aspects of one psychic state.

John Mill, reviewing various opinions about belief, comes to the conclusion that no account of it can be given:

"What," he says, "is the difference *to our minds* between thinking of a reality and representing to ourselves an imaginary picture? I confess I can see no escape from the opinion that the distinction is ultimate and primordial. There is no more difficulty in holding it to be so than in holding the difference between a sensation and an idea to be primordial. It seems almost another aspect of the same difference. . . . I cannot help thinking, therefore, that there is in the remembrance of a real fact, as distinguished from that of a thought, an element which does not consist . . . in a difference between the mere ideas which are present to the mind in the two cases. This element, howsoever we define it, constitutes belief, and is the difference between Memory and Imagination. From whatever direction we approach, this difference seems to close our path. When we arrive at it, we seem to have reached, as it were, the central point of our intellectual nature, presupposed and built upon in every attempt we make to explain the more recondite phenomena of our mental being." *

---

drance of all natural action. If I were told that the staircase was on fire and I had only a minute to escape, and the thought arose—'Have they sent for fire-engines? Is it probable that the man who has the key is on hand? Is the man a careful sort of person? Will the key be hanging on a peg? Am I thinking rightly? Perhaps they don't lock the depot'—my foot would be lifted to go down; I should be conscious to excitement that I was losing my chance; but I should be unable to stir until all these absurdities were entertained and disposed of. In the most critical moments of my life, when I ought to have been so *engrossed as to leave no room for any secondary thoughts,* I have been oppressed by the inability to be at peace. And in the most ordinary circumstances it is all the same. Let me instance the other morning I went to walk. The day was biting cold, but I was unable to proceed except by jerks. Once I got arrested, my feet in a muddy pool. One foot was lifted to go, knowing that it was not good to be standing in water, but there I was fast, the cause of detention being the discussing with myself the reasons why I should not stand in that pool." (T. S. Clouston, Clinical Lectures on Mental Diseases, 1883, p. 43. See also Berger, in Archiv f. Psychiatrie, VI. 217.)

* Note to Jas. Mill's Analysis, I. 412-423.

If the words of Mill be taken to apply to the mere sub-jective analysis of belief—to the question, What does it feel like when we have it?—they must be held, on the whole, to be correct. Belief, the sense of reality, feels like itself—that is about as much as we can say.

Prof. Brentano, in an admirable chapter of his *Psychologie*, expresses this by saying that conception and belief (which he names *judgment*) are two different fundamental psychic phenomena. What I myself have called (Vol. I, p. 275) the 'object' of thought may be comparatively simple, like "Ha! what a pain," or "It-thunders"; or it may be complex, like "Columbus-discovered-America-in-1492," or "There-exists-an-all-wise-Creator-of-the-world." In either case, however, the mere thought of the object may exist as something quite distinct from the belief in its reality. The belief, as Brentano says, presupposes the mere thought:

"Every object comes into consciousness in a twofold way, as simply thought of [*vorgestellt*] and as admitted [*anerkannt*] or denied. The relation is analogous to that which is assumed by most philosophers (by Kant no less than by Aristotle) to obtain between mere thought and desire. Nothing is ever desired without being thought of; but the desiring is nevertheless a second quite new and peculiar form of rela-tion to the object, a second quite new way of receiving it into consciousness. No more is anything judged [i.e., believed or disbelieved] which is not thought of too. But we must insist that, so soon as the object of a thought becomes the object of an assenting or rejecting judgment, our consciousness steps into an entirely new relation to-wards it. It is then twice present in consciousness, as thought of, and as held for real or denied; just as when desire awakens for it, it is both thought and simultaneously desired." (P. 266.)

The commonplace doctrine of 'judgment' is that it consists in the combination of 'ideas' by a 'copula' into a 'proposition,' which may be of various sorts, as affir-mative, negative, hypothetical, etc. But who does not see that in a disbelieved or doubted or interrogative or condi-tional proposition, the ideas are combined in the same identical way in which they are in a proposition which is solidly believed? *The way in which the ideas are combined is a part of the inner constitution of the thought's object or content.* That object is sometimes an articulated whole with relations between its parts, amongst which relations, that of predicate to subject may be one. But when we have got our object with its inner constitution thus defined in a proposition, then the question comes up regarding the object as a whole : 'Is it a real object? is this proposition a true proposition or not?' And in the answer *Yes* to *this* question lies that new psychic act which Brentano calls 'judgment,' but which I prefer to call 'belief.'

In every proposition, then, so far as it is believed, questioned, or disbelieved, four elements are to be distinguished, the subject, the predicate, and their relation (of whatever sort it be)—these form the *object* of belief—and finally the psychic attitude in which our mind stands towards the proposition taken as a whole—and this is the belief itself.*

Admitting, then, that this attitude is a state of consciousness *sui generis*, about which nothing more can be said in the way of internal analysis, let us proceed to the second way of studying the subject of belief: *Under what circumstances do we think things real?* We shall soon see how much matter this gives us to discuss.

THE VARIOUS ORDERS OF REALITY.

Suppose a new-born mind, entirely blank and waiting for experience to begin. Suppose that it begins in the form of a visual impression (whether faint or vivid is immaterial) of a lighted candle against a dark background, and nothing else, so that whilst this image lasts it constitutes the entire universe known to the mind in question. Suppose, moreover (to simplify the hypothesis), that the candle is only imaginary, and that no 'original' of it is recognized by us psychologists outside. Will this hallucinatory candle be believed in, will it have a real existence for the mind?

What possible sense (for that mind) would a suspicion have that the candle was not real? What would doubt or disbelief of it imply? When *we*, the onlooking psychologists, say the candle is unreal, we mean something quite definite, viz., that there is a world known to *us* which *is*

---

* For an excellent account of the history of opinion on this subject see A. Marty, in Vierteljahrsch. f. wiss. Phil., VII. 161 ff. (1884).

real, and to which we perceive that the candle does not belong ; it belongs exclusively to that individual mind, has no *status* anywhere else, etc. It exists, to be sure, in a fashion, for it forms the content of that mind's hallucination ; but the hallucination itself, though unquestionably it is a sort of existing fact, has no knowledge of *other* facts ; and since those *other* facts are the realities *par excellence* for us, and the only things we believe in, the candle is simply outside of our reality and belief altogether.

By the hypothesis, however, the *mind which sees the candle* can spin no such considerations as these about it, for of other facts, actual or possible, it has no inkling whatever. That candle is its all, its absolute. Its entire faculty of attention is absorbed by it. It *is,* it is *that ;* it is *there ;* no other possible candle, or quality of this candle, no other possible place, or possible object in the place, no alternative, in short, suggests itself as even conceivable ; so how can the mind help believing the candle real ? The supposition that it might possibly not do so is, under the supposed conditions, unintelligible.*

This is what Spinoza long ago announced:

"Let us conceive a boy," he said, " imagining to himself a horse, and taking note of nothing else. As this imagination involves the existence of the horse, *and the boy has no perception which annuls its existence*, he will necessarily contemplate the horse as present, nor will he be able to doubt of its existence, however little certain of it he may be. I deny that a man in so far as he imagines [*percipit*] affirms nothing. For what is it to imagine a winged horse but to affirm that the horse [that horse, namely] has wings ? For if the mind had nothing before it but the winged horse it would contemplate the same as present, would have no cause to doubt of its existence, nor any power of dissenting from its existence, unless the imagination of the winged horse were joined to an idea which contradicted [*tollit*] its existence." (Ethics, II. 49, Scholium.)

The sense that anything we think of is unreal can only come, then, when that thing is contradicted by some other

---

* We saw near the end of Chapter XIX that a candle-image taking exclusive possession of the mind in this way would probably acquire the sensational vividness. But this physiological accident is logically immaterial to the argument in the text, which ought to apply as well to the dimmest sort of mental image as to the brightest sensation.

thing of which we think. *Any object which remains uncontradicted is ipso facto believed and posited as absolute reality.*

Now, how comes it that one thing thought of can be contradicted by another? It cannot unless it begins the quarrel by saying something inadmissible about that other. Take the mind with the candle, or the boy with the horse. If either of them say, ' That candle or that horse, even when I don't see it, exists in *the outer world,*' he pushes into ' the outer world' an object which may be incompatible with everything which he otherwise knows of that world. If so, he must take his choice of which to hold by, the present perceptions or the other knowledge of the world. If he holds to the other knowledge, the present perceptions are contradicted, *so far as their relation to that world goes.* Candle and horse, whatever they may be, are not existents in outward space. They are existents, of course ; they are mental objects ; mental objects have existence as mental objects. But they are situated in their own spaces, the space in which they severally appear, and neither of those spaces is the space in which the realities called 'the outer world' exist.

Take again the horse with wings. If I merely dream of a horse with wings, my horse interferes with nothing else and has not to be contradicted. That horse, its wings, and its place, are all equally real. That horse exists no otherwise than as winged, and is moreover really there, for that place exists no otherwise than as the place of that horse, and claims as yet no connection with the other places of the world. But if with this horse I make an inroad into the *world otherwise known,* and say, for example, ' That is my old mare Maggie, having grown a pair of wings where she stands in her stall,' the whole case is altered ; for now the horse and place are identified with a horse and place otherwise known, and *what* is known of the latter objects is incompatible with what is perceived with the former. ' Maggie in her stall with wings ! Never !' The wings are unreal, then, visionary. I have dreamed a lie about Maggie in her stall.

The reader will recognize in these two cases the two sorts of judgment called in the logic-books existential and attributive respectively. 'The candle exists as an outer reality' is an existential, 'My Maggie has got a pair of wings' is an attributive, proposition;* and it follows from what was first said that *all propositions, whether attributive or existential, are believed through the very fact of being conceived, unless they clash with other propositions believed at the same time, by affirming that their terms are the same with the terms of these other propositions.* A dream-candle has existence, true enough ; but not the same existence (existence for itself, namely, or *extra mentem meam*) which the candles of waking perception have. A dream-horse has wings ; but then neither horse nor wings are the same with any horses or wings known to memory. That we can at any moment think of the same thing which at any former moment we thought of is the ultimate law of our intellectual constitution. But when we now think of it incompatibly with our other ways of thinking it, then we must choose which way to stand by, for we cannot continue to think in two contradictory ways at once. *The whole distinction of real and unreal, the whole psychology of belief, disbelief, and doubt, is thus grounded on two mental facts—first, that we are liable to think differently of the same ; and second, that when we have done so, we can choose which way of thinking to adhere to and which to disregard.*

The subjects adhered to become real subjects, the attributes adhered to real attributes, the existence adhered to real existence ; whilst the subjects disregarded become imaginary subjects, the attributes disregarded erroneous

---

* In both existential and attributive judgments a synthesis is represented. The syllable *ex* in the word Existence, *da* in the word *Dasein*, express it. 'The candle exists' is equivalent to 'The candle is *over there*.' And the 'over there' means real space, space related to other reals. The proposition amounts to saying: 'The candle is in the same space with other reals.' It affirms of the candle a very concrete predicate—namely, this relation to other particular concrete things. *Their* real existence, as we shall later see, resolves itself into their peculiar relation to *ourselves*. Existence is thus no substantive quality when we predicate it of any object ; it is a relation, ultimately terminating in ourselves, and at the moment when it terminates, becoming a *practical* relation. But of this more anon. I only wish now to indicate the superficial nature of the distinction between the existential and the attributive proposition.

attributes, and the existence disregarded an existence in no man's land, in the limbo ' where footless fancies dwell.' The real things are, in M. Taine's terminology, the *reductives* of the things judged unreal.

THE MANY WORLDS.

Habitually and practically we do not *count* these disregarded things as existents at all. For them *Væ victis* is the law in the popular philosophy ; they are not even treated as appearances ; they are treated as if they were mere waste, equivalent to nothing at all. To the genuinely philosophic mind, however, they still have existence, though not the same existence, as the real things. *As* objects of fancy, *as* errors, *as* occupants of dreamland, etc., they are in their way as indefeasible parts of life, as undeniable features of the Universe, as the realities are in their way. The total world of which the philosophers must take account is thus composed of the realities *plus* the fancies and illusions.

Two sub-universes, at least, connected by relations which philosophy tries to ascertain ! Really there are more than two sub-universes of which we take account, some of us of this one, and others of that. For there are various categories both of illusion and of reality, and alongside of the world of absolute error (i.e., error confined to single individuals) but still within the world of absolute reality (i.e., reality believed by the complete philosopher) there is the world of collective error, there are the worlds of abstract reality, of relative or practical reality, of ideal relations, and there is the supernatural world. The popular mind conceives of all these sub-worlds more or less disconnectedly ; and when dealing with one of them, forgets for the time being its relations to the rest. The complete philosopher is he who seeks not only to assign to every given object of his thought its right place in one or other of these sub-worlds, but he also seeks to determine the relation of each sub-world to the others in the total world which *is*.

The most important sub-universes commonly discriminated from each other and recognized by most of us as existing, each with its own special and separate style of existence, are the following :

(1) The world of sense, or of physical 'things' as we instinctively apprehend them, with such qualities as heat, color, and sound, and such 'forces' as life, chemical affinity, gravity, electricity, all existing as such within or on the surface of the things.

(2) The world of science, or of physical things as the learned conceive them, with secondary qualities and 'forces' (in the popular sense) excluded, and nothing real but solids and fluids and their 'laws' (i.e., customs) of motion.*

(3) The world of ideal relations, or abstract truths believed or believable by all, and expressed in logical, mathematical, metaphysical, ethical, or æsthetic propositions.

(4) The world of 'idols of the tribe,' illusions or prejudices common to the race. All educated people recognize these as forming one sub-universe. The motion of the sky round the earth, for example, belongs to this world. That motion is not a recognized item of any of the other worlds; but as an 'idol of the tribe' it really exists. For certain philosophers 'matter' exists only as an idol of the tribe. For science, the 'secondary qualities' of matter are but 'idols of the tribe.'

(5) The various supernatural worlds, the Christian heaven and hell, the world of the Hindoo mythology, the world of Swedenborg's *visa et audita*, etc. Each of these is a consistent system, with definite relations among its own parts. Neptune's trident, e.g., has no status of reality whatever in the Christian heaven; but within the classic Olympus certain definite things are true of it, whether one believe in the reality of the classic mythology as a whole or not. The various worlds of deliberate fable may be ranked with these worlds of faith—the world of the *Iliad*, that of *King Lear*, of the *Pickwick Papers*, etc.†

---

* I define the scientific universe here in the radical mechanical way. Practically, it is oftener thought of in a mongrel way and resembles in more points the popular physical world.

† It thus comes about that we can say such things as that Ivanhoe did not *really* marry Rebecca, as Thackeray *falsely* makes him do. The real Ivanhoe-world is the one which Scott wrote down for us. *In that world* Ivanhoe does *not* marry Rebecca. The objects within that world are knit together by perfectly definite relations, which can be affirmed or denied. Whilst absorbed in the novel, we turn our backs on all other

(6) The various worlds of individual opinion, as numerous as men are.

(7) The worlds of sheer madness and vagary, also indefinitely numerous.

Every object we think of gets at last referred to one world or another of this or of some similar list. It settles into our belief as a common-sense object, a scientific object, an abstract object, a mythological object, an object of some one's mistaken conception, or a madman's object; and it reaches this state sometimes immediately, but often only after being hustled and bandied about amongst other objects until it finds some which will tolerate its presence and stand in relations to it which nothing contradicts. The molecules and ether-waves of the scientific world, for example, simply kick the object's warmth and color out, they refuse to have any relations with them. But the world of 'idols of the tribe' stands ready to take them in. Just so the world of classic myth takes up the winged horse; the world of individual hallucination, the vision of the candle; the world of abstract truth, the proposition that justice is kingly, though no actual king be just. The various worlds themselves, however, appear (as aforesaid) to most men's minds in no very definitely conceived relation to each other, and our attention, when it turns to one, is apt to drop the others for the time being out of its account. Propositions concerning the different worlds are made from 'different points of view'; and in this more or less chaotic state the consciousness of most thinkers remains to the end. Each world *whilst it is attended to* is real after its own fashion; only the reality lapses with the attention.

THE WORLD OF 'PRACTICAL REALITIES.'

Each thinker, however, has dominant habits of attention; and these *practically elect from among the various worlds some one to be for him the world of ultimate realities.* From this world's objects he does not appeal. Whatever

---

worlds, and, for the time, the Ivanhoe-world remains our absolute reality. When we wake from the spell, however, we find a still more real world, which reduces Ivanhoe, and all things connected with him, to the fictive status, and relegates them to one of the sub-universes grouped under No. 5.

positively contradicts them must get into another world or die. The horse, e.g., may have wings to its heart's content, so long as it does not pretend to be the real world's horse—*that* horse is absolutely wingless. For most men, as we shall immediately see, the 'things of sense' hold this prerogative position, and are the absolutely real world's nucleus. Other things, to be sure, may be real for this man or for that—things of science, abstract moral relations, things of the Christian theology, or what not. But even for the special man, these things are usually real with a less real reality than that of the things of sense. They are taken less seriously; and the very utmost that can be said for anyone's belief in them is that it is as strong as his 'belief in his own senses.' *

In all this the everlasting partiality of our nature shows itself, our inveterate propensity to choice. For, in the strict and ultimate sense of the word existence, everything which can be thought of at all exists as *some* sort of object, whether mythical object, individual thinker's object, or object in outer space and for intelligence at large. Errors, fictions, tribal beliefs, are parts of the whole great Universe which God has made, and He must have meant all these things to be in it, each in its respective place. But for us finite creatures, "'tis to consider too curiously to consider

---

* The world of dreams is our real world whilst we are sleeping, because our attention then lapses from the sensible world. Conversely, when we wake the attention usually lapses from the dream-world and that becomes unreal. But if a dream haunts us and compels our attention during the day it is very apt to remain figuring in our consciousness as a sort of sub-universe alongside of the waking world. Most people have probably had dreams which it is hard to imagine not to have been glimpses into an actually existing region of being, perhaps a corner of the 'spiritual world.' And dreams have accordingly in all ages been regarded as revelations, and have played a large part in furnishing forth mythologies and creating themes for faith to lay hold upon. The 'larger universe,' here, which helps us to believe both in the dream and in the waking reality which is its immediate reductive, is the *total* universe, of Nature *plus* the Supernatural. The dream holds true, namely, in one half of that universe; the waking perceptions in the other half. Even to-day dream-objects figure among the realities in which some 'psychic-researchers' are seeking to rouse our belief. All our theories, not only those about the supernatural, but our philosophic and scientific theories as well, are like our dreams in rousing such different degrees of belief in different minds.

so." The mere fact of appearing as an object at all is not enough to constitute reality. That may be metaphysical reality, reality for God; but what we need is practical reality, reality for ourselves; and, to have that, an object must not only appear, but it must appear both *interesting* and *important.* The worlds whose objects are neither interesting nor important we treat simply negatively, we brand them as *un*real.

In the relative sense, then, the sense in which we contrast reality with simple *un*reality, and in which one thing is said to have *more* reality than another, and to be more believed, *reality means simply relation to our emotional and active life.* This is the only sense which the word ever has in the mouths of practical men. *In this sense, whatever excites and stimulates our interest is real;* whenever an object so appeals to us that we turn to it, accept it, fill our mind with it, or practically take account of it, so far it is real for us, and we believe it. Whenever, on the contrary, we ignore it, fail to consider it or act upon it, despise it, reject it, forget it, so far it is unreal for us and disbelieved. Hume's account of the matter was then essentially correct, when he said that belief in anything was simply the having the idea of it in a lively and active manner :

" I say, then, that belief is nothing but a more vivid, lively, forcible, firm, steady conception of an object than the imagination alone is ever able to attain. . . . It consists not in the peculiar nature or order of the ideas, but in the *manner* of their conception and in their *feeling* to the mind. I confess that it is impossible perfectly to explain this feeling or manner of conception. . . . Its true and proper name . . . is *belief*, which is a term that everyone sufficiently understands in common life. And in philosophy we can go no farther than assert that belief is something felt by the mind, which distinguishes the idea of the judgment from the fictions of the imagination.* It gives them more weight and influence ; makes them appear of greater importance ; enforces them in the mind ; gives them a superior influence on the passions, and renders them the governing principle in our actions." †

---

* Distinguishes realities from unrealities, the essential from the rubbishy and neglectable.

† Inquiry concerning Hum. Understanding, sec. v. pt. 2 (slightly transposed in my quotation).

Or as Prof. Bain puts it: "In its essential character, belief is a phase of our active nature—otherwise called the Will." *

The object of belief, then, reality or real existence, is something quite different from all the other predicates which a subject may possess. Those are properties intellectually or sensibly intuited. When we add any one of them to the subject, we increase the intrinsic content of the latter, we enrich its picture in our mind. But adding reality does not enrich the picture in any such inward way; it leaves it inwardly as it finds it, and only fixes it and stamps it in to *us.*

" The real," as Kant says, " contains no more than the possible. A hundred real dollars do not contain a penny more than a hundred possible dollars. . . . By whatever, and by however many, predicates I may think a thing, nothing is added to it if I add that the thing exists. . . . Whatever, therefore, our concept of an object may contain, we must always step outside of it in order to attribute to it existence." †

The 'stepping outside' of it is the establishment either of immediate practical relations between it and ourselves, or of relations between it and other objects with which we have immediate practical relations. Relations of this sort, which are as yet not transcended or superseded by others, are *ipso facto* real relations, and confer reality upon their objective term. *The fons et origo of all reality, whether from*

---

* Note to Jas. Mill's Analysis, I. 394.

† Critique of Pure Reason, trans. Müller, II. 515-17. Hume also: " When, after the simple conception of anything, we would conceive it as existent, we in reality make no addition to, or alteration of, our first idea. Thus, when we affirm that God is existent, we simply form the idea of such a being as He is represented to us; nor is the existence which we attribute to Him conceived by a particular idea, which we join to His other qualities, and can again separate and distinguish from them. . . . The belief of the existence joins no new idea to those which compose the ideas of the object. When I think of God, when I think of Him as existent, and when I believe Him to be existent, my idea of Him neither increases nor diminishes. But as 'tis certain there is a great difference betwixt the simple conception of the existence of an object and the belief of it, and as this difference lies not in the facts or compositions of the idea which we conceive, it follows that it must lie in the manner in which we conceive it." (Treatise of Human Nature, pt. III. sec. 7.)

the absolute or the practical point of view, is thus subjective, is ourselves. As bare logical thinkers, without emotional reaction, we give reality to whatever objects we think of, for they are really phenomena, or objects of our passing thought, if nothing more. But, *as thinkers with emotional reaction, we give what seems to us a still higher degree of reality to whatever things we select and emphasize and turn to* WITH A WILL. These are our *living* realities; and not only these, but all the other things which are intimately connected with these. Reality, starting from our Ego, thus sheds itself from point to point—first, upon all objects which have an immediate sting of interest for our Ego in them, and next, upon the objects most continuously related with these. It only fails when the connecting thread is lost. A whole system may be real, if it only hang to our Ego by one immediately *stinging* term. But what contradicts any such stinging term, even though it be another stinging term itself, is either not believed, or only believed after settlement of the dispute.

We reach thus the important conclusion that *our own reality, that sense of our own life which we at every moment possess, is the ultimate of ultimates for our belief.* 'As sure as I exist!'—this is our uttermost warrant for the being of all other things. As Descartes made the indubitable reality of the *cogito* go bail for the reality of all that the *cogito* involved, so we all of us, feeling our own present reality with absolutely coercive force, ascribe an all but equal degree of reality, first to whatever things we lay hold on with a sense of personal need, and second, to whatever farther things continuously belong with these. "Mein Jetzt und Hier," as Prof. Lipps says, "ist der letzte Angelpunkt für alle Wirklichkeit, also alle Erkenntniss."

The world of living realities as contrasted with unrealities is thus anchored in the Ego, considered as an active and emotional term.* That is the hook from which the rest dangles, the absolute support. And as from a painted

---

* I use the notion of the Ego here, as common-sense uses it. Nothing is prejudged as to the results (or absence of results) of ulterior attempts to analyze the notion.

hook it has been said that one can only hang a painted chain, so conversely, from a real hook only a real chain can properly be hung. *Whatever things have intimate and continuous connection with my life are things of whose reality I cannot doubt.* Whatever things fail to establish this connection are things which are practically no better for me than if they existed not at all.

In certain forms of melancholic perversion of the sensibilities and reactive powers, nothing touches us intimately, rouses us, or wakens natural feeling. The consequence is the complaint so often heard from melancholic patients, that nothing is believed in by them as it used to be, and that all sense of reality is fled from life. They are sheathed in india-rubber; nothing penetrates to the quick or draws blood, as it were. According to Griesinger, " I see, I hear!" such patients say, ' but the objects do not reach me, it is as if there were a wall between me and the outer world!"

" In such patients there often is an alteration of the cutaneous sensibility, such that things feel indistinct or sometimes rough and woolly. But even were this change always present, it would not completely explain the psychic phenomenon . . . which reminds us more of the alteration in our psychic relations to the outer world which advancing age on the one hand. and on the other emotions and passions, may bring about. In childhood we feel ourselves to be closer to the world of sensible phenomena, we live immediately with them and in them; an intimately vital tie binds us and them together. But with the ripening of reflection this tie is loosened, the warmth of our interest cools, things look differently to us, and we act more as foreigners to the outer world, even though we know it a great deal better. Joy and expansive emotions in general draw it nearer to us again. Everything makes a more lively impression, and with the quick immediate return of this warm receptivity for sense-impressions, joy makes us feel young again. In depressing emotions it is the other way. Outer things, whether living or inorganic, suddenly grow cold and foreign to us, and even our favorite objects of interest feel as if they belonged to us no more. Under these circumstances, receiving no longer from anything a lively impression, we cease to turn towards outer things, and the sense of inward loneliness grows upon us. . . . Where there is no strong intelligence to control this *blasé* condition, this psychic coldness and lack of interest, the issue of these states in which all seems so cold and hollow, the heart dried up, the world grown dead and empty, is often suicide or the deeper forms of insanity.*

---

* Griesinger, Mental Diseases, §§ 50, 98. The neologism we so often

THE PARAMOUNT REALITY OF SENSATIONS.

But now we are met by questions of detail. What does this stirring, this exciting power, this interest, consist in, which some objects have? which *are* those 'intimate relations' with our life which give reality? And what things stand in these relations immediately, and what others are so closely connected with the former that (in Hume's language) we 'carry our disposition' also on to them?

In a simple and direct way these questions cannot be answered at all. The whole history of human thought is but an unfinished attempt to answer them. For what have men been trying to find out, since men were men, but just those things: "Where do our true interests lie—which relations shall we call the intimate and real ones—which things shall we call living realities and which not?" A few psychological points can, however, be made clear.

Any relation to our mind at all, in the absence of a stronger relation, suffices to make an object real. The barest appeal to our attention is enough for that. Revert to the beginning of the chapter, and take the candle entering the vacant mind. The mind was waiting for just some such object to make its spring upon. It makes its spring and the candle is believed. But when the candle appears at the same time with other objects, it must run the gauntlet of their rivalry, and then it becomes a question which of the various candidates for attention shall compel belief. As a rule we believe as much as we can. We would believe everything if we only could. When objects are represented by us quite unsystematically they conflict but little with each other, and the number of them which in this chaotic manner we can believe is limitless. The primitive savage's mind is a jungle in which hallucinations, dreams, superstitions, conceptions, and sensible objects all flourish alongside of each other, unregulated except by the attention turning in this way or in that. The child's mind is the same. It is only as objects become permanent and their relations fixed that

---

hear, that an experience 'gives us a *realizing sense*' of the truth of some proposition or other, illustrates the dependence of the sense of reality upon *excitement*. Only what stirs us is 'realized.'

discrepancies and contradictions are felt and must be settled in some stable way. As a rule, the success with which a contradicted object maintains itself in our belief is proportional to several qualities which it must possess. Of these the one which would be put first by most people, because it characterizes objects of sensation, is its—

(1) Coerciveness over attention, or the mere power to possess consciousness : then follow—

(2) Liveliness, or sensible pungency, especially in the way of exciting pleasure or pain ;

(3) Stimulating effect upon the will, i.e., capacity to arouse active impulses, the more instinctive the better;

(4) Emotional interest, as object of love, dread, admiration, desire, etc. ;

(5) Congruity with certain favorite forms of contemplation—unity, simplicity, permanence, and the like ;

(6) Independence of other causes, and its own causal importance.

These characters run into each other. Coerciveness is the result of liveliness or emotional interest. What is lively and interesting stimulates *eo ipso* the will; congruity holds of active impulses as well as of contemplative forms ; causal independence and importance suit a certain contemplative demand, etc. I will therefore abandon all attempt at a formal treatment, and simply proceed to make remarks in the most convenient order of exposition.

As a whole, sensations are more lively and are judged more real than conceptions; things met with every hour more real than things seen once ; attributes perceived when awake, more real than attributes perceived in a dream. But, owing to the *diverse relations contracted by the various objects with each other*, the simple rule that the lively and permanent is the real is often enough disguised. A conceived thing may be deemed more real than a certain sensible thing, if it only be intimately related to other sensible things more vivid, permanent, or interesting than the first one. Conceived molecular vibrations, e.g., are by the physicist judged more real than felt warmth, because so intimately related to all those other facts of motion in the world which he has made his special study. Similarly, a rare thing may be deemed more real than a permanent thing if it be more widely related to other permanent things. All the occasional crucial observations of science are examples of this. A rare experience, too, is likely to be judged more real than a permanent one, if it be more interesting and exciting. Such is the sight of Saturn through a telescope; such are the occasional insights and illuminations which upset our habitual ways of thought.

But no mere floating conception, no mere disconnected rarity, ever displaces vivid things or permanent things from our belief. A conception, to prevail, must *terminate* in the world of orderly sensible experience. A rare phenomenon, to displace frequent ones, must belong with others more frequent still. The history of science is strewn with wrecks and ruins of theory—essences and principles, fluids and forces—once fondly clung to, but found to hang together with no facts of sense. And exceptional phenomena solicit our belief in vain until such time as we chance to conceive them as of kinds already admitted to exist. What science means by 'verification' is no more than this, that no object of conception shall be believed which sooner or later has not some permanent and vivid object of sensation for its *term.* Compare what was said on pages 3–7, above.

Sensible objects are thus either our realities or the tests of our realities. Conceived objects must show sensible effects or else be disbelieved. And the effects, even though reduced to relative unreality when their causes come to view (as heat, which molecular vibrations make unreal), are yet the things on which our knowledge of the causes rests. Strange mutual dependence this, in which the appearance needs the reality in order to exist, but the reality needs the appearance in order to be known!

Sensible vividness or pungency is then the vital factor in reality when once the conflict between objects, and the connecting of them together in the mind, has begun. No object which neither possesses this vividness in its own right nor is able to borrow it from anything else has a chance of making headway against vivid rivals, or of rousing in us that reaction in which belief consists. On the vivid objects we *pin,* as the saying is, our faith in all the rest; and our belief returns instinctively even to those of them from which reflection has led it away. Witness the obduracy with which the popular world of colors, sounds, and smells holds its own against that of molecules and vibrations. Let the physicist himself but nod, like Homer, and the world of sense becomes his absolute reality again.*

That things originally devoid of this stimulating power should be enabled, by association with other things which have it, to compel our belief as if they had it themselves, is a remarkable psychological fact, which since Hume's time it has been impossible to overlook.

"The vividness of the first conception," he writes, "diffuses itself along the relations and is conveyed, as by so many pipes or channels, to every idea that has any communication with the primary one. . . . Superstitious people are fond of the relics of saints and holy men, for the same reason that they seek after types and images, in order to enliven their devotion and give them a more intimate and strong conception of those exemplary lives. . . . Now, 'tis evident one of the best relics a devotee could procure would be the handiwork of a saint, and if his clothes and furniture are ever to be considered in this light, 'tis because they were once at his disposal, and were moved and affected by him; in which respect they are . . . connected with him by a shorter train of consequences than any of those from which we learn the reality of his

---

* The way in which sensations are pitted against systematized conceptions, and in which the one or the other then prevails according as the sensations are felt by ourselves or merely known by report, is interestingly illustrated at the present day by the state of public belief about 'spiritualistic' phenomena. There exist numerous narratives of movement without contact on the part of articles of furniture and other material objects, in the presence of certain privileged individuals called mediums. Such movement violates our memories, and the whole system of accepted physical 'science.' Consequently those who have not seen it either brand the narratives immediately as lies or call the phenomena 'illusions' of sense, produced by fraud or due to hallucination. But one who has actually seen such a phenomenon, under what seems to him sufficiently 'test-conditions,' will hold to his sensible experience through thick and thin, even though the whole fabric of 'science' should be rent in twain. That man would be a weak-spirited creature indeed who should allow any fly-blown generalities about 'the liability of the senses to be deceived' to bully him out of his adhesion to what for him was an indubitable experience of sight. A man may err in this obstinacy, sure enough, in any particular case. But the spirit that animates him is that on which ultimately the very life and health of Science rest.

existence. This phenomenon clearly proves that a present impression, with a relation of causation, may enliven any idea, and consequently produce belief or assent, according to the precedent definition of it. . . . It has been remarked among the Mahometans as well as Christians that those pilgrims who have seen Mecca or the Holy Land are ever after more faithful and zealous believers than those who have not had that advantage. A man whose memory presents him with a lively image of the Red Sea and the Desert and Jerusalem and Galilee can never doubt of any miraculous events which are related either by Moses or the Evangelists. The lively idea of the places passes by an easy transition to the facts which are supposed to have been related to them by contiguity, and increases the belief by increasing the vivacity of the conception. The remembrance of those fields and rivers has the same influence as a new argument. . . . The ceremonies of the Catholic religion may be considered as instances of the same nature. The devotees of that strange superstition usually plead in excuse for the mummeries with which they are upbraided that they feel the good effect of external motions and postures and actions in enlivening their devotion and quickening their fervor, which otherwise would decay, if directed entirely to distant and immaterial objects. We shadow out the objects of our faith, say they, in sensible types and images, and render them more present to us by the immediate presence of these types than it is possible for us to do merely by an intellectual view and contemplation." *

Hume's cases are rather trivial; and the things which associated sensible objects make us believe in are supposed by him to be unreal. But all the more manifest for that is the fact of their psychological influence. Who does not 'realize' more the fact of a dead or distant friend's existence, at the moment when a portrait, letter, garment or other material reminder of him is found? The whole notion of him then grows pungent and speaks to us and shakes us, in a manner unknown at other times. In children's minds, fancies and realities live side by side. But however lively their fancies may be, they still gain help from association with reality. The imaginative child identifies its *dramatis personæ* with some doll or other material object, and this evidently solidifies belief, little as it may resemble what it is held to stand for. A thing not too interesting by its own real qualities generally does the best service here. The most useful doll I ever saw was a large cucumber in the hands of a little Amazonian-Indian

---

* Treatise of Human Nature, bk. i. pt. iii. sec. 7.

girl; she nursed it and washed it and rocked it to sleep in a hammock, and talked to it all day long—there was no part in life which the cucumber did not play. Says Mr. Tylor:

"An imaginative child will make a dog do duty for a horse, or a soldier for a shepherd, till at last the objective resemblance almost disappears, and a bit of wood may be dragged about, resembling a ship on the sea or a coach on the road. Here the likeness of the bit of wood to a ship or coach is very slight indeed; but it is a thing, and can be moved about, . . . and is an evident assistance to the child in enabling it to arrange and develop its ideas. . . . Of how much use . . . may be seen by taking it away, and leaving the child nothing to play with. . . . In later years and among highly educated people the mental process which goes on in a child's playing with wooden soldiers and horses, though it never disappears, must be sought for in more complex phenomena. Perhaps nothing in after-life more closely resembles the effect of a doll upon a child than the effect of the illustrations of a tale upon a grown reader. Here the objective resemblance is very indefinite . . . yet what reality is given to the scene by a good picture. . . . Mr. Backhouse one day noticed in Van Diemen's Land a woman arranging several stones that were flat, oval, and about two inches wide, and marked in various directions with black and red lines. These, he learned, represented absent friends, and one larger than the rest stood for a fat native woman on Flinder's Island, known by the name of Mother Brown. Similar practices are found among far higher races than the ill-fated Tasmanians. Among some North American tribes a mother who has lost a child keeps its memory ever present to her by filling its cradle with black feathers and quills, and carrying it about with her for a year or more. When she stops anywhere, she sets up the cradle and talks to it as she goes about her work, just as she would have done if the dead body had been still alive within it. Here we have an image; but in Africa we find a rude doll representing the child, kept as a memorial. . . . Bastian saw Indian women in Peru who had lost an infant carrying about on their backs a wooden doll to represent it."*

To many persons among us, photographs of lost ones seem to be fetishes. They, it is true, resemble; but the fact that the mere materiality of the reminder is almost as important as its resemblance is shown by the popularity a hundred years ago of the black taffeta 'silhouettes' which are still found among family relics, and of one of which Fichte could write to his affianced: '*Die Farbe fehlt, das Auge fehlt, es fehlt der himmlische Ausdruck deiner lieblichen*

---

* Early Hist. of Mankind, p. 108.

Züge'—and yet go on worshipping it all the same. The opinion so stoutly professed by many, that language is essential to thought, seems to have this much of truth in it, that all our inward images tend invincibly to attach themselves to something sensible, so as to gain in corporeity and life. Words serve this purpose, gestures serve it, stones, straws, chalk-marks, anything will do. As soon as anyone of these things stands for the idea, the latter seems to be more real. Some persons, the present writer among the number, can hardly lecture without a black-board : the abstract conceptions must be symbolized by letters, squares or circles, and the relations between them by lines. All this symbolism, linguistic, graphic, and dramatic, has other uses too, for it abridges thought and fixes terms. But one of its uses is surely to rouse the believing reaction and give to the ideas a more living reality. As, when we are told a story, and shown the very knife that did the murder, the very ring whose hiding-place the clairvoyant revealed, the whole thing passes from fairy-land to mother-earth, so here we believe all the more, if only we see that ' the bricks are alive to tell the tale.'

So much for the prerogative position of sensations in regard to our belief. But among the sensations themselves all are not deemed equally real. The more practically important ones, the more permanent ones, and the more æsthetically apprehensible ones are selected from the mass, to be believed in most of all ; the others are degraded to the position of mere signs and suggestions of these. This fact has already been adverted to in former chapters.* The real color of a thing is that one color-sensation which it gives us when most favorably lighted for vision. So of its real size, its real shape, etc.—these are but optical sensations selected out of thousands of others, because they have æsthetic characteristics which appeal to our convenience or delight. But I will not repeat what I have already written about this matter, but pass on to our treatment of tactile and muscular sensations, as 'primary

---

* See Vol. I. pp. 285-6; Vol. II. pp. 237 ff.

qualities,' more real than those 'secondary' qualities which
eye and ear and nose reveal. Why do we thus so markedly
select the *tangible* to be the real? Our motives are not far
to seek. The tangible qualities are the least fluctuating.
When we get them at all we get them the same. The other
qualities fluctuate enormously as our relative position to
the object changes. Then, more decisive still, the tactile
properties are those most intimately connected with our
weal or woe. A dagger hurts us only when in contact with
our skin, a poison only when we take it into our mouths,
and we can only use an object for our advantage when we
have it in our muscular control. It is as tangibles, then,
that things concern us most; and the other senses, so far
as their practical use goes, do but warn us of what tangible things to expect. They are but organs of anticipatory touch, as Berkeley has with perfect clearness explained.*

Among all sensations, the *most* belief-compelling are
those productive of pleasure or of pain. Locke expressly
makes the *pleasure-* or *pain*-giving quality to be the ultimate
human criterion of anything's reality. Discussing (with a
supposed Berkeleyan before Berkeley) the notion that all
our perceptions may be but a dream, he says:

"He may please to dream that I make him this answer . . . that I
believe he will allow a very manifest difference between dreaming of
being in the fire and being actually in it. But yet if he be resolved to
appear so sceptical as to maintain that what I call being actually in the
fire is nothing but a dream, and that we cannot thereby certainly know
that any such thing as fire actually exists without us, I answer that we,
certainly finding that pleasure or pain [or emotion of any sort] follows
upon the application of certain objects to us, whose existence we perceive, or dream that we perceive by our senses, *this certainly is as great
as our happiness or misery*, beyond which we have no concernment to
know or to be." †

---

* See Theory of Vision, § 59.

† Essay, bk. IV. chap. 2, § 14. In another place: "He that sees a
candle burning and hath experimented the force of its flame by putting
his finger into it, will little doubt that this is something existing without
him, which does him harm and puts him to great pain. . . . And if our
dreamer pleases to try whether the glowing heat of a glass furnace be
barely a wandering imagination in a drowsy man's fancy by putting his
hand into it, he may, perhaps, be awakened into a certainty greater than

THE INFLUENCE OF EMOTION AND ACTIVE IMPULSE ON BELIEF.

The quality of arousing emotion, of shaking, moving us or inciting us to action, has as much to do with our belief in an object's reality as the quality of giving pleasure or pain. In Chapter XXIV I shall seek to show that our emotions probably owe their pungent quality to the bodily sensations which they involve. Our tendency to believe in emotionally exciting objects (objects of fear, desire, etc.) is thus explained without resorting to any fundamentally new principle of choice. Speaking generally, the more a conceived object *excites* us, the more reality it has. The same object excites us differently at different times. Moral and religious truths come 'home' to us far more on some occasions than on others. As Emerson says, "There is a difference between one and another hour of life in their authority and subsequent effect. Our faith comes in moments, . . . yet there is a depth in those brief moments which constrains us to ascribe more reality to them than to all other experiences." The 'depth' is partly, no doubt, the insight into wider systems of unified relation, but far more often than that it is the emotional thrill. Thus, to descend to more trivial examples, a man who has no belief in ghosts by daylight will temporarily believe in them when, alone at midnight, he feels his blood curdle at a mysterious sound or vision, his heart thumping, and his legs impelled to flee. The thought of falling when we walk along a curbstone awakens no emotion of dread; so no sense of reality attaches to it, and we are sure we shall not fall. On a precipice's edge, however, the sickening emotion which the notion of a possible fall engenders makes us believe in the latter's imminent reality, and quite unfits us to proceed.

---

he could wish, that it is something more than bare imagination. So that the evidence is as great as we can desire, being as certain to us as our pleasure or pain, i.e. happiness or misery; beyond which we have no concernment, either of knowledge or being. Such an assurance of the existence of things without us is sufficient to direct us in the attaining the good and avoiding the evil which is caused by them, which is the important concernment we have of being made acquainted with them." (*Ibid.* bk. IV. chap. 11, § 8.)

The greatest proof that a man is *sui compos* is his ability to suspend belief in presence of an emotionally exciting idea. To give this power is the highest result of education. In untutored minds the power does not exist. *Every exciting thought in the natural man carries credence with it. To conceive with passion is eo ipso to affirm.* As Bagehot says:

"The Caliph Omar burnt the Alexandrian Library, saying: ' All books which contain what is not in the Koran are dangerous. All which contain what is in it are useless !' Probably no one ever had an intenser belief in anything than Omar had in this. Yet it is impossible to imagine it preceded by an argument. His belief in Mahomet, in the Koran, and in the sufficiency of the Koran, probably came to him in spontaneous rushes of emotion ; there may have been little vestiges of argument floating here and there, but they did not justify the strength of the emotion, still less did they create it, and they hardly even excused it. . . . Probably, when the subject is thoroughly examined, conviction will be found to be one of the intensest of human emotions, and one most closely connected with the bodily state, . . . accompanied or preceded by the sensation that Scott makes his seer describe as the prelude of a prophecy :

> ' At length the fatal answer came,
> In characters of living flame—
> Not spoke in words, nor blazed in scroll,
> But borne and branded on my soul.'

A hot flash seems to burn across the brain. Men in these intense states of mind have altered all history, changed for better or worse the creed of myriads, and desolated or redeemed provinces or ages. Nor is this intensity a sign of truth, for it is precisely strongest in those points in which men differ most from each other. John Knox felt it in his anti-Catholicism ; Ignatius Loyola in his anti-Protestantism; and both, I suppose, felt it as much as it is possible to feel it." *

The reason of the belief is undoubtedly the bodily commotion which the exciting idea sets up. 'Nothing which I can feel like *that* can be false.' All our religious and supernatural beliefs are of this order. The surest warrant for immortality is the yearning of our bowels for our dear ones ; for God, the sinking sense it gives us to imagine no such Providence or help. So of our political or pecuniary hopes and fears, and things and persons dreaded and

---

* W. Bagehot, 'The Emotion of Conviction,' Literary Studies, I. 412-17.

desired. "A grocer has a full creed as to foreign policy, a young lady a complete theory of the sacraments, as to which neither has any doubt. . . . A girl in a country parsonage will be sure that Paris never can be taken, or that Bismarck is a wretch"—all because they have either conceived these things at some moment with passion, or associated them with other things which they have conceived with passion.

M. Renouvier calls this belief of a thing for no other reason than that we conceive it with passion, by the name of *mental vertigo.** Other objects whisper doubt or disbelief; but the object of passion makes us deaf to all but itself, and we affirm it unhesitatingly. Such objects are the delusions of insanity, which the insane person can at odd moments steady himself against, but which again return to sweep him off his feet. Such are the revelations of mysticism. Such, particularly, are the sudden beliefs which animate mobs of men when frenzied impulse to action is involved. Whatever be the action in point—whether the stoning of a prophet, the hailing of a conqueror, the burning of a witch, the baiting of a heretic or Jew, the starting of a forlorn hope, or the flying from a foe—the fact that to believe a certain object will *cause that action to explode* is a sufficient reason for that belief to come. The motor impulse sweeps it unresisting in its train.

The whole history of witchcraft and early medicine is a commentary on the facility with which anything which chances to be conceived is believed the moment the belief chimes in with an emotional mood. 'The cause of sickness?' When a savage asks the cause of anything he means to ask exclusively 'What is to blame?' The theoretic curiosity starts from the practical life's demands. Let some one then accuse a necromancer, suggest a charm or spell which has been cast, and no more 'evidence' is asked for. What evidence is required beyond this intimate sense of the culprit's responsibility, to which our very viscera and limbs reply?†

---

* Psychologie Rationnelle, ch. 12.

† Two examples out of a thousand :

Reid, Inquiry, ch. II. § 9: "I remember, many years ago, a white ox was brought into the country, of so enormous size that people came many

Human credulity in the way of therapeutics has similar psychological roots. If there is anything intolerable (especially to the heart of a woman), it is to do nothing when a

---

miles to see him. There happened, some months after, an uncommon fatality among women in child-bearing. Two such uncommon events, following one another, gave a suspicion of their connection, and occasioned a common opinion among the country people that the white ox was the cause of this fatality."

H. M. Stanley, Through the Dark Continent, ii. 888: "On the third day of our stay at Mowa feeling quite comfortable amongst the people, on account of their friendly bearing, I began to write in my note-book the terms for articles, in order to improve my already copious vocabulary of native words. I had proceeded only a few minutes when I observed a strange commotion amongst the people who had been flocking about me, and presently they ran away. In a short time we heard war-cries ringing loudly and shrilly over the table-land. Two hours afterwards a long line of warriors were seen descending the table-land and advancing towards our camp. There may have been between five and six hundred of them. We, on the other hand, had made but few preparations except such as would justify us replying to them in the event of the actual commencement of hostilities. But I had made many firm friends among them, and I firmly believed that I should be able to avert an open rupture. When they had assembled at about a hundred yards in front of our camp, Safeni and I walked up towards them and sat down midway. Some half-dozen of the Mowa people came near, and the shauri began.

"'What is the matter, my friends?' I asked. 'Why do you come with guns in your hands, in such numbers, as though you were coming to fight? Fight? fight us, your friends! Tut! this is some great mistake, surely.'

"Mundelé,' replied one of them, . . . 'our people saw you yesterday make marks on some tara-tara [paper]. This is very bad. Our country will waste, our goats will die, our bananas will rot, and our women will dry up. What have we done to you that you should wish to kill us? We have sold you food and we have brought you wine each day. Your people are allowed to wander where they please without trouble. Why is the Mundelé so wicked? We have gathered together to fight you if you do not burn that tara-tara now before our eyes. If you burn it we go away, and shall be your friends as heretofore.'

"I told them to rest there, and left Safeni in their hands as a pledge that I should return. My tent was not fifty yards from the spot, but while going towards it my brain was busy in devising some plan to foil this superstitious madness. My note-book contained a vast number of valuable notes. . . . I could not sacrifice it to the childish caprice of savages. As I was rummaging my book-box, I came across a volume of Shakespeare [Chandos edition] much worn, and well thumbed, and which was of the same size as my field-book; its cover was similar also, and it might be passed for the field-book, provided that no one remembered its appearance

loved one is sick or in pain. To do anything is a relief. Accordingly, whatever remedy may be suggested is a spark on inflammable soil. The mind makes its spring towards action on that cue, sends for that remedy, and for a day at least believes the danger past. Blame, dread, and hope are thus the great belief-inspiring passions, and cover among them the future, the present, and the past.

These remarks illustrate the earlier heads of the list on page 292. Whichever represented objects give us sensations, especially interesting ones, or incite our motor impulses, or arouse our hate, desire, or fear, are real enough for us. Our requirements in the way of reality terminate in our own acts and emotions, our own pleasures and pains. These are the ultimate fixities from which, as we formerly observed, the whole chain of our beliefs depends, object hanging to object, as the bees, in swarming, hang to each other until, *de proche en proche*, the supporting branch, the Self, is reached and held.

BELIEF IN OBJECTS OF THEORY.

Now the merely conceived or imagined objects which our mind represents as hanging to the sensations (causing them, etc.), filling the gaps between them, and weaving their interrupted chaos into order are innumerable. Whole systems of them conflict with other systems, and our choice of

---

too well. I took it to them. 'Is this the tara-tara, friends, that you wish burned?'

" ' Yes, yes, that is it.'

" ' Well, take it, and burn it, or keep it.'

" ' M—m. No, no, no. We will not touch it. It is fetish. You must burn it.'

" ' I ! Well, let it be so. I will do anything to please my good friends of Mowa.'

" We walked to the nearest fire. I breathed a regretful farewell to my genial companion, which, during my many weary hours of night, had assisted to relieve my mind when oppressed by almost intolerable woes, and then gravely consigned the innocent Shakespeare to the flames, heaping the brush fuel over it with ceremonious care.

" ' A h-h,' breathed the poor deluded natives sighing their relief. . . . 'There is no trouble now.' . . . And something approaching to a cheer was shouted among them, which terminated the episode of the burning of Shakespeare."

which system shall carry our belief is governed by principles which are simple enough, however subtle and difficult
may be their application to details. *The conceived system, to
pass for true, must at least include the reality of the sensible
objects in it, by explaining them as effects on us, if nothing more.
The system which includes the most of them, and definitely explains or pretends to explain the most of them, will, ceteris
paribus, prevail.* It is needless to say how far mankind still
is from having excogitated such a system. But the various
materialisms, idealisms, and hylozoisms show with what industry the attempt is forever made. It is conceivable that
several rival theories should equally well include the actual
order of our sensations in their scheme, much as the one-
fluid and two-fluid theories of electricity formulated all the
common electrical phenomena equally well. The sciences
are full of these alternatives. Which theory is then to be
believed? *That theory will be most generally believed which,
besides offering us objects able to account satisfactorily for our
sensible experience, also offers those which are most interesting,
those which appeal most urgently to our æsthetic, emotional, and
active needs.* So here, in the higher intellectual life, the
same selection among general conceptions goes on which
went on among the sensations themselves. First, a word
of their relation to our emotional and active needs—and
here I can do no better than quote from an article published some years ago :*

 "A philosophy may be unimpeachable in other respects, but either
of two defects will be fatal to its universal acceptance. First, its ultimate principle must not be one that essentially baffles and disappoints
our dearest desires and most cherished powers. A pessimistic principle
like Schopenhauer's incurably vicious Will-substance, or Hartmann's
wicked jack-at-all-trades, the Unconscious, will perpetually call forth
essays at other philosophies. Incompatibility of the future with their
desires and active tendencies is, in fact, to most men a source of more
fixed disquietude than uncertainty itself. Witness the attempts to
overcome the 'problem of evil,' the 'mystery of pain.' There is no
problem of 'good.'

 "But a second and worse defect in a philosophy than that of contradicting our active propensities is to give them no Object whatever

---

* 'Rationality, Activity, and Faith' (Princeton Review, July 1882,
pp. 64–9).

to press against. A philosophy whose principle is so incommensurate with our most intimate powers as to deny them all relevancy in universal affairs, as to annihilate their motives at one blow, will be even more unpopular than pessimism. Better face the enemy than the eternal Void ! This is why materialism will always fail of universal adoption, however well it may fuse things into an atomistic unity, however clearly it may prophesy the future eternity. For materialism denies reality to the objects of almost all the impulses which we most cherish. The real *meaning* of the impulses, it says, is something which has no emotional interest for us whatever. But what is called extradition is quite as characteristic of our emotions as of our sense. Both point to an Object as the cause of the present feeling. What an intensely objective reference lies in fear ! In like manner an enraptured man, a dreary-feeling man, are not simply aware of their subjective states ; if they were, the force of their feelings would evaporate. Both believe there is outward cause *why* they should feel as they do : either ' It is a glad world ! how good is life !' or 'What a loathsome tedium is existence !' Any philosophy which annihilates the validity of the reference by explaining away its objects or translating them into terms of no emotional pertinency leaves the mind with little to care or act for. This is the opposite condition from that of nightmare, but when acutely brought home to consciousness it produces a kindred horror. In nightmare we have motives to act, but no power : here we have powers, but no motives. A nameless *Unheimlichkeit* comes over us at the thought of there being nothing eternal in our final purposes, in the objects of those loves and aspirations which are our deepest energies. The monstrously lopsided equation of the universe and its knower, which we postulate as the ideal of cognition, is perfectly paralleled by the no less lopsided equation of the universe and the *doer*. We demand in it a *character* for which our emotions and active propensities shall be a match. Small as we are, minute as is the point by which the Cosmos impinges upon each one of us, each one desires to feel that his reaction at that point is congruous with the demands of the vast whole, that he balances the latter, so to speak, and is able to do what it expects of him. But as his abilities to ' do ' lie wholly in the line of his natural propensities ; as he enjoys reaction with such emotions as fortitude, hope, rapture, admiration, earnestness, and the like ; and as he very unwillingly reacts with fear, disgust, despair, or doubt, —a philosophy which should legitimate only emotions of the latter sort would be sure to leave the mind a prey to discontent and craving.

" It is far too little recognized how entirely the intellect is built up of practical interests. The theory of Evolution is beginning to do very good service by its reduction of all mentality to the type of reflex action. Cognition, in this view, is but a fleeting moment, a cross-section at a certain point of what in its totality is a motor phenomenon. In the lower forms of life no one will pretend that cognition is anything more than a guide to appropriate action. The germinal question concerning things brought for the first time before consciousness is not the theoretic ' What is that ?' but the practical ' Who goes there ?' or rather, as Horwicz has admirably put it, ' What is to be done ?'—' *Was fang' ich an ?* ' In all our discussions about the intelligence of lower animals the only test we use is that of their *acting* as if for a purpose. Cognition, in short, is incomplete until discharged in act. And although it is true that the later mental development, which attains its maximum through the hypertrophied cerebrum of man, gives birth to a vast amount of theoretic activity over and above that which is immediately ministerial to practice, yet the earlier claim is only postponed, not effaced, and the active nature asserts its rights to the end.

" If there be any truth at all in this view, it follows that however vaguely a philosopher may define the ultimate universal datum, he cannot be said to leave it unknown to us so long as he in the slightest degree pretends that our emotional or active attitude towards it should be of one sort rather than another. He who says, ' Life is real, life is earnest,' however much he may speak of the fundamental mysteriousness of things, gives a distinct definition to that mysteriousness by ascribing to it the right to claim from us the particular mood called seriousness, which means the willingness to live with energy, though energy bring pain. The same is true of him who says that all is vanity. Indefinable as the predicate vanity may be *in se*, it is clearly enough something which permits anæsthesia, mere escape from suffering, to be our rule of life. There is no more ludicrous incongruity than for agnostics to proclaim with one breath that the substance of things is unknowable, and with the next that the thought of it should inspire us with admiration of its glory, reverence, and a willingness to add our cooperative push in the direction towards which its manifestations seem to be drifting. The unknowable may be unfathomed, but if it make such distinct demands upon our activity, we surely are not ignorant of its essential quality.

" If we survey the field of history and ask what feature all great periods of revival, of expansion of the human mind, display in common, we shall find, I think, simply this : that each and all of them have said to the human being, ' The inmost nature of the reality is congenial to *powers* which you possess .' In what did the emancipating message of primitive Christianity consist, but in the announcement that God recognizes those weak and tender impulses which paganism had so rudely overlooked ? Take repentance : the man who can do nothing rightly can at least repent of his failures. But for paganism this faculty of repentance was a pure supernumerary, a straggler too late for the fair. Christianity took it and made it the one power within us which appealed straight to the heart of God. And after the night of the Middle Ages had so long branded with obloquy even the generous impulses of the flesh, and defined the Reality to be such that only slavish natures could commune with it, in what did the *Sursum corda !* of the Renaissance lie but in the proclamation that the archetype of verity in things laid claim on the widest activity of our whole æsthetic being? What were Luther's mission and Wesley's but appeals to powers which even the meanest of men might carry with them, faith and self-despair, but which were personal, requiring no priestly intermediation, and which brought their owner face to face with God? What caused the wild-fire influence of Rousseau but the assurance he gave that man's nature was in harmony with the nature of things, if only the paralyzing corruptions of custom would stand from between? How did Kant and Fichte, Goethe and Schiller, inspire their time with cheer, except by saying, 'Use all your powers; that is the only obedience which the universe exacts'? And Carlyle with his gospel of Work, of Fact, of Veracity, how does he move us except by saying that the universe imposes no tasks upon us but such as the most humble can perform? Emerson's creed that everything that ever was or will be is here in the enveloping Now; that man has but to obey himself—'He who will rest in what he *is*, is a part of Destiny'—is in like manner nothing but an exorcism of all scepticism as to the pertinency of one's natural faculties.

"In a word, 'Son of Man, *stand upon thy feet* and I will speak unto thee!' is the only revelation of truth to which the solving epochs have helped the disciple. But that has been enough to satisfy the greater part of his rational need. *In se* and *per se* the universal essence has hardly been more defined by any of these formulæ than by the agnostic *x;* but the mere assurance that my powers, such as they are, are not irrelevant to it, but pertinent, that it speaks to them and will in some way recognize their reply, that I can be a match for it if I will, and not a footless waif, suffices to make it rational to my feeling in the sense given above. Nothing could be more absurd than to hope for the definitive triumph of any philosophy which should refuse to legitimate, and to legitimate in an emphatic manner, the more powerful of our emotional and practical tendencies. Fatalism, whose solving word in all crises of behavior is 'All striving is vain,' will never reign supreme, for the impulse to take life strivingly is indestructible in the race. Moral creeds which speak to that impulse will be widely successful in spite of inconsistency, vagueness, and shadowy determination of expectancy. Man needs a rule for his will, and will invent one if one be not given him."

After the emotional and active needs come the intellectual and æsthetic ones. The two great æsthetic principles, of richness and of ease, dominate our intellectual as well as our sensuous life. And, *ceteris paribus,* no system which should not be rich, simple, and harmonious would have a chance of being chosen for belief, if rich, simple, and harmonious systems were also there. Into the latter we should unhesitatingly settle, with that welcoming attitude of the will in which belief consists. To quote from a remarkable book :

"This law that our consciousness constantly tends to the minimum of complexity and to the maximum of definiteness, is of great importance for all our knowledge. . . . Our own activity of attention will thus determine what we are to know and what we are to believe. If things have more than a certain complexity, not only will our limited powers of attention forbid us to unravel this complexity, but we shall strongly desire to believe the things much simpler than they are. For our thoughts about them will have a constant tendency to become as simple and definite as possible. Put a man into a perfect chaos of phenomena —sounds, sights, feelings—and if the man continued to exist, and to be rational at all, his attention would doubtless soon find for him a way to make up some kind of rhythmic regularity, which he would impute to the things about him, so as to imagine that he had discovered some laws of sequence in this mad new world. And thus, in every case where we fancy ourselves sure of a simple law of Nature, we must remember that a great deal of the fancied simplicity may be due, in the given case, not to Nature, but to the ineradicable prejudice of our own minds in favor of regularity and simplicity. All our thoughts are determined, in great measure, by this law of least effort, as it is found exemplified in our activity of attention. . . . The aim of the whole process seems to be to reach as complete and united a conception of reality as possible, a conception wherein the greatest fulness of data shall be combined with the greatest simplicity of conception. The effort of consciousness seems to be to combine the greatest richness of content with the greatest definiteness of organization."*

The richness is got by including all the facts of sense in the scheme ; the simplicity, by deducing them out of the smallest possible number of permanent and independent primordial entities : the definite organization, by assimilating these latter to ideal objects between which relations of an inwardly rational sort obtain. What these ideal objects and rational relations are will require a separate chapter to show.† Meanwhile, enough has surely been said to justify the assertion made above that no general offhand answer can be given as to which objects mankind shall choose as its realities. The fight is still under way. Our minds are yet chaotic ; and at best we make a mixture and

---

* J. Royce, The Religious Aspect of Philosophy (Boston, 1885), pp. 317–57.

† Chapter XXVIII.

a compromise, as we yield to the claim of this interest or that, and follow first one and then another principle in turn. It is undeniably true that materialistic, or so-called 'scientific,' conceptions of the universe have so far gratified the purely intellectual interests more than the mere sentimental conceptions have. But, on the other hand, as already remarked, they leave the emotional and active interests cold. *The perfect object of belief would be a God or 'Soul of the World,' represented both optimistically and moralistically (if such a combination could be), and withal so definitely conceived as to show us why our phenomenal experiences should be sent to us by Him in just the very way in which they come.* All Science and all History would thus be accounted for in the deepest and simplest fashion. The very room in which I sit, its sensible walls and floor, and the feeling the air and fire within it give me, no less than the 'scientific' conceptions which I am urged to frame concerning the mode of existence of all these phenomena when my back is turned, would then all be corroborated, not de-realized, by the ultimate principle of my belief. The World-soul sends me just those phenomena in order that I may react upon them; and among the reactions is the intellectual one of spinning these conceptions. What is beyond the crude experiences is not an *alternative* to them, but something that *means* them for me here and now. It is safe to say that, if ever such a system is satisfactorily excogitated, mankind will drop all other systems and cling to that one alone as real. Meanwhile the other systems coexist with the attempts at that one, and, all being alike fragmentary, each has its little audience and day.

I have now, I trust, shown sufficiently what the psychologic sources of the sense of reality are. Certain postulates are given in our nature; and whatever satisfies those postulates is treated as if real.* I might therefore finish the

---

* Prof. Royce puts this well in discussing idealism and the reality of an 'external' world. "If the history of popular speculation on these topics could be written, how much of cowardice and shuffling would be found in the behavior of the natural mind before the question, 'How dost thou know of an external reality.' Instead of simply and plainly answering: 'I mean by the external world in the first place something that I accept

chapter here, were it not that a few additional words will set the truth in a still clearer light.

DOUBT.

There is hardly a common man who (if consulted) would not say that things come to us in the first instance *as ideas;* and that if we take them for realities, it is because we *add something to them,* namely, the predicate of having also '*real existence outside of our thought.*' This notion that a higher faculty than the mere *having* of a conscious content is needed to make us know anything real by its means has pervaded psychology from the earliest times, and is the tradition of Scholasticism, Kantism, and Common-sense. Just as sensations must come as inward affections and then be 'extradited;' as objects of memory must appear at first as presently unrealities, and subsequently be 'projected' backwards as past realities; so conceptions must be *entia rationis* till a higher faculty uses them as windows to look beyond the ego, into the real *extra*-mental world;—so runs the orthodox and popular account.

And there is no question that this is a true account of the way in which many of our later beliefs come to pass. The logical distinction between the bare thought of an object and belief in the object's reality is often a chronological distinction as well. The having and the crediting of an

---

or demand, that I posit, postulate, actively construct on the basis of sense-data,' the natural man gives us all kinds of vague compromise answers. . . . Where shall these endless turnings and twistings have an end? . . . . . All these lesser motives are appealed to, and the one ultimate motive is neglected. The ultimate motive with the man of every-day life is the *will to have an external world.* Whatever consciousness contains, reason will persist in spontaneously adding the thought: 'But there *shall be* something beyond this.' . . . The popular assurance of an external world is the *fixed determination to make one,* now and henceforth." (Religious Aspect of Philosophy, p. 304—the italics are my own.) This immixture of the will appears most flagrantly in the fact that although external matter is doubted commonly enough, minds external to our own are never doubted. We need them too much, are too essentially social to dispense with them. Semblances of matter may suffice to react upon, but not semblances of communing souls. A psychic solipsism is too hideous a mockery of our wants, and, so far as I know, has never been seriously entertained.— Chapters IX and X of Prof. Royce's work are on the whole the clearest account of the psychology of belief with which I am acquainted.

idea do not always coalesce; for often we first suppose and
then believe; first play with the notion, frame the hypothesis, and then affirm the existence, of an object of thought.
And we are quite conscious of the succession of the two
mental acts. But these cases are none of them *primitive*
cases. They only occur in minds long schooled to doubt
by the contradictions of experience. *The primitive impulse
is to affirm immediately the reality of all that is conceived.**
When we do doubt, however, in what does the subsequent
resolution of the doubt consist? It either consists in a
purely verbal performance, the coupling of the adjectives
'real' or 'outwardly existing' (as predicates) to the thing
originally conceived (as subject); or it consists in the perception in the given case of *that for which these adjectives*, abstracted from other similar concrete cases, *stand*. But what
these adjectives stand for, we now know well. They stand
for certain relations (immediate, or through intermediaries)
to ourselves. Whatever concrete objects have hitherto stood
in those relations have been for us 'real,' 'outwardly existing.' So that when we now abstractly admit a thing to be
'real' (without perhaps going through any definite percep-

---

* "The leading fact in Belief, according to my view of it, is our Primitive Credulity. We begin by believing everything; whatever is, is true.
. . . The animal born in the morning of a summer day proceeds upon the
fact of daylight; assumes the perpetuity of that fact. Whatever it is
disposed to do, it does without misgivings. If in the morning it began a
round of operations continuing for hours, under the full benefit of daylight, it would unhesitatingly begin the same round in the evening. Its
state of mind is practically one of unbounded confidence; but, as yet, it
does not understand what confidence means.

"The pristine assurance is soon met by checks; a disagreeable experience
leading to new insight. To be thwarted and opposed is one of our earliest
and most frequent pains. It develops the sense of a distinction between
free and obstructed impulses; the unconsciousness of an open way is exchanged for consciousness; we are now said properly to believe in what
has never been contradicted, as we disbelieve in what has been contradicted.
We believe that, after the dawn of day, there is before us a continuance
of light; we do not believe that this light is to continue forever.

"Thus, the vital circumstance in belief is never to be contradicted—never
to lose *prestige*. The number of repetitions counts for little in the process:
we are as much convinced after ten as after fifty; we are more convinced
by ten unbroken than by fifty for and one against." (Bain: The Emotions
and the Will, pp. 511, 512.)

tion of its relations), it is as if we said " it belongs in the same world with those other objects." Naturally enough, we have hourly opportunities for this summary process of belief. All remote objects in space or time are believed in this way. When I believe that some prehistoric savage chipped this flint, for example, the reality of the savage and of his act makes no direct appeal either to my sensation, emotion, or volition. What I mean by my belief in it is simply my dim sense of a *continuity* between the long dead savage and his doings and the present world of which the flint forms part. It is pre-eminently a case for applying our doctrine of the 'fringe' (see Vol I. p. 258). When I think the savage with one fringe of relationship, I believe in him; when I think him without that fringe, or with another one (as, e.g., if I should class him with 'scientific vagaries' in general), I disbelieve him. The word 'real' itself is, in short, a fringe.

RELATIONS OF BELIEF AND WILL.

We shall see in Chapter XXV that will consists in nothing but a manner of attending to certain objects, or consenting to their stable presence before the mind. The objects, in the case of will, are those whose existence depends on our thought, movements of our own body for example, or facts which such movements executed in future may make real. Objects of belief, on the contrary, are those which do not change according as we think regarding them. I *will* to get up early to-morrow morning; I *believe* that I got up late yesterday morning; I *will* that my foreign bookseller in Boston shall procure me a German book and write to him to that effect. I *believe* that he will make me pay three dollars for it when it comes, etc. Now the important thing to notice is that this difference between the objects of will and belief is entirely immaterial, as far as the relation of the mind to them goes. All that the mind does is in both cases the same; it looks at the object and consents to its existence, espouses it, says 'it shall be my reality.' It turns to it, in short, in the interested active emotional way. The rest is done by nature, which in some cases *makes* the objects real which we think of in this

manner, and in other cases does not. Nature cannot change
the past to suit our thinking. She cannot change the stars
or the winds; but she *does* change our bodies to suit our
thinking, and through their instrumentality changes much
besides; so the great practical distinction between objects
which we may will or unwill, and objects which we can merely
believe or disbelieve, grows up, and is of course one of the
most important distinctions in the world. Its roots, however, do not lie in psychology, but in physiology; as the
chapter on Volition will abundantly make plain. *Will and
Belief, in short, meaning a certain relation between objects and
the Self, are two names for one and the same* PSYCHOLOGICAL
phenomenon. All the questions which arise concerning one
are questions which arise concerning the other. The causes
and conditions of the peculiar relation must be the same
in both. The free-will question arises as regards belief.
If our wills are indeterminate, so must our beliefs be, etc.
The first act of free-will, in short, would naturally be to
believe in free-will, etc. In Chapter XXVI, I shall mention
this again.

A practical observation may end this chapter. If belief
consists in an emotional reaction of the entire man on an
object, how *can* we believe at will? We cannot control our
emotions. Truly enough, a man cannot believe at will
abruptly. Nature sometimes, and indeed not very infre-
quently, produces instantaneous conversions for us. She
suddenly puts us in an active connection with objects of
which she had till then left us cold. "I realize for the first
time," we then say, "what that means!" This happens often
with moral propositions. We have often heard them; but
now they shoot into our lives; they move us; we feel their
living force. Such instantaneous beliefs are truly enough not
to be achieved by will. But *gradually* our will can lead us to
the same results by a very simple method: *we need only
in cold blood* ACT *as if the thing in question were real, and keep
acting as if it were real, and it will infallibly end by growing
into such a connection with our life that it will become real.*
It will become so knit with habit and emotion that our
interests in it will be those which characterize belief.

Those to whom 'God' and 'Duty' are now mere names can make them much more than that, if they make a little sacrifice to them every day. But all this is so well known in moral and religious education that I need say no more.*

---

* *Literature.* D. Hume: Treatise on Human Nature, part III. §§ VII–x. A. Bain: Emotions and Will, chapter on Belief (also pp. 20 ff). J. Sully: Sensation and Intuition, essay IV. J. Mill: Analysis of Human Mind, chapter XI. Ch. Renouvier: Psychologie Rationnelle, vol. II. pt. II; and Esquisse d'une Classification systématique des Doctrines Philosophiques, part VI. J. H. Newman: The Grammar of Assent. J. Venn: Some Characteristics of Belief. V. Brochard: De l'Erreur, part II. chap. VI, IX; and Revue Philosophique, XXVIII. 1. E. Rabier: Psychologie, chap XXI, Appendix. Ollé Laprune: La Certitude Morale (1881). G. F. Stout: On Genesis of Cognition of Physical Reality, in 'Mind,' Jan. 1890. J. Pikler: The Psychology of the Belief in Objective Existence (London, 1890).—Mill says that we believe present sensations; and makes our belief in all other things a matter of *association* with these. So far so good; but as he makes no mention of emotional or volitional reaction, Bain rightly charges him with treating belief as a purely intellectual state. For Bain belief is rather an incident of our active life. When a thing is such as to make us *act* on it, then we believe it, according to Bain. "But how about past things, or remote things, upon which no reaction of ours is possible? And how about belief in things which *check* action?" says Sully; who considers that we believe a thing only when "the idea of it has an inherent tendency to approximate in character and intensity to a sensation." It is obvious that each of these authors emphasizes a true aspect of the question. My own account has sought to be more complete, sensation, association, and active reaction all being acknowledged to be concerned. The most compendious possible formula perhaps would be that *our belief and attention* are the same fact. For the moment, what we attend to is reality; Attention is a motor reaction; and we are so made that sensations force attention from us. On Belief and Conduct see an article by Leslie Stephen, Fortnightly Review, July 1888.

A set of facts have been recently brought to my attention which I hardly know how to treat, so I say a word about them in this footnote. I refer to a type of experience which has frequently found a place amongst the 'Yes' answers to the 'Census of Hallucinations,' and which is generally described by those who report it as an 'impression of the presence' of someone near them, although no sensation either of sight, hearing, or touch is involved. From the way in which this experience is spoken of by those who have had it, it would appear to be an extremely definite and positive state of mind, coupled with a belief in the reality of its object quite as strong as any direct sensation ever gives. And yet *no* sensation seems to be connected with it at all. Sometimes the person whose nearness is thus impressed is a known person, dead or living, sometimes an unknown one. His attitude and situation are often very definitely impressed, and so, sometimes (though not by way of hearing), are words which he wishes to say. The phenomenon would seem to be due to a pure *conception* becoming saturated with the sort of stinging urgency which ordinarily only sensations bring. But I cannot yet persuade myself that the urgency in question consists in concomitant emotional and motor impulses. The ' impression ' may come quite suddenly and depart quickly; it may carry no emotional suggestions, and wake no motor consequences beyond those involved in attending to it. Altogether, the matter is somewhat paradoxical, and no conclusion can be come to until more definite data are obtained.

Perhaps the most curious case of the sort which I have received is the following. The subject of the observation, Mr. P., is an exceptionally intelligent witness, though the words of the narrative are his wife's.

"Mr. P. has all his life been the occasional subject of rather singular delusions or impressions of various kinds. If I had belief in the existence of latent or embryo faculties, other than the five senses, I should explain them on that ground. Being totally blind, his other perceptions are abnormally keen and developed, and given the existence of a rudimentary sixth sense, it would be only natural that this also should be more acute in him than in others. One of the most interesting of his experiences in this line was the frequent apparition of a corpse some years ago, which may be worth the attention of your Committee on that subject. At the time Mr. P. had a music-room in Boston on Beacon Street, where he used to do severe and protracted practice with little interruption. Now, all one season it was a very familiar occurrence with him while in the midst of work to feel a cold draft of air suddenly upon his face, with a prickling sensation at the roots of his hair, when he would turn from the piano, and a figure which he knew to be dead would come sliding under the crack of the door from without, flattening itself to squeeze through and rounding out again to the human form. It was of a middle-aged man, and drew itself along the carpet on hands and knees, but with head thrown back till it reached the sofa, upon which it stretched itself. It remained some moments, but vanished always if Mr. P. spoke or made a decided movement. The most singular point in the occurrence was its frequent repetition. He might expect it on any day between two and four o'clock, and it came always heralded by the same sudden cold shiver, and was invariably the same figure which went through the same movements. He afterwards traced the whole experience to strong tea. He was in the habit of taking cold tea, which always stimulates him, for lunch, and on giving up this practice he never saw this or any other apparition again. However, even allowing, as is doubtless true, that the event was a delusion of nerves first fatigued by overwork and then excited by this stimulant, there is one point which is still wholly inexplicable and highly interesting to me. Mr. P. has no memory whatever of sight, nor conception of it. It is impossible for him to form any idea of what we mean by light or color, consequently he has no cognizance of any object which does not reach his sense of hearing or of touch, though these are so acute as to give a contrary impression sometimes to other people. When he becomes aware of the presence of a person or an object, by means which seem mysterious to outsiders, he can always trace it naturally and legitimately to slight echoes, perceptible only to his keen ears, or to differences in atmospheric pressure, perceptible only to his acute nerves of touch; but with the apparition described, for the only time in his experience, he was aware of presence, size, and appearance, without the use of either of these mediums. The figure never produced the least sound nor came within a number of feet of his person, yet he knew that it was a man, that it moved, and in what direction, even that it wore a full beard, which, like the thick curly hair, was partially gray; also that it was dressed in the style of suit known as 'pepper and salt.' These points were all perfectly distinct and invariable each time. If asked how he perceived them, he will answer he cannot tell, he simply knew it, and so strongly and so distinctly that it is impossible to shake his opinion as to the exact details of the man's appearance. It would seem that in this delusion of the senses he really *saw*, as he has never done in the actual experiences of life, except in the first two years of childhood."

On cross-examining Mr. P., I could not make out that there was anything like visual imagination involved, although he was quite unable to describe in just what terms the false perception was carried on. It seemed to be more like an intensely definite *conception* than anything else, a conception to which the feeling of *present reality* was attached, but in no such shape as easily to fall under the heads laid down in my text.

CHAPTER XXII.*

WE talk of man being the rational animal; and the traditional intellectualist philosophy has always made a great point of treating the brutes as wholly irrational creatures. Nevertheless, it is by no means easy to decide just what is meant by reason, or how the peculiar thinking process called reasoning differs from other thought-sequences which may lead to similar results.

Much of our thinking consists of trains of images suggested one by another, of a sort of spontaneous revery of which it seems likely enough that the higher brutes should be capable. This sort of thinking leads nevertheless to rational conclusions, both practical and theoretical. The links between the terms are either 'contiguity' or 'similarity,' and with a mixture of both these things we can hardly be very incoherent. As a rule, in this sort of irresponsible thinking, the terms which fall to be coupled together are empirical concretes, not abstractions. A sunset may call up the vessel's deck from which I saw one last summer, the companions of my voyage, my arrival into port, etc.; or it may make me think of solar myths, of Hercules' and Hector's funeral pyres, of Homer and whether he could write, of the Greek alphabet, etc. If habitual contiguities predominate, we have a prosaic mind; if rare contiguities, or similarities, have free play, we call the person fanciful, poetic, or witty. But the thought as a rule is of matters taken in their entirety. Having been thinking of one, we find later that we are thinking of another, to which we have been lifted along, we hardly know how. If an abstract

---

* The substance of this chapter, and a good many pages of the text, originally appeared in an article entitled 'Brute and Human Intellect,' in the Journal of Speculative Philosophy for July 1878 (vol. XII. p. 236).

quality figures in the procession, it arrests our attention but for a moment, and fades into something else ; and is never very abstract. Thus, in thinking of the sun-myths, we may have a gleam of admiration at the gracefulness of the primitive human mind, or a moment of disgust at the narrowness of modern interpreters. But, in the main, we think less of qualities than of whole things, real or possible, just as we may experience them.

The upshot of it may be that we are reminded of some practical duty: we write a letter to a friend abroad, or we take down the lexicon and study our Greek lesson. Our thought is rational, and leads to a rational act, but it can hardly be called reasoning in a strict sense of the term.

There are other shorter flights of thought, single couplings of terms which suggest one another by association, which approach more to what would commonly be classed as acts of reasoning proper. Those are where a present sign suggests an unseen, distant, or future reality. Where the sign and what it suggests are both concretes which have been coupled together on previous occasions, the inference is common to both brutes and men, being really nothing more than association by contiguity. A and B, dinner-bell and dinner, have been experienced in immediate succession. Hence A no sooner falls upon the sense than B is anticipated, and steps are taken to meet it. The whole education of our domestic beasts, all the cunning added by age and experience to wild ones, and the greater part of our human knowingness consists in the ability to make a mass of inferences of this simplest sort. Our 'perceptions,' or recognitions of what objects are before us, are inferences of this kind. We feel a patch of color, and we say 'a distant house,' a whiff of odor crosses us, and we say 'a skunk,' a faint sound is heard, and we call it 'a railroad train.' Examples are needless ; for such inferences of sensations not presented form the staple and tissue of our perceptive life, and our Chapter XIX was full of them, illusory or veracious. They have been called *unconscious inferences*. Certainly we are commonly unconscious that we are inferring at all. The sign and the signified melt into what seems to us the object of a single pulse of thought. *Immediate inferences* would be a good name for these simple acts of reasoning requiring but two terms,* were it not that formal logic has already appropriated the expression for a more technical use.

'RECEPTS.'

In these first and simplest inferences the conclusion may follow so continuously upon the 'sign' that the latter is not discriminated or attended to as a separate object by the mind. Even now we can seldom define the optical signs which lead us to infer the shapes and distances of the objects which by their aid we so unhesitatingly perceive. The objects, too, when thus inferred, are *general* objects. The dog crossing a scent thinks of a deer in general, or of another dog in general, not of a particular deer or dog. To these most primitive abstract objects Dr. G. J. Romanes gives the name of *recepts* or *generic* ideas, to distinguish them from concepts and general ideas properly so called.†
They are not analyzed or defined, but only imagined.

" It requires but a slight analysis of our ordinary mental processes to prove that all our simpler ideas are group-arrangements which have been formed spontaneously or without any of that intentionally comparing, sifting, and combining process which is required in the higher departments of ideational activity. The comparing, sifting, and combining is here done, as it were, *for* the conscious agent, not *by* him. Recepts are received ; it is only concepts that require to be conceived. . . . If I am crossing a street and hear behind me a sudden shout, I do not require to wait in order to predicate to myself that there is probably a hansom-cab just about to run me down : a cry of this kind, and in those circumstances, is so intimately associated in my mind with its

---

* I see no need of assuming more than two terms in this sort of reasoning—first, the sign, and second, the thing inferred from it. Either may be complex, but essentially it is but A calling up B, and no middle term is involved. M. Binet, in his most intelligent little book, La Psychologie du Raisonnement, maintains that there are three terms. The present sensation or sign must, according to him, first evoke from the past an image which resembles it and fuses with it, and the things suggested or inferred are always the contiguous associates of this intermediate image, and not of the immediate sensation. The reader of Chapter XIX will see why I do not believe in the ' image ' in question as a distinct psychic fact.

† Mental Evolution in Man (1889), chapters III and IV. See especially pp. 68–80, and later 353, 396.

purpose, that the idea which it arouses need not rise above the level of a recept ; and the adaptive movements on my part which that idea immediately prompts are performed without any intelligent reflection. Yet, on the other hand, they are neither reflex actions nor instinctive actions ; they are what may be termed receptual actions, or actions depending on recepts." *

"How far can this kind of unnamed or non-conceptional ideation extend ?" Dr. Romanes asks ; and answers by a variety of examples taken from the life of brutes, for which I must refer to his book. One or two of them, however, I will quote :

"Houzeau writes that while crossing a wide and arid plain in Texas, his two dogs suffered greatly from thirst, and that between thirty and forty times they rushed down the hollows to search for water. The hollows were not valleys, and there were no trees in them, or any other difference in the vegetation ; and as they were absolutely dry, there could have been no smell of damp earth. The dogs behaved as if they knew that a dip in the ground offered them the best chance of finding water, and Houzeau has often witnessed the same behavior in other animals. . . .

"Mr. Darwin writes : 'When I say to my terrier in an eager voice (and I have made the trial many times), "Hi! hi! where is it ?" she at once takes it as a sign that something is to be hunted, and generally first looks quickly all round, and then rushes into the nearest thicket, to scout for any game, but finding nothing she looks up into any neighboring tree for a squirrel. Now do not these actions clearly show that she had in her mind a general idea, or concept, that some animal is to be discovered and hunted ?'" †

They certainly show this. But the idea in question is of an object *about* which nothing farther may be articulately known. The thought of it prompts to activity, but to no theoretic consequence. Similarly in the following example :

"Water-fowl adopt a somewhat different mode of alighting upon land, or even upon ice, from that which they adopt when alighting upon water; and those kinds which dive from a height (such as terns and gannets) never do so upon land or upon ice. These facts prove that the animals have one recept answering to a solid surface, and another answering to a fluid. Similarly a man will not dive from a height over hard ground or over ice, nor will he jump into water in the same way as he jumps upon dry land. In other words, like the water-fowl

---

* *Loc. cit.* p. 50. † P. 52.

he has two distinct recepts, one of which answers to solid ground, and the other to an unresisting fluid. But unlike the water-fowl he is able to bestow upon each of these receps a name, and thus to raise them both to the level of concepts. So far as the practical purposes of loco-motion are concerned, it is of course immaterial whether or not he thus raises his recepts into concepts ; but . . . for many other purposes it is of the highest importance that he is able to do this." *

IN REASONING, WE PICK OUT ESSENTIAL QUALITIES.

The chief of these purposes is *predication*, a theoretic function which, though it always leads eventually to some kind of action, yet tends as often as not to inhibit the imme-diate motor response to which the simple inferences of which we have been speaking give rise. In reasoning, A may suggest B ; but B, instead of being an idea which is simply *obeyed* by us, is an idea which suggests the distinct additional idea C. And where the train of suggestion is one of reasoning distinctively so called as contrasted with mere revery or ' associative ' sequence, the ideas bear certain inward relations to each other which we must proceed to examine with some care.

The result C yielded by a true act of reasoning is apt to be a thing voluntarily *sought*, such as the means to a proposed end, the ground for an observed effect, or the effect of an assumed cause. All these results may be thought of as concrete things, but they are *not suggested im-mediately by other concrete things*, as in the trains of simply as-sociative thought. They are linked to the concretes which precede them by intermediate steps, and these steps are formed by *general characters* articulately denoted and ex-pressly analyzed out. A thing inferred by reasoning need neither have been an habitual associate of the datum from which we infer it, nor need it be similar to it. It may be a thing entirely unknown to our previous experience, some-thing which no simple association of concretes could ever have evoked. The great difference, in fact, between that simpler kind of rational thinking which consists in the con-crete objects of past experience merely suggesting each other, and reasoning distinctively so called, is this, that

---

* *Loc. cit.* p. 74.

whilst the empirical thinking is only reproductive, reasoning is productive. An empirical, or 'rule-of-thumb,' thinker can deduce nothing from data with whose behavior and associates in the concrete he is unfamiliar. But put a reasoner amongst a set of concrete objects which he has neither seen nor heard of before, and with a little time, if he is a good reasoner, he will make such inferences from them as will quite atone for his ignorance. Reasoning helps us out of unprecedented situations—situations for which all our common associative wisdom, all the 'education' which we share in common with the beasts, leaves us without resource.

Let us make this ability to deal with NOVEL *data the technical differentia of reasoning.* This will sufficiently mark it out from common associative thinking, and will immediately enable us to say just what peculiarity it contains.

It contains analysis and abstraction. Whereas the merely empirical thinker stares at a fact in its entirety, and remains helpless, òr gets 'stuck,' if it suggests no concomitant or similar, the reasoner breaks it up and notices some one of its separate attributes. This attribute he takes to be the essential part of the whole fact before him. This attribute has properties or consequences which the fact until then was not known to have, but which, now that it is noticed to contain the attribute, it must have.

Call the fact or concrete datum S;
    the essential attribute M;
    the attribute's property P.

Then the reasoned inference of P from S cannot be made without M's intermediation. The 'essence' M is thus that third or middle term in the reasoning which a moment ago was pronounced essential. *For his original concrete S the reasoner substitutes its abstract property, M.* What is true of M, what is coupled with M, then holds true of S, is coupled with S. As M is properly one of the *parts* of the entire S, *reasoning may then be very well defined as the substitution of parts and their implications or consequences for wholes.* And the art of the reasoner will consist of two stages:

First, *sagacity*,* or the ability to discover what part, M, lies embedded in the whole S which is before him ;

Second, *learning*, or the ability to recall promptly M's consequences, concomitants, or implications.†

If we glance at the ordinary syllogism—

M is P ;
S is M ;
S is P

---

* J. Locke, Essay conc. Hum. Understanding, bk. iv. chap. ii. § 8.

† To be sagacious is to be a good observer. J. S. Mill has a passage which is so much in the spirit of the text that I cannot forbear to quote it. "The observer is not he who merely sees the thing which is before his eyes, but he who sees what parts that thing is composed of. To do this well is a rare talent. One person, from inattention, or attending only in the wrong place, overlooks half of what he sees ; another sets down much more than he sees, confounding it with what he imagines, or with what he infers; another takes note of the *kind* of all the circumstances, but being inexpert in estimating their degree, leaves the quantity of each vague and uncertain ; another sees indeed the whole, but makes such an awkward division of it into parts, throwing things into one mass which require to be separated, and separating others which might more conveniently be considered as one, that the result is much the same, sometimes even worse, than if no analysis had been attempted at all. It would be possible to point out what qualities of mind, and modes of mental culture, fit a person for being a good observer : that, however, is a question not of Logic, but of the Theory of Education, in the most enlarged sense of the term. There is not properly an Art of Observing. There may be rules for observing. But these, like rules for inventing, are properly instructions for the preparation of one's own mind ; for putting it into the state in which it will be most fitted to observe, or most likely to invent. They are, therefore, essentially rules of self-education, which is a different thing from Logic. They do not teach how to do the thing, but how to make ourselves capable of doing it. They are an art of strengthening the limbs, not an art of using them. The extent and minuteness of observation which may be requisite, and the degree of decomposition to which it may be necessary to carry the mental analysis, depend on the particular purpose in view. To ascertain the state of the whole universe at any particular moment is impossible, but would also be useless. In making chemical experiments, we do not think it necessary to note the position of the planets ; because experience has shown, as a very superficial experience is sufficient to show, that in such cases that circumstance is not material to the result : and accordingly, in the ages when man believed in the occult influences of the heavenly bodies, it might have been unphilosophical to omit ascertaining the precise condition of those bodies at the moment of the experiment." (Logic, bk. iii. chap. vii. § 1. Cf. also bk. iv. chap. ii.)

—we see that the second or minor premise, the 'subsumption' as it is sometimes called, is the one requiring the sagacity; the first or major the one requiring the fertility, or fulness of learning. Usually the learning is more apt to be ready than the sagacity, the ability to seize fresh aspects in concrete things, being rarer than the ability to learn old rules; so that, in most actual cases of reasoning, the minor premise, or the way of conceiving the subject, is the one that makes the novel step in thought. This is, to be sure, not always the case; for the fact that M carries P with it may also be unfamiliar and now formulated for the first time.

The perception that S is M is a *mode of conceiving S.* The statement that M is P is an *abstract or general proposition.* A word about both is necessary.

WHAT IS MEANT BY A MODE OF CONCEIVING.

When we conceive of S merely as M (of vermilion merely as a mercury-compound, for example), we neglect all the other attributes which it may have, and attend exclusively to this one. We mutilate the fulness of S's reality. Every reality has an infinity of aspects or properties. Even so simple a fact as a line which you trace in the air may be considered in respect to its form, its length, its direction, and its location. When we reach more complex facts, the number of ways in which we may regard them is literally endless. Vermilion is not only a mercury-compound, it is vividly red, heavy, and expensive, it comes from China, and so on, *in infinitum.* All objects are well-springs of properties, which are only little by little developed to our knowledge, and it is truly said that to know one thing thoroughly would be to know the whole universe. Mediately or immediately, that one thing is related to everything else; and to know *all* about it, all its relations need be known. But each relation forms one of its attributes, one angle by which some one may conceive it, and while so conceiving it may ignore the rest of it. A man is such a complex fact. But out of the complexity all that an army commissary picks out as important for his purposes is his property of eating so many pounds a day; the general, of marching so many miles; the chair-maker, of having such a shape; the orator, of responding to such and such feelings; the theatre-manager, of being willing to pay just such a price, and no more, for an evening's amusement. Each of these persons singles out the particular side of the entire man which has a bearing on *his* concerns, and not till this side is distinctly and separately conceived can the proper practical conclusions *for that reasoner* be drawn; and when they are drawn the man's other attributes may be ignored.

All ways of conceiving a concrete fact, if they are true ways at all, are equally true ways. *There is no property* ABSOLUTELY *essential to any one thing.* The same property which figures as the essence of a thing on one occasion becomes a very inessential feature upon another. Now that I am writing, it is essential that I conceive my paper as a surface for inscription. If I failed to do that, I should have to stop my work. But if I wished to light a fire, and no other materials were by, the essential way of conceiving the paper would be as combustible material; and I need then have no thought of any of its other destinations. It is really *all* that it is: a combustible, a writing surface, a thin thing, a hydrocarbonaceous thing, a thing eight inches one way and ten another, a thing just one furlong east of a certain stone in my neighbor's field, an American thing, etc., etc., *ad infinitum.* Whichever one of these aspects of its being I temporarily class it under, makes me unjust to the other aspects. But as I always am classing it under one aspect or another, I am always unjust, always partial, always exclusive. My excuse is necessity—the necessity which my finite and practical nature lays upon me. My thinking is first and last and always for the sake of my doing, and I can only do one thing at a time. A God, who is supposed to drive the whole universe abreast, may also be supposed, without detriment to his activity, to see all parts of it at once and without emphasis. But were our human attention so to disperse itself we should simply stare vacantly at things at large and forfeit our opportunity of doing any particular act. Mr. Warner, in his Adirondack story, shot a bear by aiming, not at his eye or heart, but 'at him gen-

erally.' But we cannot aim 'generally' at the universe ;
or if we do, we miss our game. Our scope is narrow, and
we must attack things piecemeal, ignoring the solid fulness
in which the elements of Nature exist, and stringing one
after another of them together in a serial way, to suit our
little interests as they change from hour to hour. In this,
the partiality of one moment is partly atoned for by the
different sort of partiality of the next. To me now, writing
these words, emphasis and selection seem to be the essence
of the human mind. In other chapters other qualities have
seemed, and will again seem, more important parts of psy-
chology. |

Men are so ingrainedly partial that, for common-sense
and scholasticism (which is only common-sense grown articulate), the notion that there is no one quality genuinely,
absolutely, and exclusively essential to anything is almost
unthinkable. "A thing's essence makes it *what* it is. Without an exclusive essence it would be nothing in particular,
would be quite nameless, we could not say it was this
rather than that. What you write on, for example,—why
talk of its being combustible, rectangular, and the like,
when you know that these are mere accidents, and that
what it really is, and was made to be, is just *paper* and
nothing else?" The reader is pretty sure to make some
such comment as this. But he is himself merely insisting
on an aspect of the thing which suits his own petty purpose,
that of *naming* the thing ; or else on an aspect which suits
the manufacturer's purpose, that of *producing an article
for which there is a vulgar demand.* Meanwhile the reality
overflows these purposes at every pore. Our usual purpose
with it, our commonest title for it, and the properties which
this title suggests, have in reality nothing sacramental.
They characterize *us* more than they characterize the thing.
But we are so stuck in our prejudices, so petrified intellectually, that to our vulgarest names, with their suggestions,
we ascribe an eternal and exclusive worth. The thing must
be, essentially, what the vulgarest name connotes ; what
less usual names connote, it can be only in an 'accidental'
and relatively unreal sense.*

---

* Readers brought up on Popular Science may think that the molecular

Locke undermined the fallacy. But none of his successors, so far as I know, have radically escaped it, or seen that *the only meaning of essence is teleological, and that classification and conception are purely teleological weapons of the mind.* The essence of a thing is that one of its properties which is so *important for my interests* that in comparison with it I may neglect the rest. Amongst those other things which have this important property I class it, after this property I name it, as a thing endowed with this property I conceive it; and whilst so classing, naming, and conceiving it, all other truth about it becomes to me as naught.* The properties which are important vary from man to man and from hour to hour.† Hence divers appellations and

---

structure of things is their real essence in an absolute sense, and that water is H–O–H more deeply and truly than it is a solvent of sugar or a slaker of thirst. Not a whit! It is *all* of these things with equal reality, and the only reason why *for the chemist* it is H–O–H primarily, and only secondarily the other things, is that *for his purpose of deduction and compendious definition* the H–O–H aspect of it is the more useful one to bear in mind.

* "We find that we take for granted irresistibly that each kind [of thing] has some character which distinguishes it from other classes. . . . What is the foundation of this postulate? What is the ground of this assumption that there must exist a definition which we have never seen, and which perhaps no one has seen in a satisfactory form? . . . . I reply that our conviction that there must needs be characteristic marks by which things can be defined in words is founded upon the assumption of *the necessary possibility of reasoning.*" (W. Whewell : Hist. of Scientific Ideas, bk. VIII. chap I, § 9.)

† I may quote a passage from an article entitled 'The Sentiment of Rationality,' published in vol. IV of Mind, 1879 : "What is a *conception?* It is a *teleological instrument.* It is a partial aspect of a thing which *for our purpose* we regard as its essential aspect, as the representative of the entire thing. In comparison with this aspect, whatever other properties and qualities the thing may have are unimportant accidents which we may without blame ignore. But the essence, the ground of conception, varies with the end we have in view. A substance like oil has as many different essences as it has uses to different individuals. One man conceives it as a combustible, another as a lubricator, another as a food ; the chemist thinks of it as a hydrocarbon ; the furniture-maker as a darkener of wood ; the speculator as a commodity whose market-price to-day is this and to-morrow that. The soap-boiler, the physicist, the clothes-scourer severally ascribe to it other essences in relation to their needs. Ueberweg's doctrine that the essential quality of a thing is the

conceptions for the same thing. But many objects of daily use—as paper, ink, butter, horse-car—have properties of such constant unwavering importance, and have such stereotyped names, that we end by believing that to conceive them in those ways is to conceive them in the only true way. Those are no truer ways of conceiving them than any others; they are only more important ways, more frequently serviceable ways.*

---

quality of most *worth* is strictly true; but Ueberweg has failed to note that the worth is wholly relative to the temporary interests of the conceiver. And, even, when his interest is distinctly defined in his own mind, the discrimination of the quality in the object which has the closest connection with it is a thing which no rules can teach. The only *a priori* advice that can be given to a man embarking on life with a certain purpose is the somewhat barren counsel: Be sure that in the circumstances that meet you, you attend to the *right* ones for your purpose. To pick out the right ones is the measure of the man. 'Millions,' says Hartmann, 'stare at the phenomenon before a *genialer Kopf* pounces on the concept.' The genius is simply he to whom, when he opens his eyes upon the world, the 'right' characters are the prominent ones. The fool is he who, with the same purposes as the genius, infallibly gets his attention tangled amid the accidents."

* Only if one of our purposes were itself truer than another, could one of our conceptions become the truer conception. To be a truer purpose, however, our purpose must conform more to some absolute standard of purpose in things to which our purposes ought to conform. This shows that the whole doctrine of essential characters is intimately bound up with a teleological view of the world. Materialism becomes self-contradictory when it denies teleology, and yet in the same breath calls atoms, etc., the *essential* facts. The world contains consciousness as well as atoms—and the one must be written down as just as essential as the other, in the absence of any declared purpose regarding them on the creator's part, or in the absence of any creator. As far as we ourselves go, the atoms are worth more for purposes of deduction, the consciousness for purposes of inspiration. We may fairly write the Universe in either way, thus: ATOMS-producing-consciousness; or CONSCIOUSNESS-produced-by-atoms. Atoms alone, or consciousness alone, are precisely equal mutilations of the truth. If, without believing in a God, I still continue to talk of what the world 'essentially is,' I am just as much entitled to define it as a place in which my nose itches, or as a place where at a certain corner I can get a mess of oysters for twenty cents, as to call it an evolving nebula differentiating and integrating itself. It is hard to say which of the three abstractions is the more rotten or miserable substitute for the world's concrete fulness. To conceive it merely as 'God's work' would be a similar mutilation of it, so long as we said not what God, or what kind of work. The only real truth about the world, apart from particular purposes, is the *total* truth.

So much for what is implied, when the reasoner conceives of the fact S before him as a case of which the essence is to be M. One word now as to what is involved in M's having properties, consequences, or implications, and we can go back to the study of the reasoning process again.

WHAT IS INVOLVED IN GENERAL PROPOSITIONS.

M is not a concrete, or 'self-sufficient,' as Mr. Clay would say. It is an abstract character which may exist, embedded with other characters, in many concretes. Whether it be the character of being a writing surface, of being made in America or China, of being eight inches square, or of being in a certain part of space, this is always true of it. Now we might conceive of this being a world in which all such general characters were independent of each other, so that if any one of them were found in a subject S, we never could be sure what others would be found alongside of it. On one occasion there might be P with M, on another Q, and so on. In such a world there would be no *general* sequences or coexistences, and no universal laws. Each grouping would be *sui generis;* from the experience of the past no future could be predicted; and reasoning, as we shall presently see, would be an impossibility.

But the world we live in is not one of this sort. Though many general characters seem indifferent to each other, there remain a number of them which affect constant habits of mutual concomitance or repugance. They involve or imply each other. One of them is a sign to us that the other will be found. They hunt in couples, as it were; and such a proposition as that M is P, or includes P, or precedes or accompanies P, if it prove to be true in one instance, may very likely be true in every other instance which we meet. This is, in fact, a world in which general laws obtain, in which universal propositions *are* true, and in which reasoning is therefore possible. Fortunately for us: for since we cannot handle things as wholes, but only by conceiving them through some general character which for the time we call their essence, it would be a great pity if the matter ended there, and if the general character, once picked out and in our possession, helped us to no farther advance. In

Chapter XXVIII we shall have again to consider this harmony between our reasoning faculty and the world in which
its lot is cast.*

To revert now to our symbolic representation of the
reasoning process :

$$\begin{array}{c} \text{M is P} \\ \underline{\text{S is M}} \\ \text{S is P} \end{array}$$

M is discerned and picked out for the time being to be
the essence of the concrete fact, phenomenon, or reality, S.
But M in this world of ours is inevitably conjoined with P;
so that P is the next thing that we may expect to find conjoined with the fact S. We may conclude or infer P,
through the intermediation of the M which our sagacity
began by discerning, when S came before it, to be the
essence of the case.

Now note that if P have any value or importance for us,
M was a very good character for our sagacity to pounce upon
and abstract. If, on the contrary, P were of no importance,
some other character than M would have been a better
essence for us to conceive of S by. Psychologically, as a
rule, P overshadows the process from the start. We are
seeking P, or something like P. But the bare totality of S
does not yield it to our gaze ; and casting about for some
point in S to take hold of, which will lead us to P, we hit,
if we are sagacious, upon M, because M happens to be just
the character which is knit up with P. Had we wished Q
instead of P, and were N a property of S conjoined with Q,
we ought to have ignored M, noticed N, and conceived of S
as a sort of N exclusively.

Reasoning is always for a subjective interest, to attain
some particular conclusion, or to gratify some special
curiosity. . It not only breaks up the datum placed before
it and conceives it abstractly ; it must conceive it *rightly*
too ; and conceiving it rightly means conceiving it by that
one particular abstract character which leads to the one

---

* Compare Lotze, Metaphysik, §§ 58, 67, for some instructive remarks
on ways in which the world's constitution might differ from what it actually is. Compare also Chapter XXVIII.

sort of conclusion which it is the reasoner's temporary interest to attain.*

The *results* of reasoning may be hit upon by accident.
The stereoscope was actually a result of reasoning; it is
conceivable, however, that a man playing with pictures and
mirrors might accidentally have hit upon it. Cats have been
known to open doors by pulling latches, etc. But no cat,
if the latch got out of order, could open the door again,
unless some new accident of random fumbling taught her
to associate some new total movement with the total phenomenon of the closed door. A reasoning man, however,
would open the door by first analyzing the hindrance. He
would ascertain what particular feature of the door was
wrong. The lever, e.g., does not raise the latch sufficiently
from its slot—case of insufficient elevation—raise door
bodily on hinges! Or door sticks at top by friction against
lintel—press it bodily down! Now it is obvious that a
child or an idiot might without this reasoning learn the *rule*
for opening that particular door. I remember a clock which
the maid-servant had discovered would not go unless it
were supported so as to tilt slightly forwards. She had
stumbled on this method after many weeks of groping. The
reason of the stoppage was the friction of the pendulum-
bob against the back of the clock-case, a reason which an
educated man would have analyzed out in five minutes. I

---

* Sometimes, it must be confessed, the conceiver's purpose falls short of
reasoning and the only conclusion he cares to reach is the bare naming of
the datum. "What is that?" is our first question relative to any unknown
thing. And the ease with which our curiosity is quenched as soon as we
are supplied with any sort of a name to call the object by, is ridiculous
enough. To quote from an unpublished essay by a former student of
mine, Mr. R. W. Black: "The simplest end which a thing's predicate can
serve is the satisfaction of the desire for unity itself, the mere desire that
the thing shall be the same with *something* else. Why, the other day,
when I mistook a portrait of Shakespeare for one of Hawthorne, was I not,
on psychological principles, as right as if I had correctly named it?—the
two pictures had a common essence, bald forehead, mustache, flowing
hair. Simply because the only end that could possibly be served by naming
it Hawthorne was my desire to have it so. With reference to any other end
that classification of it would not serve. And every unity, every identity,
every classification is rightly called fanciful unless it serves some other end
than the mere satisfaction, emotion, or inspiration caught by momentarily
believing in it."

have a student's lamp of which the flame vibrates most unpleasantly unless the collar which bears the chimney be raised about a sixteenth of an inch. I learned the remedy after much torment by accident, and now always keep the collar up with a small wedge. But my procedure is a mere association of two totals, diseased object and remedy. One learned in pneumatics could have named the *cause* of the disease, and thence inferred the remedy immediately. By many measurements of triangles one might find their area always equal to their height multiplied by half their base, and one might formulate an empirical law to that effect. But a reasoner saves himself all this trouble by seeing that it is the essence (*pro hac vice*) of a triangle to be the half of a parallelogram whose area is the height into the entire base. To see this he must invent additional lines; and the geometer must often draw such to get at the essential property he may require in a figure. The essence consists in some *relation of the figure to the new lines,* a relation not obvious at all until they are put in. The geometer's sagacity lies in the invention of the new lines.

THUS, THERE ARE TWO GREAT POINTS IN REASONING:

First, an extracted character is taken as equivalent to the entire datum from which it comes; and,

Second, the character thus taken suggests a certain consequence more obviously than it was suggested by the total datum as it originally came. Take them again, successively.

1. Suppose I say, when offered a piece of cloth, " I won't buy that; it looks as if it would fade," meaning merely that something about it suggests the idea of fading to my mind,—my judgment, though possibly correct, is not reasoned, but purely empirical; but, if I can say that into the color there enters a certain dye which I know to be chemically unstable, and that *therefore* the color will fade, my judgment is reasoned. The notion of the dye which is one of the parts of the cloth, is the connecting link between the latter and the notion of fading. So, again, an uneducated man will expect from past experience to see a piece of ice melt if placed near the fire, and the tip of his finger look coarse

if he views it through a convex glass. In neither of these
cases could the result be anticipated without full previous
acquaintance with the entire phenomenon. It is not a
result of reasoning.

But a man who should conceive heat as a mode of
motion, and liquefaction as identical with increased motion
of molecules; who should know that curved surfaces bend
light-rays in special ways, and that the apparent size of
anything is connected with the amount of the 'bend' of its
light-rays as they enter the eye,—such a man would make
the right inferences for all these objects, even though he
had never in his life had any concrete experience of them;
and he would do this because the ideas which we have
above supposed him to possess would mediate in his mind
between the phenomena he starts with and the conclusions
he draws. But these ideas or reasons for his conclusions
are all mere extracted portions or circumstances singled
out from the mass of characters which make up the entire
phenomena. The motions which form heat, the bending
of the light-waves, are, it is true, excessively recondite
ingredients; the hidden pendulum I spoke of above is less
so; and the sticking of a door on its sill in the earlier example would hardly be so at all. But each and all agree
in this, that they bear a *more evident relation* to the conclusion than did the immediate data in their full totality.

The difficulty is, in each case, to extract from the immediate data that particular ingredient which shall have
this very evident relation to the conclusion. Every phenomenon or so-called 'fact' has an infinity of aspects or
properties, as we have seen, amongst which the fool, or
man with little sagacity, will inevitably go astray. But no
matter for this point now. The first thing is to have seen
that every possible case of reasoning involves the extrac-
tion of a particular partial aspect of the phenomena thought
about, and that whilst Empirical Thought simply associates
phenomena in their entirety, Reasoned Thought couples
them by the conscious use of this extract.

2. And, now, to prove the second point: Why are the
couplings, consequences, and implications of extracts more

evident and obvious than those of entire phenomena? For two reasons.

First, the extracted characters are more general than the concretes, and the connections they may have are, therefore, more familiar to us, having been more often met in our experience. Think of heat as motion, and whatever is true of motion will be true of heat; but we have had a hundred experiences of motion for every one of heat. Think of the rays passing through this lens as bending towards the perpendicular, and you substitute for the comparatively unfamiliar lens the very familiar notion of a particular change in direction of a line, of which notion every day brings us countless examples.

The other reason why the relations of the extracted characters are so evident is that their properties are so *few*, compared with the properties of the whole, from which we derived them. In every concrete total the characters and their consequences are so inexhaustibly numerous that we may lose our way among them before noticing the particular consequence it behooves us to draw. But, if we are lucky enough to single out the proper character, we take in, as it were, by a single glance all its possible consequences. Thus the character of scraping the sill has very few suggestions, prominent among which is the suggestion that the scraping will cease if we raise the door; whilst the entire refractory door suggests an enormous number of notions to the mind.

Take another example. I am sitting in a railroad-car, waiting for the train to start. It is winter, and the stove fills the car with pungent smoke. The brakeman enters, and my neighbor asks him to " stop that stove smoking." He replies that it will stop entirely as soon as the car begins to move. " Why so?" asks the passenger. " It *always* does," replies the brakeman. It is evident from this 'always' that the connection between car moving and smoke stopping was a purely empirical one in the brakeman's mind, bred of habit. But, if the passenger had been an acute reasoner, he, with no experience of what that stove always did, might have anticipated the brakeman's reply, and spared his own question. Had he singled out of all the numerous points involved in a stove's not smoking the one special point of smoke pouring freely out of the stove-pipe's mouth, he would, probably, owing to the few associations of that idea, have been immediately reminded of the law that a fluid passes more rapidly out of a pipe's mouth if another fluid be at the same time streaming over that mouth; and then the rapid draught of air over the stove-pipe's mouth, which is one of the points involved in the car's motion, would immediately have occurred to him.

Thus a couple of extracted characters, with a couple of their few and obvious connections, would have formed the reasoned link in the passenger's mind between the phenomena, smoke stopping and car moving, which were only linked as wholes in the brakeman's mind. Such examples may seem trivial, but they contain the essence of the most refined and transcendental theorizing. The reason why physics grows more deductive the more the fundamental properties it assumes are of a mathematical sort, such as molecular mass or wave-length, is that the immediate consequences of these notions are so few that we can survey them all at once, and promptly pick out those which concern us.

Sagacity ; or the Perception of the Essence.

To reason, then, we must be able to extract characters,—not *any* characters, but the right characters for our conclusion. If we extract the wrong character, it will not lead to that conclusion. Here, then, is the difficulty: *How are characters extracted, and why does it require the advent of a genius in many cases before the fitting character is brought to light ?* Why cannot anybody reason as well as anybody else ? Why does it need a Newton to notice the law of the squares, a Darwin to notice the survival of the fittest ? To answer these questions we must begin a new research, and see how our insight into facts naturally grows.

All our knowledge at first is vague. When we say that a thing is vague, we mean that it has no subdivisions *ab intra*, nor precise limitations *ab extra ;* but still all the forms of thought may apply to it. It may have unity, reality, externality, extent, and what not—*thinghood*, in a word, but thinghood only as a whole.* In this vague way, probably, does the room appear to the babe who first begins to be conscious of it as something other than his moving nurse. It has no subdivisions in his mind, unless, perhaps, the window is able to attract his separate notice. In this vague way, certainly, does every entirely new experience appear to the adult. A library, a museum, a machine-shop, are mere confused wholes to the uninstructed, but the machinist, the antiquary, and the bookworm perhaps hardly notice the whole at all, so eager are they to pounce upon the details. Familiarity has in them bred discrimination. Such vague terms as 'grass,' 'mould,' and 'meat' do not exist for the botanist or the anatomist. They know too much about grasses, moulds, and muscles. A certain person said to Charles Kingsley, who was showing him the dissection of a caterpillar, with its exquisite viscera, "Why, I thought it was nothing but skin and squash!" A layman present at a shipwreck, a battle, or a fire is helpless. Discrimination has been so little awakened in him by experience that his consciousness leaves no single point of the complex situation accented and standing out for him to begin to act upon. But the sailor, the fireman, and the general know directly at what corner to take up the business. They 'see into the situation'—that is, they analyze it—with their first glance. It is full of delicately differenced ingredients which their education has little by little brought to their consciousness, but of which the novice gains no clear idea.

How this power of analysis was brought about we saw in our chapters on Discrimination and Attention. We dissociate the elements of originally vague totals by attending to them or noticing them alternately, of course. But what determines which element we shall attend to first? There are two immediate and obvious answers: first, our practical or instinctive interests; and, second, our æsthetic interests. The dog singles out of any situation its smells, and the horse its sounds, bcause they may reveal facts of practical moment, and are instinctively exciting to these several crea-

---

tures. The infant notices the candle-flame or the window, and ignores the rest of the room, because those objects give him a vivid pleasure. So, the country boy dissociates the blackberry, the chestnut, and the wintergreen, from the vague mass of other shrubs and trees, for their practical uses, and the savage is delighted with the beads, the bits of looking-glass, brought by an exploring vessel, and gives no heed to the features of the vessel itself, which is too much beyond his sphere. These æsthetic and practical interests, then, are the weightiest factors in making particular ingredients stand out in high relief. What they lay their accent on, that we notice; but what they are in themselves, we cannot say. We must content ourselves here with simply accepting them as irreducible ultimate factors in determining the way our knowledge grows.

Now, a creature which has few instinctive impulses, or interests, practical or æsthetic, will dissociate few characters, and will, at best, have limited reasoning powers; whilst one whose interests are very varied will reason much better. Man, by his immensely varied instincts, practical wants, and æsthetic feelings, to which every sense contributes, would, by dint of these alone, be sure to dissociate vastly more characters than any other animal; and accordingly we find that the lowest savages reason incomparably better than the highest brutes. The diverse interests lead, too, to a diversification of experiences, whose accumulation becomes a condition for the play of that *law of dissociation by varying concomitants* of which I treated in a former chapter (see Vol I. p. 506).

The Help given by Association by Similarity.

It is probable, also, that man's *superior association by similarity* has much to do with those discriminations of character on which his higher flights of reasoning are based. As this latter is an important matter, and as little or nothing was said of it in the chapter on Discrimination, it behooves me to dwell a little upon it here.

What does the reader do when he wishes to see in what the precise likeness or difference of two objects lies? He transfers his attention as rapidly as possible, backwards and forwards, from one to the other. The rapid alteration in consciousness shakes out, as it were, the points of difference or agreement, which would have slumbered forever unnoticed if the consciousness of the objects compared had occurred at widely distant periods of time. What does the scientific man do who searches for the reason or law embedded in a phenomenon? He deliberately accumulates all the instances he can find which have any analogy to that phenomenon; and, by simultaneously filling his mind with them all, he frequently succeeds in detaching from the collection the peculiarity which he was unable to formulate in one alone; even though that one had been preceded in his former experience by all of those with which he now at once confronts it. These examples show that the mere general fact of having occurred at some time in one's experience, with varying concomitants, is not by itself a sufficient reason for a character to be dissociated now. We need something more; we need that the varying concomitants should in all their variety be brought into consciousness *at once.* Not till then will the character in question escape from its adhesion to each and all of them and stand alone. This will immediately be recognized by those who have read Mill's Logic as the ground of Utility in his famous 'four methods of experimental inquiry,' the methods of agreement, of difference, of residues, and of concomitant variations. Each of these gives a list of analogous instances out of the midst of which a sought-for character may roll and strike the mind.

Now it is obvious that any mind in which association by similarity is highly developed is a mind which will spontaneously form lists of instances like this. Take a present case A, with a character m in it. The mind may fail at first to notice this character m at all. But if A calls up C, D, E, and F,—these being phenomena which resemble A in possessing m, but which may not have entered for months into the experience of the animal who now experiences A, why, plainly, such association performs the part of the reader's deliberately rapid comparison referred to above, and of the systematic consideration of like cases by the scientific investigator, and may lead to the noticing of *m* in an abstract way. Certainly this is obvious; and no conclusion is left to us but to assert that, after the few most powerful practical and æsthetic interests, our chief help towards noticing those special characters of phenomena, which, when once possessed and named, are used as reasons, class names, essences, or middle terms, *is this association by similarity*. Without it, indeed, the deliberate procedure of the scientific man would be impossible: he could never collect his analogous instances. But it operates of itself in highly-gifted minds without any deliberation, spontaneously collecting analogous instances, uniting in a moment what in nature the whole breadth of space and time keeps separate, and so permitting a perception of identical points in the midst of different circumstances, which minds governed wholly by the law of contiguity could never begin to attain.

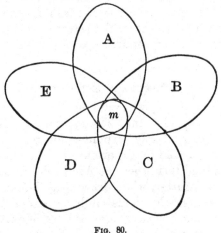

Fig. 80.

Figure 80 shows this. If *m*, in the present representation A, calls up B, C, D, and E, which are similar to A in possessing it, and calls them up in rapid succession, then *m*, being associated almost simultaneously with such varying concomitants, will 'roll out' and attract our separate notice.

If so much is clear to the reader, he will be willing to admit that the mind *in which this mode of association most prevails* will, from its better opportunity of extricating characters, be the one most prone to reasoned thinking; whilst, on the other hand, a mind in which we do not detect reasoned thinking will probably be one in which association by contiguity holds almost exclusive sway.

Geniuses are, by common consent, considered to differ from ordinary minds by an unusual development of association by similarity. One of Professor Bain's best strokes of work is the exhibition of this truth.* It applies to geniuses in the line of reasoning as well as in other lines. And as the genius is to the vulgarian, so the vulgar human mind is to the intelligence of a brute. Compared with men, it is probable that brutes neither attend to abstract characters, nor have associations by similarity. Their thoughts probably pass from one concrete object to its habitual concrete successor far more uniformly than is the case with us. In other words, their associations of ideas are almost exclusively by contiguity. It will clear up still farther our understanding of the reasoning process, if we devote a few pages to

THE INTELLECTUAL CONTRAST BETWEEN BRUTE AND MAN.

I will first try to show, by taking the best stories I can find of animal sagacity, that the mental process involved may as a rule be perfectly accounted for by mere contiguous association, based on experience. Mr. Darwin, in his ' Descent of Man,' instances the Arctic dogs, described by Dr. Hayes, who scatter, when drawing a sledge, as soon as the ice begins to crack. This might be called by some an exercise of reason. The test would be, Would the most intelligent Eskimo dogs that ever lived act so when placed upon ice for the first time together? A band of men from the tropics might do so easily. Recognizing cracking to be a sign of breaking, and seizing immediately the partial character that the point of rupture is the point of greatest

---

* See his Study of Character, chap. xv; also Senses and Intellect, ' Intellect,' chap. ii, the latter half.

strain, and that the massing of weight at a given point concentrates there the strain, a Hindoo might quickly infer that
scattering would stop the cracking, and, by crying out to
his comrades to disperse, save the party from immersion.
But in the dog's case we need only suppose that they
have individually experienced wet skins after cracking, that
they have often noticed cracking to begin when they were
huddled together, and that they have observed it to cease
when they scattered. Naturally, therefore, the sound would
redintegrate all these former experiences, including that of
scattering, which latter they would promptly renew. It
would be a case of immediate suggestion or of that 'Logic
of Recepts' as Mr. Romanes calls it, of which we spoke
above on p. 327.

A friend of the writer gave as a proof of the almost
human intelligence of his dog that he took him one day
down to his boat on the shore, but found the boat full of
dirt and water. He remembered that the sponge was up at
the house, a third of a mile distant; but, disliking to go back
himself, he made various gestures of wiping out the boat
and so forth, saying to his terrier, "Sponge, sponge; go
fetch the sponge." But he had little expectation of a result,
since the dog had never received the slightest training with
the boat or the sponge. Nevertheless, off he trotted to the
house, and, to his owner's great surprise and admiration,
brought the sponge in his jaws. Sagacious as this was, it
required nothing but ordinary contiguous association of
ideas. The terrier was only exceptional in the minuteness
of his spontaneous observation. Most terriers would have
taken no interest in the boat-cleaning operation, nor noticed what the sponge was for. This terrier, in having
picked those details out of the crude mass of his boat-expe-
rience distinctly enough to be reminded of them, was truly
enough ahead of his peers on the line which leads to human
reason. But his act was not yet an act of reasoning proper.
It might fairly have been called so if, unable to find the
sponge at the house, he had brought back a dipper or a
mop instead. Such a substitution would have shown that,
embedded in the very different appearances of these articles,
he had been able to discriminate the identical partial attri-

bute of capacity to take up water, and had reflected, "For
the present purpose they are identical." This, which the
dog did not do, any man but the very stupidest could not
fail to do.

If the reader will take the trouble to analyze the best
dog and elephant stories he knows, he will find that, in most
cases, this simple contiguous calling up of one whole by
another is quite sufficient to explain the phenomena.
Sometimes, it is true, we have to suppose the recognition of
a property or character as such, but it is then always a character which the peculiar practical interests of the animal
may have singled out. A dog, noticing his master's hat on its
peg, may possibly infer that he has not gone out. Intelligent
dogs recognize by the tone of the master's voice whether
the latter is angry or not. A dog will perceive whether
you have kicked him by accident or by design, and behave
accordingly. The character inferred by him, the particular
mental state in you, however it be represented in his
mind—it is represented probably by a 'recept' (p. 327) or
set of practical tendencies, rather than by a definite concept or idea—is still a partial character extracted from the
totality of your phenomenal being, and is his reason for
crouching and skulking, or playing with you. Dogs, moreover, seem to have the feeling of the value of their master's
personal property, or at least a particular *interest* in objects
which their master uses. A dog left with his master's coat
will defend it, though never taught to do so. I know of a
dog accustomed to swim after sticks in the water, but who
always refused to dive for stones. Nevertheless, when a fish-
basket, which he had never been trained to carry, but merely knew as his master's, fell over, he immediately dived after
it and brought it up. Dogs thus discern, at any rate so far
as to be able to act, this partial character of *being valuable*,
which lies hidden in certain things.* Stories are told of

---

* Whether the dog has the notion of your being angry or of your property being valuable in any such abstract way as *we* have these notions is
more than doubtful. The conduct is more likely an impulsive result of a
conspiracy of outward stimuli ; the beast *feels like* acting so when these
stimuli are present, though conscious of no definite reason why. The
distinction of recept and concept is useful here. Some breeds of dogs,

dogs carrying coppers to pastry-cooks to get buns, and it is said that a certain dog, if he gave two coppers, would never

e. g. collies, seem instinctively to defend their master's property. The case is similar to that of a dog's barking at people after dark, at whom he would not bark in daylight. I have heard this quoted as evidence of the dog's reasoning power. It is only, as Chapter III has shown us, the impulsive result of a summation of stimuli, and has no connection with reasoning.

In certain stages of the hypnotic trance the subject seems to lapse into the non-analytic state. If a sheet of ruled foolscap paper, or a paper with a fine monotonous ornamental pattern printed on it, be shown to the subject, and *one* of the ruled lines or elements of the pattern be pointed to for an instant, and the paper immediately removed, he will then almost always, when after a short interval the paper is presented to him again, pick out the indicated line or element with infallible correctness. The operator, meanwhile, has either to keep his eye fixed upon it, or to make sure of its position by counting, in order not to lose its place. Just so we may remember a friend's house in a street by the single character of its number rather than by its general look. The trance-subject would seem, in these instances, to surrender himself to the general look. He disperses his attention impartially over the sheet. The place of the particular line touched is part of a 'total effect' which he gets in its entirety, and which would be distorted if another line were touched instead. This total effect is lost upon the normal looker-on, bent as he is on concentration, analysis, and emphasis. What wonder, then, that, under these experimental conditions, the trance-subject excels him in touching the right line again? If he has time given him to count the line, he will excel the trance-subject ; but if the time be too short to count, he will best succeed by following the trance-method, abstaining from analysis, and being guided by the 'general look' of the line's place on the sheet. One is surprised at one's success in this the moment one gives up one's habitually analytic state of mind.

Is it too much to say that we have in this dispersion of the attention and subjection to the 'general effect' something like a relapse into the state of mind of brutes? The trance-subject never gives any other reason for his optical discriminations, save that 'it looks so.' So a man, on a road once traversed inattentively before, takes a certain turn for no reason except that he *feels* as if it must be right. He is guided by a sum of impressions, not one of which is emphatic or distinguished from the rest, not one of which is essential, not one of which is *conceived*, but all of which together drive him to a conclusion to which nothing but *that* sum-total leads. Are not some of the wonderful discriminations of animals explicable in the same way? The cow finds her own stanchions in the long stable, the horse stops at the house he has once stopped at in the monotonous street, because no other stanchions, no other house, yield impartially *all* the impressions of the previous experience. The man, however, by seeking to make some one impression characteristic and essential, prevents the rest from having their effect. So that, if the (for him) essential feature be forgotten or changed, he is too apt to be thrown off altogether, and then the brute or the trance-subject may seem to outstrip him in sagacity.

Dr. Romanes's already quoted distinction between 'receptual' and

leave without two buns. This was probably mere contiguous association, but it is *possible* that the animal noticed
the character of duality, and identified it as the same
in the coin and the cake. If so, it is the maximum of
canine abstract thinking. Another story told to the writer
is this : a dog was sent to a lumber-camp to fetch a wedge,
with which he was known to be acquainted. After half an
hour, not returning, he was sought and found biting and
tugging at the handle of an axe which was driven deeply
into a stump. The wedge could not be found. The teller
of the story thought that the dog must have had a clear
perception of the common character of serving to split
which was involved in both the instruments, and, from their
identity in this respect, inferred their identity for the purposes required.

It cannot be denied that this interpretation is a possible
one, but it seems to me far to transcend the limits of ordinary canine abstraction. The property in question was not
one which had direct personal interest for the dog, such
as that of belonging to his master is in the case of the
coat or the basket. If the dog in the sponge story had returned to the boat with a dipper it would have been no
more remarkable. It seems more probable, therefore, that
this wood-cutter's dog had also been accustomed to carry
the axe, and now, excited by the vain hunt for the wedge,
had discharged his carrying powers upon the former instrument in a sort of confusion—just as a man may pick up a
sieve to carry water in, in the excitement of putting out a
fire.*

' conceptual ' thought (published since the body of my text and my note
were written) connotes conveniently the difference which I seek to point
out. See also his Mental Evolution in Man, p. 197 ff., for proofs of the
fact that in a receptual way brutes cognize the mental states of other brutes
and men.

* This matter of confusion is important and interesting. Since confusion is mistaking the wrong part of the phenomenon for the whole, whilst
reasoning is, according to our definition, based on the substitution of the
right part for the whole, it might be said that confusion and reasoning
are generically the same process. I believe that they are so, and that the
only difference between a muddle-head and a genius is that between extracting wrong characters and right ones. In other words, a muddle-head-

Thus, then, the characters extracted by animals are very few, and always related to their immediate interests or emotions. That dissociation by varying concomitants, which in man is based so largely on association by similarity, hardly seems to take place at all in the mind of brutes. One total thought suggests to them another total thought, and they find themselves acting with propriety, they know not why. The great, the fundamental, defect of their minds seems to be the inability of their groups of ideas to break across in unaccustomed places. They are enslaved to routine, to cut-and-dried thinking; and if the most prosaic of human beings could be transported into his dog's mind, he would be appalled at the utter absence of fancy which reigns there.* Thoughts will not be found to call up their similars, but only their habitual successors. Sunsets will not suggest heroes' deaths, but supper-time. This is why man is the only metaphysical animal. To wonder why the universe should be as it is presupposes the notion of its being different, and a brute, which never reduces the actual to fluidity by breaking up its literal sequences in his imagination, can never form such a notion. He takes the world simply for granted, and never wonders at it at all.

Professor Strümpell quotes a dog-story which is probably a type of many others. The feat performed looks like abstract reasoning; but an acquaintance with all the circumstances shows it to have been a random trick learned by habit. The story is as follows:

" I have two dogs, a small, long-legged pet dog and a rather large watch-dog. Immediately beyond the house-court is the garden, into which one enters through a low lattice-gate which is closed by a latch

---

ed person is a genius spoiled in the making. I think it will be admitted that all *eminently* muddle-headed persons have the temperament of genius. They are constantly breaking away from the usual consecutions of con- cretes. A common associator by contiguity is too closely tied to routine to get muddle-headed.

* The horse is a densely stupid animal, as far as everything goes except contiguous association. We reckon him intelligent, partly because he looks so handsome, partly because he has such a wonderful faculty of contiguous association and can be so quickly moulded into a mass of set habits. Had he anything of reasoning intelligence, he would be a less faithful slave than he is.

on the yard-side. This latch is opened by lifting it. Besides this, moreover, the gate is fastened on the garden-side by a string nailed to the gate-post. Here, as often as one wished, could the following sight be observed. If the little dog was shut in the garden and he wished to get out, he placed himself before the gate and barked. Immediately the large dog in the court would hasten to him and raise the latch with his nose while the little dog on the garden-side leaped up and, catching the string in his teeth, bit it through; whereupon the big one wedged his snout between the gate and the post, pushed the gate open, and the little dog slipped through. Certainly reasoning seems here to prevail. In face of it, however, and although the dogs arrived of themselves, and without human aid, at their solution of the gate question, I am able to point out that the complete action was pieced together out of accidental experiences which the dogs followed, I might say, unconsciously. While the large dog was young, he was allowed, like the little one, to go into the garden, and therefore the gate was usually not latched, but simply closed. Now if he saw anyone go in, he would follow by thrusting his snout between gate and post, and so pushing the gate open. When he was grown I forbade his being taken in, and had the gate kept latched. But he naturally still tried to follow when anyone entered and tried in the old fashion to open it, which he could no longer do. Now it fell out that once, while making the attempt, he raised his nose higher than usual and hit the latch from below so as to lift it off its hook, and the gate unclosed. From thenceforth he made the same movement of the head when trying to open it, and, of course, with the same result. He now knew how to open the gate when it was latched.

"The little dog had been the large one's teacher in many things, especially in the chasing of cats and the catching of mice and moles; so when the little one was heard barking eagerly, the other always hastened to him. If the barking came from the garden, he opened the gate to get inside. But meanwhile the little dog, who wanted to get out the moment the gate opened, slipped out between the big one's legs, and so the appearance of his having come with the intention of letting him out arose. And that it was simply an appearance transpired from the fact that when the little dog did not succeed at once in getting out, the large one ran in and nosed about the garden, plainly showing that he had expected to find something there. In order to stop this opening of the gate I fastened a string on the garden-side which, tightly drawn, held the gate firm against the post, so that if the yard dog raised the latch and let go, it would every time fall back on to the hook. And this device was successful for quite a time, until it happened one day that on my return from a walk upon which the little dog had accompanied me I crossed the garden, and in passing through the gate the dog remained behind, and refused to come to my whistle. As it was beginning to rain, and I knew how he disliked to get wet, I closed the gate in order to punish him in this manner. But I had hardly reached the house ere he was before the gate, whining and crying most piteously, for the rain was falling faster and faster. The big dog, to whom the rain was a matter of perfect indifference, was instantly on hand and tried his utmost to open the gate, but naturally without success. Almost in despair the little dog bit at the gate, at the same time springing into the air in the attempt to jump over it, when he chanced to catch the string in his teeth ; it broke, and the gate flew open. Now he knew the secret and thenceforth bit the string whenever he wished to get out, so that I was obliged to change it.

" That the big dog in raising the latch did not in the least *know* that the latch closed the gate, that the raising of the same opened it, but that he merely repeated the automatic blow with his snout which had once had such happy consequences, transpires from the following : the gate leading to the barn is fastened with a latch precisely like the one on the garden-gate, only placed a little higher, still easily within the dog's reach. Here, too, occasionally the little dog is confined, and when he barks the big one makes every possible effort to open the gate, but it has never occurred to him to push the latch up. The brute cannot draw conclusions, that is, he cannot think." *

Other classical *differentiæ* of man besides that of being the only reasoning animal, also seem consequences of his unrivalled powers of similar association. He has, e.g., been called ' the laughing animal.' But humor has often been defined as the recognition of identities in things different. When the man in Coriolanus says of that hero that "there is no more mercy in him than there is milk in a male tiger," both the invention of the phrase and its enjoyment by the hearer depend on a peculiarly perplexing power to associate ideas by similarity.

Man is known again as 'the talking animal'; and lan-

---

* Th Schumann : Journal Daheim, No. 19, 1878. Quoted by Strümpell : Die Geisteskräfte der Menschen verglichen mit denen der Thiere (Leipzig, 1878), p. 39. Cats are notorious for the skill with which they will open latches, locks, etc. Their feats are usually ascribed to their reasoning powers. But Dr. Romanes well remarks (Mental Evolution, etc., p. 351, note) that we ought first to be sure that the actions are not due to mere association. A cat is constantly playing with things with her paws ; a trick accidentally hit upon may be retained. Romanes notes the fact that the animals most skilled in this way need not be the most generally intelligent, but those which have the best corporeal members for handling things, cat's paws, horse's lips, elephant's trunk, cow's horns. The monkey has both the corporeal and the intellectual superiority. And my deprecatory remarks on animal reasoning in the text apply far less to the quadrumana than to quadrupeds.—On the possible fallacies in interpreting animals' minds, compare C. L. Morgan in Mind, xi. 174 (1886).

guage is assuredly a capital distinction between man and brute. But it may readily be shown how this distinction merely flows from those we have pointed out, easy dissociation of a representation into its ingredients, and association by similarity.

Language is a system of *signs*, different from the things signified, but able to suggest them.

No doubt brutes have a number of such signs. When a dog yelps in front of a door, and his master, understanding his desire, opens it, the dog may, after a certain number of repetitions, get to repeat in cold blood a yelp which was at first the involuntary interjectional expression of strong emotion. The same dog may be taught to 'beg' for food, and afterwards come to do so deliberately when hungry. The dog also learns to understand the signs of men, and the word 'rat' uttered to a terrier suggests exciting thoughts of the rat-hunt. If the dog had the varied impulse to vocal utterance which some other animals have, he would probably repeat the word 'rat' whenever he spontaneously happened to think of a rat-hunt—he no doubt does have it as an auditory image, just as a parrot calls out different words spontaneously from its repertory, and having learned the name of a given dog will utter it on the sight of a different dog. In each of these separate cases the particular sign *may* be consciously noticed by the animal, as distinct from the particular thing signified, and will thus, so far as it goes, be a true manifestation of language. But when we come to man we find a great difference. *He has a deliberate intention to apply a sign to everything.* The linguistic impulse is with him generalized and systematic. For things hitherto unnoticed or unfelt, he *desires* a sign before he has one. Even though the dog should possess his 'yelp' for this thing, his 'beg' for that, and his auditory image 'rat' for a third thing, the matter with him rests there. If a fourth thing interests him for which no sign happens already to have been learned, he remains tranquilly without it and goes no further. But the man *postulates* it, its absence irritates him, and he ends by inventing it. *This* GENERAL PURPOSE *constitutes, I take it, the peculiarity of human speech, and explains its prodigious development.*

How, then, does the general purpose arise? It arises as soon as the notion of a *sign as such*, apart from any particular import, is born; and this notion is born by dissociation from the outstanding portions of a number of concrete cases of signification. The 'yelp,' the 'beg,' the 'rat,' differ as to their several imports and natures. They agree only in so far as they have the same *use*—to *be signs*, to stand for something more important than themselves. The dog whom this similarity could strike would have grasped the sign *per se* as such, and would probably thereupon become a general sign-maker, or speaker in the human sense. But how can the similarity strike him? Not without the juxtaposition of the similars (in virtue of the law we have laid down (p. 506), that in order to be segregated an experience must be repeated with varying concomitants)—not unless the 'yelp' of the dog at the moment it occurs *recalls* to him his 'beg,' by the delicate bond of their subtle similarity of use—not till then can this thought flash through his mind : " Why, yelp and beg, in spite of all their unlikeness, are yet alike in this : that they are actions, signs, which lead to important boons. Other boons, *any* boons, may then be got by other signs!" This reflection made, the gulf is passed. Animals probably never make it, because the bond of similarity is not delicate enough. Each sign is drowned in *its* import, and never awakens other signs and other imports in juxtaposition. The rat-hunt idea is too absorbingly interesting in itself to be interrupted by anything so uncontiguous to it as the idea of the 'beg for food,' or of 'the door-open yelp,' nor in their turn do these awaken the rat-hunt idea.

In the human child, however, these ruptures of contiguous association are very soon made; far off cases of sign-using arise when we make a sign now; and soon language is launched. The child in each case makes the discovery for himself. No one can help him except by furnishing him with the conditions. But as he is constituted, the conditions will sooner or later shoot together into the result.*

---

* There are two other conditions of language in the human being, additional to association by similarity, that assist its action, or rather pave the way for it. These are: first, the great natural loquacity; and, second, the

The exceedingly interesting account which Dr. Howe gives of the education of his various blind-deaf mutes illustrates this point admirably. He began to teach Laura Bridgman by gumming raised letters on various familiar articles. The child was taught by mere contiguity to pick out a certain number of particular articles when made to feel the letters. But this was merely a collection of particular signs, out of the mass of which the general purpose of *signification* had not yet been extracted by the child's mind. Dr. Howe compares his situation at this moment to that of one lowering a line to the bottom of the deep sea in which Laura's soul lay, and waiting until she should spontaneously take hold of it and be raised into the light. The moment came, 'accompanied by a radiant flash of intelligence and glow of joy'; she seemed suddenly to become aware of the general purpose imbedded in the different details of all these signs, and from that moment her education went on with extreme rapidity.

Another of the great capacities in which man has been said to differ fundamentally from the animal is that of pos-

---

great imitativeness of man. The first produces the original reflex interjectional sign; the second (as Bleek has well shown) fixes it, stamps it, and ends by multiplying the number of determinate specific signs which are a requisite preliminary to the general conscious purpose of sign-making, which I have called the characteristic human element in language. The way in which imitativeness fixes the meaning of signs is this: When a primeval man has a given emotion, he utters his natural interjection; or when (to avoid supposing that the reflex sounds are exceedingly determinate by nature) a group of such men experience a common emotion, and one takes the lead in the cry, the others cry like him from sympathy or imitativeness. Now, let one of the group hear another, who is in presence of the experience, utter the cry; he, even without the experience, will repeat the cry from pure imitativeness. But, as he repeats the sign, he will be reminded by it of his own former experience. Thus, first, he has the sign with the emotion; then, without it; then, with it again. It is :'dissociated by change of concomitants "; he feels it as a separate entity and yet as having a connection with the emotion. Immediately it becomes possible for him to couple it deliberately with the emotion, in cases where the latter would either have provoked no interjectional cry or not the same one. In a word, his mental procedure tends to *fix* this cry on *that* emotion; and when this occurs, in many instances, he is provided with a stock of signs, like the yelp, beg, rat of the dog, each of which suggests a determinate image. On this stock, then, similarity works in the way above explained.

sessing self-consciousness or reflective knowledge of himself as a thinker. But this capacity also flows from our criterion, for (without going into the matter very deeply) we may say that the brute never reflects on himself as a thinker, because he has never clearly dissociated, in the full concrete act of thought, the element of the thing thought of and the operation by which he thinks it. They remain always fused, conglomerated—just as the interjectional vocal sign of the brute almost invariably merges in his mind with the thing signified, and is not independently attended to *in se.**

Now, the dissociation of these two elements probably occurs first in the child's mind on the occasion of some error or false expectation which would make him experience the shock of difference between merely imagining a thing and getting it. The thought experienced once with the concomitant reality, and then without it or with opposite concomitants, reminds the child of other cases in which the same provoking phenomenon occurred. Thus the general ingredient of error may be dissociated and noticed *per se*, and from the notion of his error or wrong thought to that of his thought in general the transition is easy. The brute, no doubt, has plenty of instances of error and disappointment in his life, but the similar shock is in him most likely always swallowed up in the accidents of the actual case. An expectation disappointed may breed dubiety as to the realization of that particular thing when the dog next expects it. But that disappointment, that dubiety, while they are present in the mind, will *not* call up other cases, in which the material details were different, but this feature of pos-

---

* See the 'Evolution of Self-consciousness' in 'Philosophical Discussions,' by Chauncey Wright (New York: Henry Holt & Co., 1877). Dr. Romanes, in the book from which I have already quoted, seeks to show that the 'consciousness of truth as truth' and the deliberate intention to predicate (which are the characteristics of higher human reasoning) presuppose a consciousness of ideas as such, as things distinct from their objects ; and that this consciousness depends on our having made signs for them by language. My text seems to me to include Dr. Romanes's facts, and formulates them in what to me is a more elementary way, though the reader who wishes to understand the matter better should go to his clear and patient exposition also.

sible error was the same. The brute will, therefore, stop short of dissociating the general notion of error *per se*, and *a fortiori* will never attain the conception of Thought itself as such.

We may then, we think, consider it proven that *the most elementary single difference between the human mind and that of brutes lies in this deficiency on the brute's part to associate ideas by similarity*—characters, the abstraction of which depends on this sort of association, must in the brute always remain drowned, swamped in the total phenomenon which they help constitute, and never used to reason from. If a character stands out alone, it is always some obvious sensible quality like a sound or a smell which is instinctively exciting and lies in the line of the animal's propensities; or it is some obvious sign which experience has habitually coupled with a consequence, such as, for the dog, the sight of his master's hat on and the master's going out.

DIFFERENT ORDERS OF HUMAN GENIUS.

But, now, since nature never makes a jump, it is evident that we should find the lowest men occupying in this respect an intermediate position between the brutes and the highest men. And so we do. Beyond the analogies which their own minds suggest by breaking up the literal sequence of their experience, there is a whole world of analogies which they can appreciate when imparted to them by their betters, but which they could never excogitate alone. This answers the question why Darwin and Newton had to be waited for so long. The flash of similarity between an apple and the moon, between the rivalry for food in nature and the rivalry for man's selection, was too recondite to have occurred to any but exceptional minds. *Genius, then,* as has been already said, *is identical with the possession of similar association to an extreme degree.* Professor Bain says: "This I count the leading fact of genius. I consider it quite impossible to afford any explanation of intellectual originality except on the supposition of unusual energy on this point." Alike in the arts, in literature, in practical affairs, and in science, association by similarity is the prime condition of success.

But as, according to our view, there are two stages in reasoned thought, one where similarity merely *operates* to call up cognate thoughts, and another farther stage, where the bond of identity between the cognate thoughts is *noticed ;* so *minds of genius may be divided into two main sorts, those who notice the bond and those who merely obey it.* The first are the abstract reasoners, properly so called, the men of science, and philosophers—the analysts, in a word; the latter are the poets, the critics—the artists, in a word, the men of intuitions. These judge rightly, classify cases, characterize them by the most striking analogic epithets, but go no further. At first sight it might seem that the analytic mind represented simply a higher intellectual stage, and that the intuitive mind represented an arrested stage of intellectual development; but the difference is not so simple as this. Professor Bain has said that a man's advance to the scientific stage (the stage of noticing and abstracting the bond of similarity) may often be due to an *absence* of certain emotional sensibilities. The sense of color, he says, may no less determine a mind away from science than it determines it toward painting. There must be a penury in one's interest in the details of particular forms in order to permit the forces of the intellect to be concentrated on what is common to many forms.* In other words, supposing a mind fertile in the suggestion of analogies, but, at the same time, keenly interested in the particulars of each suggested image, that mind would be far less apt to single out the particular character which called up the analogy than one whose interests were less generally lively. A certain richness of the æsthetic nature may, therefore, easily keep one in the intuitive stage. All the poets are examples of this. Take Homer:

" Ulysses, too, spied round the house to see if any man were still alive and hiding, trying to get away from gloomy death. He found them all fallen in the blood and dirt, and in such number as the fish which the fishermen to the low shore, out of the foaming sea, drag with their meshy nets. These all, sick for the ocean water, are strewn around the sands, while the blazing sun takes their life from them. So there the suitors lay strewn round on one another."

* Study of Character, p. 317.

Or again:

"And as when a Mæonian or a Carian woman stains ivory with purple to be a cheek-piece for horses, and it is kept in the chamber, and many horsemen have prayed to bear it off; but it is kept a treasure for a king, both a trapping for his horse and a glory to the driver—in such wise were thy stout thighs, Menelaos, and legs and fair ankles stained with blood."

A man in whom all the accidents of an analogy rise up as vividly as this, may be excused for not attending to the ground of the analogy. But he need not on that account be deemed intellectually the inferior of a man of drier mind, in whom the ground is not as liable to be eclipsed by the general splendor. Rarely are both sorts of intellect, the splendid and the analytic, found in conjunction. Plato among philosophers, and M. Taine, who cannot quote a child's saying without describing the '*voix chantante, étonnée, heureuse*' in which it is uttered, are only exceptions whose strangeness proves the rule.

An often-quoted writer has said that Shakespeare possessed more *intellectual power* than any one else that ever lived. If by this he meant the power to pass from given premises to right or congruous conclusions, it is no doubt true. The abrupt transitions in Shakespeare's thought astonish the reader by their unexpectedness no less than they delight him by their fitness. Why, for instance, does the death of Othello so stir the spectator's blood and leave him with a sense of reconcilement? Shakespeare himself could very likely not say why; for his invention, though rational, was not ratiocinative. Wishing the curtain to fall upon a reinstated Othello, that speech about the turbaned Turk suddenly simply flashed across him as the right end of all that went before. The dry critic who comes after can, however, point out the subtle bonds of identity that guided Shakespeare's pen through that speech to the death of the Moor. Othello is sunk in ignominy, lapsed from his height from the beginning of the play. What better way to rescue him at last from this abasement than to make him for an instant identify himself in memory with the old Othello of better days, and then execute justice on his present disowned body, as he used then to smite all enemies of the State ? But Shakespeare, whose mind supplied these means, could probably not have told why they were so effective.

But though this is true, and though it would be absurd in an absolute way to say that a given analytic mind was superior to any intuitional one, yet it is none the less true that the former *represents* the higher stage. Men, taken historically, reason by analogy long before they have learned to reason by abstract characters. Association by similarity and true reasoning may have identical results. If a philosopher wishes to prove to you why you should do a certain thing, he may do so by using abstract considerations exclusively; a savage will prove the same by reminding you of a similar case in which you notoriously do as he now proposes, and this with no ability to state the *point* in which the cases are similar. In all primitive literature, in all savage oratory, we find persuasion carried on exclusively by parables and similes, and travellers in savage countries readily adopt the native custom. Take, for example, Dr. Livingstone's argument with the negro conjuror. The missionary was trying to dissuade the savage from his fetichistic ways of invoking rain. "You see," said he, "that, after all your operations, sometimes it rains and sometimes it does not, exactly as when you have not operated at all." "But," replied the sorcerer, "it is just the same with you doctors; you give your remedies, and sometimes the patient gets well and sometimes he dies, just as when you do nothing at all." To that the pious missionary replied: "The doctor does his duty, after which God performs the cure if it pleases Him." "Well," rejoined the savage, "it is just so with me. I do what is necessary to procure rain, after which God sends it or withholds it according to His pleasure." *

This is the stage in which proverbial philosophy reigns supreme. "An empty sack can't stand straight" will stand for the reason why a man with debts may lose his honesty; and "a bird in the hand is worth two in the bush" will serve to back up one's exhortations to prudence. Or we answer the question: "Why is snow white?" by saying, "For the

---

* Quoted by Renouvier, Critique Philosophique, October 19, 1879.

same reason that soap-suds or whipped eggs are white"—
in other words, instead of giving the *reason* for a fact, we
give another *example* of the same fact. This offering a similar instance, instead of a reason, has often been criticised
as one of the forms of logical depravity in men. But manifestly it is not a perverse act of thought, but only an incomplete one. Furnishing parallel cases is the necessary
first step towards abstracting the reason imbedded in
them all.

As it is with reasons, so it is with words. The first
words are probably always names of entire things and entire actions, of extensive coherent groups. A new experience in the primitive man can only be talked about by
him in terms of the old experiences which have received
names. It reminds him of certain ones from among them,
but the *points* in which it agrees with them are neither
named nor dissociated. Pure similarity must work before
the abstraction can work which is based upon it. The first
adjectives will therefore probably be total nouns embody-
ing the striking character. The primeval man will say,
not 'the bread is hard,' but 'the bread is stone'; not
'the face is round,' but 'the face is moon'; not 'the
fruit is sweet,' but 'the fruit is sugar-cane.' The first
words are thus neither particular nor general, but *vaguely*
concrete; just as we speak of an 'oval' face, a 'velvet'
skin, or an 'iron' will, without meaning to connote any
other attributes of the adjective-noun than those in which
it *does* resemble the noun it is used to qualify. After
a while certain of these adjectively-used nouns come only
to signify the particular quality for whose sake they are
oftenest used; the *entire thing* which they originally meant
receives another name, and they become true abstract
and general terms. Oval, for example, with us suggests
only shape. The first abstract qualities thus formed are,
no doubt, qualities of one and the same sense found in
different objects—as big, sweet; next analogies between
different senses, as 'sharp' of taste, 'high' of sound, etc.;
then analogies of motor combinations, or form of relation,
as simple, confused, difficult, reciprocal, relative, spontaneous, etc. The extreme degree of subtlety in analogy is

reached in such cases as when we say certain English art critics' writing reminds us of a close room in which pastilles have been burning, or that the mind of certain Frenchmen is like old Roquefort cheese. Here language utterly fails to hit upon the basis of resemblance.

Over immense departments of our thought we are still, all of us, in the savage state. Similarity operates in us, but abstraction has not taken place. We know what the present case is like, we know what it reminds us of, we have an intuition of the right course to take, if it be a practical matter. But analytic thought has made no tracks, and we cannot justify ourselves to others. In ethical, psychological, and æsthetic matters, to give a clear reason for one's judgment is universally recognized as a mark of rare genius. The helplessness of uneducated people to account for their likes and dislikes is often ludicrous. Ask the first Irish girl why she likes this country better or worse than her home, and see how much she can tell you. But if you ask your most educated friend why he prefers Titian to Paul Veronese, you will hardly get more of a reply; and you will probably get absolutely none if you inquire why Beethoven reminds him of Michael Angelo, or how it comes that a bare figure with unduly flexed joints, by the former, can so suggest the moral tragedy of life. His thought obeys a *nexus*, but cannot name it. And so it is with all those judgments of *experts*, which even though unmotived are so valuable. Saturated with experience of a particular class of materials, an expert intuitively feels whether a newly-reported fact is probable or not, whether a proposed hypothesis is worthless or the reverse. He instinctively knows that, in a novel case, this and not that will be the promising course of action. The well-known story of the old judge advising the new one never to give reasons for his decisions, "the decisions will probably be right, the reasons will surely be wrong," illustrates this. The doctor will feel that the patient is doomed, the dentist will have a premonition that the tooth will break, though neither can articulate a reason for his foreboding. The reason lies imbedded, but not yet laid bare, in all the countless previous cases dimly suggested by the actual one, all calling up the same conclusion,

which the adept thus finds himself swept on to, he knows
not how or why.

A physiological conclusion remains to be drawn. If the
principles laid down in Chapter XIV are true, then it follows that the great cerebral difference between habitual and
reasoned thinking must be this : that in the former an entire
system of cells vibrating at any one moment discharges in
its totality into another entire system, and that the order
of the discharges tends to be a constant one in time ; whilst
in the latter a part of the prior system still keeps vibrating
in the midst of the subsequent system, and the order—
which part this shall be, and what shall be its concomitants
in the subsequent system—has little tendency to fixedness
in time. This physical selection, so to call it, of one part
to vibrate persistently whilst the others rise and subside,
we found, in the chapter in question, to be the basis of
similar association. (See especially pp. 578–81.) It would
seem to be but a minor degree of that still more urgent
and importunate localized vibration which we can easiest
conceive to underlie the mental fact of interest, attention,
or dissociation. In terms of the brain-process, then, all
these mental facts resolve themselves into a single peculiarity : that of indeterminateness of connection between
the different tracts, and tendency of action to focalize
itself, so to speak, in small localities which vary infinitely
at different times, and from which irradiation may proceed in countless shifting ways. (Compare figure 80, p.
347.) To discover, or (what more befits the present stage
of nerve-physiology) to adumbrate by some possible guess,
on what chemical or molecular-mechanical fact this instable
equilibrium of the human brain may depend, should be the
next task of the physiologist who ponders over the passage
from brute to man. Whatever the physical peculiarity in
question may be, *it* is the cause why a man, whose brain
has it, reasons so much, whilst his horse, whose brain lacks
it, reasons so little. We can but bequeath the problem to
abler hands than our own.

But, meanwhile, this mode of stating the matter suggests
a couple of other inferences. The first is brief. If *focali-*

zation of brain-activity be the fundamental fact of reasonable thought, we see why intense interest or concentrated passion makes us think so much more truly and profoundly. The persistent *focalization* of motion in certain tracts is the cerebral fact corresponding to the persistent domination in consciousness of the important feature of the subject. When not 'focalized,' we are scatter-brained; but when thoroughly impassioned, we never wander from the point. None but congruous and relevant images arise. When roused by indignation or moral enthusiasm, how trenchant are our reflections, how smiting are our words! The whole network of petty scruples and by-considerations which, at ordinary languid times, surrounded the matter like a cobweb, holding back our thought, as Gulliver was pinned to the earth by the myriad Lilliputian threads, are dashed through at a blow, and the subject stands with its essential and vital lines revealed.

The last point is relative to the theory that what was acquired habit in the ancestor may become congenital tendency in the offspring. So vast a superstructure is raised upon this principle that the paucity of empirical evidence for it has alike been matter of regret to its adherents, and of triumph to its opponents. In Chapter XXVIII we shall see what we may call the whole beggarly array of proof. In the human race, where our opportunities for observation are the most complete, we seem to have no evidence whatever which would support the hypothesis, unless it possibly be the law that city-bred children are more apt to be near-sighted than country children. In the mental world we certainly do not observe that the children of great travellers get their geography lessons with unusual ease, or that a baby whose ancestors have spoken German for thirty generations will, on that account, learn Italian any the less easily from its Italian nurse. But if the considerations we have been led to are true, they explain perfectly well why this law *should not* be verified in the human race, and why, therefore, in looking for evidence on the subject, we should confine ourselves exclusively to lower animals. In them fixed habit is the essential and characteristic law of nervous action. The brain grows to the exact modes in which it has been exercised, and the inheritance of these modes—then called instincts—would have in it nothing surprising. But in man the negation of all fixed modes is the essential characteristic. He owes his whole pre-eminence as a reasoner, his whole human quality of intellect, we may say, to the facility with which a given mode of thought in him may suddenly be broken up into elements, which recombine anew. Only at the price of inheriting no settled instinctive tendencies is he able to settle every novel case by the fresh discovery by his reason of novel principles. He is, *par excellence,* the *educable* animal. If, then, the law that habits are inherited were found exemplified in him, he would, in so far forth, fall short of his human perfections; and, when we survey the human races, we actually do find that those which are most instinctive at the outset are those which, on the whole, are least educated in the end. An untutored Italian is, to a great extent, a man of the world; he has instinctive perceptions, tendencies to behavior, reactions, in a word, upon his environment, which the untutored German wholly lacks. If the latter be not drilled, he is apt to be a thoroughly loutish personage; but, on the other hand, the mere absence in his brain of definite innate tendencies enables him to advance by the development, through education, of his purely reasoned thinking, into complex regions of consciousness that the Italian may probably never approach.

We observe an identical difference between men as a whole and women as a whole. A young woman of twenty reacts with intuitive promptitude and security in all the usual circumstances in which she may be placed.* Her likes

---

* Social and domestic circumstances, that is, not material ones. Perceptions of social relations seem very keen in persons whose dealings with the material world are confined to knowing a few useful objects, principally animals, plants, and weapons. Savages and boors are often as tactful and astute socially as trained diplomatists. In general, it is probable that the consciousness of how one stands with other people occupies a relatively larger and larger part of the mind, the lower one goes in the scale of culture. Woman's intuitions, so fine in the sphere of personal relations, are seldom first-rate in the way of mechanics. All boys teach themselves how a clock goes ; few girls. Hence Dr. Whately's jest, "Woman is the unreasoning animal, and pokes the fire from on top."

and dislikes are formed; her opinions, to a great extent, the same that they will be through life. Her character is, in fact, finished in its essentials. How inferior to her is a boy of twenty in all these respects! His character is still gelatinous, uncertain what shape to assume, 'trying it on' in every direction. Feeling his power, yet ignorant of the manner in which he shall express it, he is, when compared with his sister, a being of no definite contour. But this absence of prompt tendency in his brain to set into particular modes is the very condition which insures that it shall ultimately become so much more efficient than the woman's. The very lack of preappointed trains of thought is the ground on which general principles and heads of classification grow up; and the masculine brain deals with new and complex matter indirectly by means of these, in a manner which the feminine method of direct intuition, admirably and rapidly as it performs within its limits, can vainly hope to cope with.

In looking back over the subject of reasoning, one feels how intimately connected it is with conception; and one realizes more than ever the deep reach of that principle of selection on which so much stress was laid towards the close of Chapter IX. As the art of reading (after a certain stage in one's education) is the art of skipping, so the art of being wise is the art of knowing what to overlook. The first effect on the mind of growing cultivated is that processes once multiple get to be performed by a single act. Lazarus has called this the progressive 'condensation' of thought. But in the psychological sense it is less a condensation than a loss, a genuine dropping out and throwing overboard of conscious content. Steps really sink from sight. An advanced thinker sees the relations of his topics in such masses and so instantaneously that when he comes to explain to younger minds it is often hard to say which grows the more perplexed, he or the pupil. In every university there are admirable investigators who are notoriously bad lecturers. The reason is that they never spontaneously see the subject in the minute articulate way in which the student needs to have it offered to his slow reception. They grope for the links, but the links do not come. Bowditch, who translated and annotated Laplace's Mécanique Céleste, said that whenever his author prefaced a proposition by the words 'it is evident,' he knew that many hours of hard study lay before him.

When two minds of a high order, interested in kindred subjects, come together, their conversation is chiefly remarkable for the summariness of its allusions and the rapidity of its transitions. Before one of them is half through a sentence the other knows his meaning and replies. Such genial play with such massive materials, such an easy flashing of light over far perspectives, such careless indifference to the dust and apparatus that ordinarily surround the subject and seem to pertain to its essence, make these conversations seem true feasts for gods to a listener who is educated enough to follow them at all. His mental lungs breathe more deeply, in an atmosphere more broad and vast than is their wont. On the other hand, the excessive explicitness and short-windedness of an ordinary man are as wonderful as they are tedious to the man of genius. But we need not go as far as the ways of genius. Ordinary social intercourse will do. There the charm of conversation is in direct proportion to the possibility of abridgment and elision, and in inverse ratio to the need of explicit statement. With old friends a word stands for a whole story or set of opinions. With new-comers everything must be gone over in detail. Some persons have a real mania for completeness, they must express every step. They are the most intolerable of companions, and although their mental energy may in its way be great, they always strike us as weak and second-rate. In short, the essence of plebeianism, that which separates vulgarity from aristocracy, is perhaps less a defect than an excess, the constant need to animadvert upon matters which for the aristocratic temperament do not exist. To ignore, to disdain to consider, to overlook, are the essence of the 'gentleman.' Often most provokingly so; for the things ignored may be of the deepest moral consequence. But in the very midst of our indignation with the gentleman, we have a consciousness that his preposterous inertia and negativeness in the actual emergency is, somehow or other, *allied* with his general superiority to ourselves. It is not only that the gentleman ignores considerations relative to conduct, sordid suspicions, fears, calculations, etc., which the vulgarian is fated to entertain; it is that he is silent where the vulgarian talks; that he gives nothing but results where the vulgarian is profuse of reasons; that he does not explain or apologize; that he uses one sentence instead of twenty; and that, in a word, there is an amount of *interstitial* thinking, so to call it, which it is quite impossible to get him to perform, but which is nearly all that the vulgarian mind performs at all. All this suppression of the secondary leaves the field *clear*,—for higher flights, should they choose to come. But even if they never came, what thoughts there were would still manifest the aristocratic type and wear the well-bred form. So great is our sense of harmony and ease in passing from the company of a philistine to that of an aristocratic temperament, that we are almost tempted to deem the falsest views and tastes as held by a man of the world, truer than the truest as held by a common person. In the latter the best ideas are choked, obstructed, and contaminated by the redundancy of their paltry associates. The negative conditions, at least, of an atmosphere and a free outlook are present in the former.

I may appear to have strayed from psychological analysis into æsthetic criticism. But the principle of selection is so important that no illustrations seem redundant which may help to show how great is its scope. The upshot of what I say simply is that selection implies rejection as well as choice; and that the function of ignoring, of *in*attention, is as vital a factor in mental progress as the function of attention itself.

CHAPTER XXII.

THE PRODUCTION OF MOVEMENT.

The reader will not have forgotten, in the jungle of purely inward processes and products through which the last chapters have borne him, that the final result of them all must be some form of bodily activity due to the escape of the central excitement through outgoing nerves. The whole neural organism, it will be remembered, is, physiologically considered, but a machine for converting stimuli into reactions; and the intellectual part of our life is knit up with but the middle or 'central' portion of the machine's operations. Let us now turn to consider the final or emergent operations, the bodily activities, and the forms of consciousness connected therewithal.

Every impression which impinges on the incoming nerves produces some discharge down the outgoing ones, whether we be aware of it or not. Using sweeping terms and ignoring exceptions, *we might say that every possible feeling produces a movement, and that the movement is a movement of the entire organism, and of each and all its parts.* What happens patently when an explosion or a flash of lightning startles us, or when we are tickled, happens latently with every sensation which we receive. The only reason why we do not feel the startle or tickle in the case of insignificant sensations is partly its very small amount, partly our obtuseness. Professor Bain many years ago gave the name of the Law of Diffusion to this phenomenon of general discharge, and expressed it thus: " According as an impression is accompanied with Feeling, the aroused currents diffuse themselves over the brain, leading to a general agitation of the moving organs, as well as affecting the viscera."

In cases where the feeling is strong the law is too familiar to require proof. As Prof. Bain says:

" Each of us knows in our own experience that a sudden shock of feeling is accompanied with movements of the body generally, and with other effects. When no emotion is present, we are quiescent; a slight feeling is accompanied with slight manifestations; a more intense shock has a more intense outburst. Every pleasure and every pain, and every mode of emotion, has a definite wave of effects, which our observation makes known to us; and we apply the knowledge to infer other men's feelings from their outward display. . . . The organs first and prominently affected, in the diffused wave of nervous influence, are the moving members, and of these, by preference, the features of the face (with the ears in animals), whose movements constitute the *expression* of the countenance. But the influence extends to all the parts of the moving system, voluntary and involuntary; while an important series of effects are produced on the glands and viscera—the stomach, lungs, heart ,kidneys, skin, together with the sexual and mammary organs. . . . The circumstance is seemingly universal, the proof of it does not require a citation of instances in detail; on the objectors is thrown the burden of adducing unequivocal exceptions to the law." *

There are probably no exceptions to the diffusion of every impression through the *nerve-centres*. The *effect* of the wave through the centres may, however, often be to interfere with processes, and to diminish tensions already existing there; and the outward consequences of such inhibitions may be the arrest of discharges from the inhibited regions and the checking of bodily activities already in process of occurrence. When this happens it probably is like the draining or siphoning of certain channels by currents flowing through others. When, in walking, we suddenly stand still because a sound, sight, smell, or thought catches our attention, something like this occurs. But there are cases of arrest of peripheral activity which depend, not on central inhibition, but on stimulation of centres which discharge outgoing currents of an inhibitory sort. Whenever we are startled, for example, our heart momentarily stops or slows its beating, and then palpitates with accelerated speed. The brief arrest is due to an outgoing current down the pneumogastric nerve. This nerve, when stimulated, stops or slows the heart-beats, and this

---

* Emotions and Will, pp. 4, 5.

particular effect of startling fails to occur if the nerve be cut.

In general, however, the stimulating effects of a sense-impression preponderate over the inhibitiug effects, so that we may roughly say, as we began by saying, that the wave of discharge produces an activity in all parts of the body. The task of tracing out *all* the effects of any one incoming sensation has not yet been performed by physiologists. Recent years have, however, begun to enlarge our information; and although I must refer to special treatises for the full details, I can briefly string together here a number of separate observations which prove the truth of the law of diffusion.

First take *effects upon the circulation.* Those upon the heart we have just seen. Haller long ago recorded that the blood from an open vein flowed out faster at the beat of a drum.* In Chapter III. (p. 98) we learned how instantaneously, according to Mosso, the circulation in the brain is altered by changes of sensation and of the course of thought. The effect of objects of fear, shame, and anger upon the blood-supply of the skin, especially the skin of the face, are too well known to need remark. Sensations of the higher senses produce, according to Couty and Charpentier, the most varied effects upon the pulse-rate and blood-pressure in dogs. Fig. 81, a pulse-tracing from these authors, shows the tumultuous effect on a dog's heart of hearing the screams of another dog. The changes of blood-pressure still occurred when the pneumogastric nerves were cut, showing the vaso-motor effect to be direct and not dependent on the heart. When Mosso invented that simple instrument, the *plethysmograph,* for recording the fluctuations in volume of the members of the body, what most astonished him, he says, " in the first experiments which he made in Italy, was the extreme unrest of the blood-vessels of the hand, which at every smallest emotion, whether during waking or during sleep, changed their volume in surprising fashion." † Figure 82 (from Féré ‡)

---

* Cf. Féré. Sensation et Mouvement (1887), p. 56.

† La Paura (1884), p. 117. Compare Féré : Sensation et Mouvement, chap. XVII.

‡ Revue Philosophique, XXIV. 570.

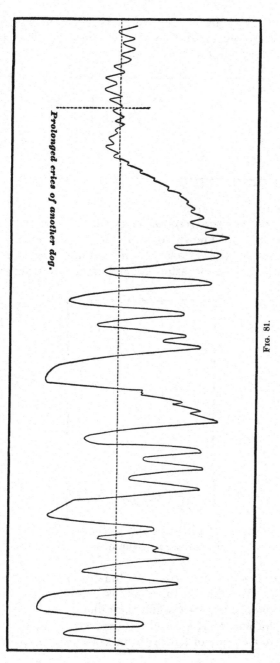

Prolonged cries of another dog.

Fig. 81.

shows the way in which the pulse of one subject was modified by the exhibition of a red light lasting from the moment marked *a* to that marked *b*.

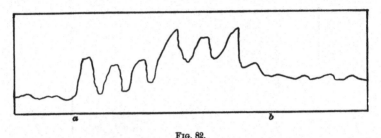

FIG. 82.

The effects upon respiration of sudden sensory stimuli are also too well known to need elaborate comment. We 'catch our breath' at every sudden sound. We 'hold our breath' whenever our attention and expectation are strongly

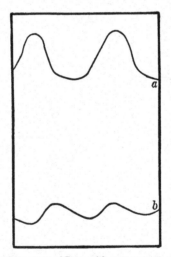

FIG. 83.—Respiratory curve of B: *a*, with eyes open; *b*, with eyes closed.

engaged, and we sigh when the tension of the situation is relieved. When a fearful object is before us we pant and cannot deeply inspire; when the object makes us angry it is, on the contrary, the act of expiration which is hard. I subjoin a couple of figures from Féré which explain them-

selves. They show the effects of light upon the breathing
of two of his hysteric patients.*

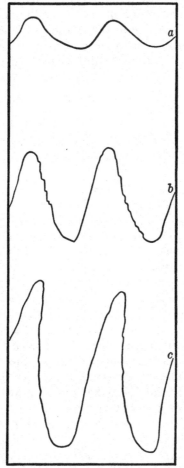

FIG. 84.—Respiratory curve of L: *a*, with yellow light; *b*, with green light; *c*, with red
light. The red has the strongest effect.

On the sweat-glands, similar consequences of sensorial
stimuli are observed. Tarchanoff, testing the condition of
the sweat-glands by the power of the skin to start a gal-

---

* Revue Phil., xxiv. pp. 566–7.—For further information about the relations between the brain and respiration, see Danilewsky's Essay in the Bio-
logisches Centralblatt, II. 690.

vanic current through electrodes applied to its surface,
found that "nearly every kind of nervous activity, from the
simplest sensations and impressions, to voluntary motions
and the highest forms of mental exertion, is accompanied
by an increased activity in the glands of the skin." * *On
the pupil* observations are recorded by Sanders which show
that a transitory dilatation follows every sensorial stimulus
applied *during sleep*, even if the stimulus be not strong
enough to wake the subject up. At the moment of awak-
ing there is a dilatation, even if strong light falls on the
eye.† The pupil of children can easily be observed to
dilate enormously under the influence of *fear*. It is said to
dilate in pain and fatigue ; and to contract, on the contrary,
in rage.

As regards *effects on the abdominal viscera*, they unquestionably exist, but very few accurate observations have
been made.‡

The bladder, bowels, and uterus respond to sensations,
even indifferent ones. Mosso and Pellicani, in their plethys-
mographic investigations on the bladder of dogs, found
all sorts of sensorial stimuli to produce reflex contractions
of this organ, independent of those of the abdominal walls.
They call the bladder 'as good an æsthesiometer as the
iris,' and refer to the not uncommon reflex effects of psychic stimuli in the human female upon this organ.§ M.
Féré has registered the contractions of the sphincter ani
which even indifferent sensations will produce. In some
pregnant women the fœtus is felt to move after almost
every sensorial excitement received by the mother. The
only natural explanation is that it is stimulated at such
moments by reflex contractions of the womb.‖ That the
glands are affected in emotion is patent enough in the case
of the tears of grief, the dry mouth, moist skin, or diar-

---

* Quoted from the report of Tarchanoff's paper (in Pflüger's Archiv,
XLVI. 46) in the American Journal of Psych., II. 652.

† Archiv f. Psychiatrie, VII. 652 ; IX. 129.

‡ Sensation et Mouvement, 57–8.

§ R. Accad. dei Lincei (1881–2). I follow the report in Hofmann u.
Schwalbe's Jahresbericht, x. II. 93.

‖ Cf. Féré, Sensation et Mouvement, chap. XIV.

rhœa of fear, the biliary disturbances which sometimes follow upon rage, etc. The watering of the mouth at the sight of succulent food is well known. It is difficult to follow the smaller degrees of all these reflex changes, but it can hardly be doubted that they exist in some degree, even where they cease to be traceable, and that all our sensations have some visceral effects. The sneezing produced by sunshine, the roughening of the skin (gooseflesh) which certain strokings, contacts, and sounds, musical or non-musical, provoke, are facts of the same order as the shuddering and standing up of the hair in fear, only of less degree.

Effects on Voluntary Muscles. Every sensorial stimulus not only sends a special discharge into certain particular muscles dependent on the special nature of the stimulus in question—some of these special discharges we have studied in Chapter XI, others we shall examine under the heads of Instinct and Emotion—but it innervates the muscles generally. M. Féré has given very curious experimental proofs of this. The strength of contraction of the subject's hand was measured by a self-registering dynamometer. Ordinarily the maximum strength, under simple experimental conditions, remains the same from day to day. But if simultaneously with the contraction the subject received a sensorial impression, the contraction was sometimes weakened, but more often increased. This reinforcing effect has received the name of *dynamogeny.* The dynamogenic value of simple *musical notes* seems to be proportional to their loudness and height. Where the notes are compounded into sad strains, the muscular strength diminishes. If the strains are gay, it is increased.—The dynamogenic value of *colored lights* varies with the color. In a subject* whose normal strength was expressed by 23, it became 24 when a blue light was

---

* The figures given are from an hysterical subject, and the differences are greater than normal. M. Féré considers that the unstable nervous system of the hysteric (' ces grenouilles de la psychologie ') shows the law on a quantitatively exaggerated scale, without altering the qualitative relations. The effects remind us a little of the influence of sensations upon minimal sensations of other orders discovered by Urbantschitsch, and reported on page 29 of this volume.

thrown on the eyes, 28 for green, 30 for yellow, 35 for orange, and 42 for red. Red is thus the most exciting color. Among *tastes,* sweet has the lowest value, next comes salt, then bitter, and finally sour, though, as M. Féré remarks, such a sour as acetic acid excites the nerves of pain and smell as well as of taste. The stimulating effects of tobacco-smoke, alcohol, beef-extract (which is innutritious), etc., etc., may be partly due to a dynamogenic action of this sort.— Of *odors,* that of musk seems to have a peculiar dynamogenic power. Fig. 85 is a copy of one of M. Féré's dynamographic tracings, which explains itself. The smaller contractions are those without stimulus; the stronger ones are due to the influence of red rays of light.

Fɪɢ. 85.

Everyone is familiar with the *patellar reflex,* or jerk upwards of the foot, which is produced by smartly tapping the tendon below the knee-pan when the leg hangs over the other knee. Drs. Weir Mitchell and Lombard have found that when other sensations come in simultaneously with the tap, the jerk is increased.* Heat, cold, pricking, itching, or faradic stimulation of the skin, sometimes strong optical impressions, music, all have this dynamogenic effect, which also results whenever voluntary movements are set up in other parts of the body, simultaneously with the tap.†

These 'dynamogenic' effects, in which one stimulation

---

* Mitchell in (Philadelphia) Medical News (Feb. 13 and 20, 1886); Lombard in American Journal of Psychology (Oct. 1887).

† Prof. H. P. Bowditch has made the interesting discovery that if the reinforcing movement be as much as 0.4 of a second late, the reinforcement fails to occur, and is transformed into a positive inhibition of the knee-jerk for retardations of between 0.4′ and 1.7′. The knee-jerk fails to be modified at all by voluntary movements made later than 1.7′ after the patellar ligament is tapped (see Boston Med. and Surg. Journ., May 31, 1888).

simply reinforces another already under way, must not be confounded with reflex acts properly so called, in which new activities are originated by the stimulus. All instinctive performances and manifestations of emotion are reflex acts. But underneath those of which we are conscious there seem to go on continually others smaller in amount, which probably in most persons might be called fluctuations of muscular *tone*, but which in certain neurotic subjects can be demonstrated ocularly. M. Féré figures some of them in the article to which I have already referred.*

Looking back over all these facts, it is hard to doubt the truth of the law of diffusion, even where verification is beyond reach. *A process set up anywhere in the centres reverberates everywhere, and in some way or other affects the organism throughout, making its activities either greater or less.* We are brought again to the assimilation which was expressed on a previous page of the nerve-central mass to a good conductor charged with electricity, of which the tension cannot be changed anywhere without changing it everywhere.

Herr Schneider has tried to show, by an ingenious and suggestive zoological review,† that all the *special* movements which highly evolved animals make are differentiated from the two originally simple movements, of contraction and expansion, in which the entire body of simple organisms takes part. The tendency to contract is the source of all the self-protective impulses and reactions which are later developed, including that of flight. The tendency to expand splits up, on the contrary, into the impulses and instincts of an aggressive kind, feeding, fighting, sexual intercourse, etc. Schneider's articles are well worth reading, if only for the careful observations on animals which they embody. I cite them here as a sort of evolutionary reason to add to the mechanical *a priori* reason why there *ought* to be the diffusive wave which our *a posteriori* instances have shown to exist.

I will now proceed to a detailed study of the more im-

---

* Revue Phil., xxiv. 572 ff.
† In the Vierteljahrschrift für wiss. Philos., iii. 294.

portant classes of movement consequent upon cerebro-mental change. They may be enumerated as—

      1) Instinctive or Impulsive Performances;

      2) Expressions of Emotion; and

      3) Voluntary Deeds;

and each shall have a chapter to itself.

CHAPTER XXIV.*

INSTINCT.

INSTINCT is usually defined as the faculty of acting in such a way as to produce certain ends, without foresight of the ends, and without previous education in the performance. That instincts, as thus defined, exist on an enormous scale in the animal kingdom needs no proof. They are the functional correlatives of structure. With the presence of a certain organ goes, one may say, almost always a native aptitude for its use.

"Has the bird a gland for the secretion of oil ? She knows instinctively how to press the oil from the gland, and apply it to the feather. Has the rattlesnake the grooved tooth and gland of poison ? He knows without instruction how to make both structure and function most effective against his enemies. Has the silk-worm the function of secreting the fluid silk ? At the proper time she winds the cocoon such as she has never seen, as thousands before have done ; and thus without instruction, pattern, or experience, forms a safe abode for herself in the period of transformation. Has the hawk talons ? She knows by instinct how to wield them effectively against the helpless quarry."†

A very common way of talking about these admirably definite tendencies to act is by naming abstractly the purpose they subserve, such as self-preservation, or defence, or care for eggs and young—and saying the animal has an instinctive fear of death or love of life, or that she has an instinct of self-preservation, or an instinct of maternity and the like. But this represents the animal as obeying abstractions which not once in a million cases is it possible it can have framed. The strict physiological way of interpret-

* This chapter has already appeared (almost exactly as now printed) in the form of magazine articles in Scribner's Magazine and in the Popular Science Monthly for 1887.

† P. A. Chadbourne : Instinct, p. 28 (New York, 1872).

ing the facts leads to far clearer results. *The actions we call instinctive all conform to the general reflex type ;* they are called forth by determinate sensory stimuli in contact with the animal's body, or at a distance in his environment. The cat runs after the mouse, runs or shows fight before the dog, avoids falling from walls and trees, shuns fire and water, etc., not because he has any notion either of life or of death, or of self, or of preservation. He has probably attained to no one of these conceptions in such a way as to react definitely upon it. He acts in each case separately, and simply because he cannot help it; being so framed that when that particular running thing called a mouse appears in his field of vision he *must* pursue ; that when that particular barking and obstreperous thing called a dog appears there he *must* retire, if at a distance, and scratch if close by ; that he *must* withdraw his feet from water and his face from flame, etc. His nervous system is to a great extent a preorganized bundle of such reactions—they are as fatal as sneezing, and as exactly correlated to their special excitants as it is to its own. Although the naturalist may, for his own convenience, class these reactions under general heads, he must not forget that in the animal it is a particular sensation or perception or image which calls them forth.

At first this view astounds us by the enormous number of special adjustments it supposes animals to possess ready-made in anticipation of the outer things among which they are to dwell. *Can* mutual dependence be so intricate and go so far? Is each thing born fitted to particular other things, and to them exclusively, as locks are fitted to their keys? Undoubtedly this must be believed to be so. Each nook and cranny of creation, down to our very skin and entrails, has its living inhabitants, with organs suited to the place, to devour and digest the food it harbors and to meet the dangers it conceals ; and the minuteness of adaptation thus shown in the way of *structure* knows no bounds. Even so are there no bounds to the minuteness of adaptation in the way of *conduct* which the several inhabitants display.

The older writings on instinct are ineffectual wastes of words, because their authors never came down to this definite and simple point of view, but smothered everything in vague wonder at the clairvoyant and prophetic power of the animals—so superior to anything in man—and at the beneficence of God in endowing them with such a gift. But God's beneficence endows them, first of all, with a nervous system; and, turning our attention to this, makes instinct immediately appear neither more nor less wonderful than all the other facts of life.

Every instinct is an impulse. Whether we shall call such impulses as blushing, sneezing, coughing, smiling, or dodging, or keeping time to music, instincts or not, is a mere matter of terminology. The process is the same throughout. In his delightfully fresh and interesting work, Der Thierische Wille, Herr G. H. Schneider subdivides impulses (*Triebe*) into sensation-impulses, perception-impulses, and idea-impulses. To crouch from cold is a sensation-impulse; to turn and follow, if we see people running one way, is a perception-impulse; to cast about for cover, if it begins to blow and rain, is an imagination-impulse. A single complex instinctive action may involve successively the awakening of impulses of all three classes. Thus a hungry lion starts to *seek* prey by the awakening in him of imagination coupled with desire; he begins to *stalk* it when, on eye, ear, or nostril, he gets an impression of its presence at a certain distance; he *springs* upon it, either when the booty takes alarm and flees, or when the distance is sufficiently reduced; he proceeds to *tear* and *devour* it the moment he gets a sensation of its contact with his claws and fangs. Seeking, stalking, springing, and devouring are just so many different kinds of muscular contraction, and neither kind is called forth by the stimulus appropriate to the other.

Schneider says of the hamster, which stores corn in its hole:

" If we analyze the propensity of storing, we find that it consists of three impulses: First, an impulse to *pick up* the nutritious object, due to perception; second, an impulse to *carry it off* into the dwelling-place, due to the idea of this latter; and third, an impulse to *lay it down* there. due to the sight of the place. It lies in the nature of the hamster that it should never see a full ear of corn without feeling a desire to strip it ; it lies in its nature to feel, as soon as its cheek-pouches are filled, an irresistible desire to hurry to its home ; and finally, it lies in its nature that the sight of the storehouse should awaken the impulse to empty the cheeks" (p. 208).

In certain animals of a low order the feeling of having executed one impulsive step is such an indispensable part of the stimulus of the next one, that the animal cannot make any variation in the order of its performance.

Now, why do the various animals do what seem to us such strange things, in the presence of such outlandish stimuli? Why does the hen, for example, submit herself to the tedium of incubating such a fearfully uninteresting set of objects as a nestful of eggs, unless she have some sort of a prophetic inkling of the result? The only answer is *ad hominem.* We can only interpret the instincts of brutes by what we know of instincts in ourselves. Why do men always lie down, when they can, on soft beds rather than on hard floors? Why do they sit round the stove on a cold day? Why, in a room, do they place themselves, ninety-nine times out of a hundred, with their faces towards its middle rather than to the wall? Why do they prefer saddle of mutton and champagne to hard-tack and ditch-water? Why does the maiden interest the youth so that everything about her seems more important and significant than anything else in the world? Nothing more can be said than that these are human ways, and that every creature *likes* its own ways, and takes to the following them as a matter of course. Science may come and consider these ways, and find that most of them are useful. But it is not for the sake of their utility that they are followed, but because at the moment of following them we feel that that is the only appropriate and natural thing to do. Not one man in a billion, when taking his dinner, ever thinks of utility. He eats because the food tastes good and makes him want more. If you ask him *why* he should want to eat more of what tastes like that, instead of revering you as a philosopher he will probably laugh at you for a fool. The connection between the savory sensation and the act it awakens is for him absolute and *selbstverständlich,* an '*a priori* synthesis' of the most perfect sort, needing no proof but its own evidence. It takes, in short, what Berkeley calls a mind debauched by learning to carry the process of making the natural seem strange, so far as to ask for the *why* of any instinctive human act. To the metaphysician alone can such questions occur as : Why do we smile, when pleased, and not scowl? Why are we unable to talk to a crowd as we talk to a single friend? Why does a particular maiden turn our wits so upside-down? The common man can only say, " *Of course* we smile, *of course* our heart palpitates at the sight of the crowd, *of course* we love the maiden, that beautiful soul clad in that perfect form, so palpably and flagrantly made from all eternity to be loved!"

And so, probably, does each animal feel about the particular things it tends to do in presence of particular objects. They, too, are *a priori* syntheses. To the lion it is the lioness which is made to be loved; to the bear, the she-bear. To the broody hen the notion would probably seem monstrous that there should be a creature in the world to whom a nestful of eggs was not the utterly fascinating and precious and never-to-be-too-much-sat-upon object which it is to her.*

Thus we may be sure that, however mysterious some animals' instincts may appear to us, our instincts will appear no less mysterious to them. And we may conclude that, to the animal which obeys it, every impulse and every step of every instinct shines with its own sufficient light, and seems at the moment the only eternally right and proper thing to do. It is done for its own sake exclusively. What volup-

---

* "It would be very simple-minded to suppose that bees follow their queen, and protect her and care for her, because they are aware that without her the hive would become extinct. The odor or the aspect of their queen is manifestly agreeable to the bees—that is why they love her so. Does not all true love base itself on agreeable perceptions much more than on representations of utility ?" (G. H. Schneider, Der Thierische Wille, p. 187.) *A priori*, there is no reason to suppose that *any* sensation might not in *some* animal cause *any* emotion and *any* impulse. To us it seems unnatural that an odor should directly excite anger or fear; or a color, lust. Yet there are creatures to which some smells are quite as frightful as any sounds, and very likely others to which color is as much a sexual irritant as form.

tuous thrill may not shake a fly, when she at last discovers the one particular leaf, or carrion, or bit of dung, that out of all the world can stimulate her ovipositor to its discharge? Does not the discharge then seem to her the only fitting thing? And need she care or know anything about the future maggot and its food?

Since the *egg-laying instincts* are simple examples to consider, a few quotations about them from Schneider may be serviceable:

" The phenomenon so often talked about, so variously interpreted, so surrounded with mystification, that an insect should always lay her eggs in a spot appropriate to the nourishment of her young, is no more marvellous than the phenomenon that every animal pairs with a mate capable of bearing posterity, or feeds on materials capable of affording him nourishment. . . . Not only the choice of a place for laying the eggs, but all the various acts for depositing and protecting them, are occasioned by the perception of the proper object, and the relation of this perception to the various stages of maternal impulse. When the burying beetle perceives a carrion, she is not only impelled to approach it and lodge her eggs in it, but also to go through the movements requisite for burying it; just as a bird who sees his hen-bird is impelled to caress her, to strut around her, dance before her, or in some other way to woo her; just as a tiger, when he sees an antelope, is impelled to stalk it, to pounce upon it, and to strangle it. When the tailor-bee cuts out pieces of rose-leaf, bends them, carries them into a caterpillar- or mouse-hole in trees or in the earth, covers their seams again with other pieces, and so makes a thimble-shaped case—when she fills this with honey and lays an egg in it, all these various appropriate expressions of her will are to be explained by supposing that at the time when the eggs are ripe within her, the appearance of a suitable caterpillar- or mouse-hole and the perception of rose-leaves are so correlated in the insect with the several impulses in question, that the performances follow as a matter of course when the perceptions take place. . . .

" The perception of the empty nest, or of a single egg, seems in birds to stand in such a close relation to the physiological functions of oviparation, that it serves as a direct stimulus to these functions, while the perception of a sufficient number of eggs has just the opposite effect. It is well known that hens and ducks lay more eggs if we keep removing them than if we leave them in the nest. The impulse to sit arises, as a rule, when a bird sees a certain number of eggs in her nest. If this number is not yet to be seen there, the ducks continue to lay, although they perhaps have laid twice as many eggs as they are accustomed to sit upon. . . . That sitting, also, is independent of any idea of purpose and is a pure perception-impulse is evident, among other things, from the fact that many birds, e.g. wild ducks, steal eggs from each other. . . . The bodily disposition to sit is, it is true, one condition [since broody hens will sit where there are no eggs], but the perception of the eggs is the other condition of the activity of the incubating impulse. The propensity of the cuckoo and of the cow-bird to lay their eggs in the nests of other species must also be interpreted as a pure perception-impulse. These birds have no bodily disposition to become broody, and there is therefore in them no connection between the perception of an egg and the impulse to sit upon it. Eggs ripen, however, in their oviducts, and the body tends to get rid of them. And since the two birds just named do not drop their eggs anywhere on the ground, but in nests, which are the only places where they may preserve the species, it might easily appear that such preservation of the species was what they had in view, and that they acted with full consciousness of the purpose. But this is not so. . . . The cuckoo is simply excited by the perception of quite determinate sorts of nest, which already contain eggs, to drop her own into them, and throw the others out, because this perception is a direct stimulus to these acts. It is impossible that she should have any notion of the other bird coming and sitting on her egg." *

INSTINCTS NOT ALWAYS BLIND OR INVARIABLE.

Remember that nothing is said yet of the origin of instincts, but only of the constitution of those that exist fully formed. How stands it with the instincts of mankind?

Nothing is commoner than the remark that Man differs from lower creatures by the almost total absence of instincts, and the assumption of their work in him by ‘reason.’ A fruitless discussion might be waged on this point by two theorizers who were careful not to define their terms. ‘Reason’ might be used, as it often has been, since Kant, not as the mere power of ‘inferring,’ but also as a name for the *tendency to obey impulses* of a certain lofty sort, such as duty, or universal ends. And ‘instinct’ might have its significance so broadened as to cover all impulses whatever, even the impulse to act from the idea of a distant fact, as well as the impulse to act from a present sensation. Were the word instinct used in this broad way, it would of course be impossible to restrict it, as we began by doing, to actions done with no prevision of an end. We must of course avoid a quarrel about words, and the facts of the case are

---

* Der Thierische Wille, pp. 282–3.

really tolerably plain. Man has a far greater variety of *impulses* than any lower animal; and any one of these impulses, taken in itself, is as 'blind' as the lowest instinct can be; but, owing to man's memory, power of reflection, and power of inference, they come each one to be felt by him, after he has once yielded to them and experienced their results, in connection with a *foresight* of those results. In this condition an impulse acted out may be said to be acted out, in part at least, *for the sake* of its results. It is obvious that *every instinctive act, in an animal with memory, must cease to be 'blind' after being once repeated*, and must be accompanied with foresight of its 'end' just so far as that end may have fallen under the animal's cognizance. An insect that lays her eggs in a place where she never sees them hatched must always do so 'blindly;' but a hen who has already hatched a brood can hardly be assumed to sit with perfect 'blindness' on her second nest. Some expectation of consequences must in every case like this be aroused; and this expectation, according as it is that of something desired or of something disliked, must necessarily either re-enforce or inhibit the mere impulse. The hen's idea of the chickens would probably encourage her to sit; a rat's memory, on the other hand, of a former escape from a trap would neutralize his impulse to take bait from anything that reminded him of that trap. If a boy sees a fat hopping-toad, he probably has incontinently an impulse (especially if with other boys) to smash the creature with a stone, which impulse we may suppose him blindly to obey. But something in the expression of the dying toad's clasped hands suggests the meanness of the act, or reminds him of sayings he has heard about the sufferings of animals being like his own; so that, when next he is tempted by a toad, an idea arises which, far from spurring him again to the torment, prompts kindly actions, and may even make him the toad's champion against less reflecting boys.

It is plain, then, that, *no matter how well endowed an animal may originally be in the way of instincts, his resultant actions will be much modified if the instincts combine with experience,* if in addition to impulses he have memories, associations, inferences, and expectations, on any considerable scale. An object O, on which he has an instinctive impulse to react in the manner A, would *directly* provoke him to that reaction. But O has meantime become for him a *sign* of the nearness of P, on which he has an equally strong impulse to react in the manner B, quite unlike A. So that when he meets O the immediate impulse A and the remote impulse B struggle in his breast for the mastery. The fatality and uniformity said to be characteristic of instinctive actions will be so little manifest that one might be tempted to deny to him altogether the possession of any instinct about the object O. Yet how false this judgment would be! The instinct about O is there; only by the complication of the associative machinery it has come into conflict with another instinct about P.

Here we immediately reap the good fruits of our simple physiological conception of what an instinct is. If it be a mere excito-motor impulse, due to the pre-existence of a certain 'reflex arc' in the nerve-centres of the creature, of course it must follow the law of all such reflex arcs. One liability of such arcs is to have their activity 'inhibited,' by other processes going on at the same time. It makes no difference whether the arc be organized at birth, or ripen spontaneously later, or be due to acquired habit, it must take its chances with all the other arcs, and sometimes succeed, and sometimes fail, in drafting off the currents through itself. The mystical view of an instinct would make it invariable. The physiological view would require it to show occasional irregularities in any animal in whom the number of separate instincts, and the possible entrance of the same stimulus into several of them, were great. And such irregularities are what every superior animal's instincts do show in abundance.*

---

* In the instincts of mammals, and even of lower creatures, the uniformity and infallibility which, a generation ago, were considered as essential characters do not exist. The minuter study of recent years has found continuity, transition, variation, and mistake, wherever it has looked for them, and decided that what is called an instinct is usually only a tendency to act in a way of which the *average* is pretty constant, but which need not be mathematically 'true.' Cf. on this point Darwin's Origin of Species: Romanes's Mental Evol., chaps. XI to XVI incl., and Appendix; W. L. Lindsay's Mind in Lower Animals, vol. I. 133–141; II. chaps. V, XX;

Wherever the mind is elevated enough to discriminate; wherever several distinct sensory elements must combine to discharge the reflex-arc; wherever, instead of plumping into action instantly at the first rough intimation of what *sort* of a thing is there, the agent waits to see which *one* of its kind it is and what the *circumstances* are of its appearance; wherever different individuals and different circumstances can impel him in different ways; wherever these are the conditions—we have a masking of the elementary constitution of the instinctive life. The whole story of our dealings with the lower wild animals is the history of our taking advantage of the way in which they judge of everything by its mere label, as it were, so as to ensnare or kill them. Nature, in them, has left matters in this rough way, and made them act *always* in the manner which would be *oftenest* right. There are more worms unattached to hooks than impaled upon them; therefore, on the whole, says Nature to her fishy children, bite at *every* worm and take your chances. But as her children get higher, and their lives more precious, she reduces the risks. Since what seems to be the same object may be now a genuine food and now a bait; since in gregarious species each individual may prove to be either the friend or the rival, according to the circumstances, of another; since any entirely unknown object may be fraught with weal or woe, *Nature implants contrary impulses to act on many classes of things*, and leaves it to slight alterations in the conditions of the individual case to decide which impulse shall carry the day. Thus, greediness and suspicion, curiosity and timidity, coyness and desire, bashfulness and vanity, sociability and pugnacity, seem to shoot over into each other as quickly, and to remain in as unstable equilibrium, in the higher birds and mammals as in man. They are all impulses, congenital, blind at first, and productive of motor reactions of a rigorously determinate sort. *Each one of them, then, is an instinct,* as instincts are commonly defined. *But they contradict each other*—'experience' in each particular oppor-

and K. Semper's Conditions of Existence in Animals, where a great many instances will be found.

tunity of application usually deciding the issue. *The animal that exhibits them loses the 'instinctive' demeanor and appears to lead a life of hesitation and choice, an intellectual life; not, however, because he has no instincts—rather because he has so many that they block each other's path.*

Thus, then, without troubling ourselves about the words instinct and reason, we may confidently say that however uncertain man's reactions upon his environment may sometimes seem in comparison with those of lower creatures, the uncertainty is probably not due to their possession of any principles of action which he lacks. *On the contrary, man possesses all the impulses that they have, and a great many more besides.* In other words, there is no material antagonism between instinct and reason. Reason, *per se,* can inhibit no impulses; the only thing that can neutralize an impulse is an impulse the other way. Reason may, however, make an *inference which will excite the imagination so as to set loose* the impulse the other way; and thus, though the animal richest in reason might be also the animal richest in instinctive impulses too, he would never seem the fatal automaton which a *merely* instinctive animal would be.

Let us now turn to human impulses with a little more detail. All we have ascertained so far is that impulses of an originally instinctive character may exist, and yet not betray themselves by automatic fatality of conduct. But in man what impulses do exist? In the light of what has been said, it is obvious that an existing impulse may not always be superficially apparent even when its object is there. And we shall see that some impulses may be masked by causes of which we have not yet spoken.

TWO PRINCIPLES OF NON-UNIFORMITY IN INSTINCTS.

Were one devising an abstract scheme, nothing would be easier than to discover from an animal's actions just how many instincts he possessed. He would react in one way only upon each class of objects with which his life had to deal; he would react in identically the same way upon every specimen of a class; and he would react invariably during his whole life. There would be no gaps among his instincts; all would come to light without perversion or disguise. But there are no such abstract animals, and no-where does the instinctive life display itself in such a way. Not only, as we have seen, may objects of the same class arouse reactions of opposite sorts in consequence of slight changes in the circumstances, in the individual object, or in the agent's inward condition; but two other principles of which we have not yet spoken, may come into play and produce results so striking that observers as eminent as Messrs. D. A. Spalding and Romanes do not hesitate to call them 'derangements of the mental constitution,' and to conclude that the instinctive machinery has got out of gear.

These principles are those

1. Of the *inhibition of instincts by habits;* and
2. Of the *transitoriness of instincts.*

Taken in conjunction with the two former principles—that the same object may excite ambiguous impulses, or *suggest* an impulse different from that which it *excites,* by suggesting a remote object—they explain any amount of departure from uniformity of conduct, without implying any getting out of gear of the elementary impulses from which the conduct flows.

1. The law of inhibition of instincts by habits is this: *When objects of a certain class elicit from an animal a certain sort of reaction, it often happens that the animal becomes partial to the first specimen of the class on which it has reacted, and will not afterward react on any other specimen.*

The selection of a particular hole to live in, of a particular mate, of a particular feeding-ground, a particular variety of diet, a particular anything, in short, out of a possible multitude, is a very wide-spread tendency among animals, even those low down in the scale. The limpet will return to the same sticking-place in its rock, and the lobster to its favorite nook on the sea-bottom. The rabbit will deposit its dung in the same corner; the bird makes its nest on the same bough. But each of these preferences carries with it an insensibility to *other* opportunities and occasions—an insensibility which can only be described physiologically as an inhibition of new impulses by the habit of old ones already formed. The possession of homes and wives of our own makes us strangely insensible to the charms of those of other people. Few of us are adventurous in the matter of food; in fact, most of us think there is something disgusting in a bill of fare to which we are unused. Strangers, we are apt to think, cannot be worth knowing, especially if they come from distant cities, etc. The original impulse which got us homes, wives, dietaries, and friends at all, seems to exhaust itself in its first achievements and to leave no surplus energy for reacting on new cases. And so it comes about that, witnessing this torpor, an observer of mankind might say that no *instinctive* propensity toward certain objects existed at all. It existed, but it existed *miscellaneously*, or as an instinct pure and simple, only before habit was formed. A habit, once grafted on an instinctive tendency, restricts the range of the tendency itself, and keeps us from reacting on any but the habitual object, although other objects might just as well have been chosen had they been the first-comers.

Another sort of arrest of instinct by habit is where the same class of objects awakens contrary instinctive impulses. Here the impulse first followed toward a given individual of the class is apt to keep him from ever awakening the opposite impulse in us. In fact, the whole class may be protected by this individual specimen from the application to it of the other impulse. Animals, for example, awaken in a child the opposite impulses of fearing and fondling. But if a child, in his first attempts to pat a dog, gets snapped at or bitten, so that the impulse of fear is strongly aroused, it may be that for years to come no dog will excite in him the impulse to fondle again. On the other hand, the greatest natural enemies, if carefully introduced to each other when young and guided at the outset by superior authority, settle down into those 'happy families' of friends which we see in our menageries. Young animals, immediately after birth, have no instinct of fear, but show their dependence by allowing themselves to be freely handled. Later, however, they grow 'wild,' and, if left to themselves, will not let man approach them. I am told by farmers in the

Adirondack wilderness that it is a very serious matter if a cow wanders off and calves in the woods and is not found for a week or more. The calf, by that time, is as wild and almost as fleet as a deer, and hard to capture without violence. But calves rarely show any particular wildness to the men who have been in contact with them during the first days of their life, when the instinct to attach themselves is uppermost, nor do they dread strangers as they would if brought up wild.

Chickens give a curious illustration of the same law. Mr. Spalding's wonderful article on instinct shall supply us with the facts. These little creatures show opposite instincts of attachment and fear, either of which may be aroused by the same object, man. If a chick is born in the absence of the hen, it

" will follow any moving object. And, when guided by sight alone, they seem to have no more disposition to follow a hen than to follow a duck or a human being. Unreflecting lookers-on, when they saw chickens a day old running after me," says Mr. Spalding, "and older ones following me for miles, and answering to my whistle, imagined that I must have some occult power over the creatures: whereas I had simply allowed them to follow me from the first. There is the instinct to follow; and the ear, prior to experience, attaches them to the right object." *

But if a man presents himself for the first time when the instinct of *fear* is strong, the phenomena are altogether reversed. Mr. Spalding kept three chickens hooded until they were nearly four days old, and thus describes their behavior :

" Each of them, on being unhooded, evinced the greatest terror to me, dashing off in the opposite direction whenever I sought to approach it. The table on which they were unhooded stood before a window, and each in its turn beat against the window like a wild bird. One of them darted behind some books, and, squeezing itself into a corner, remained cowering for a length of time. We might guess at the meaning of this strange and exceptional wildness ; but the odd fact is enough for my present purpose. Whatever might have been the meaning of this marked change in their mental constitution—had they been unhooded on the previous day they would have run to me instead of from me—it could not have been the effect of experience ; it must have resulted wholly from changes in their own organizations." †

---

* Spalding, Macmillan's Magazine, Feb. 1873, p. 287.
† *Ibid.* p. 289.

Their case was precisely analogous to that of the Adirondack calves. The two opposite instincts relative to the same object ripen in succession. If the first one engenders a habit, that habit will inhibit the application of the second instinct to that object. All animals are tame during the earliest phase of their infancy. Habits formed then limit the effects of whatever instincts of wildness may later be evolved.

Mr. Romanes gives some very curious examples of the way in which instinctive tendencies may be altered by the habits to which their first 'objects' have given rise. The cases are a little more complicated than those mentioned in the text, inasmuch as the object reacted on not only starts a habit which inhibits other kinds of impulse toward it (although such other kinds might be natural), but even modifies by its own peculiar conduct the constitution of the impulse which it actually awakens.

Two of the instances in question are those of hens who hatched out broods of chicks after having (in three previous years) hatched ducks. They strove to coax or to compel their new progeny to enter the water, and seemed much perplexed at their unwillingness. Another hen adopted a brood of young ferrets which, having lost their mother, were put under her. During all the time they were left with her she had to sit on the nest, for they could not wander like young chicks. She obeyed their hoarse growling as she would have obeyed her chickens' peep. She combed out their hair with her bill, and "used frequently to stop and look with one eye at the wriggling nestful, with an inquiring gaze, expressive of astonishment." At other times she would fly up with a loud scream, doubtless because the orphans had nipped her in their search for teats. Finally, a Brahma hen nursed a young peacock during the enormous period of *eighteen months*, and never laid any eggs during all this time. The abnormal degree of pride which she showed in her wonderful chicken is described by Dr. Romanes as ludicrous.*

---

* For the cases in full see Mental Evolution in Animals, pp. 213-217.

2. This leads us to the *law of transitoriness*, which is this : *Many instincts ripen at a certain age and then fade away.* A consequence of this law is that if, during the time of such an instinct's vivacity, objects adequate to arouse it are met with, a *habit* of acting on them is formed, which remains when the original instinct has passed away ; but that if no such objects are met with, then no habit will be formed ; and, later on in life, when the animal meets the objects, he will altogether fail to react, as at the earlier epoch he would instinctively have done.

No doubt such a law is restricted. Some instincts are far less transient than others—those connected with feeding and 'self-preservation' may hardly be transient at all, and some, after fading out for a time, recur as strong as ever, e.g., the instincts of pairing and rearing young. The law, however, though not absolute, is certainly very widespread, and a few examples will illustrate just what it means.

In the chickens and calves above mentioned, it is obvious that the instinct to follow and become attached fades out after a few days, and that the instinct of flight then takes its place, the conduct of the creature toward man being decided by the formation or non-formation of a certain habit during those days. The transiency of the chicken's instinct to follow is also proved by its conduct toward the hen. Mr. Spalding kept some chickens shut up till they were comparatively old, and, speaking of these, he says :

" A chicken that has not heard the call of the mother till until eight or ten days old then hears it as if it heard it not. I regret to find that on this point my notes are not so full as I could wish, or as they might have been. There is, however, an account of one chicken that could not be returned to the mother when ten days old. The hen followed it, and tried to entice it in every way ; still, it continually left her and ran to the house or to any person of whom it caught sight. This it persisted in doing, though beaten back with a small branch dozens of times, and, indeed, cruelly maltreated. It was also placed under the mother at night, but it again left her in the morning."

The instinct of sucking is ripe in all mammals at birth, and leads to that habit of taking the breast which, in the human infant, may be prolonged by daily exercise long beyond its usual term of a year or a year and a half. But the instinct itself is transient, in the sense that if, for any reason, the child be fed by spoon during the first few days of its life and not put to the breast, it may be no easy matter after that to make it suck at all. So of calves. If their mother die, or be dry, or refuse to let them suck for a day or two, so that they are fed by hand, it becomes hard to get them to suck at all when a new nurse is provided. The ease with which sucking creatures are weaned, by simply breaking the habit and giving them food in a new way, shows that the instinct, purely as such, must be entirely extinct.

Assuredly the simple fact that instincts are transient, and that the effect of later ones may be altered by the habits which earlier ones have left behind, is a far more philosophical explanation than the notion of an instinctive constitution vaguely 'deranged' or 'thrown out of gear.'

I have observed a Scotch terrier, born on the floor of a stable in December, and transferred six weeks later to a carpeted house, make, when he was less than four months old, a very elaborate pretence of burying things, such as gloves, etc., with which he had played till he was tired. He scratched the carpet with his forefeet, dropped the object from his mouth upon the spot, and then scratched all about it (with both fore- and hind-feet, if I remember rightly), and finally went away and let it lie. Of course, the act was entirely useless. I saw him perform it at that age, some four or five times, and never again in his life. The conditions were not present to fix a habit which should last when the prompting instinct died away. But suppose meat instead of a glove, earth instead of a carpet, hunger-pangs instead of a fresh supper a few hours later, and it is easy to see how this dog might have got into a habit of burying superfluous food, which might have lasted all his life. Who can swear that the strictly instructive part of the food-burying propensity in the wild *Canidæ* may not be as short-lived as it was in this terrier?

A similar instance is given by Dr. H. D. Schmidt* of New Orleans:

---

* Transactions of American Neurological Association, vol. i. p. 129 (1875).

"I may cite the example of a young squirrel which I had tamed, a number of years ago, when serving in the army, and when I had sufficient leisure and opportunity to study the habits of animals. In the autumn, before the winter sets in, adult squirrels bury as many nuts as they can collect, separately, in the ground. Holding the nut firmly between their teeth, they first scratch a hole in the grond, and, after pointing their ears in all directions to convince themselves that no enemy is near, they ram—the head, with the nut still between the front teeth, serving as a sledge-hammer—the nut into the ground, and then fill up the hole by means of their paws. The whole process is executed with great rapidity, and, as it appeared to me, always with exactly the same movements ; in fact, it is done so well that I could never discover the traces of the burial-ground. Now, as regards the young squirrel, which, of course, never had been present at the burial of a nut, I observed that, after having eaten a number of hickory-nuts to appease its appetite, it would take one between its teeth, then sit upright and listen in all directions. Finding all right, it would scratch upon the smooth blanket on which I was playing with it as if to make a hole, then hammer with the nut between its teeth upon the blanket, and finally perform all the motions required to fill up a hole—*in the air;* after which it would jump away, leaving the nut, of course, uncovered."

The anecdote, of course, illustrates beautifully the close relation of instinct to reflex action—a particular perception calls forth particular movements, and that is all. Dr. Schmidt writes me that the squirrel in question soon passed away from his observation. It may fairly be presumed that, if he had been long retained prisoner in a cage, he would soon have forgotten his gesticulations over the hickory-nuts.

One might, indeed, go still further with safety, and expect that, if such a captive squirrel were then set free, he would never afterwards acquire this peculiar instinct of his tribe.*

Leaving lower animals aside, and turning to human instincts, we see the law of transiency corroborated on the

* "Mr. Spalding," says Mr. Lewes (Problems of Life and Mind, prob. I. chap. II. § 22, note), "tells me of a friend of his who reared a gosling in the kitchen, away from all water ; when this bird was some months old, and was taken to a pond, it not only refused to go into the water, but when thrown in scrambled out again, as a hen would have done. Here was an instinct entirely suppressed." See a similar observation on ducklings in T. R. R. Stebbing : Essays on Darwinism (London, 1871), p. 73.

widest scale by the alternation of different interests and passions as human life goes on. With the child, life is all play and fairy-tales and learning the external properties of 'things;' with the youth, it is bodily exercises of a more systematic sort, novels of the real world, boon-fellowship and song, friendship and love, nature, travel and adventure, science and philosophy; with the man, ambition and policy, acquisitiveness, responsibility to others, and the selfish zest of the battle of life. If a boy grows up alone at the age of games and sports, and learns neither to play ball, nor row, nor sail, nor ride, nor skate, nor fish, nor shoot, probably he will be sedentary to the end of his days; and, though the best of opportunities be afforded him for learning these things later, it is a hundred to one but he will pass them by and shrink back from the effort of taking those necessary first steps the prospect of which, at an earlier age, would have filled him with eager delight. The sexual passion expires after a protracted reign; but it is well known that its peculiar manifestations in a given individual depend almost entirely on the habits he may form during the early period of its activity. Exposure to bad company then makes him a loose liver all his days; chastity kept at first makes the same easy later on. In all pedagogy the great thing is to strike the iron while hot, and to seize the wave of the pupil's interest in each successive subject before its ebb has come, so that knowledge may be got and a habit of skill acquired—a headway of interest, in short, secured, on which afterward the individual may float. There is a happy moment for fixing skill in drawing, for making boys collectors in natural history, and presently dissectors and botanists; then for initiating them into the harmonies of mechanics and the wonders of physical and chemical law. Later, introspective psychology and the metaphysical and religious mysteries take their turn; and, last of all, the drama of human affairs and worldly wisdom in the widest sense of the term. In each of us a saturation-point is soon reached in all these things; the impetus of our purely intellectual zeal expires, and unless the topic be one associated with some urgent personal need that keeps our wits constantly whetted about it, we settle into an equilibrium, and live on what we learned when our interest was fresh and instinctive, without adding to the store. Outside of their own business, the ideas gained by men before they are twenty-five are practically the only ideas they shall have in their lives. They *cannot* get anything new. Disinterested curiosity is past, the mental grooves and channels set, the power of assimilation gone. If by chance we ever do learn anything about some entirely new topic we are afflicted with a strange sense of insecurity, and we fear to advance a resolute opinion. But, with things learned in the plastic days of instinctive curiosity we never lose entirely our sense of being at home. There remains a kinship, a sentiment of intimate acquaintance, which, even when we know we have failed to keep abreast of the subject, flatters us with a sense of power over it, and makes us feel not altogether out of the pale.

Whatever individual exceptions might be cited to this are of the sort that ' prove the rule.'

To detect the moment of the instinctive readiness for the subject is, then, the first duty of every educator. As for the pupils, it would probably lead to a more earnest temper on the part of college students if they had less belief in their unlimited future intellectual potentialities, and could be brought to realize that whatever physics and political economy and philosophy they are now acquiring are, for better or worse, the physics and political economy and philosophy that will have to serve them to the end.

The natural conclusion to draw from this transiency of instincts is that *most instincts are implanted for the sake of giving rise to habits, and that, this purpose once accomplished, the instincts themselves, as such, have no raison d'être in the psychical economy, and consequently fade away.* That occasionally an instinct should fade before circumstances permit of a habit being formed, or that, if the habit be formed, other factors than the pure instinct should modify its course, need not surprise us. Life is full of the imperfect adjustment to individual cases, of arrangements which, taking the species as a whole, are quite orderly and regular. Instinct cannot be expected to escape this general risk.

SPECIAL HUMAN INSTINCTS.

Let us now test our principles by turning to human instincts in more detail. We cannot pretend in these pages to be minute or exhaustive. But we can say enough to set all the above generalities in a more favorable light. But first, what kind of motor reactions upon objects shall we count as instincts? This, as aforesaid, is a somewhat arbitrary matter. Some of the actions aroused in us by objects go no further than our own bodies. Such is the bristling up of the attention when a novel object is perceived, or the 'expression' on the face or the breathing apparatus of an emotion it may excite. These movements merge into ordinary reflex actions like laughing when tickled, or making a wry face at a bad taste. Other actions take effect upon the outer world. Such are flight from a wild beast, imitation of what we see a comrade do, etc. On the whole it is best to be catholic, since it is very hard to draw an exact line ; and call both of these kinds of activity instinctive, so far as either may be *naturally* provoked by the presence of specific sorts of outward fact.

Professor Preyer, in his careful little work, 'Die Seele des Kindes,' says "instinctive acts are in man few in number, and, apart from those connected with the sexual passion, difficult to recognize after early youth is past." And he adds, " so much the more attention should we pay to the instinctive movements of new-born babies, sucklings, and small children." That instinctive acts should be easiest *recognized* in childhood would be a very natural effect of our principles of transitoriness, and of the restrictive influence of habits once acquired; but we shall see how far they are from being 'few in number' in man. Professor Preyer divides the movements of infants into *impulsive, reflex*, and instinctive. By impulsive movements he means *random* movements of limbs, body, and voice, with no aim, and before perception is aroused. Among the first reflex movements are crying on contact with the air, *sneezing, snuffling, snoring, coughing, sighing, sobbing, gagging, vomiting, hiccuping, starting, moving the limbs when tickled, touched, or blown upon*, etc., etc.

Of the movements called by him instinctive in the child, Professor Preyer gives a full account. Herr Schneider does the same; and as their descriptions agree with each other and with what other writers about infancy say, I will base my own very brief statement on theirs.

Sucking : almost perfect at birth ; not coupled with any congenital tendency to *seek* the breast, this being a later acquisition. As we have seen, sucking is a transitory instinct.

Biting an object placed in the mouth, *chewing* and *grinding the teeth; licking* sugar ; making characteristic *grimaces* over bitter and sweet tastes ; *spitting* out.

Clasping an object which touches the fingers or toes. Later, attempts to *grasp* at an object seen at a distance. *Pointing at* such objects, and making a peculiar *sound expressive of desire*, which, in my own three children, was the first manifestation of speech, occurring many weeks before other significant sounds.

Carrying to the mouth of the object, when grasped. This instinct, guided and inhibited by the sense of taste, and combined with the instincts of biting, chewing, sucking, spitting-out, etc., and with the reflex act of swallowing, leads in the individual to a set of habits which constitute his *function of alimentation*, and which may or may not be gradually modified as life goes on.

Crying at bodily discomfort, hunger, or pain, and at solitude. *Smiling* at being noticed, fondled, or smiled at by others. It seems very doubtful whether young infants have any instinctive fear of a terrible or scowling face. I have been unable to make my own children, under a year old, change their expression when I changed mine; at most they manifested attention or curiosity. Preyer instances a *protrusion of the lips*, which, he says, may be so great as to remind one of that in the chimpanzee, as an instinctive expression of concentrated attention in the human infant.

Turning the head aside as a gesture of rejection, a gesture usually accompanied with a frown and a bending back of the body, and with holding the breath.

Holding head erect.

Sitting up.

Standing.

Locomotion. The early movements of children's limbs
are more or less symmetrical. Later a baby will move his
legs in alternation if suspended in the air. But until the
impulse to walk awakens by the natural ripening of the
nerve-centres, it seems to make no difference how often the
child's feet may be placed in contact with the ground ; the
legs remain limp, and do not respond to the sensation of
contact in the soles by muscular contractions *pressing downwards*. No sooner, however, is the standing impulse born,
than the child stiffens his legs and presses downward as
soon as he feels the floor. In some babies this is the first
locomotory reaction. In others it is preceded by the instinct to *creep*, which arises, as I can testify, often in a very
sudden way. Yesterday the baby sat quite contentedly
wherever he was put ; to-day it has become impossible to
keep him sitting at all, so irresistible is the impulse, aroused
by the sight of the floor, to throw himself forward upon his
hands. Usually the arms are too weak, and the ambitious
little experimenter falls on his nose. But his perseverance
is dauntless, and he ends in a few days by learning to travel
rapidly around the room in the quadrupedal way. The
position of the legs in 'creeping' varies much from one
child to another. My own child, when creeping, was often
observed to pick up objects from the floor with his mouth,
a phenomenon which, as Dr. O. W. Holmes has remarked,
like the early tendency to grasp with the toes, easily lends
itself to interpretation as a reminiscence of prehuman ancestral habits.

The walking instinct may awaken with no less suddenness, and its entire education be completed within a week's
compass, barring, of course, a little 'grogginess' in the
gait. Individual infants vary enormously ; but on the whole
it is safe to say that the mode of development of these
locomotor instincts is inconsistent with the account given
by the older English associationist school, of their being
results of the individual's education, due altogether to the
gradual association of certain perceptions with certain haphazard movements and certain resultant pleasures. Mr.

Bain has tried,* by describing the demeanor of new-born lambs, to show that locomotion is *learned* by a very rapid experience. But the observation recorded proves the faculty to be almost perfect from the first; and all others who have observed new-born calves, lambs, and pigs agree that in these animals the powers of standing and walking, and of interpreting the topographical significance of sights and sounds, are all but fully developed at birth. Often in animals who seem to be 'learning' to walk or fly the semblance is illusive. The awkwardness shown is not due to the fact that 'experience' has not yet been there to associate the successful movements and exclude the failures, but to the fact that the animal is beginning his attempts before the co-ordinating centres have quite ripened for their work. Mr. Spalding's observations on this point are conclusive as to birds.

"Birds," he says, " do not *learn* to fly. Two years ago I shut up five unfledged swallows in a small box, not much larger than the nest from which they were taken. The little box, which had a wire front, was hung on the wall near the nest, and the young swallows were fed by their parents through the wires. In this confinement, where they could not even extend their wings, they were kept until after they were fully fledged. . . . On going to set the prisoners free, one was found dead. . . . The remaining four were allowed to escape one at a time. Two of these were perceptibly wavering and unsteady in their flight. One of them, after a flight of some ninety yards, disappeared among some trees." No. 3 and No. 4 " never flew against anything, nor was there, in their avoiding objects, any appreciable difference between them and the old birds. No. 3 swept round the Wellingtonia, and No. 4 rose over the hedge, just as we see the old swallows doing every hour of the day. I have this summer verified these observations. Of two swallows I had similarly confined, one, on being set free, flew a yard or two close to the ground, rose in the direction of a beech-tree, which it gracefully avoided; it was seen for a considerable time sweeping round the beeches and performing magnificent evolutions in the air high above them. The other, which was observed to beat the air with its wings more than usual, was soon lost to sight behind some trees. Titmice, tomtits, and wrens I have made the subjects of similar observations, and with similar results." *

In the light of this report, one may well be tempted to make a prediction about the human child, and say that if a

---

* Senses and Intellect, 3d ed. pp. 413–675.
† Nature, XII. 507 (1875).

baby were kept from getting on his feet for two or three
weeks after the first impulse to walk had shown itself in
him,—a small blister on each sole would do the business,—
he might then be expected to walk about as well, through
the mere ripening of his nerve-centres, as if the ordinary
process of ' learning' had been allowed to occur during all
the blistered time. It is to be hoped that some scientific
widower, left alone with his offspring at the critical moment,
may ere long test this suggestion on the living subject.
Climbing on trees, fences, furniture, banisters, etc., is a well-
marked instinctive propensity which ripens after the fourth
year.

Vocalization. This may be either musical or significant.
Very few weeks after birth the baby begins to express its
spirits by emitting vowel sounds, as much during inspiration as during expiration, and will lie on its back cooing
and gurgling to itself for nearly an hour. But this singing
has nothing to do with speech. Speech is sound *significant*.
During the second year a certain number of significant
sounds are gradually acquired; but talking proper does not
set in till the instinct to *imitate sounds* ripens in the nervous
system; and this ripening seems in some children to be
quite abrupt. Then speech grows rapidly in extent and
perfection. The child imitates every word he hears uttered,
and repeats it again and again with the most evident pleasure at his new power. At this time it is quite impossible
to talk *with* him, for his condition is that of 'Echolalia,'—
instead of answering the question, he simply reiterates it.
The result is, however, that his vocabulary increases very
fast; and little by little, with teaching from above, the
young prattler understands, puts words together to express
his own wants and perceptions, and even makes intelligent
replies. From a speechless, he has become a speaking,
animal. The interesting point with regard to this instinct
is the oftentimes very sudden birth of the impulse to imitate sounds. Up to the date of its awakening the child may
have been as devoid of it as a dog. Four days later his
whole energy may be poured into this new channel. The
habits of articulation formed during the plastic age of
childhood are in most persons sufficient to inhibit the for-

mation of new ones of a fundamentally different sort—witness the inevitable 'foreign accent' which distinguishes the speech of those who learn a language after early youth.

Imitation. The child's first words are in part vocables of his own invention, which his parents adopt, and which, as far as they go, form a new human tongue upon the earth; and in part they are his more or less successful imitations of words he hears the parents use. But the instinct of *imitating gestures* develops earlier than that of imitating sounds,—unless the sympathetic crying of a baby when it hears another cry may be reckoned as imitation of a sound. Professor Preyer speaks of his child imitating the protrusion of the father's lips in its fifteenth week. The various accomplishments of infancy, making 'pat-a-cake,' saying 'bye-bye,' 'blowing out the candle,' etc., usually fall well inside the limits of the first year. Later come all the various imitative games in which childhood revels, playing 'horse,' 'soldiers,' etc., etc. And from this time onward man is essentially *the* imitative animal. His whole educability and in fact the whole history of civilization depend on this trait, which his strong tendencies to rivalry, jealousy, and acquisitiveness reinforce. '*Nil humani a me alienum puto*,' is the motto of each individual of the species; and makes him, whenever another individual shows a power or superiority of any kind, restless until he can exhibit it himself. But apart from this kind of imitation, of which the psychological roots are complex, there is the more direct propensity to speak and walk and behave like others, usually without any conscious intention of so doing. And there is the imitative tendency which shows itself in large masses of men, and produces panics, and orgies, and frenzies of violence, and which only the rarest individuals can actively withstand. This sort of imitativeness is possessed by man in common with other gregarious animals, and is an instinct in the fullest sense of the term, being a blind impulse to act as soon as a certain perception occurs. It is particularly hard not to imitate gaping, laughing, or looking and running in a certain direction, if we see others doing so. Certain mesmerized subjects must automatically imitate whatever motion their operator makes before their eyes.* A successful piece of mimicry gives to both bystanders and mimic a peculiar kind of æsthetic pleasure. The dramatic impulse, the tendency to pretend one is someone else, contains this pleasure of mimicry as one of its elements. Another element seems to be a peculiar sense of power in stretching one's own personality so as to include that of a strange person. In young children this instinct often knows no bounds. For a few months in one of my children's third year, he literally hardly ever appeared in his own person. It was always, " Play I am So-and-so, and you are So-and-so, and the chair is such a thing, and then we'll do this or that." If you called him by his name, H., you invariably got the reply, " I'm not H., I'm a hyena, or a horse-car," or whatever the feigned object might be. He outwore this impulse after a time ; but while it lasted, it had every appearance of being the automatic result of ideas, often suggested by perceptions, working out irresistible motor effects. Imitation shades into

Emulation or Rivalry, a very intense instinct, especially rife with young children, or at least especially undisguised. Everyone knows it. Nine-tenth of the work of the world is done by it. We know that if we do not do the task someone else will do it and get the credit, so we do it. It has very little connection with sympathy, but rather more with pugnacity, which we proceed in turn to consider.

Pugnacity; anger; resentment. In many respects man is the most ruthlessly ferocious of beasts. As with all gregarious animals, ' two souls,' as Faust says, ' dwell within his breast,' the one of sociability and helpfulness, the other of jealousy and antagonism to his mates. Though in a general way he cannot live without them, yet, as regards certain individuals, it often falls out that he cannot live with them either. Constrained to be a member of a tribe, he still has a right to decide, as far as in him lies, of which other members the tribe shall consist. Killing off a few

---

* See, for some excellent pedagogic remarks about *doing yourself* what you want to get your pupils to do, and not simply telling them to do it, Baumann, Handbuch der Moral (1879), p. 32 ff.

obnoxious ones may often better the chances of those that remain. And killing off a neighboring tribe from whom no good thing comes, but only competition, may materially better the lot of the whole tribe. Hence the gory cradle, the *bellum omnium contra omnes*, in which our race was reared ; hence the fickleness of human ties, the ease with which the foe of yesterday becomes the ally of to-day, the friend of to-day the enemy of to-morrow ; hence the fact that we, the lineal representatives of the successful enactors of one scene of slaughter after another, must, whatever more pacific virtues we may also possess, still carry about with us, ready at any moment to burst into flame, the smouldering and sinister traits of character by means of which they lived through so many massacres, harming others, but themselves unharmed.

Sympathy is an emotion as to whose instinctiveness psychologists have held hot debate, some of them contending that it is no primitive endowment, but, originally at least, the result of a rapid calculation of the good consequences to ourselves of the sympathetic act. Such a calculation, at first conscious, would grow more unconscious as it became more habitual, and at last, tradition and association aiding, might prompt to actions which could not be distinguished from immediate impulses. It is hardly needful to argue against the falsity of this view. Some forms of sympathy, that of mother with child, for example, are surely primitive, and not intelligent forecasts of board and lodging and other support to be reaped in old age. Danger to the child blindly and instantaneously stimulates the mother to actions of alarm or defence. Menace or harm to the adult beloved or friend excites us in a corresponding way, often against all the dictates of prudence. It is true that sympathy does not necessarily follow from the mere fact of gregariousness. Cattle do not help a wounded comrade ; on the contrary, they are more likely to dispatch him. But a dog will lick another sick dog, and even bring him food ; and the sympathy of monkeys is proved by many observations to be strong. In man, then, we may lay it down that the sight of suffering or danger to others is a direct exciter of interest, and an immediate stimulus, if no complication hinders, to acts of relief. There is nothing unaccountable or pathological about this—nothing to justify Professor Bain's assimilation of it to the 'fixed ideas' of insanity, as 'clashing with the regular outgoings of the will.' It may be as primitive as any other 'outgoing,' and may be due to a random variation selected, quite as probably as gregariousness and maternal love are, even in Spencer's opinion, due to such variations.

It is true that sympathy is peculiarly liable to inhibition from other instincts which its stimulus may call forth. The traveller whom the good Samaritan rescued may well have prompted such instinctive fear or disgust in the priest and Levite who passed him by, that their sympathy could not come to the front. Then, of course, habits, reasoned reflections, and calculations may either check or reinforce one's sympathy ; as may also the instincts of love or hate, if these exist, for the suffering individual. The hunting and pugnacious instincts, when aroused, also inhibit our sympathy absolutely. This accounts for the cruelty of collections of men hounding each other on to bait or torture a victim. The blood mounts to the eyes, and sympathy's chance is gone.*

The hunting instinct has an equally remote origin in the evolution of the race.† The hunting and the fighting in-

---

* Sympathy has been enormously written about in books on Ethics. A very good recent chapter is that by Thos. Fowler. The Principles of Morals, part II. chap. II.

† "I must now refer to a very general passion which occurs in boys who are brought up naturally, especially in the country. Everyone knows what pleasure a boy takes in the sight of a butterfly, fish, crab or other animal, or of a bird's nest, and what a strong propensity he has for pulling apart, breaking, opening, and destroying all complex objects, how he delights in pulling out the wings and legs of flies, and tormenting one animal or another, how greedy he is to steal secret dainties, with what irresistible strength the plundering of birds' nests attracts him without his having the least intention of eating the eggs or the young birds. This fact has long been familiar, and is daily remarked by teachers ; but an explanation of these impulses which follow upon a mere perception of the objects, without in most cases any representation being aroused of a future pleasure to be gained, has as yet been given by no one, and yet the impulses are very easy to explain. In many cases it will be said that the boy pulls things apart from curiosity. Quite correct : but whence comes this curiosity, this irresistible desire to open everything and see what is inside ? What makes

stinct combine in many manifestations. They both support
the emotion of anger; they combine in the fascination which
stories of atrocity have for most minds; and the utterly
blind excitement of giving the rein to our fury when our blood
is up (an excitement whose intensity is greater than that
of any other human passion save one) is only explicable as an
impulse aboriginal in character, and having more to do with
immediate and overwhelming tendencies to muscular discharge than to any possible reminiscences of effects of experience, or association of ideas. I say this here, because
the pleasure of disinterested cruelty has been thought a
paradox, and writers have sought to show that it is no
primitive attribute of our nature, but rather a resultant
of the subtile combination of other less malignant elements of mind. This is a hopeless task. If evolution and
the survival of the fittest be true at all, the destruction
of prey and of human rivals *must* have been among the
most important of man's primitive functions, the fighting
and the chasing instincts *must* have become ingrained.
Certain perceptions *must* immediately, and without the in-
tervention of inferences and ideas, have prompted emotions
and motor discharges; and both the latter must, from
the nature of the case, have been very violent, and therefore,
when unchecked, of an intensely pleasurable kind. It is just
because human bloodthirstiness is such a primitive part of
us that it is so hard to eradicate, especially where a fight
or a hunt is promised as part of the fun.*

---

the boy take the eggs from the nest and destroy them when he never thinks
of eating them ? These are effects of an hereditary instinct, so strong that
warnings and punishments are unable to counteract it." (Schneider: Der
Menschliche Wille, p. 224. See also Der Thierische Wille, pp. 180-2.)

* It is not surprising, in view of the facts of animal history and evolution, that the very special object blood should have become the stimulus
for a very special interest and excitement. That the sight of it should
make people faint is strange. Less so that a child who sees his blood flow
should forthwith become much more frightened than by the mere feeling
of the cut. Horned cattle often, though not always, become furiously
excited at the smell of blood. In some abnormal human beings the sight
or thought of it exerts a baleful fascination. "B and his father were at a
neighbor's one evening, and, while paring apples, the old man accidentally
cut his hand so severely as to cause the blood to flow profusely. B was
observed to become restless, nervous, pale, and to have undergone a peculiar

As Rochefoucauld says, there is something in the misfortunes of our very friends that does not altogether displease us ; and an apostle of peace will feel a certain vicious thrill run through him, and enjoy a vicarious brutality, as he turns to the column in his newspaper at the top of which 'Shocking Atrocity' stands printed in large capitals. See how the crowd flocks round a street-brawl! Consider the enormous annual sale of revolvers to persons, not one in a thousand of whom has any serious intention of using them, but of whom each one has his carnivorous self-consciousness agreeably tickled by the notion, as he clutches the handle of his weapon, that he will be rather a dangerous customer to meet. See the ignoble crew that escorts every great pugilist—parasites who feel as if the glory of his brutality rubbed off upon them, and whose darling hope, from day to day, is to arrange some set-to of which they may share the rapture without enduring the pains! The first blows at a prize-fight are apt to make a refined spectator sick; but his blood is soon up in favor of one party, and it will then seem as if the other fellow could not be banged and pounded and mangled enough—the refined spectator would like to reinforce the blows himself. Over the sinister orgies of blood of certain depraved and insane persons let a curtain be drawn, as well as over the ferocity with which otherwise fairly decent men may be animated, when (at the sacking of a town, for instance), the excitement of victory long de-

---

change in demeanor. Taking advantage of the distraction produced by the accident, B escaped from the house and proceeded to a neighboring farm-yard, where he cut the throat of a horse, killing it." Dr. D. H. Tuke, commenting on this man's case (Journal of Mental Science, October, 1885), speaks of the influence of blood upon him—his whole life had been one chain of cowardly atrocities—and continues : " There can be no doubt that with some individuals it constitutes a fascination. . . . We might speak of a *mania sanguinis*. Dr. Savage admitted a man from France into Bethlehem Hospital some time ago, one of whose earliest symptoms of insanity was the thirst for blood, which he endeavored to satisfy by going to an abattoir in Paris. The man whose case I have brought forward had the same passion for gloating over blood, but had no attack of acute mania. The sight of blood was distinctly a delight to him, and at any time blood aroused in him the worst elements of his nature. Instances will easily be recalled in which murderers, undoubtedly insane, have described the intense pleasure they experienced in the warm blood of children."

layed, the sudden freedom of rapine and of lust, the contagion of a crowd, and the impulse to imitate and outdo, all combine to swell the blind drunkenness of the killing-instinct, and carry it to its extreme. No! those who try to account for this from above downwards, as if it resulted from the consequences of the victory being rapidly inferred, and from the agreeable sentiments associated with them in the imagination, have missed the root of the matter. Our ferocity is blind, and can only be explained from *below.* Could we trace it back through our line of descent, we should see it taking more and more the form of a fatal reflex response, and at the same time becoming more and more the pure and direct emotion that it is.*

In childhood it takes this form. The boys who pull out grasshoppers' legs and butterflies' wings, and disembowel every frog they catch, have no *thought* at all about the matter. The creatures tempt their hands to a fascinating occupation, to which they have to yield. It is with them as with the 'boy-fiend' Jesse Pomeroy, who cut a little girl's throat, 'just to see how she'd act.' The normal provocatives of the impulse are all living beasts, great and small, toward which a contrary habit has not been formed —all human beings in whom we perceive a certain *intent* towards *us,* and a large number of human beings who offend us peremptorily, either by their look, or gait, or by some circumstance in their lives which we dislike. Inhibited by sympathy, and by reflection calling up impulses of an opposite kind, civilized men lose the habit of acting out their pugnacious instincts in a perfectly natural way, and a passing feeling of anger, with its comparatively faint bodily ex-

---

* " Bombonnel, having rolled with a panther to the border of a ravine, gets his head away from the open mouth of the animal, and by a prodigious effort rolls her into the abyss. He gets up, blinded, spitting a mass of blood, not knowing exactly what the situation is. He thinks only of one thing, that he shall probably die of his wounds, but that before dying he must take vengeance on the panther. 'I didn't think of my pain,' he tells us. '. Possessed entirely by the fury with which I was transported, I drew my hunting-knife, and not understanding what had become of the beast, I sought for her on every side in order to continue the struggle. It was in this plight that the Arabs found me when they arrived.'" (Quoted by Guyan, La Morale sans Obligation, etc., p. 210.)

pressions, may be the limit of their physical combativeness. Such a feeling as this may, however, be aroused by a wide range of objects. Inanimate things, combinations of color and sound, bad bills of fare, may in persons who combine fastidious taste with an irascible temperament produce real ebullitions of rage. Though the female sex is often said to have less pugnacity than the male, the difference seems connected more with the extent of the motor consequences of the impulse than with its frequency. Women take offence and get angry, if anything, more easily than men, but their anger is inhibited by fear and other principles of their nature from expressing itself in blows. The hunting-instinct proper seems to be decidedly weaker in them than in men. The latter instinct is easily restricted by habit to certain objects, which become legitimate 'game,' while other things are spared. If the hunting-instinct be not exercised at all, it may even entirely die out, and a man may enjoy letting a wild creature live, even though he might easily kill it. Such a type is now becoming frequent; but there is no doubt that in the eyes of a child of nature such a personage would seem a sort of moral monster.

Fear is a reaction aroused by the same objects that arouse ferocity. The antagonism of the two is an interesting study in instinctive dynamics. We both fear, and wish to kill, anything that may kill us; and the question which of the two impulses we shall follow is usually decided by some one of those *collateral circumstances* of the particular case, to be moved by which is the mark of superior mental natures. Of course this introduces uncertainty into the reaction; but it is an uncertainty found in the higher brutes as well as in men, and ought not to be taken as proof that we are less instinctive than they. Fear has bodily expressions of an extremely energetic kind, and stands, beside lust and anger, as one of the three most exciting emotions of which our nature is susceptible. The progress from brute to man is characterized by nothing so much as by the decrease in frequency of proper occasions for fear. In civilized life, in particular, it has at last become possible for large numbers of people to pass from the cradle to the grave without ever having had a pang of genuine fear. Many of us need an attack of mental disease to teach us the meaning of the word. Hence the possibility of so much blindly optimistic philosophy and religion. The atrocities of life become 'like a tale of little meaning though the words are strong;' we doubt if anything like *us* ever really was within the tiger's jaws, and conclude that the horrors we hear of are but a sort of painted tapestry for the chambers in which we lie so comfortably at peace with ourselves and with the world.

Be this as it may, fear is a genuine instinct, and one of the earliest shown by the human child. *Noises* seem especially to call it forth. Most noises from the outer world, to a child bred in the house, have no exact significance. They are simply startling. To quote a good observer, M. Perez:

"Children between three and ten months are less often alarmed by visual than by auditory impressions. In cats, from the fifteenth day, the contrary is the case. A child, three and a half months old, in the midst of the turmoil of a conflagration, in presence of the devouring flames and ruined walls, showed neither astonishment nor fear, but smiled at the woman who was taking care of him, while his parents were busy. The noise, however, of the trumpet of the firemen, who were approaching, and that of the wheels of the engine, made him start and cry. At this age I have never yet seen an infant startled at a flash of lightning, even when intense; but I have seen many of them alarmed at the voice of the thunder. . . . Thus fear comes rather by the ears than by the eyes, to the child without experience. It is natural that this should be reversed, or reduced, in animals organized to perceive danger afar. Accordingly, although I have never seen a child frightened at his first sight of fire, I have many a time seen young dogs, young cats, young chickens, and young birds frightened thereby. . . . I picked up some years ago a lost cat about a year old. Some months afterward at the onset of cold weather I lit the fire in the grate of my study, which was her reception-room. She first looked at the flame in a very frightened way. I brought her near to it. She leaped away and ran to hide under the bed. Although the fire was lighted every day, it was not until the end of the winter that I could prevail upon her to stay upon a chair near it. The next winter, however, all apprehension had disappeared. . . . Let us, then, conclude that there are hereditary dispositions to fear, which are independent of experience, but which experiences may end by attenuating very considerably. In the human infant I believe them to be particularly connected with the ear."*

---

* Psychologie de l'Enfant, pp. 72–74. In an account of a young gorilla quoted from Falkenstein, by R. Hartmann ('Anthropoid Apes,' International

The effect of noise in heightening any terror we may feel in adult years is very marked. The *howling* of the storm, whether on sea or land, is a principal cause of our anxiety when exposed to it. The writer has been interested in noticing in his own person, while lying in bed, and kept awake by the wind outside, how invariably each loud gust of it arrested momentarily his heart. A dog, attacking us, is much more dreadful by reason of the noises he makes.

Strange men, and *strange animals,* either large or small, excite fear, but especially men or animals advancing toward us in a threatening way. This is entirely instinctive and antecedent to experience. Some children will cry with terror at their very first sight of a cat or dog, and it will often be impossible for weeks to make them touch it. Others will wish to fondle it almost immediately. Certain kinds of ' vermin,' especially spiders and snakes, seem to excite a fear unusually difficult to overcome. It is impossible to say how much of this difference is instinctive and how much the result of stories heard about these creatures. That the fear of ' vermin ' ripens gradually, seemed to me to be proved in a child of my own to whom I gave a live frog once, at the age of six to eight months, and again when he was a year and a half old. The first time he seized it promptly, and holding it, in spite of its struggling, at last got its head into his mouth. He then let it crawl up his breast, and get upon his face, without showing alarm. But the second time, although he had seen no frog and heard no story about a frog between whiles, it was almost impossible to induce him to touch it. Another child, a year old, eagerly took some very large spiders into his hand. At present he is afraid, but has been exposed meanwhile to the teachings of the nursery. One of my children from her birth upwards saw daily the pet pug-dog of the house, and never betrayed the slightest fear until she was (if I recol-

---

Scientific Series, vol. LII (New York, 1886), p. 265), it is said: "He very much disliked strange noises. Thunder, the rain falling on the skylight, and especially the long-drawn note of a pipe or trumpet, threw him into such agitation as to cause a sudden affection of the digestive organs, and it became expedient to keep him at a distance. When he was slightly indisposed, we made use of this kind of music with results as successful as if we had administered purgative medicine."

lect rightly) about eight months old. Then the instinct suddenly seemed to develop, and with such intensity that familiarity had no mitigating effect. She screamed whenever the dog entered the room, and for many months remained afraid to touch him. It is needless to say that no change in the pug's unfailingly friendly conduct had anything to do with this change of feeling in the child.

Preyer tells of a young child screaming with fear on being carried near to the *sea*. The great source of terror to infancy is solitude. The teleology of this is obvious, as is also that of the infant's expression of dismay—the never-failing cry—on waking up and finding himself alone.

Black things, and especially *dark places*, holes, caverns, etc., arouse a peculiarly gruesome fear. This fear, as well as that of solitude, of being 'lost,' are explained after a fashion by ancestral experience. Says Schneider:

"It is a fact that men, especially in childhood, fear to go into a dark cavern or a gloomy wood. This feeling of fear arises, to be sure, partly from the fact that we easily suspect that dangerous beasts may lurk in these localities—a suspicion due to stories we have heard and read. But, on the other hand, it is quite sure that this fear at a certain perception is also directly inherited. Children who have been carefully guarded from all ghost-stories are nevertheless terrified and cry if led into a dark place, especially if sounds are made there. Even an adult can easily observe that an uncomfortable timidity steals over him in a lonely wood at night, although he may have the fixed conviction that not the slightest danger is near.

"This feeling of fear occurs in many men even in their own house after dark, although it is much stronger in a dark cavern or forest. The fact of such instinctive fear is easily explicable when we consider that our savage ancestors through innumerable generations were accustomed to meet with dangerous beasts in caverns, especially bears, and were for the most part attacked by such beasts during the night and in the woods, and that thus an inseparable association between the perceptions of darkness of caverns and woods, and fear took place, and was inherited." *

High places cause fear of a peculiarly sickening sort, though here, again, individuals differ enormously. The utterly blind instinctive character of the motor impulses here is shown by the fact that they are almost always

---

* Der Menschliche Wille, p. 224.

entirely unreasonable, but that reason is powerless to suppress them. That they are a mere incidental peculiarity of the nervous system, like liability to sea-sickness, or love of music, with no teleological significance, seems more than probable. The fear in question varies so much from one person to another, and its detrimental effects are so much more obvious than its uses, that it is hard to see how it could be a selected instinct. Man is anatomically one of the best fitted of animals for climbing about high places. The best psychical complement to this equipment would seem to be a 'level head' when there, not a dread of going there at all. In fact, the teleology of fear, beyond a certain point, is very dubious. Professor Mosso, in his interesting monograph, 'La Paura' (which has been translated into French), concludes that many of its manifestations must be considered pathological rather than useful; Bain, in several places, expresses the same opinion; and this, I think, is surely the view which any observer without *a priori* prejudices must take. A certain amount of timidity obviously adapts us to the world we live in, but the *fear-paroxysm* is surely altogether harmful to him who is its prey.

Fear of the supernatural is one variety of fear. It is difficult to assign any normal object for this fear, unless it were a genuine ghost. But, in spite of psychical research-societies, science has not yet adopted ghosts; so we can only say that certain *ideas* of supernatural agency, associated with real circumstances, produce a peculiar kind of horror. This horror is probably explicable as the result of a combination of simpler horrors. To bring the ghostly terror to its maximum, many usual elements of the dreadful must combine, such as loneliness, darkness, inexplicable sounds, especially of a dismal character, moving figures half discerned (or, if discerned, of dreadful aspect), and a vertiginous baffling of the expectation. This last element, which is *intellectual*, is very important. It produces a strange emotional 'curdle' in our blood to see a process with which we are familiar deliberately taking an unwonted course. Any one's heart would stop beating if he perceived his chair sliding unassisted across the floor. The lower animals appear to be sensitive to the mysteriously exceptional as

well as ourselves.   My friend Professor W. K. Brooks, of
the Johns Hopkins University, told me of his large and
noble dog being frightened into a sort of epileptic fit by a
bone being drawn across the floor by a thread which the
dog did not see.   Darwin and Romanes have given similar
experiences.*   The idea of the supernatural involves that
the usual should be set at naught.   In the witch and hob-
goblin supernatural, other elements still of fear are brought
in—caverns, slime and ooze, vermin, corpses, and the like.†
A human corpse seems normally to produce an instinctive
dread, which is no doubt somewhat due to its mysteriousness,
and which familiarity rapidly dispels.   But, in view of the
fact that cadaveric, reptilian, and underground horrors play
so specific and constant a part in many nightmares and
forms of delirium, it seems not altogether unwise to ask
whether these forms of dreadful circumstance may not at a
former period have been more normal objects of the environment than now.   The ordinary cock-sure evolutionist
ought to have no difficulty in explaining these terrors, and
the scenery that provokes them, as relapses into the
consciousness of the cave-men, a consciousness usually
overlaid in us by experiences of more recent date.

There are certain other pathological fears, and certain
peculiarities in the expression of ordinary fear, which
might receive an explanatory light from ancestral conditions, even infra-human ones.   In ordinary fear, one may

---

* Cf. Romanes, Mental Evolution, etc., p. 156.

† In the 'Overland Monthly' for 1887,' a most interesting article on
Laura Bridgman's writings has been published by Mr. E. C. Sandford.
Among other reminiscences of her early childhood, while she still knew
nothing of the sign-language, the wonderful blind deaf-mute records the
following item in her quaint language: "My father [he was a farmer and
probably did his own butchering] used to enter his kitchen bringing some
killed animals in and deposited them on one of sides of the room many
times.   As I perceived it it make me shudder with terror because I did not
know what the matter was.   I hated to approach the dead.   One morning
I went to take a short walk with my Mother.   I went into a snug house for
some time.   They took me into a room where there was a coffin.   I put
my hand in the coffin & felt something so queer.   It frightened me
unpleasantly.   I found something dead wrapped in a silk h'd'k'f so carefully.   It must have been a body that had had vitality. . . . I did not like
to venture to examine the body for I was confounded."

either run, or remain semi-paralyzed. The latter condition reminds us of the so-called death-shamming instinct shown by many animals. Dr. Lindsay, in his work 'Mind in Animals,' says this must require great self-command in those that practise it. But it is really no feigning of death at all, and requires no self-command. It is simply a terror-paralysis which has been so useful as to become hereditary. The beast of prey does not think the motionless bird, insect, or crustacean dead. He simply fails to notice them at all; because his senses, like ours, are much more strongly excited by a moving object than by a still one. It is the same instinct which leads a boy playing 'I spy' to hold his very breath when the seeker is near, and which makes the beast of prey himself in many cases motionlessly lie in wait for his victim or silently 'stalk' it, by rapid approaches alternated with periods of immobility. It is the opposite of the instinct which makes us jump up and down and move our arms when we wish to attract the notice of some one passing far away, and makes the shipwrecked sailor frantically wave a cloth upon the raft where he is floating when a distant sail appears. Now, may not the statue-like, crouching immobility of some melancholiacs, insane with general anxiety and fear of everything, be in some way connected with this old instinct? They can give no *reason* for their fear to move; but immobility makes them feel safer and more comfortable. Is not this the mental state of the 'feigning' animal?

Again, take the strange symptom which has been described of late years by the rather absurd name of *agoraphobia*. The patient is seized with palpitation and terror at the sight of any open place or broad street which he has to cross alone. He trembles, his knees bend, he may even faint at the idea. Where he has sufficient self-command he sometimes accomplishes the object by keeping safe under the lee of a vehicle going across, or joining himself to a knot of other people. But usually he slinks round the sides of the square, hugging the houses as closely as he can. This emotion has no utility in a civilized man, but when we notice the chronic agoraphobia of our domestic cats, and see the tenacious way in which many wild animals, especially rodents, cling to cover, and only venture on a dash across the open as a desperate measure—even then making for every stone or bunch of weeds which may give a momentary shelter—when we see this we are strongly tempted to ask whether such an odd kind of fear in us be not due to the accidental resurrection, through disease, of a sort of instinct which may in some of our ancestors have had a permanent and on the whole a useful part to play ?

Appropriation or *Acquisitiveness.* The beginnings of acquisitiveness are seen in the impulse which very young children display, to snatch at, or beg for, any object which pleases their attention. Later, when they begin to speak, among the first words they emphasize are ' me ' and ' mine.' * Their earliest quarrels with each other are about questions of ownership; and parents of twins soon learn that it conduces to a quiet house to buy all presents in impartial duplicate. Of the later evolution of the proprietary instinct I need not speak. Everyone knows how difficult a thing it is not to covet whatever pleasing thing we see, and how the sweetness of the thing often is as gall to us so long as it is another's. When another is in possession, the impulse to appropriate the thing often turns into the impulse to harm him—what is called *envy,* or *jealousy,* ensues. In civilized life the impulse to own is usually checked by a variety of considerations, and only passes over into action under circumstances legitimated by habit and common consent, an additional example of the way in which one instinctive tendency may be inhibited by others. A variety of the proprietary instinct is the impulse to form collections of the same sort of thing. It differs much in individuals, and shows in a striking way how instinct and habit interact. For, al-

---

* I lately saw a boy of five (who had been told the story of Hector and Achilles) teaching his younger brother, aged three, how to play Hector, wh?le he himself should play Achilles, and chase him round the walls of Troy. Having armed themselves, Achilles advanced, shouting "Where's my Patroklos ?" Whereupon the would-be Hector piped up, quite distract. ed from his *rôle,* "Where's my Patroklos? I want a Patroklos ! I want a Patroklos !"—and broke up the game. Of what kind of a thing a Patroklos might be he had, of course, no notion—enough that his brother had one, for him to claim one too.

though a collection of any given thing—like postage-stamps —need not be begun by any given person, yet the chances are that if accidentally it *be* begun by a person with the collecting instinct, it will probably be continued. The chief interest of the objects, in the collector's eyes, is that they are a collection, and that they are his. Rivalry, to be sure, inflames this, as it does every other passion, yet the objects of a collector's mania need not be necessarily such as are generally in demand. Boys will collect anything that they see another boy collect, from pieces of chalk and peach-pits up to books and photographs. Out of a hundred students whom I questioned, only four or five had never collected anything.*

The associationist psychology denies that there is any blind primitive instinct to appropriate, and would explain all acquisitiveness, in the first instance, as a desire to secure the 'pleasures' which the objects possessed may yield; and, secondly, as the association of the idea of pleasantness with the *holding* of the thing, even though the pleasure originally got by it was only gained through its expense or destruction. Thus the miser is shown to us as one who has transferred to the gold by which he may buy the goods of this life all the emotions which the goods themselves would yield; and who thereafter loves the gold for its own sake, preferring the means of pleasure to the pleasure itself. There can be little doubt that much of this analysis a broader view of the facts would have dispelled. 'The miser' is an abstraction. There are all kinds of misers. The common sort, the excessively niggardly man, simply exhibits the psychological law that the potential has often a far greater influence over our mind than the actual. A man will not marry now, because to do so puts an end to his indefinite potentialities of choice of a partner. He prefers the latter. He will not use open fires or wear his good clothes, because the day may come when he will have to use the furnace or dress in a worn-out coat, 'and then where will he be?'

---

* In 'The Nation' for September 3, 1886, President G. S. Hall has given some account of a statistical research on Boston school-boys, by Miss Wiltse, from which it appears that only nineteen out of two hundred and twenty-nine had made no collections.

For him, better the actual evil than the fear of it; and so
it is with the common lot of misers. Better to live poor
now, with the *power* of living rich, than to live rich at the
risk of losing the power. These men value their gold, not
for its own sake, but for its powers. Demonetize it, and see
how quickly they will get rid of it! The associationist theory is, as regards them, entirely at fault: they care nothing for the gold *in se.*

With other misers there combines itself with this preference of the power over the act the far more instinctive
element of the simple collecting propensity. Every one
collects money, and when a man of petty ways is smitten
with the collecting mania for this object he necessarily becomes a miser. Here again the associationist psychology
is wholly at fault. The hoarding instinct prevails widely
among animals as well as among men. Professor Silliman
has thus described one of the hoards of the California
wood-rat, made in an empty stove of an unoccupied house :

"I found the outside to be composed entirely of spikes, all laid
with symmetry, so as to present the points of the nails outward. In the
centre of this mass was the nest, composed of finely-divided fibres of
hemp-packing. Interlaced with the spikes were the following : about
two dozen knives, forks, and spoons ; all the butcher's knives, three
in number ; a large carving-knife, fork, and steel ; several large plugs
of tobacco, . . . an old purse containing some silver, matches, and
tobacco ; nearly all the small tools from the tool-closets, with several
large augers, . . . all of which must have been transported some distance, as they were originally stored in different parts of the house. . . .
The outside casing of a silver watch was disposed of in one part of
the pile, the glass of the same watch in another, and the works
in still another." *

In every lunatic asylum we find the collecting instinct
developing itself in an equally absurd way. Certain patients will spend all their time picking pins from the
floor and hoarding them. Others collect bits of thread,
buttons, or rags, and prize them exceedingly. Now, 'the
Miser' *par excellence* of the popular imagination and of
melodrama, the monster of squalor and misanthropy, is
simply one of these mentally deranged persons. His intellect may in many matters be clear, but his instincts,

---

* Quoted in Lindsay, 'Mind in Lower Animals,' vol. II. p. 151.

especially that of ownership, are insane, and their insanity has no more to do with the association of ideas than with the precession of the equinoxes. As a matter of fact his hoarding usually is directed to money; but it also includes almost anything besides. Lately in a Massachusetts town there died a miser who principally hoarded newspapers. These had ended by so filling all the rooms of his good-sized house from floor to ceiling that his living-space was restricted to a few narrow channels between them. Even as I write, the morning paper gives an account of the emptying of a miser's den in Boston by the City Board of Health. What the owner hoarded is thus described:

"He gathered old newspapers, wrapping-paper, incapacitated umbrellas, canes, pieces of common wire, cast-off clothing, empty barrels, pieces of iron, old bones, battered tin-ware, fractured pots, and bushels of such miscellany as is to be found only at the city 'dump.' The empty barrels were filled, shelves were filled, every hole and corner was filled, and in order to make more storage-room, 'the hermit' covered his store-room with a network of ropes, and hung the ropes as full as they could hold of his curious collections. There was nothing one could think of that wasn't in that room. As a wood-sawyer, the old man had never thrown away a saw-blade or a wood-buck. The bucks were rheumatic and couldn't stand up, and the saw-blades were worn down to almost nothing in the middle. Some had been actually worn in two, but the ends were carefully saved and stored away. As a coal-heaver, the old man had never cast off a worn-out basket, and there were dozens of the remains of the old things, patched up with canvas and rope-yarns, in the store-room. There were at least two dozen old hats, fur, cloth, silk, and straw," etc.

Of course there may be a great many 'associations of ideas' in the miser's mind about the things he hoards. He is a thinking being, and must associate things; but, without an entirely blind impulse in this direction behind all his ideas, such practical results could never be reached.*

Kleptomania, as it is called, is an uncontrollable impulse to appropriate, occurring in persons whose 'associations of ideas' would naturally all be of a counteracting sort.

---

* Cf. Flint, Mind, vol. I. pp. 330-333; Sully, *ibid*. p. 567. Most people probably have the *impulse* to keep bits of useless finery, old tools, pieces of once useful apparatus, etc.: but it is normally either inhibited at the outset by reflection, or, if yielded to, the objects soon grow displeasing and are thrown away.

Kleptomaniacs often promptly restore, or permit to be restored, what they have taken; so the impulse need not be to keep, but only to take. But elsewhere hoarding complicates the result. A gentleman, with whose case I am acquainted, was discovered, after his death, to have a hoard in his barn of all sorts of articles, mainly of a trumpery sort, but including pieces of silver which he had stolen from his own dining-room, and utensils which he had stolen from his own kitchen, and for which he had afterward bought substitutes with his own money.

Constructiveness is as genuine and irresistible an instinct in man as in the bee or the beaver. Whatever things are plastic to his hands, those things he must remodel into shapes of his own, and the result of the remodelling, however useless it may be, gives him more pleasure than the original thing. The mania of young children for breaking and pulling apart whatever is given them is more often the expression of a rudimentary constructive impulse than of a destructive one. 'Blocks' are the playthings of which they are least apt to tire. Clothes, weapons, tools, habitations, and works of art are the result of the discoveries to which the plastic instinct leads, each individual starting where his forerunners left off, and tradition preserving all that once is gained. Clothing, where not necessitated by cold, is nothing but a sort of attempt to remodel the human body itself—an attempt still better shown in the various tattooings, tooth-filings, scarrings, and other mutilations that are practised by savage tribes. As for habitation, there can be no doubt that the instinct to seek a sheltered nook, open only on one side, into which he may retire and be safe, is in man quite as specific as the instinct of birds to build a nest. It is not necessarily in the shape of a shelter from wet and cold that the need comes before him, but he feels less *exposed* and more at home when not altogether uninclosed than when lying all abroad. Of course the utilitarian origin of this instinct is obvious. But to stick to bare facts at present and not to trace origins, we must admit that this instinct now exists, and probably always has existed, since man was man. Habits of the most complicated kind are reared upon it. But even in the midst of these habits we see the blind instinct cropping out; as, for example, in the fact that we feign a shelter within a shelter, by backing up beds in rooms with their heads against the wall, and never lying in them the other way—just as dogs prefer to get under or upon some piece of furniture to sleep, instead of lying in the middle of the room. The first habitations were caves and leafy grottoes, bettered by the hands; and we see children to-day, when playing in wild places, take the greatest delight in discovering and appropriating such retreats and 'playing house' there.

Play. The impulse to play in special ways is certainly instinctive. A boy can no more help running after another boy who runs provokingly near him, than a kitten can help running after a rolling ball. A child trying to get into its own hand some object which it sees another child pick up, and the latter trying to get away with the prize, are just as much slaves of an automatic prompting as are two chickens or fishes, of which one has taken a big morsel into its mouth and decamps with it, while the other darts after in pursuit. All simple active games are attempts to gain the excitement yielded by certain primitive instincts, through feigning that the occasions for their exercise are there. They involve imitation, hunting, fighting, rivalry, acquisitiveness, and construction, combined in various ways; their special rules are habits, discovered by accident, selected by intelligence, and propagated by tradition; but unless they were founded in automatic impulses, games would lose most of their zest. The sexes differ somewhat in their play-impulses. As Schneider says:

"The little boy imitates soldiers, models clay into an oven, builds houses, makes a wagon out of chairs, rides on horseback upon a stick, drives nails with the hammer, harnesses his brethren and comrades together and plays the stage-driver, or lets himself be captured as a wild horse by some one else. The girl, on the contrary, plays with her doll, washes and dresses it, strokes it, clasps and kisses it, puts it to bed and tucks it in, sings it a cradle-song, or speaks with it as if it were a living being. . . . This fact that a sexual difference exists in the play-impulse, that a boy gets more pleasure from a horse and rider and a soldier than from a doll, while with the girl the opposite is the case, is proof that an hereditary connection exists between the perception of certain things (horse, doll, etc.), and the feeling of pleasure, as well as between this latter and the impulse to play." *

There is another sort of human play, into which higher æsthetic feelings enter. I refer to that love of festivities, ceremonies, ordeals, etc., which seems to be universal in our species. The lowest savages have their dances, more or less formally conducted. The various religions have their solemn rites and exercises, and civic and military power symbolize their grandeur by processions and celebrations of divers sorts. We have our operas and parties and masquerades. An element common to all these ceremonial games, as they may be called, is the excitement of concerted action as one of an organized crowd. The same acts, performed with a crowd, seem to mean vastly more than when performed alone. A walk with the people on a holiday afternoon, an excursion to drink beer or coffee at a popular 'resort,' or an ordinary ball-room, are examples of this. Not only are we amused at seeing so many strangers, but there is a distinct stimulation at feeling our share in their collective life. The perception of them is the stimulus; and our reaction upon it is our tendency to join them and do what they are doing, and our unwillingness to be the first to leave off and go home alone. This seems a primitive element in our nature, as it is difficult to trace any association of ideas that could lead up to it; although, once granting it to exist, it is very easy to see what its uses to a tribe might be in facilitating prompt and vigorous collective action. The formation of armies and the undertaking of military expeditions would be among its fruits. In the ceremonial games it is but the impulsive starting-point. What particular things the crowd then shall do, depends for the most part on the initiative of individuals, fixed by imitation and habit, and continued by tradition. The co-operation of other æsthetic pleasures with games, ceremonial or other, has a great deal to do with the selection of such as shall become stereotyped and

---

* Der Menschliche Wille, p. 205.

habitual. The peculiar form of excitement called by Professor Bain the emotion of *pursuit,* the pleasure of a *crescendo,* is the soul of many common games. The immense extent of the play-activities in human life is too obvious to be more than mentioned.*

Curiosity. Already pretty low down among vertebrates we find that any object may excite attention, provided it be only *novel,* and that attention may be followed by approach and exploration by nostril, lips, or touch. Curiosity and fear form a couple of antagonistic emotions liable to be awakened by the same outward thing, and manifestly both useful to their possessor. The spectacle of their alternation is often amusing enough, as in the timid approaches and scared wheelings which sheep or cattle will make in the presence of some new object they are investigating. I have seen alligators in the water act in precisely the same way towards a man seated on the beach in front of them—gradually drawing near as long as he kept still, frantically careering back as soon as he made a movement. Inasmuch as new objects *may* always be advantageous, it is better that an animal should not *absolutely* fear them. But, inasmuch as they may also possibly be harmful, it is better that he should not be quite indifferent to them either, but on the whole remaining on the *qui vive,* ascertain as much about them, and what they may be likely to bring forth, as he can, before settling down to rest in their presence. Some such susceptibility for being excited and irritated by the mere novelty, as such, of any movable feature of the environment must form the instinctive basis of all human curiosity; though, of course, the superstructure absorbs contributions from so many other factors of the emotional life that the original root may be hard to find. With what

---

* Professor Lazarus (Die Reize des Spieles, Berlin, 1883, p. 44) denies that we have an *instinct* to play, and says the root of the matter is the *aversion to remain unoccupied,* which substitutes a sham occupation when no real one is ready. No doubt this is true; but why the particular forms of sham occupation? The *elements* of all bodily games and of ceremonial games are given by direct excito-motor stimulations—just as when puppies chase one another and swallows have a parliament.

is called scientific curiosity, and with metaphysical wonder, the practical instinctive root has probably nothing to do. The stimuli here are not objects, but ways of conceiving objects; and the emotions and actions they give rise to are to be classed, with many other æsthetic manifestations, sensitive and motor, as *incidental* features of our mental life. The philosophic brain responds to an inconsistency or a gap in its knowledge, just as the musical brain responds to a discord in what it hears. At certain ages the sensitiveness to particular gaps and the pleasure of resolving particular puzzles reach their maximum, and then it is that stores of scientific knowledge are easiest and most naturally laid in. But these effects may have had nothing to do with the uses for which the brain was originally given; and it is probably only within a few centuries, since religious beliefs and economic applications of science have played a prominent part in the conflicts of one race with another, that they may have helped to 'select' for survival a particular type of brain. I shall have to consider this matter of incidental and supernumerary faculties in Chapter XXVIII.

Sociability and Shyness. As a gregarious animal, man is excited both by the absence and by the presence of his kind. To be alone is one of the greatest of evils for him. Solitary confinement is by many regarded as a mode of torture too cruel and unnatural for civilized countries to adopt. To one long pent up on a desert island, the sight of a human footprint or a human form in the distance would be the most tumultuously exciting of experiences. In morbid states of mind, one of the commonest symptoms is the fear of being alone. This fear may be assuaged by the presence of a little child, or even of a baby. In a case of hydrophobia known to the writer, the patient insisted on keeping his room *crowded* with neighbors all the while, so intense was his fear of solitude. In a gregarious animal, the perception that he is alone excites him to vigorous activity. Mr. Galton thus describes the behavior of the South African cattle whom he had such good opportunities for observing:

"Although the ox has little affection for, or interest in, his fellows, he cannot endure even a momentary separation from his herd. If he be separated from it by stratagem or force, he exhibits every sign of mental agony; he strives with all his might to get back again, and when he succeeds he plunges into its middle to bathe his whole body with the comfort of closest companionship." *

Man is also excited by the presence of his kind. The *bizarre* actions of dogs meeting strange dogs are not altogether without a parallel in our own constitution. We cannot meet strangers without a certain tension, or talk to them exactly as to our familiars. This is particularly the case if the stranger be an important personage. It may then happen that we not only shrink from meeting his eye, but actually cannot collect our wits or do ourselves any sort of justice in his presence.

"This odd state of mind," says Darwin,† "is chiefly recognized by the face reddening, by the eyes being averted or cast down, and by awkward, nervous movements of the body. . . . Shyness seems to depend on sensitiveness to the opinion, whether good or bad, of others, more especially with respect to external appearance. Strangers neither know nor care anything about our conduct or character, but they may, and often do, criticise our appearance. . . . The consciousness of anything peculiar, or even new, in the dress, or any slight blemish on the person, and more especially on the face—points which are likely to attract the attention of strangers—makes the shy intolerably shy.‡ On the other hand, in those cases in which conduct, and not personal appearance, is concerned, we are much more apt to be shy in the presence of acquaintances whose judgment we in some degree value than in that of strangers. . . . Some persons, however, are so sensitive that the mere act of speaking to almost any one is sufficient to rouse their self-consciousness, and a slight blush is the result. Disapprobation . . . causes shyness and blushing much more readily than does approbation. . . . Persons who are exceedingly shy are rarely shy in the presence of those with whom they are quite familiar, and of whose good opinion and sympathy they are quite assured ; for instance, a girl in presence of her mother. . . . Shyness . . . is closely related to fear ; yet it is distinct from fear in the ordinary sense. A shy man dreads the notice of strangers, but can hardly be said to be afraid of them ; he may be as bold as a hero in battle, and yet have no self-confidence about trifles in the presence of strangers. Almost every one is extremely nervous

---

* Inquiries into Human Faculty, p. 72.
† Expression of the Emotions (New York, 1873), p. 330.
‡ "The certainty that we are well dressed," a charming woman has said, "gives us a peace of heart compared to which that yielded by the consolations of religion is as nothing."

when first addressing a public assembly, and most men remain so through their lives."

As Mr. Darwin observes, a real dread of definite consequences may enter into this 'stage-fright' and complicate the shyness. Even so our shyness before an important personage may be complicated by what Professor Bain calls 'servile terror,' based on representation of definite dangers if we fail to please. But both stage-fright and servile terror may exist with the most indefinite apprehensions of danger, and, in fact, when our reason tells us there is no occasion for alarm. We must, therefore, admit a certain amount of purely instinctive perturbation and constraint, due to the consciousness that we have become objects for other people's eyes. Mr. Darwin goes on to say: " Shyness comes on at a very early age. In one of my own children, two years and three months old, I saw a trace of what certainly appeared to be shyness directed toward myself, after an absence from home of only a week." Every parent has noticed the same sort of thing. Considering the despotic powers of rulers in savage tribes, respect and awe must, from time immemorial, have been emotions excited by certain individuals; and stage-fright, servile terror, and shyness, must have had as copious opportunities for exercise as at the present time. Whether these impulses could ever have been useful, and selected for usefulness, is a question which, it would seem, can only be answered in the negative. Apparently they are pure hindrances, like fainting at sight of blood or disease, sea-sickness, a dizzy head on high places, and certain squeamishnesses of æsthetic taste. They are *incidental* emotions, in spite of which we get along. But they seem to play an important part in the production of two other propensities, about the instinctive character of which a good deal of controversy has prevailed. I refer to cleanliness and modesty, to which we must proceed, but not before we have said a word about another impulse closely allied to shyness. I mean—

Secretiveness, which, although often due to intelligent calculation and the dread of betraying our interests in some more or less definitely foreseen way, is quite as often a blind propensity, serving no useful purpose, and is so stubborn and ineradicable a part of the character as fully to deserve a place among the instincts. Its natural stimuli are unfamiliar human beings, especially those whom we respect. Its reactions are the arrest of whatever we are saying or doing when such strangers draw nigh, coupled often with the pretense that we were not saying or doing that thing, but possibly something different. Often there is added to this a disposition to mendacity when asked to give an account of ourselves. With many persons the first impulse, when the door-bell rings, or a visitor is suddenly announced, is to scuttle out of the room, so as not to be 'caught.' When a person at whom we have been looking becomes aware of us, our immediate impulse may be to look the other way, and pretend we have not seen him. Many friends have confessed to me that this is a frequent phenomenon with them in meeting acquaintances in the street, especially unfamiliar ones. The bow is a secondary correction of the primary feint that we do not see the other person. Probably most readers will recognize in themselves, at least, the *start*, the nascent disposition, on many occasions, to act in each and all of these several ways. That the 'start' is neutralized by second thought proves it to come from a deeper region than thought. There is unquestionably a native impulse in every one to conceal love-affairs, and the acquired impulse to conceal pecuniary affairs seems in many to be almost equally strong. It is to be noted that even where a given habit of concealment is reflective and deliberate, its motive is far less often definite prudence than a vague aversion to have one's sanctity invaded and one's personal concerns fingered and turned over by other people. Thus, some persons will never leave anything with their name written on it, where others may pick it up—even in the woods, an old envelope must not be thrown on the ground. Many cut all the leaves of a book of which they may be reading a single chapter, so that no one shall know which one they have singled out, and all this with no *definite* notion of harm. The impulse to conceal is more apt to be provoked by superiors than by equals or inferiors. How differently do boys talk together when their parents are not by! Servants see more of their masters' characters than masters of servants'. * Where we conceal from our equals and familiars, there is probably always a definite element of prudential prevision involved. *Collective* secrecy, mystery, enters into the emotional interest of many games, and is one of the elements of the importance men attach to freemasonries of various sorts, being delightful apart from any end.

Cleanliness. Seeing how very filthy savages and exceptional individuals among civilized people may be, philosophers have doubted whether any genuine instinct of cleanliness exists, and whether education and habit be not responsible for whatever amount of it is found. Were it an instinct, its stimulus would be dirt, and its characteristic reaction the shrinking from contact therewith, and the cleaning of it away after contact had occurred. Now, if some animals are cleanly, men *may* be so, and there can be no doubt that some kinds of matter *are* natively repugnant, both to sight, touch, and smell—excrementitious and putrid things, blood, pus, entrails, and diseased tissues, for example. It is true that the shrinking from contact with these things may be inhibited very easily, as by a medical education; and it is equally true that the impulse to clean them away may be inhibited by so slight an obstacle as the thought of the coldness of the ablution, or the necessity of getting up to perform it. It is also true than an impulse to cleanliness, habitually checked, will become obsolete fast enough. But none of these facts prove the impulse never to have been

---

* Thackeray, in his exquisite Roundabout Paper, 'On a Chalk-Mark on the Door,' says: "You get truth habitually from equals only; so, my good Mr. Holyshade, don't talk to me about the habitual candor of the young Etonian of high birth, or I have my own opinion of *your* candor or discernment when you do. No. Tom Bowling is the soul of honor, and has been true to Black-eyed Syousan since the last time they parted at Wapping Old Stairs; but do you suppose Tom is perfectly frank, familiar, and above-board in his conversation with Admiral Nelson, K.C.B.? There are secrets, prevarications, fibs, if you will, between Tom and the admiral—between your crew (of servants) and *their* captain. I know I hire a worthy, clean, agreeable, and conscientious male or female hypocrite at so many guineas a year to do so and so for me. Were he other than hypocrite, I would send him about his business."

there.* It seems to be there in all cases; and then to be particularly amenable to outside influences, the child having his own degree of squeamishness about what he shall touch or eat, and later being either hardened or made more fastidious still by the habits he is forced to acquire and the examples among which he lives.

Examples get their hold on him in this way, that a particularly evil-smelling or catarrhal or lousy comrade is rather offensive to him, and that he sees the odiousness in another of an amount of dirt to which he would have no spontaneous objection if it were on his own skin. That *we dislike in others things which we tolerate in ourselves* is a law of our æsthetic nature about which there can be no doubt. But as soon as generalization and reflection step in, this judging of others leads to a new way of regarding ourselves. "Who taught you politeness? The impolite," is, I believe, a Chinese proverb. The concept, 'dirty fellow,' which we have formed, becomes one under which we personally shrink from being classed; and so we 'wash up,' and set ourselves right, at moments when our social self-consciousness is awakened, in a manner toward which no strictly instinctive native prompting exists. But the standard of cleanliness attained in this way is not likely to go beyond the mutual tolerance for one another of the members of the tribe, and hence may comport a good deal of actual filth.

Modesty, Shame. Whether there be an instinctive impulse to hide certain parts of the body and certain acts is perhaps even more open to doubt than whether there be an instinct of cleanliness. Anthropologists have denied it, and in the utter shamelessness of infancy and of many savage tribes have seemed to find a good basis for their views. It must, however, be remembered that infancy proves nothing, and that, as far as sexual modesty goes, the sexual impulse itself works directly against it at times of excitement, and with reference to certain people; and that habits of immodesty

---

* The insane symptom called "mysophobia," or dread of foulness, which leads a patient to wash his hands perhaps a hundred times a day, hardly seems explicable without supposing a primitive impulse to clean one's self of which it is, as it were, the convulsive exaggeration.

contracted with those people may forever afterwards inhibit any impulse to be modest towards *them.* This would account for a great deal of actual immodesty, even if an original modest impulse were there. On the other hand, the modest impulse, if it do exist, must be admitted to have a singularly ill-defined sphere of influence, both as regards the presences that call it forth, and as regards the acts to which it leads. Ethnology shows it to have very little backbone of its own, and to follow easily fashion and example. Still, it is hard to see the ubiquity of *some* sort of tribute to shame, however perverted—as where female modesty consists in covering the face alone, or immodesty in appearing before strangers unpainted—and to believe it to have no impulsive root whatever. Now, what may the impulsive root be? I believe that, for one thing, it is shyness, the feeling of dread that unfamiliar persons, as explained above, may inspire us withal. Such persons are the original stimuli to our modesty.* But the actions of modesty are quite different from the actions of shyness. They consist of the restraint of certain bodily functions, and of the covering of certain parts; and why do such particular actions necessarily ensue? That there *may* be in the human animal, as such, a 'blind' and immediate automatic impulse to such restraints and coverings in respect-inspiring presences is a possibility difficult of actual disproof. But it seems more likely, from the facts, that the actions of modesty are suggested to us in a roundabout way; and that, even more than those of cleanliness, they arise from the application in the second instance to ourselves of judgments primarily passed upon our mates. It is not easy to believe that, even among the nakedest savages, an unusual degree of cynicism and indecency in an individual should not beget a certain degree of contempt, and cheapen him in his neighbor's eyes. Human nature is sufficiently homo-

---

* "We often find modesty coming in only in the presence of foreigners, especially of clothed Europeans. Only before these do the Indian women in Brazil cover themselves with their girdle, only before these do the women on Timor conceal their bosom. In Australia we find the same thing happening." (Th. Waitz, Anthropologie der Naturvölker, vol. I. p. 358.) The author gives bibliographical references, which I omit.

geneous for us to be sure that everywhere reserve must inspire some respect, and that persons who suffer every liberty
are persons whom others disregard. Not to be like such
people, then, would be one of the first resolutions suggested by social self-consciousness to a child of nature just
emerging from the unreflective state. And the resolution
would probably acquire effective pungency for the first
time when the social self-consciousness was sharpened into
a real fit of shyness by some person being present whom it
was important not to disgust or displease. Public opinion
would of course go on to build its positive precepts upon
this germ; and, through a variety of examples and experiences, the ritual of modesty would grow, until it reached
the New England pitch of sensitiveness and range, making
us say stomach instead of belly, limb instead of leg, retire
instead of go to bed, and forbidding us to call a female dog
by name.

At bottom this amounts to the admission that, though
in some shape or other a natural and inevitable feature of
human life, modesty need not necessarily be an instinct in
the pure and simple excito-motor sense of the term.

Love. Of all propensities, the sexual impulses bear on
their face the most obvious signs of being instinctive, in
the sense of blind, automatic, and untaught. The teleology
they contain is often at variance with the wishes of the individuals concerned; and the actions are performed for no
assignable reason but because Nature urges just that way.
Here, if ever, then, we ought to find those characters of
fatality, infallibility, and uniformity, which, we are told,
make of actions done from instinct a class so utterly apart.
But is this so? The facts are just the reverse: the sexual
instinct is particularly liable to be checked and modified
by slight differences in the individual stimulus, by the
inward condition of the agent himself, by habits once acquired, and by the antagonism of contrary impulses operating on the mind. One of these is the ordinary shyness
recently described; another is what might be called the
anti-sexual instinct, the instinct of personal isolation, the
actual repulsiveness to us of the idea of intimate contact

with most of the persons we meet, especially those of our own sex.* Thus it comes about that this strongest passion of all, so far from being the most 'irresistible,' may, on the contrary, be the hardest one to give rein to, and that individuals in whom the inhibiting influences are potent may pass through life and never find an occasion to have it gratified. There could be no better proof of the truth of that proposition with which we began our study of the instinctive life in man, that irregularity of behavior may come as well from the possession of too many instincts as from the lack of any at all.

The instinct of personal isolation, of which we have spoken, exists more strongly in men with respect to one another, and more strongly in women with respect to men. In women it is called coyness, and has to be positively overcome by a process of wooing before the sexual instinct inhibits it and takes its place. As Darwin has shown in his book on the 'Descent of Man and Sexual Selection,' it has played a vital part in the amelioration of all higher animal types, and is to a great degree responsible for whatever degree of chastity the human race may show. It illustrates strikingly, however, the law of the inhibition of instincts by habits—for, once broken through with a given person, it is not apt to assert itself again ; and habitually broken through, as by prostitutes, with various persons, it may altogether decay. Habit also fixes it in us toward certain individuals : nothing is so particularly displeasing as the notion of close personal contact with those whom we have long known in a respectful and distant way. The fondness of the ancients and of modern Orientals for forms of unnatural vice, of which the notion affects us with horror, is probably a mere case of the way in which this instinct may be inhibited by habit. We can hardly suppose that the ancients had by gift of Nature a propensity of which we are devoid, and were all victims of what is now a pathological aberration limited to individuals. It is more probable that with them the instinct of physical aver-

---

* To most of us it is even unpleasant to sit down in a chair still warm from occupancy by another person's body. To many, hand-shaking is disagreeable.

sion toward a certaiñ class of objects was inhibited early in life by *habits,* formed under the influence of *example;* and that then a kind of sexual appetite, of which very likely most men possess the germinal possibility, developed itself in an unrestricted way. That the development of it in an abnormal way may check its development in the normal way, seems to be a well-ascertained medical fact. And that the direction of the sexual instinct towards one individual tends to inhibit its application to other individuals, is a law, upon which, though it suffers many exceptions, the whole *régime* of monogamy is based. These details are a little unpleasant to discuss, but they show so beautifully the correctness of the general principles in the light of which our review has been made, that it was impossible to pass them over unremarked.

Jealousy is unquestionably instinctive.

Parental Love is an instinct stronger in woman than in man, at least in the early childhood of its object. I need do little more than quote Schneider's lively description of it as it exists in her :

"As soon as a wife becomes a mother her whole thought and feeling, her whole being, is altered. Until then she had only thought of her own well-being, of the satisfaction of her vanity ; the whole world appeared made only for her ; everything that went on about her was only noticed so far as it had personal reference to herself ; she asked of every one that he should appear interested in her, pay her the requisite attention, and as far as possible fulfil her wishes. Now, however, the centre of the world is no longer herself, but her child. She does not think of her own hunger, she must first be sure that the child is fed. It is nothing to her that she herself is tired and needs rest, so long as she sees that the child's sleep is disturbed ; the moment it stirs she awakes, though far stronger noises fail to arouse her now. She, who formerly could not bear the slightest carelessness of dress, and touched everything with gloves, allows herself to be soiled by the infant, and does not shrink from seizing its clouts with her naked hands. Now, she has the greatest patience with the ugly, piping cry-baby (*Schreihals*), whereas until now every discordant sound, every slightly unpleasant noise, made her nervous. Every limb of the still hideous little being appears to her beautiful, every movement fills her with delight. She has, in one word, transferred her entire egoism to the child, and lives only in it. Thus, at least, it is in all unspoiled, naturally-bred mothers, who, alas ! seem to be growing rarer; and thus it is with all the higher animal-mothers. The maternal joys of a cat, for example, are not to be disguised. With an expression of infinite comfort she stretches out her fore-legs to offer her teats to her children, and moves her tail with delight when the little hungry mouths tug and suck. . . . But not only the contact, the bare look of the offspring affords endless delight, not only because the mother thinks that the child will some day grow great and handsome and bring her many joys, but because she has received from Nature an instinctive love for her children. She does not herself know why she is so happy, and why the look of the child and the care of it are so agreeable, any more than the young man can give an account of why he loves a maiden, and is so happy when she is near. Few mothers, in caring for their child, think of the proper purpose of maternal love for the preservation of the species. Such a thought may arise in the father's mind ; seldom in that of the mother. The latter feels only . . . that it is an everlasting delight to hold the being which she has brought forth protectingly in her arms, to dress it, to wash it, to rock it to sleep, or to still its hunger."

So far the worthy Schneider, to whose words may be added this remark, that the passionate devotion of a mother —ill herself, perhaps—to a sick or dying child is perhaps the most simply beautiful moral spectacle that human life affords. Contemning every danger, triumphing over every difficulty, outlasting all fatigue, woman's love is here invincibly superior to anything that man can show.

These are the most prominent of the tendencies which are worthy of being called instinctive in the human species.*

---

* Some will, of course, find the list too large, others too small. With the boundaries of instinct fading into reflex action below, and into acquired habit or suggested activity above, it is likely that there will always be controversy about just what to include under the class-name. Shall we add the propensity to walk along a curbstone, or any other narrow path, to the list of instincts ? Shall we subtract secretiveness, as due to shyness or to fear ? Who knows? Meanwhile our physiological method has this inestimable advantage, that such questions of limit have neither theoretical nor practical importance. The facts once noted, it matters little how they are named. Most authors give a shorter list than that in the text. The phrenologists add adhesiveness, inhabitiveness, love of approbation, etc., etc., to their list of ' sentiments,' which in the main agree with our list of instincts. Fortlage, in his System der Psychologie, classes among the *Triebe* all the vegetative physiological functions. Santlus (Zur Psychologie der Menschlichen Triebe, Leipsic, 1864) says there are at bottom but three instincts, that of ' Being,' that of ' Function,' and that of ' Life,' The ' Instinct of Being ' he subdivides into *animal*, embracing the activities of

It will be observed that *no other mammal, not even the monkey, shows so large an array.* In a perfectly-rounded development, every one of these instincts would start a habit toward certain objects and inhibit a habit toward certain others. Usually this is the case; but, in the one-sided development of civilized life, it happens that the timely age goes by in a sort of starvation of objects, and the individual then grows up with gaps in his psychic constitution which future experiences can never fill. Compare the accomplished gentleman with the poor artisan or trades-man of a city: during the adolescence of the former, objects appropriate to his growing interests, bodily and mental, were offered as fast as the interests awoke, and, as a consequence, he is armed and equipped at every angle to meet the world. Sport came to the rescue and completed his education where real things were lacking. He has tasted of the essence of every side of human life, being sailor, hunter, athlete, scholar, fighter, talker, dandy, man of affairs, etc., all in one. Over the city poor boy's youth no such golden opportunities were hung, and in his man-hood no desires for most of them exist. Fortunate it is for him if gaps are the only anomalies his instinctive life pre-sents; perversions are too often the fruit of his unnatural bringing up.

---

all the senses; and *psychical,* embracing the acts of the intellect and of the ' transempiric consciousness.' The ' Instinct of Function ' he divides into *sexual, inclinational* (friendship, attachment, honor); and *moral* (re-ligion, philanthropy, faith, truth, moral freedom, etc.). The ' Instinct of Life ' embraces *conservation* (nutrition, motion); *sociability* (imitation, juridical and ethical arrangements); and *personal interest* (love of inde-pendence and freedom, acquisitiveness, self-defence). Such a muddled list as this shows how great are the advantages of the physiological analysis we have used.

CHAPTER XXV.*

THE EMOTIONS.

In speaking of the instincts it has been impossible to keep them separate from the emotional excitements which go with them. Objects of rage, love, fear, etc., not only prompt a man to outward deeds, but provoke characteristic alterations in his attitude and visage, and affect his breathing, circulation, and other organic functions in specific ways. When the outward deeds are inhibited, these latter emotional expressions still remain, and we read the anger in the face, though the blow may not be struck, and the fear betrays itself in voice and color, though one may suppress all other sign. *Instinctive reactions and emotional expressions thus shade imperceptibly into each other. Every object that excites an instinct excites an emotion as well.* Emotions, however, fall short of instincts, in that the emotional reaction usually terminates in the subject's own body, whilst the instinctive reaction is apt to go farther and enter into practical relations with the exciting object.

Emotional reactions are often excited by objects with which we have no practical dealings. A ludicrous object, for example, or a beautiful object are not necessarily objects to which we *do* anything; we simply laugh, or stand in admiration, as the case may be. The class of emotional, is thus rather larger than that of instinctive, impulses, commonly so called. Its stimuli are more numerous, and its expressions are more internal and delicate, and often less practical. The physiological plan and essence of the two classes of impulse, however, is the same.

As with instincts, so with emotions, the mere memory or imagination of the object may suffice to liberate the excite-

---

* Parts of this chapter have already appeared in an article published in 1884 in Mind.

ment. One may get angrier in thinking over one's insult than at the moment of receiving it; and we melt more over a mother who is dead than we ever did when she was living. In the rest of the chapter I shall use the word *object* of emotion indifferently to mean one which is physically present or one which is merely thought of.

It would be tedious to go through a complete list of the reactions which characterize the various emotions. For that the special treatises must be referred to. A few examples of their variety, however, ought to find a place here. Let me begin with the manifestations of Grief as a Danish physiologist, C. Lange, describes them : *

"The chief feature in the physiognomy of grief is perhaps its paralyzing effect on the voluntary movements. This effect is by no means as extreme as that which fright produces, being seldom more than that degree of weakening which makes it cost an effort to perform actions usually done with ease. It is, in other words, a feeling of weariness; and (as in all weariness) movements are made slowly, heavily, without strength, unwillingly, and with exertion, and are limited to the fewest possible. By this the grieving person gets his outward stamp : he walks slowly, unsteadily, dragging his feet and hanging his arms. His voice is weak and without resonance, in consequence of the feeble activity of the muscles of expiration and of the larynx. He prefers to sit still, sunk in himself and silent. The tonicity or 'latent innervation' of the muscles is strikingly diminished. The neck is bent, the head hangs ('bowed down' with grief), the relaxation of the cheek- and jaw-muscles makes the face look long and narrow, the jaw may even hang open. The eyes appear large, as is always the case where the *orbicularis* muscle is paralyzed, but they may often be partly covered by the upper lid which droops in consequence of the laming of its own *levator*. With this condition of weakness of the voluntary nerve- and muscle-apparatus of the whole body, there coexists, as aforesaid, just as in all states of similar motor weakness, a subjective feeling of weariness and heavi·ness, of something which weighs upon one ; one feels 'downcast,' 'oppressed,' 'laden,' one speaks of his 'weight of sorrow,' one must 'bear up' under it, just as one must 'keep down' his anger. Many there are who 'succumb' to sorrow to such a degree that they literally cannot stand upright, but sink or lean against surrounding objects, fall on their knees, or, like Romeo in the monk's cell, throw themselves upon the earth in their despair.

"But this weakness of the entire voluntary motor apparatus (the so-called apparatus of 'animal' life) is only one side of the physiology of grief. Another side, hardly less important, and in its consequences

---

* Ueber Gemüthsbewegungen, uebersetzt von H. Kurella (Leipzig, 1887).

perhaps even more so, belongs to another subdivision of the motor apparatus, namely, the involuntary or 'organic' muscles, especially those which are found in the walls of the blood-vessels, and the use of which is, by contracting, to diminish the latter's calibre. These muscles and their nerves, forming together the 'vaso-motor apparatus,' act in grief contrarily to the voluntary motor apparatus. Instead of being paralyzed, like the latter, the vascular muscles are more strongly contracted than usual, so that the tissues and organs of the body become anæmic. The immediate consequence of this bloodlessness is pallor and shrunkenness, and the pale color and collapsed features are the peculiarities which, in connection with the relaxation of the visage, give to the victim of grief his characteristic physiognomy, and often give an impression of emaciation which ensues too rapidly to be possibly due to real disturbance of nutrition, or waste uncompensated by repair. Another regular consequence of the bloodlessness of the skin is a feeling of cold, and shivering. A constant symptom of grief is sensitiveness to cold, and difficulty in keeping warm. In grief, the inner organs are unquestionably anæmic as well as the skin. This is of course not obvious to the eye, but many phenomena prove it. Such is the diminution of the various secretions, at least of such as are accessible to observation. The mouth grows dry, the tongue sticky, and a bitter taste ensues which, it would appear, is only a consequence of the tongue's dryness. [The expression 'bitter sorrow' may possibly arise from this.] In nursing women the milk diminishes or altogether dries up. There is one of the most regular manifestations of grief, which apparently contradicts these other physiological phenomena, and that is the weeping, with its profuse secretion of tears, its swollen reddened face, red eyes, and augmented secretion from the nasal mucous membrane."

Lange goes on to suggest that this may be a reaction from a previously contracted vaso-motor state. The explanation seems a forced one. The fact is that there are changeable expressions of grief. The weeping is as apt as not to be immediate, especially in women and children. Some men can never weep. The tearful and the dry phases alternate in all who can weep, sobbing storms being followed by periods of calm; and the shrunken, cold, and pale condition which Lange describes so well is more characteristic of a severe settled sorrow than of an acute mental pain. Properly we have two distinct emotions here, both prompted by the same object, it is true, but affecting different persons, or the same person at different times, and *feeling* quite differently whilst they last, as anyone's consciousness will testify. There is an excitement during the crying fit which is not without a certain pungent pleasure of its own; but it would take a genius for felicity to discover any dash of redeeming quality in the feeling of dry and shrunken sorrow.—Our author continues:

" If the smaller vessels of the lungs contract so that these organs become anæmic, we have (as is usual under such conditions) the feeling of insufficient breath, and of oppression of the chest, and these tormenting sensations increase the sufferings of the griever, who seeks relief by long drawn sighs, instinctively, like every one who lacks breath from whatever cause.*

---

* The bronchial tubes may be contracted as well as the ramifications of the pulmonary artery. Professor J. Henle has, amongst his Anthropologische Vorträge, an exquisite one on the ' Natural History of the Sigh,' in which he represents our inspirations as the result of a battle between the red muscles of our skeleton, ribs, and diaphragm, and the white ones of the lungs, which seek to narrow the calibre of the air-tubes. "In the normal state the former easily conquer, but under other conditions they either conquer with difficulty or are defeated. . . . The contrasted emotions express themselves in similarly contrasted wise, by spasm and paralysis of the unstriped muscles, and for the most part alike in all the organs which are provided with them, as arteries, skin, and bronchial tubes. The contrast among the emotions is generally expressed by dividing them into exciting and depressing ones. It is a remarkable fact that the depressing emotions, like fear, horror, disgust, increase the contraction of these smooth muscles, whilst the exciting emotions, like joy, anger, etc., make them relax. Contrasts of temperature act similarly, cold like the depressing, and warmth like the exciting, emotions. Cold produces pallor and gooseflesh, warmth smooths out the skin and widens the vessels. If one notices the uncomfortable mood brought about by strained expectation, anxiety before a public address, vexation at an unmerited affront, etc., one finds that the suffering part of it concentrates itself principally in the chest, and that it consists in a soreness, hardly to be called pain, felt in the middle of the breast and due to an unpleasant resistance which is offered to the movements of inspiration, and sets a limit to their extent. The insufficiency of the diaphragm is obtruded upon consciousness, and we try by the aid of the external voluntary chest-muscles to draw a deeper breath. [This is the sigh.] If we fail, the unpleasantness of the situation is increased, for then to our mental distress is added the corporeally repugnant feeling of lack of air, a slight degree of suffocation. If, on the contrary, the outer muscles overcome the resistance of the inner ones, the oppressed breast is lightened. We think we speak symbolically when we speak of a stone weighing on our heart, or of a burden rolled from off our breast. But really we only express the exact fact, for we should have to raise the entire weight of the atmosphere (about 820 kilog.) at each inspiration, if the air did not balance it by streaming into our lungs." (P. 55.) It must not be forgotten that an inhibition of the inspiratory centre similar to that produced by exciting the superior laryngeal nerve may possibly play a part in these phenomena. For a very interesting discussion of the respiratory difficulty and its connec-

" The anæmia of the brain in grief is shown by intellectual inertia, dullness, a feeling of mental weariness, effort, and indisposition to work, often by sleeplessness. Indeed it is the anæmia of the motor centres of the brain which lies at the bottom of all that weakening of the voluntary powers of motion which we described in the first instance."

My impression is that Dr. Lange simplifies and universalizes the phenomena a little too much in this description, and in particular that he very likely overdoes the anæmia-business. But such as it is, his account may stand as a favorable specimen of the sort of descriptive work to which the emotions have given rise.

Take next another emotion, Fear, and read what Mr. Darwin says of its effects :

" Fear is often preceded by astonishment, and is so far akin to it that both lead to the senses of sight and hearing being instantly aroused. In both cases the eyes and mouth are widely opened and the eyebrows raised. The frightened man at first stands like a statue, motionless and breathless, or crouches down as if instinctively to escape observation. The heart beats quickly and violently, so that it palpitates or knocks against the ribs ; but it is very doubtful if it then works more efficiently than usual, so as to send a greater supply of blood to all parts of the body ; for the skin instantly becomes pale as during incipient faintness. This paleness of the surface, however, is probably in large part, or is exclusively, due to the vaso-motor centre being affected in such a manner as to cause the contraction of the small arteries of the skin. That the skin is much affected under the sense of great fear, we see in the marvellous manner in which perspiration immediately exudes from it. This exudation is all the more remarkable, as the surface is then cold, and hence the term, a cold sweat ; whereas the sudorific glands are properly excited into action when the surface is heated. The hairs also on the skin stand erect, and the superficial muscles shiver. In connection with the disturbed action of the heart the breathing is hurried. The salivary glands act imperfectly; the mouth becomes dry and is often opened and shut. I have also noticed that under slight fear there is strong tendency to yawn. One of the best marked symptoms is the trembling of all the muscles of the body ; and this is often first seen in the lips. From this cause, and from the dryness of the mouth, the voice becomes husky or indistinct or may altogether fail. ' Obstupui steteruntque comæ, et vox faucibus hæsit.' . . . As fear increases into an agony of terror, we behold, as under all violent emotions, diversified results. The heart beats wild-

tion with anxiety and fear, see ' A Case of Hydrophobia ' by the lamented Thos. B. Curtis in the Boston Med. and Surg. Journal, Nov. 7 and 14, 1878, and remarks thereon by James J. Putnam, *ibid*. Nov. 21.

ly or must fail to act and faintness ensue ; there is a death-like pallor ;
the breathing is labored ; the wings of the nostrils are widely dilated ;
there is a gasping and convulsive motion of the lips, a tremor on the
hollow cheek, a gulping and catching of the throat ; the uncovered and
protruding eyeballs are fixed on the object of terror ; or they may roll
restlessly from side to side, *huc illuc volens oculos totumque pererrat.*
The pupils are said to be enormously dilated. All the muscles of the
body may become rigid or may be thrown into convulsive movements.
The hands are alternately clenched and opened, often with a twitching
movement. The arms may be protruded as if to avert some dreadful
danger, or may be thrown wildly over the head. The Rev. Mr. Hagen-
auer has seen this latter action in a terrified Australian. In other cases
there is a sudden and uncontrollable tendency to headlong flight; and
so strong is this that the boldest soldiers may be seized with a sudden
panic." *

Finally take Hatred, and read the synopsis of its possible
effects as given by Sig. Mantegazza : †

"Withdrawal of the head backwards, withdrawal of the trunk ;
projection forwards of the hands, as if to defend one's self against the
hated object ; contraction or closure of the eyes ; elevation of the upper
lip and closure of the nose,—these are all elementary movements of turning away. Next threatening movements, as : intense frowning ; eyes
wide open ; display of teeth ; grinding teeth and contracting jaws ;
opened mouth with tongue advanced ; clenched fists ; threatening action
of arms ; stamping with the feet ; deep inspirations—panting ; growling
and various cries ; automatic repetition of one word or syllable ; sudden weakness and trembling of voice ; spitting. Finally, various miscellaneous reactions and vaso-motor symptoms: general trembling ; con-
vulsions of lips and facial muscles, of limbs and of trunk; acts of violence
to one's self, as biting fist or nails ; sardonic laughter ; bright redness
of face ; sudden pallor of face ; extreme dilatation of nostrils ; standing up of hair on head."

Were we to go through the whole list of emotions which
have been named by men, and study their organic manifestations, we should but ring the changes on the elements
which these three typical cases involve. Rigidity of this
muscle, relaxation of that, constriction of arteries here, dilatation there, breathing of this sort or that, pulse slowing
or quickening, this gland secreting and that one dry, etc.,
etc. We should, moreover, find that our descriptions had no

---

* Origin of the Emotions, Darwin, pp. 290-2.
† La Physionomie et l'Expression des Sentiments (Paris, 1885), p. 140.

absolute truth ; that they only applied to the average man ;
that every one of us, almost, has some personal idiosyncrasy
of expression, laughing or sobbing differently from his
neighbor, or reddening or growing pale where others do
not.   We should find a like variation in the objects which
excite emotion in different persons.   Jokes at which one
explodes with laughter nauseate another, and seem blas-
phemous to a third ; and occasions which overwhelm me with
fear or bashfulness are just what give you the full sense of
ease and power.   The internal shadings of emotional feeling, moreover, merge endlessly into each other.   Language
has discriminated some of them, as hatred, antipathy, ani-
mosity, dislike, aversion, malice, spite, vengefulness, ab-
horrence, etc., etc. ; but in the dictionaries of synonyms we
find these feelings distinguished more by their severally
appropriate objective stimuli than by their conscious or
subjective tone.

The result of all this flux is that the merely descriptive
literature of the emotions is one of the most tedious parts
of psychology.   And not only is it tedious, but you feel
that its subdivisions are to a great extent either fictitious
or unimportant, and that its pretences to accuracy are a
sham.   But unfortunately there is little psychological writing about the emotions which is not merely descriptive.
As emotions are described in novels, they interest us, for
we are made to share them.   We have grown acquainted
with the concrete objects and emergencies which call
them forth, and any knowing touch of introspection which
may grace the page meets with a quick and feeling
response.   Confessedly literary works of aphoristic philosophy also flash lights into our emotional life, and give us a
fitful delight.   But as far as "scientific psychology" of the
emotions goes, I may have been surfeited by too much
reading of classic works on the subject, but I should as
lief read verbal descriptions of the shapes of the rocks on
a New Hampshire farm as toil through them again.   They
give one nowhere a central point of view, or a deductive
or generative principle.   They distinguish and refine and
specify *in infinitum* without ever getting on to another logical level.   Whereas the beauty of all truly scientific work

is to get to ever deeper levels. Is there no way out from this level of individual description in the case of the emotions? I believe there is a way out, but I fear that few will take it.

The trouble with the emotions in psychology is that they are regarded too much as absolutely individual things. So long as they are set down as so many eternal and sacred psychic entities, like the old immutable species in natural history, so long all that *can* be done with them is reverently to catalogue their separate characters, points, and effects. But if we regard them as products of more general causes (as 'species' are now regarded as products of heredity and variation), the mere distinguishing and cataloguing becomes of subsidiary importance. Having the goose which lays the golden eggs, the description of each egg already laid is a minor matter. Now the general causes of the emotions are indubitably physiological. Prof. C. Lange, of Copenhagen, in the pamphlet from which I have already quoted, published in 1885 a physiological theory of their constitution and conditioning, which I had already broached the previous year in an article in Mind. None of the criticisms which I have heard of it have made me doubt its essential truth. I will therefore devote the next few pages to explaining what it is. I shall limit myself in the first instance to what may be called the *coarser* emotions, grief, fear, rage, love, in which every one recognizes a strong organic reverberation, and afterwards speak of the *subtler* emotions, or of those whose organic reverberation is less obvious and strong.

EMOTION FOLLOWS UPON THE BODILY EXPRESSION IN THE COARSER EMOTIONS AT LEAST.

Our natural way of thinking about these coarser emotions is that the mental perception of some fact excites the mental affection called the emotion, and that this latter state of mind gives rise to the bodily expression. My theory, on the contrary, is that *the bodily changes follow directly the perception of the exciting fact, and that our feeling of the same changes as they occur* IS *the emotion.* Common-sense says, we lose our fortune, are sorry and weep; we meet a bear, are frightened and run; we are insulted by a rival, are angry and strike. The hypothesis here to be defended says that this order of sequence is incorrect, that the one mental state is not immediately induced by the other, that the bodily manifestations must first be interposed between, and that the more rational statement is that we feel sorry because we cry, angry because we strike, afraid because we tremble, and not that we cry, strike, or tremble, because we are sorry, angry, or fearful, as the case may be. Without the bodily states following on the perception, the latter would be purely cognitive in form, pale, colorless, destitute of emotional warmth. We might then see the bear, and judge it best to run, receive the insult and deem it right to strike, but we should not actually *feel* afraid or angry.

Stated in this crude way, the hypothesis is pretty sure to meet with immediate disbelief. And yet neither many nor far-fetched considerations are required to mitigate its paradoxical character, and possibly to produce conviction of its truth.

To begin with, no reader of the last two chapters will be inclined to doubt the fact that *objects do excite bodily changes* by a preorganized mechanism, or the farther fact that *the changes are so indefinitely numerous and subtle that the entire organism may be called a sounding-board,* which every change of consciousness, however slight, may make reverberate. The various permutations and combinations of which these organic activities are susceptible make it abstractly possible that no shade of emotion, however slight, should be without a bodily reverberation as unique, when taken in its totality, as is the mental mood itself. The immense number of parts modified in each emotion is what makes it so difficult for us to reproduce in cold blood the total and integral expression of any one of them. We may catch the trick with the voluntary muscles, but fail with the skin, glands, heart, and other viscera. Just as an artificially imitated sneeze lacks something of the reality, so the attempt to imitate an emotion in the absence of its normal instigating cause is apt to be rather 'hollow.'

The next thing to be noticed is this, that *every one of the bodily changes, whatsoever it be, is* FELT, *acutely or obscurely, the moment it occurs.* If the reader has never paid attention to this matter, he will be both interested and astonished to learn how many different local bodily feelings he can detect in himself as characteristic of his various emotional moods. It would be perhaps too much to expect him to arrest the tide of any strong gust of passion for the sake of any such curious analysis as this; but he can observe more tranquil states, and that may be assumed here to be true of the greater which is shown to be true of the less. Our whole cubic capacity is sensibly alive; and each morsel of it contributes its pulsations of feeling, dim or sharp, pleasant, painful, or dubious, to that sense of personality that every one of us unfailingly carries with him. It is surprising what little items give accent to these complexes of sensibility. When worried by any slight trouble, one may find that the focus of one's bodily consciousness is the contraction, often quite inconsiderable, of the eyes and brows. When momentarily embarrassed, it is something in the pharynx that compels either a swallow, a clearing of the throat, or a slight cough; and so on for as many more instances as might be named. Our concern here being with the general view rather than with the details, I will not linger to discuss these, but, assuming the point admitted that every change that occurs must be felt, I will pass on.

I now proceed to urge the vital point of my whole theory, which is this: *If we fancy some strong emotion, and then try to abstract from our consciousness of it all the feelings of its bodily symptoms, we find we have nothing left behind,* no 'mind-stuff' out of which the emotion can be constituted, and that a cold and neutral state of intellectual perception is all that remains. It is true that, although most people when asked say that their introspection verifies this statement, some persist in saying theirs does not. Many cannot be made to understand the question. When you beg them to imagine away every feeling of laughter and of tendency to laugh from their consciousness of the ludicrousness of an object, and then to tell you what the feeling of its ludicrousness would be like, whether it be anything more than the perception that the object belongs to the class 'funny,' they persist in replying that the thing proposed is a physical impossibility, and that they always *must* laugh if they see a funny object. Of course the task proposed is not the practical one of seeing a ludicrous object and annihilating one's tendency to laugh. It is the purely speculative one of subtracting certain elements of feeling from an emotional state supposed to exist in its fulness, and saying what the residual elements are. I cannot help thinking that all who rightly apprehend this problem will agree with the proposition above laid down. What kind of an emotion of fear would be left if the feeling neither of quickened heart-beats nor of shallow breathing, neither of trembling lips nor of weakened limbs, neither of goose-flesh nor of visceral stirrings, were present, it is quite impossible for me to think. Can one fancy the state of rage and picture no ebullition in the chest, no flushing of the face, no dilatation of the nostrils, no clenching of the teeth, no impulse to vigorous action, but in their stead limp muscles, calm breathing, and a placid face? The present writer, for one, certainly cannot. The rage is as completely evaporated as the sensation of its so-called manifestations, and the only thing that can possibly be supposed to take its place is some cold-blooded and dispassionate judicial sentence, confined entirely to the intellectual realm, to the effect that a certain person or persons merit chastisement for their sins. In like manner of grief: what would it be without its tears, its sobs, its suffocation of the heart, its pang in the breastbone? A feelingless cognition that certain circumstances are deplorable, and nothing more. Every passion in turn tells the same story. A purely disembodied human emotion is a nonentity. I do not say that it is a contradiction in the nature of things, or that pure spirits are necessarily condemned to cold intellectual lives; but I say that for *us*, emotion dissociated from all bodily feeling is inconceivable. The more closely I scrutinize my states, the more persuaded I become that whatever moods, affections, and passions I have are in very truth constituted by, and made up of, those bodily changes which we ordinarily call their expression or consequence; and the more it seems to me that if I were to become corporeally anæsthetic, I should be excluded from the life of the affections, harsh and tender alike, and drag out an existence of merely cognitive or intellectual form. Such an existence, although it seems to have been the ideal of ancient sages, is too apathetic to be keenly sought after by those born after the revival of the worship of sensibility, a few generations ago.

Let not this view be called materialistic. It is neither more nor less materialistic than any other view which says that our emotions are conditioned by nervous processes. No reader of this book is likely to rebel against such a saying so long as it is expressed in general terms; and if any one still finds materialism in the thesis now defended, that must be because of the special processes invoked. They are *sensational* processes, processes due to inward currents set up by physical happenings. Such processes have, it is true, always been regarded by the platonizers in psychology as having something peculiarly base about them. But our emotions must always be *inwardly* what they are, whatever be the physiological ground of their apparition. If they are deep, pure, worthy, spiritual facts on any conceivable theory of their physiological source, they remain no less deep, pure, spiritual, and worthy of regard on this present sensational theory. They carry their own inner measure of worth with them; and it is just as logical to use the present theory of the emotions for proving that sensational processes need not be vile and material, as to use their vileness and materiality as a proof that such a theory cannot be true.

If such a theory is true, then each emotion is the resultant of a sum of elements, and each element is caused by a physiological process of a sort already well known. The elements are all organic changes, and each of them is the reflex effect of the exciting object. Definite questions now immediately arise—questions very different from those which were the only possible ones without this view. Those were questions of classification : "Which are the proper genera of emotion, and which the species under each?" or of description: "By what expression is each emotion characterized?" The questions now are *causal:* Just what changes does this object and what changes does that object excite?" and "How come they to excite these particular changes and not others?" We step from a superficial to a deep order of inquiry. Classification and description are the lowest stage of science. They sink into the background the moment questions of genesis are formulated, and remain important only so far as they facilitate our answering these. Now the moment the genesis of an emotion is accounted for, as the arousal by an object of a lot of reflex acts which are forthwith felt, *we immediately see why there is no limit to the number of possible different emotions which may exist, and why the emotions of different individuals may vary indefinitely,* both as to their constitution and as to objects which call them forth. For there is nothing sacramental or eternally fixed in reflex action. Any sort of reflex effect is possible, and reflexes actually vary indefinitely, as we know.

"We have all seen men dumb, instead of talkative, with joy; we have seen fright drive the blood into the head of its victim, instead of making him pale; we have seen grief run restlessly about lamenting, instead of sitting bowed down and mute; etc., etc., and this naturally enough, for one and the same cause can work differently on different men's blood-vessels (since these do not always react alike), whilst moreover the impulse on its way through the brain to the vaso-motor centre is differently influenced by different earlier impressions in the form of recollections or associations of ideas." *

In short, *any classification of the emotions is seen to be as true and as 'natural' as any other,* if it only serves some purpose; and such a question as "What is the 'real' or 'typical' expression of anger, or fear?" is seen to have no objective meaning at all. Instead of it we now have the question as to how any given 'expression' of anger or fear may have come to exist; and that is a real question of physiological mechanics on the one hand, and of history on the other, which (like all real questions) is in essence answerable, although the answer may be hard to find. On a later page I shall mention the attempts to answer it which have been made.

DIFFICULTY OF TESTING THE THEORY EXPERIMENTALLY.

I have thus fairly propounded what seems to me the most fruitful way of conceiving of the emotions. It must

---

* Lange, *op. cit.* p. 75.

be admitted that it is so far only a hypothesis, only *possibly* a true conception, and that much is lacking to its definitive proof. The only way coercively to *dis*prove it, however, would be to take some emotion, and then exhibit qualities of feeling in it which should be *demonstrably* additional to all those which could possibly be derived from the organs affected at the time. But to detect with certainty such purely spiritual qualities of feeling would obviously be a task beyond human power. We have, as Professor Lange says, absolutely no immediate criterion by which to distinguish between spiritual and corporeal feelings; and, I may add, the more we sharpen our introspection, the more *localized* all our qualities of feeling become (see above, Vol. I. p. 300) and the more difficult the discrimination consequently grows.*

A positive proof of the theory would, on the other hand, be given if we could find a subject absolutely anæsthetic inside and out, but not paralytic, so that emotion-inspiring objects might evoke the usual bodily expressions from him, but who, on being consulted, should say that no subjective emotional affection was felt. Such a man would be like one who, because he eats, appears to bystanders to be hungry, but who afterwards confesses that he had no appetite at all. Cases like this are extremely hard to find. Medical literature contains reports, so far as I know, of but three. In the famous one of Remigius Leins no mention is made by the reporters of his emotional condition. In Dr. G. Winter's case † the patient is said to be inert and phlegmatic, but no particular attention, as I learn from Dr. W., was paid to his psychic condition. In the extraordinary case reported by Professor Strumpell (to which I must refer later in another connection) ‡ we read that the patient, a shoemaker's apprentice of fifteen, entirely anæsthetic, inside

---

* Professor Höffding, in his excellent treatise on Psychology, admits (p. 342) the mixture of bodily sensation with purely spiritual affection in the emotions. He does not, however, discuss the difficulties of discerning the spiritual affection (nor even show that he has fairly considered them) in his contention that it exists.

† Ein Fall von allgemeiner Anaesthesie (Heidelberg, 1882).

‡ Ziemssen's Deutsches Archiv für klinische Medicin, xxii. 321.

and out, with the exception of one eye and one ear, had shown *shame* on the occasion of soiling his bed, and *grief*, when a formerly favorite dish was set before him, at the thought that he could no longer taste its flavor. Dr. Strumpell is also kind enough to inform me that he manifested *surprise, fear*, and *anger* on certain occasions. In observing him, however, no such theory as the present one seems to have been thought of; and it always remains possible that, just as he satisfied his natural appetites and necessities in cold blood, with no inward feeling, so his emotional expressions may have been accompanied by a quite cold heart.* Any new case which turns up of generalized anæsthesia ought to be carefully examined as to the inward emotional sensibility as distinct from the 'expressions' of emotion which circumstances may bring forth.

Objections Considered.

Let me now notice a few objections. The replies will make the theory still more plausible.

First Objection. There is no real evidence, it may be said,

---

* The not very uncommon cases of hysterical hemianæsthesia are not complete enough to be utilized in this inquiry. Moreover, the recent researches, of which some account was given in Chapter IV, tend to show that hysterical anæsthesia is not a real absence of sensibility, but a ' dissociation,' as M. Pierre Janet calls it, or splitting-off of certain sensations from the rest of the person's consciousness, this *rest* forming the self which remains connected with the ordinary organs of expression. The split-off consciousness forms a secondary self ; and M. Janet writes me that he sees no reason why sensations whose ' dissociation ' from the body of consciousness makes the patient practically anæsthetic, might not, nevertheless, contribute to the emotional life of the patient. They do still contribute to the function of locomotion; for in his patient L. there was no ataxia in spite of the anæsthesia. M. Janet writes me, apropos of his anæsthetic patient L., that she seemed to ' suffer by hallucination.' " I have often pricked or burned her without warning, and when she did not see me. She never moved, and evidently perceived nothing. But if afterwards in her movements she caught sight of her wounded arm, and *saw* on her skin a little drop of blood resulting from a slight cut, she would begin to cry out and lament as if she suffered a great deal. ' My blood flows,' she said one day ; 'I *must be* suffering a great deal!' She suffered by hallucination. This sort of suffering is very general in hysterics. It is enough for them to receive the slightest hint of a modification in their body, when their imagination fills up the rest and invents changes that were not felt.' See the remarks published at a later date in Janet's Automatisme Psychologique, pp. 214–15.

for the assumption that particular perceptions *do* produce wide-spread bodily effects by a sort of immediate physical influence, antecedent to the arousal of an emotion or emotional idea?

Reply. There is most assuredly such evidence. In listening to poetry, drama, or heroic narrative we are often surprised at the cutaneous shiver which like a sudden wave flows over us, and at the heart-swelling and the lachrymal effusion that unexpectedly catch us at intervals. In listening to music the same is even more strikingly true. If we abruptly see a dark moving form in the woods, our heart stops beating, and we catch our breath instantly and before any articulate idea of danger can arise. If our friend goes near to the edge of a precipice, we get the well-known feeling of 'all-overishness,' and we shrink back, although we positively *know* him to be safe, and have no distinct imagination of his fall. The writer well remembers his astonishment, when a boy of seven or eight, at fainting when he saw a horse bled. The blood was in a bucket, with a stick in it, and, if memory does not deceive him, he stirred it round and saw it drip from the stick with no feeling save that of childish curiosity. Suddenly the world grew black before his eyes, his ears began to buzz, and he knew no more. He had never heard of the sight of blood producing faintness or sickness, and he had so little repugnance to it, and so little apprehension of any other sort of danger from it, that even at that tender age, as he well remembers, he could not help wondering how the mere physical presence of a pailful of crimson fluid could occasion in him such formidable bodily effects.

Professor Lange writes:

"No one has ever thought of separating the emotion produced by an unusually loud sound from the true inward affections. No one hesitates to call it a sort of fright, and it shows the ordinary signs of fright. And yet it is by no means combined with the idea of danger, or in any way occasioned by associations, memories, or other mental processes. The phenomena of fright follow the noise immediately without a trace of 'spiritual' fear. Many men can never grow used to standing beside a cannon when it is fired off, although they perfectly know that there is danger neither for themselves nor for others—the bare sound is too much for them." *

* *Op. cit.* p. 63.

Imagine two steel knife-blades with their keen edges crossing each other at right angles, and moving to and fro. Our whole nervous organization is ' on-edge ' at the thought; and yet what emotion can be there except the unpleasant nervous feeling itself, or the dread that more of it may come? The entire fund and capital of the emotion here is the senseless bodily effect which the blades immediately arouse. This case is typical of a class: where an ideal emotion seems to precede the bodily symptoms, it is often nothing but an anticipation of the symptoms themselves. One who has already fainted at the sight of blood may witness the preparations for a surgical operation with uncontrollable heart-sinking and anxiety. He anticipates certain feelings, and the anticipation precipitates their arrival. In cases of morbid terror the subjects often confess that what possesses them seems, more than anything, to be fear of the fear itself. In the various forms of what Professor Bain calls 'tender emotion,' although the appropriate object must usually be directly contemplated before the emotion can be aroused, yet sometimes thinking of the symptoms of the emotion itself may have the same effect. In sentimental natures the thought of 'yearning' will produce real 'yearning.' And, not to speak of coarser examples, a mother's imagination of the caresses she bestows on her child may arouse a spasm of parental longing.

In such cases as these we see plainly how the emotion both begins and ends with what we call its effects or manifestations. It has no mental *status* except as either the vivid feeling of the manifestations, or the idea of them; and the latter thus constitute its entire material, and sum and substance. And these cases ought to make us see how in all cases the feeling of the manifestations may play a much deeper part in the constitution of the emotion than we are wont to suppose.

The best proof that the immediate cause of emotion is a physical effect on the nerves is furnished by *those pathological cases in which the emotion is objectless*. One of the chief merits, in fact, of the view which I propose seems to be that we can so easily formulate by its means pathological cases and normal cases under a common scheme. In every asylum we find examples of absolutely unmotived fear, anger, melancholy, or conceit; and others of an equally unmotived apathy which persists in spite of the best of outward reasons why it should give way. In the former cases we must suppose the nervous machinery to be so 'labile' in some one emotional direction that almost every stimulus (however inappropriate) causes it to upset in that way, and to engender the particular complex of feelings of which the psychic body of the emotion consists. Thus, to take one special instance, if inability to draw deep breath, fluttering of the heart, and that peculiar epigastric change felt as 'precordial anxiety,' with an irresistible tendency to take a somewhat crouching attitude and to sit still, and with perhaps other visceral processes not now known, all spontaneously occur together in a certain person; his feeling of their combination *is* the emotion of dread, and he is the victim of what is known as morbid fear. A friend who has had occasional attacks of this most distressing of all maladies tells me that in his case the whole drama seems to centre about the region of the heart and respiratory apparatus, that his main effort during the attacks is to get control of his inspirations and to slow his heart, and that the moment he attains to breathing deeply and to holding himself erect, the dread, *ipso facto*, seems to depart.*

The emotion here is nothing but the feeling of a bodily state, and it has a purely bodily cause.

---

* It must be confessed that there are cases of morbid fear in which objectively the heart is not much perturbed. These, however, fail to prove anything against our theory, for it is of course possible that the cortical centres normally percipient of dread as a complex of cardiac and other organic sensations due to real bodily change, should become *primarily* excited in brain-disease, and give rise to an hallucination of the changes being there,—an hallucination of dread, consequently, coexistent with a comparatively calm pulse, etc. I say it is possible, for I am ignorant of observations which might test the fact. Trance, ecstasy, etc., offer analogous examples,—not to speak of ordinary dreaming. Under all these conditions one may have the liveliest subjective feelings, either of eye or ear, or of the more visceral and emotional sort, as a result of pure nerve-central activity, and yet, as I believe, with complete peripheral repose.

" All physicians who have been much engaged in general practice have seen cases of dyspepsia in which constant low spirits and occasional attacks of terror rendered the patient's condition pitiable in the extreme. I have observed these cases often, and have watched them closely, and I have never seen greater suffering of any kind than I have witnessed during these attacks. . . . Thus, a man is suffering from what we call nervous dyspepsia. Some day, we will suppose in the middle of the afternoon, without any warning or visible cause, one of these attacks of terror comes on. The first thing the man feels is great but vague discomfort. Then he notices that his heart is beating much too violently. At the same time shocks or flashes as of electrical discharges, so violent as to be almost painful, pass one after another through his body and limbs. Then in a few minutes he falls into a condition of the most intense fear. He is not afraid of anything ; he is simply afraid. His mind is perfectly clear. He looks for a cause of his wretched condition, but sees none. Presently his terror is such that he trembles violently and utters low moans ; his body is damp with perspiration; his mouth is perfectly dry ; and at this stage there are no tears in his eyes, though his suffering is intense. When the climax of the attack is reached and passed, there is a copious flow of tears, or else a mental condition in which the person weeps upon the least provocation. At this stage a large quantity of pale urine is passed. Then the heart's action becomes again normal, and the attack passes off." *

Again :

" There are outbreaks of rage so groundless and unbridled that all must admit them to be expressions of disease. For the medical layman hardly anything can be more instructive than the observation of such a pathological attack of rage, especially when it presents itself pure and unmixed with other psychical disturbances. This happens in that rather rare disease named transitory mania. The patient predisposed to this—otherwise an entirely reasonable person—will be attacked suddenly without the slightest outward provocation, and thrown (to use the words of the latest writer on the subject, O. Schwartzer, Die transitorische Tobsucht, Wien, 1880), ' into a paroxysm of the wildest rage, with a fearful and blindly furious impulse to do violence and destroy.' He flies at those about him; strikes, kicks, and throttles whomever he can catch ; dashes every object about which he can lay his hands on; breaks and crushes what is near him; tears his clothes; shouts, howls, and roars, with eyes that flash and roll, and shows meanwhile all those symptoms of vaso-motor congestion which we have learned to know as the concomitants of anger. His face is red, swollen, his cheeks hot, his eyes protuberant and their whites bloodshot, the heart beats vio-

---

*·R. M. Bucke: Man's Moral Nature (N. Y., 1879), p. 97.

lently, the pulse marks 100–120 strokes a minutes. The arteries of the neck are full and pulsating, the veins are swollen, the saliva flows. The fit lasts only a few hours, and ends suddenly with a sleep of from 8 to 12 hours, on waking from which the patient has entirely forgotten what has happened." *

In these (outwardly) causeless emotional conditions the particular paths which are explosive are discharged by any and every incoming sensation. Just as, when we are seasick, every smell, every taste, every sound, every sight, every movement, every sensible experience whatever, augments our nausea, so the morbid terror or anger is increased by each and every sensation which stirs up the nerve-centres. Absolute quiet is the only treatment for the time. It seems impossible not to admit that in all this the bodily condition takes the lead, and that the mental emotion follows. The *intellect* may, in fact, be so little affected as to play the cold-blooded spectator all the while, and note the absence of a real object for the emotion.†

A few words from Henle may close my reply to this first objection :

"Does it not seem as if the excitations of the bodily nerves met the ideas half way, in order to raise the latter to the height of emotions? [Note how justly this expresses our theory !] That they do so is proved by the cases in which particular nerves, when specially irritable, share in the emotion and determine its quality. When one is suffering from an open wound, any grievous or horrid spectacle will cause pain in the

---

* Lange, *op. cit.* p. 61.

† I am inclined to think that in some hysteriform conditions of grief, rage, etc., the visceral disturbances are less strong than those which go to outward expression. We have then a tremendous verbal display with a hollow inside. Whilst the bystanders are wrung with compassion, or pale with alarm, the subject all the while lets himself go, but feels his insincerity, and wonders how long he can keep up the performance. The attacks are often surprisingly sudden in their onset. The treatment here is to intimidate the patient by a stronger will. Take out your temper, if he takes out his—"Nay, if thou'lt mouth, I'll rant as well as thou." These are the cases of apparently great bodily manifestation with comparatively little real subjective emotion, which may be used to throw discredit on the theory advanced in the text.—It is probable that the *visceral* manifestations in these cases are quite disproportionately slight, compared with those of the vocal organs. The subject's state is somewhat similar to that of an actor who does not feel his part.

wound. In sufferers from heart-disease there is developed a psychic excitability, which is often incomprehensible to the patients themselves, but which comes from the heart's liability to palpitate. I said that the very quality of the emotion is determined by the organs disposed to participate in it. Just as surely as a dark foreboding, rightly grounded on inference from the constellations, will be accompanied by a feeling of oppression in the chest, so surely will a similar feeling of oppression, when due to disease of the thoracic organs, be accompanied by ground-less forebodings. So small a thing as a bubble of air rising from the stomach through the œsophagus, and loitering on its way a few minutes and exerting pressure on the heart, is able during sleep to occasion a nightmare, and during waking to produce a vague anxiety. On the other hand, we see that joyous thoughts dilate our blood-vessels, and that a suitable quantity of wine, because it dilates the vessels, also dis·poses us to joyous thoughts. If both the jest and the wine work to-gether, they supplement each other in producing the emotional effect, and our demands on the jest are the more modest in proportion as the wine takes upon itself a larger part of the task." *

Second Objection. If our theory be true, a necessary corollary of it ought to be this : that any voluntary and cold-blooded arousal of the so-called manifestations of a special emotion ought to give us the emotion itself. Now this (the objection says) is not found to be the case. An actor can perfectly simulate an emotion and yet be inwardly cold ; and we can all pretend to cry and not feel grief ; and feign laughter without being amused.

Reply. In the majority of emotions this test is inapplicable ; for many of the manifestations are in organs over which we have no voluntary control. Few people in pretending to cry can shed real tears, for example. But, within the limits in which it can be verified, experience corroborates rather than disproves the corollary from our theory, upon which the present objection rests. Every one knows how panic is increased by flight, and how the giving way to the symptoms of grief or anger increases those passions themselves. Each fit of sobbing makes the sorrow more acute, and calls forth another fit stronger still, until at last repose only ensues with lassitude and with the

---

* *Op. cit.* p. 72.—Lange lays great stress on the neurotic drugs, as parts of his proof that influences of a physical nature upon the body are the first thing in order in the production of emotions.

apparent exhaustion of the machinery. In rage, it is notorious how we 'work ourselves up' to a climax by repeated outbreaks of expression. Refuse to express a passion, and it dies. Count ten before venting your anger, and its occasion seems ridiculous. Whistling to keep up courage is no mere figure of speech. On the other hand, sit all day in a moping posture, sigh, and reply to everything with a dismal voice, and your melancholy lingers. There is no more valuable precept in moral education than this, as all who have experience know : if we wish to conquer undesirable emotional tendencies in ourselves, we must assiduously, and in the first instance cold-bloodedly, go through the *outward movements* of those contrary dispositions which we prefer to cultivate. The reward of persistency will infallibly come, in the fading out of the sullenness or depression, and the advent of real cheerfulness and kindliness in their stead. Smooth the brow, brighten the eye, contract the dorsal rather than the ventral aspect of the frame, and speak in a major key, pass the genial compliment, and your heart must be frigid indeed if it do not gradually thaw !

This is recognized by all psychologists, only they fail to see its full import. Professor Bain writes, for example :

" We find that a feeble [emotional] wave . . . is suspended inwardly by being arrested outwardly ; the currents of the brain and the agitation of the centres die away if the external vent is resisted at every point. It is by such restraint that we are in the habit of suppressing pity, anger, fear, pride—on many trifling occasions. If so, it is a fact that the suppression of the actual movements has a tendency to suppress the nervous currents that incite them, so that the external quiescence is followed by the internal. The effect would not happen in any case *if there were not some dependence of the cerebral wave upon the free outward vent or manifestation.* . . . By the same interposition we may summon up a dormant feeling. By acting out the external manifestations, we gradually infect the nerves leading to them, and finally waken up the diffusive current by a sort of action *ab extra.* . . . Thus it is that we are sometimes able to assume a cheerful tone of mind by forcing a hilarious expression.*

---

* Emotions and Will, pp. 361-2.

We have a mass of other testimony of similar effect.
Burke, in his treatise on the Sublime and Beautiful, writes
as follows of the physiognomist Campanella :

" This man, it seems, had not only made very accurate observations
on human faces, but was very expert in mimicking such as were in any
way remarkable.   When he had a mind to penetrate into the inclinations
of those he had to deal with, he composed his face, his gesture, and his
whole body, as nearly as he could, into the exact similitude of the person he intended to examine ; and then carefully observed what turn of
mind he seemed to acquire by the change.   So that, says my author, he
was able to enter into the dispositions and thoughts of people as effectually as if he had been changed into the very men.   I have often observed [Burke now goes on in his own person] that, on mimicking the
looks and gestures of angry, or placid, or frightened, or daring men, I
have involuntarily found my mind turned to that passion whose appearance I strove to imitate ; nay, I am convinced it is hard to avoid it,
though one strove to separate the passion from its corresponding gestures." *

Against this it is to be said that many actors who perfectly mimic the outward appearances of emotion in face,
gait, and voice declare that they feel no emotion at all.
Others, however, according to Mr. Wm. Archer, who has
made a very instructive statistical inquiry among them,
say that the emotion of the part masters them whenever
they play it well.†   Thus :

" 'I often turn pale,' writes Miss Isabel Bateman, 'in scenes of
terror or great excitement.   I have been told this many times, and I
can feel myself getting very cold and shivering and pale in thrilling
situations.'   'When I am playing rage or terror,' writes Mr. Lionel
Brough, 'I believe I do turn pale.   My mouth gets dry, my tongue
cleaves to my palate.   In Bob Acres, for instance (in the last act), I

---

* Quoted by Dugald Stewart, Elements, etc. (Hamilton's ed.), iii. 140.
Fechner (Vorschule der Aesthetik, 156) says almost the same thing of himself : "One may find by one's own observation that the *imitation* of the
bodily expression of a mental condition makes us understand it much
better than the merely looking on. . . . When I walk behind some one
whom I do not know, and imitate as accurately as possible his gait and
carriage, I get the most curious impression of feeling as the person himself
must feel.   To go tripping and mincing after the fashion of a young woman puts one, so to speak, in a feminine mood of mind."

† 'The Anatomy of Acting,' in Longman's Magazine, vol. xi. pp. 266,
375, 498 (1888), since republished in book form.

have to continually moisten my mouth, or I shall become inarticulate. I have to "swallow the lump," as I call it.' All artists who have had much experience of emotional parts are absolutely unanimous. . . . 'Playing with the brain,' says Miss Alma Murray, 'is far less fatiguing than playing with the heart. An adventuress taxes the physique far less than a sympathetic heroine. Muscular exertion has comparatively little to do with it.' . . . 'Emotion while acting,' writes Mr. Howe, ' will induce perspiration much more than physical exertion. I always perspired profusely while acting Joseph Surface, which requires little or no exertion.' . . . 'I suffer from fatigue,' writes Mr. Forbes Robertson, 'in proportion to the amount of emotion I may have been called upon to go through, and not from physical exertion.' . . . 'Though I have played Othello,' writes Mr. Coleman, ' ever since I was seventeen (at nineteen I had the honor of acting the Moor to Macready's Iago), husband my resources as I may, this is the one part, the part of parts, which always leaves me physically prostrate. I have never been able to find a pigment that would stay on my face, though I have tried every preparation in existence. Even the titanic Edwin Forrest told me that he was always knocked over in Othello, and I have heard Charles Kean, Phelps, Brooke, Dillion, say the same thing. On the other hand, I have frequently acted Richard III. without turning a hair.' " *

The explanation for the discrepancy amongst actors is probably that which these quotations suggest. The *visceral and organic* part of the expression can be suppressed in some men, but not in others, and on this it is probable that the chief part of the felt emotion depends. Coquelin and the other actors who are inwardly cold are probably able to affect the dissociation in a complete way. Prof. Sikorsky of Kieff has contributed an important article on the facial expression of the insane to the Neurologisches Centralblatt for 1887. Having practised facial mimicry himself a great deal, he says :

" When I contract my facial muscles in any mimetic combination, *I feel no emotional excitement*, so that the mimicry is in the fullest sense of the word artificial, although quite irreproachable from the expressive point of view." †

We find, however, from the context that Prof. S.'s practice before the mirror has developed in him such a virtuosity in the control of his facial muscles that he can entirely disregard their natural association and contract them in any order of grouping, on either side of the face isolatedly,

---

and each one alone. Probably in him the facial mimicry is an entirely restricted and localized thing, without sympathetic changes of any sort elsewhere.

Third Objection. Manifesting an emotion, so far from increasing it, makes it cease. Rage evaporates after a good outburst; it is *pent-up* emotions that "work like madness in the brain."

Reply. The objection fails to discriminate between what is felt *during* and what is felt *after* the manifestation. *During* the manifestation the emotion is always felt. In the normal course of things this, being the natural channel of discharge, exhausts the nerve-centres, and emotional calm ensues. But if tears or anger are simply suppressed, whilst the object of grief or rage remains unchanged before the mind, the current which would have invaded the normal channels turns into others, for it must find some outlet of escape. It may then work different and worse effects later on. Thus vengeful brooding may replace a burst of indignation ; a dry heat may consume the frame of one who fain would weep, or he may, as Dante says, turn to stone within ; and then tears or a storming fit may bring a grateful relief. This is when the current is strong enough to strike into a pathological path when the normal one is dammed. When this is so, an immediate outpour may be best. But here, to quote Prof. Bain again :

" There is nothing more implied than the fact that an emotion may be too strong to be resisted, and we only waste our strength in the endeavor. If we are really able to stem the torrent, there is no more reason for refraining from the attempt than in the case of weaker feelings. And undoubtedly the *habitual* control of the emotions is not to be attained without a systematic restraint, extended to weak and strong."

When we teach children to repress their emotional talk and display, it is not that they may *feel* more—quite the reverse. It is that they may *think* more ; for, to a certain extent, whatever currents are diverted from the regions below, must swell the activity of the thought-tracts of the brain. In apoplexies and other brain injuries we get the opposite condition—an obstruction, namely, to the passage of currents among the thought-tracts, and with this an increased tendency of objects to start downward currents into the organs of the body. The consequence is tears, laughter, and temper-fits, on the most insignificant provocation, accompanying a proportional feebleness in logical thought and the power of volitional attention and decision,— just the sort of thing from which we try to wean our child. It is true that we say of certain persons that "they would feel more if they expressed less." And in another class of persons the explosive energy with which passion manifests itself on critical occasions seems correlated with the way in which they bottle it up during the intervals. But these are only eccentric types of character, and within each type the law of the last paragraph prevails. The sentimentalist is so constructed that 'gushing' is his or her normal mode of expression. Putting a stopper on the 'gush' will only to a limited extent cause more 'real' activities to take its place; in the main it will simply produce listlessness. On the other hand, the ponderous and bilious 'slumbering volcano,' let him repress the expression of his passions as he will, will find them expire if they get no vent at all; whilst if the rare occasions multiply which he deems worthy of their outbreak, he will find them grow in intensity as life proceeds. On the whole, I cannot see that this third objection carries any weight.

If our hypothesis is true, it makes us realize more deeply than ever how much our mental life is knit up with our corporeal frame, in the strictest sense of the term. Rapture, love, ambition, indignation, and pride, considered as feelings, are fruits of the same soil with the grossest bodily sensations of pleasure and of pain. But the reader will remember that we agreed at the outset to affirm this only of what we then called the 'coarser' emotions, and that those inward states of emotional sensibility which appeared devoid at first sight of bodily results should be left out of our account. We must now say a word or two about these latter feelings, the 'subtler' emotions, as we then agreed to call them.

THE SUBTLER EMOTIONS.

These are the moral, intellectual, and æsthetic feelings. Concords of sounds, of colors, of lines, logical consistencies, teleological fitnesses, affect us with a pleasure that seems ingrained in the very form of the representation itself, and to borrow nothing from any reverberation surging up from the parts below the brain. The Herbartian psychologists have distinguished feelings due to the *form* in which ideas may be arranged. A mathematical demonstration may be as 'pretty,' and an act of justice as 'neat,' as a drawing or a tune, although the prettiness and neatness seem to have nothing to do with sensation. We have, then, or some of us seem to have, genuinely *cerebral* forms of pleasure and displeasure, apparently not agreeing in their mode of production with the 'coarser' emotions we have been analyzing. And it is certain that readers whom our reasons have hitherto failed to convince will now start up at this admission, and consider that by it we give up our whole case. Since musical perceptions, since logical ideas, can immediately arouse a form of emotional feeling, they will say, is it not more natural to suppose that in the case of the so-called 'coarser' emotions, prompted by other kinds of objects, the emotional feeling is equally immediate, and the bodily expression something that comes later and is added on?

In reply to this we must immediately insist that æsthetic emotion, *pure and simple*, the pleasure given us by certain lines and masses, and combinations of colors and sounds, is an absolutely sensational experience, an optical or auricular feeling that is primary, and not due to the repercussion backwards of other sensations elsewhere consecutively aroused. To this simple primary and immediate pleasure in certain pure sensations and harmonious combinations of them, there may, it is true, be *added* secondary pleasures; and in the practical enjoyment of works of art by the masses of mankind these secondary pleasures play a great part. The more *classic* one's taste is, however, the less relatively important are the secondary pleasures felt to be in comparison with those of the primary sensation as it comes in.* Classicism and romanticism have their battles over this point. Complex suggestiveness, the awakening of

---

* Even the feelings of the lower senses may have this secondary escort, due to the arousing of associational trains which reverberate. A flavor may fairly shake us by the ghosts of 'banquet halls deserted,' which it suddenly calls up; or a smell may make us feel almost sick with the waft it brings over our memory of 'gardens that are ruins, and pleasure-houses that are dust.' "In the Pyrenees," says M. Guyau, "after a summer-day's tramp carried to the extreme of fatigue, I met a shepherd and asked him for some milk. He went to fetch from his hut, under which a brook ran, a jar of milk plunged in the water and kept at a coldness which was almost icy. In drinking this fresh milk *into which all the mountain had put its perfume,* and of which each savory swallow seemed to give new life, I certainly experienced a series of feelings which the word *agreeable* is insufficient to designate. It was like a pastoral symphony, apprehended by the taste instead of by the ear" (quoted by F. Paulhan from 'Les Problèmes de l'Æsthétique Contemporaine, p. 63).—Compare the dithyrambic about whiskey of Col. R. Ingersoll, to which the presidential campaign of 1888 gave such notoriety : "I send you some of the most wonderful whiskey that ever drove the skeleton from a feast or painted landscapes in the brain of man. It is the mingled souls of wheat and corn. In it you will find the sunshine and shadow that chase each other over the billowy fields, the breath of June, the carol of the lark, the dews of the night, the wealth of summer, and autumn's rich content—all golden with imprisoned light. Drink it, and you will hear the voice of men and maidens singing the 'Harvest Home,' mingled with the laughter of children. Drink it, and you will feel within your blood the star-lit dawns, the dreamy, tawny dusks of many perfect days. For forty years this liquid joy has been within the happy staves of oak, longing to touch the lips of man."—It is in this way that I should reply to Mr. Gurney's criticism on my theory. My "view," this writer says (Mind, ix. 425), "goes far to confound the two things which in my opinion it is the prime necessity of musical psychology to distinguish —the effect chiefly sensuous of mere streams or masses of finely colored sound, and the distinctive musical emotion to which the *form* of a sequence of sound, its melodic and harmonic individuality, even realized in complete silence, is the vital and essential object. It is with the former of these two very different things that the physical reactions, the stirring of the hair— the tingling and the shiver—are by far most markedly connected. . . . If I may speak of myself, there is plenty of music from which I have received as much emotion in silent representation as when presented by the finest orchestra; but it is with the latter condition that I almost exclusively associate the cutaneous tingling and hair-stirring. But to call my enjoyment of the *form,* of the *note-after-note*ness of a melody a mere critical 'judgment of right' [see below, p. 472] would really be to deny to me the power of expressing a fact of simple and intimate expression in English. It is quint-essentially emotion. . . . Now there are hundreds of other bits of music . . . . which I judge to be *right* without receiving an iota of the emotion. For purposes of emotion they are to me like geometrical demonstrations or

vistas of memory and association, and the stirring of our flesh with picturesque mystery and gloom, make a work of art *romantic*. The classic taste brands these effects as coarse and tawdry, and prefers the naked beauty of the optical and auditory sensations, unadorned with frippery or foliage. To the romantic mind, on the contrary, the immediate beauty of these sensations seems dry and thin. I am of course not discussing which view is right, but only showing that the discrimination between the primary feeling of beauty, as a pure incoming sensible quality, and the secondary emotions which are grafted thereupon, is one that must be made.

These secondary emotions themselves are assuredly for the most part constituted of other incoming sensations aroused by the diffusive wave of reflex effects which the beautiful object sets up. A glow, a pang in the breast, a shudder, a fulness of the breathing, a flutter of the heart, a shiver down the back, a moistening of the eyes, a stirring in the hypogastrium, and a thousand unnamable symptoms besides, may be felt the moment the beauty *excites* us. And these symptoms also result when we are excited by moral perceptions, as of pathos, magnanimity, or courage. The voice breaks and the sob rises in the struggling chest, or the nostril dilates and the fingers tighten, whilst the heart beats, etc., etc.

As far as *these ingredients* of the subtler emotions go, then, the latter form no exception to our account, but rather an additional illustration thereof. In all cases of intellectual or moral rapture we find that, unless there be coupled a bodily reverberation of some kind with the mere

---

like acts of integrity performed in Peru." The Beethoven-rightness of which Gurney then goes on to speak, as something different from the Clementi-rightness (even when the respective pieces are only heard in idea), is probably a purely *auditory-sensational* thing. The Clementi-rightness also ; only, for reasons impossible to assign, the Clementi form does not give the same sort of purely auditory satisfaction as the Beethoven form, and might better be described perhaps negatively as *non-wrong*, i.e., free from positively unpleasant acoustic quality. In organizations as musical as Mr. Gurney's, purely acoustic form gives so intense a degree of sensible pleasure that the lower bodily reverberation is of no account. But I repeat that I see nothing in the facts which Mr. Gurney cites, to lead one to believe in an emotion divorced from *sensational processes* of any kind.

thought of the object and cognition of its quality; unless we actually laugh at the neatness of the demonstration or witticism; unless we thrill at the case of justice, or tingle at the act of magnanimity; our state of mind can hardly be called emotional at all. It is in fact a mere intellectual perception of how certain things are to be called—neat, right, witty, generous, and the like. Such a judicial state of mind as this is to be classed among awarenesses of truth; it is a *cognitive* act. As a matter of fact, however, the moral and intellectual cognitions hardly ever do exist thus unaccompanied. The bodily sounding-board is at work, as careful introspection will show, far more than we usually suppose. Still, where long familiarity with a certain class of effects, even æsthetic ones, has blunted mere emotional excitability as much as it has sharpened taste and judgment, we do get the intellectual emotion, if such it can be called, pure and undefiled. And the dryness of it, the paleness, the absence of all glow, as it may exist in a thoroughly expert critic's mind, not only shows us what an altogether different thing it is from the 'coarser' emotions we considered first, but makes us suspect that almost the entire difference lies in the fact that the bodily sounding-board, vibrating in the one case, is in the other mute. "Not so very bad" is, in a person of consummate taste, apt to be the highest limit of approving expression. "*Rien ne me choque*" is said to have been Chopin's superlative of praise of new music. A sentimental layman would feel, and ought to feel, horrified, on being admitted into such a critic's mind, to see how cold, how thin, how void of human significance, are the motives for favor or disfavor that there prevail. The capacity to make a nice spot on the wall will outweigh a picture's whole content; a foolish trick of words will preserve a poem; an utterly meaningless fitness of sequence in one musical composition set at naught any amount of 'expressiveness' in another.

I remember seeing an English couple sit for more than an hour on a piercing February day in the Academy at Venice before the celebrated 'Assumption' by Titian; and when I, after being chased from room to room by the cold, concluded to get into the sunshine as fast as possible and let the pictures go, but before leaving drew reverently near to them to learn with what superior forms of susceptibility they might be endowed, all I overheard was the woman's voice murmuring : " What a *deprecatory* expression her face wears ! What self-abneg*ation !* How *unworthy* she feels of the honor she is receiving !" Their honest hearts had been kept warm all the time by a glow of spurious sentiment that would have fairly made old Titian sick. Mr. Ruskin somewhere makes the (for him terrible) admission that religious people as a rule care little for pictures, and that when they do care for them they generally prefer the worst ones to the best. Yes! in every art, in every science, there is the keen perception of certain relations being *right* or not, and there is the emotional flush and thrill consequent thereupon. And these are two things, not one. In the former of them it is that experts and masters are at home. The latter accompaniments are bodily commotions that they may hardly feel, but that may be experienced in their fulness by *crétins* and philistines in whom the critical judgment is at its lowest ebb. The 'marvels' of Science, about which so much edifying popular literature is written, are apt to be 'caviare' to the men in the laboratories. And even divine Philosophy itself, which common mortals consider so 'sublime' an occupation, on account of the vastness of its data and outlook, is too apt to the practical philosopher himself to be but a sharpening and tightening business, a matter of 'points,' of screwing down things, of splitting hairs, and of the 'intent' rather than the 'extent' of conceptions. Very little emotion here!—except the effort of setting the attention fine, and the feeling of ease and relief (mainly in the breathing apparatus) when the inconsistencies are overcome and the thoughts run smoothly for a while. Emotion and cognition seem then parted even in this last retreat ; and cerebral processes are almost feelingless, so far as we can judge, until they summon help from parts below.

NO SPECIAL BRAIN-CENTRES FOR EMOTION.

If the neural process underlying emotional consciousness be what I have now sought to prove it, the physiology of the brain becomes a simpler matter than has been hitherto supposed. Sensational, associational, and motor elements are all that the organ need contain. The physiologists who, during the past few years, have been so industriously exploring the brain's functions, have limited their explanations to its cognitive and volitional performances. Dividing the brain into sensory and motor centres, they have found their division to be exactly paralleled by the analysis made by empirical psychology of the perceptive and volitional parts of the mind into their simplest elements. But the emotions have been so ignored in all these researches that one is tempted to suppose that if these investigators were asked for a theory of them in brain-terms, they would have to reply, either that they had as yet bestowed no thought upon the subject, or that they had found it so difficult to make distinct hypotheses that the matter lay among the problems of the future, only to be taken up after the simpler ones of the present should have been definitively solved.

And yet it is even now certain that of two things concerning the emotions, one must be true. Either separate and special centres, affected to them alone, are their brain-seat, or else they correspond to processes occurring in the motor and sensory centres already assigned, or in others like them, not yet known. If the former be the case, we must deny the view that is current, and hold the cortex to be something more than the surface of 'projection' for every sensitive spot and every muscle in the body. If the latter be the case, we must ask whether the emotional *process* in the sensory or motor centre be an altogether peculiar one, or whether it resembles the ordinary perceptive processes of which those centres are already recognized to be the seat. Now if the theory I have defended be true, the latter alternative is all that it demands. Supposing the cortex to contain parts, liable to be excited by changes in each special sense-organ, in each portion of the skin, in each muscle, each joint, and each viscus, and to contain absolutely nothing else, we still have a scheme capable of representing the process of the emotions. An object falls on a sense-organ, affects a cortical part, and is perceived;

or else the latter, excited inwardly, gives rise to an idea of the same object. Quick as a flash, the reflex currents pass down through their preordained channels, alter the condition of muscle, skin, and viscus; and these alterations, perceived, like the original object, in as many portions of the cortex, combine with it in consciousness and transform it from an object-simply-apprehended into an object-emotionally-felt. No new principles have to be invoked, nothing postulated beyond the ordinary reflex circuits, and the local centres admitted in one shape or another by all to exist.

EMOTIONAL DIFFERENCES BETWEEN INDIVIDUALS.

The revivability in memory of the emotions, like that of all the feelings of the lower senses, is very small. We can remember that we underwent grief or rapture, but not just how the grief or rapture felt. This difficult *ideal* revivability is, however, more than compensated in the case of the emotions by a very easy *actual* revivability. That is, we can produce, not remembrances of the old grief or rapture, but new griefs and raptures, by summoning up a lively thought of their exciting cause. The cause is now only an idea, but this idea produces the same organic irradiations, or almost the same, which were produced by its original, so that the emotion is again a reality. We have 'recaptured' it. Shame, love, and anger are particularly liable to be thus revived by ideas of their object. Professor Bain admits * that "in their strict character of emotion proper, they [the emotions] have the minimum of revivability; but being always incorporated with the sensations of the higher senses, they share in the superior revivability of sights and sounds." But he fails to point out that the revived sights and sounds may be *ideal* without ceasing to be distinct; whilst the emotion, to be distinct, must become real again. Prof. Bain seems to forget that an 'ideal emotion' and a real emotion prompted by an ideal object are two very different things.

---

* In his chapter on 'Ideal Emotion,' to which the reader is referred for farther details on this subject.

An emotional temperament on the one hand, and a lively imagination for objects and circumstances on the other, are thus the conditions, necessary and sufficient, for an abundant emotional life. No matter how emotional the temperament may be, if the imagination be poor, the occasions for touching off the emotional trains will fail to be realized, and the life will be *pro tanto* cold and dry. This is perhaps a reason why it may be better that a man of thought should not have too strong a visualizing power. He is less likely to have his trains of meditation disturbed by emotional interruptions. It will be remembered that Mr. Galton found the members of the Royal Society and of the French Academy of Sciences to be below par in visualizing power. If I may speak of myself, I am far less able to visualize now, at the age of 46, than in my earlier years; and I am strongly inclined to believe that the relative sluggishness of my emotional life at present is quite as much connected with this fact as it is with the invading torpor of hoary eld, or with the omnibus-horse routine of settled professional and domestic life. I say this because I occasionally have a flash of the old stronger visual imagery, and I notice that the emotional commentary, so to call it, is then liable to become much more acute than is its present wont. Charcot's patient, whose case is given above on p. 58 ff., complained of his incapacity for emotional feeling after his optical images were gone. His mother's death, which in former times would have wrung his heart, left him quite cold; largely, as he himself suggests, because he could form no definite visual image of the event, and of the effect of the loss on the rest of the family at home.

One final generality about the emotions remains to be noted : *They blunt themselves by repetition more rapidly than any other sort of feeling.* This is due not only to the general law of 'accommodation' to their stimulus which we saw to obtain of all feelings whatever, but to the peculiar fact that the 'diffusive wave' of reflex effects tends always to become more narrow. It seems as if it were essentially meant to be a provisional arrangement, on the basis of which precise and determinate reactions might arise. The more we exercise ourselves at anything, the fewer muscles we employ; and just so, the oftener we meet an object, the more definitely we think and behave about it; and the less is the organic perturbation to which it gives rise. The first time we saw it we could perhaps neither act nor think at all, and had no reaction but organic perturbation. The emotions of startled surprise, wonder, or curiosity were the result. Now we look on with absolutely no emotion.* This tendency to economy in the nerve-paths through which our sensations and ideas discharge, is the basis of all growth in efficiency, readiness, and skill. Where would the general, the surgeon, the presiding chairman, be, if their nerve-currents kept running down into their viscera, instead of keeping up amid their convolutions? But what they gain for practice by this law, they lose, it must be confessed, for feeling. For the world-worn and experienced man, the sense of pleasure which he gets from the free and powerful flow of thoughts, overcoming obstacles as they arise, is the only compensation for that freshness of the heart which he once enjoyed. This free and powerful flow means that brain-paths of association and memory have more and more organized themselves in him, and that through them the stimulus is drafted off into nerves which lead merely to the writing finger or the speaking tongue.† The trains of *intellectual* association, the memories, the logical relations, may,

---

* Those feelings which Prof. Bain calls 'emotions of relativity,' excitement of novelty, wonder, rapture of freedom, sense of power, hardly survive any repetition of the experience. But as the text goes on to explain, and as Goethe as quoted by Prof. Höffding says, this is because "the soul is inwardly grown larger without knowing it, and can no longer be filled by that first sensation. The man thinks that he has lost, but really he has gained. What he has lost in rapture, he has gained in inward growth." "It is," as Prof. Höffding himself adds, in a beautiful figure of speech, "with our virgin feelings, as with the first breath drawn by the new-born child, in which the lung expands itself so that it can never be emptied to the same degree again. No later breath can feel just like that first one." On this whole subject of emotional blunting, compare Höffding's Psychologie, vi. E., and Bain's Emotions and Will, chapter iv. of the first part.

† M. Fr. Paulhan, in a little work full of accurate observations of detail (Les Phénomènes Affectifs et les Lois de leur Apparition), seems to me rather to turn the truth upside down by his formula that emotions are due to an inhibition of impulsive tendencies. *One* kind of emotion, namely, uneasiness, annoyance, distress, does occur when any definite impulsive tendency is checked, and all of M. P.'s illustrations are drawn from this

however, be voluminous in the extreme. Past emotions may be among the things remembered. The more of all these trains an object can set going in us, the richer our cognitive intimacy with it is. This cerebral sense of richness seems itself to be a source of pleasure, possibly even apart from the *euphoria* which from time to time comes up from respiratory organs. If there *be* such a thing as a purely spiritual emotion, I should be inclined to restrict it to this cerebral sense of abundance and ease, this feeling, as Sir W. Hamilton would call it, of unimpeded and not overstrained activity of thought. Under ordinary conditions, it is a fine and serene but not an excited state of consciousness. In certain intoxications it becomes exciting, and it may be intensely exciting. I can hardly imagine a more frenzied excitement than that which goes with the consciousness of seeing absolute truth, which characterizes the coming to from nitrous-oxide drunkenness. Chloroform, ether, and alcohol all produce this deepening sense of insight into truth ; and with all of them it may be a 'strong' emotion; but then there also come with it all sorts of strange bodily feelings and changes in the incoming sensibilities. I cannot see my way to affirming that the emotion is independent of these. I will concede, however, that if its independence is anywhere to be maintained, these theoretic raptures seem the place at which to begin the defence.

THE GENESIS OF THE VARIOUS EMOTIONS.

On a former page (pp. 453–4) I said that two questions, and only two, are important, if we regard the emotions as constituted by feelings due to the diffusive wave.

(1) *What special diffusive effects do the various special objective and subjective experiences excite?* and

(2) *How come they to excite them?*

The works on physiognomy and expression are all of them attempts to answer question 1. As is but natural, the

---

sort. The other emotions are themselves primary impulsive tendencies, of a diffusive sort (involving, as M. P. rightly says, a *multiplicité des phénomènes*); and just in proportion as more and more of these multiple tendencies are checked, and replaced by some few narrow forms of discharge, does the original emotion tend to disappear.

effects upon the face have received the most careful attention. The reader who wishes details additional to those
given above on pp. 443–7 is referred to the works mentioned in the note below.*

As regards question 2, some little progress has of recent
years been made in answering it. Two things are certain :

a. The facial muscles of expression are not given us
simply for expression's sake ;†

b. Each muscle is not affected to some one emotion exclusively, as certain writers have thought.

Some movements of expression can be accounted for
as *weakened repetitions of movements which formerly* (when
they were stronger) *were of utility to the subject.* Others
are similarly weakened repetitions of movements which
under other conditions were *physiologically necessary effects.*
Of the latter reactions the respiratory disturbances in
anger and fear might be taken as examples—organic
reminiscences, as it were, reverberations in imagination
of the blowings of the man making a series of combative
efforts, of the pantings of one in precipitate flight. Such
at least is a suggestion made by Mr. Spencer which has
found approval. And he also was the first, so far as I
know, to suggest that other movements in anger and fear
could be explained by the nascent excitation of formerly
useful acts.

" To have in a slight degree," he says, "such psychical states as accompany the reception of wounds, and are experienced during flight, is
to be in a state of what we call fear. And to have in a slight degree
such psychical states as the processes of catching, killing, and eating
imply, is to have the desires to catch, kill, and eat. That the propensities to the acts are nothing else than nascent excitations of the

---

* A list of the older writings on the subject is given in Mantegazza's
work, La Physionomie et l'Expression, chap. I ; others in Darwin's first
chapter. Bell's Anatomy of Expression, Mosso's La Paura, Piderit's
Wissenschaftliches System der Mimik und Physiognomik, Duchenne's
Mécanisme de la Physionomie Humaine, are, besides Lange and Darwin,
the most useful works with which I am acquainted. Compare also Sully:
Sensation and Intuition, chap. II.

† One must remember, however, that just in so far forth as sexual
selection may have played a part in determining the human organism, selection of expressive faces must have increased the average mobility of the
human countenance.

psychical state involved in the acts, is proved by the natural language of the propensities. Fear, when strong, expresses itself in cries, in efforts to escape, in palpitations, in tremblings; and these are just the manifestations that go along with an actual suffering of the evil feared. The destructive passion is shown in a general tension of the muscular system, in gnashing of teeth and protrusion of the claws, in dilated eyes and nostrils, in growls; and these are weaker forms of the actions that accompany the killing of prey. To such objective evidences every one can add subjective evidences. Every one can testify that the psychical state called fear consists of mental representations of certain painful results; and that the one called anger consists of mental representations of the actions and impressions which would occur while inflicting some kind of pain."*

About fear I shall have more to say presently. Meanwhile the principle of *revival in weakened form of reactions useful in more violent dealings with the object inspiring the emotion,* has found many applications. So slight a symptom as the snarl or sneer, the one-sided uncovering of the upper teeth, is accounted for by Darwin as a survival from the time when our ancestors had large canines, and unfleshed them (as dogs now do) for attack. Similarly the raising of the eyebrows in outward attention, the opening of the mouth in astonishment, come, according to the same author, from the utility of these movements in extreme cases. The raising of the eyebrows goes with the opening of the eye for better vision; the opening of the mouth with the intensest listening, and with the rapid catching of the breath which precedes muscular effort. The distention of the nostrils in anger is interpreted by Spencer as an echo of the way in which our ancestors had to breathe when, during combat, their "mouth was filled up by a part of an antagonist's body that had been seized (!)." The trembling of fear is supposed by Mantegazza to be for the sake of warming the blood(!). The reddening of the face and neck is called by Wundt a compensatory arrangement for relieving the brain of the blood-pressure which the simultaneous excitement of the heart brings with it. The effusion of tears is explained both by this author and by Darwin to be a blood-withdrawing agency of a similar sort. The contraction of the muscles around the eyes, of which the primitive use is to

---

* Psychol., § 213.

protect those organs from being too much gorged with blood during the screaming fits of infancy, survives in adult life in the shape of the frown, which instantly comes over the brow when anything difficult or displeasing presents itself either to thought or action.

" As the habit of contracting the brows has been followed by infants during innumerable generations, at the commencement of every crying or screaming fit," says Darwin, " it has become firmly associated with the incipient sense of something distressing or disagreeable. Hence, under similar circumstances, it would be apt to be continued during maturity, although never then developed, into a crying fit. Screaming or weeping begins to be voluntarily restrained at an early period of life, whereas frowning is hardly ever restrained at any age." *

The intermittent expirations which constitute laughter have, according to Dr. Hecker, the purpose of counteracting the anæmia of the brain, which he supposes to be brought about by the action of the joyous or comic stimulus upon the vaso-motor nerves.† A smile is the weak vestige of a laugh. The tight closure of the mouth in all effort is useful for retaining the air in the lungs so as to fix the chest and give a firm basis of insertion for the muscles of the flanks. Accordingly, we see the lips compress themselves upon every slight occasion of resolve. The blood-pressure has to be high during the sexual embrace ; hence the palpi-

---

* Weeping in childhood is almost as regular a symptom of anger as it is of grief, which would account (on Darwin's principles) for the frown of anger. Mr. Spencer has an account of the angry frown as having arisen through the survival of the fittest, by its utility in keeping the sun out of one's eyes when engaged in mortal combat (!). (Principle of Psychology, II. 546.) Professor Mosso objects to any explanation of the frown by its utility for vision, that it is coupled, during emotional excitement, with a dilatation of the pupil which is very unfavorable for distinct vision, and that this ought to have been weeded out by natural selection, if natural selection had the power to fix the frown (see La Paura, chap. IX. § VI). Unfortunately this very able author speaks as if all the emotions affected the pupil in the same way. Fear certainly does make it dilate. But Gratiolet is quoted by Darwin and others as saying that the pupils *contract* in anger. I have made no observations of my own on the point, and Mosso's earlier paper on the pupil (Turin, 1875) I have not seen. I must repeat, with Darwin, that we need more minute observations on this subject.

† Physiologie u. Psychologie des Lachens und des Komischen (Berlin, 1873), pp. 13 15

tations, and hence also the tendency to caressing action, which accompanies tender emotion in its fainter forms. Other examples might be given; but these are quite enough to show the scope of the principle of revival of useful action in weaker form.

Another principle, to which Darwin perhaps hardly does sufficient justice, may be called the principle of *reacting similarly to analogous-feeling stimuli.* There is a whole vocabulary of descriptive adjectives common to impressions belonging to different sensible spheres—experiences of all classes are *sweet,* impressions of all classes *rich* or *solid,* sensations of all classes *sharp.* Wundt and Piderit accordingly explain many of our most expressive reactions upon moral causes as symbolic gustatory movements. As soon as any experience arises which has an affinity with the feeling of sweet, or bitter, or sour, the same movements are executed which would result from the taste in point.* "All the states of mind which language designates by the metaphors bitter, harsh, sweet, combine themselves, therefore, with the corresponding mimetic movements of the mouth." Certainly the emotions of disgust and satisfaction do express themselves in this mimetic way. Disgust is an incipient regurgitation or retching, limiting its expression often to the grimace of the lips and nose ; satisfaction goes with a sucking smile, or tasting motion of the lips. In Mantegazza's loose if learned work, the attempt is made, much less successfully, to bring in the eye and ear as additional sources of symbolically expressive reaction. The ordinary gesture of negation—among us, moving the head about its axis from side to side—is a reaction originally used by babies to keep disagreeables from getting into their mouth, and may be observed in perfection in any nursery.†

---

* These movements are explained teleologically, in the first instance, by the efforts which the tongue is forced to make to adapt itself to the better perception or avoidance of the sapid body. (Cf. Physiol. Psych., II. 423.)

† Professor Henle derives the negative wag of the head from an incipient shudder, and remarks how fortunate is the abbreviation, as when a lady declines a partner in the ballroom. The clapping of the hands for applause he explains as a symbolic abridgment of an embrace. The pro-

It is now evoked where the stimulus is only an unwelcome idea. Similarly the nod forward in affirmation is after the analogy of taking food into the mouth. The connection of the expression of moral or social disdain or dislike, especially in women, with movements having a perfectly definite original olfactory function, is too obvious for comment. Winking is the effect of any threatening surprise, not only of what puts the eyes in danger; and a momentary aversion of the eyes is very apt to be one's first symptom of response to an unexpectedly unwelcome proposition.—These may suffice as examples of movements expressive from analogy.

But if certain of our emotional reactions can be explained by the two principles invoked—and the reader will himself have felt how conjectural and fallible in some of the instances the explanation is—there remain many reactions which cannot so be explained at all, and these we must write down for the present as purely idiopathic effects of the stimulus. Amongst them are the effects on the viscera and internal glands, the dryness of the mouth and diarrhœa and nausea of fear, the liver-disturbances which sometimes produce jaundice after excessive rage, the urinary secretion of sanguine excitement, and the bladder-contraction of apprehension, the gaping of expectancy, the 'lump in the throat' of grief, the tickling there and the swallowing of embarrassment, the 'precordial' anxiety' of dread, the changes in the pupil, the various sweatings of the skin, cold or hot, local or general, and its flushings, together with other symptoms which probably exist but are too hidden to have been noticed or named. It seems as if even the changes of blood-pressure and heart-beat during emotional excitement might, instead of being teleologically determined, prove to be purely mechanical or physiological outpourings through the easiest drainage-channels—the pneumogastrics and sympathetic nerves happening under ordinary circumstances to be such channels.

---

trusion of the lips (*der prüfende Zug*) which goes with all sorts of dubious and questioning states of mind is derived by Dr. Piderit from the *tasting* movement which we can see on any one's mouth when deciding whether a wine is good or not.

Mr. Spencer argues that the *smallest* muscles must be such channels; and instances the tail in dogs, cats, and birds, the ears in horses, the crest in parrots, the face and fingers in man, as the first organs to be moved by emotional stimuli.* This principle (if it be one) would apply still more easily to the muscles of the smaller arteries (though not exactly to the heart); whilst the great variability of the circulatory symptoms would also suggest that they are determined by causes into which utility does not enter. The quickening of the heart lends itself, it is true, rather easily to explanation by inherited habit, organic memory of more violent excitement; and Darwin speaks in favor of this view (see his Expression, etc., pp. 74–5). But, on the other hand, we have so many cases of reaction which are indisputably pathological, as we may say, and which could never be serviceable or derived from what was serviceable, that I think we should be cautious about pushing our explanations of the varied heart-beat too far in the teleological direction. Trembling, which is found in many excitements besides that of terror, is, *pace* Mr. Spencer and Sig. Mantegazza, quite pathological. So are terror's other strong symptoms. Professor Mosso, as the total result of his study, writes as follows:

" We have seen that the graver the peril becomes, the more do the reactions which are positively harmful to the animal prevail in number and inefficacy. We already saw that the trembling and the palsy make it incapable of flight or defence ; we have also convinced ourselves that in the most decisive moments of danger we are less able to see [or to think] than when we are tranquil. In face of such facts we must admit that the phenomena of fear cannot all be accounted for by ' selection.' Their extreme degrees are morbid phenomena which show an imperfection in the organism. We might almost say that Nature had not been

---

* *Loc. cit.* § 497. Why a dog's face-muscles are not more mobile than they are Mr. Spencer fails to explain, as also why different stimuli should innervate these small muscles in such different ways, if easy drainage be the only principle involved. Charles Bell accounted for the special part played by the facial muscles in expression by their being *accessory muscles of respiration*, governed by nerves whose origin is close to the respiratory centre in the medulla oblongata. They are an adjuvant of *voice*, and like it their function is *communication*. (See Bell's Anatomy of Expression, Appendix by Alexander Shaw.)

able to frame a substance which should be excitable enough to compose the brain and spinal marrow, and yet which should not be so excited by exceptional stimulation as to overstep in its reactions those physiological bounds which are useful to the conservation of the creature." *

Professor Bain, if I mistake not, had long previously commented upon fear in a similar way.

Mr. Darwin accounts for many emotional expressions by what he calls the principle of antithesis. In virtue of this principle, if a certain stimulus prompted a certain set of movements, then a contrary-feeling stimulus would prompt exactly the opposite movements, although these might otherwise have neither utility nor significance. It is in this wise that Darwin explains the expression of impotence, raised eyebrows, and shrugged shoulders, dropped arms and open palms, as being the antithesis of the frowning brow, the thrown-back shoulders, and clenched fists of rage, which is the emotion of power. No doubt a certain number of movements can be formulated under this law ; but whether it expresses a *causal* principle is more than doubtful. It has been by most critics considered the least successful of Darwin's speculations on this subject.

To sum up, we see the reason for a few emotional reactions ; for others a possible species of reason may be guessed ; but others remain for which no plausible reason can even be conceived. These may be reactions which are purely mechanical results of the way in which our nervous centres are framed, reactions which, although permanent in us now, may be called accidental as far as their origin goes. In fact, in an organism as complex as the nervous system there *must* be many such reactions, incidental to others evolved for utility's sake, but which would never themselves have been evolved independently, for any utility they might possess. Sea-sickness, the love of music, of the various intoxicants, nay, the entire æsthetic life of man, we have already traced to this accidental origin. It would be foolish to suppose that none of the reactions called emotional could have arisen in this *quasi*-accidental way.

---

* La Paura, Appendice, p. 295.

This is all I have to say about the emotions. If one should seek to name each particular one of them of which the human heart is the seat, it is plain that the limit to their number would lie in the introspective vocabulary of the seeker, each race of men having found names for some shade of feeling which other races have left undiscriminated. If then we should seek to break the emotions, thus enumerated, into groups, according to their affinities, it is again plain that all sorts of groupings would be possible, according as we chose this character or that as a basis, and that all groupings would be equally real and true. The only question would be, does this grouping or that suit our purpose best? The reader may then class the emotions as he will, as sad or joyous, sthenic or asthenic, natural or acquired, inspired by animate or inanimate things, formal or material, sensuous or ideal, direct or reflective, egoistic or non-egoistic, retrospective, prospective or immediate, organismally or environmentally initiated, or what more besides. All these are divisions which have been actually proposed. Each of them has its merits, and each one brings together some emotions which the others keep apart. For a fuller account, and for other classificatory schemes, I refer to the Appendix to Bain's Emotions and the Will, and to Mercier's, Stanley's, and Read's articles on the Emotions, in Mind, vols. IX, X, and XI. In vol. IX. p. 421 there is also an article by the lamented Edmund Gurney in criticism of the view which in this chapter I continue to defend.

CHAPTER XXVI.*

DESIRE, wish, will, are states of mind which everyone knows, and which no definition can make plainer. We desire to feel, to have, to do, all sorts of things which at the moment are not felt, had, or done. If with the desire there goes a sense that attainment is not possible, we simply *wish* ; but if we believe that the end is in our power, we *will* that the desired feeling, having, or doing shall be real; and real it presently becomes, either immediately upon the willing or after certain preliminaries have been fulfilled.

The only ends which follow *immediately* upon our willing seem to be movements of our own bodies. Whatever *feelings* and *havings* we may will to get, come in as results of preliminary movements which we make for the purpose. This fact is too familiar to need illustration; so that we may start with the proposition that the only *direct* outward effects of our will are bodily movements. The mechanism of production of these voluntary movements is what befalls us to study now. The subject involves a good many separate points which it is difficult to arrange in any continuous logical order. I will treat of them successively in the mere order of convenience ; trusting that at the end the reader will gain a clear and connected view.

The movements we have studied hitherto have been automatic and reflex, and (on the first occasion of their performance, at any rate) unforeseen by the agent. The movements to the study of which we now address ourselves, being desired and intended beforehand, are of course done

---

* Parts of this chapter have appeared in an essay called " The Feeling of Effort," published in the Anniversary Memoirs of the Boston Society of Natural History, 1880 ; and parts in Scribner's Magazine for Feb. 1888.

with full prevision of what they are to be. It follows from this that *voluntary movements must be secondary, not primary functions of our organism.* This is the first point to understand in the psychology of Volition. Reflex, instinctive, and emotional movements are all primary performances. The nerve-centres are so organized that certain stimuli pull the trigger of certain explosive parts; and a creature going through one of these explosions for the first time undergoes an entirely novel experience. The other day I was standing at a railroad station with a little child, when an express-train went thundering by. The child, who was near the edge of the platform, started, winked, had his breathing convulsed, turned pale, burst out crying, and ran frantically towards me and hid his face. I have no doubt that this youngster was almost as much astonished by his own behavior as he was by the train, and more than I was, who stood by. Of course if such a reaction has many times occurred we learn what to expect of ourselves, and can then foresee our conduct, even though it remain as involuntary and uncontrollable as it was before. But if, in voluntary action properly so-called, the act must be foreseen, it follows that no creature not endowed with divinatory power can perform an act voluntarily for the first time. Well, we are no more endowed with prophetic vision of what movements lie in our power, than we are endowed with prophetic vision of what sensations we are capable of receiving. As we must wait for the sensations to be given us, so we must wait for the movements to be performed involuntarily,* before we can frame ideas of what either of these things are. We learn all our possibilities by the way of experience. When a particular movement, having once occurred in a random, reflex, or involuntary way, has left an image of itself in the memory, then the movement can be desired again, proposed as an end, and deliberately willed. But it is impossible to see how it could be willed before.

---

* I am abstracting at present for simplicity's sake, and so as to keep to the elements of the matter, from the learning of acts by seeing others do them.

A supply of ideas of the various movements that are possible left in the memory by experiences of their involuntary perform- ance is thus the first prerequisite of the voluntary life.

Now the same movement involuntarily performed may leave many different kinds of ideas of itself in the memory. If performed by another person, we of course *see* it, or we *feel* it if the moving part strikes another part of our own body. Similarly we have an auditory image of its effects if it produces sounds, as for example when it is one of the movements made in vocalization, or in playing on a musical instrument. All these *remote* effects of the movement, as we may call them, are also produced by movements which we ourselves perform ; and they leave innumerable ideas in our mind by which we distinguish each movement from the rest. It *looks* distinct; it *feels* distinct to some distant part of the body which it strikes; or it *sounds* dis- tinct. These remote effects would then, rigorously speak- ing, suffice to furnish the mind with the supply of ideas required.

But in addition to these impressions upon remote or- gans of sense, we have, whenever we perform a movement ourselves, another set of impressions, those, namely, which come up from the parts that are actually moved. These *kinæsthetic* impressions, as Dr. Bastian has called them, are so many *resident* effects of the motion. Not only are our muscles supplied with afferent as well as with efferent nerves, but the tendons, the ligaments, the articular sur- faces, and the skin about the joints are all sensitive, and, being stretched and squeezed in ways characteristic of each particular movement, give us as many distinctive feelings as there are movements possible to perform.

It is by these resident impressions that we are made conscious of *passive movements*—movements communicated to our limbs by others. If you lie with closed eyes, and another person noiselessly places your arm or leg in any arbitrarily chosen attitude, you receive an accurate feeling of what attitude it is, and can immediately reproduce it yourself in the arm or leg of the opposite side. Similarly a man waked suddenly from sleep in the dark is aware of how he finds himself lying. At least this is what happens when the nervous apparatus is normal. But in cases of disease we sometimes find that the resident impressions do not normally excite the centres, and that then the sense of attitude is lost. It is only recently that pathologists have begun to study these anæsthesias with the delicacy which they require ; and we have doubtless yet a great deal to learn about them. The skin may be anæsthetic, and the muscles may not feel the cramp-like pain which is produced by faradic currents sent through them, and yet the sense of passive movement may be retained. It seems, in fact, to persist more obstinately than the other forms of sensibility, for cases are comparatively common in which all the other feelings in the limb but this one of attitude are lost. In Chapter XX I have tried to make it appear that the articular surfaces are probably the most important source of the resident kinæsthetic feelings. But the determination of their special organ is indifferent to our present quest. It is enough to know that the existence of these feelings cannot be denied.

When the feelings of passive movement as well as all the other feelings of a limb are lost, we get such results as are given in the following account by Professor A. Strümpell of his wonderful anæsthetic boy, whose only sources of feeling were the right eye and the left ear : *

" Passive movements could be imprinted on all the extremities to the greatest extent, without attracting the patient's notice. Only in violent forced hyperextension of the joints, especially of the knees, there arose a dull vague feeling of strain, but this was seldom precisely localized. We have often, after bandaging the eyes of the patient, carried him about the room, laid him on a table, given to his arms and legs the most fantastic and apparently the most inconvenient attitudes, without his having a suspicion of it. The expression of astonishment in his face, when all at once the removal of the handkerchief revealed his situation, is indescribable in words. Only when his head was made to hang away down he immediately spoke of dizziness, but could not assign its ground. Later he sometimes inferred from the sounds connected with the manipulation that something special was being done with him . . . . He had no feelings of muscular fatigue. If, with his eyes shut, we told him to raise his arm and to keep it up, he did so without trouble. After one or two minutes, however, the arm began to

* Deutsches Archiv f. Klin. Medicin, XXII. 321.

tremble and sink without his being aware of it. He asserted still his ability to keep it up. . . . Passively holding still his fingers did not affect him. He thought constantly that he opened and shut his hand, whereas it was really fixed."

Or we read of cases like this :

" Voluntary movements cannot be estimated the moment the patient ceases to take note of them by his eyes. Thus, after having made him close his eyes, if one asks him to move one of his limbs either wholly or in part, he does it but cannot tell whether the effected movement is large or small, strong or weak, or even if it has taken place at all. And when he opens his eyes after moving his leg from right to left, for example, he declares that he had a very inexact notion of the extent of the effected movement. . . . If, having the intention of executing a certain movement, *I prevent him*, he does not perceive it, and supposes the limb to have taken the position he intended to give it." *

Or this :

"The patient, when his eyes were closed in the middle of an unpractised movement, remained with the extremity in the position it had when the eyes closed and did not complete the movement properly. Then after some oscillations the limb gradually sank by reason of its weight (the sense of fatigue being absent). Of this the patient was not aware, and wondered, when he opened his eyes, at the altered position of his limb." †

A similar condition can be readily reproduced experimentally in many hypnotic subjects. All that is needed is to tell a suitably predisposed person during the hypnotic trance that he cannot feel his limb, and he will be quite unaware of the attitudes into which you may throw it.‡

All these cases, whether spontaneous or experimental, show the absolute need of *guiding sensations* of some kind for the successful carrying out of a concatenated series of movements. It is, in fact, easy to see that, just as where the chain of movements is automatic (see above, Vol. I. p. 116), each later movement of the chain has to be discharged by the impression which the next earlier one makes in being

---

* Landry : Mémoire sur la Paralysie du Sens Musculaire, Gazette des Hôpitaux, 1855, p. 270.

† Tåkacs : Ueber die Verspätung der Empfindungsleitung, Archiv für Psychiatrie, Bd. x. Heft 2, p. 533. Concerning all such cases see the re marks made above on pp. 205-6.

‡ Proceedings of American Soc. for Psychical Research, p. 95.

executed, so also, where the chain is voluntary, we need to know at each movement just *where we are in it,* if we are to will intelligently what the next link shall be. A man with no feeling of his movements might lead off never so well, and yet be sure to get lost soon and go astray.* But patients like those described, who get no kinæsthetic impressions, can still be guided by the sense of sight. Thus Strümpell says of his boy:

"One could always observe how his eye was directed first to the object held before him, then to his own arm; and how it never ceased

---

* In reality the movement cannot even be *started* correctly in some cases without the kinæsthetic impression. Thus Dr. Strümpell relates how turning over the boy's hand made him bend the little finger instead of the forefinger, when his eye was closed. "Ordered to point, e.g., towards the left with his left arm, the arm was usually raised straight forward, and then wandered about in groping uncertainty, sometimes getting the right position and then leaving it again. Similarly with the lower limbs. If the patient, lying in bed, had, immediately after the tying of his eyes, to lay the left leg over the right, it often happened that he moved it farther over towards the left, and that it lay over the side of the bed in apparently the most intolerably-uncomfortable position. The turning of the head, too, from right to left, or towards certain objects known to the patient, only ensued correctly when the patient, immediately before his eye was bandaged, specially refreshed his perception as to what the required movement was to be." In another anæsthetic of Dr. Strümpell's (described in the same essay) the arm could not be moved *at all* unless the eyes were opened, however energetic the volition. The variations in these hysteric cases are great. Some patients cannot move the anæsthetic part *at all* when the eyes are closed. Others move it perfectly well, and can even write continuous sentences with the anæsthetic hand. The causes of such differences are as yet incompletely unexplored. M. Binet suggests (Revue Philosophique, xxv. 478) that in those who cannot move the hand at all the sensation of light is required as a 'dynamogenic' agent (see above, p. 377); and that in those who can move it skilfully the anæsthesia is only a pseudo-insensibility and that the limb is in reality governed by a dissociated or secondary consciousness. This latter explanation is certainly correct. Professor G. E. Müller (Pflüger's Archiv, xlv. 90) invokes the fact of individual differences of imagination to account for the cases who cannot write at all. Their kinæsthetic images properly so called may be weak, he says, and their optical images insufficiently powerful to supplement them without a 'fillip' from sensation. Janet's observation that hysteric anæsthesias may carry amnesias with them would perfectly legitimate Müller's supposition. What we now want is a minute examination of the individual cases. Meanwhile Binet's article above referred to, and Bastian's paper in Brain for April 1887, contain important discussions of the question. In a later note I shall return to the subject again (see p. 520).

to follow the latter during its entire movement. All his voluntary movements took place under the unremitting lead of the eye, which as an indispensable guide, was never untrue to its functions."

So in the Landry case :

" With his eyes open, he easily opposes the thumb to each of the other fingers ; with his eyes closed, the movement of opposition occurs, but the thumb only by chance meets the finger which it seeks. With his eyes open he is able, without hesitation, to bring his two hands together ; but when his eyes are closed his hands seek one another in space, and only meet by chance."

In Charles Bell's well-known old case of anæsthesia the woman could only hold her baby safely in her arms so long as she looked at it. I have myself reproduced a similar condition in two hypnotic subjects whose arm and hand were made anæsthetic without being paralyzed. They could write their names when looking, but not when their eyes were closed. The modern mode of teaching deaf mutes to articulate consists in making them attentive to certain laryngeal, labial, thoracic, and other sensations, the reproduction of which becomes a guide to their vocalization. Normally it is the remoter sensations which we receive by the ear which keep us from going astray in our speech. The phenomena of aphasia show this to be the usual case.*

This is perhaps all that need be said about the existence of passive sensations of movement and their indispensableness for our voluntary activity. We may consequently set it down as certain that, *whether or no there be anything else in the mind at the moment when we consciously will a certain act, a mental conception made up of memory-images of these sensations, defining which special act it is, must be there.*

Now *is there anything else in the mind when we will to do an act ?* We must proceed in this chapter from the simpler to the more complicated cases. My first thesis accordingly is, that *there need be nothing else,* and that *in perfectly simple vol-*

---

* Professor Beaunis found that the accuracy with which a certain tenor sang was not lost when his vocal cords were made anæsthetic by cocain. He concludes that the guiding sensations here are resident in the laryngeal muscles themselves. They are much more probably in the ear. (Beaunis, Les Sensations Internes (1889), p. 253).

untary acts there is nothing else, in the mind but the kinæsthetic idea, thus defined, of what the act is to be.

A powerful tradition in Psychology will have it that something additional to these images of passive sensation is essential to the mental determination of a voluntary act. There must, of course, be a special current of energy going out from the brain into the appropriate muscles during the act; and this outgoing current (it is supposed) must have in each particular case a feeling *sui generis* attached to it, or else (it is said) the mind could never tell which particular current, the current to this muscle or the current to that one, was the right one to use. This feeling of the current of out-going energy has received from Wundt the name of the *feeling of innervation.* *I disbelieve in its existence,* and must proceed to criticise the notion of it, at what I fear may to some prove tedious length.

At first sight there is something extremely plausible in the feeling of innervation. The passive feelings of move-ment with which we have hitherto been dealing all come after the movement's performance. But wherever a move-ment is difficult and precise, we become, as a matter of fact, acutely aware *in advance* of the amount and direction of energy which it is to involve. One has only to play ten-pins or billiards, or throw a ball, to catch his will in the act, as it were, of balancing tentatively its possible efforts, and ideally rehearsing various muscular contractions nearly correct, until it gets just the right one before it, when it says 'Now go!' This premonitory weighing feels so much like a succession of tentative sallyings forth of power into the outer world, followed by correction just in time to avoid the irrevocable deed, that the notion that *outgoing* nerve-currents rather than mere vestiges of former passive sensi-bility accompany it, is a most natural one to entertain.

We find accordingly that most authors have taken the existence of feelings of innervation as a matter of course. Bain, Wundt, Helmholtz, and Mach defend them most explicitly. But in spite of the authority which such writers deservedly wield, I cannot help thinking that they are in this instance wrong,—that the discharge into the motor nerves is insentient, and that *all our ideas of movement,* including those of the effort which it requires, as well as those of its direction, its extent, its strength, and its velocity, *are images of peripheral sensations, either ' remote,' or resident in the moving parts, or in other parts which sympathetically act with them in consequenceof the ' diffusive wave.'*

A priori, as I shall show, there is no reason why there should be a consciousness of the motor discharge, and there is a reason why there should not be such a consciousness. The *presumption* is thus against the existence of the feeling of innervation ; and the burden of proving it falls upon those who believe in it. If the positive empirical evidence which they offer prove also insufficient, then their case falls to the ground, and the feeling in question must be ruled out of court.

In the first place, then, let me show that *the assumption of the feeling of innervation is unnecessary.*

I cannot help suspecting that the scholastic prejudice that ' the effect must be already in some way *contained in* the cause ' has had something to do with making psychologists so ready to admit the feeling of innervation. The outgoing current being the effect, what psychic antecedent could contain or prefigure it better than a feeling of it ? But if we take a wide view, and consider the psychic antecedents of our activities at large, we see that the scholastic maxim breaks down everywhere, and that its verification in this instance would rather violate than illustrate the general rule. In the diffusive wave, in reflex action, and in emotional expression, the movements which are the effects are in no manner contained by anticipation in the stimuli which are their cause. The latter are subjective sensations or objective perceptions, which do not in the slightest degree resemble or prefigure the movements. But we get them, and, presto ! there the movements are ! They are knocked out of us, they surprise us. It is just cause for wonder, as our chapter on Instinct has shown us, that such bodily consequences should follow such mental antecedents. We explain the mystery *tant bien que mal* by our evolutionary theories, saying that lucky variations and heredity have gradually brought it about that this particular pair of terms should have grown into a uniform sequence. Meanwhile why any state of consciousness *at all* should precede a movement, we know not—the two things seem so essentially discontinuous. But if a state of consciousness there must be, why then it may, for aught we can see, as easily be one sort of a state as another. It is swallowing a camel and straining at a gnat for a man (all of whose muscles will on certain occasions contract at a sudden touch or sound) to suppose that on another occasion the idea of the feelings about to be produced by their contraction is an insufficient mental signal for the latter, and to insist that an additional antecedent is needed in the shape of 'a feeling of the outgoing discharge.'

No! for aught we can see, and in the light of general analogy, the kinæsthetic ideas, as we have defined them, or images of incoming feelings of attitude and motion, are as *likely* as any feelings of innervation are, to be the last psychic antecedents and determiners of the various currents downwards into the muscles from the brain. The question " What *are* the antecedents and determinants?" is a question of fact, to be decided by whatever empirical evidence may be found.*

---

* As the feeling of heat, for example, is the last psychic antecedent of sweating, as the feeling of bright light is that of the pupil's contraction, as the sight or smell of carrion is that of the movements of disgust, as the remembrance of a blunder may be that of a blush, so the idea of a movement's sensible effects might be that of the movement itself. It is true that the idea of sweating will not commonly make us sweat, nor that of blushing make us blush. But in certain nauseated states the idea of vomiting will make us vomit; and a kind of sequence which is in this case realized only exceptionally might be the rule with the so-called voluntary muscles. It all depends on the nervous connections between the centres of ideation and the discharging paths. These may differ from one sort of centre to another. They do differ somewhat from one individual to another. Many persons never blush at the idea of their blunders, but only when the actual blunder is committed; others blush at the idea; and some do not blush at all. According to Lotze, with some persons " It is possible to weep at will by trying to recall that peculiar feeling in the trigeminal nerve which habitually precedes tears. Some can even succeed in sweating voluntarily, by the lively recollection of the characteristic skin-sensations, and the voluntary reproduction of an indescribable sort of feeling of relaxation, which ordinarily precedes the flow of perspiration." (Med. Psych., p. 303.) The commoner type of exceptional case is that in which the idea of the *stimulus*, not that of the effects, provokes the effects. Thus we

But before considering the empirical evidence, let me go on to show that there is *a certain a priori reason why the kinœsthetic images* OUGHT *to be the last psychic antecedents of the outgoing currents, and why we should expect these currents to be insentient; why, in short, the soi-disant feelings of inner-vation should* NOT *exist.*

It is a general principle in Psychology that consciousness deserts all processes where it can no longer be of use. The tendency of consciousness to a minimum of complication is in fact a dominating law. The law of parsimony in logic is only its best known case. We grow unconscious of every feeling which is useless as a sign to lead us to our ends, and where one sign will suffice others drop out, and that one remains, to work alone. We observe this in the whole history of sense-perception, and in the acquisition of every art. We ignore which eye we see with, because a fixed mechanical association has been formed between our motions and each retinal image. Our motions are the ends of our seeing, our retinal images the signals to these ends. If each retinal image, whichever it be, can suggest automatically a motion in the right direction, what need for us to know whether it be in the right eye or the left?

---

read of persons who contract their pupils at will by strongly imagining a brilliant light. A gentleman once informed me (strangely enough I cannot recall who he was, but I have an impression of his being a medical man) that he could sweat at will by imagining himself on the brink of a precipice. The sweating palms of fear are sometimes producible by imagining a terrible object (cf. Manouvrier in Rev. Phil., xxii. 203). One of my students, whose eyes were made to water by sitting in the dentist's chair before a bright window, can now shed tears by imagining that situation again. One might doubtless collect a large number of idiosyncratic cases of this sort. They teach us how greatly the centres vary in their power to discharge through certain channels. All that we need, now, to account for the differences observed between the psychic antecedents of the voluntary and involuntary movements is that centres producing ideas of the movement's sensible effects should be able to instigate the former, but be out of gear with the latter, unless in exceptional individuals. The famous case of Col. Townsend, who could stop his heart at will, is well known. See, on this whole matter, D. H. Tuke: Illustrations of the Influence of the Mind on the Body, chap. xiv. § 3; also J. Braid: Observations on Trance or Human Hybernation (1850). The latest reported case of voluntary control of the heart is by Dr. S. A. Pease, in Boston Medical and Surgical Journal, May 30, 1889.

That knowledge would be superfluous complication. So in acquiring any art or voluntary function. The marksman ends by thinking only of the exact position of the goal, the singer only of the perfect sound, the balancer only of the point of the pole whose oscillations he must counteract. The associated mechanism has become so perfect in all these persons that each variation in the thought of the end is functionally correlated with the one movement fitted to bring the latter about. Whilst they were tyros, they thought of their means as well as their end: the marksman of the position of his gun or bow, or the weight of his stone ; the pianist of the visible position of the note on the keyboard; the singer of his throat or breathing; the balancer of his feet on the rope, or his hand or chin under the pole. But little by little they succeeded in dropping all this supernumerary consciousness, and they became secure in their movements exactly in proportion as they did so.

Now if we analyze the nervous mechanism of voluntary action, we shall see that by virtue of this principle of parsimony in consciousness the motor discharge *ought* to be devoid of sentience. If we call the immediate psychic antecedent of a movement the latter's *mental cue*, all that is needed for invariability of sequence on the movement's part is a *fixed connection* between each several mental cue, and one particular movement. For a movement to be produced with perfect precision, it suffices that it obey instantly its own mental cue and nothing else, and that this mental cue be incapable of awakening any other movement. Now the *simplest* possible arrangement for producing voluntary movements would be that the memory-images of the movement's distinctive peripheral effects, whether resident or remote,* themselves should severally constitute the mental cues, and that no other psychic facts should intervene or be mixed up with them. For a million different voluntary movements, we should then need a million dis-

---

* Prof. Harless, in an article which in many respects forestalls what I have to say (Der Apparat des Willens, in Fichte's Zeitschrift f. Philos., Bd. 38, 1861), uses the convenient word *Effectsbild* to designate these images.

tinct processes in the brain-cortex (each corresponding to the idea or memory-image of one movement), and a million distinct paths of discharge. Everything would then be unambiguously determined, and if the idea were right, the movement would be right too. Everything *after* the idea might then be quite insentient, and the motor discharge itself could be unconsciously performed.

The partisans of the feeling of innervation, however, say that the motor discharge itself must be felt, and that it, and not the idea of the movement's distinctive effects, must be the proper mental cue. Thus the principle of parsimony is sacrificed, and all economy and simplicity are lost. For what can be gained by the interposition of this relay of feeling between the idea of the movement and the movement? Nothing on the score of economy of nerve-tracts; for it takes just as many of them to associate a million ideas of movement with a million motor centres, each with a specific feeling of innervation attached to its discharge, as to associate the same million ideas with a million insentient motor centres. And nothing on the score of precision; for the only conceivable way in which the feelings of innervation might further precision would be by giving to a mind whose idea of a movement was vague, a sort of halting stage with sharper imagery on which to collect its wits before uttering its *fiat.* But not only are the conscious discriminations between our kinæsthetic ideas much sharper than any one pretends the shades of difference between feelings of innervation to be, but even were this not the case, it is impossible to see how a mind with its idea vaguely conceived could tell out of a lot of *Innervations-gefühle*, were they never so sharply differentiated, which one fitted that idea exactly, and which did not. A sharply conceived idea will, on the other hand, *directly* awaken a distinct movement as easily as it will awaken a distinct feeling of innervation. If feelings can go astray through vagueness, surely the fewer steps of feeling there are interposed the more securely we shall act. We ought then, on *a priori* grounds alone, to regard the *Innervationsgefühl* as a pure encumbrance, and to presume that the peripheral ideas of movement are sufficient mental cues.

The presumption being thus against the feelings of innervation, those who defend their existence are bound to prove it by positive evidence. The evidence might be direct or indirect. If we could introspectively feel them as something plainly distinct from the peripheral feelings and ideas of movement which nobody denies to be there, that would be evidence both direct and conclusive. Unfortunately it does not exist.

There is no introspective evidence of the feeling of innervation. Wherever we look for it and think we have grasped it, we find that we have really got a peripheral feeling or image instead—an image of the way in which we feel when the innervation is over, and the movement is in process of doing or is done. Our idea of raising our arm, for example, or of crooking our finger, is a sense, more or less vivid, of how the raised arm or the crooked finger feels. There is no other mental material out of which such an idea might be made. We cannot possibly have any idea of our ears' motion until our ears have moved; and this is true of every other organ as well.

Since the time of Hume it has been a commonplace in psychology that we are only conversant with the outward results of our volition, and not with the hidden inner machinery of nerves and muscles which are what it primarily sets at work.* The believers in the feeling of innervation readily admit this, but seem hardly alive to its consequences. It seems to me that one immediate consequence ought to be to make us doubt the existence of the feeling in dispute. Whoever says that in raising his arm he is ignorant of how many muscles he contracts, in what order of sequence, and in what degrees of intensity, expressively avows a colossal amount of unconsciousness of the processes of motor discharge. Each separate muscle at any rate cannot have its distinct feeling of innervation. Wundt,† who makes such enormous use of these hypo-

---

* The best modern statement I know is by Jaccoud: Des Paraplégies et de l'Ataxie du Mouvement (Paris, 1864), p. 591.

† Leidesdorf u. Meynert's Vierteljsch. f. Psychiatrie, Bd. I. Heft I. S. 36–7 (1867). Physiologische Psychologie, 1st ed. S. 316.

thetical feelings in his psychologic construction of space, is himself led to admit that they have no differences of quality, but feel alike in all muscles, and vary only in their degrees of intensity. They are used by the mind as guides, not of *which* movement, but of *how strong* a movement, it is making, or shall make. But does not this virtually surrender their existence altogether? *

For if anything be obvious to introspection it is that the degree of strength of our muscular contractions is completely revealed to us by afferent feelings coming from the muscles themselves and their insertions, from the vicinity of the joints, and from the general fixation of the larynx, chest, face, and body, in the phenomenon of effort, objectively considered. When a certain degree of energy of contraction rather than another is thought of by us, this complex aggregate of afferent feelings, forming the material of our thought, renders absolutely precise and distinctive our mental image of the exact strength of movement to be made, and the exact amount of resistance to be overcome.

Let the reader try to direct his will towards a particular movement, and then notice what *constituted* the direction of the will. Was it anything over and above the notion of the different feelings to which the movement when effected would give rise? If we abstract from these feelings, will any sign, principle, or means of orientation be left by which the will may innervate the right muscles with the right intensity, and not go astray into the wrong ones? Strip off these images of result, and so far from leaving us with a complete assortment of directions into which our will may launch itself, you leave our consciousness in an absolute and total vacuum. If I will to write "Peter" rather than "Paul," it is the thought of certain digital sensations, of certain alphabetic sounds, of certain appearances on the paper, and of no others, which immediately precedes the motion of my pen.

---

* Professor Fouillée, who defends them in the Revue Philosophique, XXVIII, 561 ff., also admits (p. 574) that they are the same whatever be the movement, and that all our discrimination of *which* movement we are innervating is afferent, consisting of sensations after, and of sensory images before, the act.

If I will to utter the word *Paul* rather than *Peter*, it is the thought of my voice falling on my ear, and of certain muscular feelings in my tongue, lips, and larynx, which guide the utterance. All these are incoming feelings, and between the thought of them, by which the act is mentally specified with all possible completeness, and the act itself, there is no room for any third order of mental phenomenon. There is indeed the *fiat*, the element of consent, or resolve that the act shall ensue. This, doubtless, to the reader's mind, as to my own, constitutes the essence of the voluntariness of the act. This *fiat* will be treated of in detail farther on. It may be entirely neglected here, for it is a constant coefficient, affecting all voluntary actions alike, and incapable of serving to distinguish them. No one will pretend that its quality varies according as the right arm, for example, or the left is used.

An anticipatory image, then, of the sensorial consequences of a movement, plus (on certain occasions) the fiat that these consequences shall become actual, is the only psychic state which introspection lets us discern as the forerunner of our voluntary acts. There is no introspective evidence whatever of any still later or concomitant feeling attached to the efferent discharge. The various degrees of difficulty with which the fiat is given form a complication of the utmost importance, to be discussed farther on.

Now the reader may still shake his head and say: " But can you seriously mean that all the wonderfully exact adjustment of my action's strength to its ends is not a matter of outgoing innervation? Here is a cannon-ball, and here a pasteboard box: instantly and accurately I lift each from the table, the ball not refusing to rise because my innervation was too weak, the box not flying abruptly into the air because it was too strong. Could representations of the movement's different sensory effects in the two cases be so delicately foreshadowed in the mind? or being there, is it credible that they should, all unaided, so delicately graduate the stimulation of the unconscious motor centres to their work?" Even so! I reply to both queries. We have a most extremely delicate foreshadowing of the sensory effects. Why else the start of surprise that runs through us if some one has filled the light-seeming box with sand before we try to lift it, or has substituted for the cannon-ball which we know a painted wooden imitation? *Surprise* can only come from getting a sensation which differs from the one we expect. But the truth is that when we know the objects well, the very slightest difference from the expected weight will surprise us, or at least attract our notice. With unknown objects we begin by expecting the weight made probable by their appearance. The expectation of this sensation innervates our lift, and we 'set' it rather small at first. An instant verifies whether it is too small. Our expectation rises, i.e., we think in a twinkling of a setting of the chest and teeth, a bracing of the back, and a more violent feeling in the arms. Quicker than thought we have them, and with them the burden ascends into the air.[*] Bernhardt[†] has shown in a rough experimental way that our estimation of the amount of a resistance is as delicately graduated when our wills are passive, and our limbs made to contract by direct local faradization, as when we our-

---

[*] Cf. Souriau in Rev. Philosophique, xxii. 454.—Professor G. E. Müller thus describes some of his experiments with weights: If, after lifting a weight of 3000 grams a number of times we suddenly get a weight of only 500 grams to lift, "this latter weight is then lifted with a velocity which strikes every onlooker, so that the receptacle for the weight with all its contents often flies high up as if it carried the arm along with it, and the energy with which it is raised is sometimes so entirely out of proportion to the weight itself, that the contents of the receptacle is slung out upon the table in spite of the mechanical obstacles which such a result has to overcome. A more palpable proof that the trouble here is a wrong adaptation of the motor impulse could not be given." Pflüger's Archiv, xlv. 47. Compare also p. 57, and the quotation from Hering on the same page.

[†] Archiv für Psychiatrie, iii. 618–635. Bernhardt strangely enough seems to think that what his experiments disprove is the existence of afferent muscular feelings, not those of efferent innervation—apparently because he deems that the peculiar thrill of the electricity ought to overpower all other afferent feelings from the part. But it is far more natural to interpret his results the other way, even aside from the certainty yielded by other evidence that passive muscular feelings exist. This other evidence, after being compendiously summed up by Sachs in Reichert und Du Bois' Archiv (1874), pp. 174–188, is, as far as the anatomical and physiological grounds go, again thrown into doubt by Mays, Zeitschrift f. Biologie, Bd. xx.

selves innervate them. Ferrier * has repeated and verified
the observations. They admit of no great precision, and
too much stress should not be laid upon them either way;
but at the very least they tend to show that no added delicacy would accrue to our perception from the consciousness
of the efferent process, even if it existed.

Since there is no direct introspective evidence for the
feelings of innervation, is there any indirect or circumstantial evidence? Much is· offered ; but on critical examination it bréaks down. Let us see what it is. Wundt says
that were our motor feelings of an afferent nature,

"it ought to be expected that they would increase and diminish with
the amount of outer or inner work actually effected in contraction.
This, however, is not the case, but the strength of the motor sensation
is purely proportional to the strength of the *impulse* to movement,
which starts from the central organ innervating the motor nerves.
This may be proved by observations made by physicians in cases of
morbid alteration in the muscular effect. A patient whose arm or leg
is half paralyzed, so that he can only move the limb with great effort,
has a distinct feeling of this effort : the limb seems to him heavier than
before, appearing as if weighted with lead ; he has, therefore, a sense
of more work effected than formerly, and yet the effected work is either
the same or even less. Only he must, to get even this effect, exert a
stronger innervation, a stronger motor impulse, than formerly." †

In complete paralysis, also, patients will be conscious
of putting forth the greatest exertion to move a limb which
remains absolutely still upon the bed, and from which of
course no afferent muscular or other feelings can come.‡

But Dr. Ferrier in his Functions of the Brain (Am. Ed.

---

* Functions of the Brain, p. 228.

‡ Vorlesungen über Menschen und Thierseele, I. 222.

‡ In some instances we get an opposite result. Dr. H. Charlton Bastian
(British Medical Journal (1869), p. 461, note), says :

"Ask a man whose lower extremities are completely paralyzed, whether,
when he ineffectually wills to move either of these limbs, he is conscious
of an expenditure of energy in any degree proportionate to that which he
would have experienced if his muscles had naturally responded to his volition. He will tell us rather that he has a sense only of his utter power-
lessness, and that his volition is a mere mental act, carrying with it no feelings of expended energy such as he is accustomed to experience when his
muscles are in powerful action, and from which action and its consequences
alone, as I think, he can derive any adequate notion of resistance."

pp. 222–4) disposes very easily of this line of argument. He says:

" It is necessary, however, to exclude movements *altogether* before such an explanation [as Wundt's] can be adopted. Now, though the hemiplegic patient cannot move his paralyzed limb, though he is conscious of trying hard, yet he will be found to be making powerful muscular exertion of some kind. Vulpian has called attention to the fact, and I have repeatedly verified it, that when a hemiplegic patient is desired to close his paralyzed fist, in his endeavors to do so he unconsciously performs this action with the sound one. It is, in fact, almost impossible to exclude such a source of complication, and unless this is taken into account very erroneous conclusions as to the cause of the sense of effort may be drawn. In the fact of muscular contraction and the concomitant centripetal impressions, even though the action is not such as is desired, the conditions of the consciousness of effort exist without our being obliged to regard it as depending on central innervation or outgoing currents.

" It is, however, easy to make an experiment of a simple nature which will satisfactorily account for the sense of effort, even when these unconscious contractions of the other side, such as hemiplegics make, are entirely excluded.

" If the reader will extend his right arm and hold his forefinger in the position required for pulling the trigger of a pistol, he may without actually moving his finger, but by simply making believe, experience a consciousness of energy put forth. Here, then, is a clear case of consciousness of energy without actual contraction of the muscles either of the one hand or the other, and without any perceptible bodily strain. If the reader will again perform the experiment, and pay careful attention to the condition of his respiration, he will observe that his consciousness of effort coincides with a fixation of the muscles of his chest, and that in proportion to the amount of energy he feels he is putting forth, he is keeping his glottis closed and actively contracting his respiratory muscles. Let him place his finger as before, and *continue breathing* all the time, and he will find that however much he may direct his attention to his finger, he will experience not the slightest trace of consciousness of effort until he has actually moved the finger itself, and then it is referred locally to the muscles in action. It is only when this essential and ever-present respiratory factor is, as it has been, overlooked, that the consciousness of effort can with any degree of plausibility be ascribed to the outgoing current. In the contraction of the respiratory muscles there are the necessary conditions of centripetal impressions, and these are capable of originating the general sense of effort. When these active efforts are withheld, no consciousness of effort ever arises, except in so far as it is conditioned by the local contraction of the group of muscles towards which the attention is directed, or by other muscular contractions called unconsciously into play in the attempt.

" I am unable to find a single case of consciousness of effort which is not explicable in one or other of the ways specified. In all instances the consciousness of effort is conditioned by the actual fact of muscular contraction. That it is dependent on centripetal impressions generated by the act of contraction, I have already endeavored to show. When the paths of the centripetal impressions or the cerebral centres of the same are destroyed, there is no vestige of a muscular sense. That the central organs for the apprehension of the impressions originating from muscular contraction are different from those which send out the motor impulse, has already been established. But when Wundt argues that this cannot be so, because then the sensation would always keep pace with the energy of muscular contraction, he overlooks the important factor of the fixation of the respiratory muscles, which is the basis of the general sense of effort in all its varying degrees."

To these remarks of Ferrier's I have nothing to add.* Any one may verify them, and they prove conclusively that the consciousness of muscular exertion, being impossible without movement *effected somewhere*, must be an afferent and not an efferent sensation; a consequence, and not an antecedent, of the movement itself. An idea of the amount of muscular exertion requisite to perform a certain movement can consequently be nothing other than an anticipatory image of the movement's sensible effects.

---

* Münsterberg's words may be added : " In lifting an object in the hand I can discover no sensation of volitional energy I perceive in the first place a slight tension about the head, but that this results from a contraction in the head muscles, and not from a feeling of the brain-discharge, is shown by the simple fact that I get the tension on the right side of the head when I move the right arm, whereas the motor discharge takes place in the opposite side of the brain. . . . In maximal contractions of body- and limb-muscles there occur, as if it were to reinforce them, those special contractions of the muscles of the face [especially frowning and clinching teeth] and those tensions of the skin of the head. These sympathetic movements, felt particularly on the side which makes the effort, are perhaps the immediate ground why we ascribe our awareness of maximal contraction to the region of the head, and call it a consciousness of force, instead of a peripheral sensation." (Die Willenshandlung (1888), pp. 73, 82.) Herr Münsterberg's work is a little masterpiece, which appeared after my text was written. I shall have repeatedly to refer to it again, and cordially recommend to the reader its most thorough refutation of the Innervations-gefühl-theory.

Driven thus from the body at large, where next shall the circumstantial evidence for the feeling of innervation lodge itself? Where but in the muscles of the eye, from which small retreat it judges itself inexpugnable. Nevertheless, that fastness too must fall, and by the lightest of bombardments. But, before trying the bombardment, let us recall our general principles about optical vertigo, or illusory appearance of movement in objects.

We judge that an object moves under two distinct sets of circumstances:

1. When its image moves on the retina, and we know that the eye is still.

2. When its image is stationary on the retina, and we know that the eye is moving. In this case we feel that we *follow* the object.

In either of these cases a mistaken judgment about the state of the eye will produce optical vertigo.

If in case 1 we think our eye is still when it is really moving, we get a movement of the retinal image which we judge to be due to a real outward motion of the object. This is what happens after looking at rushing water, or through the windows of a moving railroad car, or after turning on one's heel to giddiness. The eyes, without our intending to move them, go through a series of involuntary rotations, continuing those they were previously obliged to make to keep objects in view. If the objects had been whirling by to our right, our eyes when turned to stationary objects will still move slowly towards the right. The retinal image upon them will then move like that of an object passing to the left. We then try to catch it by voluntarily and rapidly rotating the eyes to the left, when the involuntary impulse again rotates the eyes to the right, continuing the apparent motion; and so the game goes on. (See above, pp. 89–91.)

If in case 2 we think our eyes moving when they are in reality still, we shall judge that we are following a moving object when we are but fixating a steadfast one. Illusions of this kind occur after sudden and complete paralysis of special eye muscles, and the partisans of feelings of efferent innervation regard them as *experimenta crucis*. Helmholtz writes : *

" When the external rectus muscle of the right eye, or its nerve, is paralyzed, the eye can no longer be rotated to the right side. So long as the patient turns it only to the nasal side it makes regular movements, and he perceives correctly the position of objects in the visual field. So soon, however, as he tries to rotate it outwardly, i.e., towards the right, it ceases to obey his will, stands motionless in the middle of its course, and the objects appear flying to the right, although position of eye and retinal image are unaltered.†

" In such a case the exertion of the will is followed neither by actual movement of the eye, nor by contraction of the muscle in question, nor even by increased tension in it. The act of will *produced absolutely no effect* beyond the nervous system, and yet we judge of the direction of the line of vision as if the will had exercised its normal effects. We believe it to have moved to the right, and since the retinal image is unchanged, we attribute to the object the same movement we have erroneously ascribed to the eye. . . . These phenomena leave no room for doubt that we only judge the direction of the line of sight by the effort of will with which we strive to change the position of our eyes. There are also certain weak feelings in our eyelids, . . . and furthermore in excessive lateral rotations we feel a fatiguing strain in the muscles. But all these feelings are too faint and vague to be of use in the perception of direction. We feel then what impulse of the will, and how strong a one, we apply to turn our eye into a given position."

Partial paralysis of the same muscle, *paresis*, as it has been called, seems to point even more conclusively to the same inference, that the will to innervate is felt independently of all its afferent results. I will quote the account given by a recent authority, ‡ of the effects of this accident:

" When the nerve going to an eye muscle, e.g., the external rectus of one side, falls into a state of paresis, the first result is that the same volitional stimulus, which under normal circumstances would have perhaps rotated the eye to its extreme position outwards, now is competent to effect only a moderate outward rotation, say of 20°. If now, shutting the sound eye, the patient looks at an object situated just so far out-

---

* Physiologische Optik, p. 600.

† [The left and sound eye is here supposed covered. If both eyes look at the same field there are double images which still more perplex the judgment. The patient, however, learns to see correctly before many days or weeks are over.—W. J.]

‡ Alfred Graefe, in Handbuch der gesammten Augenheilkunde, Bd. VI. pp. 18-21.

wards from the paretic eye that this latter must turn 20° in order to see it distinctly, the patient will feel as if he had moved it not only 20° towards the side, but into its extreme lateral position, for the impulse of innervation requisite for bringing it into view is a perfectly conscious act, whilst the diminished state of contraction of the paretic muscle lies for the present out of the ken of consciousness. The test proposed by von Graefe, of localization by the sense of touch, serves to render evident the error which the patient now makes. If we direct him to touch rapidly the object looked at, with the fore-finger of the hand of the same side, the line through which the finger moves will not be the line of sight directed 20° outward, but will approach more nearly to the extreme possible outward line of vision."

A stone-cutter with the external rectus of the left eye paralyzed, will strike his hand instead of his chisel with his hammer, until experience has taught him wisdom.

It appears as if here the judgment of direction *could* only arise from the excessive innervation of the rectus when the object is looked at. All the afferent feelings must be identical with those experienced when the eye is sound and the judgment is correct. The eyeball is rotated just 20° in the one case as in the other, the image falls on the same part of the retina, the pressures on the eyeball and the tensions of the skin and conjunctiva are identical. There is only one feeling which *can* vary, and lead us to our mistake. That feeling must be the effort which the will makes, moderate in the one case, excessive in the other, but in both cases an efferent feeling, pure and simple.

Beautiful and clear as this reasoning seems to be, it is based on an incomplete inventory of the afferent data. The writers have all omitted to consider what is going on in the *other eye.* This is kept covered during the experiments, to prevent double images, and other complications. But if its condition under these circumstances be examined, it will be found to present changes which must result in strong afferent feelings. And the taking account of these feelings demolishes in an instant all the conclusions which the authors from whom I have quoted base upon their supposed absence. This I will now proceed to show.*

---

* Professor G. E. Müller (Zur Grundlegung der Psychophysik (1878), p. 318, was the first to explain the phenomenon after the manner advocated

Take first the case of complete paralysis and assume the right eye affected. Suppose the patient desires to rotate his gaze to an object situated in the extreme right of the field of vision. As Hering has so beautifully shown, both eyes move by a common act of innervation, and in this instance both move towards the right. But the paralyzed right eye stops short in the middle of its course, the object still appearing far to the right of its fixation point. The left sound eye, meanwhile, although covered, continues its rotation until the extreme rightward limit thereof has been reached. To an observer looking at both eyes the left will seem to squint. Of course this continued and extreme rotation produces afferent feelings of rightward motion in the eyeball, which momentarily overpower the faint feelings of central position in the diseased and uncovered eye. The patient feels by his left eyeball as if he were following an object which by his right retina he perceives he does not overtake. All the conditions of optical vertigo are here present: the image stationary on the retina, and the erroneous conviction that the eyes are moving.

The objection that a feeling in the left eyeball ought not to produce a conviction that the right eye moves, will be considered in a moment. Let us meanwhile turn to the

---

in the text. Still unacquainted with his book, I published my own similar explanation two years later.

"Professor Mach in his wonderfully original little work 'Beiträge zur Analyse der Empfindungen,' p. 57, describes an artificial way of getting translocation, and explains the effect likewise by the feeling of innervation. "Turn your eyes," he says, "as far as possible towards the left and press against the right sides of the orbits two large lumps of putty. If you then try to look as quickly as possible towards the right, this succeeds, on account of the incompletely spherical form of the eyes, only imperfectly, and the objects consequently appear translocated very considerably towards the right. The *bare will* to look rightwards gives to all images on the retina a greater *rightwards value*, to express it shortly. The experiment is at first surprising."—I regret to say that I cannot myself make it succeed—I know not for what reason. But even where it does succeed it seems to me that the conditions are much too complicated for Professor Mach's theoretic conclusions to be safely drawn. The putty squeezed into the orbit, and the pressure of the eyeball against it must give rise to peripheral sensations *strong* enough, at any rate (if only of the right kind), to justify any amount of false perception of our eyeball's position, quite apart from the innervation feelings which Professsor Mach supposes to coexist.

case of simple paresis with apparent translocation of the field.

Here the right eye succeeds in fixating the object, but observation of the left eye will reveal to an observer the fact that it squints just as violently inwards as in the former case. The direction which the finger of the patient takes in pointing to the object, is the direction of this squinting and covered left eye. As Graefe says (although he fails to seize the true import of his own observation), "It appears to have been by no means sufficiently noticed how significantly the direction of the line of sight of the secondarily deviating eye [i.e., of the left,] and the line of direction of the pointed finger agree."

The translocation would, in a word, be perfectly explained could we suppose that the sensation of a certain degree of rotation in the left eyeball were able to suggest to the patient the position of an object whose image falls on the right retina alone.* Can, then, a feeling in one eye

---

* An illusion in principle exactly analogous to that of the patient under discussion can be produced experimentally in anyone in a way which Hering has described in his Lehre von Binocularen Sehen, pp. 12–14. I will quote Helmholtz's account of it, which is especially valuable as coming from a believer in the *Innervationsgefühl*: "Let the two eyes first look parallel, then let the right eye be closed whilst the left still looks at the infinitely distant object *a*. The directions of both eyes will thus remain unaltered, and *a* will be seen in its right place. Now accommodate the left eye for a point *f* [a needle in Hering's experiment] lying on the optical axis between it and *a*, only very near. The position of the left eye and its optical axis, as well as the place of the retinal image upon it . . . are wholly unaltered by this movement. But the consequence is that an apparent movement of the object occurs—a movement towards the left. As soon as we accommodate again for distance the object returns to its old place. Now what alters itself in this experiment is only the position of the closed right eye : its optical axis, when the effort is made to accommodate for the point *f*, also converges towards this point. . . . Conversely it is possible for me to make my optical axes diverge, even with closed eyes, so that in the above experiment the right eye should turn far to the right of *a*. This divergence is but slowly reached, and gives me therefore no illusory movement. But when I suddenly relax my effort to make it, and the right optical axis springs back to the parallel position, I immediately see the object which the left eye fixates shift its position towards the left. Thus not only the position of the seeing eye *a*, but also that of the closed eye *b*, influences our judgment of the direction in which the seen object

be confounded with a feeling in the other? It most assuredly can, for not only Donders and Adamük, by their
vivisections, but Hering by his exquisite optical experiments,
have proved that the apparatus of innervation for both
eyes is single, and that they function as one organ—a
double eye, according to Hering, or what Helmholtz calls
a *Cyclopenauge.* The retinal feelings of this double organ,
singly innervated, are naturally undistinguished as respects
our knowing whether they belong to the left retina or to
the right. We use them only to tell us where their objects
lie. It takes long practice directed specially *ad hoc* to
teach us on which retina the sensations severally fall. Similarly the different sensations which arise from the positions of the eyeballs are used exclusively as signs of the
position of objects ; an object directly fixated being localized habitually at the intersection of the two optical axes,
but without any separate consciousness on our part that
the position of one axis is different from another. All we
are aware of is a consolidated feeling of a certain 'strain'
in the eyeballs, accompanied by the perception that just
so far in front and so far to the right or to the left there is
an object which we see. So that a 'muscular' process in
one eye is as likely to combine with a retinal process in the
other eye to effect a perceptive judgment, as two processes
in one eye are likely so to combine.

Another piece of circumstantial evidence for the feelings
of innervation is that adduced by Professor Mach, as follows :

"If we stand on a bridge, and look at the water flowing beneath,
we usually feel ourselves at rest, whilst the water seems in motion.
Prolonged looking at the water, however, commonly has for its result
to make the bridge with the observer and surroundings suddenly seem
to move in the direction opposed to that of the water, whilst the water
itself assumes the appearance of standing still. The *relative* motion of
the objects is in both cases the same, and there must therefore be some

lies. The open eye remaining fixed, and the closed eye moving towards
the right or left, the object seen by the open eye appears also to move towards the right or left." (Physiol. Optik, pp. 607-8.)

adequate *physiological* ground why sometimes one, sometimes the other part of them is felt to move. In order to investigate the matter conveniently, I had the simple apparatus constructed which is represented in Fig. 86. An oil-cloth with a simple pattern is horizontally stretched over two cylinders (each 2 metres long and 3 feet apart) and kept in uniform motion by the help of a crank. Across the cloth, and some 30 cm. above it, is

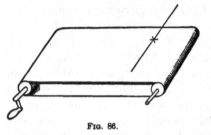

FIG. 86.

stretched a string, with a knot *x*, which serves as a fixation-point for the eye of the observer. If the observer *follow* with his eyes the pattern of the cloth as it moves, he sees it in movement, himself and the surroundings at rest. But if he looks at the *knot*, he soon feels as if the entire room were moving contrary to the direction of the cloth, whilst the latter seems to stand still. This change in the mode of looking comes about in more or less time according to one's momentary disposition, but usually it takes but a few seconds. If one once understands the point, one can make the two appearances alternate at will. Every following of the oil-cloth makes the observer stationary ; every fixation of the knot or *inattention to the oil-cloth, so that its pattern becomes blurred*, sets him in apparent motion." *

Professor Mach proceeds to explain the phenomenon as follows:

" Moving objects exert, as is well known, a peculiar motor stimulation upon the eye, they draw our attention and our look after them. If the look really follows them . . . we assume that they move. But if the eye, instead of following the moving objects, remains steadfastly at rest, it must be that the constant stimulus to motion which it receives is neutralized by an equally constant current of innervation flowing into its motor apparatus. But this is just what would happen if the steadfastly fixated point were itself moving uniformly in the other direction, and we were following it with our eyes. When this comes about, whatever motionless things are looked at must appear in motion." †

The knot *x*, the string, we ourselves, and all our sta-

---

* Beiträge zur Analyse der Empfindungen, p. 65.
† P. 68.

tionary surroundings thus appear in movement, according
to Mach, because we are constantly innervating our eyeballs to resist the *drag* exerted upon them by the pattern
or the flowing waves. I have myself repeated the observation many times above flowing streams, but have never succeeded in getting the full illusion as described by Mach.
I gain a sense of the movement of the bridge and of my
own body, but the river never seems absolutely to stop : it
still moves in one direction, whilst I float away in the other.
But, be the illusion partial or complete, a different explanation of it from Professor Mach's seems to me the
more natural one to adopt. The illusion is said to cease
when, our attention being fully fixed on the moving oil-cloth,
we perceive the latter for what it is; and to recommence, on
the contrary, when we perceive the oil-cloth as a vaguely
moving background behind an object which we directly
fixate and whose position with regard to our own body is
unchanged. This, however, is the sort of consciousness
which we have whenever we are ourselves borne in a vehicle,
on horseback, or in a boat. As we and our belongings go
one way, the *whole background* goes the other. I should
rather, therefore, explain Professor Mach's illusion as
similar to the illusion at railroad-stations described above
on page 90. The other train moves, but it makes ours seem
to move, because, filling the window as it does, it stands for
the time being as the total background. So here, the
water or oil-cloth stands for us as background *überhaupt*
whenever we seem to ourselves to be moving over it. The
relative motion felt by the retina is assigned to that one of
its components which we look at more in itself and less as
a mere *repoussoir*. This may be the knot above the oil-
cloth or the bridge beneath our feet, or it may be, on the
other hand, the oil-cloth's pattern or the surface of the
swirling stream. Similar changes may be produced in the
apparent motion of the moon and the clouds through which
it shines, by similarly altering the attention. Such alterations, however, in our conception of which part of the visual field is substantive object and which part background,
seem to have no connection with feelings of innervation. I

cannot, therefore, regard the observation of Prof. Mach as any proof that the latter feelings exist.*

The circumstantial evidence for the feeling of innervation thus seems to break down like the introspective evidence. But not only can we rebut experiments intended to prove it, we can also adduce experiments which disprove it. A person who moves a limb voluntarily must innervate it in any case, and if he feels the innervation he ought to be able to use the feeling to define what his limb is about, even though the limb itself were anæsthetic. If, however, the limb be totally anæsthetic, it turns out that he does not know at all how much work it performs in its contraction—in other words, he has no perception of the amount of innervation which he exerts. A patient examined by Messrs. Gley and Marillier beautifully showed this. His entire arms, and his trunk down to the navel, were insensible both superficially and deeply, but his arms were not paralyzed :

"We take three stone bottles—two of them are empty and weigh each 250 grams; the third is full of mercury and weighs 1850 grams. We ask L . . . to estimate their weight and tell us which is heaviest. He declares that he finds them all three alike. With many days of interval we made two series of six experiments each. The result was always the same. The experiment, it need hardly be said, was arranged in

---

* I owe the interpretation in the text to my friend and former student, Mr. E. S. Drown, whom I set to observe the phenomenon before I had observed it myself. Concerning the vacillations in our interpretation of relative motion over retina and skin, see above, p. 173.

Herr Münsterberg gives additional reasons against the feeling of innervation, of which I will quote a couple. First, our ideas of movement are all *faint* ideas, resembling in this the copies of sensations in memory. Were they feelings of the outgoing discharge, they would be original states of consciousness, not copies ; and ought by analogy to be *vivid* like other original states.—Second, our unstriped muscles yield no feelings in contracting, nor can they be contracted at will, differing thus in *two* peculiarities from the voluntary muscles. What more natural than to suppose that the two peculiarities hang together, and that the reason why we cannot contract our intestines, for example, at will, is, that we have no memory-images of how their contraction feels ? Were the supposed innervation-feeling always the 'mental cue,' one doesn't see why we might not have it even where, as here, the contractions themselves are unfelt, and why it might not bring the contractions about. (Die Willenshandlung, pp. 87-8.)

such wise that he could be informed neither by sight nor by hearing. He even declared, holding in his hand the bottleful of mercury, that he found it to have no weight. . . . We place successively in his hand (his eyes being still bandaged) a piece of modelling wax, a stick of hard wood, a thick India-rubber tube, a newspaper folded up lengthwise and rumpled, and we make him squeeze these several objects. He feels no difference of resistance and does not even perceive that anything is in his hand." *

M. Gley in another place † quotes experiments by Dr. Bloch which prove that the sense which we have of our limbs' position owes absolutely nothing to the feeling of innervation put forth. Dr. Bloch stood opposite the angle of a screen whose sides made an angle of about 90°, and tried to place his hands symmetrically, or so that both should fall on corresponding spots of the two screen-sides, which were marked with squares for the purpose. The average error being noted, one hand was then passively carried by an assistant to a spot on its screen-side, and the other actively sought the corresponding spot on the opposite side. The accuracy of the correspondence proved to be as great as when both arms were innervated voluntarily, showing that the consciousness of innervation in the first of the two experiments added nothing to the sense of the limbs' position. Dr. Bloch then tried, pressing a certain number of pages of a book between the thumb and fore-finger of one hand, to press an equal number between the same fingers of the other hand. He did this just as well when the fingers in question were drawn apart by India-rubber bands as when they were uninterfered with, showing that the physiologically much greater innervation-current required in the former case had no effect upon the conscious-ness of the movement made, so far as its spatial character at any rate was concerned.‡

---

* Revue Philosophique, XXIII. 442.

† *Ibid.* XX. 604.

‡ Herr Sternberg (Pflüger's Archiv, XXXVII. p. 1) thinks that he proves the feeling of innervation by the fact that when we have willed to make a movement we generally think that it is made. We have already seen some of the facts on pp. 105–6, above. S. cites from Exner the fact that if we put a piece of hard rubber between our back teeth and bite, our front teeth seem actually to approach each other, although it is physically impossible

On the whole, then, it seems as probable as anything can well be, that these feelings of innervation do not exist.

for them to do so. He proposes the following experiment: Lay the palm of the hand on a table with the forefinger overlapping its edge and flexed back as far as possible, whilst the table keeps the other fingers extended; then try to flex the terminal joint of the forefinger without looking. You do not do it, and yet you think that you do. Here again the innervation, according to the author, is felt as an executed movement. It seems to me, as I said in the previous place, that the illusion is in all these cases due to the inveterate association of ideas. Normally our will to move has always been followed by the sensation that we *have* moved, except when the simultaneous sensation of an external resistance was there. The result is that where we feel no external resistance, and the muscles and tendons tighten, the invariably associated idea is intense enough to be hallucinatory. In the experiment with the teeth, the resistance customarily met with when our masseters contract is a soft one. We do not close our teeth on a thing like hard rubber once in a million times; so when we do so, we imagine the habitual result.—Persons with *amputated limbs* more often than not continue to feel them as if they were still there, and can, moreover, give themselves the feeling of moving them at will. The life-long sensorial associate of the idea of 'working one's toes,' e.g. (uncorrected by any opposite sensation, since no real sensation of non-movement can come from non-existing toes), follows the idea and swallows it up. The man thinks that his toes are 'working' (cf. Proceedings of American Soc. for Psych. Research, p. 249).

Herr Loeb also comes to the rescue of the feeling of innervation with observations of his own made after my text was written, but they convince me no more than the arguments of others. Loeb's facts are these (Pflüger's Archiv, XLIV. p. 1): If we stand before a vertical surface, and if, with our hands *at different heights*, we *simultaneously* make with them what seem to us equally extensive movements, that movement always turns out really shorter which is made with the arm whose muscles (in virtue of the arm's position) are already the more contracted. The same result ensues when the arms are laterally unsymmetrical. Loeb assumes that both arms contract by virtue of a common innervation, but that although this innervation is relatively less effective upon the more contracted arm, our *feeling* of its equal strength overpowers the disparity of the incoming sensations of movement which the two limbs send back, and makes us think that the spaces they traverse are the same. "The sensation of the extent and direction of our voluntary movements depends accordingly upon the impulse of our will to move, and not upon the feelings set up by the motion in the active organ." Now if this is the elementary law which Loeb calls it, why does it only manifest its effect when both hands are moving simultaneously? Why not when the *same* hand makes *successive* movements? and especially why not when both hands move symmetrically or at the same level, but *one of them is weighted?* A weighted hand surely requires a stronger innervation than an unweighted one to move an equal distance upwards; and yet, as Loeb confesses, we do not tend to overestimate the path which it traverses under these circumstances. The fact is that the illusion which Loeb

If the motor cells are distinct structures, they are as insentient as the motor nerve-trunks are after the posterior roots are cut. If they are not distinct structures, but are only the last sensory cells, those at the 'mouth of the funnel,' * then their consciousness is that of kinæsthetic ideas and sensations merely, and this consciousness accompanies the *rise* of activity in them rather than its discharge. The entire content and material of our consciousness—consciousness of movement, as of all things else—is thus of peripheral origin, and came to us in the first instance through the peripheral nerves. If it be asked what we gain by this sensationalistic conclusion, I reply that we gain at any rate simplicity and uniformity. In the chapters on Space, on Belief, on the Emotions, we found sensation to be a much richer thing than is commonly supposed; and this chapter seems at this point to fall into line with those. Then, as for sensationalism being a degrading belief, which abolishes all inward originality and spontaneity, there is this

---

has studied is a complex resultant of many factors. One of them, it seems to me, is an instinctive tendency to *revert to the type of the bilateral movements of childhood.* In adult life we move our arms for the most part in alternation ; but in infancy the free movements of the arms are almost always similar on both sides, symmetrical when the direction of motion is horizontal, and with the hands on the same level when it is vertical. The most natural innervation, when the movements are rapidly performed, is one which takes the movement back to this form. Our *estimation* meanwhile of the lengths severally traversed by the two hands is mainly based, as such estimations with closed eyes usually are (see Loeb's own earlier paper, *Untersuchungen über den Fühlraum der Hand,* in Pflüger's Archiv, xli. 107), upon the apparent velocity and duration of the movement. The duration is the same for both hands, since the movements begin and end simultaneously. The velocities of the two hands are under the experimental conditions almost impossible of comparison. It is well known how imperfect a discrimination of *weights* we have when we 'heft' them simultaneously, one in either hand; and G. E. Müller has well shown (Pflüger's Archiv, xlv. 57) that the velocity of the lift is the main factor in determining our judgment of weight. It is hardly possible to conceive of more unfavorable conditions for making an accurate comparison of the length of two movements than those which govern the experiments which are under discussion. The only prominent sign is the duration, which would lead us to infer the equality of the two movements. We consequently deem them equal, though a native tendency in our motor centres keeps them from being so.

* This is by no means an unplausible opinion. See Vol I. p. 65.

to be said, that the advocates of inward spontaneity may be turning their backs on its real citadel, when they make a fight, on its behalf, for the consciousness of energy put forth in the outgoing discharge. Let there be no such consciousness ; let all our thoughts of movements be of sensational constitution; still in the emphasizing, choosing, and espousing of one of them rather than another, in the saying to it, 'be thou the reality for me,' there is ample scope for our inward initiative to be shown. Here, it seems to me, the true line between the passive materials and the activity of the spirit should be drawn. It is certainly false strategy to draw it between such ideas as are connected with the outgoing and such as are connected with the incoming neural wave.*

If the ideas by which we discriminate between one movement and another, at the instant of deciding in our mind which one we shall perform, are always of sensorial origin, then the question arises, "Of which sensorial order need they be?" It will be remembered that we distinguished two orders of kinæsthetic impression, the *remote* ones, made by the movement on the eye or ear or distant skin, etc., and the *resident* ones, made on the moving parts themselves, muscles, joints, etc. Now do resident images, exclusively, form what I have called the mental cue, or will remote ones equally suffice?

There can be no doubt whatever that the mental cue may be either an image of the resident or of the remote kind. Although, at the outset of our learning a movement, it would seem that the resident feelings must come strongly before consciousness (cf. p. 487), later this need not be the case. The rule, in fact, would seem to be that they tend to lapse

---

* Maine de Biran, Roger Collard, Sir John Herschel, Dr. Carpenter, Dr. Martineau, all seem to posit a force-sense by which, in becoming aware of an outer resistance to our will, we are taught the existence of an outer world. I hold that every peripheral sensation gives us an outer world. An insect crawling on our skin gives us as 'outward' an impression as a hundred pounds weighing on our back.—I have read M. A. Bertrand's criticism of my views (La Psychologie de l'Effort, 1889); but as he seems to think that I deny the *feeling* of effort altogether, I can get no profit from it, despite his charming way of saying things.

more and more from consciousness, and that the more practised we become in a movement, the more 'remote' do the ideas become which form its mental cue. What we are *interested* in is what sticks in our consciousness; everything else we get rid of as quickly as we can. Our resident feelings of movement have no substantive interest for us at all, as a rule. What interest us are the ends which the movement is to attain. Such an end is generally an outer impression on the eye or ear, or sometimes on the skin, nose, or palate. Now let the idea of the end associate itself definitely with the right motor innervation, and the thought of the innervation's *resident* effects will become as great an encumbrance as we formerly concluded that the feeling of the innervation itself would be. The mind does not need it; the end alone is enough.

The idea of the end, then, tends more and more to make itself all-sufficient. Or, at any rate, if the kinæsthetic ideas are called up at all, they are so swamped in the vivid kinæsthetic feelings by which they are immediately overtaken that we have no time to be aware of their separate existence. As I write, I have no anticipation, as a thing distinct from my sensation, of either the look or the digital feel of the letters which flow from my pen. The words chime on my mental *ear*, as it were, before I write them, but not on my mental eye or hand. This comes from the rapidity with which often-repeated movements follow on their mental cue. An end consented to as soon as conceived innervates directly the centre of the first movement of the chain which leads to its accomplishment, and then the whole chain rattles off *quasi*-reflexly, as was described on pp. 115–6 of Vol. I.

The reader will certainly recognize this to be true in all fluent and unhesitating voluntary acts. The only special fiat there is at the outset of the performance. A man says to himself, "I must change my shirt," and involuntarily he has taken off his coat, and his fingers are at work in their accustomed manner on his waistcoat-buttons, etc.; or we say, "I must go downstairs," and ere we know it we have risen, walked, and turned the handle of the door;—all through the idea of an end coupled with a series of guiding

sensations which successively arise. It would seem indeed
that we fail of accuracy and certainty in our attainment of
the end whenever we are preoccupied with much ideal consciousness of the means. We walk a beam the better the
less we think of the position of our feet upon it. We pitch
or catch, we shoot or chop the better the less tactile and
muscular (the less resident), and the more exclusively optical,
(the more remote) our consciousness is. Keep your *eye* on
the place aimed at, and your hand will fetch it; think of
your hand, and you will very likely miss your aim. Dr.
Southard found that he could touch a spot with a pencil-
point more accurately with a visual than with a tactile
mental cue. In the former case he looked at a small
object and closed his eyes before trying to touch it. In
the latter case he *placed* it with closed eyes, and then after
removing his hand tried to touch it again. The average
error with touch (when the results were most favorable)
was 17.13 mm. With sight it was only 12.37 mm.*—All
these are plain results of introspection and observation.
By what neural machinery they are made possible we need
not, at this present stage, inquire.

In Chapter XVIII we saw how enormously individuals
differ in respect to their mental imagery. In the type of
imagination called *tactile* by the French authors, it is probable that the kinæsthetic ideas are more prominent than in
my account. We must not expect too great a uniformity
in individual accounts, nor wrangle overmuch as to which
one 'truly' represents the process.†

---

* Bowditch and Southard in Journal of Physiology, vol. III. No. 3. It
was found in these experiments that the maximum of accuracy was reached
when two seconds of time elapsed between locating the object by eye or
hand and starting to touch it. When the mark was located with one
hand, and the other hand had to touch it, the error was considerably
greater than when the same hand both located and touched it.

† The same caution must be shown in discussing pathological cases.
There are remarkable discrepancies in the effects of peripheral anæsthesia
upon the voluntary power. Such cases as I quoted in the text (p. 490) are
by no means the only type. In those cases the patients could move their
limbs accurately when the eyes were open, and inaccurately when they
were shut. In other cases, however, the anæsthetic patients *cannot move
their limbs at all* when the eyes are shut. (For reports of two such cases see
Bastian in 'Brain,' Binet in Rev. Philos., xxv. 478.) M. Binet explains

I trust that I have now made clear what that 'idea of a movement' is which must precede it in order that it be voluntary. It is not the thought of the innervation which the movement requires. It is the anticipation of the movement's sensible effects, resident or remote, and sometimes very remote indeed. Such anticipations, to say the least, determine *what* our movements shall be. I have spoken all along as if they also might determine *that* they shall be. This, no doubt, has disconcerted many readers, for it certainly seems as if a special fiat, or consent to the movement were required in addition to the mere conception of it, in many cases of volition ; and this fiat I have altogether left out of my account. This leads us to the next point in the

these (hysterical) cases as requiring the 'dynamogenic' stimulus of light (see above, p. 377). They *might*, however, be cases of such congenitally defective optical imagination that the 'mental cue' was normally 'tactile ;' and that when this tactile cue failed through functional inertness of the kinæsthetic centres, the only optical cue strong enough to determine the discharge had to be an actual *sensation* of the eye.—There is still a third class of cases in which the limbs have lost all sensibility, even for movements passively imprinted, but in which voluntary movements can be accurately executed even when the eyes are closed. MM. Binet and Féré have reported some of these interesting cases, which are found amongst the hysterical hemianæsthetics. They can, for example, write accurately at will, although their eyes are closed and they have no feeling of the writing taking place, and many of them do not know when it begins or stops. Asked to write repeatedly the letter *a*, and then say how many times they have written it, some are able to assign the number and some are not. Some of them admit that they are guided by visual imagination of what is being done. Cf. Archives de Physiologie, Oct. 1887, pp. 363-5. Now it would seem at first sight that feelings of outgoing innervation must exist in these cases and be kept account of. There are no other guiding impressions, either immediate or remote, of which the patient is conscious ; and unless feelings of innervation be there, the writing would seem miraculous. But if such feelings are present in these cases, and suffice to direct accurately the succession of movements, why do they not suffice in those other anæsthetic cases in which movement becomes disorderly when the eyes are closed. *Innervation* is there, or there would be no movement ; why is the *feeling* of the innervation gone ? The truth seems to be, as M. Binet supposes (Rev. Philos., xxiii. p. 479), that these cases are not arguments for the feeling of innervation. They are pathological curiosities ; and the patients are not really anæsthetic, but are victims of that curious dissociation or splitting-off of one part of their consciousness from the rest which we are just begin to understand, thanks to Messrs. Janet, Binet, and Gurney, and in which the split-off part (in this case the kinæsthetic sensations) may nevertheless remain to produce its usual effects. Compare what was said above, p. 491.

psychology of the Will. It can be the more easily treated now that we have got rid of so much tedious preliminary matter.

IDEO-MOTOR ACTION.

The question is this : *Is the bare idea of a movement's sensible effects its sufficient mental cue (p. 497), or must there be an additional mental antecedent, in the shape of a fiat, decision, consent, volitional mandate, or other synonymous phenomenon of consciousness, before the movement can follow ?*

I answer : Sometimes the bare idea is sufficient, but sometimes an additional conscious element, in the shape of a fiat, mandate, or express consent, has to intervene and precede the movement. The cases without a fiat constitute the more fundamental, because the more simple, variety. The others involve a special complication, which must be fully discussed at the proper time. For the present let us turn to *ideo-motor action*, as it has been termed, or the sequence of movement upon the mere thought of it, as the type of the process of volition.

Wherever movement follows *unhesitatingly and immediately* the notion of it in the mind, we have ideo-motor action. We are then aware of nothing between the conception and the execution. All sorts of neuro-muscular processes come between, of course, but we know absolutely nothing of them. We think the act, and it is done ; and that is all that introspection tells us of the matter. Dr. Carpenter, who first used, I believe, the name of ideo-motor action, placed it, if I mistake not, among the curiosities of our mental life. The truth is that it is no curiosity, but simply the normal process stripped of disguise. Whilst talking I become conscious of a pin on the floor, or of some dust on my sleeve. Without interrupting the conversation I brush away the dust or pick up the pin. I make no express resolve, but the mere perception of the object and the fleeting notion of the act seem of themselves to bring the latter about. Similarly, I sit at table after dinner and find myself from time to time taking nuts or raisins out of the dish and eating them. My dinner properly is over, and in the heat of the conversation I am hardly aware of what I do, but the perception of the fruit and the fleeting notion that I may eat it seem fatally to bring the act about. There is certainly no express fiat here ; any more than there is in all those habitual goings and comings and rearrangements of ourselves which fill every hour of the day, and which incoming sensations instigate so immediately that it is often difficult to decide whether not to call them reflex rather than voluntary acts. We have seen in Chapter IV that the intermediary terms of an habitual series of acts leading to an end are apt to be of this *quasi*-automatic sort. As Lotze says :

" We see in writing or piano-playing a great number of very complicated movements following quickly one upon the other, the instigative representations of which remained scarcely a second in consciousness, certainly not long enough to awaken any other volition than the general one of resigning one's self without reserve to the passing over of representation into action. All the acts of our daily life happen in this wise : Our standing up, walking, talking, all this never demands a distinct impulse of the will, but is adequately brought about by the pure flux of thought." *

In all this the determining condition of the unhesitating and resistless sequence of the act seems to be *the absence of any conflicting notion in the mind.* Either there is nothing else at all in the mind, or what is there does not conflict. The hypnotic subject realizes the former condition. Ask him what he is thinking about, and ten to one he will reply ' nothing.' The consequence is that he both believes everything he is told, and performs every act that is suggested. The suggestion may be a vocal command, or it may be the performance before him of the movement required. Hypnotic subjects in certain conditions repeat whatever they

---

* Medicinische Psychologie, p. 293. In his admirably acute chapter on the Will this author has most explicitly maintained the position that what we call muscular exertion is an afferent and not an efferent feeling ; " We must affirm universally that in the muscular feeling we are not sensible of the *force* on its way to produce an effect, but only of the *sufferance* already produced in our movable organs, the muscles, after the force has, in a manner unobservable by us, exerted upon them its causality " (p. 311). How often the battles of psychology have to be fought over again, each time with heavier armies and bigger trains, though not always with such able generals !

hear you say, and imitate whatever they see you do. Dr. Féré says that certain waking persons of neurotic type, if one repeatedly close and open one's hand before their eyes, soon begin to have corresponding feelings in their own fingers, and presently begin irresistibly to execute the movements which they see. Under these conditions of 'preparation' Dr. Féré found that his subjects could squeeze the hand-dynamometer much more strongly than when abruptly invited to do so. A few *passive* repetitions of a movement will enable many enfeebled patients to execute it actively with greater strength. These observations beautifully show how the mere quickening of kinæsthetic ideas is equivalent to a certain amount of tension towards discharge in the centres.*

We know what it is to get out of bed on a freezing morning in a room without a fire, and how the very vital principle within us protests against the ordeal. Probably most persons have lain on certain mornings for an hour at a time unable to brace themselves to the resolve. We think how late we shall be, how the duties of the day will suffer; we say, "I *must* get up, this is ignominious," etc.; but still the warm couch feels too delicious, the cold outside too cruel, and resolution faints away and postpones itself again and again just as it seemed on the verge of bursting the resistance and passing over into the decisive act. Now how do we *ever* get up under such circumstances? If I may generalize from my own experience, we more often than not get up without any struggle or decision at all. We suddenly find that we *have* got up. A fortunate lapse of consciousness occurs; we forget both the warmth and the cold; we fall into some revery connected with the day's life, in the course of which the idea flashes across us, "Hollo! I must lie here no longer"—an idea which at that lucky instant awakens no contradictory or paralyzing suggestions, and consequently produces immediately its appropriate motor effects. It was our acute consciousness of both the warmth and the cold during the period of struggle,

---

* Ch. Féré: Sensation et Mouvement (1887), chapter III.

which paralyzed our activity then and kept our idea of rising in the condition of *wish* and not of *will*. The moment these inhibitory ideas ceased, the original idea exerted its effects.

This case seems to me to contain in miniature form the data for an entire psychology of volition. It was in fact through meditating on the phenomenon in my own person that I first became convinced of the truth of the doctrine which these pages present, and which I need here illustrate by no farther examples.* The reason why that doctrine is not a self-evident truth is that we have so many ideas which *do not* result in action. But it will be seen that in every such case, without exception, that is because other ideas simultaneously present rob them of their impulsive power. But even here, and when a movement is inhibited from *completely* taking place by contrary ideas, it will *incipiently* take place. To quote Lotze once more :

"The spectator accompanies the throwing of a billiard-ball, or the thrust of the swordsman, with slight movements of his arm; the untaught narrator tells his story with many gesticulations; the reader while absorbed in the perusal of a battle-scene feels a slight tension run through his muscular system, keeping time as it were with the actions he is reading of. These results become the more marked the more we are absorbed in thinking of the movements which suggest them; they grow fainter exactly in proportion as a complex consciousness, under the dominion of a crowd of other representations, withstands the passing over of mental contemplation into outward action."

The ' willing-game,' the exhibitions of so-called 'mind-reading,' or more properly muscle-reading, which have lately grown so fashionable, are based on this incipient obedience of muscular contraction to idea, even when the deliberate intention is that no contraction shall occur.†

---

* Professor A. Bain (Senses and Intellect, pp. 336–48) and Dr. W. B. Carpenter (Mental Physiology, chap. VI) give examples in abundance.

† For a full account, by an expert, of the 'willing-game,' see Mr. Stuart Cumberland's article: A Thought-reader's Experiences in the Nineteenth century, XX. 867. M. Gley has given a good example of ideo-motor action in the Bulletins de la Société de Psychologie Physiologique for 1889. Tell a person to think intently of a certain name, and saying that you will then force her to write it, let her hold a pencil, and do you yourself hold her hand. She will then probably trace the name involuntarily, believing that you are forcing her to do it.

We may then lay it down for certain that *every repre-sentation of a movement awakens in some degree the actual movement which is its object; and awakens it in a maximum degree whenever it is not kept from so doing by an antagonis-tic representation present simultaneously to the mind.*

The express fiat, or act of mental consent to the move-ment, comes in when the neutralization of the antagonistic and inhibitory idea is required. But that there is no express fiat needed when the conditions are simple, the reader ought now to be convinced. Lest, however, he should still share the common prejudice that voluntary action without 'exertion of will-power' is Hamlet with the prince's part left out, I will make a few farther remarks. The first point to start from in understanding voluntary action, and the possible occurrence of it with no fiat or express resolve, is the fact that consciousness is *in its very nature impulsive.** We do not have a sensation or a thought and then have to *add* something dynamic to it to get a movement. Every pulse of feeling which we have is the correlate of some neural activity that is already on its way to instigate a movement. Our sensations and thoughts are but cross-sections, as it were, of currents whose essential consequence is motion, and which no sooner run in at one nerve than they run out again at another. The popular notion that mere conscious-ness as such is not essentially a forerunner of activity, that the latter must result from some superadded 'will-force,' is a very natural inference from those special cases in which we think of an act for an indefinite length of time without the action taking place. These cases, however, are not the norm; they are cases of inhibition by antagonistic

---

* I abstract here from the fact that a certain *intensity* of the conscious-ness is required for its impulsiveness to be effective in a complete degree. There is an inertia in the motor processes as in all other natural things. In certain individuals, and at certain times (disease, fatigue), the inertia is unusually great, and we may then have ideas of action which produce no visible act, but discharge themselves into merely nascent dispositions to activity or into emotional expression. The inertia of the motor parts here plays the same rôle as is elsewhere played by antagonistic ideas. We shall consider this restrictive inertia later on; it obviously introduces no essen-tial alteration into the law which the text lays down.

thoughts. When the blocking is released we feel as if an inward spring were let loose, and this is the additional impulse or *fiat* upon which the act effectively succeeds. We shall study anon the blocking and its release. Our higher thought is full of it. But where there is no blocking, there is naturally no hiatus between the thought-process and the motor discharge. *Movement is the natural immediate effect of feeling, irrespective of what the quality of the feeling may be. It is so in reflex action, it is so in emotional expression, it is so in the voluntary life.* Ideo-motor action is thus no paradox, to be softened or explained away. It obeys the type of all conscious action, and from it one must start to explain action in which a special fiat is involved.

It may be remarked in passing, that the inhibition of a movement no more involves an express effort or command than its execution does. Either of them *may* require it. But in all simple and ordinary cases, just as the bare presence of one idea prompts a movement, so the bare presence of another idea will prevent its taking place. Try to feel as if you were crooking your finger, whilst keeping it straight. In a minute it will fairly tingle with the imaginary change of position; yet it will not sensibly move, because *its not really moving* is also a part of what you have in mind. Drop *this* idea, think of the movement purely and simply, with all brakes off; and, presto! it takes place with no effort at all.

A waking man's behavior is thus at all times the resultant of two opposing neural forces. With unimaginable fineness some currents among the cells and fibres of his brain are playing on his motor nerves, whilst other currents, as unimaginably fine, are playing on the first currents, damming or helping them, altering their direction or their speed. The upshot of it all is, that whilst the currents must always end by being drained off through *some* motor nerves, they are drained off sometimes through one set and sometimes through another; and sometimes they keep each other in equilibrium so long that a superficial observer may think they are not drained off at all. Such an observer must remember, however, that from the physiological point of view a gesture, an expression of the brow, or an expulsion of the breath are movements as much as an act of locomotion is. A king's breath slays as well as an assassin's blow ; and the outpouring of those currents which the magic imponderable streaming of our ideas accompanies need not always be of an explosive or otherwise physically conspicuous kind.

ACTION AFTER DELIBERATION.

We are now in a position to describe *what happens in deliberate action,* or when the mind is the seat of many ideas related to each other in antagonistic or in favorable ways.* One of the ideas is that of an act. By itself this idea would prompt a movement ; some of the additional considerations, however, which are present to consciousness block the motor discharge, whilst others, on the contrary, solicit it to take place. The result is that peculiar feeling of inward unrest known as *indecision.* Fortunately it is too familiar to need description, for to describe it would be impossible. As long as it lasts, with the various objects before the attention, we are said to *deliberate ;* and when finally the original suggestion either prevails and makes the movement take place, or gets definitively quenched by its antagonists, we are said to *decide,* or to *utter our voluntary fiat* in favor of one or the other course. The reinforcing and inhibiting ideas meanwhile are termed the *reasons* or *motives* by which the decision is brought about.

The process of deliberation contains endless degrees of complication. At every moment of it our consciousness is of an extremely complex object, namely the existence of the whole set of motives and their conflict, as explained on p. 275 of Vol. I. Of this object, the totality of which is realized more or less dimly all the while, certain parts stand out more or less sharply at one moment in the

---

* I use the common phraseology here for mere convenience' sake. The reader who has made himself acquainted with Chapter IX will always understand, when he hears of many ideas simultaneously present to the mind and acting upon each other, that what is really meant is a mind with one idea before it, of many objects, purposes, reasons, motives related to each other, some in a harmonious and some in an antagonistic way. With this caution I shall not hesitate from time to time to fall into the popular Lockian speech, erroneous though I believe it to be.

foreground, and at another moment other parts, in consequence of the oscillations of our attention, and of the ' associative ' flow of our ideas. But no matter how sharp the
foreground-reasons may be, or how imminently close to
bursting through the dam and carrying the motor consequences their own way, the background, however dimly felt,
is always there ; and its presence (so long as the indecision
actually lasts) serves as an effective check upon the irrevocable discharge. The deliberation may last for weeks or
months, occupying at intervals the mind. The motives
which yesterday seemed full of urgency and blood and life
to-day feel strangely weak and pale and dead. But as little
to-day as to-morrow is the question finally resolved. Something tells us that all this is provisional ; that the weakened
reasons will wax strong again, and the stronger weaken ;
that equilibrium is unreached ; that testing our reasons, not
obeying them, is still the order of the day, and that we
must wait awhile, patient or impatiently, until our mind
is made up ' for good and all.' This inclining first to one
then to another future, both of which we represent as possible, resembles the oscillations to and fro of a material
body within the limits of its elasticity. There is inward
strain, but no outward rapture. And this condition,
plainly enough, is susceptible of indefinite continuance, as
well in the physical mass as in the mind. If the elasticity
give way, however, if the dam ever do break, and the currents burst the crust, vacillation is over and decision is
irrevocably there.

The decision may come in either of many modes. I
will try briefly to sketch the most characteristic types of it,
merely warning the reader that this is only an introspective
account of symptoms and phenomena, and that all questions of causal agency, whether neural or spiritual, are rele-
gated to a later page.

The particular reasons for or against action are of course
infinitely various in concrete cases. But certain motives
are more or less constantly in play. One of these is *im-
patience of the deliberative state;* or to express it otherwise,
proneness to act or to decide merely because action and

decision are, as such, agreeable, and relieve the tension of doubt and hesitancy. Thus it comes that we will often take any course whatever which happens to be most vividly before our minds, at the moment when this impulse to decisive action becomes extreme.

Against this impulse we have the *dread of the irrevocable,* which often engenders a type of character incapable of prompt and vigorous resolve, except perhaps when surprised into sudden activity. These two opposing motives twine round whatever other motives may be present at the moment when decision is imminent, and tend to precipitate or retard it. The conflict of these motives so far as they alone affect the matter of decision is a conflict as to *when* it shall occur. One says ' now,' the other says ' not yet.'

Another constant component of the web of motivation is the impulse to persist in a decision once made. There is no more remarkable difference in human character than that between resolute and irresolute natures. Neither the physiological nor the psychical grounds of this difference have yet been analyzed. Its symptom is that whereas in the irresolute all decisions are provisional and liable to be reversed, in the resolute they are settled once for all and not disturbed again. Now into every one's deliberations the representation of one alternative will often enter with such sudden force as to carry the imagination with itself exclusively, and to produce an apparently settled decision in its own favor. These premature and spurious decisions are of course known to everyone. They often seem ridiculous in the light of the considerations that succeed them. But it cannot be denied that in the resolute type of character the accident that one of them has once been made does afterwards enter as a motive additional to the more genuine reasons why it should not be revoked, or if provisionally revoked, why it should be made again. How many of us persist in a precipitate course which, but for a moment of heedlessness, we might never have entered upon, simply because we hate to ' change our mind.'

FIVE TYPES OF DECISION.

Turning now to the form of the decision itself, we may distinguish four chief types. The first may be called *the reasonable type.* It is that of those cases in which the arguments for and against a given course seem gradually and almost insensibly to settle themselves in the mind and to end by leaving a clear balance in favor of one alternative, which alternative we then adopt without effort or constraint. Until this rational balancing of the books is consummated we have a calm feeling that the evidence is not yet all in, and this keeps action in suspense. But some day we wake with the sense that we see the thing rightly, that no new light will be thrown on the subject by farther delay, and that the matter had better be settled *now.* In this easy transition from doubt to assurance we seem to ourselves almost passive; the 'reasons which decide us appearing to flow in from the nature of things, and to owe nothing to our will. We have, however, a perfect sense of being *free*, in that we are devoid of any feeling of coercion. The conclusive reason for the decision in these cases usually is the discovery that we can refer the case to a *class* upon which we are accustomed to act unhesitatingly in a certain stereotyped way. It may be said in general that a great part of every deliberation consists in the turning over of all the possible modes of *conceiving* the doing or not doing of the act in point. The moment we hit upon a conception which lets us apply some principle of action which is a fixed and stable part of our Ego, our state of doubt is at an end. Persons of authority, who have to make many decisions in the day, carry with them a set of heads of classification, each bearing its motor consequence, and under these they seek as far as possible to range each new emergency as it occurs. It is where the emergency belongs to a species without precedent, to which consequently no cut-and-dried maxim will apply, that we feel most at a loss, and are distressed at the indeterminateness of our task. As soon, however, as we see our way to a familiar classification, we are at ease again. *In action as in reasoning, then, the great thing is the quest of the right conception.* The concrete dilemmas do not come to us with labels gummed upon their backs. We may name them by many names. The wise man is he who succeeds in finding the name which suits the needs of the particular occasion best. A 'reasonable' character is one who has a store of stable and worthy ends, and who does not decide about an action till he has calmly ascertained whether it be ministerial or detrimental to any one of these.

In the next two types of decision, the final fiat occurs before the evidence is all 'in.' It often happens that no paramount and authoritative reason for either course will come. Either seems a case of a Good, and there is no umpire as to which good should yield its place to the other. We grow tired of long hesitation and inconclusiveness, and the hour may come when we feel that even a bad decision is better than no decision at all. Under these conditions it will often happen that some accidental circumstance, supervening at a particular movement upon our mental weariness, will upset the balance in the direction of one of the alternatives, to which then we feel ourselves committed, although an opposite accident at the same time might have produced the opposite result.

In the *second type* of case our feeling is to a certain extent that of letting ourselves drift with a certain indifferent acquiescence in a direction accidentally determined *from without*, with the conviction that, after all, we might as well stand by this course as by the other, and that things are in any event sure to turn out sufficiently right.

In the third type the determination seems equally accidental, but it comes from within, and not from without. It often happens, when the absence of imperative principle is perplexing and suspense distracting, that we find ourselves acting, as it were, automatically, and as if by a spontaneous discharge of our nerves, in the direction of one of the horns of the dilemma. But so exciting is this sense of motion after our intolerable pent-up state, that we eagerly throw ourselves into it. 'Forward now!' we inwardly cry, 'though the heavens fall.' This reckless and exultant espousal of an energy so little premeditated by us that we feel rather like passive spectators cheering on the display of some extraneous force than like voluntary agents, is a type of decision too abrupt and tumultuous to occur often in humdrum and cool-blooded natures. But it is probably frequent in persons of strong emotional endowment and unstable or vacillating character. And in men of the world-shaking type, the Napoleons, Luthers, etc., in whom tenacious passion combines with ebullient activity, when by any chance the passion's outlet has been dammed by scruples or apprehensions, the resolution is probably often of this catastrophic kind. The flood breaks quite unexpectedly through the dam. That it should so often do so is quite sufficient to account for the tendency of these characters to a fatalistic mood of mind. And the fatalistic mood itself is sure to reinforce the strength of the energy just started on its exciting path of discharge.

There is a *fourth form* of decision, which often ends deliberation as suddenly as the third form does. It comes when, in consequence of some outer experience or some inexplicable inward charge, *we suddenly pass from the easy and careless to the sober and strenuous mood*, or possibly the other way. The whole scale of values of our motives and impulses then undergoes a change like that which a change of the observer's level produces on a view. The most sobering possible agents are objects of grief and fear. When one of these affects us, all 'light fantastic' notions lose their motive power, all solemn ones find theirs multiplied many-fold. The consequence is an instant abandonment of the more trivial projects with which we had been dallying, and an instant practical acceptance of the more grim and earnest alternative which till then could not extort our mind's consent. All those 'changes of heart,' 'awakenings of conscience,' etc., which make new men of so many of us, may be classed under this head. The character abruptly rises to another 'level,' and deliberation comes to an immediate end.*

---

* My attention was first emphatically called to this class of decisions by my colleague, Professor C. C. Everett.

In the *fifth and final type* of decision, the feeling that the evidence is all in, and that reason has balanced the books, may be either present or absent. But in either case we feel, in deciding, as if we ourselves by our own wilful act inclined the beam; in the former case by adding our living effort to the weight of the logical reason which, taken alone, seems powerless to make the act discharge; in the latter by a kind of creative contribution of something instead of a reason which does a reason's work. The slow dead heave of the will that is felt in these instances makes of them a class altogether different subjectively from all the three preceding classes. What the heave of the will betokens metaphysically, what the effort might lead us to infer about a will-power distinct from motives, are not matters that concern us yet. Subjectively and phenomenally, the *feeling of effort*, absent from the former decisions, accompanies these. Whether it be the dreary resignation for the sake of austere and naked duty of all sorts of rich mundane delights, or whether it be the heavy resolve that of two mutually exclusive trains of future fact, both sweet and good, and with no strictly objective or imperative principle of choice between them, one shall forevermore become impossible, while the other shall become reality, it is a desolate and acrid sort of act, an excursion into a lonesome moral wilderness. If examined closely, its chief difference from the three former cases appears to be that in those cases the mind at the moment of deciding on the triumphant alternative dropped the other one wholly or nearly out of sight, whereas here both alternatives are steadily held in view, and in the very act of murdering the vanquished possibility the chooser realizes how much in that instant he is making himself lose. It is deliberately driving a thorn into one's flesh; and the sense of *inward effort* with which the act is accompanied is an element which sets the fourth type of decision in strong contrast with the previous three varieties, and makes of it an altogether peculiar sort of mental phenomenon. The immense majority of human decisions are decisions without effort. In comparatively few of them, in most people, does effort accompany the final act. We are, I think, misled into supposing that effort is more frequent than it is, by the fact that *during deliberation* we so often have a feeling of how great an effort it would take to make a decision *now.* Later, after the decision has made itself with ease, we recollect this and erroneously suppose the effort also to have been made then.

The existence of the effort as a phenomenal fact in our consciousness cannot of course be doubted or denied. Its significance, on the other hand, is a matter about which the gravest difference of opinion prevails. Questions as momentous as that of the very existence of spiritual causality, as vast as that of universal predestination or free-will, depend on its interpretation. It therefore becomes essential that we study with some care the conditions under which the feeling of volitional effort is found.

THE FEELING OF EFFORT.

When, awhile back (p. 526), I said that *consciousness* (or the neural process which goes with it) *is in its very nature impulsive,* I added in a note the proviso that *it must be sufficiently intense.* Now there are remarkable differences in the power of different sorts of consciousness to excite movement. The intensity of some feelings is practically apt to be below the discharging point, whilst that of others is apt to be above it. By practically apt, I mean apt under ordinary circumstances. These circumstances may be habitual inhibitions, like that comfortable feeling of the *dolce far niente* which gives to each and all of us a certain dose of laziness only to be overcome by the acuteness of the impulsive spur; or they may consist in the native inertia, or internal resistance, of the motor centres themselves making explosion impossible until a certain inward tension has been reached and overpast. These conditions may vary from one person to another and in the same person from time to time. The neural inertia may wax or wane, and the habitual inhibitions dwindle or augment. The intensity of particular thought-processes and stimulations may also change independently, and particular paths of association grow more pervious or less so. There thus result great possibilities of alteration in the actual impulsive efficacy of particular motives compared with others. It is where the normally less efficacious motive becomes more efficacious and the normally more efficacious one less so that actions ordinarily effortless, or abstinences ordinarily easy, either become impossible or are effected, if at all, by the expenditure of effort. A little more description will make it plainer what these cases are.

There is a certain normal ratio in the impulsive power of different sorts of motive, which characterizes what may be called ordinary healthiness of will, and which is departed from only at exceptional times or by exceptional individuals. The states of mind which normally possess the most impulsive quality are either those which represent objects of passion, appetite, or emotion—objects of instinctive reaction, in short; or they are feelings or ideas of pleasure or of pain; or ideas which for any reason we have grown accustomed to obey so that the habit of reacting on them is ingrained; or finally, in comparison with ideas of remoter objects, they are ideas of objects present or near in space and time. Compared with these various objects, all far-off considerations, all highly abstract conceptions, unaccustomed reasons, and motives foreign to the instinctive history of the race, have little or no impulsive power. They prevail, when they ever do prevail, *with effort; and the normal,* as distinguished from the pathological, *sphere of effort is thus found wherever non-instinctive motives to behavior are to rule the day.*

Healthiness of will moreover requires a certain amount of complication in the process which precedes the fiat or the act. Each stimulus or idea, at the same time that it wakens its own impulse, must arouse other ideas (associated and consequential) with their impulses, and action must follow, neither too slowly nor too rapidly, as the resultant of all the forces thus engaged. Even when the decision is very prompt, there is thus a sort of preliminary survey of the field and a vision of which course is best before the fiat comes. And where the will is healthy, *the vision must be right* (i.e., the motives must be on the whole in a normal or not too unusual ratio to each other), *and the action must obey the vision's lead.*

Unhealthiness of will may thus come about in many ways. The action may follow the stimulus or idea too rapidly, leaving no time for the arousal of restraining associates—*we then have a precipitate will.* Or, although the associates may come, the ratio which the impulsive and inhibitive forces normally bear to each other may be distorted, and we then have *a will which is perverse.* The perversity, in turn, may be due to either of many causes—too much intensity, or too little, here; too much or too little inertia there; or elsewhere too much or too little inhibitory power. *If we compare the outward symptoms of perversity together, they fall into two groups,* in one of which normal actions are impossible, and in the other abnormal ones are irrepressible. Briefly, *we may call them respectively the obstructed and the explosive will.*

It must be kept in mind, however, that since the resultant action is always due to the *ratio* between the obstructive and the explosive forces which are present, we never can tell by the mere outward symptoms to what *elementary* cause the perversion of a man's will may be due, whether to an increase of one component or a diminution of the other. One may grow explosive as readily by losing the usual brakes as by getting up more of the impulsive steam ; and one may find things impossible as well through the enfeeblement of the original desire as through the advent of new lions in the path. As Dr. Clouston says, " the driver may be so weak that he cannot control well-broken horses, or the horses may be so hard-mouthed that no driver can pull them up." In some concrete cases (whether of explosive or of obstructed will) it is difficult to tell whether the trouble is due to inhibitory or to impulsive change. Generally, however, we can make a plausible guess at the truth.

THE EXPLOSIVE WILL.

There is a normal type of character, for example, in which impulses seem to discharge so promptly into movements that inhibitions get no time to arise. These are the 'dare-devil' and 'mercurial' temperaments, overflowing with animation, and fizzling with talk, which are so common in the Latin and Celtic races, and with which the cold-blooded and long-headed English character forms so marked a contrast. Monkeys these people seem to us, whilst we seem to them reptilian. It is quite impossible to judge, as between an obstructed and an explosive individual, which has the greatest sum of vital energy. An explosive Italian with good perception and intellect will cut a figure as a perfectly tremendous fellow, on an inward capital that could be tucked away inside of an obstructed Yankee and hardly let you know that it was there. He will be the king of his company, sing all the songs and make all the speeches, lead the parties, carry out the practical jokes, kiss all the girls, fight the men, and, if need be, lead the forlorn hopes and enterprises, so that an onlooker would think he has more life in his little finger than can exist in the whole body of a correct judicious fellow. But the judicious fellow all the while may have all these possibilities and more besides, ready to break out in the same or even a more violent way, if only the brakes were taken off. It is the absence of scruples, of consequences, of considerations, the extraordinary simplification of each moment's mental outlook, that gives to the explosive individual such motor energy and ease; it need not be the greater intensity of any of his passions, motives, or thoughts. As mental evolution goes on, the complexity of human consciousness grows ever greater, and with it the multiplication of the inhibitions to which every impulse is exposed. But this predominance of inhibition has a bad as well as a good side; and if a man's impulses are in the main orderly as well as prompt, if he has courage to accept their consequences, and intellect to lead them to a successful end, he is all the better for his hair-trigger organization, and for not being 'sicklied o'er with the pale cast of thought.' Many of the most successful military and revolutionary characters in history have belonged to this simple but quick-witted impulsive type. Problems come much harder to reflective and inhibitive minds. They can, it is true, solve much vaster problems; and they can avoid many a mistake to which the men of impulse are exposed. But when the latter do not make mistakes, or when they are always able to retrieve them, theirs is one of the most engaging and indispensable of human types.*

In infancy, and in certain conditions of exhaustion as well as in peculiar pathological states, the inhibitory power may fail to arrest the explosions of the impulsive discharge. We have then an explosive temperament temporarily realized in an individual who at other times may be of a relatively obstructed type. I cannot do better here than copy a few pages from Dr. Clouston's excellent work : †

"Take a child of six months, and there is absolutely no such brain-power existent as mental inhibition ; no desire or tendency is stopped by a mental act. . . . At a year old the rudiments of the great faculty of self-control are clearly apparent in most children. They will resist the desire to seize the gas-flame, they will not upset the milk-jug, they will obey orders to sit still when they want to run about, all through a higher mental inhibition. But the power of control is just as gradual a development as the motions of the hands. . . . Look at a more complicated act, that will be recognized by any competent physiologist to be automatic and beyond the control of any ordinary inhibitory power, e.g., irritate and tease a child of one or two years sufficiently, and it will suddenly strike out at you ; suddenly strike at a man, and he will either perform an act of defence or offence, or both, quite automatically, and without power of controlling himself. Place a bright tempting toy before a child of a year, and it will be instantly appropriated. Place cold water before a man dying of thirst, and he will take and drink it without power of doing otherwise. Ex-

---

* In an excellent article on The 'Mental Qualities of an Athlete' in the Harvard Monthly, vol. vi. p. 43, Mr. A. T. Dudley assigns the first place to the rapidly impulsive temperament. "Ask him how, in some complex trick, he performed a certain act, why he pushed or pulled at a certain instant, and he will tell you he does not know ; he did it by instinct ; or rather his nerves and muscles did it of themselves. . . . Here is the distinguishing feature of the good player : the good player, confident in his training and his practice, in the critical game trusts entirely to his impulse, and does not think out every move. The poor player, unable to trust his impulsive actions, is compelled to think carefully all the time. He thus not only loses the opportunities through his slowness in comprehending the whole situation, but, being compelled to think rapidly all the time, at critical points becomes confused ; while the first-rate player, not trying to reason, but acting as impulse directs, is continually distinguishing himself and plays the better under the greater pressure."

† T. S. Clouston, Clinical Lectures on Mental Diseases (London 1883), pp. 310–318.

haustion of nervous energy always lessens the inhibitory power. Who is not conscious of this? 'Irritability' is one manifestation of this. Many persons have so small a stock of reserve brain-power—that most valuable of all brain-qualities—that it is soon used up, and you see at once that they lose their power of self-control very soon. They are angels or demons just as they are fresh or tired. That surplus store of energy or resistive force which provides, in persons normally constituted, that moderate excesses in all directions shall do no great harm so long as they are not too often repeated, not being present in these people, overwork, over-drinking, or small debauches leave them at the mercy of their morbid impulses without power of resistance. . . . Woe to the man who uses up his surplus stock of brain-inhibition too near the bitter end, or too often ! . . . The physiological word inhibition can be used synonymously with the psychological and ethical expression self-control, or with the will when exercised in certain directions. It is the characteristic of most forms of mental disease for self-control to be lost, but this loss is usually part of a general mental affection with melancholic, maniacal, demented, or delusional symptoms as the chief manifestation of the disease. There are other cases, not so numerous, where the loss of the power of inhibition is the chief and by far the most marked symptom. . . . I shall call this form 'Inhibitory Insanity.' Some of these cases have uncontrollable impulses to violence and destruction, others to homicide, others to suicide prompted by no depressed feelings, others to acts of animal gratification (satyriasis, nymphomania, erotomania, bestiality), others to drinking too much alcohol (dipsomania), others towards setting things on fire (pyromania), others to stealing (kleptomania), and others towards immoralities of all sorts. The impulsive tendencies and morbid desires are innumerable in kind. Many of these varieties of Insanity have been distinguished by distinct names. To dig up and eat dead bodies (necrophilism), to wander from home and throw off the restraints of society (planomania), to act like a wild beast (lycanthropia), etc. Action from impulse in all these directions may take place from a loss of controlling power in the higher regions of the brain, or from an over-development of energy in certain portions of the brain, which the normal power of inhibition cannot control. The driver may be so weak that he cannot control well-broken horses, or the horses may be so hard-mouthed that no driver can pull them up. Both conditions may arise from purely cerebral disorder . . . . or may be reflex. . . . The *ego*, the man, the will, may be non-existent for the time. The most perfect examples of this are murders done during somnambulism or epileptic unconsciousness, or acts done in the hypnotic state. There is no conscious desire to attain the object at all in such cases. In other cases there is consciousness and memory present, but no power of restraining action. The simplest example of this is where an imbecile or dement, seeing something glittering, appropriates it to himself, or when he commits indecent sexual acts. Through disease a previously sane and vigorous-minded person may get into the same state. The motives that would lead other persons not to do such acts do not operate in such persons. I have known a man steal who said he had no intense longing for the article he appropriated at all, at least consciously, but his will was in abeyance, and he could not resist the ordinary desire of possession common to all human nature."

It is not only those technically classed imbeciles and dements who exhibit this promptitude of impulse and tardiness of inhibition. Ask half the common drunkards you know why it is that they fall so often a prey to temptation, and they will say that most of the time they cannot tell. It is a sort of vertigo with them. Their nervous centres have become a sluice-way pathologically unlocked by every passing conception of a bottle and a glass. They do not thirst for the beverage; the taste of it may even appear repugnant; and they perfectly foresee the morrow's remorse. But when they think of the liquor or see it, they find themselves preparing to drink, and do not stop themselves: and more than this they cannot say. Similarly a man may lead a life of incessant love-making or sexual indulgence, though what spurs him thereto seems rather to be suggestions and notions of possibility than any overweening strength in his affections or lusts. He may even be physically impotent all the while. The paths of natural (or it may be unnatural) impulse are so pervious in these characters that the slightest rise in the level of innervation produces an overflow. It is the condition recognized in pathology as 'irritable weakness.' The phase known as nascency or latency is so short in the excitement of the neural tissues that there is no opportunity for strain or tension to accumulate within them; and the consequence is that with all the agitation and activity, the amount of real feeling engaged may be very small. The hysterical temperament is the play-ground *par excellence* of this unstable equilibrium. One of these subjects will be filled with what seems the most genuine and settled aversion to a certain line of conduct, and the very next *instant* follow the stirring of temptation and plunge in it up to the neck. Professor Ribot well gives the name of 'Le Règne des Caprices' to the chapter in which he describes the hysterical temperament in his interesting little monograph 'The Diseases of the Will.'

Disorderly and impulsive conduct may, on the other hand, come about where the neural tissues preserve their proper inward tone, and where the inhibitory power is normal or even unusually great. In such cases *the strength of the impulsive idea is preternaturally exalted,* and what would be for most people the passing suggestion of a possibility becomes a gnawing, craving urgency to act. Works on insanity are full of examples of these morbid insistent ideas, in obstinately struggling against which the unfortunate victim's soul often sweats with agony, ere at last it gets swept away. One instance will stand for many; M. Ribot quotes it from Calmeil : *

" Glénadal, having lost his father in infancy, was brought up by his mother, whom he adored. At sixteen, his character, till then good and docile, changed. He became gloomy and taciturn. Pressed with questions by his mother, he decided at last to make a confession. ' To you,' said he, ' I owe everything ; I love you with all my soul ; yet for some time past an incessant idea drives me to kill you. Prevent so terrible a misfortune from happening, in case some day the temptation should overpower me : allow me to enlist.' Notwithstanding pressing solicitations, he was firm in his resolve, went off, and was a good soldier. Still a secret impulse stimulated him without cessation to desert in order to come home and kill his mother. At the end of his term of service the idea was as strong as on the first day. He enlisted for another term. The murderous instinct persisted, but substituted another victim. He no longer thought of killing his mother—the horrible impulse pointed day and night towards his sister-in-law. In order to resist the second impulse, he condemned himself to perpetual exile. At this time one of his old neighbors arrived in the regiment. Glénadal confesses all his trouble. ' Be at rest,' said the other. ' Your crime is impossible ; your sister-in-law has just died.' At these words Glénadal rises like a delivered captive. Joy fills his heart. He travels to the home of his childhood, unvisited for so many years. But as he arrives he sees his sister-in-law living. He gives a cry, and the terrible impulse seizes him again as a prey. That very evening he makes his brother tie him fast. ' Take a solid rope, bind me like a wolf in the barn, and go and tell Dr. Calmeil. . . .' From him he got admission to an insane asylum. The evening before his entrance he wrote to the director of the establishment : ' Sir, I am to become an inmate of your house. I shall behave there as if I were in the regiment. You will think me cured. At moments perhaps I shall pretend to be so. Never believe me. Never let me out on any pretext. If I beg to be released, double

---

* In his Maladies de la Volonté, p. 77.

your watchfulness; the only use I shall make of my liberty will be to commit a crime which I abhor.' " *

The craving for drink in real dipsomaniacs, or for opium or chloral in those subjugated, is of a strength of which normal persons can form no conception. "Were a keg of rum in one corner of a room and were a cannon constantly discharging balls between me and it, I could not refrain from passing before that cannon in order to get the rum ;" "If a bottle of brandy stood at one hand and the pit of hell yawned at the other, and I were convinced that I should be pushed in as sure as I took one glass, I could not refrain :" such statements abound in dipsomaniacs' mouths. Dr. Mussey of Cincinnati relates this case :

" A few years ago a tippler was put into an almshouse in this State. Within a few days he had devised various expedients to procure rum, but failed. At length, however, he hit upon one which was successful. He went into the wood-yard of the establishment, placed one hand upon the block, and with an axe in the other, struck it off at a single blow. With the stump raised and streaming he ran into the house and cried, ' Get some rum! get some rum! my hand is off!' In the confusion and bustle of the occasion a bowl of rum was brought, into which he plunged the bleeding member of his body, then raising the bowl to his mouth, drank freely, and exultingly exclaimed, ' Now I am satisfied.' Dr. J. E. Turner tells of a man who, while under treatment for inebriety, during four weeks secretly drank the alcohol from six jars containing morbid specimens. On asking him why he had committed this loathsome act, he replied: ' Sir, it is as impossible for me to control this diseased appetite as it is for me to control the pulsations of my heart.'" †

The passion of love may be called a monomania to which all of us are subject, however otherwise sane. It can coexist with contempt and even hatred for the ' object ' which inspires it, and whilst it lasts the whole life of the man is altered by its presence. Alfieri thus describes the struggles of his unusually powerful inhibitive power with his abnormally excited impulses toward a certain lady :

"Contemptible in my own eyes, I fell into such a state of melancholy as would, if long continued, inevitably have led to insanity or

---

* For other cases of ' impulsive insanity,' see H. Maudsley's Responsibility in Mental Disease, pp. 133–170, and Forbes Winslow's Obscure Diseases of the Mind and Brain, chapters VI, VII, VIII.

† Quoted by G. Burr, in an article on the Insanity of Inebriety in the N. Y. Psychological and Medico-Legal Journal, Dec. 1874.

death. I continued to wear my disgraceful fetters till towards the end of January, 1775, when my rage, which had hitherto so often been restrained within bounds, broke forth with the greatest violence. On returning one evening from the opera (the most insipid and tiresome amusement in Italy), where I had passed several hours in the box of the woman who was by turns the object of my antipathy and my love, I took the firm determination of emancipating myself forever from her yoke. Experience had taught me that flight, so far from enabling me to persevere in my resolutions, tended on the contrary to weaken and destroy them: I was inclined therefore to subject myself to a still more severe trial, imagining from the obstinacy and peculiarity of my character that I should succeed most certainly by the adoption of such measures as would compel me to make the greatest efforts. I determined never to leave the house, which, as I have already said, was exactly opposite that of the lady; to gaze at her windows, to see her go in and out every day, to listen to the sound of her voice, though firmly resolved that no advances on her part, either direct or indirect, no tender remembrances, nor in short any other means which might be employed, should ever again tempt me to a revival of our friendship. I was determined to die or liberate myself from my disgraceful thraldom. In order to give stability to my purpose, and to render it impossible for me to waver without the imputation of dishonor, I communicated my determination to one of my friends, who was greatly attached to me, and whom I highly esteemed. He had lamented the state of mind into which I had fallen, but not wishing to give countenance to my conduct, and seeing the impossibility of inducing me to abandon it, he had for some time ceased to visit at my house. In the few lines which I addressed to him, I briefly stated the resolution I had adopted, and as a pledge of my constancy I sent him a long tress of my ugly red hair. I had purposely caused it to be cut off in order to prevent my going out, as no one but clowns and sailors then appeared in public with short hair. I concluded my billet by conjuring him to strengthen and aid my fortitude by his presence and example. Isolated in this manner in my own house, I prohibited all species of intercourse, and passed the first fifteen days in uttering the most frightful lamentations and groans. Some of my friends came to visit me, and appeared to commiserate my situation, perhaps because I did not myself complain: but my figure and whole appearance bespoke my sufferings. Wishing to read something I had recourse to the gazettes, whole pages of which I frequently ran over without understanding a single word. . . I passed more than two months till the end of March 1775, in a state bordering on frenzy; but about this time a new idea darted into my mind, which tended to assuage my melancholy."

This was the idea of poetical composition, at which Alfieri describes his first attempts, made under these diseased circumstances, and goes on:

" The only good that occurred to me from this whim was that of gradually detaching me from love, and of awakening my reason which had so long lain dormant. I no longer found it necessary to cause myself to be tied with cords to a chair, in order to prevent me from leaving my house and returning to that of my lady. This had been one of the expedients I devised to render myself wise by force. The cords were concealed under a large mantle in which I was enveloped, and only one hand remained at liberty. Of all those who came to see me, not one suspected I was bound down in this manner. I remained in this situation for whole hours; Elias, who was my jailer, was alone intrusted with the secret. He always liberated me, as he had been enjoined, whenever the paroxysms of my rage subsided. Of all the whimsical methods which I employed, however, the most curious was that of appearing in masquerade at the theatre towards the end of the carnival. Habited as Apollo. I ventured to present myself with a lyre, on which I played as well as I was able and sang some bad verses of my own composing. Such effrontery was diametrically opposite to my natural character. The only excuse I can offer for such scenes was my inability to resist an imperious passion. I felt that it was necessary to place an insuperable barrier between its object and me; and I saw that the strongest of all was the shame to which I should expose myself by renewing an attachment which I had so publicly turned into ridicule." *

Often the insistent idea is of a trivial sort, but it may wear the patient's life out. His hands feel dirty, they must be washed. He *knows* they are not dirty ; yet to get rid of the teasing idea he washes them. The idea, however, returns in a moment, and the unfortunate victim, who is not in the least deluded *intellectually*, will end by spending the whole day at the wash-stand. Or his clothes are not 'rightly' put on ; and to banish the thought he takes them off and puts them on again, till his toilet consumes two or three hours of time. Most people have the potentiality of this disease. To few has it not happened to conceive, after getting into bed, that they may have forgotten to lock the front door, or to turn out the entry gas. And few of us have not on some occasion got up to repeat the performance, less because they believed in the reality of its omission than because only so could they banish the worrying doubt and get to sleep.†

---

* Autobiography, Howells' edition (1877), pp. 192–6.

† See a paper on Insistent and Fixed Ideas by Dr. Cowles in American Journal of Psychology, I. 222 ; and another on the so-called Insanity of Doubt by Dr. Knapp, *ibid.* III. 1. The latter contains a partial bibliography of the subject.

THE OBSTRUCTED WILL.

In striking contrast with the cases in which inhibition is insufficient or impulsion in excess are those in which impulsion is insufficient or inhibition of in excess. We all know the condition described on p. 404 of Vol. I, in which the mind for a few moments seems to lose its focussing power and to be unable to rally its attention to any determinate thing. At such times we sit blankly staring and do nothing. The objects of consciousness fail to touch the quick or break the skin. They are there, but do not reach the level of effectiveness. This state of non-efficacious presence is the normal condition of *some* objects, in all of us. Great fatigue or exhaustion may make it the condition of almost all objects ; and an apathy resembling that then brought about is recognized in asylums under the name of *abulia* as a symptom of mental disease. The healthy state of the will requires, as aforesaid, both that vision should be right, and that action should obey its lead. But in the morbid condition in question the vision may be wholly unaffected, and the intellect clear, and yet the act either fails to follow or follows in some other way. " *Video meliora proboque, deteriora sequor* " is the classic expression of the latter condition of mind. The former it is to which the name *abulia* peculiarly applies. The patients, says Guislain,

"are able to will inwardly, mentally, according to the dictates of reason. They experience the desire to act, but they are powerless to act as they should. . . . Their will cannot overpass certain limits : one would say that the force of action within them is blocked up : the *I will* does not transform itself into impulsive volition, into active determination. Some of these patients wonder themselves at the impotence with which their will is smitten. If you abandon them to themselves, they pass whole days in their bed or on a chair. If one speaks to them or excites them, they express themselves properly though briefly ; and judge of things pretty well." *

In Chapter XXI, as will be remembered, it was said that the sentiment of reality with which an object appealed to the mind is proportionate (amongst other things) to its efficacy as a stimulus to the will. Here we get the

---

* Quoted by Ribot, *op cit.* p. 39.

obverse side of the truth. Those ideas, objects, considerations, which (in these lethargic states) fail to *get to* the will, fail to draw blood, seem, in so far forth, distant and unreal. The connection of the reality of things with their effectiveness as motives is a tale that has never yet been fully told. The moral tragedy of human life comes almost wholly from the fact that the link is ruptured which normally should hold between vision of the truth and action, and that this pungent sense of effective reality will not attach to certain ideas. Men do not differ so much in their mere feelings and conceptions. Their notions of possibility and their ideals are not as far apart as might be argued from their differing fates. No class of them have better sentiments or feel more constantly the difference between the higher and the lower path in life than the hopeless failures, the sentimentalists, the drunkards, the schemers, the 'dead-beats,' whose life is one long contradiction between knowledge and action, and who, with full command of theory, never get to holding their limp characters erect. No one eats of the fruit of the tree of knowledge as they do ; as far as moral insight goes, in comparison with them, the orderly and prosperous philistines whom they scandalize are sucking babes. And yet their moral knowledge, always there grumbling and rumbling in the background,—discerning, commenting, protesting, longing, half resolving,—never wholly resolves, never gets its voice out of the minor into the major key, or its speech out of the subjunctive into the imperative mood, never breaks the spell, never takes the helm into its hands. In such characters as Rousseau and Restif it would seem as if the lower motives had all the impulsive efficacy in their hands. Like trains with the right of way, they retain exclusive possession of the track. The more ideal motives exist alongside of them in profusion, but they never get switched on, and the man's conduct is no more influenced by them than an express train is influenced by a wayfarer standing by the roadside and calling to be taken aboard. They are an inert accompaniment to the end of time ; and the consciousness of inward hollowness that accrues from habitually seeing the better only to do the worse, is one of the saddest feelings one can bear with him through this vale of tears.

We now see at one view when it is that effort complicates volition. It does so whenever a rarer and more ideal impulse is called upon to neutralize others of a more instinctive and habitual kind; it does so whenever strongly explosive tendencies are checked, or strongly obstructive conditions overcome. The *âme bien née*, the child of the sunshine, at whose birth the fairies made their gifts, does not need much of it in his life. The hero and the neurotic subject, on the other hand, do. Now our spontaneous way of conceiving the effort, under all these circumstances, is as an active force adding its strength to that of the motives which ultimately prevail. When outer forces impinge upon a body, we say that the resultant motion is in the line of least resistance, or of greatest traction. But it is a curious fact that our spontaneous language never speaks of volition with effort in this way. Of course if we proceed *a priori* and define the line of least resistance as the line that is followed, the physical law must also hold good in the mental sphere. But we *feel*, in all hard cases of volition, as if the line taken, when the rarer and more ideal motives prevail, were the line of greater resistance, and as if the line of coarser motivation were the more pervious and easy one, even at the very moment when we refuse to follow it. He who under the surgeon's knife represses cries of pain, or he who exposes himself to social obloquy for duty's sake, feels as if he were following the line of greatest temporary resistance. He speaks of conquering and overcoming his impulses and temptations.

But the sluggard, the drunkard, the coward, never talk of their conduct in that way or say they resist their energy, overcome their sobriety, conquer their courage, and so forth. If in general we class all springs of action as propensities on the one hand and ideals on the other, the sensualist never says of his behavior that it results from a victory over his ideals, but the moralist always speaks of his as a victory over his propensities. The sensualist uses terms of inactivity, says he forgets his ideals, is deaf to duty, and so forth; which terms seem to imply that the ideal motives *per se* can be annulled without energy or effort, and that the strongest mere traction lies in the line of the propensities. The ideal impulse appears, in comparison with this, a still small voice which must be artificially reinforced to prevail. Effort is what reinforces it, making things seem as if, while the force of propensity were essentially a fixed quantity, the ideal force might be of various amount. But what determines the amount of the effort when, by its aid, an ideal motive becomes victorious over a great sensual resistance? The very greatness of the resistance itself. If the sensual propensity is small, the effort is small. The latter is *made great* by the presence of a great antagonist to overcome. And if a brief definition of ideal or moral action were required, none could be given which would better fit the appearances than this: *It is action in the line of the greatest resistance.*

The facts may be most briefly symbolized thus, P standing for the propensity, I for the ideal impulse, and E for the effort:

$$I \text{ } per \text{ } se < P.$$
$$I + E > P.$$

In other words, if E adds itself to I, P immediately offers the least resistance, and motion occurs in spite of it.

But the E does not seem to form an integral part of the I. It appears adventitious and indeterminate in advance. We can make more or less as we please, and *if* we make enough we can convert the greatest mental resistance into the least. Such, at least, is the impression which the facts spontaneously produce upon us. But we will not discuss the truth of this impression at present; let us rather continue our descriptive detail.

PLEASURE AND PAIN AS SPRINGS OF ACTION.

Objects and thoughts of objects start our action, but the pleasures and pains which action brings modify its course and regulate it; and later the thoughts of the pleasures and the pains acquire themselves impulsive and inhibitive power. Not that the thought of a pleasure need be itself a pleasure, usually it is the reverse—*nessun maggior dolore*—as Dante says—and not that the thought of pain need be a pain, for, as Homer says, "griefs are often afterwards an entertainment." But as present pleasures are tremendous reinforcers, and present pains tremendous inhibitors of whatever action leads to them, so the thoughts of pleasures and pains take rank amongst the thoughts which have most impulsive and inhibitive power. The precise relation which these thoughts hold to other thoughts is thus a matter demanding some attention.

If a movement feels agreeable, we repeat and repeat it as long as the pleasure lasts. If it hurts us, our muscular contractions at the instant stop. So complete is the inhibition in this latter case that it is almost impossible for a man to cut or mutilate himself slowly and deliberately—his hand invincibly refusing to bring on the pain. And there are many pleasures which, when once we have begun to taste them, make it all but obligatory to keep up the activity to which they are due. So widespread and searching is this influence of pleasures and pains upon our movements that a premature philosophy has decided that these are our only spurs to action, and that wherever they seem to be absent, it is only because they are so far on among the 'remoter' images that prompt the action that they are overlooked.

This is a great mistake, however. Important as is the influence of pleasures and pains upon our movements, they are far from being our only stimuli. With the manifestations of instinct and emotional expression, for example, they have absolutely nothing to do. Who smiles for the pleasure of the smiling, or frowns for the pleasure of the frown? Who blushes to escape the discomfort of not blushing? Or who in anger, grief, or fear is actuated to the movements which he makes by the pleasures which they yield? In all these cases the movements are discharged fatally by the *vis a tergo* which the stimulus exerts upon a nervous system framed to respond in just that way. The objects of our rage, love, or terror, the occasions of our tears and smiles, whether they be present to our senses, or whether they be merely represented in idea, have this peculiar sort of impulsive power. The *impulsive quality* of mental states is an attribute behind which we cannot go. Some states of mind have more of it than others, some have it in this direction, and some in that. Feelings of pleasure and pain have it, and perceptions and imaginations of fact have it, but neither have it exclusively or peculiarly. It is of the essence of all consciousness (or of the neural process which underlies it) to instigate movement of some sort. That with one creature and object it should be of one sort, with others of another sort, is a problem for evolutionary history to explain. However the actual impulsions may have arisen, they must now be described as they exist; and those persons obey a curiously narrow teleological superstition who think themselves bound to interpret them in every instance as effects of the secret solicitancy of pleasure and repugnancy of pain.*

---

* The silliness of the old-fashioned pleasure-philosophy *saute aux yeux*. Take, for example, Prof. Bain's explanation of sociability and parental love by the pleasures of touch : "Touch is the fundamental and generic sense. . . . Even after the remaining senses are differentiated, the primary sense continues to be a leading susceptibility of the mind. The soft warm touch, if not a first-class influence, is at least an approach to that. The combined power of soft contact and warmth amounts to a considerable pitch of massive pleasure ; while there may be subtle influences not reducible to these two heads, such as we term, from not knowing anything about them, magnetic or electric. The sort of thrill from taking a baby in arms is something beyond mere warm touch ; and it may rise to the ecstatic height, in which case, however, there may be concurrent sensations and ideas. . . . In mere tender emotion not sexual, there is nothing but the sense of touch to gratify, unless we assume the occult magnetic influences. . . . In a word, our love pleasures begin and end in sensual contact. Touch is both the alpha and omega of affection. As the terminal and satisfying sensation, the *ne plus ultra*, it must be a pleasure of the highest degree. . . . Why should a more lively feeling grow up towards a fellow-being than towards a perennial fountain ? [This 'should' is simply delicious from the more modern evolutionary point of view.] It must be that there is a source of pleasure in the companionship of other sentient creatures, over and above the help afforded by them in obtaining the necessaries of life. To account for this, I can suggest nothing but the primary and independent pleasure of the animal embrace." [Mind, this is said not of the sexual interest, but of 'Sociability at Large.'] "For this pleasure every creature is disposed to pay something, even when it is only fraternal. A certain

It might be that to *reflection* such a narrow teleology would justify itself, that pleasures and pains might seem the only *comprehensible and reasonable* motives for action, the only motives on which we *ought* to act. That is an *ethical* proposition, in favor of which a good deal may be said. But it is not a *psychological* proposition ; and nothing follows from it as to the motives upon which as a matter of fact we *do* act. These motives are supplied by innumerable objects, which innervate our voluntary muscles by a process as automatic as that by which they light a fever in our breasts. If the thought of pleasure can impel to action, surely other thoughts may. Experience only can decide which thoughts do. The chapters on Instinct and Emotion have shown us that their name is legion ; and with this verdict we ought to remain contented, and not seek an illusory simplification at the cost of half the facts.

If in these our *first* acts pleasures and pains bear no part, as little do they bear in our last acts, or those artificially acquired performances which have become habitual.

---

amount of material benefit imparted is a condition of the full heartiness of a responding embrace, the complete fruition of this primitive joy. In the absence of those conditions the pleasure of giving . . . can scarcely be accounted for ; we know full well that, without these helps, it would be a very meagre sentiment in beings like ourselves. . . . It seems to me that there must be at the [parental instinct's] foundation that intense pleasure in the embrace of the young which we find to characterize the parental feeling throughout. Such a pleasure once created would associate itself with the prevailing features and aspects of the young, and give to all of these their very great interest. For the sake of the pleasure, the parent discovers the necessity of nourishing the subject of it, and comes to regard the ministering function as a part or condition of the delight " (Emotions and Will, pp. 126, 127, 132, 133, 140). Prof. Bain does not explain why a satin cushion kept at about 98° F. would not on the whole give us the pleasure in question more cheaply than our friends and babies do. It is true that the cushion might lack the 'occult magnetic influences.' Most of us would say that neither a baby's nor a friend's skin would possess them, were not a tenderness already there. The youth who feels ecstasy shoot through him when by accident the silken palm or even the ' vesture's hem ' of his idol touches him, would hardly feel it were he not hard hit by Cupid in advance. The love creates the ecstasy, not the ecstasy the love. And for the rest of us can it possibly be that all our social virtue springs from an appetite for the sensual pleasure of having our hand shaken, or being slapped on the back ?

All the daily routine of life, our dressing and undressing, the coming and going from our work or carrying through of its various operations, is utterly without mental reference to pleasure and pain, except under rarely realized conditions. It is ideo-motor action. As I do not breathe for the pleasure of the breathing, but simply find that I *am* breathing, so I do not write for the pleasure of the writing, but simply because I have once begun, and being in a state of intellectual excitement which keeps venting itself in that way, find that I *am* writing still. Who will pretend that when he idly fingers his knife-handle at the table, it is for the sake of any pleasure which it gives him, or pain which he thereby avoids. We do all these things because at the moment we cannot help it; our nervous systems are so shaped that they overflow in just that way; and for many of our idle or purely 'nervous' and fidgety performances we can assign absolutely no *reason* at all.

Or what shall be said of a shy and unsociable man who receives point-blank an invitation to a small party? The thing is to him an abomination; but your presence exerts a compulsion on him, he can think of no excuse, and so says yes, cursing himself the while for what he does. He is unusually *sui compos* who does not every week of his life fall into some such blundering act as this. Such instances of *voluntas invita* show not only that our acts cannot all be conceived as effects of represented pleasure, but that they cannot even be classed as cases of represented *good*. The class 'goods' contains many more generally influential motives to action than the class 'pleasants.' Pleasures often attract us only because we deem them goods. Mr. Spencer, e.g., urges us to court pleasures for their influence upon health, which comes to us as a good. But almost as little as under the form of pleasures do our acts invariably appear to us under the form of *goods*. All diseased impulses and pathological fixed ideas are instances to the contrary. It is the very badness of the act that gives it then its vertiginous fascination. Remove the prohibition, and the attraction stops. In my university days a student threw himself from an upper entry window of one of the college buildings and was nearly killed. Another student, a friend of my own, had to pass the window daily in coming and going from his room, and experienced a dreadful temptation to imitate the deed. Being a Catholic, he told his director, who said, ' All right! if you must, you must,' and added, ' Go ahead and do it,' thereby instantly quenching his desire. This director knew how to minister to a mind diseased. But we need not go to minds diseased for examples of the occasional tempting-power of simple badness and unpleasantness as such. Every one who has a wound or hurt anywhere, a sore tooth, e.g., will ever and anon press it just to bring out the pain. If we are near a new sort of stink, we must sniff it again just to verify once more how bad it is. This very day I have been repeating over and over to myself a verbal jingle whose mawkish silliness was the secret of its haunting power. I loathed yet could not banish it.

Believers in the pleasure-and-pain theory must thus, if they are candid, make large exceptions in the application of their creed. Action from ' fixed ideas ' is accordingly a terrible stumbling-block to the candid Professor Bain. Ideas have in his psychology no impulsive but only a ' guiding' function, whilst

" The proper stimulus of the will, namely, some variety of pleasure and pain, is needed to give the impetus. . . . The intellectual link is not sufficient for causing the deed to rise at the beck of the idea (except in case of an 'idée fixe') ; " but " should any *pleasure* spring up or be continued, by performing an action that we clearly conceive, the causation is then complete ; both the directing and the moving powers are present." *

Pleasures and pains are for Professor Bain the ' *genuine* impulses of the will.' †

" Without an antecedent of pleasurable or painful feeling—actual or ideal, primary or derivative—the will cannot be stimulated. Through

---

* Emotion and Will, p. 352. But even Bain's own description belies his formula, for the idea appears as the ' moving ' and the pleasure as the ' directing ' force.

† P. 398.

all the disguises that wrap up what we call motives, something of one or other of these two grand conditions can be detected."*

Accordingly, where Professor Bain finds an exception to this rule, he refuses to call the phenomenon a 'genuinely voluntary impulse.' The exceptions, he admits, 'are those furnished by never-dying spontaneity, habits, and fixed ideas.' † Fixed ideas 'traverse the proper course of volition.' ‡

" *Disinterested impulses* are wholly distinct from the attainment of pleasure and the avoidance of pain. . . . The theory of disinterested action, in the only form that I can conceive it, supposes that the action of the will and the attainment of happiness do not square throughout."§

Sympathy " has this in common with the Fixed Idea, that it clashes with the regular outgoings of the will in favor of our pleasures." ‖

Prof. Bain thus admits all the essential facts. Pleasure and pain are motives of only part of our activity. But he prefers to give to that part of the activity exclusively which these feelings prompt the name of ' *regular* outgoings ' and ' *genuine* impulses ' of the will, ¶ and to treat all the rest as mere paradoxes and anomalies, of which nothing rational can be said. This amounts to taking one species of a genus, calling it alone by the generic name, and ordering the other co-ordinate species to find what names they may. At bottom this is only verbal play. How much more conducive to clearness and insight it is to take the *genus* ' springs of action ' and treat it as a whole ; and then to distinguish within it the species ' pleasure and pain ' from whatever other species may be found !

There is, it is true, a complication in the relation of pleasure to action, which partly excuses those who make it the exclusive spur. This complication deserves some notice at our hands.

An impulse which discharges itself immediately is generally quite *neutral* as regards pleasure or pain—the breath-

---

ing impulse, for example. If such an impulse is arrested, however, by an extrinsic force, a great feeling of *uneasiness* is produced—for instance, the dyspnœa of asthma. And in proportion as the arresting force is then overcome, *relief* acrues—as when we draw breath again after the asthma subsides. The relief is a pleasure and the uneasiness a pain ; and thus it happens that round all our impulses, merely as such, there twine, as it were, secondary possibilities of pleasant and painful feeling, involved in the manner in which the act is allowed to occur. These *pleasures and pains of achievement, discharge, or fruition* exist, no matter what the original spring of action be. We are glad when we have successfully got ourselves out of a danger, though the thought of the gladness was surely not what suggested to us to escape. To have compassed the steps towards a proposed sensual indulgence also makes us glad, and this gladness is a pleasure additional to the pleasure originally proposed. On the other hand, we are chagrined and displeased when any activity, however instigated, is hindered whilst in process of actual discharge. We are 'uneasy' till the discharge starts up again. And this is just as true when the action is neutral, or has nothing but pain in view as its result, as when it was undertaken for pleasure's express sake. The moth is probably as annoyed if hindered from getting into the lamp-flame as the *roué* is if interrupted in his debauch ; and we are chagrined if prevented from doing some quite unimportant act which would have given us no noticeable pleasure if done, merely because the prevention itself is disagreeable.

Let us now call the pleasure *for the sake* of which the act may be done the *pursued pleasure*. It follows that, even when no pleasure is pursued by an act, the act itself may be the *pleasantest line* of conduct when once the impulse has begun, on account of the incidental pleasure which then attends its successful achievement and the pain which would come of interruption. A *pleasant act* and an act *pursuing a pleasure* are in themselves, however, two perfectly distinct conceptions, though they coalesce in one concrete phenomenon whenever a pleasure is deliberately pursued. I cannot help thinking that it is the *confusion of pursued pleasure with mere pleasure of achievement* which makes the pleasure-theory of action so plausible to the ordinary mind. We feel an impulse, no matter whence derived; we proceed to act; if hindered, we feel displeasure; and if successful, relief. Action *in the line of the present impulse* is always for the time being the pleasant course; and the ordinary hedonist expresses this fact by saying that we act for the *sake* of the pleasantness involved. But who does not see that for this sort of pleasure to be possible, *the impulse must be there already as an independent fact?* The pleasure of successful performance is the *result* of the impulse, not its *cause*. You cannot have your pleasure of achievement unless you have managed to get your impulse under headway beforehand by some previous means.

It is true that on special occasions (so complex is the human mind) *the pleasure of achievement may itself become a pursued pleasure;* and these cases form another point on which the pleasure-theory is apt to rally. Take a foot-ball game or a fox-hunt. Who in cold blood wants the fox for its own sake, or cares whether the ball be at this goal or that? We know, however, by experience, that if we can once rouse a certain impulsive excitement in ourselves, whether to overtake the fox, or to get the ball to one particular goal, the successful venting of it over the counteracting checks will fill us with exceeding joy. We therefore get ourselves deliberately and artificially into the hot impulsive state. It takes the presence of various instinct-arousing conditions to excite it; but little by little, once we are in the field, it reaches its paroxysm; and we reap the reward of our exertions in that pleasure of successful achievement which, far more than the dead fox or the goal-got ball, was the object we originally pursued. So it often is with duties. Lots of actions are done with heaviness all through, and not till they are completed does pleasure emerge, in the joy of being done with them. Like Hamlet we say of each such successive task,

> " O cursed spite,
> That ever I was born to set it right ! "

and then we often add to the original impulse that set us on, this additional one, that " we shall feel so glad when well through with it," that thought also having its impulsive spur. But because a pleasure of achievement *can* thus become a pursued pleasure upon occasion, it does not follow that everywhere and always that pleasure must be what is pursued. This, however, is what the pleasure-philosophers seem to suppose. As well might they suppose, because no steamer can go to sea without incidentally consuming coal, and because some steamers may occasionally go to sea to *try* their coal, that therefore no steamer *can* go to sea for any other motive than that of coal-consumption.*

As we need not act for the sake of gaining the pleasure of achievement, so neither need we act for the sake of escaping the uneasiness of arrest. This uneasiness is altogether due to the fact that the act is *already tending to occur* on other grounds. And these original grounds are what impel to its continuance, even though the uneasiness of the arrest may upon occasion add to their impulsive power.

To conclude, I am far from denying the exceeding prominence and importance of the part which pleasures and pains, both felt and represented, play in the motivation of our conduct. But I must insist that it is no exclusive part, and that co-ordinately with these mental object innumerable others have an exactly similar impulsive and inhibitive power.†

If one must have a single name for the condition upon which the impulsive and inhibitive quality of objects depends, one had better call it their *interest*. 'The interest-

---

* How much clearer Hume's head was than that of his disciples' ! "It has been proved beyond all controversy that even the passions commonly esteemed selfish carry the Mind beyond self directly to the object ; that though the satisfaction of these passions gives us enjoyment, yet the prospect of this enjoyment is not the cause of the passions but, on the contrary, the passion is antecedent to the enjoyment, and without the former the latter could never possibly exist," etc. (Essay on the Different Species of Philosophy, § 1, note near the end.)

† In favor of the view in the text, one may consult H. Sidgwick, Methods of Ethics, book I. chap. IV; T. H. Green, Prolegomena to Ethics, bk. III. chap. I. p. 179; Carpenter, Mental Physiol., chap VI , J. Martineau, Types of Ethical Theory, part II, bk. I, chap. II. i, and bk. II, branch I. chap. I. i. § 3. Against it see Leslie Stephen, Science of Ethics. chap. II. § II ; H. Spencer, Data of Ethics, §§ 9–15; D. G. Thompson, System of Psychology, part IX, and Mind, VI. 62. Also Bain, Senses and Intellect, 338–44 ; Emotions and Will, 436.

ing' is a title which covers not only the pleasant and the painful, but also the morbidly fascinating, the tediously haunting, and even the simply habitual, inasmuch as the attention usually travels on habitual lines, and what-we-at-tend-to and what-interests-us are synonymous terms. It seems as if we ought to look for the secret of an idea's impulsiveness, not in any peculiar relations which it may have with paths of motor discharge,—for *all* ideas have relations with some such paths,—but rather in a preliminary phe-nomenon, the *urgency, namely, with which it is able to compel attention and dominate in consciousness.* Let it once so dominate, let no other ideas succeed in displacing it, and what-ever motor effects belong to it by nature will inevitably occur—its impulsion, in short, will be given to boot, and will manifest itself as a matter of course. This is what we have seen in instinct, in emotion, in common ideo-motor action, in hypnotic suggestion, in morbid impulsion, and in *voluntas invita,*—the impelling idea is simply the one which possesses the attention. It is the same where pleasure and pain are the motor spurs—they drive other thoughts from con-sciousness at the same time that they instigate their own characteristic 'volitional' effects. And this is also what happens at the moment of the *fiat,* in all the five types of 'decision' which we have described. In short, one does not see any case in which the steadfast occupancy of conscious-ness does not appear to be the prime condition of impulsive power. It is still more obviously the prime condition of inhibitive power. What checks our impulses is the mere thinking of reasons to the contrary—it is their bare presence to the mind which gives the veto, and makes acts, otherwise seductive, impossible to perform. If we could only *forget* our scruples, our doubts, our fears, what exultant energy we should for a while display!

WILL IS A RELATION BETWEEN THE MIND AND ITS 'IDEAS.'

In closing in, therefore, after all these preliminaries, upon the more *intimate* nature of the volitional process, we find ourselves driven more and more exclusively to con-sider the conditions which make ideas prevail in the mind.

With the prevalence, once there as a fact, of the motive idea the *psychology* of volition properly stops. The movements which ensue are exclusively physiological phenomena, following according to physiological laws upon the neura events to which the idea corresponds. The *willing* terminates with the prevalence of the idea ; and whether the act then follows or not is a matter quite immaterial, so far as the willing itself goes. I will to write, and the act follows. I will to sneeze, and it does not. I will that the distant table slide over the floor towards me ; it also does not. My willing representation can no more instigate my sneezing-centre than it can instigate the table to activity. But in both cases it is as true and good willing as it was when I willed to write.* In a word, volition is a psychic or moral fact pure and simple, and is absolutely completed when the stable state of the idea is there. The supervention of motion is a supernumerary phenomenon depending on executive ganglia whose function lies outside the mind.

In St. Vitus' dance, in locomotor ataxy, the representation of a movement and the consent to it take place normally. But the inferior executive centres are deranged, and although the ideas discharge them, they do not discharge them so as to reproduce the precise sensations anticipated. In aphasia the patient has an image of certain words which he wishes to utter, but when he opens his mouth he hears himself making quite unintended sounds. This may fill him with rage and despair—which passions only show how

---

* This sentence is written from the author's own consciousness. But many persons say that where they disbelieve in the effects ensuing, as in the case of the table, they cannot will it. They " cannot exert a volition that a table should move." This personal difference may be partly verbal. Different people may attach different connotations to the word 'will.' But I incline to think that we differ psychologically as well. When one knows that he has no power, one's desire of a thing is called a *wish* and not a will. The sense of impotence inhibits the volition. Only by abstracting from the thought of the impossibility am I able energetically to imagine strongly the table sliding over the floor, make the bodily ' effort ' which I do, and to will it to come towards me. It may be that some people are unable to perform this abstraction, and that the image of the table stationary on the floor inhibits the contradictory image of its moving, which is the object to be willed.

intact his will remains. Paralysis only goes a step farther. The associated mechanism is not only deranged but altogether broken through. The volition occurs, but the hand remains as still as the table. The paralytic is made aware of this by the absence of the expected change in his afferent sensations. He tries harder, i.e., he mentally frames the sensation of muscular ' effort,' with consent that it shall occur. It does so : he frowns, he heaves his chest, he clinches his other fist, but the palsied arm lies passive as before.*

We thus find that *we reach the heart of our inquiry into volition when we ask by what process it is that the thought of any given object comes to prevail stably in the mind.* Where thoughts prevail without effort, we have sufficiently studied in the several chapters on sensation, association, and attention, the laws of their advent before consciousness and of their stay. We will not go over that ground again, for we know that interest and association are the words, let their worth be what it may, on which our explanations must perforce rely. Where, on the other hand, the prevalence of the thought is accompanied by the phenomenon of effort, the case is much less clear. Already in the chapter on attention we postponed the final consideration of voluntary attention with effort to a later place. We have now brought things to a point at which we see that attention with effort is all that any case of volition implies. *The essential achievement of the will, in short, when it is most ' voluntary,' is to* ATTEND *to a difficult object and hold it fast before the mind.* The so-doing *is* the *fiat ;* and it is a mere physiological incident that when the object is thus attended to, immediate motor consequences should ensue. A *resolve,* whose contemplated motor consequences are not to ensue until some possibly far distant future condition shall have been fulfilled, involves all the psychic elements of a motor fiat except the word ' *now ;*' and it is the same with many of

---

* A normal palsy occurs during sleep. We will all sorts of motions in our dreams, but seldom perform any of them. In nightmare we become conscious of the non-performance, and make a muscular ' effort.' This seems then to occur in a restricted way, limiting itself to the occlusion of the glottis and producing the respiratory anxiety which wakes us up.

our purely theoretic beliefs. We saw in effect in the appropriate chapter, how in the last resort belief means only a peculiar sort of occupancy of the mind, and relation to the self felt in the thing believed ; and we know in the case of many beliefs how constant an effort of the attention is required to keep them in this situation and protect them from displacement by contradictory ideas.* (Compare above, p. 321.)

Effort of attention is thus the essential phenomenon of will.† Every reader must know by his own experience that this is so, for every reader must have felt some fiery passion's grasp. What constitutes the difficulty for a man laboring under an unwise passion of acting as if the passion

---

* Both resolves and beliefs have of course immediate motor consequences of a quasi-emotional sort, changes of breathing, of attitude, internal speech movements, etc.; but these movements are not the *objects* resolved on or believed. The movements in common volition are the objects willed.

† This *volitional* effort pure and simple must be carefully distinguished from the *muscular* effort with which it is usually confounded. The latter consists of all those peripheral feelings to which a muscular 'exertion' may give rise. These feelings, whenever they are massive and the body is not 'fresh,' are rather disagreeable, especially when accompanied by stopped breath, congested head, bruised skin of fingers, toes, or shoulders, and strained joints. And it is only *as thus disagreeable* that the mind must make its *volitional* effort in stably representing their reality and consequently bringing it about That they happen to be made real by muscular activity is a purely accidental circumstance. A soldier standing still to be fired at expects disagreeable sensations from his muscular passivity. The action of his will, in sustaining the expectation, is identical with that required for a painful muscular effort. What is hard for both is *facing an idea as real*.

Where much muscular effort is not needed or where the 'freshness' is very great, the volitional effort is not required to sustain the idea of movement, which comes then and stays in virtue of association's simpler laws. More commonly, however, muscular effort involves volitional effort as well. Exhausted with fatigue and wet and watching, the sailor on a wreck throws himself down to rest. But hardly are his limbs fairly relaxed, when the order 'To the pumps!' again sounds in his ears. Shall he, can he, obey it ? Is it not better just to let his aching body lie, and let the ship go down if she will? So he lies on, till, with a desperate heave of the will, at last he staggers to his legs, and to his task again. Again, there are instances where the fiat demands great volitional effort though the muscular exertion be insignificant, e.g., the getting out of bed and bathing one's self on a cold morning.

were unwise ? Certainly there is no physical difficulty. It is as easy physically to avoid a fight as to begin one, to pocket one's money as to squander it on one's cupidities, to walk away from as towards a coquette's door. The difficulty is mental; it is that of getting the idea of the wise action to stay before our mind at all. When any strong emotional state whatever is upon us the tendency is for no images but such as are congruous with it to come up. If others by chance offer themselves, they are instantly smothered and crowded out. If we be joyous, we cannot keep thinking of those uncertainties and risks of failure which abound upon our path ; if lugubrious, we cannot think of new triumphs, travels, loves, and joys ; nor if vengeful, of our oppressor's community of nature with ourselves. The cooling advice which we get from others when the fever-fit is on us is the most jarring and exasperating thing in life. Reply we cannot, so we get angry ; for by a sort of self-preserving instinct which our passion has, it feels that these chill objects, if they once but gain a lodgment, will work and work until they have frozen the very vital spark from out of all our mood and brought our airy castles in ruin to the ground. Such is the inevitable effect of reasonable ideas over others —*if they can once get a quiet hearing ;* and passion's cue accordingly is always and everywhere to prevent their still small voice from being heard at all. "Let me not think of that ! Don't speak to me of that !" This is the sudden cry of all those who in a passion perceive some sobering considerations about to check them in mid-career. " *Hæc tibi erit janua leti,*" we feel. There is something so icy in this cold-water bath, something which seems so hostile to the movement of our life, so purely negative, in Reason, when she lays her corpse-like finger on our heart and says, "Halt! give up ! leave off ! go back ! sit down !" that it is no wonder that to most men the steadying influence seems, for the time being, a very minister of death.

The strong-willed man, however, is the man who hears the still small voice unflinchingly, and who, when the death-bringing consideration comes, looks at its face, consents to its presence, clings to it, affirms it, and holds it fast, in spite of the host of exciting mental images which rise in revolt against it and would expel it from the mind. Sustained in this way by a resolute effort of attention, the difficult object erelong begins to call up its own congerers and associates and ends by changing the disposition of the man's consciousness altogether. And with his consciousness, his action changes, for the new object, once stably in possesion of the field of his thoughts, infallibly produces its own motor effects. The difficulty lies in the gaining possession of that field. Though the spontaneous drift of thought is all the other way, the attention must be kept strained on that one object until at last it *grows*, so as to maintain itself before the mind with ease. This strain of the attention is the fundamental act of will. And the will's work is in most cases practically ended when the bare presence to our thought of the naturally unwelcome object has been secured. For the mysterious tie between the thought and the motor centres next comes into play, and, in a way which we cannot even guess at, the obedience of the bodily organs follows as a matter of course.

In all this one sees how the immediate point of application of the volitional effort lies exclusively in the mental world. The whole drama is a mental drama. The whole difficulty is a mental difficulty, a difficulty with an object of our thought. If I may use the word *idea* without suggesting associationist or Herbartian fables, I will say that it is an idea to which our will applies itself, an idea which if we let it go would slip away, but which we will not let go. Consent to the idea's undivided presence, this is effort's sole achievement. Its only function is to get this feeling of consent into the mind. And for this there is but one way. The idea to be consented to must be kept from flickering and going out. It must be held steadily before the mind until it *fills* the mind. Such filling of the mind by an idea, with its congruous associates, *is* consent to the idea and to the fact which the idea represents. If the idea be that, or include that, of a bodily movement of our own, then we call the consent thus laboriously gained a motor volition. For Nature here 'backs' us instantaneously and follows up our inward willingness by outward changes on her own part. She does this in no other instance. Pity she should not have been more generous, nor made a world whose other parts were as immediately subject to our will!

On page 531, in describing the 'reasonable type' of decision, it was said that it usually came when the right conception of the case was found. Where, however, the right conception is an anti-impulsive one, the whole intellectual ingenuity of the man usually goes to work to crowd it out of sight, and to find names for the emergency, by the help of which the dispositions of the moment may sound sanctified, and sloth or passion may reign unchecked. How many excuses does the drunkard find when each new temptation comes! It is a new brand of liquor which the interests of intellectual culture in such matters oblige him to test; moreover it is poured out and it is sin to waste it; or others are drinking and it would be churlishness to refuse; or it is but to enable him to sleep, or just to get through this job of work; or it isn't drinking, it is because he feels so cold; or it is Christmas-day; or it is a means of stimulating him to make a more powerful resolution in favor of abstinence than any he has hitherto made; or it is just this once, and once doesn't count, etc., etc., *ad libitum*—it is, in fact, anything you like except *being a drunkard*. *That* is the conception that will not stay before the poor soul's attention. But if he once gets able to pick out that way of conceiving, from all the other possible ways of conceiving the various opportunities which occur, if through thick and thin he holds to it that this is being a drunkard and is nothing else, he is not likely to remain one long. The effort by which he succeeds in keeping the right *name* unwaveringly present to his mind proves to be his saving moral act.*

Everywhere then the function of the effort is the same: to keep affirming and adopting a thought which, if left to itself, would slip away. It may be cold and flat when the spontaneous mental drift is towards excitement, or great and arduous when the spontaneous drift is towards repose. In the one case the effort has to inhibit an explosive, in the

---

* Cf. Aristotle's Nichomachæan Ethics, VII. 3 ; also a discussion of the doctrine of 'The Practical Syllogism' in Sir A. Grant's edition of this work, 2d ed. vol. I. p. 212 ff.

other to arouse an obstructed will. The exhausted sailor on a wreck has a will which is obstructed. One of his ideas is that of his sore hands, of the nameless exhaustion of his whole frame which the act of farther pumping involves, and of the deliciousness of sinking into sleep. The other is that of the hungry sea ingulfing him. "Rather the aching toil!" he says; and it becomes reality then, in spite of the inhibiting influence of the relatively luxurious sensations which he gets from lying still. But exactly similar in form would be his consent to lie and sleep. Often it is the thought of sleep and what leads to it which is the hard one to keep before the mind. If a patient afflicted with insomnia can only control the whirling chase of his thoughts so far as to think of _nothing at all_ (which can be done), or so far as to imagine one letter after another of a verse of scripture or poetry spelt slowly and monotonously out, it is almost certain that here, too, specific bodily effects will follow, and that sleep will come. The trouble is to keep the mind upon a train of objects naturally so insipid. _To sustain a representation, to think_, is, in short, the only moral act, for the impulsive and the obstructed, for sane and lunatics alike. Most maniacs know their thoughts to be crazy, but find them too pressing to be withstood. Compared with them the sane truths are so deadly sober, so cadaverous, that the lunatic cannot bear to look them in the face and say, "Let these alone be my reality!" But with sufficient effort, as Dr. Wigan says,

"Such a man can for a time _wind himself up_, as it were, and determine that the notions of the disordered brain shall not be manifested. Many instances are on record similar to that told by Pinel, where an inmate of the Bicêtre, having stood a long cross-examination, and given every mark of restored reason, signed his name to the paper authorizing his discharge 'Jesus Christ,' and then went off into all the vagaries connected with that delusion. In the phraseology of the gentleman whose case is related in an early part of this [Wigan's] work he had 'held himself tight' during the examination in order to attain his object; this once accomplished he 'let himself down' again, and, if even _conscious_ of his delusion, could not control it. I have observed with such persons that it requires a considerable time to wind themselves up to the pitch of complete self-control, that the effort is a painful tension of the mind. . . . When thrown off their guard by any accidental remark or worn out by the length of the examination, they

let themselves go, and cannot gather themselves up again without preparation. Lord Erskine relates the story of a man who brought an
action against Dr. Munro for confining him without cause. He underwent the most rigid examination by the counsel for the defendant without discovering any appearance of insanity, till a gentleman asked him
about a princess with whom he corresponded in cherry-juice, and he
became instantly insane."*

To sum it all up in a word, *the terminus of the psychological process in volition, the point to which the will is directly applied, is always an idea.* There are at all times *some* ideas
from which we shy away like frightened horses the moment
we get a glimpse of their forbidding profile upon the
threshold of our thought. *The only resistance which our
will can possibly experience is the resistance which such an idea
offers to being attended to at all.* To attend to it is the volitional act, and the only inward volitional act which we ever
perform.

I have put the thing in this ultra-simple way because I
want more than anything else to emphasize the fact that
volition is primarily a relation, not between our Self and

---

* The Duality of the Mind, pp. 141–2. Another case from the same
book (p 123): "A gentleman of respectable birth, excellent education,
and ample fortune, engaged in one of the highest departments of trade,
. . . and being induced to embark in one of the plausible speculations of
the day . . . was utterly ruined. Like other men he could bear a sudden
overwhelming reverse better than a long succession of petty misfortunes,
and the way in which he conducted himself on the occasion met with unbounded admiration from his friends. He withdrew, however, into rigid
seclusion, and being no longer able to exercise the generosity and indulge
the benevolent feelings which had formed the happiness of his life, made
himself a substitute for them by daydreams, gradually fell into a state of
irritable despondency, from which he only gradually recovered with the
loss of reason. He now fancied himself possessed of immense wealth, and
gave without stint his imaginary riches. He has ever since been under
gentle restraint, and leads a life not merely of happiness, but of bliss ; con-
verses rationally, reads the newspapers, where every tale of distress attracts
his notice, and being furnished with an abundant supply of blank checks,
he fills up one of them with a munificent sum, sends it off to the sufferer,
and sits down to his dinner with a happy conviction that he has earned the
right to a little indulgence in the pleasures of the table ; and yet, on a
serious conversation with one of his old friends, he is quite conscious of
his real position, but the conviction is so exquisitely painful that *he will
not let himself believe it.*"

extra-mental matter (as many philosophers still maintain), but between our Self and our own states of mind. But when, a short while ago, I spoke of the filling of the mind with an idea as being equivalent to consent to the idea's object, I said something which the reader doubtless questioned at the time, and which certainly now demands some qualification ere we pass beyond.

It is unqualifiedly true that if any thought *do* fill the mind exclusively, such filling is consent. The thought, for that time at any rate, carries the man and his will with it. But it is not true that the thought *need* fill the mind exclusively for consent to be there; for we often consent to things whilst thinking of other things, even of hostile things; and we saw in fact that precisely what distinguishes our 'fifth type' of decision from the other types (see p. 534) is just this coexistence with the triumphant thought of other thoughts which would inhibit it but for the effort which makes it prevail. The effort to *attend* is therefore only a part of what the word 'will' covers; it covers also the effort to *consent* to something to which our attention is not quite complete. Often, when an object has gained our attention exclusively, and its motor results are just on the point of setting in, it seems as if the sense of their imminent irrevocability were enough of itself to start up the inhibitory ideas and to make us pause. Then we need a new stroke of effort to break down the sudden hesitation which seizes upon us, and to persevere. So that although attention is the first and fundamental thing in volition, *express consent to the reality of what is attended to* is often an additional and quite distinct phenomenon involved.

The reader's own consciousness tells him of course just what these words of mine denote. And I freely confess that I am impotent to carry the analysis of the matter any farther, or to explain in other terms of what this consent consists. It seems a subjective experience *sui generis*, which we can designate but not define. We stand here exactly where we did in the case of belief. When an idea *stings* us in a certain way, makes as it were a certain electric connection with our self, we believe that it *is* a reality. When it stings us in another way, makes another connection with our Self, we say, *let it be* a reality. To the word 'is' and to the words 'let it be' there correspond peculiar attitudes of consciousness which it is vain to seek to explain. The indicative and the imperative moods are as much ultimate categories of thinking as they are of grammar. The 'quality of reality' which these moods attach to things is not like other qualities. It is a relation to our life. It means *our* adoption of the things, *our* caring for them, *our* standing by them. This at least is what it practically means for us; what it may mean beyond that we do not know. And the transition from merely considering an object as possible, to deciding or willing it to be real; the change from the fluctuating to the stable personal attitude concerning it; from the 'don't care' state of mind to that in which 'we mean business,' is one of the most familiar things in life. We can partly enumerate its conditions; and we can partly trace its consequences, especially the momentous one that when the mental object is a movement of our own body, it realizes itself outwardly when the mental change in question has occurred. But the change itself as a subjective phenomenon is something which we can translate into no simpler terms.

THE QUESTION OF 'FREE-WILL.'

Especially must we, when talking about it, rid our mind of the fabulous warfare of separate agents called 'ideas.' The brain-processes may be agents, and the thought as such may be an agent. But what the ordinary psychologies call 'ideas' are nothing but parts of the total *object* of representation. All that is before the mind at once, no matter how complex a system of things and relations it may be, is one object for the thought. Thus, 'A-and-B-and-their-mutual-incompatibility-and-the-fact-that-one-alone-can-be-true-or-can-become-real-notwithstanding-the-probability-or-desirability-of-both' may be such a complex object; and where the thought is deliberative its object has always some such form as this. When, now, we pass from deliberation to decision, that total object undergoes a change. We either dismiss A altogether and its relations to B, and think of B exclusively; or after thinking of both as possibilities, we next think that A is impossible, and that B is or forthwith shall be real. In either case a *new* object is before our thought; and where effort exists, *it* is where the change from the first object to the second one is hard. Our thought seems to turn in this case like a heavy door upon its hinges ; only, so far as the effort feels spontaneous, it turns, not as if by some one helping, but as if by an inward activity, born for the occasion, of its own.

The psychologists who discussed 'the muscular sense' at the international congress at Paris in 1889 agreed at the end that they needed to come to a better understanding in regard to this appearance of internal activity at the moment when a decision is made. M. Fouillée, in an article which I find more interesting and suggestive than coherent or conclusive,* seems to resolve our sense of activity into that of our very *existence as thinking entities.* At least so I translate his words.† But we saw in Chapter X how hard it is to lay a verifying finger plainly upon the thinking process as such, and to distinguish it from certain objects of the stream. M. Fouillée admits this ; but I do not think he fully realizes how strong would be the position of a man who should suggest (see Vol. I. p. 301) that the feeling of moral activity itself which accompanies the advent of cer- tain 'objects' before the mind is nothing but certain other objects,—constrictions, namely, in the brows, eyes, throat, and breathing apparatus, present then, but absent from other pulses of subjective change. Were this the truth, then a part, at any rate, of the activity of which we become aware in effort would seem merely to be that of our body ; and many thinkers would probably thereupon conclude that this 'settles the claims' of inner activity, and dismisses the whole notion of such a thing as a superfluity in psy- chological science.

I cannot see my way to so extreme a view; even al- though I must repeat the confession made on pp. 296–7 of Vol. I, that I do not *fully* understand how we come to our unshakable belief that thinking exists as a special kind of

---

* 'Le Sentiment de l'Effort, et la Conscience de l'Action,' in Revue Philosophique, xxviii. 561. † P. 577.

immaterial process alongside of the material processes of the world. It is certain, however, that only by *postulating* such thinking do we make things currently intelligible; and it is certain that no psychologist has as yet denied the *fact* of thinking, the utmost that has been denied being its dynamic power. But if we postulate the fact of the thinking at all, I believe that we must postulate its power as well; nor do I see how we can rightly equalize its power with its mere existence, and say (as M. Fouillée seems to say) that for the thought-process to *go on at all* is an activity, and an activity everywhere the same; for certain steps forward in this process seem *prima facie* to be passive, and other steps (as where an object comes with effort) seem *prima facie* to be active in a supreme degree. If we admit, therefore, that our thoughts *exist*, we ought to admit that they exist after the fashion in which they appear, as things, namely, that supervene upon each other, sometimes with effort and sometimes with ease; the only questions being, is the effort where it exists a fixed function of the *object*, which the latter imposes on the thought? or is it such an independent 'variable' that with a constant object more or less of it may be made?

It certainly appears to us indeterminate, and as if, even with an unchanging object, we might make more or less, as we choose. If it be really indeterminate, our future acts are ambiguous or unpredestinate: in common parlance, *our wills are free*. If the amount of effort be not indeterminate, but be related in a fixed manner to the objects themselves, in such wise that whatever object at any time fills our consciousness was from eternity bound to fill it then and there, and compel from us the exact effort, neither more nor less, which we bestow upon it,—then our wills are not free, and all our acts are foreordained. *The question of fact in the free-will controversy is thus extremely simple.* It relates solely to the amount of effort of attention or consent which we can at any time put forth. Are the duration and intensity of this effort fixed functions of the object, or are they not? Now, as I just said, it *seems* as if the effort were an independent variable, as if we might exert more or less of it in any given case. When a man has let his thoughts go **for**

days and weeks until at last they culminate in some particularly dirty or cowardly or cruel act, it is hard to persuade him, in the midst of his remorse, that he might not
have reined them in ; hard to make him believe that this
whole goodly universe (which his act so jars upon) required
and exacted it of him at that fatal moment, and from eternity
made aught else impossible. But, on the other hand, there
is the certainty that all his *effortless* volitions are resultants
of interests and associations whose strength and sequence are
mechanically determined by the structure of that physical
mass, his brain ; and the general continuity of things and
the monistic conception of the world may lead one irresistibly to postulate that a little fact like effort can form no
real exception to the overwhelming reign of deterministic
law. Even in effortless volition we have the consciousness
of the alternative being also possible. This is surely a delusion here ; why is it not a delusion everywhere ?

My own belief is that the question of free-will is insoluble on strictly psychologic grounds. After a certain
amount of effort of attention has been given to an idea, it
is manifestly impossible to tell whether either more or less
of it *might* have been given or not. To tell that, we should
have to ascend to the antecedents of the effort, and defining them with mathematical exactitude, prove, by laws of
which we have not at present even an inkling, that the
only amount of sequent effort which could *possibly* comport
with them was the precise amount which actually came.
Measurements, whether of psychic or of neural quantities,
and deductive reasonings such as this method of proof implies, will surely be forever beyond human reach. No serious psychologist or physiologist will venture even to suggest a notion of how they might be practically made. We
are thrown back therefore upon the crude evidences of introspection on the one hand, with all its liabilities to deception, and, on the other hand, upon *a priori* postulates
and probabilities. He who loves to balance nice doubts
need be in no hurry to decide the point. Like Mephis-
topheles to Faust, he can say to himself, " *dazu hast du noch
eine lange Frist,*" for from generation to generation the
reasons adduced on both sides will grow more voluminous,

and the discussion more refined. But if our speculative delight be less keen, if the love of a *parti pris* outweighs that of keeping questions open, or if, as a French philosopher of genius says, *"l'amour de la vie qui s'indigne de tant de discours,"* awakens in us, craving the sense of either peace or power,—then, taking the risk of error on our head, we must project upon one of the alternative views the attribute of reality for us; we must so fill our mind with the idea of it that it becomes our settled creed. The present writer does this for the alternative of freedom, but since the grounds of his opinion are ethical rather than psychological, he prefers to exclude them from the present book.*

A few words, however, may be permitted about the logic of the question. The most that any argument can do for determinism is to make it a clear and seductive conception, which a man is foolish not to espouse, so long as he stands by the great scientific postulate that the world must be one unbroken fact, and that prediction of all things without exception must be ideally, even if not actually, possible. It is a *moral* postulate about the Universe, the postulate that *what ought to be can be, and that bad acts cannot be fated, but that good ones must be possible in their place*, which would lead one to espouse the contrary view. But when scientific and moral postulates war thus with each other and objective proof is not to be had, the only course is voluntary choice, for scepticism itself, if systematic, is also voluntary choice. If, meanwhile, the will *be* undetermined, it would seem only fitting that the belief in its indetermination should be voluntarily chosen from amongst other possible beliefs. Freedom's first deed should be to affirm itself. We ought never to hope for any other method of getting at the truth if indeterminism be a fact. Doubt of this particular truth will therefore probably be open to us to the end of time, and the utmost that a

---

* They will be found indicated, in somewhat popular form, in a lecture on 'The Dilemma of Determinism,' published in the Unitarian Review (of Boston) for September 1884 (vol. XXII. p. 193).

believer in free-will can *ever* do will be to show that the deterministic arguments are not coercive. That they are seductive, I am the last to deny; nor do I deny that effort may be needed to keep the faith in freedom, when they press upon it, upright in the mind.

There is a *fatalistic argument* for determinism, however, which is radically vicious. When a man has let himself go time after time, he easily becomes impressed with the enormously preponderating influence of circumstances, hereditary habits, and temporary bodily dispositions over what might seem a spontaneity born for the occasion. "All is fate," he then says; "all is resultant of what pre-exists. Even if the moment seems original, it is but the instable molecules passively tumbling in their preappointed way. It is hopeless to resist the drift, vain to look for any new force coming in; and less, perhaps, than anywhere else under the sun is there anything really mine in the decisions which I make." This is really no argument for simple determinism. There runs throughout it the sense of a force which might make things otherwise from one moment to another, if it were only strong enough to breast the tide. A person who feels the *impotence* of free effort in this way has the acutest notion of what is meant by it, and of its possible independent power. How else could he be so conscious of its absence and of that of its effects? But genuine determinism occupies a totally different ground; not the *impotence* but the *unthinkability* of free-will is what it affirms. It admits something phenomenal *called* free effort, which *seems* to breast the tide, but it claims this as a *portion of the tide*. The variations of the effort cannot be independent, it says; they cannot originate *ex nihilo*, or come from a fourth dimension; they are mathematically fixed functions of the ideas themselves, which are the tide. Fatalism, which conceives of effort clearly enough as an independent variable that *might* come from a fourth dimension, if it *would* come but that *does not* come, is a very dubious ally for determinism. It strongly imagines that very *possibility* which determinism denies.

But what, quite as much as the inconceivability of absolutely independent variables, persuades modern men

of science that their efforts must be predetermined, is the
continuity of the latter with other phenomena whose pre-
determination no one doubts. Decisions with effort merge
so gradually into those without it that it is not easy to say
where the limit lies. Decisions without effort merge again
into ideo-motor, and these into reflex acts ; so that the
temptation is almost irresistible to throw the formula
which covers so many cases over absolutely all. Where
there is effort just as where there is none, the ideas themselves which furnish the matter of deliberation are brought
before the mind by the machinery of association. And
this machinery is essentially a system of arcs and paths,
a reflex system, whether effort be amongst its incidents or
not. The reflex way is, after all, the universal way of
conceiving the business. The feeling of *ease* is a passive
result of the way in which the thoughts unwind themselves.
Why is not the feeling of effort the same? Professor
Lipps, in his admirably clear deterministic statement, so
far from admitting that the feeling of effort testifies to an
increment of force exerted, explains it as a sign that force
is lost. We speak of effort, according to him, whenever a
force expends itself (wholly or partly) in neutralizing
another force, and so fails of its own possible outward
effect. The outward effect of the antagonistic force, however, also fails in corresponding measure, " so that there is
no effort without counter-effort, . . . and effort and counter-effort signify only that causes are mutually robbing
each other of effectiveness." * Where the forces are ideas,
both sets of them, strictly speaking, are the seat of effort—
both those which tend to explode, and those which tend to
check them. We, however, call the more abundant mass
of ideas *ourselves;* and, talking of its effort as *our* effort, and
of that of the smaller mass of ideas as the *resistance,*† we
say that our effort sometimes overcomes the resistances
offered by the inertias of an obstructed, and sometimes

---

* See Grundtatsachen des Seelenlebens, pp. 594–5 ; and compare the
conclusion of our own chapter on Attention, Vol. I. pp. 448–454.

† Thus at least I interpret Prof. Lipps's words : " Wir wissen us natur-
gemäss in jedem Streben umsomehr aktiv, je mehr unser *ganzes* Ich bei
dem Streben betheiligt ist," u. s. w. (p. 601).

those presented by the impulsions of an explosive, will. Really both effort and resistance are ours, and the identification of our *self* with one of these factors is an illusion and a trick of speech. I do not see how anyone can fail (especially when the mythologic dynamism of separate 'ideas,' which Professor Lipps cleaves to, is translated into that of brain-processes) to recognize the fascinating simplicity of some such view as his. Nor do I see why *for scientific purposes* one need give it up even if indeterminate amounts of effort really do occur. Before their indeterminism, science simply *stops.* She can abstract from it altogether, then; for in the impulses and inhibitions with which the effort has to cope there is already a larger field of uniformity than she can ever practically cultivate. Her prevision will never foretell, even if the effort be completely predestinate, the actual way in which each individual emergency is resolved. Psychology will be Psychology,* and Science Science, as much as ever (as much and no more) in this world, whether free-will be true in it or not. Science, however, must be constantly reminded that her purposes are not the only purposes, and that the order of uniform causation which she has use for, and is therefore right in postulating, may be enveloped in a wider order, on which she has no claims at all.

We can therefore leave the free-will question altogether out of our account. As we said in Chapter VI (p. 453), the operation of free effort, if it existed, could only be to hold some one ideal object, or part of an object, a little longer or a little more intensely before the mind. Amongst the alternatives which present themselves as *genuine possi-*

---

* Such ejaculations as Mr. Spencer's: "Psychical changes either conform to law or they do not. If they do not, this work, in common with all works on the subject, is sheer nonsense: no science of Psychology is possible" (Principles of Psychology, i. 503),—are beneath criticism. Mr. Spencer's work, like all the other 'works on the subject,' treats of those general conditions of *possible* conduct within which all our real decisions must fall no matter whether their effort be small or great. However closely psychical changes may conform to law, it is safe to say that individual histories and biographies will never be written in advance no matter how 'evolved' psychology may become.

bles, it would thus make one effective.* And although such quickening of one idea might be *morally and historically momentous,* yet, if considered *dynamically,* it would be an operation amongst those physiological infinitesimals which calculation must forever neglect.

But whilst eliminating the question about the amount of

---

* *Caricatures* of the kind of supposition which free will demands abound in deterministic literature. The following passage from John Fiske's Cosmic Philosophy (pt. II. chap. XVII) is an example: "If volitions arise without cause, it necessarily follows that we cannot infer from them the character of the antecedent states of feeling. If, therefore, a murder has been committed, we have *a priori* no better reason for suspecting the worst enemy than the best friend of the murdered man. If we see a man jump from a fourth-story window, we must beware of too hastily inferring his insanity, since he may be merely exercising his free-will; the intense love of life implanted in the human breast being, as it seems, unconnected with attempts at suicide or at self-preservation. We can thus frame no theory of human actions whatever. The countless empirical maxims of every-day life, the embodiment as they are of the inherited and organized sagacity of many generations, become wholly incompetent to guide us; and nothing which any one may do ought ever to occasion surprise. The mother may strangle her first-born child, the miser may cast his long-treasured gold into the sea, the sculptor may break in pieces his lately-finished statue, in the presence of no other feelings than those which before led them to chersish, to hoard, and to create.

"To state these conclusions is to refute their premise. Probably no defender of the doctrine of free-will could be induced to accept them, even to save the theorem with which they are inseparably wrapped up. Yet the dilemma cannot be avoided. Volitions are either caused or they are not. If they are not caused, an inexorable logic brings us to the absurdities just mentioned. If they are caused, the free-will doctrine is annihilated. . . . In truth, the immediate corollaries of the free-will doctrine are so shocking, not only to philosophy but to common-sense, that were not accurate thinking a somewhat rare phenomenon, it would be inexplicable how any credit should ever have been given to such a dogma. This is but one of the many instances in which by the force of words alone men have been held subject to chronic delusion. . . . Attempting, as the free-will philosophers do, to destroy the science of history, they are compelled by an inexorable logic to pull down with it the cardinal principles of ethics, politics, and jurisprudence. Political economy, if rigidly dealt with on their theory, would fare little better; and psychology would become chaotic jargon. . . . The denial of causation is the affirmation of chance, and 'between the theory of Chance and the theory of Law there can be no compromise, no reciprocity, no borrowing and lending.' To write history on any method furnished by the free-will doctrine would be utterly impossible."—All this comes from Mr. Fiske's not distinguishing between the possibles which really tempt a man and those which tempt him not at all. Free-will, like psychology, deals with the former possibles exclusively.

our effort as one which psychology will never have a practical call to decide, I must say one word about the extraordinarily intimate and important character which the phenomenon of effort assumes in our own eyes as individual men. Of course we measure ourselves by many standards. Our strength and our intelligence, our wealth and even our good luck, are things which warm our heart and make us feel ourselves a match for life. But deeper than all such things, and able to suffice unto itself without them, is the sense of the amount of effort which we can put forth. Those are, after all, but effects, products, and reflections of the outer world within. But the effort seems to belong to an altogether different realm, as if it were the substantive thing which we *are*, and those were but externals which we *carry*. If the 'searching of our heart and reins' be the purpose of this human drama, then what is sought seems to be what effort we can make. He who can make none is but a shadow; he who can make much is a hero. The huge world that girdles us about puts all sorts of questions to us, and tests us in all sorts of ways. Some of the tests we meet by actions that are easy, and some of the questions we answer in articulately formulated words. But the deepest question that is ever asked admits of no reply but the dumb turning of the will and tightening of our heartstrings as we say, " *Yes, I will even have it so!* " When a dreadful object is presented, or when life as a whole turns up its dark abysses to our view, then the worthless ones among us lose their hold on the situation altogether, and either escape from its difficulties by averting their attention, or if they cannot do that, collapse into yielding masses of plaintiveness and fear. The effort required for facing and consenting to such objects is beyond their power to make. But the heroic mind does differently. To it, too, the objects are sinister and dreadful, unwelcome, incompatible with wished-for things. But it can face them if necessary, without for that losing its hold upon the rest of life. The world thus finds in the heroic man its worthy match and mate; and the effort which he is able to put forth to hold himself erect and keep his heart unshaken is the direct measure of his worth

and function in the game of human life. He can *stand* this
Universe. He can meet it and keep up his faith in it in
presence of those same features which lay his weaker brethren low. He can still find a zest in it, not by 'ostrich-like
forgetfulness,' but by pure inward willingness to face the
world with those deterrent objects there. And hereby he
becomes one of the masters and the lords of life. He must
be counted with henceforth; he forms a part of human
destiny. Neither in the theoretic nor in the practical
sphere do we care for, or go for help to, those who have
no head for risks, or sense for living on the perilous edge.
Our religious life lies more, our practical life lies less, than
it used to, on the perilous edge. But just as our courage
is so often a reflex of another's courage, so our faith is apt
to be, as Max Müller somewhere says, a faith in some one
else's faith. We draw new life from the heroic example.
The prophet has drunk more deeply than anyone of the cup
of bitterness, but his countenance is so unshaken and he
speaks such mighty words of cheer that his will becomes
our will, and our life is kindled at his own.

Thus not only our morality but our religion, so far as
the latter is deliberate, depend on the effort which we can
make. "*Will you or won't you have it so?*" is the most prob-
ing question we are ever asked; we are asked it every hour
of the day, and about the largest as well as the smallest,
the most theoretical as well as the most practical, things.
We answer by *consents or non-consents* and not by words.
What wonder that these dumb responses should seem our
deepest organs of communication with the nature of things!
What wonder if the effort demanded by them be the measure of our worth as men! What wonder if the amount
which we accord of it be the one strictly underived and
original contribution which we make to the world!

THE EDUCATION OF THE WILL.

The education of the will may be taken in a broader or a
narrower sense. In the broader sense, it means the whole
of one's training to moral and prudential conduct, and of
one's learning to adapt means to ends, involving the 'association of ideas,' in all its varieties and complications, to-

gether with the power of inhibiting impulses irrelevant to the ends desired, and of initiating movements contributory thereto. It is the acquisition of these latter powers which I mean by the education of the will in the narrower sense. And it is in this sense alone that it is worth while to treat the matter here.*

Since a willed movement is a movement preceded by an idea of itself, the problem of the will's education is the problem of how the idea of a movement can arouse the movement itself. This, as we have seen, is a secondary kind of process; for framed as we are, we can have no *a priori* idea of a movement, no idea of a movement which we have not already performed. Before the idea can be generated, the movement must have occurred in a blind, unexpected way, and left its idea behind. *Reflex, instinctive,* or *random execution* of a *movement* must, in other words, precede its voluntary execution. Reflex and instinctive movements have already been considered sufficiently for the purposes of this book. 'Random' movements are mentioned so as to include *quasi*-accidental reflexes from inner causes, or movements possibly arising from such overflow of nutrition in special centres as Prof. Bain postulates in his explanation of those 'spontaneous discharges' by which he sets such great store in his derivation of the voluntary life.†

Now *how can the sensory process which a movement has previously produced, discharge, when excited again, into the centre for the movement itself?* On the movement's original occurrence the motor discharge came first and the sensory process second; now in the voluntary repetition the sensory process (excited in weak or 'ideational' form) comes first, and the motor discharge comes second. To tell how this comes to pass would be to answer the problem of the education of the will in physiological terms. Evidently the problem is that of the formation of *new paths;* and the

---

* On the education of the Will from a pedagogic point of view, see an article by G. Stanley Hall in the Princeton Review for November 1882, and some bibliographic references there contained.

† See his Emotions and Will, 'The Will,' chap. I. I take the name of random movements from Sully, Outlines of Psychology, p. 593.

only thing to do is to make hypotheses, till we find some which seem to cover all the facts.

How is a fresh path ever formed? All paths are paths of discharge, and the discharge always takes place in the direction of least resistance, whether the cell which discharges be 'motor' or 'sensory.' The *connate* paths of least resistance are the paths of instinctive reaction; and I submit as my first hypothesis that *these paths all run one way, that is from 'sensory' cells into 'motor' cells and from motor cells into muscles, without ever taking the reverse direction.* A motor cell, for example, never awakens a sensory cell directly, but only through the incoming current caused by the bodily movements to which its discharge gives rise. And a sensory cell *always* discharges or normally tends to discharge towards the motor region. Let this direction be called the 'forward' direction. I call the law an hypothesis, but really it is an indubitable truth. No impression or idea of eye, ear, or skin comes to us without occasioning a movement, even though the movement be no more than the accommodation of the sense-organ; and all our trains of sensation and sensational imagery have their terms alternated and interpenetrated with motor processes, of most of which we practically are unconscious. Another way of stating the rule is to say that, primarily or connately, all currents through the brain run towards the Rolandic region, and that there they run out, and never return upon themselves. From this point of view the distinction of sensory and motor cells has no fundamental significance. All cells are motor; we simply call those of the Rolandic region, those nearest the mouth of the funnel, the motor cells *par excellence.*

A corollary of this law is that 'sensory' cells do not awaken each other connately; that is, that no one sensible property of things has any tendency, in advance of experience, to awaken in us the idea of any other sensible properties which in the nature of things may go with it. *There is no a priori calling up of one 'idea' by another;* the only *a priori* couplings are of ideas with movements. All suggestions of one sensible fact by another take place by secondary paths which experience has formed.

The diagram (Fig. 87) shows what happens in a nervous system ideally reduced to the fewest possible terms. A stimulus reaching the sense-organ awakens the sensory cell, S ; this by the connate or instinctive path discharges the motor cell, M, which makes the muscle contract; and the contraction arouses the second sensory cell, K, which

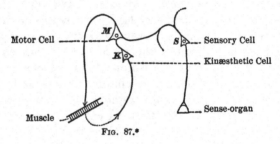

Motor Cell _ _ _ _   *S* _ _ Sensory Cell

_ _ Kinæsthetic Cell

_ _ Sense-organ

Muscle _ _

Fig. 87.*

may be the organ either of a 'resident' or 'kinæsthetic,' or of a 'remote,' sensation. (See above, p. 488.) This cell K again discharges into M. If this were the entire nervous mechanism, the movement, once begun, would be self-maintaining, and would stop only when the parts were exhausted. And this, according to M. Pierre Janet, is what actually happens in *catalepsy.* A cataleptic patient is anæsthetic, speechless, motionless. Consciousness, so far as we can judge, is abolished. Nevertheless the limbs will retain whatever position is impressed upon them from without, and retain it so long that if it be a strained and unnatural position, the phenomenon is regarded by Charcot as one of the few conclusive tests against hypnotic subjects shamming, since hypnotics can be made catalep-

---

* This figure and the following ones are purely schematic, and must not be supposed to involve any theory about protoplasmatic and axis-cylinder processes. The latter, according to Golgi and others, emerge from the base of the cell, and each cell has but one. They alone form a nervous network. The reader will of course also understand that none of the hypothetical constructions which I make from now to the end of the chapter are proposed as definite accounts of what happens. All I aim at is to make it clear in some more or less symbolic fashion that the formation of new paths, the learning of habits, etc., is in *some* mechanical way conceivable. Compare what was said in Vol. I. p. 81, note.

tic, and then keep their limbs outstretched for a length of time quite unattainable by the waking will. M. Janet thinks that in all these cases the outlying ideational processes in the brain are temporarily thrown out of gear. The kinæsthetic sensation of the raised arm, for example, is produced in the patient when the operator raises the arm, this sensation discharges into the motor cell, which through the muscle reproduces the sensation, etc., the currents running in this closed circle until they grow so weak, by exhaustion of the parts, that the member slowly drops. We may call this circle from the muscle to K, from K to M, and from M to the muscle again, the 'motor circle.' *We should all be cataleptics and never stop a muscular contraction once begun, were it not that other processes simultaneously going on inhibit the contraction. Inhibition is therefore not an occasional accident; it is an essential and unremitting element of our cerebral life.* It is interesting to note that Dr. Mercier, by a different path of reasoning, is also led to conclude that we owe to outside inhibitions exclusively our power to arrest a movement once begun.*

One great inhibiter of the discharge of K into M seems to be the painful or otherwise displeasing quality of the sensation itself of K; and conversely, when this sensation is distinctly pleasant, that fact tends to further K's discharge into M, and to keep the primordial motor circle agoing. Tremendous as the part is which pleasure and pain play in our psychic life, we must confess that absolutely nothing is known of their cerebral conditions. It is hard to imagine them as having special centres; it is harder still to invent peculiar forms of process in each and every centre, to which these feelings may be due. And let one try as one will to represent the cerebral activity in exclusively mechanical terms, I, for one, find it quite impossible to enumerate what seem to be the facts and yet to make no mention of the psychic side which they possess. However it be with other drainage currents and discharges, the drainage currents and discharges of the brain are not purely physical facts. They are *psycho-physical* facts, and the

---

* The Nervous System and the Mind (1888), pp. 75-6.

spiritual quality of them seems a codeterminant of their mechanical effectiveness. If the mechanical activities in a cell, as they increase, give pleasure, they seem to increase all the more rapidly for that fact; if they give displeasure, the displeasure seems to dampen the activities. The psychic side of the phenomenon thus seems, somewhat like the applause or hissing at a spectacle, to be an encouraging or adverse *comment* on what the machinery brings forth. The soul *presents* nothing herself; *creates* nothing; is at the mercy of the material forces for all *possibilities;* but amongst these possibilities she *selects;* and by reinforcing one and checking others, she figures not as an 'epiphenomenon,' but as something from which the play gets moral support. I shall therefore never hesitate to invoke the efficacy of the conscious comment, where no strictly mechanical reason appears why a current escaping from a cell should take one path rather than another.* But the *existence* of the current, and its *tendency* towards either path, I feel bound to account for by mechanical laws.

Having now considered a nervous system reduced to its lowest possible terms, in which all the paths are connate, and the possibilities of inhibition not extrinsic, but due solely to the agreeableness or disagreeableness of the feeling aroused, let us turn to the conditions under which new paths may be formed. Potentialities of new paths are furnished by the fibres which connect the sensory cells amongst themselves; but these fibres are not originally pervious, and have to be made so by a process which I proceed hypothetically to state as follows: *Each discharge from a sensory cell in the forward direction† tends to drain the cells lying behind the discharging one of whatever tension they may possess. The drainage from the rearward cells is what for the first time makes the fibres pervious. The result is a new-formed 'path,' running from the cells which were 'rearward' to the cell which was 'forward' on that occasion; which path, if on future occasions the rearward cells are independently excited, will tend to carry off their activity in the same direction so as to excite the*

---

* Compare Vol. I. pp. 137, 142.

† That is, the direction towards the motor cells.

forward cell, and will deepen itself more and more every time it is used.

Now the 'rearward cells,' so far, stand for all the sensory cells of the brain other than the one which is discharging ; but such an indefinitely broad path would practically be no better than no path, so here I make a third hypothesis, which, taken together with the others, seems to me to cover all the facts. It is that *the deepest paths are formed from the most drainable to the most draining cells; that the most drainable cells are those which have just been discharging ; and that the most draining cells are those which are now discharging or in which the tension is rising towards the point of discharge.** Another diagram, Fig. 88, will make the matter clear. Take the operation represented by the previous diagram at the moment when, the muscular contraction having occurred, the cell K is discharging forward into M. Through the dotted line *p* it will, according to our third hypothesis, drain S (which, in the supposed case, has just dis-

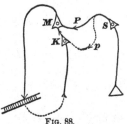

Fig. 88.

charged into M by the connate path P, and caused the muscular contraction), and the result is that *p* will now remain as a new path open from S to K. When next S is excited from without it will tend not only to discharge into M, but into K as well. K thus gets excited directly by S *before* it gets excited by the incoming current from the muscle ; or, translated into psychic terms : *when a sensation has once produced a movement in us, the next time we have the sensation, it tends to suggest the idea of the movement, even before the movement occurs.*†

---

* This brain-scheme seems oddly enough to give a certain basis of reality to those hideously fabulous performances of the Herbartian *Vorstellungen.* Herbart says that when one idea is inhibited by another it fuses with that other and thereafter helps it to ascend into consciousness. Inhibition is thus the basis of association in both schemes, for the 'draining' of which the text speaks is tantamount to an inhibition of the activity of the cells which are drained, which inhibition makes the inhibited revive the inhibiter on later occasions.

† See the luminous passage in Münsterberg : Die Willenshandlung, pp. 144-5.

The same principles also apply to the relations of K and M. M, lying in the forward direction, drains K, and the path KM, even though it be no primary or a connate path, becomes a secondary or habitual one. Hereafter K may be aroused in any way whatsoever (not as before from S or from without) and still it will tend to discharge into M ; or, to express it again in psychic terms, *the idea of the movement M's sensory effects will have become an immediately antecedent condition to the production of the movement itself.*

Here, then, we have the answer to our original question of how a sensory process which, the first time it occurred, was the effect of a movement, can later figure as the movement's cause.

It is obvious on this scheme that the cell which we have marked K may stand for the seat of either a resident or a remote sensation occasioned by the motor discharge. It may indifferently be a tactile, a visual, or an auditory cell. The idea of how the arm *feels* when raised may cause it to rise ; but no less may the idea of some *sound* which it makes in rising, or of some *optical* impression which it produces. Thus we see that the 'mental cue' may belong to either of various senses ; and that what our diagrams lead us to infer is what really happens ; namely, that in our movements, such as that of speech, for example, in some of us it is the tactile, in others the acoustic, *Effectsbild,* or memory-image, which seems most concerned in starting the articulation (Vol. I. pp. 54–5). The *primitive* ' starters,' however, of all our movements are not *Effectsbilder* at all, but sensations and objects, and subsequently ideas derived therefrom.

Let us now turn to the more complex and serially concatenated movements which oftenest meet us in real life. The object of our will is seldom a single muscular contraction ; it is almost always an orderly sequence of contractions, ending with a sensation which tells us that the goal is reached. But the several contractions of the sequence are not each distinctly willed ; each earlier one seems rather, by the sensation it produces, to call its follower up, after the fashion described in Chapter VI, where we spoke of habitual concatenated movements being due to a series of secondarily organized reflex arcs (Vol. I. p. 116). The first contraction is the one distinctly willed, and after willing it we let the rest of the chain rattle off of its own accord. How now is such an orderly concatenation of movements originally learned? or in other words, how are paths formed for the first time between one motor centre and another, so that the discharge of the first centre makes the others discharge in due order all along the line ?

The phenomenon involves a rapid alternation of motor discharges and resultant afferent impressions, for as long a time as it lasts. They must be associated in one definite order; and the order must once have been *learned*, i.e., it must have been picked out and held to more and more exclusively out of the many other random orders which first presented themselves. The random afferent impressions fell out, those that felt right were selected and grew together in the chain. A chain which we actively teach ourselves by stringing a lot of right-feeling impressions together differs in no essential respect from a chain which we passively learn from someone else who gives us impressions in a certain order. So to make our ideas more precise, let us take a particular concatenated movement for an example, and let it be the recitation of the alphabet, which someone in our childhood taught us to say by heart.

What we have seen so far is how the idea of the sound or articulatory feeling of A may make us say 'A,' that of B, 'B,' and so on. But what we now want to see is *why the sensation that A is uttered should make us say ' B,' why the sensation that B is uttered should make us say 'C,' and so on.*

To understand this we must recall what happened when we first learned the letters in their order. Someone repeated A, B, C, D to us over and over again, and we imitated the sounds. Sensory cells corresponding to each letter were awakened in succession in such wise that each one of them (by virtue of our second law) must have 'drained' the cell just previously excited and left a path by which that cell tended ever afterwards to discharge into the cell that drained it. Let S^a, S^b, S^c in figure 89 stand for three of these cells. Each later one of them, as it discharges motorwards, draws a current from the previous one, S^b from S^a, and S^c from S^b. Cell S^b having thus drained S^a, if S^a ever gets excited again, it tends to discharge into S^b; whilst

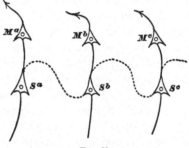

Fɪɢ. 89.

S^c having drained S^b, S^b later discharges into S^c, etc., etc. —all through the dotted lines. Let now the idea of the letter A arise in the mind, or, in other words, let S^a be aroused: what happens? A current runs from S^a not only into the motor cell M^a for pronouncing that letter, but also into the cell S^b. When, a moment later, the effect of M^a's discharge comes back by the afferent nerve and re-excites S^a, this latter cell is inhibited from discharging again into M^a and reproducing the 'primordial motor circle' (which

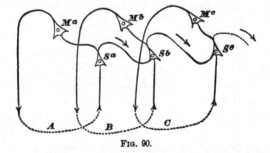

Fɪɢ. 90.

in this case would be the continued utterance of the letter A), by the fact that the process in S^b, already under headway and tending to discharge into its own motor associate M^b, is, *under the existing conditions*, the stronger drainage-channel for S^a's excitement. The result is that M^b discharges and the letter B is pronounced; whilst at the same time S^c receives some of S^b's overflow; and, a moment later when the sound of B enters the ear, discharges into the motor cell for pronouncing C, by a repetition of the same mechanism as before; and so on *ad libitum.* Figure 90 represents the entire set of processes involved.

The only thing that one does not immediately see is the reason why 'under the existing conditions' the path from S^a to S^b should be the stronger drainage-channel for S^a's excitement. If the cells and fibres in the figure constituted the entire brain we might suppose either a mechanical or a psychical reason. The mechanical reason might lie in a general law that cells like S^b and M^b, whose excitement is in a rising phase, are stronger drainers than cells like M^a, which have just discharged; or it might lie in the fact that an irradiation of the current beyond S^b into S^c and M^c has already begun also; and in a still farther law that drainage tends in the direction of the widest irradiations. Either of these suppositions would be a sufficient mechanical reason why, having once said A, we should not say it again. But we must not forget that the process has a psychical side, nor close our eyes to the possibility that the *sort of feeling* aroused by incipient currents may be the reason why certain of them are instantly inhibited and others helped to flow. There is no doubt that before we have uttered a single letter, the general intention to recite the alphabet is already there; nor is there any doubt that to that intention corresponds a widespread premonitory rising of tensions along the entire system of cells and fibres which are later to be aroused. So long as this rise of tensions *feels good*, so long every current which increases it is furthered, and every current which diminishes it is checked; and this may be the chief one of the 'existing conditions' which make the drainage-channel from S^a to S^b temporarily so strong.*

The new paths between the sensory cells of which we have studied the formation are paths of 'association,' and we now see why associations run always in the forward

---

* L. Lange's and Münsterberg's experiments with 'shortened' or 'muscular' reaction-time (see Vol. I. p. 432) show how potent a fact dynamically this anticipatory preparation of a whole set of possible drainage-channels is.

direction ; why, for example, we cannot say the alphabet
backward, and why, although S^b discharges into S^c, there
is no tendency for S^c to discharge into S^b, or at least no
more than for it to discharge into S^a.* The first-formed
paths had, according to the principles which we invoked,
to run from cells that had just discharged to those that
were discharging ; and now, to get currents to run the other
way, we must go through a new learning of our letters with
their order reversed. There will *then* be two sets of asso-
ciation-pathways, either of them possible, between the sensible cells. I represent them in Fig. 91, leaving out the
motor features for simplicity's sake. The dotted lines are
the paths in the backward direction, newly organized from

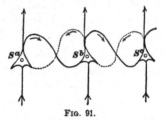

FIG. 91.

the reception by the ear of the letters in the order C B A.
   The same principles will explain the formation of new
paths successively concatenated to no matter how great an
extent, but it would obviously be folly to pretend to illustrate by more intricate examples. I will therefore only
bring back the case of the child and flame (Vol. I. p. 25), to
show how easily it admits of explanation as a ' purely cortical
transaction ' (*ibid.* p. 80). The sight of the flame stimulates the cortical centre S^1 which discharges by an instinctive reflex path into the centre M^1 for the grasping-move-

---

* Even as the proofs of these pages are passing through my hands, I
receive Heft 2 of the Zeitschrift für Psychologie u. Physiologie der Sin-
nesorgane, in which the irrepressible young Münsterberg publishes experiments to show that there is no association between successive ideas,
apart from intervening movements. As my explanations have assumed that
an earlier excited *sensory* cell drains a later one, his experiments and inferences would, if sound, upset all my hypotheses. I therefore can (at this
late moment) only refer the reader to Herr M.'s article, hoping to review
the subject again myself in another place.

ment. This movement produces the feeling of burn, as its effects come back to the centre S²; and this centre by a

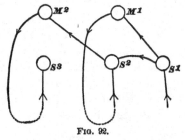

Fig. 92.

second connate path discharges into M², the centre for withdrawing the hand. The movement of withdrawal stimulates the centre S³, and this, as far as we are concerned, is the last thing that happens. Now the next time the child sees the candle, the cortex is in possession of the secondary paths which the first experience left behind. S², having been stimulated immediately after S¹, drained the latter, and now S¹ discharges into S² before the discharge of M¹ has had time to occur; in other words, the sight of the flame suggests the idea of the burn before it produces its own natural reflex effects. The result is an inhibition of M¹, or an overtaking of it before it is completed, by M².—The characteristic physiological feature in all these acquired systems of paths lies in the fact that the new-formed sensory irradiations keep *draining things forward,* and so breaking up the ' motor circles ' which would otherwise accrue. But, even apart from catalepsy, we see the ' motor circle ' every now and then come back. An infant learning to execute a simple movement at will, without regard to other movements beyond it, keeps repeating it till tired. How reiteratively they babble each new-learned word! And we adults often catch ourselves reiterating some meaningless word over and over again, if by chance we once begin to utter it ' absent-mindedly,' that is, without thinking of any ulterior train of words to which it may belong.

One more observation before closing these already too protracted physiological speculations. Already (Vol. I. p. 71) I have tried to shadow forth a reason why collateral innervation should establish itself after loss of brain-tissue, and why incoming stimuli should find their way out again, after an interval, by their former paths. I can now explain this a little better. Let S¹ be the dog's hearing-centre when he receives the command 'Give your paw.' This *used* to discharge into the motor centre M¹, of whose discharge S² represents the kinæsthetic effect; but now M¹ has been destroyed by an operation, so that S¹ discharges as it can, into other movements of the body, whimpering, raising the wrong paw, etc. The kinæsthetic centre S² meanwhile has

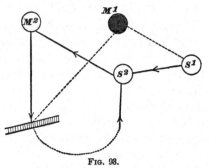

Fig. 98.

been awakened by the order S¹, and the poor animal's mind tingles with expectation and desire of certain incoming sensations which are entirely at variance with those which the really executed movements give. None of the latter sensations arouse a 'motor circle,' for they are displeasing and inhibitory. But when, by random accident, S¹ and S² *do* discharge into a path leading through M², by which the *paw is again given*, and S² is excited at last from without as well as from within, there are no inhibitions and the 'motor circle' is formed: S¹ discharges into M² over and over again, and the path from the one spot to the other is so much deepened that at last it becomes organized as the regular channel of efflux when S¹ is aroused. No other path has a chance of being organized in like degree.

CHAPTER XXVII.

HYPNOTISM.

MODES OF OPERATING, AND SUSCEPTIBILITY.

THE 'hypnotic,' 'mesmeric,' or 'magnetic' trance *can be induced in various ways*, each operator having his pet method. The simplest one is to leave the subject seated by himself, telling him that if he close his eyes and relax his muscles and, as far as possible, think of vacancy, in a few minutes he will 'go off.' On returning in ten minutes you may find him effectually hypnotized. Braid used to make his subjects look at a bright button held near their forehead until their eyes spontaneously closed. The older mesmerists made 'passes' in a downward direction over the face and body, but without contact. Stroking the skin of the head, face, arms and hands, especially that of the region round the brows and eyes, will have the same effect. Staring into the eyes of the subject until the latter droop; making him listen to a watch's ticking; or simply making him close his eyes for a minute whilst you describe to him the feeling of falling into sleep, 'talk sleep' to him, are equally efficacious methods in the hands of some operators; whilst with trained subjects any method whatever from which they have been led by previous suggestion to expect results will be successful.* The touching of an object

---

* It should be said that the methods of leaving the patient to himself, and that of the simple verbal suggestion of sleep (the so-called Nancy method introduced by Dr. Liébault of that place), seem, wherever applicable, to be the best, as they entail none of the after-inconveniences which occasionally follow upon straining his eyes. A new patient should not be put through a great variety of different suggestions in immediate succession. He should be waked up from time to time, and then rehypnotized to avoid mental confusion and excitement. Before finally waking a subject you should *undo* whatever delusive suggestions you may have implanted in him, by telling him that they are all gone, etc., and that you are now going to restore him to his natural state. Headache, languor, etc., which sometimes fol-

which they are told has been 'magnetized,' the drinking of 'magnetized' water, the reception of a letter ordering them to sleep, etc., are means which have been frequently employed. Recently M. Liégeois has hypnotized some of his subjects at a distance of 1½ kilometres by giving them an intimation to that effect through a telephone. With some subjects, if you tell them in advance that at a certain hour of a certain day they will become entranced, the prophecy is fulfilled. Certain hysterical patients are immediately thrown into hypnotic catalepsy by any violent sensation, such as a blow on a gong or the flashing of an intense light in their eyes. Pressure on certain parts of the body (called *zones hypnogènes* by M. Pitres) rapidly produces hypnotic sleep in some hysterics. These regions, which differ in different subjects, are oftenest found on the forehead and about the root of the thumbs. Finally, persons in ordinary sleep may be transferred into the hypnotic condition by verbal intimation or contact, performed so gently as not to wake them up.

Some operators appear to be more successful than others in getting control of their subjects. I am informed that Mr. Gurney (who made valuable contributions to the theory of hypnotism) was never able himself to hypnotize, and had to use for his observations the subjects of others. On the other hand, Liébault claims that he hypnotizes 92 per cent of all comers, and Wetterstrand in Stockholm says that amongst 718 persons there proved to be only 18 whom he failed to influence. Some of this disparity is unquestionably due to differences in the personal 'authority' of the operator, for the prime condition of success is that the subject should confidently *expect* to be entranced. Much also depends on the operator's tact in interpreting the physiognomy of his subjects, so as to give the right commands, and 'crowd it on' to the subject, at just the propitious moments. These conditions account for the fact that operators grow more

---

low the first trance or two, must be banished at the outset, by the operator strongly assuring the subject that such things *never* come from hypnotism, that the subject *must not* have them, etc.

successful the more they operate. Bernheim says that whoever does not hypnotize 80 per cent of the persons whom he tries has not yet learned to operate as he should. Whether certain operators have over and above this a peculiar 'magnetic power' is a question which I leave at present undecided.* Children under three or four, and insane persons, especially idiots, are unusually hard to hypnotize. This seems due to the impossibility of getting them to fix their attention continuously on the idea of the coming trance. All ages above infancy are probably equally hypotizable, as are all races and both sexes. A certain amount of mental training, sufficient to aid concentration of the attention, seems a favorable condition, and so does a certain momentary indifference or passivity as to the result. Native strength or weakness of 'will' have absolutely nothing to do with the matter. Frequent trances enormously increase the susceptibility of a subject, and many who resist at first succumb after several trials. Dr. Moll says he has more than once succeeded after forty fruitless attempts. Some experts are of the opinion that every one is hypnotizable essentially, the only difficulty being the more habitual presence in some individuals of hindering mental preoccupations, which, however, may suddenly at some moment be removed.

The trance may be dispelled instantaneously by saying in a rousing voice, 'All right, wake up!' or words of similar purport. At the Salpêtrière they awaken subjects by blowing on their eyelids. Upward passes have an awakening effect; sprinkling cold water ditto. Anything will awaken a patient who expects to be awakened by that thing. Tell him that he will wake after counting five, and he will do so. Tell him to waken in five minutes, and he is very likely to do so punctually, even though he interrupt thereby some exciting histrionic performance which you may have suggested.—As Dr. Moll says, any theory which pretends to

---

* Certain facts would seem to point that way. Cf., e.g., the case of the man described by P. Despine, Étude Scientifique sur le Somnambulisme, p. 286 ff.

explain the physiology of the hypnotic state must keep account of the fact that so simple a thing as hearing the word ' wake! ' will end it.

THEORIES ABOUT THE HYPNOTIC STATE.

The intimate nature of the hypnotic condition, when once induced, can hardly be said to be understood. Without entering into details of controversy, one may say that three main opinions have been held concerning it, which we may call respectively the theories of

1. Animal magnetism ;
2. of Neurosis ; and finally of
3. Suggestion.

According to the *animal-magnetism theory* there is a direct passage of force from the operator to the subject, whereby the latter becomes the former's puppet. This theory is nowadays given up as regards all the ordinary hypnotic phenomena, and is only held to by some persons as an explanation of a few effects exceptionally met with.

According to the *neurosis-theory,* the hypnotic state is a peculiar pathological condition into which certain predisposed patients fall, and in which special physical agents have the power of provoking special symptoms, quite apart from the subjects mentally expecting the effect. Professor Charcot and his colleagues at the Salpêtrière hospital admit that this condition is rarely found in typical form. They call it then *le grand hypnotisme,* and say that it accompanies the disease hystero-epilepsy. If a patient subject to this sort of hypnotism hear a sudden loud noise, or look at a bright light unexpectedly, she falls into the *cataleptic* trance. Her limbs and body offer no resistance to movements communicated to them, but retain permanently the attitudes impressed. The eyes are staring, there is insensibility to pain, etc., etc. If the eyelids be forcibly closed, the cataleptic gives place to the *lethargic* condition, characterized by apparent abolition of consciousness, and absolute muscular relaxation except where the muscles are kneaded or the tendons struck by the operator's hand, or certain nerve-trunks are pressed upon. Then the muscles in question, or those supplied by the same nerve-trunk enter into a more or less steadfast tonic contraction. Charcot calls this symptom by the name of neuro-muscular hyperexcitability. The lethargic state may be *primarily* brought on by fixedly looking at anything, or by pressure on the closed eyeballs. Friction on the top of the head will make the patient pass from either of the two preceding conditions into the *somnambulic* state, in which she is alert, talkative, and susceptible to all the suggestions of the operator. The somnambulic state may also be induced primarily, by fixedly looking at a small object. In this state the accurately limited muscular contractions characteristic of lethargy do not follow upon the above-described manipulations, but instead of them there is a tendency to rigidity of entire regions of the body, which may upon occasion develop into general tetanus, and which is brought about by gently touching the skin or blowing upon it. M. Charcot calls this by the name of cutaneo-muscular hyperexcitability.

Many other symptoms, supposed by their observers to be independent of mental expectation, are described, of which I only will mention the more interesting. Opening the eyes of a patient in lethargy causes her to pass into catalepsy. If one eye only be opened, the corresponding half of the body becomes cataleptic, whilst the other half remains in lethargy. Similarly, rubbing one side of the head may result in a patient becoming hemilethargic or hemicataleptic and hemisomnambulic. The approach of a magnet (or certain metals) to the skin causes these half-states (and many others) to be transferred to the opposite sides. Automatic repetition of every sound heard ('*echolalia*') is said to be produced by pressure on the lower cervical vertebræ or on the epigastrium. *Aphasia* is brought about by rubbing the head over the region of the speech-centre. Pressure behind the occiput determines *movements of imitation*. Heidenhain describes a number of curious automatic tendencies to movement, which are brought about by stroking various portions of the vertebral column. Certain other symptoms have been frequently noticed, such as a flushed face and cold hands, brilliant and congested eyes, dilated pupils. Dilated reti-

nal vessels and spasm of the accommodation are also reported.

The theory of Suggestion denies that there is any special
hypnotic *state* worthy of the name of trance or neurosis.
All the symptoms above described, as well as those to be
described hereafter, are results of that mental susceptibility which we all to some degree possess, of yielding
assent to outward suggestion, of affirming what we strongly
conceive, and of acting in accordance with what we are
made to expect. The bodily symptoms of the Salpétrière
patients are all of them results of expectation and training.
The first patients accidentally did certain things which
their doctors thought typical and caused to be repeated.
The subsequent subjects 'caught on' and followed the
established tradition. In proof of this the fact is urged
that the classical three stages and their grouped symptoms
have *only* been reported as spontaneously occurring, so far,
at the Salpétrière, though they may be superinduced by
deliberate suggestion, in patients anywhere found. The
ocular symptoms, the flushed face, accelerated breathing,
etc., are said not to be symptoms of the passage into the
hypnotic state as such, but merely consequences of the
strain on the eyes when the method of looking at a bright
object is used. They are absent in the subjects at Nancy,
where simple verbal suggestion is employed. The various
reflex effects (aphasia, echolalia, imitation, etc.) are but
habits induced by the influence of the operator, who unconsciously urges the subject into the direction in which he
would prefer to have him go. The influence of the magnet,
the opposite effects of upward and downward passes, etc.,
are similarly explained. Even that sleepy and inert condition, the advent of which seems to be the prime condition of
farther symptoms being developed, is said to be merely due
to the fact that the mind expects it to come ; whilst its influence on the other symptoms is not physiological, so to speak,
but psychical, its own easy realization by suggestion simply
encouraging the subject to expect that ulterior suggestions
will be realized with equal ease. The radical defenders of
the suggestion-theory are thus led to deny the very exist-

ence of the hypnotic state, in the sense of a peculiar trance-like condition which deprives the patient of spontaneity and makes him passive to suggestion from without. The trance itself is only one of the suggestions, and many subjects in fact can be made to exhibit the other hypnotic phenomena without the preliminary induction of this one.

The theory of suggestion may be said to be quite triumphant at the present day over the neurosis-theory as held at the Salpétrière, with its three states, and its definite symptoms supposed to be produced by physical agents apart from co-operation of the subject's mind. But it is one thing to say this, and it is quite another thing to say that there is no peculiar physiological condition whatever worthy of the name of hypnotic trance, no peculiar state of nervous equilibrium, 'hypotaxy,' 'dissociation,' or whatever you please to call it, during which the subject's susceptibility to outward suggestion is greater than at ordinary times. All the facts seem to prove that, until this trance-like state is assumed by the patient, suggestion produces very insignificant results, but that, when it is once assumed, there are no limits to suggestion's power. The state in question has many affinities with ordinary sleep. It is probable, in fact, that we all pass through it transiently whenever we fall asleep; and one might most naturally describe the usual relation of operator and subject by saying that the former keeps the latter suspended between waking and sleeping by talking to him enough to keep his slumber from growing profound, and yet not in such a way as to wake him up. A hynotized patient, *left to himself*, will either fall sound asleep or wake up entirely. The difficulty in hypnotizing refractory persons is that of catching them at the right moment of transition and making it permanent. Fixing the eyes and relaxing the muscles of the body produce the hypnotic state just as they facilitate the advent of sleep. The first stages of ordinary sleep are characterized by a peculiar dispersed attitude of the attention. Images come before consciousness which are entirely incongruous with our ordinary beliefs and habits of thought. The latter either vanish altogether or withdraw, as it were, inertly into the background of the mind, and let the incongruous images reign alone. These images acquire, moreover, an exceptional vivacity; they become first 'hypnagogic hallucinations,' and then, as the sleep grows deeper, dreams. Now the 'mono-ideism,' or else the impotency and failure to 'rally' on the part of the background-ideas, which thus characterize somnolescence, are unquestionably the result of a special physiological change occurring in the brain at that time. Just so that similar mono-ideism, or dissociation of the reigning fancy from those other thoughts which might possibly act as its 'reductives,' which characterize the hypnotic consciousness, must equally be due to a special cerebral change. The term 'hypnotic trance,' which I employ, tells us nothing of what the change is, but it marks the fact that it exists, and is consequently a useful expression. The great vivacity of the hypnotic images (as gauged by their motor effects), the oblivion of them when normal life is resumed, the abrupt awakening, the recollection of them again in subsequent trances, the anæsthesia and hyperæsthesia which are so frequent, all point away from our simple waking credulity and 'suggestibility' as the type by which the phenomena are to be interpreted, and make us look rather towards sleep and dreaming, or towards those deeper alterations of the personality known as automatism, double consciousness, or 'second' personality for the true analogues of the hypnotic trance.* Even the best hypnotic subjects pass through life without any one suspecting them to possess such a remarkable susceptibility, until by deliberate experiment it is made manifest. The operator fixes their eyes or their attention a short time to develop the propitious phase, holds them in it by his talk, and *the state being there,* makes them the puppets of all his suggestions. But no ordinary suggestions of waking life ever took such control of their mind.

---

* The state is not *identical* with sleep, however analogous in certain respects. The lighter stages of it, particularly, differ from sleep and dreaming, inasmuch as they are characterized almost exclusively by *muscular* inabilities and compulsions, which are not noted in ordinary somnolescence, and the *mind*, which is confused in somnolescence, may be quite clearly conscious, in the lighter state of trance, of all that is going on.

The suggestion-theory may therefore be approved as correct, provided we grant the trance-state as its prerequisite. The three states of Charcot, the strange reflexes of Heidenhain, and all the other bodily phenomena which have been called direct consequences of the trance-state itself, are not such. They are products of suggestion, the trance-state having no particular outward symptoms of its own; but without the trance-state there, those particular suggestions could never have been successfully made.*

THE SYMPTOMS OF THE TRANCE.

This accounts for the altogether indefinite array of symptoms which have been gathered together as characteristic of the hypnotic state. The law of habit dominates hypnotic subjects even more than it does waking ones. Any sort of personal peculiarity, any trick accidentally fallen into in the first instance by some one subject, may, by attracting attention, become stereotyped, serve as a pattern for imitation, and figure as the type of a school. The first subject trains the operator, the operator trains the succeeding subjects, all of them in perfect good faith conspiring together to evolve a perfectly arbitrary result. With the extraordinary perspicacity and subtlety of perception which subjects often display for all that concerns the operator with whom they are *en rapport*, it is hard to keep them ignorant of anything which he expects. Thus it happens that one easily verifies on new subjects what one has already seen on old ones, or any desired symptom of which one may have heard or read.

The symptoms earliest observed by writers were all thought to be typical. But with the multiplication of ob-

---

* The word 'suggestion' has been bandied about too much as if it explained all mysteries: When the subject obeys it is by reason of the 'operator's suggestion'; when he proves refractory it is in consequence of an 'auto-suggestion' which he has made to himself, etc., etc. What explains everything explains nothing; and it must be remembered that what *needs* explanation here is the fact that in a certain condition of the subject suggestions operate as they do *at no other time;* that through them functions are affected which ordinarily elude the action of the waking will ; and that usually all this happens in a condition of which no after-memory remains.

served phenomena, the importance of most particular symptoms as marks of the state has diminished. This lightens very much our own immediate task. Proceeding to enumerate the symptoms of the hypnotic trance, I may confine myself to those which are intrinsically interesting, or which differ considerably from the normal functions of man.

First of all comes *amnesia.* In the earlier stages of hypnotism the patient remembers what has happened, but with successive sittings he sinks into a deeper condition, which is commonly followed by complete loss of memory. He may have been led through the liveliest hallucinations and dramatic performances, and have exhibited the intensest apparent emotion, but on waking he can recall nothing at all. The same thing happens on waking from sleep in the midst of a dream—it quickly eludes recall. But just as we may be *reminded* of it, or of parts of it, by meeting persons or objects which figured therein, so on being adroitly prompted, the hypnotic patient will often remember what happened in his trance. One cause of the forgetfulness seems to be the disconnection of the trance performances with the system of waking ideas. Memory requires a continuous train of association. M. Delbœuf, reasoning in this way, woke his subjects in the midst of an action begun during trance (washing the hands, e.g.), and found that they then remembered the trance. The act in question bridged over the two states. But one can often make them remember by merely telling them during the trance that they *shall* remember. Acts of one trance, moreover, are usually recalled, either spontaneously or at command, during another trance, provided that the contents of the two trances be not mutually incompatible.

Suggestibility. The patient believes everything which his hypnotizer tells him, and does everything which the latter commands. Even results over which the will has normally no control, such as sneezing, secretion, reddening and growing pale, alterations of temperature and heartbeat, menstruation, action of the bowels, etc., may take place in consequence of the operator's firm assertions during the hypnotic trance, and the resulting conviction on the part of the subject, that the effects will occur. Since almost all the phenomena yet to be described are effects of this heightened suggestibility, I will say no more under the general head, but proceed to illustrate the peculiarity in detail.

Effects on the voluntary muscles seem to be those most easily got; and the ordinary routine of hypnotizing consists in provoking them first. Tell the patient that he cannot open his eyes or his mouth, cannot unclasp his hands or lower his raised arm, cannot rise from his seat, or pick up a certain object from the floor, and he will be immediately smitten with absolute impotence in these regards. The effect here is generally due to the *involuntary contraction* of antagonizing muscles. But one can equally well suggest *paralysis*, of an arm for example, in which case it will hang perfectly placid by the subject's side. Cataleptic and tetanic rigidity are easily produced by suggestion, aided by handling the parts. One of the favorite shows at public exhibitions is that of a subject stretched stiff as a board with his head on one chair and his heels on another. The cataleptic retention of impressed attitudes differs from voluntary assumption of the same attitude. An arm voluntarily held out straight will drop from fatigue after a quarter of an hour at the utmost, and before it falls the agent's distress will be made manifest by oscillations in the arm, disturbances in the breathing, etc. But Charcot has shown that an arm held out in hypnotic catalepsy, though it may as soon descend, yet does so slowly and with no accompanying vibration, whilst the breathing remains entirely calm. He rightly points out that this shows a profound physiological change, and is proof positive against simulation, as far as this symptom is concerned. A cataleptic attitude, moreover, may be held for many hours. — Sometimes an expressive attitude, clinching of the fist, contraction of the brows, will gradually set up a sympathetic action of the other muscles of the body, so that at last a *tableau vivant* of fear, anger, disdain, prayer, or other emotional condition, is produced with rare perfection. This effect would seem to be due to the suggestion of the mental state by the first contraction. Stammering, aphasia, or inability to utter certain words, pronounce certain letters, are readily producible by suggestion.

Hallucinations of all the senses and *delusions* of every conceivable kind can be easily suggested to good subjects. The emotional effects are then often so lively, and the pantomimic display so expressive, that it is hard not to believe in a certain 'psychic hyper-excitability,' as one of the concomitants of the hypnotic condition. You can make the subject think that he is freezing or burning, itching or covered with dirt, or wet; you can make him eat a potato for a peach, or drink a cup of vinegar for a glass of champagne; * ammonia will smell to him like cologne water; a chair will be a lion, a broom-stick a beautiful woman, a noise in the street will be an orchestral music, etc., etc., with no limit except your powers of invention and the patience of the lookers on.† Illusions and hallucinations form the *pieces de résistance* at public exhibitions. The comic effect is at its climax when it is successfully suggested to the subject that his personality is changed into that of a baby, of a street boy, of a young lady dressing for a party, of a stump orator, or of Napoleon the Great. He may even be transformed into a beast, or an inanimate thing like a chair or a carpet, and in every case will act out all the details of the part with a sincerity and intensity seldom seen at the theatre. The excellence of the performance is in these cases the best reply to the suspicion that the subject may be shamming—so skilful a shammer must long since have found his true function in life upon the stage. Hallucinations and histrionic delusions generally go with a certain depth of the trance, and are followed

---

* A complete fit of drunkenness may be the consequence of the suggested champagne. It is even said that real drunkenness has been cured by suggestion.

† The suggested hallucination may be followed by a negative after-image, just as if it were a real object. This can be very easily verified with the suggested hallucination of a colored cross on a sheet of white paper. The subject, on turning to another sheet of paper, will see a cross of the complementary color. Hallucinations have been shown by MM. Binet and Féré to be doubled by a prism or mirror, magnified by a lens, and in many other ways to behave optically like real objects. These points have been discussed already on p. 128 ff.

by complete forgetfulness. The subject awakens from them at the command of the operator with a sudden start of surprise, and may seem for a while a little dazed.

Subjects in this condition will receive and execute suggestions of crime, and act out a theft, forgery, arson, or murder. A girl will believe that she is married to her hypnotizer, etc. It is unfair, however, to say that in these cases the subject is a pure puppet with no spontaneity. His spontaneity is certainly not in abeyance so far as things go which are harmoniously associated with the suggestion given him. He takes the text from his operator; but he may amplify and develop it enormously as he acts it out. His spontaneity is lost only for those systems of ideas which *conflict* with the suggested delusion. The latter is thus 'systematized'; the rest of consciousness is shut off, excluded, dissociated from it. In extreme cases the rest of the mind would seem to be actually abolished and the hypnotic subject to be literally a changed personality, a being in one of those 'second' states which we studied in Chapter X. But the reign of the delusion is often not as absolute as this. If the thing suggested be too intimately repugnant, the subject may strenuously resist and get nervously excited in consequence, even to the point of having an hysterical attack. The conflicting ideas slumber in the background and merely permit those in the foreground to have their way until a *real* emergency arises; then they assert their rights. As M. Delbœuf says, the subject surrenders himself good-naturedly to the performance, stabs with the pasteboard dagger you give him because he knows what it is, and fires off the pistol because he knows it has no ball; but for a real murder he would not be your man. It is undoubtedly true that subjects are often well aware that they are acting a part. They know that what they do is absurd. They know that the hallucination which they see, describe, and act upon, is not really there. They may laugh at themselves; and they always recognize the abnormality of their state when asked about it, and call it 'sleep.' One often notices a sort of mocking smile upon them, as if they were playing a comedy, and they may even say on 'coming to' that they were shamming all the while. These facts have misled ultra-skeptical people so far as to make them doubt the genuineness of any hypnotic phenomena at all. But, save the consciousness of 'sleep,' they do not occur in the deeper conditions; and when they do occur they are only a natural consequence of the fact that the 'monoideism' is incomplete. The background-thoughts still exist, and have the power of *comment* on the suggestions, but no power to inhibit their motor and associative effects. A similar condition is frequent enough in the waking state, when an impulse carries us away and our 'will' looks on wonderingly like an impotent spectator. These 'shammers' continue to sham in just the same way, every new time you hypnotize them, until at last they are forced to admit that if shamming there be, it is something very different from the free voluntary shamming of waking hours.

Real sensations may be abolished as well as false ones suggested. Legs and breasts may be amputated, children born, teeth extracted, in short the most painful experiences undergone, with no other anæsthetic than the hypnotizer's assurance that no pain shall be felt. Similarly morbid pains may be annihilated, neuralgias, toothaches, rheumatisms cured. The sensation of hunger has thus been abolished, so that a patient took no nourishment for fourteen days. The most interesting of these suggested anæsthesias are those limited to certain objects of perception. Thus a subject may be made blind to a certain person and to him alone, or deaf to certain words but to no others.* In this case the anæsthesia (or *negative hallucination*, as it has been called) is apt to become *systematized*. Other things related to the person to whom one has been made blind may also be shut out of consciousness. What he says is not heard, his contact is not felt, objects which he takes from his pocket are not seen, etc. Objects which he screens are seen as if he were transparent. Facts about him are forgotten, his name is not recognized when pronounced. Of course there is great variety in the com-

---

* M. Liégeois explains the common exhibition-trick of making the subject unable to get his arms into his coat-sleeves again after he has taken his coat off, by an anæsthesia to the necessary parts of the coat.

pleteness of this systematic extension of the suggested anæsthesia, but one may say that some tendency to it always exists. When one of the subjects' own limbs is made anæsthetic, for example, memories as well as sensations of its movements often seem to depart. An interesting degree of the phenomenon is found in the case related by M. Binet of a subject to whom it was suggested that a certain M. C. was invisible. She still saw M. C., but saw him as a stranger, having lost the memory of his name and his existence.—Nothing is easier than to make subjects forget their own name and condition in life. It is one of the suggestions which most promptly succeed, even with quite fresh ones. A systematized amnesia of certain periods of one's life may also be suggested, the subject placed, for instance, where he was a decade ago with the intervening years obliterated from his mind.

The mental condition which accompanies these systematized anæsthesias and amnesias is a very curious one. The anæsthesia is not a genuine sensorial one, for if you make a real red cross (say) on a sheet of white paper invisible to an hypnotic subject, and yet cause him to look fixedly at a dot on the paper on or near the cross, he will, on transferring his eye to a blank sheet, see a bluish-green after-image of the cross. This proves that it has impressed his sensibility. He has *felt* it, but not *perceived* it. He had actively ignored it, refused to recognize it, as it were. Another experiment proves that he must *distinguish* it first in order thus to ignore it. Make a stroke on paper or blackboard, and tell the subject it is not there, and he will see nothing but the clean paper or board. Next, he not looking, surround the original stroke with other strokes exactly like it, and ask him what he sees. He will point out one by one all the new strokes and omit the original one every time, no matter how numerous the new strokes may be, or in what order they are arranged. Similarly, if the original single stroke to which he is blind be *doubled* by a prism of sixteen degrees placed before one of his eyes (both being kept open), he will say that he now sees *one* stroke, and point in the direction in which the image seen through the prism lies.

Obviously, then, he is not blind to the *kind* of stroke in the least. He is blind only to one individual stroke of that kind in a particular position on the board or paper,— that is, to a particular complex object; and, paradoxical as it may seem to say so, he must distinguish it with great accuracy from others like it, in order to remain blind to it when the others are brought near. He 'apperceives' it, as a preliminary to not seeing it at all! How to conceive of this state of mind is not easy. It would be much simpler to understand the process, if adding new strokes made the first one visible. There would then be two different objects apperceived as totals,—paper with one stroke, paper with two strokes; and, blind to the former, he would see all that was *in* the latter, because he would have apperceived it as a different total in the first instance.

A process of this sort occurs sometimes (not always) when the new strokes, instead of being mere repetitions of the original one, are lines which combine with it into a total object, say a human face. The subject of the trance then may regain his sight of the line to which he had previously been blind, by seeing it as part of the face.

When by a prism before one eye a previously invisible line has been made visible to that eye, and the other eye is closed or screened, *its* closure makes no difference ; the line still remains visible. But if *then* the prism is removed, the line will disappear even to the eye which a moment ago saw it, and both eyes will revert to their original blind state.

We have, then, to deal in these cases neither with a sensorial anæsthesia, nor with a mere failure to notice, but with something much more complex ; namely, an active counting out and positive exclusion of certain objects. It is as when one 'cuts' an acquaintance, 'ignores' a claim, or 'refuses to be influenced' by a consideration of whose existence one remains aware. Thus a lover of Nature in America finds himself able to overlook and ignore entirely the board- and rail-fences and general roadside raggedness, and revel in the beauty and picturesqueness of the other elements of the landscape, whilst to a newly-arrived European the fences are so aggressively present as to spoil enjoyment.

Messrs. Gurney, Janet, and Binet have shown that the ignored elements are preserved in a split-off portion of the subjects' consciousness which can be tapped in certain ways, and made to give an account of itself (see Vol. I. p. 209).

Hyperæsthesia of the senses is as common a symptom as anæsthesia. On the skin two points can be discriminated at less than the normal distance. The sense of touch is so delicate that (as M. Delbœuf informs me) a subject after simply poising on her finger-tips a blank card drawn from a pack of similar ones can pick it out from the pack again by its 'weight.' We approach here the line where, to many persons, it seems as if something more than the ordinary senses, however sharpened, were required in explanation. I have seen a coin from the operator's pocket repeatedly picked out by the subject from a heap of twenty others,* by its greater 'weight' in the subject's language.—Auditory hyperæsthesia may enable a subject to hear a watch tick, or his operator speak, in a distant room.—One of the most extraordinary examples of visual hyperæsthesia is that reported by Bergson, in which a subject who seemed to be reading through the back of a book held and looked at by the operator, was really proved to be reading the image of the page reflected on the latter's cornea. The same subject was able to discriminate with the naked eye details in a microscopic preparation. Such cases of ' hyperæsthesia of vision ' as that reported by Taguet and Sauvaire, where subjects could see things mirrored by non-reflecting bodies, or through opaque pasteboard, would seem rather to belong to ' psychical research ' than to the present category.—The ordinary test of visual hyperacuteness in hypnotism is the favorite trick of giving a subject the hallucination of a picture on a blank sheet of card-board, and then mixing the latter with a lot of other similar sheets. The subject will always find the picture on the original sheet again, and recognize infallibly if it has been turned

---

* Precautions being taken against differences of temperature and other grounds of suggestion.

over, or upside down, although the bystanders have to resort to artifice to identify it again. The Subject notes peculiarities on the card, too small for waking observation to detect.* If it be said that the spectators guide him by their manner, their breathing, etc., that is only another proof of his hyperæsthesia; for he undoubtedly *is* conscious of subtler personal indications (of his operator's mental states especially) than he could notice in his waking state. Examples of this are found in the so-called 'magnetic *rapport*.' This is a name for the fact that in deep trance, or in lighter trance whenever the suggestion is made, the subject is deaf and blind to everyone but the operator or those spectators to whom the latter expressly awakens his senses. The most violent appeals from anyone else are for him as if non-existent, whilst he obeys the faintest signals on the part of his hypnotizer. If in catalepsy, his limbs will retain their attitude only when the operator moves them; when others move them they fall down, etc. A more remarkable fact still is that the patient will often answer anyone whom his operator touches, or at whom he even points his finger, in however concealed a manner. All which is rationally explicable by expectation and suggestion, if only it be farther admitted that his senses are acutely sharpened for all the operator's movements.† He often shows great anxiety and restlessness if the latter is out of the room. A favorite experiment of Mr. E. Gurney's was to put the subject's hands through an opaque screen, and cause the operator to point at one finger. *That* finger presently grew insensible or rigid. A bystander pointing simultaneously at another finger, never made that insensible or rigid. Of course the elective *rapport* with their operator had been developed in these

---

* It should be said, however, that the bystander's ability to discriminate unmarked cards and sheets of paper from each other is much greater than one would naturally suppose.

† I must repeat, however, that we are here on the verge of possibly unknown forces and modes of communication. Hypnotization at a distance, with no grounds for expectation on the subject's part that it was to be tried, seems pretty well established in certain very rare cases. See in general, for information on these matters, the Proceedings of the Soc. for Psych. Research, *passim*.

trained subjects during the hypnotic state, but the phenomenon then occurred in some of them during the waking state, even when their consciousness was absorbed in animated conversation with a fourth party.* I confess that when I saw these experiments I was impressed with the necessity for admitting between the *emanations* from different people differences for which we have no name, and a discriminative sensibility for them of the nature of which we can form no clear conception, but which seems to be developed in certain subjects by the hypnotic trance.—The enigmatic reports of the effect of magnets and metals, even if they be due, as many contend, to unintentional suggestion on the operator's part, certainly involve hyperæsthetic perception, for the operator seeks as well as possible to conceal the moment when the magnet is brought into play, and yet the subject not only finds it out that moment in a way difficult to understand, but may develop effects which (in the first instance certainly) the operator did not expect to find. Unilateral contractures, movements, paralyses, hallucinations, etc., are made to pass to the other side of the body, hallucinations to disappear, or to change to the complementary color, suggested emotions to pass into their opposites, etc. Many Italian observations agree with the French ones, and the upshot is that if unconscious suggestion lie at the bottom of this matter, the patients show an enormously exalted power of divining what it is they are expected to do. This hyperæsthetic perception is what concerns us now.† Its *modus* cannot yet be said to be defined.

---

* Here again the perception in question must take place below the threshold of ordinary consciousness, possibly in one of those split-off selves or 'second' states whose existence we have so often to recognize.

† I myself verified many of the above effects of the magnet on a blindfolded subject on whom I was trying them for the first time, and whom I believe to have never heard of them before. The moment, however, an opaque screen was added to the blindfolding, the effects ceased to coincide with the approximation of the magnet, so that it looks as if visual perception had been instrumental in producing them. The subject passed from my observation, so that I never could clear up the mystery. Of course I gave him consciously no hint of what I was looking for.

Changes in the nutrition of the tissues may be produced by suggestion. These effects lead into therapeutics—a subject which I do not propose to treat of here. But I may say that there seems no reasonable ground for doubting that in certain chosen subjects the suggestion of a congestion, a burn, a blister, a raised papule, or a bleeding from the nose or skin, may produce the effect. Messrs. Beaunis, Berjon, Bernheim, Bourru, Burot, Charcot, Delbœuf, Dumontpallier, Focachon, Forel, Jendrássik, Krafft-Ebing, Liébault, Liégeois, Lipp, Mabille, and others have recently vouched for one or other of these effects. Messrs. Delbœuf and Liégeois have annulled by suggestion, one the effects of a burn, the other of a blister. Delbœuf was led to his experiments after seeing a burn on the skin produced by suggestion, at the Salpétrière, by reasoning that if the idea of a pain could produce inflammation it must be because pain was itself an inflammatory irritant, and that the abolition of it from a real burn ought therefore to entail the absence of inflammation. He applied the actual cautery (as well as vesicants) to symmetrical places on the skin, affirming that no pain should be felt on one of the sides. The result was a dry scorch on that side, with (as he assures me) no after-mark, but on the other side a regular blister with suppuration and a subsequent scar. This explains the innocuity of certain assaults made on subjects during trance. To test simulation, recourse is often had to sticking pins under their finger-nails or through their tongue, to inhalations of strong ammonia, and the like. These irritations, when not felt by the subject, seem to leave no after-consequences. One is reminded of the reported non-inflammatory character of the wounds made on themselves by dervishes in their pious orgies. On the other hand, the reddenings and bleedings of the skin along certain lines, suggested by tracing lines or pressing objects thereupon, put the accounts handed down to us of the stigmata of the cross appearing on the hands, feet, sides, and forehead of certain Catholic mystics in a new light. As so often happens, a fact is denied until a welcome interpretation comes with it. Then it is admitted readily enough; and evidence judged quite insufficient to back a claim, so long as the church had an interest in making it, proves to

be quite sufficient for modern scientific enlightenment, the
moment it appears that a reputed saint can thereby be
classed as 'a case of hystero-epilepsy.'

There remain two other topics, viz., post-hypnotic effects
of suggestion, and effects of suggestion in the waking
state.

Post-hypnotic, or deferred, suggestions are such as are
given to the patients during trance, to take effect after waking. They succeed with a certain number of patients even
when the execution is named for a remote period—months
or even a year, in one case reported by M. Liégeois. In
this way one can make the patient feel a pain, or be paralyzed, or be hungry or thirsty, or have an hallucination,
positive or negative, or perform some fantastic action after
emerging from his trance. The effect in question may be
ordered to take place not immediately, but after an interval
of time has elapsed, and the interval may be left to the
subject to measure, or may be marked by a certain signal.
The moment the signal occurs, or the time is run out, the
subject, who until then seems in a perfectly normal waking
condition, will experience the suggested effect. In many
instances, whilst thus obedient to the suggestion, he
seems to fall into the hypnotic condition again. This is
proved by the fact that the moment the hallucination or suggested performance is over he forgets it, denies all knowledge of it, and so forth; and by the further fact that he is
'suggestable' during its performance, that is, will receive
new hallucinations, etc., at command. A moment later and
this suggestibility has disappeared. It cannot be said, however, that relapse into the trance is an absolutely necessary
condition for the post-hypnotic carrying out of commands,
for the subject may be neither suggestible nor amnesic, and
may struggle with all the strength of his will against the
absurdity of this impulse which he feels rising in him, he
knows not why. In these cases, as in most cases, he forgets
the circumstance of the impulse having been suggested to
him in a previous trance; regards it as arising within himself; and often improvises, as he yields to it, some more or
less plausible or ingenious motive by which to justify it to

the lookers-on. He acts, in short, with his usual sense of personal spontaneity and freedom ; and the disbelievers in the freedom of the will have naturally made much of these cases in their attempts to show it to be an illusion.

The only really mysterious feature of these deferred suggestions is the patient's absolute ignorance during the interval preceding their execution that they have been deposited in his mind. They will often surge up at the preappointed time, even though you have vainly tried a while before to make him recall the circumstances of their production. The most important class of post-hypnotic suggestions are, of course, those relative to the patient's health—bowels, sleep, and other bodily functions. Among the most *interesting* (apart from the hallucinations) are those relative to future trances. One can determine the hour and minute, or the signal, at which the patient will of his own accord lapse into trance again. One can make him susceptible in future to another operator who may have been unsuccessful with him in the past. Or more important still in certain cases, one can, by suggesting that certain persons shall never be able hereafter to put him to sleep, remove him for all future time from hypnotic influences which might be dangerous. This, indeed, is the simple and natural safeguard against those 'dangers of hypnotism' of which uninstructed persons talk so vaguely. A subject who knows himself to be ultra-susceptible should never allow himself to be entranced by an operator in whose moral delicacy he lacks complete confidence ; and he can use a trusted operator's suggestions to protect himself against liberties which others, knowing his weakness, might be tempted to take with him.

The mechanism by which the command is retained until the moment for its execution arrives is a mystery which has given rise to much discussion. The experiments of Gurney and the observations of M. Pierre Janet and others on certain hysterical somnabulists seem to prove that it is stored up in consciousness ; not simply organically registered, but that *the consciousness which thus retains it is split off, dissociated from the rest of the subject's mind.* We have here, in short, an experimental production of one of those 'second' states of the personality of which we have spoken so often. Only here the second state coexists as well as alternates with the first. Gurney had the brilliant idea of *tapping* this second consciousness by means of the planchette. He found that certain persons, who were both hypnotic subjects and automatic writers, would if their hands were placed on a planchette (after being wakened from a trance in which they had received the suggestion of something to be done at a later time) write out unconsciously the order, or something connected with it. This shows that something inside of them, which could express itself through the hand alone, was continuing to think of the order, and possibly of it alone. These researches have opened a new vista of possible experimental investigations into the so-called ' second' states of the personality.

Some subjects seem almost as obedient to suggestion in the waking state as in sleep, or even more so, according to certain observers. Not only muscular phenomena, but changes of personality and hallucinations are recorded as the result of simple affirmation on the operator's part, without the previous ceremony of 'magnetizing' or putting into the ' mesmeric sleep.' These are all trained subjects, however, so far as I know, and the affirmation must apparently be accompanied by the patient concentrating his attention and gazing, however briefly, into the eyes of the operator. It is probable therefore that an extremely rapidly induced condition of trance is a prerequisite for success in these experiments.

I have now made mention of all the more important phenomena of the hypnotic trance. Of their therapeutic or forensic bearings this is not the proper place to speak. The recent literature of the subject is quite voluminous, but much of it consists in repetition. The best compendious work on the subject is ' Der Hypnotismus,' by Dr. A. Moll (Berlin, 1889 ; and just translated into English, N. Y., 1890), which is extraordinarily complete and judicious. The other writings most recommendable are subjoined in the note.*

---

* Binet and Féré, ' Animal Magnetism,' in the International Scientific Series ; A. Bernheim, ' Suggestive Therapeutics ' (N.Y., 1889); J. Liegeois,

Most of them contain a historical sketch and much bibliography. A complete bibliography has been published by M. Dessoir (Berlin, 1888).

' De la Suggestion ' (1889) ; E. Gurney, two articles in Mind, vol. ix.—In the recent revival of interest in the history of this subject, it seems a pity that the admirably critical and scientific work of Dr. John Kearsley Mitchell of Philadelphia should remain relatively so unknown. It is quite worthy to rank with Braid's investigations. See "Five Essays" by the above author, edited by S. Weir Mitchell, Philadelphia, 1859, pp. 141–274.

CHAPTER XXVIII.

NECESSARY TRUTHS AND THE EFFECTS OF EXPERIENCE.

In this final chapter I shall treat of what has sometimes been called *psychogenesis*, and try to ascertain just how far the connections of things in the outward environment can account for our tendency to think of, and to react upon, certain things in certain ways and in no others, even though personally we have had of the things in question no experience, or almost no experience, at all. It is a familiar truth that some propositions are *necessary*. We *must* attach the predicate 'equal' to the subject 'opposite sides of a parallelogram' if we think those terms together at all, whereas we need not in any such way attach the predicate 'rainy,' for example, to the subject 'to-morrow.' The dubious sort of coupling of terms is universally admitted to be due to 'experience'; the certain sort is ascribed to the 'organic structure' of the mind. This structure is in turn supposed by the so-called *apriorists* to be of transcendental origin, or at any rate not to be explicable by experience; whilst by evolutionary empiricists it is supposed to be also due to experience, only not to the experience of the individual, but to that of his ancestors as far back as one may please to go. Our emotional and instinctive tendencies, our irresistible impulses to couple certain movements with the perception or thought of certain things, are also features of our connate mental structure, and like the necessary judgments, are interpreted by the apriorists and the empiricists in the same warring ways.

I shall try in the course of the chapter to make plain three things:

1) That, taking the word experience as it is universally understood, the experience of the race can no more account

for our necessary or *a priori* judgments than the experience of the individual can ;

2) That there is no good evidence for the belief that our instinctive reactions are fruits of our ancestors' education in the midst of the same environment, transmitted to us at birth.

3) That the features of our organic mental structure cannot be explained at all by our conscious intercourse with the outer environment, but must rather be understood as congenital variations, ' accidental ' * in the first instance, but then transmitted as fixed features of the race.

On the whole, then, the account which the apriorists give of the *facts* is that which I defend ; although I should contend (as will hereafter appear) for a naturalistic view of their *cause.*

The first thing I have to say is that all schools (however they otherwise differ) must allow that the *elementary qualities* of cold, heat, pleasure, pain, red, blue, sound, silence, etc., are original, innate, or *a priori* properties of our subjective nature, even though they should require the touch of experience to waken them into actual consciousness, and should slumber, to all eternity, without it.

This is so on either of the two hypotheses we may make concerning the relation of the feelings to the realities at whose touch they become alive. For in the first place, if a feeling do *not* mirror the reality which wakens it and to which we say it corresponds, if it mirror no reality whatever outside of the mind, it of course is a purely mental product. By its very definition it can be nothing else. But in the second place, even if it *do* mirror the reality exactly, still it *is* not that reality itself, it is a duplication of it, the result of a mental reaction. And that the mind should have the power of reacting in just that duplicate way can only be stated as a *harmony* between its nature and the nature of the truth outside of it, a harmony whereby it follows that the qualities of both parties match.

---

* ' Accidental ' in the Darwinian sense, as belonging to a cycle of causation inaccessible to the present order of research.

The originality of these *elements* is not, then, a question for dispute. *The warfare of philosophers is exclusively relative to their* FORMS OF COMBINATION. The empiricist maintains that these forms can only follow the order of combination in which the elements were originally awakened by the impressions of the external world; the apriorists insist, on the contrary, that *some* modes of combination, at any rate, follow from the natures of the elements themselves, and that no amount of experience can modify this result.

WHAT IS MEANT BY EXPERIENCE?

The phrase 'organic mental structure' names the matter in dispute. Has the mind such a structure or not? Are its contents *arranged* from the start, or is the arrangement they may possess simply due to the shuffling of them by experience in an absolutely plastic bed? Now the first thing to make sure of is that when we talk of 'experience,' we attach a definite meaning to the word. *Experience means experience of something foreign supposed to impress us,* whether spontaneously or in consequence of our own exertions and acts. Impressions, as we well know, affect certain orders of sequence and coexistence, and the mind's habits copy the habits of the impressions, so that our images of things assume a time- and space-arrangement which resembles the time- and space-arrangements outside. To uniform outer coexistences and sequences correspond constant conjunctions of ideas, to fortuitous coexistences and sequences casual conjunctions of ideas. We are sure that fire will burn and water wet us, less sure that thunder will come after lightning, not at all sure whether a strange dog will bark at us or let us go by. In these ways experience moulds us every hour, and makes of our minds a mirror of the time- and space-connections between the things in the world. The principle of habit within us so *fixes* the copy at last that we find it difficult even to imagine how the outward order could possibly be different from what it is, and we continually divine from the present what the future is to be. These habits of transition, from one thought to another, are features of mental structure which were lacking in us at birth; we can see their growth under experience's moulding finger, and we can see how often experience undoes her own work, and for an earlier order substitutes a new one. '*The order of experience,*' in this matter of the time- and space-conjunctions of things, is thus an indisputably *vera causa* of our forms of thought. It is our educator, our sovereign helper and friend; and its name, standing for something with so real and definite a use, ought to be kept sacred and encumbered with no vaguer meaning.

If *all* the connections among ideas in the mind could be interpreted as so many combinations of sense-data wrought into fixity in this way from without, then experience in the common and legitimate sense of the word would be the sole fashioner of the mind.

The empirical school in psychology has in the main contended that they can be so interpreted. Before our generation, it was the experience of the individual only which was meant. But when one nowadays says that the human mind owes its present shape to experience, he means the experience of ancestors as well. Mr. Spencer's statement of this is the earliest emphatic one, and deserves quotation in full : *

"The supposition that the inner cohesions are adjusted to the outer persistences by *accumulated* experience of those outer persistences is in harmony with all our actual knowledge of mental phenomena. Though in so far as reflex actions and instincts are concerned, the experience-hypothesis seems insufficient; yet its seeming insufficiency occurs only where the evidence is beyond our reach. Nay, even here such few facts as we can get point to the conclusion that automatic psychical connections result from the registration of *experiences continued for numberless generations.*

"In brief, the case stands thus : It is agreed that all psychical relations, save the absolutely indissoluble, are determined by experiences. Their various strengths are admitted, other things equal, to be proportionate to the *multiplication of experiences.* It is an unavoidable

---

* The passage is in § 207 of the Principles of Psychology, at the end of the chapter entitled 'Reason.' I italicize certain words in order to show that the essence of this explanation is to demand *numerically frequent* experiences. The bearing of this remark will later appear. (Cf. pp. 641–2, *infra.*)

corollary that an *infinity of experiences* will produce a psychical relation that is indissoluble. Though such infinity of experiences cannot be received by a single individual, yet it may be received by the succession of individuals forming a race. And if there is a transmission of induced tendencies in the nervous system, it is inferrible that *all psychical relations whatever*, from the necessary to the fortuitous, result from the experiences of the corresponding external relations ; and are so brought into harmony with them.

" Thus, the experience-hypothesis furnishes an adequate solution. The genesis of instinct, the development of memory and reason out of it, and the consolidation of rational actions and inferences into instinctive ones, are alike explicable on the *single principle* that the cohesion between psychical states is proportionate to the *frequency* with which the relation between the answering external phenomena has been *repeated in experience.*

" The *universal law* that, other things equal, the cohesion of psychical states is proportionate to the *frequency* with which they have followed one another in experience, supplies an explanation of the so-called ' forms of thought,' as soon as it is supplemented by the law that *habitual* psychical successions entail some hereditary tendency to such successions, which, under persistent conditions, will become cumulative in generation after generation. We saw that the establishment of those compound reflex actions called instincts is comprehensible on the principle that inner relations are, by *perpetual repetition*, organized into correspondence with outer relations. We have now to observe that the establishment of those consolidated, those indissoluble, those instinctive mental relations constituting our ideas of Space and Time is comprehensible on the same principle. For if even to external relations that are *often* experienced during the life of a single organism, answering internal relations are established that become next to automatic— if such a combination of psychical changes as that which guides a savage in hitting a bird with an arrow becomes, by constant repetition, so organized as to be performed almost without thought of the processes of adjustment gone through—and if skill of this kind is so far transmissible that particular races of men become characterized by particular aptitudes, which are nothing else than partially-organized psychical connections ; then, if there exist certain external relations which are experienced by all organisms at all instants of their waking lives— relations which are absolutely constant, absolutely universal—there will be established answering internal relations that are absolutely constant, absolutely universal. Such relations we have in those of Space and Time. The organization of subjective relations adjusted to these objective relations has been cumulative, not in each race of creatures only, but throughout successive races of creatures ; and such subjective relations have, therefore, become more consolidated than all others. Being experienced in every perception and every action of each creature, these connections among outer existences must, for this reason too, be responded to by connections among inner feelings, that are, above all others, indissoluble. As the substrata of all other relations in the *non-ego*, they must be responded to by conceptions that are the substrata of all other relations in the *ego*. Being the *constant and infinitely-repeated* elements of thought, they must become the automatic elements of thought—the elements of thought which it is impossible to get rid of —the 'forms of intuition.'

" Such, it seems to me, is the only possible reconciliation between the experience-hypothesis and the hypothesis of the transcendentalists; neither of which is tenable by itself. Insurmountable difficulties are presented by the Kantian doctrine (as we shall hereafter see) ; and the antagonist doctrine, taken alone, presents difficulties that are equally insurmountable. To rest with the unqualified assertion that, antecedent to experience, the mind is a blank, is to ignore the questions—whence comes the power of organizing experiences ? whence arise the different degrees of that power possessed by different races of organisms, and different individuals of the same race ? If, at birth, there exists nothing but a passive receptivity of impressions, why is not a horse as educable as a man ? Should it be said that language makes the difference, then why do not the cat and the dog, reared in the same household, arrive at equal degrees and kinds of intelligence ? Understood in its current form, the experience-hypothesis implies that the presence of a definitely-organized nervous system is a circumstance of no moment —a fact not needing to be taken into account ! Yet it is the all-important fact—the fact to which, in one sense, the criticisms of Leibnitz and others pointed—the fact without which an assimilation of experiences is inexplicable. Throughout the animal kingdom in general, the actions are dependent on the nervous structure. The physiologist shows us that each reflex movement implies the agency of certain nerves and ganglia ; that a development of complicated instincts is accompanied by complication of the nervous centres and their commissural connections ; that the same creature in different stages, as larva and imago for example, changes its instincts as its nervous structure changes ; and that as we advance to creatures of high intelligence, a vast increase in the size and in the complexity of the nervous system takes place. What is the obvious inference ? It is that the ability to co-ordinate impressions and to perform the appropriate actions always implies the pre-existence of certain nerves arranged in a certain way. What is the meaning of the human brain ? It is that the many *established* relations among its parts stand for so many *established* relations among the psychical changes. Each of the constant connections among the fibres of the cerebral masses answers to some *constant connection* of phenomena in the experiences of the race. Just as the organized arrangement subsisting between the sensory nerves of the nostrils and the motor nerves of the respiratory muscles not only makes possible a sneeze, but also, in the newly-born infant, implies sneezings to be hereafter performed ; so, all the organized arrangements subsisting among the nerves of the infant's brain not only make possible certain combinations of impressions, but also imply that such combinations will hereafter be made—imply that there are answering combinations in the outer world—imply a preparedness to cognize these combinations—imply faculties of comprehending them. It is true that the resulting compound psychical changes do not take place with the same readiness and automatic precision as the simple reflex action instanced—it is true that some individual experiences seem required to establish them. But while this is partly due to the fact that these combinations are highly involved, extremely varied in their modes of occurrence, made up therefore of psychical relations less completely coherent, and hence need further repetitions to perfect them ; it is in a much greater degree due to the fact that at birth the organization of the brain is incomplete, and does not cease its spontaneous progress for twenty or thirty years afterwards. Those who contend that knowledge results wholly from the experiences of the individual, ignoring as they do the mental evolution which accompanies the autogenous development of the nervous system, fall into an error as great as if they were to ascribe all bodily growth and structure to exercise, forgetting the innate tendency to assume the adult form. Were the infant born with a full-sized and completely-constructed brain, their position would be less untenable. But, as the case stands, the gradually-increasing intelligence displayed throughout childhood and youth is more attributable to the completion of the cerebral organization than to the individual experiences—a truth proved by the fact that in adult life there is sometimes displayed a high endowment of some faculty which, during education, was never brought into play. Doubtless, experiences received by the individual furnish the concrete materials for all thought. Doubtless, the organized and semi-organized arrangements existing among the cerebral nerves can give no knowledge until there has been a presentation of the external relations to which they correspond. And doubtless the child's daily observations and reasonings aid the formation of those involved nervous connections that are in process of spontaneous evolution ; just as its daily gambols aid the development of its limbs. But saying this is quite a different thing from saying that its intelligence is wholly *produced* by its experiences. That is an utterly inadmissible doctrine—a doctrine which makes the presence of a brain meaningless—a doctrine which makes idiotcy unaccountable.

" In the sense, then, that there exist in the nervous system certain pre-established relations answering to relations in the environment, there is truth in the doctrine of ' forms of intuition'—not the truth which its defenders suppose, but a parallel truth. Corresponding to absolute external relations, there are established in the structure of the nervous system absolute internal relations—relations that are potentially present before birth in the shape of definite nervous connections ; that are antecedent to, and independent of, individual experiences ; and that are automatically disclosed along with the first cognitions. And, as here understood, it is not only these fundamental relations which are thus predetermined, but also hosts of other relations of a more or less constant kind, which are congenitally represented by more or less complete nervous connections. But these predetermined internal relations, though independent of the experiences of the individual, are not independent of experiences in general : they have been determined by the experiences of preceding organisms. The corollary here drawn from the general argument is that the human brain is an organized register of *infinitely-numerous* experiences received during the evolution of life, or rather during the evolution of that series of organisms through which the human organism has been reached. The effects of the most *uniform and frequent* of these experiences have been successively bequeathed, principal and interest ; and have slowly amounted to that high intelligence which lies latent in the brain of the infant— which the infant in after-life exercises and perhaps strengthens or further complicates—and which, with minute additions, it bequeaths to future generations. And thus it happens that the European inherits from twenty to thirty cubic inches more brain than the Papuan. Thus it happens that faculties, as of music, which scarcely exist in some inferior human races, become congenital in superior ones. Thus it happens that out of savages unable to count up to the number of their fingers, and speaking a language containing only nouns and verbs, arise at length our Newtons and Shakspeares."

This is a brilliant and seductive statement, and it doubtless includes a good deal of truth. Unfortunately it fails to go into details ; and when the details are scrutinized, as they soon must be by us, many of them will be seen to be inexplicable in this simple way, and the choice will then remain to us either of denying the experiential origin of certain of our judgments, or of enlarging the meaning of the word experience so as to include these cases among its effects.

TWO MODES OF ORIGIN OF BRAIN STRUCTURE.

If we adopt the former course we meet with a controversial difficulty. The 'experience-philosophy' has from time immemorial been the opponent of theological modes of thought. The word experience has a halo of anti-supernaturalism about it; so that if anyone express dissatisfaction with any function claimed for it, he is liable to be treated as if he could only be animated by loyalty to the catechism, or in some way have the interests of obscurantism at heart. I am entirely certain that, on this ground alone, what I have ereloing to say will make this a sealed chapter to many of my readers. "He denies experience!" they will exclaim, "denies science; believes the mind created by miracle; is a regular old partisan of innate ideas! That is enough! we'll listen to such antediluvian twaddle no more." Regrettable as is the loss of readers capable of such wholesale discipleship, I feel that a definite meaning for the word experience is even more important than their company. 'Experience' does not mean every natural, as opposed to every supernatural, cause. It means a particular sort of natural agency, alongside of which other more recondite natural agencies may perfectly well exist. With the scientific animus of anti-supernaturalism we ought to agree, but we ought to free ourselves from its verbal idols and bugbears.

Nature has many methods of producing the same effect. She may make a 'born' draughtsman or singer by tipping in a certain direction at an opportune moment the molecules of some human ovum; or she may bring forth a child ungifted and make him spend laborious but successful years at school. She may make our ears ring by the sound of a bell, or by a dose of quinine ; make us see yellow by spreading a field of buttercups before our eyes, or by mixing a little santonine powder with our food ; fill us with terror of certain surroundings by making them really dangerous, or by a blow which produces a pathological alteration of our brain. It is obvious that we need two words to designate these two modes of operating. *In the one case the natural agents produce perceptions which take cognizance of the agents themselves ; in the other case, they produce perceptions which take cognizance of something else.* What is taught to the mind by the 'experience,' in the first case, is the *order of the experience itself*—the 'inner relation' (in Spencer's phrase) 'corresponds' to the 'outer relation' which produced it, by remembering and knowing the latter. But in the case of the *other* sort of natural agency, what is taught to the mind has nothing to do with the agency itself, but with some different outer relation altogether. A diagram will express the alternatives. B stands for our human brain in the midst of the world. All the little *o*'s

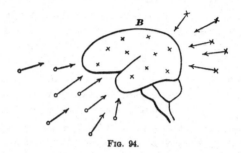

Fig. 94.

with arrows proceeding from them are natural objects (like sunsets, etc.), which impress it through the senses, and in the strict sense of the word give it *experience,* teaching it by habit and association what is the order of their ways. All the little *x*'s inside the brain and all the little *x*'s outside of it are other natural objects and processes (in the ovum, in the blood, etc.), which equally modify the brain, but mould it to no cognition of *themselves.* The *tinnitus aurium* discloses no properties of the quinine; the musical endowment teaches no embryology; the morbid dread (of solitude, perhaps) no brain-pathology; but the way in which a dirty sunset and a rainy morrow hang together in the mind copies and teaches the sequences of sunsets and rainfall in the outer world.

In zoological evolution we have two modes in which an animal race may grow to be a better match for its environment.

First, the so-called way of ' adaptation,' in which the environment may itself modify its inhabitant by exercising, hardening, and habituating him to certain sequences, and these habits may, it is often maintained, become hereditary.

Second, the way of 'accidental variation,' as Mr. Darwin termed it, in which certain young are born with peculiarities that help them and their progeny to survive. That variations of *this* sort tend to become hereditary, no one doubts.

The first mode is called by Mr. Spencer direct, the second indirect, equilibration. Both equilibrations must of course be natural and physical processes, but they belong to entirely different physical spheres. The direct influences are obvious and accessible things. The causes of variation in the young are, on the other hand, molecular and hidden. The direct influences are the animal's 'experiences,' in the widest sense of the term. Where what is influenced by them is the *mental* organism, they are *conscious* experiences, and become the *objects* as well as the causes of their effects. That is, the effect consists in a tendency of the experience itself to be remembered, or to have its elements thereafter coupled in imagination just as they were coupled in the experience. In the diagram these experiences are represented by the o's exclusively. The x's, on the other hand, stand for the indirect causes of mental modification—causes of which we are not immediately conscious as such, and which are not the direct *objects* of the effects they produce. Some of them are molecular accidents before birth ; some of them are collateral and remote combinations, unintended combinations, one might say, of more direct effects wrought in the unstable and intricate brain-tissue. Such a result is unquestionably the susceptibility to music, which some individuals possess at the present day. It has no zoological utility ; it corresponds to no object in the natural environment; it is a pure *incident* of having a hearing organ, an incident depending on such instable and inessential conditions that one brother may have it and another brother not. Just so with the susceptibility to sea-sickness, which, so far from being engendered by long experience of its 'object' (if a heaving deck can be called its object) is erelong annulled thereby. Our higher æsthetic, moral, and intellectual life seems made up of affections of this collateral and incidental sort, which have entered the mind by the back stairs, as it were, or rather have not entered the mind at all, but got surreptitiously born in the house. No one can successfully treat of psychogenesis, or the factors of mental evolution, without distinguishing between these two ways in which the mind is assailed.

The way of 'experience' proper is the front door, the door of the five senses. The agents which affect the brain in this way immediately become the mind's *objects*. The other agents do not. It would be simply silly to say of two men with perhaps equal effective skill in drawing, one an untaught natural genius, the other a mere obstinate plodder in the studio, that both alike owe their skill to their 'experience.' The reasons of their several skills lie in wholly disparate natural cycles of causation.*

I will then, with the reader's permission, *restrict the word 'experience' to processes which influence the mind by the front-door-way of simple habits and association.* What the back-door-effects may be will probably grow clearer

---

* Principles of Biology, part III. chaps. XI, XII.—Goltz and Loeb have found that dogs become mild in character when their occipital, and fierce when their frontal, brain-lobes are cut off. "A dog which originally was cross in an extreme degree, never suffering himself to be touched, and even refusing, after two days' fasting, to take a piece of bread from my hand, became, after a bilateral operation on the occipital lobes, perfectly trustful and harmless. He underwent five operations on these parts. . . . Each one of them made him more good-natured; so that at last (just as Goltz observed of his dogs) he would let other dogs take away the very bones which he was gnawing" (Loeb, Pflüger's Archiv, XXXIX. 300). A course of kind treatment and training might have had a similar effect. But how absurd to call two such different causes by the same name, and to say both times that the beast's 'experience of outer relations' is what educates him to good-nature. This, however, is virtually what all writers do who ignore the distinction between the 'front-door' and the 'back-door' manners of producing mental change.

One of the most striking of these back-door affections is *susceptibility to the charm of drunkenness*. This (taking drunkenness in the broadest sense, as teetotalers use the word) is one of the deepest functions of human nature. Half of both the poetry and the tragedy of human life would vanish if alcohol were taken away. As it is, the thirst for it is such that in the United States the cash-value of its sales amounts to that of the sales of meat and of bread put together. And yet what ancestral 'outer relation' is responsible for this peculiar reaction of ours? The only 'outer relation' could be the alcohol itself, which, comparatively speaking, came into the environment but yesterday, and which, so far from creating, is tending to eradicate, the love of itself from our mental structure, by letting only those families of men survive in whom it is not strong. The love of drunkenness is a purely accidental susceptibility of a brain, evolved for entirely different uses, and its causes are to be sought in the molecular realm, rather than in any possible order of 'outer relations.'

as we proceed; so I will pass right on to a scrutiny of the actual mental structure which we find.

THE GENESIS OF THE ELEMENTARY MENTAL CATEGORIES.

We find: 1. Elementary sorts of sensation, and feelings of personal activity;

2. Emotions; desires; instincts; ideas of worth; æsthetic ideas;

3. Ideas of time and space and number;

4. Ideas of difference and resemblance, and of their degrees.

5. Ideas of causal dependence among events; of end and means; of subject and attribute.

6. Judgments affirming, denying, doubting, supposing any of the above ideas.

7. Judgments that the former judgments logically involve, exclude, or are indifferent to, each other.

Now we may postulate at the outset that all these forms of thought have a *natural* origin, if we could only get at it. That assumption must be made at the outset of every scientific investigation, or there is no temptation to proceed. But the first account of their origin which we are likely to hit upon is a snare. All these mental affections are ways of knowing objects. Most psychologists nowadays believe that the objects first, in some natural way, engendered a brain from out of their midst, and then imprinted these various cognitive affections upon it. But how? The ordinary evolutionist answer to this question is exceedingly simple-minded. The idea of most speculators seems to be that, since it suffices *now* for us to become acquainted with a complex object, that it should be simply *present* to us often enough, so it must be fair to assume universally that, with time enough given, the *mere presence* of the various objects and relations to be known must end by bringing about the latter's cognition, and that in this way all mental structure was from first to last evolved. Any ordinary Spencerite will tell you that just as the experience of blue objects wrought into our mind the color blue, and hard objects got it to feel hardness, so the presence of large and small objects in the world gave it the notion of size, moving objects made it aware of motion, and objective successions taught it time. Similarly in a world with different impressing things, the mind had to acquire a sense of difference, whilst the like parts of the world as they fell upon it kindled in it the perception of similarity. Outward sequences which sometimes held good, and sometimes failed, naturally engendered in it doubtful and uncertain forms of expectation, and ultimately gave rise to the disjunctive forms of judgment; whilst the hypothetic form, 'if *a*, then *b*,' was sure to ensue from sequences that were invariable in the outer world. On this view, if the outer order suddenly were to change its elements and modes, we should have no faculties to cognize the new order by. At most we should feel a sort of frustration and confusion. But little by little the new presence would work on us as the old one did; and in course of time another set of psychic categories would arise, fitted to take cognizance of the altered world.

This notion of the outer world inevitably building up a sort of mental duplicate of itself if we only give it time, is so easy and natural in its vagueness that one hardly knows how to start to criticise it. One thing, however, is obvious, namely that *the manner in which we now become acquainted with complex objects need not in the least resemble the manner in which the original elements of our consciousness grew up.* Now, it is true, a new sort of animal need only be present to me, to impress its image permanently on my mind; but this is because I am already in possession of categories for knowing each and all of its several attributes, and of a memory for retracing the order of their conjunction. I now have preformed categories for all possible objects. The objects need only awaken these from their slumber. But it is a very different matter to account for the categories themselves. I think we must admit that the origin of the various elementary feelings is a recondite history, even after some sort of neural tissue is there for the outer world to begin its work on. The mere existence of things to be known is even now not, as a rule, sufficient to bring about a knowledge of them. Our abstract and general discoveries usually come to us as lucky fancies; and it is only *après coup* that we find that they correspond to some reality. What immediately produced them were previous thoughts, with which, and with the brain-processes of which, that reality had naught to do.

Why may it not have been so of the original elements of consciousness, sensation, time, space, resemblance, difference, and other relations? Why may they not have come into being by the back-door method, by such physical processes as lie more in the sphere of morphological accident, of inward summation of effects, than in that of the 'sensible presence' of objects? Why may they not, in short, be pure *idiosyncrasies*, spontaneous variations, fitted by good luck (those of them which have survived) to take cognizance of objects (that is, to steer us in our active dealings with them), without being in any intelligible sense immediate derivatives from them? I think we shall find this view gain more and more plausibility as we proceed.*

All these elements are subjective duplicates of outer objects. They *are* not the outer objects. The secondary qualities among them are not supposed by any educated person even to resemble the objects. Their *nature* depends more on the reacting brain than on the stimuli which touch it off. This is even more palpably true of the natures of pleasure and pain, effort, desire and aversion, and of such feelings as those of cause and substance, of denial and of

---

* Mr. Grant Allen, in a brilliant article entitled Idiosyncrasy (Mind, VIII. 493), seeks to show that accidental morphological changes in the brain cannot possibly be imagined to result in any mental change of a sort which would *fit the animal to its environment*. If spontaneous variation ever works on the brain, its product, says Mr. Allen, ought to be an idiot or a raving madman, not a minister and interpreter of Nature. Only the environment can change us in the direction of accommodation *to itself*. But I think we ought to know a little better just what the molecular changes in the brain are on which thought depends, before we talk so confidently about what the effect can be of their possible variations. Mr. Allen, it should be said, has made a laudable effort to conceive them distinctly. To me his conception remains too purely anatomical. Meanwhile this essay and another by the same author in the Atlantic Monthly are probably as serious attempts as any that have been made towards applying the Spencerian theory in a radical way to the facts of human history.

doubt. Here then is a native wealth of inner forms whose origin is shrouded in mystery, and which at any rate were not simply 'impressed' from without, in any intelligible sense of the verb 'to impress.'

Their *time- and space-relations*, however, *are* impressed from without—for two outer things at least the evolutionary psychologist must believe to resemble our thoughts of them, these are the time and space in which the objects lie. *The time- and space-relations between things do stamp copies of themselves within.* Things juxtaposed in space impress us, and continue to be thought, in the relation in which they exist there. Things sequent in time, ditto. And thus, through experience in the legitimate sense of the word, there can be truly explained an immense number of our mental habitudes, many of our abstract beliefs, and all our ideas of concrete things, and of their ways of behavior. Such truths as that fire burns and water wets, that glass refracts, heat melts snow, fishes live in water and die on land, and the like, form no small part of the most refined education, and are the all-in-all of education amongst the brutes and lowest men. Here the mind is passive and tributary, a servile copy, fatally and unresistingly fashioned from without. It is the merit of the associationist school to have seen the wide scope of these effects of neighborhood in time and space ; and their exaggerated applications of the principle of mere neighborhood ought not to blind us to the excellent service it has done to Psychology in their hands. As far as a large part of our thinking goes, then, it can intelligibly be formulated as a mere lot of *habits* impressed upon us from without. The degree of cohesion of our inner relations, is, in this part of our thinking, proportionate, in Mr. Spencer's phrase, to the degree of cohesion of the outer relations ; the causes and the objects of our thought are one ; and we are, in so far forth, what the materialistic evolutionists would have us altogether, mere offshoots and creatures of our environment, and naught besides.*

---

* In my own previous chapters on habit, memory, association, and perception, justice has been done to all these facts.

But now the plot thickens, for the images impressed upon our memory by the outer stimuli are not restricted to the mere time- and space-relations, in which they originally came, but revive in various manners (dependent on the intricacy of the brain-paths and the instability of the tissue thereof), and form secondary combinations such as the *forms of judgment*, which, taken *per se*, are not congruent either with the forms in which reality exists or in those in which experiences befall us, but which may nevertheless be explained by the way in which experiences befall in a mind gifted with memory, expectation, and the possibility of feeling doubt, curiosity, belief, and denial. The conjunctions of experience befall more or less invariably, variably, or never. The idea of one term will then engender a fixed, a wavering, or a negative expectation of another, giving affirmative, the hypothetical, disjunctive, interrogative, and negative judgments, and judgments of actuality and possibility about certain things. The separation of attribute from subject in all judgments (which violates the way in which nature exists) may be similarly explained by the piecemeal order in which our perceptions come to us, a vague nucleus growing gradually more detailed as we attend to it more and more. These particular secondary mental forms have had ample justice done them by associationists from Hume downwards.

Associationists have also sought to account for discrimination, abstraction, and generalization by the rates of frequency in which attributes come to us conjoined. With much less success, I think. In the chapter on Discrimination, I have, under the "law of dissociation by varying concomitants," sought to explain as much as possible by the passive order of experience. But the reader saw how much was left for active interest and unknown forces to do. In the chapter on Imagination I have similarly striven to do justice to the ' blended image ' theory of generalization and abstraction. So I need say no more of these matters here.

THE GENESIS OF THE NATURAL SCIENCES.

Our ' scientific ' ways of thinking the outer reality are highly abstract ways. The essence of things for science is not to be what they seem, but to be atoms and molecules moving to and from each other according to strange laws. Nowhere does the account of inner relations produced by outer ones in proportion to the frequency with which the latter have been met, more egregiously break down than in the case of scientific conceptions. The order of scientific thought is quite incongruent either with the way in which reality exists or with the way in which it comes before us. Scientific thought goes by selection and emphasis exclusively. We break the solid plenitude of fact into separate essences, conceive generally what only exists particularly, and by our classifications leave nothing in its natural neighborhood, but separate the contiguous, and join what the poles divorce. The reality *exists* as a *plenum.* All its parts are contemporaneous, each is as real as any other, and each as essential for making the whole just what it is and nothing else. But we can neither experience nor think this *plenum.* What we experience, what *comes before us,* is a chaos of fragmentary impressions interrupting each other ; * what we *think* is an abstract system of hypothetical data and laws.†

---

* " The order of nature, as perceived at a first glance, presents at every instant a chaos followed by another chaos. We must decompose each chaos into single facts. We must learn to see in the chaotic antecedent a multitude of distinct antecedents, in the chaotic consequent ₁a multitude of distinct consequents. This, supposing it done, will not of itself tell us on which of the antecedents each consequent is invariably attendant. To determine that point, we must endeavor to effect a separation of the facts from one another, not in our minds only, but in nature. The mental analysis, however, must take place first. And every one knows that in the mode of performing it, one intellect differs immensely from another." (J. S. Mill, Logic, bk. III. chap. VII. § 1.)

† I quote from an address entitled ' Reflex Action and Theism,' published in the ' Unitarian Review ' for November 1881, and translated in the Critique Philosophique for January and February 1882. "The conceiving or theorizing faculty works exclusively for the sake of ends that do not exist at all in the world of the impressions received by way of our senses, but are set by our emotional and practical subjectivity. It is a transformer of the world of our impressions into a totally different world, the world of our conception ; and the transformation is effected in the interests of our volitional nature, and for no other purpose whatsoever. Destroy the volitional nature, the definite subjective purposes, preferences, fondnesses for certain effects, forms, orders, and not the slightest motive would remain for the brute order of our experience to be remodelled at all. But, as we have the elaborate volitional constitution we do have, the re-

This sort of scientific algebra, little as it immediately resembles the reality given to us, turns out (strangely

---

modelling must be effected, there is no escape. The world's contents are *given* to each of us in an order so foreign to our subjective interests that we can hardly by an effort of the imagination picture to ourselves what it is like. We have to break that order altogether, and by picking out from it the items that concern us, and connecting them with others far away, which we say 'belong' with them, we are able to make out definite threads of sequence and tendency, to foresee particular liabilities and get ready for them, to enjoy simplicity and harmony in the place of what was chaos. Is not the sum of your actual experience taken at this moment and impartially added together an utter chaos ? The strains of my voice, the lights and shades inside the room and out, the murmur of the wind, the ticking of the clock, the various organic feelings you may happen individually to possess, do these make a whole at all ? Is it not the only condition of your mental sanity in the midst of them that most of them should become nonexistent for you, and that a few others—the sounds, I hope, which I am uttering—should evoke from places in your memory, that have nothing to do with this scene, associates fitted to combine with them in what we call a rational train of thought ?—rational because it leads to a conclusion we have some organ to appreciate. We have no organ or faculty to appreciate the simply given order. The real world as it is given at this moment is the sum total of all its beings and events now. But can we think of such a sum ? Can we realize for an instant what a cross-section of all existence at a definite point of time would be ? While I talk and the flies buzz, a sea gull catches a fish at the mouth of the Amazon, a tree falls in the Adirondack wilderness, a man sneezes in Germany, a horse dies in Tartary, and twins are born in France. What does that mean ? Does the contemporaneity of these events with each other and with a million more as disjointed as they form a rational bond between them, and unite them into anything that means for us a world ? Yet just such a collateral contemporaneity, and nothing else, is the *real* order of the world. It is an order with which we have nothing to do but to get away from it as fast as possible. As I said, we break it : we break it into histories, and we break it into arts, and we break it into sciences ; and then we begin to feel at home. We make ten thousand separate serial orders of it. On any one of these, we may react as if the rest did not exist. We discover among its parts relations that were never given to sense at all,—mathematical relations, tangents, squares, and roots and logarithmic functions,—and out of an infinite number of these we call certain ones essential and lawgiving, and ignore the rest. Essential these relations are, but only *for our purpose*, the other relations being just as real and present as they ; and our purpose is to *conceive simply* and to *foresee* Are not simple conception and prevision subjective ends, pure and simple ? They are the ends of what we call science ; and the miracle of miracles, a miracle not yet exhaustively cleared up by any philosophy, is that the given order lends itself to the remodelling. It shows itself plastic to many of our scientific, to many of our æsthetic, to many of our practical purposes and ends." Cf. also Hodgson : Philos. of Refl., ch. v ; Lotze : Logik, §§ 342–351 ; Sigwart : Logik, §§ 60–63, 105.

enough) applicable to it. That is, it yields expressions which, at given places and times, can be translated into real values, or interpreted as definite portions of the chaos that falls upon our sense. It becomes thus a practical guide to our expectations as well as a theoretic delight. But I do not see how any one with a sense for the facts can possibly call our systems immediate results of 'experience' in the ordinary sense. Every scientific conception is in the first instance a 'spontaneous variation' in some one's brain.* For one that proves useful and applicable there are a thousand that perish through their worthlessness. Their genesis is strictly akin to that of the flashes of poetry and sallies of wit to which the instable brain-paths equally give rise. But whereas the poetry and wit (like the science of the ancients) are their 'own excuse for being,' and have to run the gauntlet of no farther test, the 'scientific' conceptions must prove their worth by being 'verified.' This test, however, is the cause of their *preservation*, not that of their production; and one might as well account for the origin of Artemus Ward's jokes by the 'cohesion' of subjects with predicates in proportion to the 'persistence of the outer relations' to which they 'correspond' as to treat the genesis of scientific conceptions in the same ponderously unreal way.

The most persistent outer relations which science believes in are never matters of experience at all, but have to be disengaged from under experience by a process of elimination, that is, by ignoring conditions which are always present. The *elementary* laws of mechanics, physics, and chemistry are all of this sort. The principle of uniformity in nature is of this sort; it has to be *sought* under and in spite of the most rebellious appearances; and our convic-

---

* In an article entitled 'Great Men, Great Thoughts, and the Environment,' published in the Atlantic Monthly for October 1880, the reader will find some ampler illustrations of these remarks. I have there tried to show that both mental and social evolution are to be conceived after the Darwinian fashion, and that the function of the environment properly so called is much more that of *selecting* forms, produced by invisible forces, than *producing* of such forms,—producing being the only function thought of by the pre-Darwinian evolutionists, and the only one on which stress is laid by such contemporary ones as Mr. Spencer and Mr. Allen.

tion of its truth is far more like a religious faith than like assent to a demonstration. The only cohesions which experience in the literal sense of the word produces in our mind are, as we contended some time back, the proximate laws of nature, and habitudes of concrete things, that heat melts ice, that salt preserves meat, that fish die out of water, and the like.* Such 'empirical truths' as these we

---

* "It is perfectly true that our world of experience begins with such associations as lead us to expect that what has happened to us will happen again. These associations lead the babe to look for milk from its nurse and not from its father, the child to believe that the apple he sees will taste good; and whilst they make him wish for it, they make him fear the bottle which contains his bitter medicine. But whereas a part of these associations grows confirmed by frequent repetition, another part is destroyed by contradictory experiences; and the world becomes divided for us into two provinces, one in which we are at home and anticipate with confidence always the same sequences; another filled with alternating, variable, accidental occurrences.

" . . . Accident is, in a wide sphere, such an every-day matter that we need not be surprised if it sometimes invades the territory where order is the rule. And one personification or another of the capricious power of chance easily helps us over the difficulties which further reflection might find in the exceptions. Yes, indeed, Exception has a peculiar fascination; it is a subject of astonishment, a θαῦμα, and the credulity with which in this first stage of pure association we adopt our supposed rules is matched by the equal credulity with which we adopt the miracles that interfere with them.

"The whole history of popular beliefs about nature refutes the notion that the thought of an universal physical order can possibly have arisen through the purely passive reception and association of particular perceptions. Indubitable as it is that all men infer from known cases to unknown, it is equally certain that this procedure, if restricted to the phenomenal materials that spontaneously offer themselves, would never have led to the belief in a general uniformity, but only to the belief that law and lawlessness rule the world in motley alternation. From the point of view of strict empiricism nothing exists but the sum of particular perceptions with their coincidences on the one hand, their contradictions on the other.

"That there is more order in the world than appears at first sight is not discovered till the order is looked for. The first impulse to look for it proceeds from practical needs: where ends must be attained, we must know trustworthy means which infallibly possess a property or produce a result. But the practical need is only the first occasion for our reflection on the conditions of a true knowledge; even were there no such need, motives would still be present to carry us beyond the stage of mere association. For not with an equal interest, or rather with an equal lack of interest, does man contemplate those natural processes in which like is joined to like, and those in which like and unlike are joined; the former processes

admitted to form an enormous part of human wisdom. The 'scientific' truths have to harmonize with these truths, or be given up as useless; but they arise in the mind in no such passive associative way as that in which the simpler truths arise. Even those experiences which are used to prove a scientific truth are for the most part artificial experiences of the laboratory gained after the truth itself has been conjectured. Instead of experiences engendering the 'inner relations,' the inner relations are what engender the experiences here.

What happens in the brain after experience has done its utmost is what happens in every material mass which has been fashioned by an outward force,—in every pudding or mortar, for example, which I may make with my hands. The fashioning from without brings the elements into collocations which set new internal forces free to exert their effects in turn. And the random irradiations and resettlements of our ideas, which *supervene upon experience,* and constitute our free mental play, are due entirely to these secondary internal processes, which vary enormously from brain to brain, even though the brains be exposed to exactly the same 'outer relations.' The higher thought-processes owe their being to causes which correspond far more to the sourings and fermentations of dough, the setting of mortar, or the subsidence of sediments in mixtures, than to the manipulations by which these physical aggregates came to be compounded. Our study of similar association and reasoning taught us that the whole superiority of man depended on the facility with which in his brain the paths worn by the most frequent outer cohesions could be ruptured. The causes of the instability, the reasons why now this point and now that become in him the seat of rupture,

---

harmonize with the conditions of his thinking, the latter do not; in the former his concepts, judgments, inferences apply to realities, in the latter they have no such application. And thus the intellectual satisfaction which at first comes to him without reflection, at last excites in him the conscious wish to find realized throughout the entire phenomenal world those rational continuities, uniformities, and necessities which are the fundamental element and guiding principle of his own thought." (C. Sigwart: Logik, II. 380-2.)

we saw to be entirely obscure. (Vol. I. p. 580; Vol. II. p. 364.) The only clear thing about the peculiarity seems to be its interstitial character, and the certainty that no mere appeal to man's 'experience' suffices to explain it.

When we pass from scientific to æsthetic and ethical systems, every one readily admits that, although the elements are matters of experience, the peculiar forms of relation into which they are woven are incongruent with the order of passively received experience. The world of æsthetics and ethics is an ideal world, a Utopia a world which the outer relations persist in contradicting, but which we as stubbornly persist in striving to make actual. Why do we thus invincibly crave to alter the given order of nature? Simply because other relations among things are far more interesting to us and more charming than the mere rates of frequency of their time- and space-conjunctions. These other relations are all secondary and brain-born, 'spontaneous variations' most of them, of our sensibility, whereby certain elements of experience, and certain arrangements in time and space, have acquired an agreeableness which otherwise would not have been felt. It is true that habitual arrangements may also become agreeable. But this agreeableness of the merely habitual is felt to be a mere ape and counterfeit of real inward fitness; and one sign of intelligence is never to mistake the one for the other.

There are then ideal and inward relations amongst the objects of our thought which can in no intelligible sense whatever be interpreted as reproductions of the order of outer experience. In the æsthetic and ethical realms they conflict with its order—the early Christian with his kingdom of heaven, and the contemporary anarchist with his abstract dream of justice, will tell you that the existing order must perish, root and branch, ere the true order can come. Now the peculiarity of those relations among the objects of our thought which are dubbed 'scientific' is this, that although they no more are inward *reproductions* of the outer order than the ethical and æsthetic relations are, yet they do not conflict with that order, but, once having sprung up by the play of the inward forces, are found—some of them at least, namely the only ones which have survived long enough **to** be matters of record—to be *congruent* with the time- and space-relations which our impressions affect.

In other words, though nature's materials lend themselves slowly and discouragingly to our translation of them into ethical forms, but more readily into æsthetic forms; to translation into scientific forms they lend themselves with relative ease and completeness. The translation, it is true, will probably never be ended. The perceptive order does not give way, nor the right conceptive substitute for it arise, at our bare word of command.* It is often a deadly fight; and many a man of science can say, like Johannes Müller, after an investigation, ' *Es klebt Blut an der Arbeit.*' But victory after victory makes us sure that the essential doom of our enemy is defeat.†

---

* Cf. Hodgson : Philosophy of Reflection, book ii, chap. v.

† The aspiration to be 'scientific' is such an idol of the tribe to the present generation, is so sucked in with his mother's milk by every one of us, that we find it hard to conceive of a creature who should not feel it, and harder still to treat it freely as the altogether peculiar and one-sided subjective interest which it is. But as a matter of fact, few even of the cultivated members of the race have shared it ; it was invented but a generation or two ago. In the middle ages it meant only impious magic ; and the way in which it even now strikes orientals is charmingly shown in the letter of a Turkish cadi to an English traveller asking him for statistical information, which Sir A. Layard prints at the end of his 'Nineveh and Babylon.' The document is too full of edification not to be given in full. It runs thus :

" *My Illustrious Friend, and Joy of my Liver !*

" The thing you ask of me is both difficult and useless. Although I have passed all my days in this place, I have neither counted the houses nor inquired into the number of the inhabitants ; and as to what one person loads on his mules and the other stows away in the bottom of his ship, that is no business of mine. But, above all, as to the previous history of this city, God only knows the amount of dirt and confusion that the infidels may have eaten before the coming of the sword of Islam. It were unprofitable for us to inquire into it.

" O my soul ! O my lamb ! seek not after the things which concern thee not. Thou camest unto us and we welcomed thee : go in peace.

" Of a truth thou hast spoken many words and there is no harm done, for the speaker is one and the listener is another. After the fashion of thy people thou hast wandered from one place to another, until thou art happy and content in none. We (praise be to God) were born here, and never desire to quit it. Is it possible, then, that the idea of a general intercourse

THE GENESIS OF THE PURE SCIENCES.

I have now stated in general terms the relation of the natural sciences to experience strictly so called, and shall complete what I have to say by reverting to the subject on a later page. At present I will pass to the so-called *pure* or *a priori sciences* of Classification, Logic, and Mathematics. My thesis concerning these is that they are even less than the natural sciences effects of the order of the world as it comes to our experience. THE PURE SCIENCES EXPRESS RESULTS OF COMPARISON *exclusively ; comparison is not a conceivable effect of the order in which outer impressions are experienced— it is one of the house-born* (p. 627) *portions of our mental structure ; therefore the pure sciences form a body of propositions with whose genesis experience has nothing to do.*

First, consider the nature of comparison. *The relations of resemblance and difference among things have nothing to do with the time- and space-order in which we may experience the latter.* Suppose a hundred beings created by God and gifted with the faculties of memory and comparison. Suppose that upon each of them the same lot of sensations are imprinted, but in different orders. Let some

---

between mankind should make any impression on our understandings ? God forbid !

"Listen, O my son ! There is no wisdom equal unto the belief in God ! He created the world, and shall we liken ourselves unto Him in seeking to penetrate into the mysteries of His creation ? Shall we say, Behold this star spinneth round that star, and this other star with a tail goeth and cometh in so many years ! Let it go ! He from whose hand it came will guide and direct it.

"But thou wilt say unto me, Stand aside, O man, for I am more learned than thou art, and have seen more things. If thou thinkest that thou art in this respect better than I am, thou art welcome. I praise God that I seek not that which I require not. Thou art learned in the things I care not for ; and as for that which thou has seen, I spit upon it. Will much knowledge create thee a double belly, or wilt thou seek Paradise with thine eyes ?

"O my friend ! if thou wilt be happy, say, There is no God but God ! Do no evil, and thus wilt thou fear neither man nor death ; for surely thine hour will come !

"The meek in spirit (El Fakir)
"IMAUM ALI ZADI."

of them have no single sensation more than once. Let some have this one and others that one repeated. Let every conceivable permutation prevail. And then let the magic-lantern show die out, and keep the creatures in a void eternity, with naught but their memories to muse upon. Inevitably in their long leisure they will begin to play with the items of their experience and rearrange them, make classificatory series of them, place gray between white and black, orange between red and yellow, and trace all other degrees of resemblance and difference. And this new construction will be absolutely identical in all the hundred creatures, the diversity of the sequence of the original experiences having no effect as regards this rearrangement. Any and every form of sequence will give the same result, because the result expresses the relation between the *inward natures* of the sensations; and to that the question of their outward succession is quite irrelevant. Black will differ from white just as much in a world in which they always come close together as in one in which they always come far apart; just as much in one in which they appear rarely as in one in which they appear all the time.

But the advocate of ' persistent outer relations' may still return to the charge : These *are* what make us so sure that white and black differ, he may say; for in a world where sometimes black resembled white and sometimes differed from it, we could never be so sure. It is because in this world black and white have *always* differed that the sense of their difference has become a necessary form of thought. The pair of colors on the one hand and the sense of difference on the other, inseparably experienced, not only by ourselves but by our ancestors, have become inseparably connected in the mind. Not through any essential structure of the mind, which made difference the only possible feeling which they could arouse ; no, but because they simply *did* differ so often that at last they begat in us an impotency to imagine them doing anything else, and made us accept such a fabulous account as that just presented, of creatures to whom a single experience would suffice to make us feel the neccessariness of this relation.

I know not whether Mr. Spencer would subscribe to this or not ;—nor do I care, for there are mysteries which press more for solution than the meaning of this vague writer's words. But to me such an explanation of our difference-judgment is absolutely unintelligible. We now find black and white different, the explanation says, *because we have always have so found them.* But why should we always have so found them ? Why should difference have popped into our heads so invariably with the thought of them ? There must have been either a subjective or an objective reason. The subjective reason can only be that our minds were so constructed that a sense of difference was the only sort of conscious transition possible between black and white; the objective reason can only be that difference was always there, with these colors, outside the mind as an objective fact. The subjective reason explains outer frequency by inward structure, not inward structure by outer frequency ; and so surrenders the experience-theory. The objective reason simply says that if an outer difference is there the mind must needs know it—which is no explanation at all, but a mere appeal to the fact that somehow the mind does know what is there.

The only clear thing to do is to give up the sham of a pretended explanation, and to fall back on the fact that the sense of difference *has* arisen, in some natural manner doubtless, but in a manner which we do not understand. It was by the back-stairs way, at all events ; and, from the very first, happened to be the only mode of reaction by which consciousness could feel the transition from one term to another of what (in *consequence* of this very reaction) we now call a contrasted pair.

In noticing the differences and resemblances of things, and their degrees, the mind feels its own activity, and has given the name of *comparison* thereto. It need not compare its materials, but if once roused to do so, it can compare them with but one result, and this a fixed consequence of the nature of the materials themselves. Difference and resemblance are thus relations between ideal objects, or conceptions as such. To learn whether black and white differ,

I need not consult the world of experience at all; the mere ideas suffice. *What I mean* by black differs from *what I mean* by white, whether such colors exist *extra mentem meam* or not. If they ever do so exist, they *will* differ. White things may blacken, but the black of them will differ from the white of them, so long as I mean anything definite by these three words.*

I shall now in what follows call all propositions which express time- and space-relations empirical propositions; and I shall give the name of rational propositions to all propositions which express the results of a comparison. The latter denomination is in a sense arbitrary, for resemblance and difference are not usually held to be the only rational relations between things. I will next proceed to show, however, how many other rational relations commonly supposed distinct can be resolved into these, so that my definition of rational propositions will end, I trust, by proving less arbitrary than it now appears to be.

SERIES OF EVEN DIFFERENCE AND MEDIATE COMPARISON.

In Chapter XII we saw that the mind can at successive moments *mean the same*, and that it gradually comes into possession of a stock of permanent and fixed meanings, ideal objects, or conceptions, some of which are universal qualities, like the black and white of our example, and some, individual things. We now see that not only are the objects permanent mental possessions, but the results of their comparison are permanent too. The objects and their differences together form an immutable system. *The same objects, compared in the same way, always give the same results;*

---

* "Though a man in a fever should from sugar have a bitter taste which at another time would produce a sweet one, yet the idea of bitter in that man's mind would be as clear and distinct from the idea of sweet as if he had tasted only gall. Nor does it make any more confusion between the two ideas of sweet and bitter that the same sort of body produces at one time one and at another time another idea by the taste, than it makes a confusion in two ideas of white and sweet, or white and round, that the same piece of sugar produces them both in the mind at the same time." Locke's Essay, bk. II. ch. XI. § 3.

if the result be not the same, then the objects are not those originally meant.

This last principle, which we may call the *axiom of constant result,* holds good throughout all our mental operations, not only when we compare, but when we add, divide, class, or infer a given matter in any conceivable way. Its most general expression would be "*the Same operated on in the same way gives the Same.*" In mathematics it takes the form of "equals added to, or subtracted from, equals give equals," and the like. We shall meet with it again.

The next thing which we observe is that *the operation of comparing may be repeated on its own results ;* in other words, that we can think of the various resemblances and differences which we find and compare them with each other, making differences and resemblances of a higher order. *The mind thus becomes aware of sets of similar differences, and forms series of terms with the same kind and amount of difference between them, terms which, as they succeed each other, maintain a constant direction of serial increase.* This sense of constant direction in a series of operations we saw in Chapter XIII (p. 490) to be a cardinal mental fact. "A differs from B differs from C differs from D, etc.," makes a *series* only when the differences are in the same direction. In any such difference-series all terms differ in just the same way from their predecessors. The numbers 1, 2, 3, 4, 5, . . . the notes of the chromatic scale in music, are familiar examples. As soon as the mind grasps such a series as a whole, it perceives that *two terms taken far apart differ more than two terms taken near together,* and that any one term differs more from a remote than from a near successor, and this no matter what the terms may be, or what the sort of difference may be, provided it is always the same sort.

This PRINCIPLE OF MEDIATE COMPARISON might be briefly (though obscurely) expressed by the formula "*more than the more is more than the less*"—the words *more* and *less* standing simply for degrees of increase along a constant direction of differences. Such a formula would cover all possible cases, as, earlier than early is earlier than late, worse than bad is worse than good, east of east is east of west; etc., etc., *ad libitum.** Symbolically, we might write it as $a < b < c < d \ldots$ and say that any number of intermediaries may be expunged without obliging us to alter anything in what remains written.

The principle of mediate comparison is only one form of a law which holds in many series of homogeneously related terms, the law that *skipping intermediary terms leaves relations the same.* This AXIOM OF SKIPPED INTERMEDIARIES or of TRANSFERRED RELATIONS occurs, as we soon shall see, in logic as the fundamental principle of inference, in arithmetic as the fundamental property of the number-series, in geometry as that of the straight line, the plane and the parallel. *It seems to be on the whole the broadest and deepest law of man's thought.*

In certain lists of terms the result of comparison may be to find no-difference, or equality in place of difference. Here also intermediaries may be skipped, and mediate comparison be carried on with the general result expressed by the *axiom of mediate equality,* "equals of equals are equal," which is the great principle of the mathematical sciences. This too as a result of the mind's mere acuteness, and in utter independence of the order in which experiences come associated together. Symbolically, again : $a = b = c = d \ldots$, with the same consequence as regards expunging terms which we saw before.

CLASSIFICATORY SERIES.

Thus we have a rather intricate system of necessary and immutable *ideal truths of comparison,* a system applicable to terms *experienced* in any order of sequence or frequency, or even to terms never experienced or to be experienced, such as the mind's imaginary constructions would be. These truths of comparison result in *Classifications.* It is, for some unknown reason, a great æsthetic delight for the mind to break the order of experience, and class its materials in serial orders, proceeding from step to step of difference, and to contemplate untiringly the crossings and inosculations of the

---

* Cf. Bradley, Logic, p. 226.

series among themselves. The first steps in most of the sciences are purely classificatory. Where facts fall easily into rich and intricate series (as plants and animals and chemical compounds do), the mere sight of the series fill the mind with a satisfaction *sui generis ;* and a world whose *real* materials naturally lend themselves to serial classification is *pro tanto* a more rational world, a world with which the mind will feel more intimate, than with a world in which they do not. By the pre-evolutionary naturalists, whose generation has hardly passed away, classifications were supposed to be ultimate insights into God's mind, filling us with adoration of his ways. The fact that Nature lets us make them was a proof of the presence of his Thought in her bosom. So far as the facts of experience can *not* be serially classified, therefore, so far experience fails to be rational in *one* of the ways, at least, which we crave.

THE LOGIC-SERIES.

Closely akin to the function of comparison is that of *judging, predicating, or subsuming.* In fact, these elementary intellectual functions run into each other so, that it is often only a question of practical convenience whether we shall call a given mental operation by the name of one or of the other. Comparisons result in groups of like things ; and presently (through discrimination and abstraction) in conceptions of the *respects* in which the likenesses obtain. The groups are *genera* or *classes,* the respects are *characters* or *attributes.* The attributes again may be compared, forming genera of higher orders, and their characters singled out ; so that we have a new sort of series, *that of predication, or of kind including kind.* Thus horses are quadrupeds, quadrupeds animals, animals machines, machines liable to wear out, etc. In such a series as this the several couplings of terms may have been made out originally at widely different times and under different circumstances. But memory may bring them together afterwards ; and whenever it does so, our faculty of apprehending serial increase makes us conscious of them as a single system of successive terms united by the same relation.*

Now whenever we become thus conscious, we may become aware of an additional relation which is of the highest intellectual importance, inasmuch as upon it the whole structure of logic is reared. *The principle of mediate predication or subsumption* is only the axiom of skipped intermediaries applied to a series of successive predications. It expresses the fact that any earlier term in the series stands to any later term in the same relation in which it stands to any intermediate term; in other words, that *whatever has an attribute has all the attributes of that attribute;* or more briefly still, that *whatever is of a kind is of that kind's kind.* A little explanation of this statement will bring out all that it involves.

We learned in the chapter on Reasoning what our great motive is for abstracting attributes and predicating them. It is that our varying practical purposes require us to lay hold of different angles of the reality at different times. But for these we should be satisfied to 'see it whole,' and always alike. The purpose, however, makes one aspect essential; so, to avoid dispersion of the attention, we treat the reality as if for the time being it were nothing but that aspect, and we let its supernumerary determinations go. In short, we substitute the aspect for the whole real thing. *For our purpose* the aspect *can* be substituted for the whole, and the two treated as the same; and the word *is* (which couples the whole with its aspect or attribute in the categoric judgment) expresses (among other things) the identifying operation performed. The predication-series a is b, b is c, c is d, ... closely resembles for certain practical purposes the equation-series $a = b$, $b = c$, $c = d$, etc.

But what is our purpose in predicating? Ultimately, it may be anything we please; but proximately and immediately, it is always the gratification of a certain curi-

---

* This apprehension of them as forming a single system is what Mr. Bradley means by the act of *construction* which underlies all reasoning. The awareness, which then supervenes, of the additional relation of which I speak in the next paragraph of my text, is what this author calls the act of *inspection.* Cf. Principles of Logic, bk. II. pt. I. chap. III.

osity as to whether the object in hand is or is not *of a kind* connected with that ultimate purpose. Usually the connection is not obvious, and we only find that the object S is of a kind connected with P, after first finding that it is of a kind M, which itself is connected with P. Thus, to fix our ideas by an example, we have a curiosity (our ultimate purpose being conquest over nature) as to how Sirius may move. It is not obvious whether Sirius is a kind of thing which moves in the line of sight or not. When, however, we find it to be a kind of thing in whose spectrum the hydrogen-line is shifted, and when we reflect that *that* kind of thing is a kind of thing which moves in the line of sight; we conclude that Sirius does so move. Whatever Sirius's attribute is, Sirius is ; its adjective's adjective can supersede its own adjective in our thinking, and this with no loss to our knowledge, *so long as we stick to the definite purpose in view.*

Now please note that this elimination of intermediary kinds and transfer of *is*'s along the line, results from our insight into the very meaning of the word *is*, and into the constitution of any series of terms connected by that relation. It has naught to do with what any particular thing is or is not; but, *whatever* any given thing may be, we see that it also is whatever *that* is, indefinitely. To grasp in one view a succession of *is*'s is to apprehend this relation between the terms which they connect ; just as to grasp a list of successive equals is to apprehend their *mutual* equality throughout. The principle of mediate subsumption thus expresses relations of ideal objects as such. It can be discovered by a mind left at leisure with any set of meanings (however originally obtained), of which some are predicable of others. The moment we string them in a serial line, that moment we see that we can drop intermediaries, use remote terms just like near ones, and put a genus in the place of a species. This shows that *the principle of mediate subsumption has nothing to do with the particular order of our experiences, or with the outer coexistences and sequences of terms.* Were it a mere outgrowth of habit and association, we should be forced to regard it as having no universal validity ; for every hour of the day we meet things which we consider to be of this kind or of that, but later learn that they have none of the kind's properties, that they *do not* belong to the kind's kind. Instead, however, of correcting the principle by these cases, we correct the cases by the principle. We say that if the thing we named an M has not M's properties, then we were either mistaken in calling it an M, or mistaken about M's properties ; or else that it is no longer M, but has changed. But we never say that it is an M without M's properties ; for by conceiving a thing as of the kind M I mean that it *shall* have M's properties, be of M's kind, even though I should never be able to find in the real world anything which is an M. The principle emanates from my perception of what a lot of successive is's *mean.* This perception can no more be confirmed by one set, or weakened by another set, of outer facts, than the perception that black is not white can be confirmed by the fact that snow never blackens, or weakened by the fact that photographer's paper blackens as soon as you lay it in the sun.

The abstract scheme of successive predications, extended indefinitely, with all the possibilities of substitution which it involves, is thus an immutable system of truth which flows from the very structure and form of our thinking. *If* any real terms ever do fit into such a scheme, they will obey its laws ; *whether* they do is a question as to nature's facts, the answer to which can only be empirically ascertained. *Formal logic* is the name of the Science which traces in skeleton form all the remote relations of terms connected by successive *is*'s with each other, and enumerates their possibilities of mutual substitution. To our principle of mediate subsumption she has given various formulations, of which the best is perhaps this broad expression, that *the same can be substituted for the same in any mental operation.**

The ordinary logical series contains but three terms

---

* Realities fall under this only so far as they prove to *be* the same. So far as they cannot be substituted for each other, for the purpose in hand, so far they are not the same ; though for other purposes and in other respects they might be substituted, and then be treated as the same. Apart from purpose, of course; no realities ever are absolutely and exactly the same.

—"Socrates, man, mortal." But we also have ' Sorites ' —Socrates, man, animal, machine, run down, mortal, etc.— and it violates psychology to represent these as syllogisms with terms suppressed. The ground of there being any logic at all is our power to grasp any series as a whole, and the more terms it holds the better. This synthetic consciousness of an uniform direction of advance through a multiplicity of terms is, apparently, what the brutes and lower men cannot accomplish, and what gives to us our extraordinary power of ratiocinative thought. The mind which can grasp a string of *is*'s as a whole—the objects linked by them may be ideal or real, physical, mental, or symbolic, indifferently— - :n also apply to it the principle of skipped intermediaries. *The logic-list is thus in its origin and essential nature just like those graded classificatory lists which we erewhile described.* The ' rational proposition' which lies at the basis of all reasoning, the *dictum de omni et nullo* in all the various forms in which it may be expressed, the fundamental law of thought, is thus *only the result of the function of comparison* in a mind which has come by some lucky variation to apprehend a series of more than two terms at once.* So far, then, *both Systematic Classification and Logic are seen to be incidental results of the mere capacity for discerning difference and likeness,* which capacity is a thing with which the *order of experience*, properly so styled, has absolutely nothing to do.

But how comes it (it may next be asked) when systematic classifications have so little ultimate theoretic importance—for the conceiving of things according to their mere degrees of resemblance always yields to other modes of conceiving when these can be obtained—that the logical relations among things should form such a mighty engine for dealing with the facts of life?

Chapter XXII already gave the reason (see p. 335, above). This world *might* be a world in which all things differed, and in which what properties there were were

---

* A mind, in other words, which has got *beyond* the merely *dichotomic* style of thought which Wundt alleges to be the essential form of human thinking (Physiol. Psych., II. 312).

ultimate and had no farther predicates. In such a world there would be as many kinds as there were separate things. We could never subsume a new thing under an old kind ; or if we could, no consequences would follow. Or, again, this might be a world in which innumerable things were of a kind, but in which no concrete thing remained of the same kind long, but all objects were in a flux. Here again, though we could subsume and infer, our logic would be of no practical use to us, for the subjects of our propositions would have changed whilst we were talking. In such worlds, logical relations would obtain, and be known (doubtless) as they are now, but they would form a merely theoretic scheme and be of no use for the conduct of life. But our world is no such world. It is a very peculiar world, and plays right into logic's hands. *Some* of the things, at least, which it contains are of the same kind as other things ; *some* of them remain always of the kind of which they once were ; and some of the properties of them cohere indissolubly and are always found together. *Which* things these latter things are we learn by experience in the strict sense of the word, and the results of the experience are embodied in 'empirical propositions.' Whenever such a thing is met with by us now, our sagacity notes it to be of a certain kind ; our learning immediately recalls that kind's kind, and then *that* kind's kind, and so on ; so that a moment's thinking may make us aware that the thing is of a kind so remote that we could never have directly perceived the connection. The flight to this last kind *over the heads of the intermediaries* is the essential feature of the intellectual operation here. Evidently it is a pure outcome of our sense for apprehending serial increase ; and, unlike the several propositions themselves which make up the series (and which may all be empirical), it has nothing to do with the time- and space-order in which the things have been experienced.

MATHEMATICAL RELATIONS.

So much for the *a priori* necessities called systematic classification and logical inference. The other couplings of data which pass for *a priori* necessities of thought are the *mathematical* judgments, and certain metaphysical propositions. These latter we shall consider farther on. As regards the mathematical judgments, they are all ' rational propositions ' in the sense defined on p. 644, for they express results of comparison and nothing more. The mathematical sciences deal with similarities and equalities exclusively, and not with coexistences and sequences. Hence they have, in the first instance, no connection with the order of experience. The comparisons of mathematics are between numbers and extensive magnitudes, giving rise to arithmetic and geometry respectively.

Number seems to signify primarily the strokes of our attention in discriminating things. These strokes remain in the memory in groups, large or small, and the groups can be compared. The discrimination is, as we know, psychologically facilitated by the mobility of the thing as a total (p. 173). But within each thing we discriminate parts ; so that the number of things which any one given phenomenon may be depends in the last instance on our way of taking it. A globe is one, if undivided ; two, if composed of hemispheres. A sand-heap is one thing, or twenty thousand things, as we may choose to count it. We amuse ourselves by the counting of *mere* strokes, to form rhythms, and these we compare and name. Little by little in our minds the number-series is formed. This, like all lists of terms in which there is a direction of serial increase, carries with it the sense of those mediate relations between its terms which we expressed by the axiom "the more than the more is more than the less." That axiom seems, in fact, only a way of stating that the terms do form an increasing series. But, in addition to this, we are aware of certain other relations among our strokes of counting. We may interrupt them where we like, and go on again. All the while we feel that the interruption does not alter the strokes themselves. We may count 12 straight through ; or count 7 and pause, and then count 5, but still the strokes will be the same. We thus distinguish between our acts of counting and those of interrupting or grouping, as between an unchanged matter and an operation of mere shuffling performed on it. The matter is the original units or strokes ;

which all modes of grouping or combining simply give us back unchanged. In short, *combinations of numbers are combinations of their units,* which is the fundamental axiom of arithmetic,* leading to such consequences as that $7 + 5 = 8 + 4$ because both $= 12$. The general axiom of mediate equality, that equals of equals are equal, comes in here.† The principle of constancy in our meanings, when applied to strokes of counting, also gives rise to the axiom that the same number, operated on (interrupted, grouped) in the same way will always give the same result or be the same. How shouldn't it? Nothing is supposed changed.

Arithmetic and its fundamental principles are thus independent of our experiences or of the order of the world. The matter of arithmetic is *mental matter;* its principles flow from the fact that the matter forms a series, which can be cut into by us wherever we like without the matter changing. The empiricist school has strangely tried to interpret the truths of number as results of coexistences among outward things. John Mill calls number a physical property of things. 'One,' according to Mill, means one sort of passive sensation which we receive, 'two' another, 'three' a third. The same things, however, can give us different number-sensations. Three things arranged thus, ○ ○ ○, for example, impress us differently from three things arranged thus, ○°○. But experience tells us that every real object-group which can be arranged in one of these ways can always be arranged in the other also, and that $2 + 1$ and 3 are thus modes of numbering things which 'coexist' invariably with each other. The indefeasibility of our belief in their 'coexistence' (which is Mill's word for their equivalence) is due solely to the enormous amount of experience we have of it. For all things, whatever other sensations they may give us, give us at any rate number-sensations. Those number-sensations which the same thing may be successively made to arouse are the numbers which we deem

---

* Said to be expressed by Grassman in the fundamental Axiom of Arithmetic $(a + b) + 1 = a + (b + 1)$.

† Compare Helmholtz's more technically expressed Essay 'Zählen u. Messen,' in the Philosophische Aufsätze, Ed. Zeller gewidmet (Leipzig, 1887), p. 17.

equal to each other; those which the same thing refuses to arouse are those which we deem unequal.

This is as clear a restatement as I can make of Mill's doctrine.* And its failure is written upon its front. Woe to arithmetic, were such the only grounds for its validity! The same real things are countable in numberless ways, and pass from one numerical form, not only to its equivalent (as Mill implies), but to its other, as the sport of physical accidents or of our mode of attending may decide. How could our notion that one and one are eternally and necessarily two ever maintain itself in a world where every time we add one drop of water to another we get not two but one again? in a world where every time we add a drop to a crumb of quicklime we get a dozen or more?— had it no better warrant than such experiences? At most we could then say that one and one are *usually* two. Our arithmetical propositions would never have the confident tone which they now possess. That confident tone is due to the fact that they deal with abstract and ideal numbers exclusively. *What we mean* by one plus one *is* two; we *make* two out of it; and it would mean two still even in a world where *physically* (according to a conceit of Mill's) a third thing was engendered every time one thing came together with another. We are masters of our meanings, and discriminate between the things we mean and our ways of taking them, between our strokes of numeration themselves, and our bundlings and separatings thereof.

Mill ought not only to have said, " All things are numbered." He ought, in order to prove his point, to have shown that they are *unequivocally* numbered, which they notoriously are not. Only the abstract numbers themselves are unequivocal, only those which we create mentally and hold fast to as ideal objects always the same. A concrete natural thing can always be numbered in a great variety of ways. " We need only conceive a thing divided into four equal parts (and all things may be conceived as so divided)," as

---

* For the original statements, cf. J. S. Mill's Logic, bk. ii. chap. vi. §§ 2, 3; and bk. iii. chap. xxiv. § 5.

Mill is himself compelled to say, to find the number four in it, and so on.

The relation of numbers to experience is just like that of 'kinds' in logic. So long as an experience will keep its kind we can handle it by logic. So long as it will keep its number we can deal with it by arithmetic. *Sensibly*, however, things are constantly changing their numbers, just as they are changing their kinds. They are forever breaking apart and fusing. Compounds and their elements are never numerically identical, for the elements are sensibly many and the compounds sensibly one. Unless our arithmetic is to remain without application to life, we must somehow *make* more numerical continuity than we spontaneously find. Accordingly Lavoisier discovers his weight-units which remain the same in compounds and elements, though volume-units and quality-units all have changed. A great discovery! And modern science outdoes it by denying that compounds exist at all. There is no such thing as 'water' for 'science;' that is only a handy name for H_2 and O when they have got into the position H-O-H, and then affect our senses in a novel way. The modern theories of atoms, of heat, and of gases are, in fact, only intensely artificial devices for gaining that constancy in the numbers of things which sensible experience will not show. "Sensible things are not the things for me," says Science, "because in their changes they will not keep their numbers the same. Sensible qualities are not the qualities for me, because they can with difficulty be numbered at all. These hypothetic atoms, however, are the things, these hypothetic masses and velocities are the qualities for me; they will stay numbered all the time."

By such elaborate inventions, and at such a cost to the imagination, do men succeed in making for themselves a world in which real things shall be coerced *per fas aut nefas* under arithmetical law.

The other branch of mathematics is *geometry*. Its objects are also ideal creations. Whether nature contain circles or not, I can know what I mean by a circle and can stick to my meaning; and when I mean two circles I mean two things of an identical kind. The axiom of constant results (see above, p. 645) holds in geometry. The same forms, treated in the same way (added, subtracted, or compared), give the same results—how shouldn't they? The axioms of mediate comparison (p. 645), of logic (p. 648), and of number (p. 654) all apply to the forms which we imagine in space, inasmuch as these resemble or differ from each other, form kinds, and are numerable things. But in addition to these general principles, which are true of space-forms only as they are of other mental conceptions, there are certain axioms relative to space-forms exclusively, which we must briefly consider.

Three of them give marks of identity among straight lines, planes, and parallels. Straight lines which have two points, planes which have three points, parallels to a given line which have one point, in common, coalesce throughout. Some say that the certainty of our belief in these axioms is due to repeated experiences of their truth; others that it is due to an intuitive acquaintance with the properties of space. It is neither. We experience lines enough which pass through two points only to separate again, only we won't call them straight. Similarly of planes and parallels. We have a definite idea of what we mean by each of these words; and when something different is offered us, we see the difference. Straight lines, planes, and parallels, as they figure in geometry, are mere inventions of our faculty for apprehending serial increase. The farther continuations of these forms, we say, *shall* bear the same relation to their last visible parts which these did to still earlier parts. It thus follows (from that axiom of skipped intermediaries which obtains in all regular series) that parts of these figures separated by other parts must agree in direction, just as contiguous parts do. This uniformity of direction throughout is, in fact, all that makes us care for these forms, gives them their beauty, and stamps them into fixed conceptions in our mind. But obviously if two lines, or two planes, with a common segment, were to part company beyond the segment, it could only be because the direction of at least one of them had changed. Parting company in lines and planes *means* changing direction, means assuming a new relation to the parts that pre-exist; and assuming a new relation means ceasing to be straight or plane. If we mean by a parallel a line that will never meet a second line; and if we have one such line drawn through a point, any third line drawn through that point which does not coalesce with the first must be inclined to it, and if inclined to it must approach the second, i.e., cease to be parallel with it. No properties of outlying space need come in here: only a definite conception of uniform direction, and constancy in sticking to one's point.

The other two axioms peculiar to geometry are that figures can be moved in space without change, and that no variation in the way of subdividing a given amount of space alters its total quantity.* This last axiom is similar to what we found to obtain in numbers. 'The whole is equal to its parts' is an abridged way of expressing it. A man is not the same biological whole if we cut him in two at the neck as if we divide him at the ankles; but geometrically he is the same whole, no matter in which place we cut him. The axiom about figures being movable in space is rather a postulate than an axiom. *So far as they are* so movable, then certain fixed equalities and differences obtain between forms, *no matter where placed.* But if translation through space warped or magnified forms, then the relations of equality, etc., would always have to be expressed with a position-qualification added. A geometry as absolutely certain as ours could be invented on the supposition of such a space, if the laws of its warping and deformation were fixed. It would, however, be much more complicated than our geometry, which makes the simplest possible supposition; and finds, luckily enough, that it is a supposition with which the space of our experience seems to agree.

By means of these principles, all playing into each other's hands, the mutual equivalences of an immense number of forms can be traced, even of such as at first sight bear hardly any resemblance to each other. We move and

---

* The subdivision itself consumes none of the space. In all practical experience our subdivisions do consume space. They consume it in our geometrical figures. But for simplicity's sake, in geometry we postulate subdivisions which violate experience and consume none of it.

turn them mentally, and find that parts of them will super-pose. We add imaginary lines which subdivide or enlarge them, and find that the new figures resemble each other in ways which show us that the old ones are equivalent too. We thus end by expressing all sorts of forms in terms of other forms, enlarging our knowledge of the kinds of things which certain other kinds of things are, or to which they are equivalent.

The result is a new system of mental objects which can be treated as identical for certain purposes, a new series of *is*'s almost indefinitely prolonged, just like the series of equivalencies among numbers, part of which the multiplication-table expresses. And all this is in the first instance regardless of the coexistences and sequences of nature, and regardless of whether the figures we speak of have ever been outwardly experienced or not.

CONSCIOUSNESS OF SERIES IS THE BASIS OF RATIONALITY.

Classification, logic, and mathematics all result, then, from the mere play of the mind comparing its conceptions, no matter whence the latter may have come. The essential condition for the formation of all these sciences is that we should have grown capable of apprehending series as such, and of distinguishing them as homogeneous or hetero-geneous, and as possessing definite directions of what I have called 'increase.' This consciousness of series is a human perfection which has been gradually evolved, and which varies amazingly from one man to another. No accounting for it as a result of habitual associations among outward impressions, so we must simply ascribe it to the factors, whatever they be, of inward cerebral growth. Once this consciousness attained to, however, *mediate* thought be-comes possible ; with our very awareness of a series may go an awareness that dropping terms out of it will leave identical relations between the terms that remain ; and thus arises a perception of relations between things so naturally separate that we should otherwise never have compared them together at all.

The axiom of skipped intermediaries applies, however, only to certain particular series, and among them to those which we have considered, in which the recurring relation is either of difference, of likeness, of kind, of numerical addition, or of prolongation in the same linear or plane direction. It is therefore not a purely formal law of thinking, but flows from the nature of the matters thought about. It will not do to say universally that in all series of homogeneously related terms the remote members are related to each other as the near ones are; for that will often be untrue. The series A is not B is not C is not D . . . does not permit the relation to be traced between remote terms. From two negations no inference can be drawn. Nor, to become more concrete, does the lover of a woman generally love her beloved, or the contradictor of a contradictor contradict whomever he contradicts. The slayer of a slayer does not slay the latter's victim ; the acquaintances or enemies of a man need not be each other's acquaintances or enemies ; nor are two things which are on top of a third thing necessarily on top of each other.

All skipping of intermediaries and transfer of relations occurs within homogeneous series. But not all homogeneous series allow of intermediaries being skipped and relations transferred. It depends on which series they are, on what relations they contain.* Let it not be said that it is a mere matter of verbal association, due to the fact that language sometimes permits us to transfer the *name* of a relation over skipped intermediaries, and sometimes does not ; as where we call men 'progenitors' of their remote as well as of their immediate posterity, but refuse to call them 'fathers' thereof. There are relations which are *intrinsically* transferable, whilst others are not. The relation of *condition*, e.g., is intrinsically transferable. What conditions a condition conditions what it conditions—" cause of cause is cause of effect." The relations of negation and *frustration*, on the other hand, are not transferable : what frustrates a frustration does not frustrate what it frustrates. No changes of terminology would annul the intimate difference between these two cases.

* Cf. A. de Morgan : Syllabus of a proposed System of Logic (1860), pp. 46-56.

Nothing but the clear sight of the ideas themselves shows whether the axiom of skipped intermediaries applies to them or not. Their connections, immediate and remote, flow from their inward natures. We try to consider them in certain ways, to bring them into certain relations, and we find that sometimes we can and sometimes we cannot. *The question whether there are or are not inward and essential connections between conceived objects as such, really is the same thing as the question whether we can get any new perception from mentally coupling them together, or pass from one to another by a mental operation which gives a result.* In the case of some ideas and operations we get a result; but no result in the case of others. Where a result comes, it is due exclusively to the *nature* of the ideas and of the operation. Take blueness and yellowness, for example. We can operate on them in some ways, but not in other ways. We can compare them; but we cannot add one to or subtract it from the other. We can refer them to a common kind, color; but we cannot make one a kind of the other, or infer one from the other. This has nothing to do with experience. For we *can* add blue *pigment* to yellow *pigment*, and subtract it again, and get a result both times. Only we know perfectly that this is no addition or subtraction of the blue and yellow qualities or natures themselves.*

There is thus no denying the fact that *the mind is filled with necessary and eternal relations which it finds between certain of its ideal conceptions, and which form a determinate system, independent of the order of frequency in which experience may have associated the conception's originals in time and space.*

Shall we continue to call these sciences 'intuitive,' 'innate,' or '*a priori*' bodies of truth, or not?† Personally

---

* Cf. Locke's Essay, bk. II. chap. XVII § 6.

† Some readers may expect me to plunge into the old debate as to whether the *a priori* truths are 'analytic' or 'synthetic.' It seems to me that the distinction is one of Kant's most unhappy legacies, for the reason that it is impossible to make it sharp. No one will say that such analytic judgments as "equidistant lines can nowhere meet" are *pure* tautologies. The predicate is a somewhat new way of conceiving as well as of naming the subject. There is *something* 'ampliative' in our greatest truisms, our state of mind is richer after than before we have uttered them. This

I should like to do so. But I hesitate to use the terms,
on account of the odium which controversial history has
made the whole of their connotation for many worthy persons. The most politic way not to alienate these readers
is to flourish the name of the immortal Locke. For in truth
I have done nothing more in the previous pages than to
make a little more explicit the teachings of Locke's fourth
book :

"The immutability of the same relations between the same immutable things is now the idea that shows him that if the three angles of
a triangle were once equal to two right angles, they will always be
equal to two right ones. And hence he comes to be certain that what
was once true in the case is always true ; what ideas once agreed will
always agree . . . Upon this ground it is that particular demonstrations
in mathematics afford general knowledge. If, then, the perception
that the same ideas will eternally have the same habitudes and relations
be not a sufficient ground of knowledge, there could be no knowledge
of general propositions in mathematics. . . . All general knowledge
lies only in our own thoughts, and consists barely in the contemplation of
our abstract ideas. Wherever we perceive any agreement or disagree-
ment amongst them, there we have general knowledge ; and by putting
the names of those ideas together accordingly in propositions, can with
certainty pronounce general truths. . . . What is once known of such
ideas will be perpetually and forever true. So that, as to all general
knowledge, we must search and find it only in our own minds and it is
only the examining of our own ideas that furnisheth us with that.
Truths belonging to essences of things (that is, to abstract ideas) are

---

being the case, the question "at what point does the new state of mind
cease to be *implicit* in the old ?" is too vague to be answered. The only
sharp way of defining synthetic propositions would be to say that they express a relation between *two data* at least. But it is hard to find any proposition which cannot be construed as doing this. Even verbal definitions
do it. Such painstaking attempts as that latest one by Mr. D. G. Thompson to prove all necessary judgments to be analytic (System of Psychology,
II. pp. 232 ff.) seem accordingly but *nugæ difficiles*, and little better than
wastes of ink and paper. All philosophic interest vanishes from the
question, the moment one ceases to ascribe to *any a priori* truths
(whether analytic or synthetic) that "legislative character for all possible
experience" which Kant believed in. We ourselves have denied such
legislative character, and contended that it was for experience itself to
prove whether its data can or cannot be assimilated to those ideal terms
between which *a priori* relations obtain. The analytic-synthetic debate is
thus for us devoid of all significance. On the whole, the best recent treatment of the question known to me is in one of A. Spir's works, his Denken
und Wirklichkeit, I think, but I cannot now find the page.

eternal, and are to be found out only by the contemplation of those essences. . . . Knowledge is the consequence of the ideas (be they what they will) that are in our minds, producing there certain general propositions. . . . Such propositions are therefore called 'eternal truths,' . . . because, being once made about abstract ideas so as to be true, they will, whenever they can be supposed to be made again, at any time past or to come, by a mind having those ideas, always actually be true. For names being supposed to stand perpetually for the same ideas, and the same ideas having immutably the same habitudes one to another, propositions concerning any abstract ideas that are once true must needs be eternal verities."

But what are these eternal verities, these 'agreements,' which the mind discovers by barely considering its own fixed meanings, except what I have said?—relations of likeness and difference, immediate or mediate, between the terms of certain series. Classification is serial comparison, logic mediate subsumption, arithmetic mediate equality of different bundles of attention-strokes, geometry mediate equality of different ways of carving space. None of these eternal verities has anything to say about facts, about what is or is not in the world. Logic does not say whether Socrates, men, mortals or immortals *exist;* arithmetic does not tell us where her 7's, 5's, and 12's are to be *found;* geometry affirms not that circles and rectangles are *real.* All that these sciences make us sure of is, that *if* these things are anywhere to be found, the eternal verities will obtain of them. Locke accordingly never tires of telling us that the

"universal propositions of whose truth or falsehood we can have certain knowledge, concern not existence. . . . These universal and self-evident principles, being only our constant, clear, and distinct knowledge of our own ideas more general or comprehensive, can assure us of nothing that passes without the mind; their certainty is founded only upon the knowledge of each idea by itself, and of its distinction from others; about which we cannot be mistaken whilst they are in our minds. . . . The mathematician considers the truth and properties belonging to a rectangle or circle only as they are in idea in his own mind. For it is possible he never found either of them existing mathematically, i.e., precisely true, in his life. But yet the knowledge he has of any truths or properties belonging to a circle, or any other mathematical figure, are nevertheless true and certain even of real things existing; because real things are no farther concerned nor intended to be meant by any such propositions, than as things really agree to those archetypes in his mind. Is it true of the idea of a triangle, that its three angles are equal to two right ones ? It is true also of a triangle wherever it really exists. Whatever other figure exists that is not exactly answerable to that idea in his mind is not at all concerned in that proposition. And therefore he is certain all his knowledge concerning such ideas is real knowledge: because, intending things no farther than they agree with those his ideas, he is sure what he knows concerning those figures when they have barely an ideal existence in his mind will hold true of them also when they have a real existence in matter." But "that any or what bodies do exist, that we are left to our senses to discover to us as far as they can." *

Locke accordingly distinguishes between ' mental truth ' and 'real truth.' † The former is intuitively certain ; the latter dependent on experience. Only *hypothetically* can we affirm intuitive truths of real things—by *supposing*, namely, that real things exist which correspond exactly with the ideal subjects of the intuitive propositions.

If our senses corroborate the supposition all goes well. But note the strange descent in Locke's hands of the dignity of *a priori* propositions. By the ancients they were considered, without farther question, to reveal the constitution of Reality. Archetypal things existed, it was assumed, in the relations in which we had to think them. The mind's necessities were a warrant for those of Being; and it was not till Descartes' time that scepticism had so advanced (in 'dogmatic' circles) that the warrant must itself be warranted, and the veracity of the Deity invoked as a reason for holding fast to our natural beliefs.

But the intuitive propositions of Locke leave us as regards outer reality none the better for their possession. We still have to "go to our senses" to find what the reality is. The vindication of the intuitionist position is thus a barren victory. The eternal verities which the very structure of our mind lays hold of do not necessarily themselves lay hold on extra-mental being, nor have they, as Kant pretended later,‡ a legislating character even

---

* Book IV. chaps. IX. § 1; VII. 14.

† Chap. v. §§ 6, 8.

‡ Kant, by the way, made a strange tactical blunder in his way of showing that the forms of our necessary thought are underived from experience. He insisted on thought-forms with which experience largely *agrees*, forgetting that the only forms which could not by any possibility

for all possible experience. They are primarily interesting only as subjective facts. They stand waiting in the mind, forming a beautiful ideal network; and the most we can say is that we *hope* to discover realities over which the network may be flung so that ideal and real may coincide.

And this brings us back to ' science ' from which we diverted our attention so long ago (see p. 640). Science thinks she has discovered the objective realities in question. Atoms and ether, with no properties but masses and velocities expressible by numbers, and paths expressible by analytic formulas, these at last are things over which the mathematico-logical network may be flung, and by supposing which instead of sensible phenomena science becomes yearly more able to manufacture for herself a world about which rational propositions may be framed. Sensible phenomena are pure delusions for the mechanical philosophy. The ' things ' and qualities we instinctively believe in do not exist. The only realities are swarming solids in everlasting motion, undulatory or continued, whose expressionless and meaningless changes of position form the history of the world, and are deducible from initial collocations and habits of movement hypothetically assumed. Thousands of years ago men started to cast the chaos of nature's sequences and juxtapositions into a form that might seem intelligible. Many were their ideal prototypes of rational order : teleological and æsthetic ties between things, causal and substantial bonds, as well as logical and mathematical relations. The most promising of these ideal systems at first were of course the richer ones, the sentimental ones. The baldest and least promising were the mathematical ones; but the history of the latter's application is a history of steadily advancing successes, whilst that of the sentimentally richer

---

be the results of experience would be such as experience *violated.* The first thing a Kantian ought to do is to discover forms of judgment to which *no* order in ' things ' runs parallel. These would indeed be features native to the mind. I owe this remark to Herr A. Spir, in whose ' Denken und Wirklichkeit ' it is somewhere contained. I have myself already to some extent proceeded, and in the pages which follow shall proceed still farther, to show the originality of the mind's structure in this way.

systems is one of relative sterility and failure.* Take those
aspects of phenomena which interest you as a human being
most, and class the phenomena as perfect and imperfect, as
ends and means to ends, as high and low, beautiful and ugly,
positive and negative, harmonious and discordant, fit and
unfit, natural and unnatural, etc., and barren are all your
results.   In the ideal world the kind 'precious' has characteristic properties.   What is precious should be preserved ; unworthy things should be sacrificed for its sake ;
exceptions made on its account ; its preciousness is a reason for other things' actions, and the like.   But none of
these things need happen to your ' precious ' object in the
real world.   Call the things of nature as much as you like
by sentimental, moral, and æsthetic names, no natural
consequences follow from the naming.   They may be of
the kinds you allege, but they are not of ' *the kind's kind;*
and the last great system-maker of this sort, Hegel, was
obliged explicitly to repudiate logic in order to make any
inferences at all from the names he called things by.

But when you give things mathematical and mechanical
names and call them just so many solids in just such positions, describing just such paths with just such velocities,
all is changed.   Your sagacity finds its reward in the verification by nature of all the deductions which you may next
proceed to make.   Your ' things ' realize all the *consequences*
of the names by which you classed them.   The modern
mechanico-physical philosophy of which we are all so
proud, because it includes the nebular cosmogony, the
conservation of energy, the kinetic theory of heat and

---

* Yet even so late as Berkeley's time one could write: " As in reading
other books a wise man will choose to fix his thoughts on the sense and
apply it to use, rather than lay them out in grammatical remarks on the
language : so in perusing the volume of nature methinks it is beneath the
dignity of the mind to affect an exactness in reducing each particular phenomenon to general rules, or showing how it follows from them.   We
should propose to ourselves nobler views, namely, to recreate and exalt the
mind with a prospect of the beauty, order, extent, and variety of natural
things : hence, by proper inferences, to enlarge our notions of the grandeur, wisdom, and beneficence of the Creator," etc., etc., etc.   (Principles
of Human Knowledge, § 109.)

gases, etc., etc., begins by saying that the *only* facts are collocations and motions of primordial solids, and the only laws the changes of motion which changes in collocation bring. The ideal which this philosophy strives after is a mathematical world-formula, by which, if all the collocations and motions at a given moment were known, it would be possible to reckon those of any wished-for future moment, by simply considering the necessary geometrical, arithmetical, and logical implications. Once we have the world in this bare shape, we can fling our net of *a priori* relations over all its terms, and pass from one of its phases to another by inward thought-necessity. Of course it is a world with a very minimum of rational *stuff*. The sentimental facts and relations are butchered at a blow. But the rationality yielded is so superbly complete in *form* that to many minds this atones for the loss, and reconciles the thinker to the notion of a purposeless universe, in which all the things and qualities men love, *dulcissima mundi nomina*, are but illusions of our fancy attached to accidental clouds of dust which the eternal cosmic weather will dissipate as carelessly as it has formed them.

The popular notion that 'Science' is forced on the mind *ab extra*, and that our interests have nothing to do with its constructions, is utterly absurd. The craving to believe that the things of the world belong to kinds which are related by inward rationality together, is the parent of Science as well as of sentimental philosophy; and the original investigator always preserves a healthy sense of how plastic the materials are in his hands.

"Once for all," says Helmholtz in beginning that little work of his which laid the foundations of the 'conservation of energy,' "it is the task of the physical sciences to seek for laws by which particular processes in nature may be referred to general rules, and deduced from such again. Such rules (for example the laws of reflection or refraction of light, or that of Mariotte and Gay-Lussac for gas-volumes) are evidently nothing but generic-concepts for embracing whole classes of phenomena. The search for them is the business of the experimental division of our Science. Its theoretic division, on the other hand, tries to discover the unknown causes of processes from their visible effects; tries to understand them by the law of causality. . . . The ultimate goal of theoretic physics is to find the last *unchanging* causes of the processes in Nature. Whether all processes be really ascribable to such causes, whether, in other words, *nature be completely intelligible*, or whether there be changes which would elude the law of a necessary causality, and fall into a realm of spontaneity or freedom, is not here the place to determine ; but at any rate it is clear that the Science whose aim it is to make nature appear intelligible [*die Natur zu begreifen*] must start with the *assumption* of her intelligibility, and draw consequences in conformity with this assumption, until irrefutable facts show the limitations of this method. . . . The postulate that natural phenomena must be reduced to changeless ultimate causes next shapes itself so that *forces unchanged by time* must be found to be these causes. Now in Science we have already found portions of matter with changeless forces (indestructible qualities), and called them (chemical) elements. If, then, we imagine the world composed of elements with inalterable qualities, the only changes that can remain possible in such a world are spatial changes, i.e. movements, and the only outer relations which can modify the action of the forces are spatial too or, in other words, the forces are motor forces dependent for their effect only on spatial relations. More exactly still : The phenomena of nature must be reduced to [*zurückgeführt*, conceived as, classed as] motions of material points with inalterable motor forces acting according to space-relations alone. . . . But points have no mutual space-relations except their distance, . . . and a motor force which they exert upon each other can cause nothing but a change of distance—i.e. be an attractive or a repulsive force. . . . And its intensity can only depend on distance. So that at last the task of Physics resolves itself into this, to refer phenomena to inalterable attractive and repulsive forces whose intensity varies with distance. The solution of this task would at the same time be the condition of Nature's complete intelligibility." *

The subjective interest leading to the assumption could not be more candidly expressed. What makes the assumption ' scientific ' and not merely poetic, what makes a Helmholtz and his kin *discoverers*, is that the things of Nature turn out to act as if they *were* of the kind assumed. They behave as such mere drawing and driving atoms would behave ; and so far as they have been distinctly enough translated into molecular terms to test the point, so far a certain fantastically ideal object, namely, the mathematical sum containing their mutual distances and velocities, is found to be constant throughout all their movements. This sum is called the total energy of the molecules considered. Its con-

---

* Die Erhaltung der Kraft (1847), pp. 2–6.

stancy or ' conservation' gives the name to the hypothesis of molecules and central forces from which it was logically deduced.

Take any other mathematico-mechanical theory and it is the same. They are all translations of sensible experiences into other forms, substitutions of items between which ideal relations of kind, number, form, equality, etc., obtain, for items between which no such relations obtain; coupled with declarations that the experienced form is false and the ideal form true, declarations which are justified by the appearance of new sensible experiences at just those times and places at which we logically infer that their ideal correlates ought to be. Wave-hypotheses thus make us predict rings of darkness and color, distortions, dispersions, changes of pitch in sonorous bodies moving from us, etc.; molecule-hypotheses lead to predictions of vapor-density, freezing point, etc.,—all which predictions fall true.

Thus the world grows more orderly and rational to the mind, which passes from one feature of it to another by deductive necessity, as soon as it conceives it as made up of so few and so simple phenomena as bodies with no properties but number and movement to and fro.

METAPHYSICAL AXIOMS.

But alongside of these ideal relations between terms which the world verifies, there are other ideal relations not as yet so verified. I refer to those propositions (no longer expressing mere results of comparison) which are formulated in such metaphysical and æsthetic axioms as "The Principle of things is one;" "The quantity of existence is unchanged;" "Nature is simple and invariable;" "Nature acts by the shortest ways;" "*Ex nihilo nihil fit;*" "Nothing can be evolved which was not involved;" "Whatever is in the effect must be in the cause;" "A thing can only work where it is;" "A thing can only affect another of its own kind;" "*Cessante causa, cessat et effectus;*" "Nature makes no leaps;" "Things belong to discrete and permanent kinds;" "Nothing is or happens without a reason;" "The world is throughout rationally intelligible;" etc.,

etc., etc. Such principles as these, which might be multiplied to satiety,* are properly to be called *postulates of rationality*, not propositions of fact. If nature *did* obey them, she *would* be *pro tanto* more intelligible ; and we seek meanwhile so to conceive her phenomena as to show that she does obey them. To a certain extent we succeed. For example, instead of the 'quantity of existence' so vaguely postulated as unchanged, Nature allows us to suppose that curious sum of distances and velocities which for want of a better term we call 'energy.' For the effect being 'contained in the cause,' nature lets us substitute ' the effect *is* the cause,' so soon as she lets us conceive both effect and cause as the same molecules, in two successive positions.— But all around these incipient successes (as all around the molecular world, so soon as we add to it as its 'effects' those illusory 'things' of common-sense which we had to butcher for its sake), there still spreads a vast field of irrationalized fact whose items simply *are* together, and from one to another of which we can pass by no ideally 'rational' way.

It is not that these more metaphysical postulates of rationality are absolutely barren—though barren enough they were when used, as the scholastics used them, as immediate propositions of fact.† They have a fertility as

---

* Perhaps the most influential of all these postulates is that the nature of the world must be such that sweeping statements may be made about it.

† Consider, e.g., the use of the axioms ' *nemo potest supra seipsum,*' and ' *nemo dat quod non habet,*' in this refutation of 'Darwinism,' which I take from the much-used scholastic compendium of Logic and Metaphysics of Liberatore, 3d ed. (Rome, 1880): "Hæc hypothesis . . . aperte contradicit principiis Metaphysicæ, quæ docent essentias rerum esse immutabiles, et effectum non posse superare causam. Et sane, quando, juxta Darwin, species inferior se evolvit in superiorem, unde trahit maiorem illam nobilitatem? Ex ejus carentia. At nihil dat quod non habet ; et minus gignere nequit plus, aut negatio positionem. Præterea in transformatione quæ fingitur, natura prioris speciei, servatur aut destruitur? Si primum, mutatio erit tantum accidentalis, qualem reapse videmus in diversis stirpibus animantium. Sin alterum asseritur, ut reapse fert hypothesis darwiniana, res tenderet ad seipsam destruendam ; cum contra omnia naturaliter tendant ad sui conservationem, et nonnisi per actionem contrarii agentis corruant." It is merely a question of fact whether these ideally proper relations do or do not obtain between animal and vegetable ancestors and descendants. If they do not, what happens? simply this, that we cannot continue to class animal and vegetal facts under the *kinds* between which

ideals, and keep us uneasy and striving always to recast the world of sense until its lines become more congruent with theirs. Take for example the principle that 'nothing can happen without a cause.' We have no definite idea of what we mean by cause, or of what causality consists in. But the principle expresses a demand for *some* deeper sort of inward connection between phenomena than their merely habitual time-sequence seems to us to be. The word 'cause' is, in short, an altar to an unknown god; an empty pedestal still marking the place of a hoped-for statue. *Any* really inward belonging-together of the sequent terms, if discovered, would be accepted as what the word cause was meant to stand for. So we seek, and seek; and in the molecular systems we find a sort of inward belonging in the notion of identity of matter with change of collocation. Perhaps by still seeking we may find other sorts of inward belonging, even between the molecules and those 'secondary qualities,' etc., which they produce upon our minds.

It cannot be too often repeated that the triumphant application of any one of our ideal systems of rational relations to the real world justifies our hope that other systems may be found also applicable. Metaphysics should take heart from the example of physics, simply confessing that hers is the longer task. Nature *may* be remodelled, nay, certainly will be remodelled, far beyond the point at present reached. Just how far?—is a question which only the whole future history of Science and Philosophy can answer.* Our task being Psychology, we cannot even cross the threshold of that larger problem.

Besides the mental structure which results in such

---

those ideal relations obtain. Thus, we can no longer call animal breeds by the name of 'species'; cannot call generating a kind of 'giving,' or treat a descendant as an 'effect' of his ancestor. The ideal scheme of terms and relations can remain, if you like; but it must remain purely mental, and without application to life, which 'gangs its ain gait' regardless of ideal schemes. Most of us, however, would prefer to doubt whether such abstract axioms as that 'a thing cannot tend to its own destruction' express ideal relations of an important sort at all.

* Compare A. Riehl: Der Philosophische Kriticismus, Bd. ii. Thl. i. Abschn. i. Cap. iii. § 6.

metaphysical principles as those just considered, there is a mental structure which expresses itself in

ÆSTHETIC AND MORAL PRINCIPLES.

The æsthetic principles are at bottom such axioms as that a note sounds good with its third and fifth, or that potatoes need salt. We are once for all so made that when certain impressions come before our mind, one of them will seem to call for or repel the others as its companions. To a certain extent the principle of habit will explain these æsthetic connections. When a conjunction is repeatedly experienced, the cohesion of its terms grows grateful, or at least their disruption grows unpleasant. But to explain *all* æsthetic judgments in this way would be absurd; for it is notorious how seldom natural experiences come up to our æsthetic demands. Many of the so-called metaphysical principles are at bottom only expressions of æsthetic feeling. Nature is simple and invariable; makes no leaps, or makes nothing but leaps; is rationally intelligible; neither increases nor diminishes in quantity; flows from one principle, etc., etc.,—what do all such principles express save our sense of how pleasantly our intellect would feel if it had a Nature of that sort to deal with? The subjectivity of which feeling is of course quite compatible with Nature also turning out objectively to be of that sort, later on.

The *moral* principles which our mental structure engenders are quite as little explicable *in toto* by habitual experiences having bred inner cohesions. Rightness is not *mere* usualness, wrongness not *mere* oddity, however numerous the facts which might be invoked to prove such identity. Nor are the moral judgments those most invariably and emphatically impressed on us by public opinion. The most characteristically and peculiarly moral judgments that a man is ever called on to make are in unprecedented cases and lonely emergencies, where no popular rhetorical maxims can avail, and the hidden oracle alone can speak; and it speaks often in favor of conduct quite unusual, and suicidal as far as gaining popular approbation goes. The forces which conspire to this resultant are subtle harmonies and discords between the

elementary ideas which form the data of the case. Some of
these harmonies, no doubt, have to do with habit; but
in respect to most of them our sensibility must assuredly
be a phenomenon of supernumerary order, correlated with
a brain-function quite as secondary as that which takes
cognizance of the diverse excellence of elaborate musical
compositions. No more than the higher musical sensibility can the higher moral sensibility be accounted for by the
frequency with which outer relations have cohered.* Take
judgments of justice or equity, for example. Instinctively,
one judges everything differently, according as it pertains
to one's self or to some one else. Empirically one notices
that everybody else does the same. But little by little
there dawns in one the judgment "nothing can be right for
me which would not be right for another similarly placed;"
or "the fulfilment of my desires is intrinsically no more imperative than that of anyone else's;" or "what it is reasonable that another should do for me, it is also reasonable
that I should do for him;" † and forthwith the whole mass
of the habitual gets overturned. It gets *seriously* overturned only in a few fanatical heads. But its overturning
is due to a back-door and not to a front-door process.
Some minds are preternaturally sensitive to logical consistency and inconsistency. When they have ranked a
thing under a kind, they *must* treat it as of that kind's
kind, or feel all out of tune. In many respects we do class
ourselves with other men, and call them and ourselves by
a common name. They agree with us in having the same
Heavenly Father, in not being consulted about their birth,

---

* As one example out of a thousand of exceptionally delicate idiosyncrasy in this regard, take this: "I must quit society. I would rather undergo twice the danger from beasts and ten times the danger from rocks.
It is not pain, it is not death, that I dread,—it is the hatred of a man; there
is something in it so shocking that I would rather submit to any injury
than incur or increase the hatred of a man by revenging it. . . . . Another
sufficient reason for suicide is that I was this morning out of temper with
Mrs. Douglas (for no fault of hers). I did not betray myself in the least,
but I reflected that to be exposed to the possibility of such an event once a
year, was evil enough to render life intolerable. The disgrace of using an
impatient word is to me overpowering." (Elton Hammond, quoted in
Henry Crabb Robinson's Diary, vol. I. p. 424.)

† Compare H. Sidgwick, Methods of Ethics, bk. III. chap. XIII. § 3.

in not being themselves to thank or blame for their natural gifts, in having the same desires and pains and pleasures, in short in a host of fundamental relations. Hence, *if these things be our essence*, we should be substitutable for other men, and they for us, in any proposition in which either of us is involved. The more fundamental and common the essence chosen, and the more simple the reasoning,* the more wildly radical and unconditional will the justice be which is aspired to. Life is one long struggle between conclusions based on abstract ways of conceiving cases, and opposite conclusions prompted by our instinctive perception of them as individual facts. The logical stickler for justice always seems pedantic and mechanical to the man who goes by tact and the particular instance, and who usually makes a poor show at argument. Sometimes the abstract conceiver's way is better, sometimes that of the man of instinct. But just as in our study of reasoning we found it impossible to lay down any mark whereby to distinguish *right* conception of a concrete case from *confusion* (see pp. 336, 350), so here we can give no general rule for deciding when it is morally useful to treat a concrete case as *sui generis*, and when to lump it with others in an abstract class.†

---

* A gentleman told me that he had a conclusive argument for opening the Harvard Medical School to women. It was this: "Are not women human?"—which major premise of course had to be granted. "Then are they not entitled to all the rights of humanity?" My friend said that he had never met anyone who could successfully meet this reasoning.

† You reach the Mephistophelian point of view as well as the point of view of justice by treating cases as if they belonged rigorously to abstract classes. Pure rationalism, complete immunity from prejudice, consists in refusing to see that the case before one is absolutely unique. It is always possible to treat the country of one's nativity, the house of one's fathers, the bed in which one's mother died, nay, the mother herself if need be, on a naked equality with all other specimens of so many respective genera. It shows the world in a clear frosty light from which all fuliginous mists of affection, all swamp-lights of sentimentality, are absent. Straight and immediate action becomes easy then—witness a Napoleon's or a Frederick's career. But the question always remains, "Are not the mists and vapors *worth* retaining?" The illogical refusal to treat certain concretes by the mere law of their genus has made the drama of human history. The obstinate insisting that tweedledum is *not* tweedledee is the bone and marrow of life. Look at the Jews and the Scots, with their miserable factions and sec-

An adequate treatment of the way in which we come by our æsthetic and moral judgments would require a separate chapter, which I cannot conveniently include in this book. Suffice it that these judgments express inner harmonies and discords between objects of thought; and that whilst outer cohesions frequently repeated will often seem harmonious, all harmonies are not thus engendered, but our feeling of many of them is a secondary and incidental function of the mind. Where harmonies are asserted of the real world, they are obviously mere postulates of rationality, so far as they transcend experience. Such postulates are exemplified by the ethical propositions that the individual and universal good are one, and that happiness and goodness are bound to coalesce in the same subject.

SUMMARY OF WHAT PRECEDES.

I will now sum up our progress so far by a short summary of the most important conclusions which we have reached.

---

tarian disputes, their loyalties and patriotisms and exclusions,—their annals now become a classic heritage, because men of genius took part and sang in them. A thing is important if any one *think* it important. The process of history consists in certain folks becoming possessed of the mania that certain special things are important infinitely, whilst other folks cannot agree in the belief. The Shah of Persia refused to be taken to the Derby Day, saying "It is already known to me that one horse can run faster than another." He made the question "*which* horse?" immaterial. Any question can be made immaterial by subsuming all its answers under a common head. Imagine what college ball-games and races would be if the teams were to forget the absolute distinctness of Harvard from Yale and think of both as One in the higher genus College. The sovereign road to indifference, whether to evils or to goods, lies in the thought of the higher genus. "When we have meat before us," says Marcus Aurelius, seeking indifference to *that* kind of good, "we must receive the impression that this is the dead body of a fish, and this is the dead body of a bird or of a pig; and again that this Falernian is only a little grape-juice, and this purple robe some sheep's wool dyed with the blood of a shell-fish. Such, then, are these impressions, and they reach the things themselves and penetrate them, and we see what kind of things they are. Just in the same way ought we to act through life, and where there are things which appear most worthy of our approbation, we ought to lay them bare and look at their worthlessness and strip them of all the words by which they are exalted." (Long's Translation, vi. 13.)

The mind has a native structure in this sense, that certain of its objects, if considered together in certain ways, give definite results ; and that no other ways of considering, and no other results, are possible if the same objects be taken.

The results are 'relations' which are all expressed by judgments of subsumption and of comparison.

The judgments of subsumption are themselves subsumed under the *laws of logic.*

Those of comparison are expressed in *classifications*, and in the *sciences of arithmetic and geometry.*

Mr. Spencer's opinion that our consciousness of classificatory, logical, and mathematical relations between ideas is due to the frequency with which the corresponding 'outer relations' have impressed our minds, is unintelligible.

Our consciousness of these relations, no doubt, has a natural genesis. But it is to be sought rather in the inner forces which have made the brain grow, than in any mere paths of 'frequent' association which outer stimuli may have ploughed in that organ.

But let our sense for these relations have arisen as it may, the relations themselves form a fixed system of lines of cleavage, so to speak, in the mind, by which we naturally pass from one object to another ; and the objects connected by these lines of cleavage are often not connected by any regular time- and space-associations. We distinguish, therefore, between the empirical order of things, and this their rational order of comparison ; and, so far as possible, we seek to translate the former into the latter, as being the more congenial of the two to our intellect.

Any classification of things into kinds (especially if the kinds form series, or if they successively involve each other) is a more rational way of conceiving the things than is that mere juxtaposition or separation of them as individuals in time and space which is the order of their crude perception. Any assimilation of things to terms between which such classificatory relations, with their remote and mediate transactions, obtain, is a way of bringing the things into a more rational scheme.

Solids in motion are such terms ; and the mechanical

philosophy is only a way of conceiving nature so as to arrange its items along some of the more natural lines of cleavage of our mental structure.

Other natural lines are the moral and æsthetic relations. Philosophy is still seeking to conceive things so that these relations also may seem to obtain between them.

As long as things have not successfully been so conceived, the moral and æsthetic relations obtain only between *entia rationis,* terms in the mind; and the moral and æsthetic principles remain but postulates, not propositions, with regard to the real world outside.

There is thus a large body of *a priori* or intuitively necessary truths. As a rule, these are truths of *comparison* only, and in the first instance they express relations between merely mental terms. Nature, however, acts as if some of her realities were identical with these mental terms. So far as she does this, we can make *a priori* propositions concerning natural fact. The aim of both science and philosophy is to make the identifiable terms more numerous. So far it has proved easier to identify nature's things with mental terms of the mechanical than with mental terms of the sentimental order.

The widest postulate of rationality is that the world *is* rationally intelligible throughout, after the pattern of *some* ideal system. The whole war of the philosophies is over that point of faith. Some say they can see their way already to the rationality; others that it is hopeless in any other but the mechanical way. To some the very fact that there is a world at all seems irrational. Nonentity would be a more natural thing than existence, for these minds. One philosopher at least says that the relatedness of things to each other is irrational anyhow, and that a world of relations can never be made intelligible.*

With this I may be assumed to have completed the programme which I announced at the beginning of the chapter, so far as the *theoretic* part of our organic mental struc-

---

* "*An sich, in seinem eignen Wesen, ist jedes reale Object mit sich selbst identisch und unbedingt*"—that is, the "*allgemeinste Einsicht a priori,*" and the "*allgemeinste aus Erfahrung*" is "*Alles erkennbare ist bedingt.*" (A. Spir : Denken und Wirklichkeit. Compare also Herbart and Hegel.)

ture goes. It can be due neither to our own nor to our ancestors' experience. I now pass to those practical parts of our organic mental structure. Things are a little different here ; and our conclusion, though it lies in the same direction, can be by no means as confidently expressed.

To be as short and simple as possible, I will take the case of instincts, and, supposing the reader to be familiar with Chapter XXIV, I will plunge *in medias res.*

THE ORIGIN OF INSTINCTS.

Instincts must have been either

1) Each specially created in complete form, or
2) Gradually evolved.

As the first alternative is nowadays obsolete, I proceed directly to the second. The two most prominent suggestions as to the way in which instincts may have been evolved are associated with the names of Lamarck and Darwin.

Lamarck's statement is that animals have *wants,* and contract, to satisfy them, *habits* which transform themselves gradually into so many propensities which they can neither resist nor change. These *propensities,* once acquired, propagate themselves by way of transmission to the young, so that they come to exist in new individuals, anteriorly to all exercise. Thus are the same emotions, the same habits, the same *instincts,* perpetuated without variation from one generation to another, so long as the outward conditions of existence remain the same.* Mr. Lewes calls this the theory of ' lapsed intelligence.' Mr. Spencer's words are clearer than Lamarck's, so that I will quote from him : †

---

* Philosophie Zoölogique, 3me partie, chap. v., ' de l'Instinct.'

† It should be said that Mr. Spencer's most formal utterance about instinct is in his Principles of Psychology, in the chapter under that name. Dr. Romanes has reformulated and criticised the doctrine of this chapter in his Mental Evolution in Animals, chapter xvii. I must confess my inability to state its vagueness in intelligible terms. It treats instincts as a further development of reflex actions, and as forerunners of intelligence,— which is probably true of many. But when it ascribes their formation to the mere ' multiplication of experiences,' which, at first simple, mould the nervous system to ' correspond to outer relations ' by simple reflex actions, and, afterwards complex, make it ' correspond ' by ' compound reflex actions,' it becomes too mysterious to follow without more of a key than is given. The whole thing becomes perfectly simple if we suppose the reflex actions to be accidental inborn idiosyncrasies preserved.

"Setting out with the unquestionable assumption, that every new form of emotion making its appearance in the individual or the race is a modification of some pre-existing emotion, or a compounding of several pre-existing emotions, we should be greatly aided by knowing what always are the pre-existing emotions. When, for example, we find that very few, if any, of the lower animals show any love of accumulation, and that this feeling is absent in infancy ; when we see that an infant in arms exhibits anger, fear, wonder, while yet it manifests no desire of permanent possession ; and that a brute which has no acquisitive emotion can nevertheless feel attachment, jealousy, love of approbation,—we may suspect that the feeling which property satisfies is compounded out of simpler and deeper feelings. We may conclude that as when a dog hides a bone there must exist in him a prospective gratification of hunger, so there must similarly, at first, in all cases where anything is secured or taken possession of, exist an ideal excitement of the feeling which that thing will gratify. We may further conclude that when the intelligence is such that a variety of objects come to be utilized for different purposes ; when, as among savages, divers wants are satisfied through the articles appropriated for weapons, shelter, clothing, ornament,—the act of appropriating comes to be one constantly involving agreeable associations, and one which is therefore pleasurable, irrespective of the end subserved. And when, as in civilized life, the property acquired is of a kind not conducing to one order of gratifications, but is capable of ministering to all gratifications, the pleasure of acquiring property grows more distinct from each of the various pleasures subserved—is more completely differentiated into a separate emotion.* It is well known that on newly-discovered islands not inhabited by man, birds are so devoid of fear as to allow themselves to be knocked over with sticks, but that in the course of genera-

---

* This account of acquisitiveness differs from our own. Without denying the associationist account to be a true description of a great deal of our proprietary feeling, we admitted in addition an entirely primitive form of desire. (See above, p. 422ff.) The reader must decide as to the plausibilities of the case. Certainly appearances are in favor of there being in us *some* cupidities quite disconnected with the ulterior uses of the things appropriated. The source of their fascination lies in their appeal to our æsthetic sense, and we wish thereupon simply to *own* them. Glittering, hard, metallic, odd, pretty things ; curious things especially ; natural objects that look as if they were artificial, or that mimic other objects,—these form a class of things which human beings snatch at as magpies snatch rags. They simply fascinate us. What house does not contain some drawer or cupboard full of senseless odds and ends of this sort, with which nobody knows what to do, but which a blind instinct saves from the ash-barrel ? Witness people returning from a walk on the sea-shore or in the woods, each carrying some *lusus naturæ* in the shape of stone or shell, or strip of bark or odd-shaped fungus, which litter the house and grow daily more unsightly, until at last reason triumphs over blind propensity and sweeps them away.

tions they acquire such a dread of man as to fly on his approach, and that this dread is manifested by young as well as old. Now unless this change be ascribed to the killing off of the least fearful, and the preservation and multiplication of the more fearful, which, considering the small number killed by man, is an inadequate cause, it must be ascribed to accumulated experiences, and each experience must be held to have a share in producing it. We must conclude that in each bird that escapes with injuries inflicted by man, or is alarmed by the outcries of other members of the flock, . . . there is established an association of ideas between the human aspect and the pains, direct and indirect, suffered from human agency. And we must further conclude that the state of consciousness which impels the bird to take flight is at first nothing more than an ideal reproduction of those painful impressions which before followed man's approach ; that such ideal reproduction becomes more vivid and more massive as the painful experiences, direct or sympathetic, increase ; and that thus the emotion, in its incipient state, is nothing else than an aggregation of the revived pains before experienced. As, in the course of generations, the young birds of this race begin to display a fear of man before they have been injured by him, it is an unavoidable inference that the nervous system of the race has been organically modified by these experiences ; we have no choice but to conclude that when a young bird is thus led to fly, it is because the impression produced on its senses by the approaching man entails, through an incipiently reflex action, a partial excitement of all those nerves which, in its ancestors, had been excited under the like conditions ; that this partial excitement has its accompanying painful consciousness ; and that the vague painful consciousness thus arising constitutes emotion proper—*emotion undecomposable into specific experiences, and therefore seemingly homogeneous. If such be the explanation of the fact in this case, then it is in all cases. If the emotion is so generated here, then it is so generated throughout.* If so, we must perforce conclude that the emotional modifications displayed by different nations, and those higher emotions by which civilized are distinguished from savage, are to be accounted for on the same principle. And, concluding this, we are led strongly to suspect that the emotions in general have severally thus originated." *

Obviously the word 'emotion' here means instinct as well,—the actions we call instinctive are expressions or manifestations of the emotions whose genesis Mr. Spencer describes. Now if habit could thus bear fruit outside the individual life, and if the modifications so painfully acquired by the parents' nervous systems could be found ready-made at birth in those of the young, it would be hard

* Review of Bain in H. Spencer: Illustrations of Universal Progress (New York 1864), pp. 311, 315.

to overestimate the importance, both practical and theoretical, of such an extension of its sway. In principle, instincts would then be assimilated to 'secondarily-automatic' habits, and the origin of many of them out of tentative experiments made during ancestral lives, perfected by repetition, addition, and association through successive generations, would be a comparatively simple thing to understand.

Contemporary students of instinct have accordingly been alert to discover all the facts which would seem to establish the possibility of such an explanation. The list is not very long, considering what a burden of conclusions it has to bear. Let acquisitiveness and fear of man, as just argued for by Spencer, lead it off. Other cases of the latter sort are the increased shyness of the woodcock noticed to have occurred within sixty years' observation by Mr. T. A. Knight, and the greater shyness everywhere shown by large than by small birds, to which Darwin has called attention. Then we may add—

The propensities of 'pointing,' 'retrieving,' etc., in sporting dogs, which seem partly, at any rate, to be due to training, but which in well-bred stock are all but innate. It is in these breeds considered bad for a litter of young if its sire or dam have not been trained in the field.

Docility of domestic breeds of horses and cattle.

Tameness of young of tame rabbit—young wild rabbits being invincibly timid.

Young foxes are most wary in those places where they are most severely hunted.

Wild ducks, hatched out by tame ones, fly off. But if kept close for some generations, the young are said to become tame.*

Young savages at a certain age will revert to the woods.

English greyhounds taken to the high plateau of Mexico could not at first run well, on account of rarefied air. Their whelps entirely got over the difficulty.

Mr. Lewes somewhere † tells of a terrier pup whose parents had been taught to 'beg,' and who constantly

---

* Ribot : De l'Hérédité, 2me éd. p. 26.

† Quoted (without reference) in Spencer's Biology, vol. I. p. 247.

threw himself spontaneously into the begging attitude. Darwin tells of a French orphan-child, brought up out of France, yet *shrugging* like his ancestors.*

Musical ability often increases from generation to generation in the families of musicians.

The hereditarily epileptic guinea-pigs of Brown-Séquard, whose parents had become epileptic through surgical operations on the spinal cord or sciatic nerve. The adults often lose some of their hind toes, and the young, in addition to being epileptic, are frequently born with the corresponding toes lacking. The offspring of guinea-pigs whose cervical sympathetic nerve has been cut on one side will have the ear larger, the eyeball smaller, etc., just like their parents after the operation. Puncture of the 'restiform body' of the medulla will, in the same animal, congest and enlarge one eye, and cause gangrene of one ear. In the young of such parents the same symptoms occur.

Physical refinement, delicate hands and feet, etc., appear in families well-bred and rich for several generations.

The 'nervous' temperament also develops in the descendants of sedentary brain-working people.

Inebriates produce offspring in various ways degenerate.

Nearsightedness is produced by indoor occupation for generations. It has been found in Europe much more frequent among schoolchildren in towns than among children of the same age in the country.

These latter cases are of the inheritance of structural rather than of functional peculiarities. But as structure gives rise to function it may be said that the principle is the same. Amongst other inheritances of adaptive† structural change may be mentioned:

The 'Yankee' type.

Scrofula, rickets, and other diseases of bad conditions of life.

The udders and permanent milk of the domestic breeds of cow.

---

* Expression of Emotions (N. Y.), p. 287.

† 'Adaptive' changes are those produced by the direct effect of outward conditions on an organ or organism. Sunburned complexion, horny hands, muscular toughness, are illustrations.

The 'fancy' rabbit's ears, drooping through lack of need to erect them. Dog's, ass's, etc., in some breeds ditto.

The obsolete eyes of mole and various cave-dwelling animals.

The diminished size of the wing-bones of domesticated ducks, due to ancestral disuse of flight.*

These are about all the facts which, by one author or another, have been invoked as evidence in favor of the 'lapsed intelligence' theory of the origin of instincts.

Mr. Darwin's theory is that of the natural selection of accidentally produced tendencies to action.

"It would," says he, " be the most serious error to suppose that the greater number of instincts have been acquired by habit in one generation, and then transmitted by inheritance in succeeding generations. It can clearly be shown that the most wonderful instincts with which we are acquainted, namely, those of the hive-bee and of many ants, could not possibly have been thus acquired.† It will be universally admitted that instincts are as important as corporeal structure for the welfare of each species, under its present conditions of life. Under changed conditions of life, it is at least possible that slight modifications of instinct might be profitable to a species ; and if it can be shown that instincts do vary ever so little, then I can see no difficulty in natural selection preserving and continually accumulating variations of instinct to any extent that may be profitable. It is thus, as I believe, that all the most complex and wonderful instincts have arisen. . . . I believe that the effects of habit are of quite subordinate importance to the effects of the natural selection of what may be called accidental variations of instincts ;—that is, of variations produced by the same unknown causes which produce slight deviations of bodily structure." ‡

The evidence for Mr. Darwin's view is too complex to be given in this place. To my own mind it is quite convincing. If, with the Darwinian theory in mind, one re-reads

---

* For these and other facts cf. Th. Ribot: De l'Hérédité ; W. B. Carpenter: Contemporary Review, vol. 21, p. 295, 779, 867 ; H. Spencer: Princ. of Biol. pt. II. ch. v, VIII, IX, X ; pt. III. ch. XI, XII ; C. Darwin: Animals and Plants under Domestication, ch. XII, XIII, XIV ; Sam'l Butler: Life and Habit ; T. A. Knight: Philos. Trans. 1837 ; E. Dupuy: Popular Science Monthly, vol. XI. p. 332 ; F. Papillon : Nature and Life, p. 330 ; Crothers, in Pop. Sci. M., Jan. (or Feb.) 1889.

† [Because, being exhibited by neuter insects, the effects of mere practice cannot accumulate from one generation to another.—W. J.]

‡ Origin of Species, chap. VII.

the list of examples given in favor of the Lamarckian theory, one finds that many of the cases are irrelevant, and that some make for one side as well as for the other. This is so obvious in many of the cases that it is needless to point it out in detail. The shrugging child and the begging pup, e.g., prove somewhat too much. They are examples so unique as to suggest spontaneous variation rather than inherited habit. In other cases the observations much need corroboration, e.g., the effects of not training for a generation in sporting dogs and race-horses, the difference between young wild rabbits born in captivity and young tame ones, the cumulative effect of many generations of captivity on wild ducks, etc.

Similarly, the increased wariness of the large birds, of those on islands frequented by men, of the woodcock, of the foxes, may be due to the fact that the bolder families have been killed off, and left none but the naturally timid behind, or simply to the individual experience of older birds being imparted by example to the young so that a new *educational tradition* has occurred.—The cases of physical refinement, nervous temperament, Yankee type, etc., also need much more discriminating treatment than they have yet received from the Lamarckians. There is no real evidence that physical refinement and nervosity tend to accumulate from generation to generation in aristocratic or intellectual families; nor is there any that the change in that direction which Europeans transplanted to America undergo is not all completed in the first generation of children bred on our soil. To my mind, the facts all point that way. Similarly the better breathing of the greyhounds born in Mexico was surely due to a post-natal adaptation of the pups' thorax to the rarer air.

Distinct neurotic *degeneration* may undoubtedly accumulate from parent to child, and as the parent usually in this case grows worse by his own irregular habits of life, the temptation lies near to ascribe the child's deterioration to this cause. This, again, is a hasty conclusion. For neurotic degeneration is unquestionably a disease whose original causes are unknown; and like other 'accidental variations' it is hereditary. But it ultimately ends in sterility; and it seems to me quite unfair to draw any conclusions from its natural history in favor of the transmission of acquired peculiarities. Nor does the degeneration of the children of alcoholics prove anything in favor of their having inherited the shattered nervous system which the alcohol has induced in their parents : because the poison usually has a chance to directly affect their own bodies before birth, by acting on the germinal matter from which they are formed whilst it is still nourished by the alcoholized blood of the parent. In many cases, however, the parental alcoholics are themselves degenerates neurotically, and the drink-habit is only a symptom of their disease, which in some form or other they also propagate to their children.

There remain the inherited mutilations of the guinea-pig. But these are such startling exceptions to the ordinary rule with animals that they should hardly be used as examples of a typical process. The docility of domestic cattle is certainly in part due to man's selection, etc., etc. In a word, the proofs form rather a beggarly array.

Add to this that the writers who have tried to carry out the theory of transmitted habit with any detail are always obliged *somewhere* to admit inexplicable variation. Thus Spencer allows that

" Sociality can begin only where, through some slight variation, there is less tendency than usual for the individuals to disperse. . . . That slight variations of mental nature, sufficient to initiate this process, may be fairly assumed, all our domestic animals show us: differences in their characters and likings are conspicuous. Sociality having thus commenced, and survival of the fittest tending ever to maintain and increase it, it will be further strengthened by the inherited effects of habit.'·* Again, in writing of the pleasure of pity, Mr. Spencer says : " This feeling is not one that has arisen through the inherited effects of experiences, but belongs to a quite different group, traceable to the survival of the fittest simply—to the natural selection of incidental variations. In this group are included all the bodily appetites, together with those simpler instincts, sexual and parental, by which every race is maintained ; and which must exist before the higher processes of mental evolution can commence." †

The inheritance of tricks of manner and trifling peculiarities, such as handwriting, certain odd gestures when pleased, peculiar movements during sleep, etc., have also been quoted in favor of the theory of transmission of acquired habits. Strangely enough ; for of all things in the world these tricks seem most like idiosyncratic variations. They are usually defects or oddities which the education of the individual, the pressure of what is really *acquired* by him, would counteract, but which are too native to be repressed, and breaks through all artificial barriers, in his children as well as in himself.

I leave my text practically just as it was written in 1885. I proceeded at that time to draw a tentative conclusion to the effect that the origin of *most* of our instincts must certainly be deemed fruits of the back-door method of genesis, and not of ancestral experience in the proper meaning of the term. Whether acquired ancestral habits played any part at all in their production was still an open question in which it would be as rash to affirm as to deny. Already before that time, however, Professor Weismann of Freiburg had begun a very serious attack upon the Lamarckian theory,* and his polemic has at last excited such a widespread interest among naturalists that the whilom almost unhesitatingly accepted theory seems almost on the point of being abandoned.

I will therefore add some of Weismann's criticisms of the supposed evidence to my own. In the first place, he has a captivating theory of descent of his own,† which makes him think it *a priori* impossible that any peculiarity acquired during lifetime by the parent should be transmitted to the germ. Into the nature of that theory this is not the place to go. Suffice to say that it has made him a keener critic of Lamarck's and Spencer's theory than he otherwise might have been. The only way in which the germinal products can be influenced whilst in the body of the parent is, according to Weismann, by good or bad nutrition. Through this they may degenerate in various ways or lose vitality altogether. They may also be infected through the blood by small-pox, syphilis, or other virulent diseases, and otherwise be poisoned. But peculiarities of neural structure and habit in the parents *which the parents themselves were not*

---

* Ueber die Vererbung (Jena, 1883). Prof. Weismann's Essays on Heredity have recently (1889) been published in English in a collected form.

† Best expressed in the Essay on the *Continuitat des Keimplasmas* (1885).

born with, they can never acquire unless perhaps accidentally through some coincidental variation of their own. *Accidental* variations develop of course into idiosyncrasies which tend to pass to later generations in virtue of the well-known law which no one doubts.

Referring to the often-heard assertion that the increase of talent found in certain families from one generation to another is due to the transmitted effects of *exercise* of the faculty concerned (the Bachs, the Bernoullis, Mozart, etc.), he sensibly remarks, that the talent being kept in exercise, it ought to have gone on growing for an indefinite number of generations. As a matter of fact, it quickly reaches a maximum, and then we hear no more of it, which is what happens always when an idiosyncrasy is exposed to the effects of miscellaneous intermarriage.

The hereditary epilepsy and other degenerations of the operated guinea-pigs are explained by Professor Weismann as results of *infection* of the young by the parent's blood. The latter he supposes to undergo a pathologic change in consequence of the original traumatic injury. The obsolescence of disused organs he explains very satisfactorily, without invoking any transmission of the direct effects of disuse, by his theory of *panmixy,* for which I must refer to his own writings. Finally, he criticises searchingly the stories we occasionally hear of inherited mutilations in animals (dogs' ears and tails, etc.), and cites a prolonged series of experiments of his own on mice, which he bred for many generations, cutting off both parental tails each time, without interfering in the least with the length of tail with which the young continued to be born.

The strongest argument, after all, in favor of the Lamarckian theory remains the *a priori* one urged by Spencer in his little work (much the solidest thing, by the way, which he has ever written) 'The Factors of Organic Evolution.'

Since, says Mr. Spencer, the accidental variations of all parts of the body are independent of each other, if the entire organization of animals were due to such accidental variations alone, the amount of mutual adaptation and harmony that we now find there could hardly possibly have come about in any finite time. We must rather suppose that the divers varying parts *brought* the other parts into harmony with themselves by *exercising them ad hoc*, and that the effects of the exercise remained and were passed on to the young. This forms, of course, a great *presumption* against the all-sufficiency of the view of selection of accidental variations exclusively. But it must be admitted that in favor of the contrary view, that adaptive changes are inherited, we have as yet perhaps not one single unequivocal item of positive proof.

I must therefore end this chapter on the genesis of our mental structure by reaffirming my conviction that the so-called Experience-philosophy has failed to prove its point. No more if we take ancestral experiences into account than if we limit ourselves to those of the individual after birth, can we believe that the couplings of terms within the mind are simple copies of corresponding couplings impressed upon it by the environment. This indeed is true of a small part of our cognitions. But so far as logical and mathematical, ethical, æsthetical, and metaphysical propositions go, such an assertion is not only untrue but altogether unintelligible; for these propositions say nothing about the time- and space-order of things, and it is hard to understand how such shallow and vague accounts of them as Mill's and Spencer's could ever have been given by thinking men.

The causes of our mental structure are doubtless natural, and connected, like all our other peculiarities, with those of our nervous structure. Our interests, our tendencies of attention, our motor impulses, the æsthetic, moral, and theoretic combinations we delight in, the extent of our power of apprehending schemes of relation, just like the elementary relations themselves, time, space, difference and similarity, and the elementary kinds of feeling, have all grown up in ways of which at present we can give no account. Even in the clearest parts of Psychology our insight is insignificant enough. And the more sincerely one seeks to trace the actual course of *psychogenesis*, the steps by which as a race we may have come by the peculiar mental attributes which we possess, the more clearly one perceives " the slowly gathering twilight close in utter night."

INDEX.

INDEX.